ISBN 978-1-330-45872-3
PIBN 10065174

1 MONTH OF
FREE
READING

at

www.ForgottenBooks.com

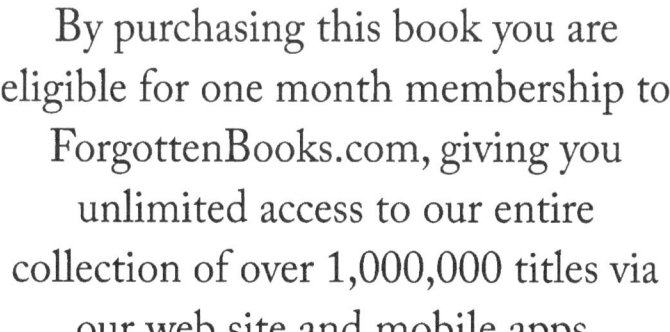

By purchasing this book you are eligible for one month membership to ForgottenBooks.com, giving you unlimited access to our entire collection of over 1,000,000 titles via our web site and mobile apps.

To claim your free month visit:

www.forgottenbooks.com/free65174

English
Français
Deutsche
Italiano
Español
Português

www.forgottenbooks.com

Mythology Photography **Fiction**
Fishing Christianity **Art** Cooking
Essays Buddhism Freemasonry
Medicine **Biology** Music **Ancient
Egypt** Evolution Carpentry Physics
Dance Geology **Mathematics** Fitness
Shakespeare **Folklore** Yoga Marketing
Confidence Immortality Biographies
Poetry **Psychology** Witchcraft
Electronics Chemistry History **Law**
Accounting **Philosophy** Anthropology
Alchemy Drama Quantum Mechanics
Atheism Sexual Health **Ancient History**
Entrepreneurship Languages Sport
Paleontology Needlework Islam
Metaphysics Investment Archaeology
Parenting Statistics Criminology
Motivational

HISTORY OF ENGLAND

L. VON RANKE

London

MACMILLAN AND CO.

PUBLISHERS TO THE UNIVERSITY OF

Oxford

A

HISTORY OF ENGLAND

PRINCIPALLY

IN THE SEVENTEENTH CENTURY

BY

LEOPOLD VON RANKE

VOLUME IV

Oxford

AT THE CLARENDON PRESS

1875

CONTENTS.

BOOK XVI.

THE LATER YEARS OF CHARLES II, 1675—1685.
WHIGS AND TORIES.

BOOK XVII.

REIGN OF JAMES II, FEBRUARY 1685 TO SEPTEMBER 1688.

BOOK XVIII.

THE FALL OF JAMES II IN ITS CONNEXION WITH THE EUROPEAN CONFLICTS WHICH MARKED THE CLOSE OF 1688.

BOOK XIX.

COMPLETION OF THE REVOLUTION IN THE THREE KINGDOMS, 1688—1691.

BOOK XVI.

THE LATER YEARS OF CHARLES II, 1675–1685.

WHIGS AND TORIES.

NEITHER a republic nor an absolute monarchy was seriously contemplated in England at this period. There were still many men in whom the passions of the fanatics and republicans continued to work; but the general feeling of the nation was opposed to their return at any time to power. And Charles II could never flatter himself that he would acquire such an authority as Louis XIV possessed in France. For he had been restored by Parliament, and we have seen how Parliament, though at first devoted to his authority and allied with him, gradually took up a position of resistance.

The questions of the day were of a constitutional nature, and were concerned with determining the limits of the authority of the Crown and of the two Houses in accordance with the Parliamentary constitution; and it is precisely this question of limitation, at this time practically undetermined, that lends a new and general interest to affairs.

Parliament calls the King's ministers to account; the King, if the decision is contrary to his inclination, makes difficulties about dismissing them from his service.

Parliament lays claim to the control over the expenditure of the moneys granted by it; the King reserves the right of examining the account books himself, and judging about them.

The King has on the whole free scope, as he is not compelled to summon Parliament every year. He can at his will adjourn or dissolve it ; but the dissolution gives him a prospect of such unfavourable results that he recoils from it ; and the adjournment embitters men's tempers.

Parliament, by granting the crown insufficient revenues, has placed it under the necessity of seeking Parliamentary assistance, not only in very extraordinary cases, but in the ordinary course of things as well ; the King does not hesitate to emancipate himself, by means of foreign subsidies, from this duty which is to him the most burdensome of all.

Already Parliament in different cases has exercised a decided influence upon foreign affairs; the King considers the main point of his prerogative to consist in determining with unconditional authority, his relations with foreign powers.

Parliament has accompanied the restoration of the Anglican Church with exclusive privileges, oppressive to every diverging opinion ; the King looks upon it as a right and duty to restrict these privileges.

Though we have seen how all these points of dispute originated in the circumstances and affairs of England, and so took their peculiar form, yet they have a general meaning which reaches beyond the persons concerned, their weaknesses, errors, and transgressions; they are questions to a certain extent inevitable. For if monarchy is to have any meaning of its own, and otherwise it would be useless to the constitution, it cannot renounce the freedom of individual judgment, without which no one would choose to live. But on the other hand, a Parliament which once feels its power, will hardly reconcile itself to the necessity of remaining subordinate to an external will. The opposition lies in the nature of the two powers, each of which strives, in accordance with its inward impulse, after an authority which, if obtained, would destroy the freedom of action enjoyed by the other, and hamper its self-consciousness.

This became most strikingly apparent in the religious question. Without doubt Parliament was within its rights, to a greater degree even than it was aware, when it opposed the intrusive advance of Catholicism, by the restoration of which the monarchy hoped to establish once for all the royal supremacy. Charles II had now submitted, but near to him stood his brother, the heir to the throne, who adhered to the Catholic faith with unwavering zeal. Was the country calmly to submit to the dangers which the Established Church would run on the accession of a prince who held these views? Or should the heir to the monarchy allow Parliament to set him measure and limit in the most private and personal of all matters, his religion? Or if not, how were the complications, which might be expected, to be safely avoided?

But whilst the expectation of this great contest, in which the future of Great Britain was involved, filled the horizon, political action was at the same time excited day by day by continental relations and their changes.

The European war had taken another direction, now that a great continental alliance had come to the support of the Dutch. For Louis XIV this could not be in itself disagreeable, for it gave him the opportunity of returning to the most important of all his schemes, and the one which has had most effect upon posterity,—the extension of the French boundary on the East. He not only opposed to the forces of the allies, which were in themselves superior, his well-practised and well-commanded army, but he knew also how to occupy them on another side, by awakening enemies in their rear, Swedes, Poles, Hungarians, and Turks. Still even so he would with difficulty have resisted his opponents, if England had joined with them as Parliament continually demanded. To keep King Charles on their side, the French never wearied of representing to him that Parliament aimed at interfering in his government and overthrowing his ministers: must it not be, they urged, the chief maxim of a prince to carry out his will under all circumstances, and to maintain his ministers? for otherwise the next attack might be directed against himself. And if Charles II asked for subsidies, they were always inclined to consent, for French money, even in the time of war, could not be better employed than in neutralising the English Parliament[1]. But with all his submission to France, Charles II could not shut his eyes to his relations with the

---

1 Ruvigny, Jan. 27, 1675: 'Que les finances du roi ne pouvoient pas être mieux employées qu'à la destruction d'un puissant ennemi qui soutenoit tous les autres.'

other European powers, and to the position which the English kingdom held in the world; his financial necessities also perpetually awakened in him the desire to stand well with Parliament. He wavered, according to his custom, from one side to the other, as his advantage required. Whether he would follow this or that impulse, formed always one of the most important elements in determining the fate of Europe and the Parliamentary difficulties at home.

CHAPTER I.

THE French influence did not at first extend so far that King Charles would have allowed himself to be restrained from summoning Parliament. The French offers, even an autograph letter which Louis XIV wrote for that purpose[1], had, this time, no effect upon him. For he could have no doubt that an understanding with Parliament, if it could be brought about without loss to the crown, was far preferable to a French alliance. Charles II said to the French ambassador, that he must give Parliament another trial, but that he would defend the outworks of the crown against all its attacks; he would not allow it to interfere either with his ministers or with the succession to the kingdom, or let it meddle with political matters[2]; he would never allow himself to be separated from the King of France: Parliament might still be very useful; should he see that nothing could be done with it, he would decide upon dissolution. On the 13th April, 1675, the fourteenth session of Parliament was opened.

The King had from the first determined on a change in the conduct of affairs. Buckingham had retired; Arlington fell into disfavour immediately after the first debates, in which

---

[1] 'Tendre et pleine d'amitié'; such is Charles II's opinion: but Ruvigny, February 24, adds—'il est persuadé que les affaires seroient ruinées s'il éloignoit encore le parlement.'

[2] 'Que le parlement fasse aucune entreprise contre ses droits—parle d'alliance, de traités de succession, de paix, de guerre ou d'attaquer les ministres.' Ruvigny, March 3.

his friends took up a factious position. The King no longer
asked his advice, and no longer attended to him when he
gave his opinion unasked.

The chief ground for this lay in the fact that Arlington's
advice had led to the most serious complications, and the
King was of opinion that he would not be able to do
anything with Parliament, unless he avoided all Catholic
tendencies. The man he now trusted was Thomas Osborne,
Earl of Danby, whom he had raised to be Lord Treasurer,
and who, in his administration of this office, in which he
discovered unexpected financial resources, won his especial
favour. But even in this, Danby became convinced that it
was impossible to administer the state without agreement
with the Commons, and this again could not be attained if
their religious sentiments were resisted. Already beforehand
he had planned the publication of a declaration against
Catholics and Nonconformists, to which Arlington could never
have consented; from the first he had been excluded from
the discussions about it ; besides Danby, only the old Presbyterian, Lauderdale took part in it. It was in accordance with
this that the speech from the throne joined to the demand of
subsidies for the restoration of the navy the most express
assurances in favour of religious uniformity.

For only by this means was further progress considered
possible. Thomas Osborne had been one of the chief opponents of Lord Chancellor Clarendon ; as Lord Treasurer he
returned, if not to Clarendon's system, at least to his principal
ideas. He wished to attempt the union of the Anglican
interest with the maintenance of the prerogative.

He himself belonged to a Royalist family, which in the civil
wars had suffered great losses, and had never been indemnified
for them ; his wife was the granddaughter of the Lord
Lindsay who perished fighting most bravely at the battle
of Edgehill. He had, as it were, an inherited right to favour
and advancement from the King. But he also neglected no
means of advancing himself. When Buckingham rose into
power he was one of his most zealous adherents ; the Duke

---

[1] Reresby (Memoirs 176) ascribes this also to Buckingham : they may, without
knowing it, have co-operated.

of York claims to have recommended him as Lord Treasurer[1]: still this did not keep him, when once he had entered
upon his high office, from turning away with equal decision from
both; he took up his position midway between the patron
of the Dissenters and the head of the Catholics. Only by
closely uniting the crown with the bishops and the Anglican
gentry, to whom he himself belonged, did he see any possibility of forming a compact administrative power. He was
a minister who could still prevail upon himself, in reality
against his better judgment, to follow the King in his doubtful policy, and to be responsible for him in the embarrassments
which it produced: adapting himself to circumstances, not
particular in the choice of means, in his private life as little
correct as most others, he still occupied himself with wide
and comprehensive schemes, maintained them with perse-
verance, and even knew how to convert the King to them:
Danby was of greater importance in the general development
of English affairs than is usually supposed.

Early in the session a bill for security against disaffected
persons was introduced, which perfectly expresses his sentiments[1]. According to it the declaration already imposed
upon the clergy, to the effect that all resistance to the King
and his officials was illegal, and that no attempt would be
made to introduce any change into the government of Church
and State, was now prescribed for lay officials also, and even
for members of Parliament. It is easy to see what this
involved. The laws enacting unconditional obedience in civil
matters and uniformity in religion, would have been most
closely united and permanently established; the Presbyterians, who had been carried in continually increasing numbers
in chance elections, would have been obliged to retire from
the Lower, and the Catholics from the Upper House; the
power of the state would have been concentrated in the
hands of the Anglicans; Parliament and Government would
have been united into one single dominant party. Danby
made it known, that in that case the government would
make common cause with Parliament in foreign politics also.

---

[1] The no resisting test. Parliamentary History iv. 715.

England would have become united in the Anglican-Pro-
testant interest. His friends said that he had been induced
by the bishops to make these proposals, but the bishops
declared that he himself had taken the initiative. If he
succeeded he would become unassailable.

The immediate result of the reading of the bill in the
Upper House, where it was first introduced, was an outcry
of indignation. Lord Bristol exclaimed that it ought to be
burnt. How entirely the claim of the Lords, that their right
to a seat and a vote in Parliament was due to their birth,
was abolished, if its exercise were to be made conditional upon
an oath of this kind! Some other influential lords united
with Bristol in a protest against the further progress of the
bill. In spite of this it was taken into consideration by a
committee of the whole House. Here many urgent objections were made to it. It was affirmed that the very nature
of a limited monarchy subjected it to the necessary fear of
resistance ; for by this means the Prince was prevented
from forming for himself a special interest in opposition to
his people. Further it was affirmed that it belonged to the
nature of a legislative power to take into consideration
changes of government. There was a return to the doctrine
of the Long Parliament, that a distinction exists between
the king in theory and the king in practice, and the system
of the Anglican Church, as well as the bishops' claim to
a divine right, was attacked with a zeal which recalled those
times. But as the bishops themselves possessed seats and
votes, and numbered not a few adherents amongst the lay
lords, and also had the authority of the government on their
side, all these objections produced no particular effect [1]. Some
changes were made in the resolutions : it was conceded that
no one should be excluded from Parliament for refusing to
take the oath ; but what was substituted was little better,
that those who refused the oath should be liable to a penalty
of £500, and that for each session. Such an amendment
could pacify no one.

---

[1] Ruvigny, June 21 : 'Les évêques étant joints avec plusieurs Seigneurs ont paru
superieurs dans la chambre haute.'

These resolutions contain the strongest manifestations of the Anglican and monarchical idea which had yet appeared. The King renounced his Catholic tendencies in contradiction to his brother, who declared himself opposed to the bill. Protestantism was to be the foundation of the government, but a Protestantism entirely royalist in politics; the theory of non-resistance which the Presbyterians rejected was to become the doctrine of the state, and was alone to grant full civil rights.

It lies in the nature of things that such a proposal should awaken the most active opposition. The French ambassador often alludes to a society of confederate lords to which Buckingham, Wharton, Ogle and Shaftesbury belonged; the last-named peer must be looked upon as its intellectual chief. In their opposition to the doctrine of non-resistance, they were the natural allies of the Presbyterians, whose leader was Lord Hollis: they may be looked upon as the first Whigs, although this term was not imported from Scotland till a few years later. They took up again the tendencies which they had formerly defended against Lord Chancellor Clarendon, and for the sake of which they had separated themselves from the Catholic-minded administration. Danby's policy was undoubtedly Protestant, but it bore an analogy to the exclusive privileges which in France and in the domains of the house of Austria were attached to the confession of Catholicism. These lords opposed the minister through personal dislike, and his policy through political conviction.

In the Upper House, as we have shown, they effected nothing; in the Lower House they had adherents, but it was thought that the bill, as it had passed in the Upper House, would also pass in the Commons, where the Cavaliers, who were on the Church side, were in the majority. What means of opposition existed?

Between the Upper and the Lower House a dispute broke out which made their co-operation impossible. It was generally supposed at the time that Shaftesbury, to avoid the danger, had purposely inflamed the quarrel. And it is true that those lords who opposed the bill set themselves, in the course of this dispute, against every possible reconciliation.

But the two occurrences have also in themselves an internal connexion.

The Upper House had exercised, in a case in which a member of the Lower House was the defendant, the right which belonged to it, as the supreme judicature of the kingdom, of receiving appeals from the decisions of the courts of justice. The Commons asserted against this the protection of their privileges.

Lord Shaftesbury then proclaimed himself the most zealous defender of the rights of the Upper House, and that from the general point of view of the necessity of aristocratic institutions. For, he said, there had never yet been a king, who had not supported himself either on a standing army or on the aristocracy. If the country did not wish to fall under a military power it must maintain its aristocracy. It would be unjustifiable if the Lords allowed themselves to be deprived of their right to the supreme judicature, for that was the life and soul of the House; it was just as good a right as any other in the country; as good as that by which the meanest man in the country possessed his cottage. From this point of view, of justly acquired rights and possessions, Shaftesbury combatted the idea of the divine right of the crown. For such a right could have been restricted by no human laws; the laws would be rules which the existing king approved of; they would not have an universal value; Magna Charta would lose its worth, for no king would be able to subject to an obligation the divine right of his successors. For this reason also he insisted upon the right of resistance, and upon the privilege of each individual to defend his rights should they be attacked. 'I will,' he exclaimed, 'serve my prince as a peer, but will not in any way destroy the peerage to serve him [1].'

We see that these old Whigs started with the most intense sense of their aristocratic rights. Whether it was intentional or no, the King found himself obliged, by the growing dispute between the two Houses, to prorogue Parliament from the 9th

[1] [Shaftesbury's speech was made on October 20, 1675, in the fifteenth session, not in the fourteenth before the prorogation of the 9th of June. Parliamentary Debates. Grey's Debates. Echard.]—Editor.

of June until October, without having attained his object in the most important matter.

Still Charles II declared himself not dissatisfied with the result of the debates; for it had not been found possible to detach his policy from that of France, or to overthrow his ministers, either Danby who had been attacked, or Lauderdale who was still threatened with an old accusation. The French ambassador on the other hand, remarked that the Parliamentary session had all the same been harmful both for affairs in general and for those of England in particular; it had kept alive in the allies the hope that they would be able to find a support in the English Parliament, and so had prevented them from consenting to the peace which Louis XIV offered: had the peace been once concluded, Louis would have been able to assist the King of England with more considerable means against his refractory subjects.

To keep England true to the French alliance was all the same necessary for the French, as their campaign just then took an unfavourable turn. The death of Turenne at Sasbach (July 27) was in itself equal to the loss of a battle; the French found themselves obliged immediately afterwards to retreat across the Rhine; then the courage of the allies awoke; the expelled Duke of Lorraine had the good fortune, a short time before his death, to see his soldiers triumph over the French (at the Bridge of Konzer, August 11), in consequence of which Treves also was wrested from the French.

In this state of affairs it was of decisive importance to Louis XIV either to keep England on his side, as far as she then was—for English troops still served under his standard—or anyhow not to let her go over to the side of his enemies. He was very ready to make it possible for King Charles to do without the grants of his Parliament. But about this a question arose. Should another prorogation follow, perhaps until the ensuing spring, so that at least the preparations for the summer campaign might be made without the participation of England, or was it not more advisable to await the meeting of Parliament at the appointed time, and if Charles II could do nothing with it, to assure him of a sufficient support for several years, on the condition that he should dissolve Parliament at once? After some consideration Louis XIV preferred the latter course [1]; it seemed better to deliver himself once for all, or at least for a long time, from this continual agitation; and he prevailed on the King of England to take the same view. It was agreed that Parliament should be assembled at the appointed time, and then should be called upon by the King to pay him the necessary subsidies; if then it made its supplies conditional upon a breach with France, it was to be dissolved, but in this case Louis XIV bound himself to pay King Charles an annual subsidy of 500,000 louis d'or—a moderate sum, which would be very well laid out should it enable him, at an important moment, to neutralise the English power.

The coalition on its side turned to Parliament. The Dutch ambassador, Van Beuningen, took a large house in Westminster so as to entertain his friends there; his persuasive power and his ingenuity caused the French ambassador serious anxiety. The French court had also enabled him, while Parliament existed, to make a House, as the term was; Louis XIV put at his disposal considerable means fo bribing the members.

In the summer of 1675 arrived the Spanish ambassador, Don Pedro Ronquillo, a man full of zeal in the cause of the European alliance against France, and of proud confidence in himself; he had made it his peculiar task to excite the members of Parliament against the policy of the King and the existing ministers; he also was provided with some means for bribing [2].

In the Parliamentary policy of the government the Lord Treasurer introduced a change, by entering less than his predecessors had done into relation with the leaders of parties, and more with their individual members, who were thus put into a position of immediate dependence upon him: he also thought it advisable to attach them to himself by means of money.

The sight of this corruption on all sides causes a feeling of

---

[1] Louis XIV to Ruvigny, August 27, 1675; already printed in Mignet iii. 360.

[2] Memorias historicas y politicas; from his papers in the archives at Brussels.

disgust. The English Parliament seems to offer itself as a wrestling-ground for foreign influences, like the Polish and Swedish diets. Meanwhile her own affairs still continued to be of the chief importance to England. It was principally the opposition to the Lord Treasurer, and to his whole scheme of internal policy, which provided the European coalition with friends in Parliament. So also in the case of the King, the actual cement of his alliance with the French was not merely the money; what bound him to them was that they made it possible for him to maintain his prerogative. The internal and external disputes merged in one another.

Of great importance to both was the new (the fifteenth) session of Parliament, which 'was opened on the 13th of October, 1675.

In the speech from the throne the King thought well to confess that hitherto he had not managed his expenditure in the best way possible; still he was not so extravagant as was said, and for the future things should be better: he demanded supplies to cover the loans which burdened the revenues, and to refit the navy. On the other hand, in the Lower House, on the very first day of the session, two bills of very opposite tendency were proposed, which affected respectively the court and the administration most directly and most sensibly; one for the exclusion of all Papists from Parliament, and the other for the appropriation of the collective receipts of the customs for the navy.

Don Pedro Ronquillo accounts it as an honour to himself that he insisted that the proposals of the government should be taken into consideration without delay, from anxiety lest otherwise, through the influence of the court, many votes, which at present might be counted upon, should be lost. Especially he directed his warnings against consenting to vote money to pay off loans, for by that means the King would become master of his revenues and would employ them to the advantage of France [1].

---

[1] In his letter dated October 28 he describes it as his intention, tener S. M. Brca en yndigencia y falta de dinero.'

As early as the 18th of October there ensued a decisive debate about the loans. They were reckoned at some £800,000 and were produced by the expenses of the last war, which never could be calculated in advance; but their payment was declared to be absolutely necessary, because the condition of the English forces was miserable; it would be impossible to prevent the King of France from landing in England with an army of 30,000 men. So spoke the friends of the government. Their opponents reminded them that Parliament had been opposed to the last war; was it now after the event to undertake its expenses? Should it by its subsidies afford means to continue the maintenance of an expensive court, or, as once before, of a pernicious policy? Coventry thought that there was no reason to dread a French attack upon England; for the interests of the allied powers would prevent them from allowing it. They knew very well that Parliament inclined towards them, the King's ministers on the other hand leant towards France; they would not be at all glad to see the ministers obtain free power of action by the relief of the revenues[1].

It was principally political reasons and suppositions which came under discussion. The one party wished to know that the kingdom had been made capable of defence, so as to resist whatever might happen. The others wished not to rescue the government from its embarrassments, and not to be guilty of enabling it to support France. Opinions wavered. The proposal for the reimbursement of the loans was at last rejected, but only by a majority of seven votes, 172 against 165. Don Pedro Ronquillo goes so far as to attribute to himself the credit of this vote; at least it was quite in accordance with the views of Spain and its allies.

Matters could not be pushed so far as regards the navy, for it would have made a bad impression in the country if there had been no disposition to do anything for it. £300,000 was granted to build twenty ships. But the opposition determined to entrust the administration of this money, not to the Treasury, but to the London Exchequer; for that was much

---

[1] Speeches of Meres, Powle, Birch. Grey's Debates iii. 307.

more secure than the Treasury, and they wanted to give the King ships, not money. This proposition seemed likely to be accepted; the members of the government inquired of the King what were his views; he enjoined them to oppose it with all their power[1]. Their principal argument was, that it looked like the beginning of an opposition government; soon Parliament would have one treasurer, and the King another: Pepys demonstrated that under the King, and especially under the existing treasurer, more ships would be built than under any other administration in the same time. Once more the government carried the day; by a small majority the resolution was passed to entrust the Treasury with the sum voted. The opponents insisted, all the more emphatically, that the money should be especially accounted for. The Treasury officials were threatened with punishment if it were not really used for the appointed purpose. A still greater innovation was also contemplated. Parliament was reminded that the receipts of the customs were originally destined for the navy, and that there never would be a navy until this appropriation was again renewed; this must be at once included in the bill before them. In vain it was objected that this brought together two entirely different things, and took away from the King more than it gave him, as most of the loans had been raised upon the customs' receipts, and so the administration would be made as good as impossible; the King would be deprived of his daily bread and left without a shilling. But the whole current of opinion set in this direction. The object was, to make it impossible for the government to interfere in the European war otherwise than according to the will of Parliament, which often broke out into violent outcries against France. The increase of the French fleet was to be opposed by the improvement of the English; and there was a great inclination to strike a blow at the royal household as it was then constituted. There was express mention made of Alice Perrers, in Edward III's time, and the effect of the mistrust which Parliament had exhibited towards her. On the 11th of November the resolution was passed, even by a considerable

---

[1] Ruvigny, 5th November.

majority—for in money matters discontent was most easily
aroused—that the appropriation of the customs to the navy
should not only be enacted, but also inserted at once in the
bill* for the new subsidies; from which it followed that this
grant itself would become invalid, unless the King accepted
the appropriation of the customs.

Through this resolution runs a vein of animosity; it could
not be carried out without putting the court and the administration into the greatest confusion.

At the same time the dispute between the two Houses had
broken out again with violence. The Commons turned to the
citizens of London to demand from them sympathy in their
cause, which was the cause of the people; on the other hand
the Lords affirmed, that the declaration of the Commons was
contrary to the laws and the constitution. This discord gave
the King occasion, on the 22nd of November, to adjourn
Parliament again. He did not go so far as to order the
dissolution of the Lower House, in accordance with his
promise to the French; for then the agitation about the new
elections would begin at once: but it was an unprecedented
suspension of parliamentary sessions which he announced; he
prorogued Parliament for fifteen months, from November
1675 till February 1676/7.

It is true, the case contemplated in the agreement with
France had not exactly occurred; it was not, nominally, on
account of foreign affairs, but on account of home questions
that the King closed Parliament; he only prorogued and did
not dissolve it. The French court, for one moment, wished to
maintain that only in the case of a dissolution was it bound
to the payment of the stipulated sum, and now might at least
count upon some abatement. But the English government
demanded the entire sum which had already been entered
into the receipt account[1]; the only question was, when the
payment would follow. The ambassador Ruvigny did not
consider it advisable even to allude to any objection; he
feared, by so doing, to awaken the opponents of France in the

---

[1] Ruvigny, December 5, 1675: ' Le roi d'Angleterre a fait entrer dans l'estat qu'il
a fait de sa recette, les 100 m. L. st.' So far then there had been agreement.

court itself. The Lord Treasurer had, after all, only consented hesitatingly and out of necessity to the agreement. Louis XIV acceded to the representations made to him : the payments were to be quarterly.

Infinitely more important to him was the neutrality of England than the sums of money which he paid.

CHAPTER II.

THE adjournment of Parliament was a decisive step for European politics. Occupied with the war against Sweden, and robbed at the same time of the help of England, the allies were not capable of accomplishing much against Louis XIV. Their successes were limited to the capture of Philipsburg. On the other hand the French maintained their hold upon Maestricht; they took Aire, Bonchain, Condé, and, what was most important to them, were able, at the beginning of the year 1677, to strike a decisive blow against Valenciennes. Their most splendid success in the year 1676 was obtained at sea. The Dutch had joined with the Spaniards to defend Sicily; three times the allied squadrons were beaten by the French, who, with a comparatively untried fleet, remained masters of the Mediterranean.

Whilst Louis XIV filled the world with the fame of the French arms, and maintained his preponderance in the face of a great continental coalition, Charles II gave himself up to the enjoyments of peace. He gave his desires full scope, and they became, as is so often the case with princes, the subject of calculation and intrigue.

In January 1676 there arrived in London Hortensia, the niece of Cardinal Mazarin, of whose marriage with Charles II there had formerly been so much talk. She had been married by her uncle to Armand de la Meilleraye, who took the title of Duke of Mazarin, but she had left him again, because he indulged too much for her taste in religious rhapsodies; she now came from Italy to England, ostensibly to visit her

cousin, the Duchess of York. It seems as if a party in opposition to the existing government, with which the Duchess
of Portsmouth stood on good terms, wished to try if the
King's former inclination to this lady might not be again
awakened, and so through her a different policy gain influence
over him. Arlington, who some time ago had again quarrelled with the Duchess, was thought capable of lending his
hand to this scheme. One of his friends, Montague, went
to meet the new arrival, and acted as her escort[1]. She appeared in male attire; amongst her suite a little Moor, who
accompanied her, attracted general attention. She took up
her abode in St. James's, and managed, according to her
custom, to assemble round her at the English court a
brilliant company. She was still beautiful, at least to the
French she appeared more beautiful than any English
woman; she had a smattering of literary cultivation and
a gift for conversation, which visibly exercised an attractive
power upon the King. The French ambassador took upon
himself one day to warn him against her charms; he was a
little afraid of her[2]. Madame de Mazarin thought that she
had a cause of complaint against Louis XIV, because in her
matrimonial disputes he had taken her husband's part; it was
expected that, if she gained any influence over Charles II,
she would use it to the disadvantage of the French King,
were it only to make him feel that he ought to have shown
her more consideration.

In reality however the King's inclinations at that time
were directed towards another quarter. Ruvigny's successor,
Courtin, took great credit to himself for having established
friendly relationships between the two ladies who were considered to be rivals, but who both belonged to France. The
way in which this was brought about is characteristic. One
day two other ladies at the court invited themselves as his
guests, on condition that each might bring a friend. One

---

[1] Ruvigny, January 2, 1676: 'il a ses desseins.'

[2] 'Il nous a fort assuré, qu'il ne se laisseroit pas gagner; mais elle est belle:
il luy parle plus volontiers qu'à personne, qu'il va rencontrer dans son chemin'
(June 8).

brought the Duchess of Portsmouth, the other the Duchess
of Mazarin. The two ladies found themselves unexpectedly
together, and were purposely left alone; a short conversation dispelled every cloud between them; hand in hand, and
in good temper, they returned to the company.

Though reassured in this quarter, the Duchess of Portsmouth, conscious that she was no longer in her first bloom,
still had the sorrow of seeing that Charles II was by no
means faithful to her.

What scenes then occurred! One day, during a visit of
Courtin's, her heart overflowed; whilst she thought of the
King's faithlessness[1] her words were interrupted by sighs,
and she wept loud and passionately: all the time her two
waiting-women stood leaning against the wall, their eyes fixed
rigidly upon the floor. Courtin sought to comfort the Duchess;
above all he represented to her that she must submit to the
King, and take care of the boy whom she had borne him; he
was called the Duke of Richmond.

Lady Castlemaine, who now bore the title of Duchess of
Cleveland, had long ago been thrown into the background with
the King. She went just then with her two sons, one of
whom was Arlington's son-in-law, to live in France, according
to her rank, but with greater economy. We are reminded
of the first lines of Dryden's Absalom and Achitophel, when
we learn that Nell Gwyn also had two sons by the King.
She lived at that time at Windsor, and by her lively wit
always exercised a certain influence over the King. By the
people she was almost beloved, as the King's Protestant mistress; the Duchess of Portsmouth, as the Catholic mistress,
was extremely unpopular[2]. She was able also, in spite of
his infidelities, to maintain herself always in the King's
favour, who liked to see society at her house. For the French
ambassadors, it was an object of policy to maintain this
relationship, for it was in the Duchess's apartments that they

---

[1] Courtin, whose letters begin in June 1676, remarks about this 'chagrin, que
les fréquentes visites du roi d'Angleterre chez Mme. de Sussex lui causent tous les
jours.'

[2] Cunningham, The Story of Nell Gwyn, p. 120.

saw the King most unreservedly; they did not forget to gratify the lady herself from time to time with delicate attentions, with charming and sometimes even costly presents.

Louis XIV, as is well known, lived also in similar relationships. But with him everything had more propriety and method; he kept his politics and his sensualities farther apart. For he set before himself splendid ends, and employed consistent diligence to attain them; his personal pride supplied him with a kind of force, and he possessed the gift—for I consider it an inborn gift—of commanding obedience. Charles II, with his affable and easy manner, was not entirely deficient in this quality; he had as much intelligence as Louis XIV, or even more: it is also a mistake to think that his excesses estranged him from public affairs; he was what is called a roué, a man of pleasure, but still a man who wished to achieve something in the world. The principal difference between the two men lies in the point of view from which they acted. Louis XIV had constantly before his eyes the extension and security of the French frontier on the east and north, the acquisition of the Spanish monarchy, and the religious and political independence of his kingdom: the internal opponents of his crown had been conquered before his time; he need only keep them down. Charles II had taken as his aim the reestablishment of the royal authority. To be obliged to submit the prerogative to the influence of Parliament seemed to him to give only imperfect enjoyment of the crown, and in consequence of the vacillations of parliamentary parties and resolutions, to afford no security: to conquer this opposition was the aim of his life, an aim which in reality always remained the same, and which he pursued through ceaseless perplexities. He continually returned to this point, and always in a different way; he had no hesitation in shaping his external relations to suit home affairs. Louis XIV represented his country, and carried with him men's sympathies for his aims; Charles II always held a party-position in his kingdom, and whilst wishing to maintain this position, was always falling into a troublesome contest with an element which rested upon ancient right, had public opinion in its favour, and was already too powerful for him. The faults of Louis XIV disappeared in the light of his great successes, and he was admired in spite of them. On the other hand, Charles II excited against himself the independent feeling of his people, both in foreign and in home affairs; from his faults the evils which occurred seemed to spring.

During the fortunate progress of the French arms, attention was called, in the course of the year 1676, even in the court of Charles II, to the consequent danger which might ensue for England herself. Charles II then replied, that this very power of France made it advisable to avoid all hostilities with her. He felt only one anxiety, that was, lest the French should conclude a treaty with the United Netherlands to the disadvantage of England. We would be justified in calling his care for trade and naval power the second aim of Charles II: naval jealousy of Holland lay deep in his soul; he felt no continental jealousy of France. To prepare the way for a comprehensive treaty of alliance, which was always under discussion, Charles II proposed that a personal engagement should be made by the two Kings, that neither would enter into union with a third state without the consent of the other. In France this was agreed to, because nothing was more dreaded than an understanding between Holland and England. But with a merely general consent the English on their side were not content: Danby raised new scruples. He only accepted the scheme for the treaty when the engagement made by the two Princes, not to enter upon any new treaties without consulting one another, was expressly extended to the Netherlands also. Danby and Lauderdale examined the treaty and negotiated about it; they had all the share in it which ministers usually have in the conclusion of state treaties, but they had scruples about signing it, because it might some time or other turn out to be very dangerous for them[1]. The King himself thought the deepest

---

[1] Ruvigny, February 17, 1676: 'Le grand trésorier a été voir le duc de Lauderdale, à qui il a représenté le péril, qu'il y auroit pour leurs têtes, s'ils étoient seuls à délibérer sur le traité et à le signer.' They demand that the other ministers also should be informed about it. But the King refuses; he will not even sign any full powers of treating for which the Gieat Seal would be necessary: 'Qu'il avoit

secrecy necessary, on the ground that he had accepted the position of a mediator at the congress at Nimuegen, and with this a separate treaty with one of the great belligerent powers agreed badly. He copied with his own hand the treaty, as it had now been drawn up, and then signed it in the presence of the French ambassador, who informs us that the King himself lighted the taper to melt the wax upon which he then pressed his privy seal.

The French ambassador remarks, that this result was of especial importance, because the King was thereby pledged, and this must in time react upon the nation also. He always urged the dissolution of Parliament, which so decidedly set itself against both the prerogative and the French interest. A new one, he thought, would not be worse, and might be better.

From an opposite side a similar proposal was made to the King. The allied lords, of whom we have spoken, were far from having obtained that influence to which they aspired. By new elections, which would principally bring Presbyterians into the House, they might hope to win entire preponderance. They gave the King to understand that the new Parliament, if he granted freedom of conscience, would bring order into his finances, and above all would pay his debts.

Under this twofold pressure the question which had already been so often raised, whether Parliament was not at last really to be dissolved, was once more deliberated on all sides: in the end however, the old reasons against it once more prevailed. The King was afraid of a considerable increase of Presbyterians, and especially of an opposition on points of principle, whilst after all the existing assembly agreed with him on the fundamental principles of the royalist party. He remarked that during the last session he had wanted only a small number of votes to insure a majority on the disputed points. Danby left no means untried to secure the necessary votes for the

---

resolu de signer le traité de sa main et d'y apposer son cachet en ma presence, si V. M. l'assuroit par un billet écrit de sa main qu'elle a signé ce traité et qu'elle y a mis le cachet, il le recevroit avec plus de confiance, que si un de ses ministres y auroit été temoin.'

next session, and this still seemed possible. During the last half of the year, all the measures of the government were directed to this object.

A treaty of commerce, which was brought about between France and England in November 1676, principally aimed at calming the antipathies which the privateer war of the French had awakened in the capital. On the ground, or under the pretext, that an understanding existed between the great merchant firms of Amsterdam and London, a considerable number of English vessels had been seized, and because their cargo did not consist of English, but of Dutch goods, they had been condemned by the French prize-court. The French were informed that, if this were not put a stop to, a storm would break out in Parliament, which the King would not be able to resist for a fortnight : Louis XIV might, if he liked, invade Scotland; that would not injure him so much with the English Parliament as a violation of London's commercial interests. Upon this the French determined to publish an ordinance, which distinctly forbade the seizure of English, Scottish, or Irish ships provided with a pass by the King of England or by the custom office, or even by civil magistrates in the three kingdoms. On the urgent demand of the English, the French government granted them this concession, even for a period extending beyond the conclusion of the present war.

The result has shown that even this concession, which the French made very unwillingly, did not procure them as many friends as they expected. But the minister, in consequence of this advantageous agreement, was enabled with greater security tɔ face Parliament, on which all eyes were now fixed. What aided him in this was the unpopularity of the existing House. It was considered quite inadmissible that a certain number of men should remain for so many years invested with the right to represent the counties and corporations, whilst the opinion and confidence of their constituencies had altered : the constitution of England demanded frequent and fresh Parliaments. The minister took Parliament under his protection against these attacks. We know that he caused the author of a pamphlet, in which the Lower House was attacked, to be arrested, and would not even admit him to bail. With this intent the political discussions in the coffee-houses were also watched.

These were the contests which, on the reopening of Parliament, first led to an entire change of position.

With such means much effect cannot be produced on the public mind. Immediately before the expiration of the adjournment, in spite of all precautions, thousands of copies of two fly-leaves were distributed, in which the assertion was put forward that the Lower House, by the excessive length of its prorogation, was in deed and truth already dissolved. For an act of Edward III prescribed annual Parliaments, and its regulations had been always silently retained in later alterations; in decisive contradiction to this stood the last prorogation, 'which ordered the Parliament not to meet within a year, but some months after. Wherefore this last prorogation of Parliament is void and null.... Parliament cannot meet by virtue of such a prorogation': the new Parliament was no longer a Parliament.

And now, on the 15th of February, 1676/7, as soon as the opening speeches had been made, before even a proposal was made or a debate begun, these views were advanced in both Houses of Parliament.

In the Upper House Buckingham brought forward the question with his usual wit and energy[1]. He ventured to say that if the King in this case broke the law, then in a word there existed no law in England; the King might then abrogate the Magna Charta and the Statute de tallagio non concedendo, he might deprive every one of his property. Whether he was quite serious in this might indeed be doubted. The allied lords, who saw clearly that they would not have a majority in this session, had taken up this idea to procure the dissolution of Parliament. But, even in their own circle, by no means every one was fully convinced of the justice of their arguments. Salisbury, Wharton, above all Shaftesbury,

---

[1] In the Journal of the Lords there was at first mention made of these discussions. After the resolution passed in 1680 they were cancelled but not destroyed.

supported Buckingham; but Hollis, who after all, as leader
of the Presbyterians, had the greatest interest in the matter,
was silent: Halifax brought forward many arguments in
Buckingham's favour, but at last summed up against him;
the remaining lords were decidedly opposed. It was asserted
that the old statute had never yet been so interpreted, and
that in its application especial regard ought to be had to
existing custom; but if it were so interpreted now, at most
this would only amount to a grievance; it would be impossible
to declare subsequent Parliaments illegal because former ones
had not been summoned.

In the Lower House the same question was agitated by
Lord Cavendish, who demanded that the act of Edward III
should be laid before the House; but it was objected that,
according to this supposition, the Lower House did not rightfully exist, and therefore had not even the right to have
these acts laid before it or to take them into consideration:
how was it to deliberate about the question whether it existed
or not? The reading of a bill, for the introduction of which
leave had been already given in the last session, was proceeded
with, and the business of the House actually began.

Now however it becomes evident how much the Lord
Treasurer had gained by this. His enemies seemed to be also
the enemies of the existing Parliament, and he was its ally.
Suddenly again in possession of the majority, he conceived
the idea of using the favourable moment by returning his
opponents' attack. On the very first day of session, Lord
Freshville, who had at the time a seat in the Upper House,
joined with Lord Arundel in remarking, that the contempt with
which the existing Parliament was treated by the Lords called
for censure, and brought forward a motion on the subject: on
the following day a resolution was passed. Buckingham put
himself on his defence, but he felt at once that he no longer
met with approval, and retired unobserved. The House decided that the four Lords must ask pardon for their mis-
demeanour against Parliament: Salisbury, who had expressed
himself moderately, was to do so from his seat with uncovered
head; Shaftesbury, on the other hand, who had spoken with
the greatest vehemence, was to do so kneeling at the bar;

they were to ask pardon of the King and the House for having spoken with contempt of Parliament. As they refused to submit to this, they were condemned to be confined in the Tower at the pleasure of the King and the House. In the case of Salisbury, Shaftesbury, and Wharton, this was at once carried out[1]; they only entreated that their cooks might accompany them, as though they would otherwise run a risk of poison. The King, who was present, regarded this imputation as a new and heavy offence; but he himself desired that their request should be granted. The next day Buckingham excused his absence with a jest, and he also was taken to the Tower.

This occurrence completed the ascendency of the leading minister. The allied lords, from whom the opposition hitherto had proceeded, were obliged to take up their abode in the Tower, and were thus excluded, if not entirely from all influence, still from daily and direct influence on Parliamentary proceedings.

In the Lower House the demands of the government were agreed to, in spite of the resistance of the old opposition, which was even itself convinced that the position of European affairs made an increase of the naval power necessary; it was doubly objectionable that English seamen should take service in the French fleet, because they were not occupied at home. Still the old opposition did not mean to advance beyond the former grant of £300,000 for twenty ships. But the officials of the Admiralty demonstrated that it was better at once to take in hand the construction of thirty ships. It made a certain impression when Pepys called attention to the service done by the Stuarts to the navy, as for instance by Charles I, with whose great men-of-war the Commonwealth had been able to resist the Dutch, and especially by Charles II, who gave as much as he possibly could both for the construction of ships and the equipment of officers. 'The King has not spent this year on the navy less than £400,000. I will give it under my hand, that that hand may witness against my head if it be not so[2].' The

---

[1] Courtin adds to them Lademar (Latimer) also.

[2] 'Most august is the King's seminary for seamen.' Pepys' speech, Grey's Debates iv. 118. Still the feeling always remained that the payment was a 'necessitas necessitata': in reality so much was not necessary.

most zealous adherents of the crown wished to go still further. In consequence of an understanding between them and their moderate friends, a grant of £600,000 was carried.

When it was considered how this sum was to be raised, and the ships not only built but maintained, the idea again arose of decreeing in the money-bill at the same time the appropriation of the customs to the needs of the navy. But it was affirmed, with still greater emphasis than before, that, in so doing, two distinct things were confused; for in accepting a money-bill the King only expressed his thanks; if they chose to compel him at the same time to give his consent to a bill which imposed restrictions on him, they would injure the constitution which reserved to the King a veto. For this right men had fought and shed their blood; the freedom of the King was the freedom of Parliament; they must maintain it, otherwise they would return to the errors of the Long Parliament, whose decrees it had been necessary to annul [1]. The final resolution was, that no decision about the appropriation of the customs to the navy should be introduced into the money-bill.

The possibility of such an appropriation was still kept in view, but already a great success had been won by the fact that the new grant was saddled with no condition, and that regarding the appropriation of the customs the King's right of assent had not been prejudiced.

Whilst, however, in this manner Parliament and government approached nearer one another in questions of finance (which are always the most urgent), the idea prevailed that it was possible to discover means of accommodating the other questions also, with which men's minds were occupied.

With the consent of the Duke of York, the Lord Treasurer introduced into the Upper House a bill for the better securing of the Protestant religion, in case a Catholic should ascend the English throne. In this bill, naturally, it was again provided that the Prince should undertake no innovation in religion without the consent of Parliament; for how could Parliament

---

[1] March 5, G. Downing's speech. Grey's Debates 184. 'That power (not to be dissolved) they obtained tacked to a money-bill.'

have allowed its legislative power to be restricted on this point? But the most important point was to limit the royal prerogative as regards the appointment to bishoprics. It was intended in this matter to extend the Test Act to the crown also. The oath drawn up against the acceptance of transubstantiation was to be tendered to the successor of the throne by the Primate, and if he refused to take it, the right of presentation to the vacant ecclesiastical dignities was to be held by a commission, composed of the highest ecclesiastics, who were to present the names of three persons to the Prince, out of whom he should choose one. Without attracting much attention this bill was carried in the Lords. In the Lower House also it reached its second reading. But in every word the debate shows with what anxiety, even then, the Duke of York's accession to the throne was contemplated. And however closely the Lower House might be allied with the clergy, it still did not wish that they should become too powerful. It was feared that the bishops might in the end allow themselves to be led over to Catholicism by a determined king. The proposal was made, in all seriousness, that bishoprics should be given to none but married men, for they alone were thought safe; only in upholding a point which the Popes could never concede, was the security of the Protestant religion seen.

The most lively differences, and even open quarrels, were excited in the House by the debates about continental affairs. Just at the moment when Parliament re-assembled, the King of France succeeded in taking Valenciennes; immediately afterwards Cambray and St. Omer, after the Prince of Orange had been beaten back at Montcassel, fell also into his hands; he might be looked upon as master of the Spanish Netherlands (March and April 1677). At this the old antipathy necessarily revived in Parliament with redoubled strength. All other grievances, said Coventry, were trifles in comparison; now only did it become apparent how powerful France was in Europe: peace once concluded, she would find an expedition against England practicable; then the intrusion of Popery might also without fail be expected. The Spanish ambassador, Salinas, and his colleague, Fonseca, did not neglect to fan the flame. An address was published, in which the Upper House also joined, calling upon the King to calm the anxieties of his kingdom by fitting alliances. He was advised to enter into the Great Alliance, and no secret was made of the desire that he should take part in its war against France: promises were given of most vigorous support.

This put King Charles into the most violent passion. That Parliament wished to give him advice in the administration of foreign affairs, and that too under the influence of a foreign embassy, he considered as an insult to his honour. In conversation with Salinas he had let fall, according to his custom, contemptuous words about his opponents in Parliament; the ambassador did not keep them to himself, and this enabled the King, without much ceremony, to expel him from the country. After some disagreeable bickerings, over which it is not worth while to delay any longer, he adjourned also this session of Parliament in displeasure [1].

At an audience of Beuningen, who also alluded to the sympathies of Parliament in favour of an alliance with the allied powers, he threw his handkerchief into the air with the exclamation, 'I care just that for Parliament.'

But how strange, and yet how exactly like Charles II, was it, that whilst rejecting the demands of his Parliament with insulting contempt, he had himself decided to do with his own hand exactly what they demanded: he thought that he saw before him circumstances, by the skilful use of which he might satisfy the Parliament and the people, and might at the same time raise himself to be master of the situation in England and even in Europe.

---

[1] On this point the reports of the Brandenburg ambassador, Schwerin, are also valuable. In Orlich's extracts their contents are to be found; still the original form is preferable.

CHAPTER III.

DYNASTIC AND POLITICAL ALLIANCE OF CHARLES II WITH THE PRINCE OF ORANGE.

CHARLES II's connexion with France was in itself by no means so close as it had been before and during the war of 1672. At that time all his ambition was bound up with it; he flattered himself that he would humble Holland, and by the accomplishment of his Catholic scheme, gain the mastery over Parliament. Now the whole position of affairs was different; peace had been concluded with Holland and the Catholic scheme abandoned; the old ministers had fallen, and their successors again paid attention to the public temper. Thanks to the very advantages which France procured from the alliance with England, the continuation of that alliance offered day by day greater difficulties; the national feeling opposed it all the more passionately.

If formerly the dynastic considerations in favour of the Prince of Orange had contributed to the alliance with France, this connexion also was now quite changed. The Prince disdained a union with the two Kings, but made this difference, that he set himself up as the opponent of Louis XIV, while on the other hand he was intent upon drawing Charles II over to his side. We know how the internal affairs of England tended to incline the King towards him, how he felt himself moved to propose to the Prince a marriage with his niece.

The Prince had not yet accepted this proposal, but had never lost sight of it for a moment. Before beginning the campaign of 1676, he talked about it one day at the peace congress with the English ambassador Temple, whom he had summoned to his side in his garden at Hondslarsdyk. He did not disguise from him that, even from England, he received warnings against it, because it would attach him too much to the court, which just then by its conduct was precipitating itself into the greatest dangers. Temple rejoined that in his opinion the English crown already rested on firm ground, on account of the universal dislike to any other constitution; between the Prince and the King however there naturally existed a close connexion; one might do the other the greatest harm or procure for him the greatest advantage; for the Prince it would be a great gain if he drew another step nearer to the crown, and in all appearance became the nearest to it. The Prince also inquired concerning the personal qualities of the Lady Mary; for a wife, he said, who should give him disturbances at home would be unbearable. Temple, who knew the governess of the Princess, bore the highest testimony to her, so far as her youth allowed any judgment in the matter [1].

We see what was passing in the Prince's mind. He still put off a decisive step. As yet his general position was not quite secure; now for the first time it acquired firmer outlines according to the universal law, through effort and the resistance which it provoked. The commission which the Prince received, after the revival of the office of supreme Statholder, to set in order the three provinces of Utrecht, Guelders, and Overyssel, which had been estranged during the war, seemed to open to him the way to sovereignty. At the first diet which the province of Guelders held through his permission, the estates, nobles and towns passed a resolution to offer to the Prince, whom God had wonderfully raised for their deliverance, the rule over them, with the title of Duke of Guelders and Count of Zutphen[2]. William answered that, before he accepted the proposal, he must first hear the other provinces. In them however this proposal awakened the greatest anxiety; it was felt that the approval of such an extensive

---

[1] Temple, Memoirs, chap. ii.; Works ii. 335.

[2] Resolution des états de Gueldre, 19 Janv. 1675; in Samson's Histoire de Guillaume III, iii. 375. The event itself we find more clearly related in Wagenaar (Bd. lv.), whom Grovestins (iii. 16) has taken as his foundation.

change in one province seemed to infer an inclination in all the others to imitate it. The first founder of independence had, it is true, at one time been saluted as Count of Holland and Zeeland. That in these provinces a like tendency still existed, the friends at least of the house of Orange always positively affirmed; one day at Zuylestin, in the presence of the Prince, although much to his vexation, his health was drunk as Count of Holland. But in reality republican principles, once held even indispensable to the progress of commerce, had since then taken the deepest root in Holland and Zeeland. The Prince's question was answered with the advice that he should follow the example of Gideon, to whom Israel after its deliverance offered the sovereignty, but who refused it. The Prince's answer to Zeeland[1] shows how deeply he felt himself wounded by the want of confidence shown towards him[2], but he gave up the intention. He explained to the estates of Guelders that he could not accept their offer, because it would awaken jealousy. He refused the princely title, but gave to the three provinces an organisation by which he acquired a kind of sovereignty. In the remaining provinces the attempt had already excited men's minds; the repressed aristocratic party obtained once more a standing ground. Offence was now taken at the independent manner with which the Prince had been accustomed, in times of danger, to administer military and even financial affairs: it was said that he conducted himself as if everything belonged to him; men even became suspicious of his moral qualities. There again broke out, between the tendencies which inclined to monarchy and those which were purely republican, the strife which had from time to time thrown the Republic into the most violent agitation, and had so often revived under different fórms.

But now it also befell the Prince that the scanty results

---

[1] Réponse du Prince d'Orange aux Etats de Zeelande, 18 Mars, 1675; in Samson iii. 396.

[2] Letter from Middleburg, May 1677 : 'The Prince of Orange lost the affecting of the chief men and of the people. They find him daily more and more dissembling covert and sailing in his word and promises. No account given by him of any money; disposes of all as of his own.'

of the campaign in the year 1676 interrupted his good understanding with the allies. His failure to relieve Bouchain by
a resolute attack upon the French, he attributed to the hindrances put in his way by the Spaniards ; that he had then
failed to take Maestricht he ascribed to the non-arrival of
the German auxiliary troops, and to the Emperor's lack of
zeal ; but the loss of the battle of Montcassel was evidently
more the fault of the Netherland troops ; that Charleroi had
not been taken, the Spaniards ascribed to the ill-will of
William himself. For in military disasters those concerned
always throw the blame upon one another. The Spaniards
spoke of the Prince as a traitor, coming as he did of a traitorous stock.

Meanwhile in the Netherlands a universal desire for peace
spread on all sides. Men were not only weary of the allies,
but thought that they perceived in the conduct of the war
the one-sided interest of the Statholder, which they were
determined to resist.

Under these circumstances, his position being neither quite
secure nor quite satisfactory, the Prince turned his eyes to
his uncle in Great Britain. As early as the beginning of the
year 1677, he caused overtures to be made through Temple ;
in June of that year he sent over to him his most confidential
servant, Bentinck : it was agreed that at the end of the
campaign the Prince himself should go to England [1].

Charles II greeted with joy these approaches of his nephew.
In the Prince's quarrels with Spain he saw the opportunity
of acting in accordance with the wishes of his people and
with the necessities of his own position, without thereby sub-
mitting to the demands of Parliament, which had no idea
of the real situation of affairs.

In September 1677 the Prince arrived in Newmarket,
whither the English court was in the habit of retiring after
the business of Parliament. He took care not to mix himself

---

[1] In a collection at the British Museum, Add. 21, 492, which contains a number
of original documents, and deserves a place as a supplement to Groen, we find,
'J'ai une joie extreme de ce, que le roi a temoigné, qu'il consentira qu' à la fin de la
campagne je fasse un tour à Angleterre—si en avant ce temps je n'ay la tête
cassée.'

up with the prevailing party divisions; from his old friend Arlington he kept as far aloof as possible. Danby, the minister now in power, was perhaps even more actively attached to his interests, and met his wishes half way. At first he avoided speaking of political affairs; it was only reported that he spoke unfavourably of the Spaniards, by whom he had been left in the lurch. The King returned a few days sooner from Newmarket to Westminster, on purpose to give the Prince an opportunity of making the acquaintance of the Princess. William of Orange had, as was mentioned, one especial motive. He knew well that he would be an exacting husband, and he wished above all to convince himself that he need not expect domestic discomfort from his future wife. The Princess Mary, who was then fifteen years old, left on him the impression that such would not be the case, but that she would attach herself entirely to him; he did not hesitate to ask the Duke of York for his daughter's hand.

The Duke's attention had long ago been drawn by the French court to the danger which he might one day incur from a son-in-law who should follow an entirely different political and religious direction, and have his own party in England: he was told that Louis XIV looked on the Prince of Orange as his chief enemy. Still this produced at the time no impression. The Duke, indeed, said that it was not he himself, but his daughter, who was to marry the Prince of Orange; marriages had often occurred in royal houses without producing any change of policy. At the same time he had a good reason for giving way; the creation of a hope of the Prince's succession in England (although only uncertain, for the Duke's wife was still young) might be advantageous to him, so far as it tended to weaken the immediate opposition to his succession to the throne. The King said that there was one party which aroused ambitious hopes in the Prince of Orange, by which they hoped to gain him, but this marriage would teach him to see his future greatness only in friendship with the King of England, and in a firm attachment to his interest. By a union of the whole royal house, to which the Prince also belonged, its opponents were to be deprived of the hope which they grounded upon its divisions.

But the external politics of Europe played as great a part in forming this union as did the internal politics of England. The King of England withdrew a step from his alliance with France, and formed the intention of bringing about, in concert with the Prince of Orange, universal peace upon durable conditions acceptable to all parties. Many negotiations were carried on, in which the King declared his opinion that Louis XIV, if he once had peace, would adhere to it: this the Prince and Temple disputed; at last it was agreed to establish the following basis for peace :—restoration of Alsace and Lorraine, and in return cession of Franche Comté; in the Netherlands, the restoration to the Spaniards of nine places which they had lost, amongst others Valenciennes and Condé, so as to form a secure bulwark for the Belgian country and for eastern Europe. The Prince undertook to secure the consent of the Spaniards, the King that of the French. This idea was almost the same as that which had prevailed in the Triple Alliance, but was more comprehensive and better founded; the King of England had no longer to come to an understanding with a Grand Pensionary whom he hated from the bottom of his soul, but with a Prince united to his house by new and intimate ties; even then, the intention of the naval powers had been to allow Franche Comté to pass to France, and this had only been prevented by Castelrodrigo's far-seeing policy.

On receiving the King's consent, the Prince had announced his betrothal to the States-General; on his return with his young wife he was greeted with popular rejoicings.

Still stronger perhaps was the impression in England itself, where fears were already entertained that the young Princess might be married to the Dauphin, and by that means the right of succession to the English crown transferred to the house of Bourbon, so that England would incur the danger of becoming in time a French province[1]. The King received

---

[1] W. Temple to John Temple, Nov. 1677 (Works iv. 366), mentions the 'apprehensions of some greater matches that might befall us, with consequences ill enough to posterity as well as to the present age.'

visits from members of the Parliamentary opposition who came to express their gratitude. He said, he hoped that he had now convinced them that he did not mean to change the religion and government of England.

Now, however, he had at once to face the question, what form his relations to his former ally, Louis XIV, would assume.

Charles II had by no means the intention of breaking with France, because he drew nearer to the Prince of Orange ; on the contrary, the whole idea of his policy tended to such an alliance with his neighbours as would make it impossible for any one of them to exercise an influence adverse to himself over the internal affairs of England. He thought that he had enough influence with Louis XIV to prevail on him to accept the conditions of peace on which he and the Prince had agreed. On this account he did not, as had been first decided, send to France Temple, who might be looked upon as an adherent of the allies, but rather Lord Duras, now made Earl of Feversham, by birth a Frenchman, a member of the house of Durfort-Duras. Duras enjoyed the confidence of the Duke of York, and was considered French in his sympathies. Through him Charles II entreated the King of France to accept the conditions which he proposed, for even then the peace would be one of the most glorious and advantageous which a European prince had ever concluded. If he, the King of England, had hitherto looked at the progress of the French power without jealousy, still he could not let it go further without being regarded in England as a traitor to his own crown. Moreover Louis XIV might do something for his sake.

Charles II was thoroughly assured that the King of France would remember the inestimable advantages, which so far he had derived from their good understanding, and would at the same time take into consideration the position of the English crown, which, if it rigidly maintained its present policy, might awaken an opposition which it could not be able to resist.

He was soon to realise how much he deceived himself.

Louis XIV kept in vivid distinctness before his eyes his great aim, the acquisition of a northern and eastern frontier,

such as would for ever secure his country, and especially his
capital, from foreign attacks: he thought that he was just
on the point of obtaining this object, when the proposals
brought by Lord Duras ran counter to it; he did not feel the
slightest inclination to accept them out of consideration for
Charles II and his prerogatives. He answered by proposing
a truce, during which negotiations might be carried on for
a general peace; but although it was evident that even the
negotiations about the truce, which would have to be carried
on both in Vienna and Madrid, required considerable time,
he had not any intention on that account of restraining the
course of his arms. On the contrary, at that very moment,
in December 1677, his troops had occupied St. Ghislain,
which till now had been of the greatest importance for the
defence of Mons; there was no doubt that he would at once
advance further. In the midst of the festivities which greeted
him on his return, the Prince of Orange was disagreeably
startled by this news.

Under the impression produced by the negative answer and
the late capture—an impression not less strong in England
than in Holland—the plenipotentiaries of the two powers, on
January 10, 1678 (N. S.), agreed upon a treaty of alliance, to
bring about peace on a basis to which, in its main points, the
Prince and the King had consented, and which will presently
be stated in detail. They are convinced that the King of
Spain will agree to their proposals, which aim at procuring for
the Spanish Netherlands a secure barrier against France. If
the King of France should refuse to do so, the two naval
powers will unite all their forces to compel him to it; peace
once brought about, a guarantee is to be established in the
most secure way imaginable; and thus the repose of Christendom will be assured [1].

Charles II still paid so much consideration to France as
to put off for a fortnight the general opening of Parliament,
which had again been summoned, so as to leave time for
further negotiations. When this delay led to nothing, he
opened Parliament on the 28th of January, 1677/8, with a

---

[1] This treaty is taken from Du Mont.

speech, in which, as regarded the alliance which had just been concluded, he announced his intention of enforcing peace by arms if he could procure it in no other way. This corresponded to the sentiments which Parliament had always openly held ; another of its demands was also satisfied by the recall of the English troops which were still in the service of the French.

Upon this the outbreak of war between England and France was seriously expected. A letter from the leading English minister invited the Prince of Orange to enter into consultations about common measures for the war in which, in the following spring, England would be as deeply engaged as Holland herself[1]. The union of England with the opponents of France seemed to be imminent, and a consequent change in the whole relations of Europe.

It was thought at the time, and afterwards, that King Charles was not serious in these demonstrations. And who indeed would vouch for his general truthfulness? But in this case the interest of his crown, which he always kept in sight throughout his political vagaries, lay in this direction ; not indeed in the war itself, which was only the less welcome alternative, but in an energetic mediation for a peace in accordance with his proposals. A durable establishment of the frontier of the Netherlands seemed desirable also to assuage the unruliness of the English Parliament, which threatened otherwise to interfere even in the management of external affairs, and the same purpose was also served by the new dynastic alliance with the house of Orange. But still another idea on this point occupied the King's mind. For energetic mediátion, no less than for actual war, was the establishment of a standing army necessary ; and if such an army were formed, its influence upon Parliament would certainly strengthen the royal authority. Charles II had himself hinted at this in confidential circles ; though he had no desire to oppose Parliament, or put it on one side, still his idea was to induce it to make the concessions which his financial

---

[1] Danby to the Prince of Orange, Dec. 8, 1677 : 'The fault will now lie on your side of the water, if you have not either the peace upon the terms proposed, or us engaged as deep in the war as yourselves.' Danby's Letters 162.

position demanded, and then for a time to dispense with it. In this way he would have gained a great position in Europe, the acquisition of which he always regarded as one of his aims, if not the principal one. The new alliance between Holland and England was designed with the same view as the Triple Alliance had formerly been.

Parliament agreed with delight to this anti-French policy of the King's. The zeal of a considerable majority in the Lower House, who demanded the re-establishment of the terms of the Peace of the Pyrenees, had to be restrained rather than encouraged. On the 5/15th of February a resolution was passed, to support the King with money in behalf of the alliance which he had just concluded with the confederate states for the purpose of resisting the French supremacy; on the 6th, it was further resolved that, for this purpose, ninety ships should be equipped, and on the 8th, thirty-two regiments—twenty-six of infantry, four of cavalry, and two of dragoons—were added; ten days later the proposals which aimed at a more moderate vote of money were rejected, and it was decided to raise £1,000,000, to enable the King to proceed to actual war with France; for this purpose, on February 23, the imposition of a poll-tax was agreed to, from which no one who did not receive alms was to be exempted. A prohibition of French merchandise, as strict as it was extensive, accompanied these resolutions. The fact that Louis XIV, just when things were in this position, succeeded in taking so important a place as Ghent, caused the warlike spirit to prevail over all demonstrations of opposition. A regiment of English troops was transported to Ostend, the Spanish government allowing it under these circumstances; some battalions were sent on to Bruges. These were the oldest and most trustworthy of the English troops. An encounter was all the more expected, because it would be of importance to the King of France to annihilate these choice troops. The Duke of York, as late as the 1st of April, 1678, expressed to his son-in-law his opinion that the war would break out, for he knew the temper of the French. The Prince of Orange had taken up a position at Boom, so as to cover the Scheldt and Antwerp, though only with very indifferent forces; the

Duke assured him that he might expect speedy succour from England, the levies were already making the best possible progress [1].

But would the King of France, now that everything seemed to have been decided, allow a renewed outbreak of the war, by which all his previous successes might be endangered?

---

[1] The correspondence between James and William was first communicated in part by Dalrymple; Grovestins and Groen have completed it.

CHAPTER IV.

NOT by force of arms only was Louis XIV accustomed to meet his enemies; it was one of his maxims to raise up on his own side their natural opponents, internal as well as external. Feeling himself, if not endangered—he was still too strong for that—yet hampered in the execution of his plans, by the alliance between Charles II and the Prince of Orange, he had entered into connexion with their political opponents in both countries.

It is an important event in English history, not only that this should have happened, but, still more, that it should have happened as it did.

As long as Charles II adhered to the French alliance, and Parliament desired an alliance against him, Barrillon had attempted, by managing influential members and sparing no money in so doing, to restrain the impulse of the majority. Now when the King himself drew closer to the majority, we cannot wonder that the ambassador still continued his endeavours. He represented to his court, that any money he might give to such members as would be influenced by it would be very well laid out. Had nothing more been involved in this than the money, we should only have to do with an ordinary human weakness, of which there would be no need to give a detailed account. But the connexions which Barrillon sought to make, and for the most part succeeded in making, have a much wider bearing.

By the alliance of Charles II with the Prince of Orange the

Prince's former friends in England were, as he clearly foresaw, disagreeably affected ; for it was brought about by the minister whom they hated, and whose importance they did not at all like to see increased.

In other respects Danby's system of allying the monarchy with the Anglican Church had made great progress during the session, from which the chief opposing lords had been excluded. These lords had indeed since then returned to their seats, and had agreed to make the explanations required of them. Their old friends, who wished to introduce a popular system, gathered round them again ; they had a support in the Presbyterians, but they could cherish no great hopes, should Danby succeed by his Protestant and anti-French sentiments in allaying the opposition which till now had been shown him by the majority. In that case it became indeed possible that the Duke of York would be recognised as successor under restricted conditions, that the new system would be perfected and secured for ever by the establishment of an armed force, and perhaps by an advantage gained over France. Each of them saw in this a personal danger.

The lords were in this temper when Barrillon caused proposals to be made to them. This was done by a former secretary of Arlington's, who was also connected with the Presbyterians ; but principally by the younger Ruvigny, who came to London about the negotiations which still continued between the two courts, and, without awakening notice, visited the old acquaintances of his father and the families with which he was connected. The lords did not reject the overtures of the French. But it was not their intention only to serve the King of France and await what might then occur ; they conceived the idea of using this connexion as a means towards their political objects. Ruvigny consulted with Buckingham, Russell, and Hollis. The first said to him that King Louis XIV must consent to be in future a friend of the nation, to defend them in their old rights, and to stand by them in all their interests [1] ; then in the impending

---

[1] Barrillon, Feb. 7 : 'Si on voulût faire entendre que le dessein du roi (de France) est, d'être des amis de la nation et de la maintenir dans tous ses droits et ses

questions they would also stand on his side.   Hollis and
Russell added that they would not be content with indefinite
declarations, they demanded some firm security.   With this
information Ruvigny proceeded to his King's camp at Ghent.

It was a very remarkable relationship, though perhaps not
unique, into which the French embassy now entered.   It still
carried on the communications between the two Kings;
Ruvigny took the respective proposals backwards and forwards.   Barrillon maintained his former connexion with the
Duchess of Portsmouth, who dreaded nothing so much as an
interruption of the friendly relations between Louis XIV
and Charles II.   She occupied herself with trying to discover
some means of accommodation; this was one of her subjects
of conversation with Charles II; they might be seen sitting
together over a map of the Netherlands, considering what
might or might not be granted to the King of France.
Whilst in this manner the old friendship seemed to prevail,
Barrillon was weighing the individual characters of those
members of Parliament with whom it would be most advantageous to unite against the existing policy of the King: in
February he remarked that he had promised money to some,
but on condition that the declaration of war should be prevented; for without real results he would not agree to any
payment[1].

In the meanwhile Ruvigny returned from Louis XIV's camp.
The King of France had once more rejected Charles II's proposals, and on the other hand had consented that the English
lords should receive the security they demanded.   Ruvigny
failed in his attempts with Hollis, who took a different
point of view, but with Russell he succeeded in coming to •
an agreement on the subject. Russell refused any fellowship
with men who received money from the ambassador; he was
most pleased at learning that at that moment a real under-

---

privilèges, il étoit sûr que la France auroit dans son parti tous ceux, qui se sont
toujours opposés aux desseins du roi d'Angleterre.'

[1] Feb. 24: 'Les Anglois avec qui j'ay relation, me font espérer de trainer les
affaires encore quelque tems.   J'ai redoublé mes soins pour les encourager.   Je
me suis advancé de promettre des recompenses effectives à condition expresse
d'empêcher la guerre.'

standing no longer existed between the two Kings: Ruvigny
assured him that Louis was far from having any intention of
making Charles II an absolute monarch. This at once brought
another motive into play. Russell, as well as Shaftesbury
and Buckingham, wished for the dissolution of the existing
Parliament [1], for only in a new Parliament could they find
any sympathy for the ideas they cherished. But the dissolution seemed only possible through the influence of Louis XIV.
That he gave notice of his intention to aid in this object, since
the Parliament was also extremely odious to him, was a thing
that had been much desired. Russell's plan now was, to put
the King of England once more under the necessity of seeking the friendship of Louis XIV, so that Louis might use his
influence for this purpose. But he called attention to the
fact, that this plan could only meet with success if it were
kept secret; for otherwise the members of Parliament would
employ every means to frustrate it. Without any consideration of any kind he would attack the Lord Treasurer, and
even the Duke of York and the remaining great Catholics:
he did not hide his project of bringing about the exclusion of
the Duke of York and the Catholic lords from the Upper
House.

We recognise the ideas of the systematic opposition:—
dissolution of the Lower House with its Anglican sympathies
—destruction of the Catholic element in the Upper House—
attack upon the Duke of York—fall of the minister: all
through the help of the French King, to whom in return such
services only were rendered as were otherwise in accordance
with the views of the opposition.

They could not exactly oppose the declaration of war
against France, as they had formerly themselves proposed

---

[1] Milord Roussel dit à M. de Ruvigny, que luy et tous ses amis ne souhaitoient
autre chose que la cassation du parlement, qu'ils savoient, qu'elle ne pouvoit venir
que du côté de France, que puisqu'il les assuroit que c'étoit le dessein de S. M. d'y
travailler ils se voyoient obligés de se fier en luy et faire tout leur possible pour
obliger le roi d'Angleterre à rechercher encore une fois son amitié et mettre par ce
moyen S. M. en état de contribuer à leur satisfaction.' Mémoire de Barrillon,
14 Mai. In Dalrymple ii. 158, and in Lord John Russell's Life of William Russell,
ch. vi. 103, other motives for this are here mentioned which have been overlooked.

it, but they sought by indirect means to hinder it[1]. In the party disputes such violent expressions were let fall, that the King sometimes feared an intention to force him into war, so as to rule him all the more easily in the perplexities which would consequently arise, and to subject the crown to Parliament. On his side the Duke of York made known his fear that the declaration of war would lead to a persecution of the Catholics. Whilst they entertained the intention of declaring themselves against France, they were already afraid of the consequences. The King, who even under these cir-cumstances was assured by the French ambassador of the support of France, in case he were obliged to prorogue his Parliament, did not entirely reject his offer of help. There was once more talk of a money payment, if peace were con-cluded upon the conditions proposed by the King of France. Charles II said that, in the existing temper of the nation, he would then have to fear a rebellion, from which he could only be protected by very considerable support. Against his opinion, and with an express protest that it was not by his advice, the Lord Treasurer let himself be persuaded to confer on the matter with the French ambassador. He named a sum of 6,000,000 livres (tournois) annually for three years as his probable demand.

How in all this are open negotiations and secret intentions intermingled! The French wished to persuade the King of England to peace and the dissolution of Parliament, by pro-mises on the one hand, and by stirring up the opposition against him on the other; this dissolution was all important for the allied lords, they regarded on that account even a good understanding between the two Kings as desirable, whilst openly they still spoke in favour of the war. And now Charles II was embarrassed: whilst he pursued a direction hostile to France, and threatened her with war, he was still afraid of detaching himself from her; in spite of all his pre-cautions and his cleverness, he had no suspicion of the con-

---

[1] 'Ils employent toute leur industrie pour éluder la guerre par des longeurs affectées. Autrefois ils proposèrent la guerre, parcequ'ils croyoient, qu'on ne la feroit pas: présentement quand ils voyent, qu'on y est assez disposé, ils ont une grande envie de la traverser.' Barrillon, March 3.

nexion between the French and the opposition in Parliament; he sought support from France against those very men with whom she had allied herself.

But, whilst England was thus embarrassed, the French policy was even still more successful in Holland: the Prince became sensible of the reaction caused by the affair at Guelders, which had given fresh life to the aristocratic party[1]. The multitude may have greeted his marriage with joy, but the aristocrats had no pleasure in the dynastic union which he thus concluded. The treaty, concluded under the joint influence of the King and the Prince, met with no approval from them, and was in their eyes suspicious. Estrades, who even after his dismissal remained in communication with his friends, called their attention to the fact that the new alliance gave the sovereignty to the house of Orange; the existence of a secret article was hinted at, in which the two states were said to have agreed to support each other against their respective rebels, and this might have serious results; we hear of secret friends of the old ambassador who employed themselves actively in spreading abroad the intent of the English league. The result was that the alliance was not ratified by the States-General.

For the patrician burgomasters and representatives in the Netherlands were far more powerful than the lords of the opposition in England, since they undoubtedly possessed a share of the chief power; they turned away from the proposals agreed on between the Prince and King Charles, and inclined to those made by France. .

No one denied that the former were the more beneficial, but still there was no inclination to continue the war to secure them. The capture of Ghent had, moreover, a depressing effect; for what exertions would be necessary to recover from the victorious King his booty, and what danger lay in leaving it in his hands! But it was precisely this which he promised to give up if peace were concluded. The ultimatum presented by Louis XIV at Nimuegen, reserved indeed great

---

[1] In Mignet iv. 546. 'Son Altesse,' as is said in another letter, 'donne grande jalousie et s'attire mille malédictions.'

advantages for himself, but contained an offer to give back eight considerable towns, amongst which was Ghent; it was well received in Holland. Two parties, which till now had divided the town of Amsterdam, joined in approving of the French proposals; the example of the most powerful town was followed by the rest. A stately deputation was despatched to the camp of Louis XIV and found him at Wetteren; a truce for six weeks was agreed on, for the purpose of securing during that time the acceptance in their integrity of the conditions proposed by him. In vain the Prince of Orange opposed it. He prevailed upon himself to address a conciliatory letter to Louis XIV.

In the meanwhile the King of England had also submitted to what was inevitable. To avoid becoming dependent on Parliament he yielded, in return for the promise of the six millions of livres tournois, to the hard conditions which the French imposed upon him. He accepted their proposals of peace, and promised not only to dissolve Parliament, but also, what was still more important for Louis XIV, to disband his military forces. These were just the points in which the French interests coincided with the wishes of the lords; these were the very demands they had made.

This was the position of affairs; the schemes of the King and the Prince were shattered by the influence of the French on their opponents at home: at Nimuegen great exertions were being made for the complete establishment of the peace, which even the Spaniards no longer opposed; when suddenly, on the very spot, a difficulty arose which threatened to throw everything back again.

To a question asked by the Spanish ambassador in Nimuegen, with regard to the time at which the promised restoration of the eight places which had not been ceded to France might be expected, the French ambassador answered without reserve, that it must be delayed until the countries and territories taken from Sweden during the course of the war by the Elector of Brandenburg had been restored. For whilst Louis XIV concluded a favourable peace, he did not wish to see those ruined through whose alliance he had obtained his great advantages. But it was not in this way that the Dutch and the Spaniards had understood the conditions which they accepted. They did not wish to make the establishment of the frontier, in which they saw their future security, depend upon the chance of persuading the Emperor and the Empire to agree, in contradiction to a promise made to the Elector of Brandenburg, to the establishment of the Swedish dominion in Germany, and upon the Elector's own submission.

In Holland the news of this demand made a most decidedly unfavourable impression. The common talk at the street corners was that the peace would consequently turn out a hoax. Louis XIV would keep the strongholds, or at least demolish them; under the excuse of the Swedish misunderstandings, he might begin the war again at any moment. In all the towns a different temper spread from that which had formerly prevailed.

Still stronger was the reaction in England. With a kind of joyful haste Charles II seized this new prospect of a breach, not so much on account of European interests or out of sympathy for Brandenburg, but because he saw in it the means of avoiding the oppressive obligation of dismissing his troops, which was being imposed upon him from two different sides, and of returning to the policy which he had planned in concert with the Prince of Orange. He did not lose an hour in making it known to the Lords, who were just about to discuss the dismissal of the troops; they resolved that it should be put off for another month. In the Committee for Foreign Affairs there was only one opinion about the inadmissibility of the French demands, and the necessity of resisting them at any price. Temple was sent back to Holland without delay, and as he undertook the commission because he thought matters were now in earnest, his word, in which the Dutch put confidence, produced a great impression. On the 26th of July a new compact was formed, in which the two powers united to fix a period of only a fortnight, within which the King of France must abandon his lofty pretensions; if not they would carry on war against him until he should be driven to re-establish the Peace of the Pyrenees, or at least to accept the conditions which had formerly been proposed to him on the part of England. The policy of Charles II and the Prince of Orange were again in the ascendant.

Once more by this means war seemed to be imminent; the previous delay was even looked upon as advantageous, since it had given time to exercise the crews meanwhile, and to send a reinforcement of troops to the Netherlands. After the Spanish ambassador, who to his own astonishment received marks of favour, and the confidant of the Duke of York, Lord Duras, had convinced themselves on the spot that a favourable result might be expected, the King's natural son, the Duke of Monmouth, was sent thither with the order, at the expiration of the appointed interval, to unite with the Prince of Orange, who had likewise taken the field; it was decided to maintain Mons by a common effort. There were skirmishes at sea between the French and English ships, such as had formerly preceded an open breach. Charles II refused to ratify the treaty which had been last agreed upon with France, because there could no longer be any question of dismissal of the troops under circumstances like the present, and he did not think fit to prorogue Parliament.

By this turn of affairs no one was more confounded than the lords of the opposition, the friends of France in both Houses. They observed that it was of no use to them for France to demand the dismissal of the troops, because that made the King take the side of the confederates, nor. for France to raise difficulties with regard to the peace, because that gave him an excuse for keeping the troops together: until the army was disbanded no friend of France would be able to do her any service, but, when peace was once established, Charles II would be able to undertake nothing against the friends of liberty, who were also the friends of France; the nation would then rather rebel than endure that[1]. In a word, the English opposition demanded that their ally, Louis XIV, should give way.

I feel no doubt that, on this occasion, this consideration

---

[1] Barrillon, July 25: 'Ceux, en faveur desquels V. M auroit voulu obtenir le licentiement des troupes, ne seroient pas en état, de rendre aucun service. Ceux, qui sont les plus amateurs de la liberté du pays, désirent fort la paix.'

influenced the King of France; moreover just then an expedient was suggested to him from England, which made it possible for him to yield a step with honour.

Together with the Swedish plenipotentiary at the congress of Nimuegen, Olivenkranz, who was at that time in London, an agent from Holstein, Du Cros, also took a great part in the negotiations in the name of Sweden. We learn that he was in the confidence of the French ambassador, of the Duchess of Portsmouth, and of the Earl of Sunderland, who all now most urgently desired the conclusion of peace[1]. The expedient hit upon in London was, that Sweden herself should liberate the King of France from that strict obligation. Without being empowered by his court, Olivenkranz went to Nimuegen, and expressed his opinion to the French ambassador that that obligation only concerned the general peace, and not special treaties, the only aim of which was the diminution of the number of the enemies of the two powers. Later Olivenkranz was called to account by his government for his unauthorised conduct. Louis XIV however seized the expedient with delight; the internal relations of England were now matters of consideration for him. Barrillon had called his attention to the fact, that it was not at all his interest to repel the friends of freedom and support absolute government in England. The appointed time had not expired when Louis XIV authorised his ambassadors to withdraw from the condition which till now had been attached to the evacuation of the strongholds. They did not lose a moment in making use of this permission, as they were convinced that otherwise it would be impossible to prevent the renewal of the war, which, thanks to the participation of England, would become doubly dangerous; they even went further in accessory points than they were empowered to do by Louis XIV. Then the Dutch could not refuse to confirm the projected treaty, to the effect that they would remain neutral in the struggle between Germany and the North. After a conference of five hours, on the appointed day (July 31/Aug. 10), the plenipotentiaries of each party united in signing the peace as it stood.

---

[1] Temple's Memoirs (Works i. 465).

In this the duplicity of Charles II once more appeared in a glaring light. He persuaded himself to advise the Swedish ambassador to adopt this line of conduct, not because he wished for peace, as he says in a letter, for it was already his opinion that Louis XIV was inclined to give way anyhow; he only wished to enjoy the credit with him of having caused the Swedish suggestions to be made.

This did not prevent him from ordering in the same breath the exchange of the ratifications of the Dutch agreement, which contemplated a state of war; this took place after the peace had been already concluded. But as yet peace was not generally believed in; four days even after it had been signed, a bloody encounter in the field took place.

The French were besieging Mons, and for a long while it had been the intention of the confederates at least to provision the place, which apparently would be otherwise obliged to surrender: on the day on which the peace was signed at Nimuegen, the Prince of Orange set himself in motion with his army, which had been joined by the English, who had come over under Monmouth's command; on the 4/14th of August, he fell in with Marshal Luxemburg, who had taken up a strong position at St. Denys. The Marshal knew that peace was concluded, but from a feeling of military honour he would not inform the Prince of the fact. The Prince as yet knew nothing about it; he attacked the French with vigour and won some successes, which were honourable for him without being decisive; the next day the news reached him[1]. Luxemburg also received orders to suspend hostilities.

The two commanders hereupon ceased their fighting, but the fact that blood had once more been shed gave rise to the universal opinion that war was even now more probable than peace. All the hopes of the allies awoke. At the English court and in London this prospect was greeted with delight. The government sent some more regiments to the Netherlands;

---

[1] When the Prince in his letter to Fagel says, Aug 15, 'Je puis déclarer devant Dieu, que. je n'ai appris la nouvelle de la signature de la paix qu'aujourd'hui à midi' (Grovestins iii. 164), I believe it unconditionally. Gourville's account (Coll Pet lii 482) must rest upon a misunderstanding.

the Duke of York wished to go over himself, and asked his son-in-law to give him notice of the fitting opportunity.

Charles II sought to hold the States-General to the compact concluded with him. He reminded them that the peace signed at Nimuegen did not correspond to the agreement made between them ; in the one France reserved to herself some exceptions from the evacuation of strongholds which had been determined on in the other ; this very reservation introduced the case foreseen by them, and brought their treaty into force. He called upon them not to ratify the peace, and promised that three days after receiving news of their refusal he would declare war against France. His exhortations were energetically supported by the Prince and his adherents.

If the peace were to be ratified, France must give up every reservation which she had therein made to the disadvantage of Spain. Once more Louis *XIV* gave way ; for it was necessary to deprive the intrigues of the King of England and the Prince of Orange of every excuse. By the mediation of the plenipotentiaries of the Republic, who inclined to peace, an accommodation was brought about which contented the Spaniards; and after this difficulty had been removed, the peace was ratified by the States-General (September 9/19, 1678). A new French ambassador appeared at the Hague ; he was commissioned to assure the Republic that his King would defend it from the ambition of the Prince of Orange and the schemes of the King of England.

Barrillon had incessantly reminded the King of France how closely his interests were allied with those of the English opposition ; he praised the services which it had rendered in preventing Charles II from taking part in the war against France ; and if it were Charles II's chief object to keep his troops under arms and so to subject England to his rule, Louis XIV should remember that it would not be his interest that the strength of England should be united in one hand [1].

---

[1] September 8: 'Les interests de V.M. ne paraissent pas être de laisser établir l'autorité royale (en Angleterre) de manière que toutes ses forces et sa puissance soient unies.'

By means of his ambassador, Louis XIV entered into new
connexions with the party leaders. It was only as a political
move that he gave way in the peace negotiations, and took
care to keep on his side the domestic opponents of the Prince
as well as of the King.

Their aim had been to take into their own hand the
decision of European affairs. As matters had turned out,
this decision was far more dependent on the union of
Louis XIV with the aristocracy in Holland and the opposition
lords in England.

But all was not yet concluded, as neither the Emperor nor
the other Princes of the Empire had accepted the peace;
on the contrary, the Elector of Brandenburg, trusting in the
imposing and well-disciplined army which he kept in the field,
urged with great zeal the continuation of the war. In England there was at one time an idea of making common cause
with the Swedes, for the chief thing was to avoid laying down
arms; but it was still more likely, and in the Privy Council
was seriously taken into consideration, that they should
in preference join the Elector of Brandenburg, and the other
German Princes, for the maintenance of the conquests made
from the Swedes. The proposal was made that by a grant
of considerable subsidies the Emperor should be put into a
position to continue the war [1].

In face of the strength of the Parliamentary opposition
there was little prospect of attaining this. Also it was not
so important for the government to produce a different
settlement of European affairs, as to make use of the continuance of disturbances to avoid disbanding the army.

Parliament had been adjourned in July: when it met again
on October 21/31, the King raised the question whether it
was a suitable moment for reducing the land and sea forces.
This was then discussed in greater detail by the Chancellor.
He demonstrated how necessary it had been to keep the

---

[1] Barrillon, September 26: 'On a informé (de la part du roi) quelques membres
du parlement, que s'ils vouloient donner de subsides à l'empereur, il continueroit de
faire la guerre à V. M. et que le roi de Danemark, l'électeur de Brandebourg, l'evesque
de Munster et les Princes de Brunswik s'uniroient à l'Angleterre pour conserver
ce qu'ils ont pris sur la Suède.'

troops together, and how greatly this had contributed to save the Spanish Netherlands ; that the money granted for disbanding the troops had been spent instead in carrying on the armament, needed no excuse, for it had been unavoidable. And even now the position of affairs required that they should continue to be ready for war. For what the allies recognised with gratitude, the protection afforded to the Netherlands, was looked on with quite different eyes by the other side. Nothing would be more gratifying to the enemies of England, than that she should be afraid of maintaining herself in a posture of defence [1].

Still, in spite of all that had passed, the government held to the old idea of making animosity to France a motive of its internal policy. As yet Danby had made no change in his system. If he maintained the armed force, he still believed he would be able, whilst protecting the Duke of York, to carry out his plans in favour of the Anglican Church, to uphold the prerogative, and to overpower his personal enemies.

But already signs had appeared, such as were alluded to in the speech from the throne, which threw the whole nation into agitation ; no man could calculate what effects they might have.

---

[1] ' Nothing in the world would more gratify our enemys, than to see us afraid of maintaining ourselves in a posture of defence, which is the only posture they are afraid to find us in.' Journals of Lords xiii. 294.

CHAPTER V.

DENUNCIATION OF A JESUIT CONSPIRACY. LAST SESSION
OF THE PARLIAMENT OF THE RESTORATION.

ONE day in August 1678, Charles II was walking in
St. James's Park, when an old acquaintance, by name Kirkby,
approached, and warned him not to separate himself from
his companions, for there was a plot against his life; he might
easily be shot even on this walk. Being ordered to come to
Whitehall in the evening to give fuller information, Kirkby
brought with him a London clergyman of Puritan opinions,
Israel Tonge by name, who gave the King detailed information about a Jesuit conspiracy, which was all the more credible as it came from a man who had just apostatised from the
Order, Titus Oates. Tonge had written against the morality
of the Jesuits; Oates affirmed that he had been commissioned to put him out of the way in consequence; but instead
of killing him he had made friends with him. He was in
possession of very offensive letters or extracts from letters.
Tonge first showed him their object and their full bearing.
In the information which Tonge communicated to the King,
he was so far himself concerned, and anyhow it was well
calculated to excite attention and anxiety[1].

These extracts were taken from the correspondence of
English Jesuits, who lived in London, with members of the
old Jesuit seminaries on the Continent, such as the Rector

---

[1] Titus Oates, his narrative, Journals of Lords xiii. 313 : this unites the original
information (forty-three points) and the later additions with some new evidence given
on cross-examination. ' The Jesuits unmasked,' and a similar pamphlet by Tonge,
appeared in 1678.

of St. Omer, the Procurator in Madrid and the Provincial in London : Oates had opened the letters which had been entrusted to him to deliver, and so had succeeded in gaining much additional information which he wrote down.

What at once becomes clear from all this may be easily imagined. The entire world of zealous Catholics, and especially the Order, had been much agitated when Charles II, from whom they had hoped for restoration, quarrelled with Louis XIV and took a direction in favour of Protestantism. There is no doubt that since then he had been spoken of in the seminaries in the most depreciatory language. The Jesuits themselves have charged Oates with having, in a sermon at St. Omer, made merry, in a scurrilous tone, at the uncertain religious bearing of Charles II [1]. St. Thomas Becket's day was begun with sermons against the supremacy and the oath of allegiance, as it was worded in England. Oates affirms that the King was described as a black bastard, that the legitimacy of his birth was disputed, and talked of as a deception which must no longer be tolerated. From other judicial depositions, independent of Oates, we learn that even in many English counties the King was spoken of in similar language : he was a heretic and excommunicated ; also on account of his evil life he deserved to live no longer ; whoever killed him might hope to be called a saint, for after his death, under his successor, a reform ·in England in favour of Catholicism might justly be hoped for.

Not only seditious utterances, but also hostile acts were mentioned in the information. Oates named members of the Order, who had been sent by it to the Presbyterians in Scotland, professing to belong to them, for the purpose of exhorting them to take up arms ; he declared that he knew of preparations in Ireland for opening a port to the King of France, as soon as the war between him and Charles II should break out ; he added that attempts were made to

---

[1] Statement of Haggerstone in the trial of Oates for perjury 1685. He said, 'that King Charles halted betwixt two opinions, and a stream of popery went between his legs.' State Trials x. 1113.

convince the Emperor, the King of Spain and the Governor Villahermosa in Brussels, that Charles II had no honourable intentions in his approaches to them, but only aimed at making his nephew an absolute Prince in Holland.

But the most important point was the denunciation of a plot devised by the Jesuits, for the immediate assassination of the King of England; at a meeting of English and foreign Jesuits in an inn in London, April 24, 1678—at which Oates affirmed that he had himself been present—this resolution had been formally adopted [1]. The meeting had in reality taken place, but it was engaged only on the private business of the Order: with regard to Oates, it has been almost certainly proved that at that time he was not in London at all. The Duke's confessor, a Jesuit, who had received letters, the contents of which bordered on high treason, had the presence of mind to bring them forward unasked; they were most probably forged. About the plans that had been formed for the re-establishment of Catholicism in England upon the death of the King, Oates made statements which contradict the actual position of affairs; they are without doubt false. Oates had been from his youth up notorious for the most shameless untruthfulness. He had a passion for startling people and giving himself importance by boastful and lying exaggerations, which he spiced with invective on every side, and confirmed with wild oaths: he was a small man with a short neck [2] and a mouth strikingly out of proportion; people were careful not to contradict him, as they were afraid of quarrelling with him. He mixed up what he knew with what he only guessed, or what seemed to him serviceable for his schemes, and he was believed by all. His successful shamelessness stirred up emulators, of whom Bedlow was one. But still it cannot be affirmed that all that they alleged was mere invention. 'There was some truth in it,' as Dryden says, 'but mixed with lies.' Moreover the fact that much of what they said as to matters which no one suspected proved true, led people to accept also the monstrous things they gave

---

[1] Statements of Stephen Dugdale. State Trials vii. 1230.
[2] North's Examen 225.

out. Coleman's correspondence, which Oates first described
and afterwards discovered, especially forwarded this impression ; its contents, relating to the bearings of the various
parties, will presently be spoken of. To this must be added,
that the public temper was at that time very sensitive in
this direction. In Louis XIV's undertakings religious intentions were at once presupposed ; the advantages which he
derived from the peace of Nimuegen seemed to be so many
disadvantages for Protestantism, and especially for England.
The name of Jesuit had been hated and even feared since the
times of Queen Elizabeth. It made no matter to the English
that the Order no longer held by Spain but by France ; men
thought there was danger of a new Gunpowder Plot and a
new fire in the city. As all that was well-grounded in Oates'
statements originated in the excitement of the Catholic world
caused by the impossibility of depending upon Charles II, so
the reason why his exaggerations found credence lay in the
corresponding excitement of the Protestants about the progress of the great Catholic power. The Popish Plot appears
as a symptom of the violent antipathies once more excited
between the creeds.

The King would rather have suppressed the matter, for he
was displeased at the fact that there was so much talk about
attacks on his life, which might inspire others with like
thoughts. Of Danby also, whom many wished to regard as
the secret originator of the denunciation, we know that he
at first treated Oates with a certain contempt[1]. Still the
information could not be entirely suppressed ; from other
sides also more of the same kind flowed in[2]. If the matter
had acquired publicity in another manner, it would have been
still more dangerous ; if the government itself took it in hand
it might perhaps be useful to it.

The King alluded to the matter in his opening speech,
although cautiously ; the Chancellor spoke of it most definitely
as one of the unjustifiable practices, by which it was intended
to introduce a strange religion into the country. The excite-

---

[1] So Barillon affirms, Dec. 26.

[2] Compare the very alarming letter of the Archbishop of Canterbury, Somers
Tracts, viii. 59.

ment into which men's minds had been thrown by the mere
report was increased to a kind of tumultuous pity and wild
terror by an occurrence which, till this hour, has not been
cleared up; a justice of the peace, who had taken part in the
preparation of the examination, was found murdered. The
man received a funeral which became a Protestant demonstration, before which the Catholics shut themselves up
in their houses; on the other hand two sturdy men stood by
the side of the preacher who spoke the funeral address,
as if the orator himself had to fear the fate of the victim
whom he mourned [1].

On the demand of Parliament, which it did not seem
advisable to oppose, the government published a proclamation,
by which all Catholics were banished from Westminster and
London, except such householders and fathers of families as
would take the oaths of allegiance and supremacy. The
military patents which had been given to the Catholics had
to be withdrawn; the Secretary of State who had signed
them barely escaped punishment. The King was entreated
to keep none in his guard who had not taken the test oath, to
let no Papists come to his court, still less hold any place in
his kitchen or cellar. Any one who doubted the immediate
danger of the King would have been regarded as a religous
and political heretic [2].

But against whom was this animosity likely to be directed,
if not against the Catholic members of the legislative
assembly? A bill was introduced, and reached its third
reading, by which Catholics were to be excluded from
both Houses of Parliament. After an examination of Tonge
and Oates by the Lower House itself, on account of their
information, five Catholic lords, Arundel, Powis, Stafford,
Petre, and Bellasis, whom they accused of participation,
were confined in the Tower. Bellasis was pointed out
as the future commander of the Popish army. Charles II
laughed at it, for the man could hardly keep his feet; how
was he to command an army? He observed how improbable

---

[1] North's Examen 203. No one had contradicted the report.

[2] Paoli Sarotti (secretario Veneto), 24 Oct. 1678: 'Né si puo aprir bocca in
favore de' cattolici senza correre qualche rischio '

and indeed impossible were many things in the denunciations, but here and there again a statement produced an impression upon him.

We shall not follow in detail the trials, which now for a time occupied both Houses of Parliament, the courts of justice, the juries, and through them the nation : from the accusations, defences, and counter-accusations, little that is historically certain emerges; it is horrible to see the long list of executions of those who confessed nothing. It is, as it were, a natural phenomenon in politics, showing the Protestant Parliamentary spirit defending itself, with all possible means which self-preservation put into its hands, against the opposing influence of the Jesuit-Catholic faction, as it had formerly done against the republican and fanatical sects.   But the position assumed by the two contending political parties, deserves careful attention. The tumult in men's minds did not originate with them, but they sought to make use of it.

As the Chancellor hinted that it would tend to the security of Protestantism if the King were thought to be in personal danger through its opponents, so the Lord Treasurer believed that, in the general excitement, the means would be secured by which King and religion, whose cause was identical, might be placed in safety : he hoped that the dismissal of the troops would not be insisted upon.

That this result was feared by the other side also, is evident from Barrillon's remark, that he would, and must, resist Danby's artifices; he also knew other clever people who were of opinion that the Treasurer would not carry his point in this way. .

But the best means for setting to work to separate the court and religion lay in the above-mentioned correspondence, which was found at Coleman's house, although it was dated some years back. It disclosed not only a secret understanding between the Catholic party and the French ambassador for the sake of influencing Parliament, but in it was stated, in so many words, that the Duke of York's object was directed towards obtaining at some future day, through the intervention of the Pope and the help of France and Spain, possession of his rights; after which he would show all possible favour to the Catholics [1]. Coleman was the Duchess of York's secretary; his letters left no doubt that the Duke of York agreed with them. Circumstances had changed since then; the Duke's disposition was rather anti-French; but how was this to be discérned in Parliament in the excitement of the day? The lords of the opposition, whose hostility was directed especially against the Duke, determined to use the circumstances to make·a decisive attack upon him. It was the important matter out of which the future fortunes of England were to develop; it was the question between hereditary monarchy and the religion of the country: in the midst of the general tumultuous commotion caused by religious differences, this question, from a kind of necessity, gradually came to the front.

As yet it had at the same time the form of a ministerial party question, about which the lords took counsel even with the French ambassador.

To him it was all-important to overthrow Danby and disband the army. Halifax, who now belonged to the union, and Buckingham, represented to him that, to obtain this object, the best means would be an attack upon the Duke. For the government, they said, could then either take him under its protection, or let him fall: either course would be destructive to it. In the first case, they would break with Parliament and find no support there; in the second case, the Duke would take up a hostile position towards the minister: he could no longer oppose, as he had hitherto done, the disbanding of the army, at the head of which he even now, with the consent of the minister, aspired to renew the war [2]. Barrillon let himself be persuaded; strange to say the lords, with the

---

[1] Coleman to the Internuntio, Sept. 4, 1674.

[2] Barrillon, Oct. 27: 'Si le tresorier donnoit la main et secondoit la chaleur du parlement, la persécution (des catholiques) se trouveroit si forte, qu'elle envellopperoit le duc d'York et lui feroit voir, qu'il a esté trompé par le grand tresorier, et qu'il faut pour sesauver qu'il ait recours à la protection de V. Mé; et qu'après s'être declaré directement contre ce ministre, il abandonne tous les desseins de guerre qu'il a eu, et celui de la conservation de l'armée.'

approval of the representative of France, began their attack
upon the Duke and his succession.

On the 1st of November a conference was held between the
two Houses, and it was resolved to take into consideration, in
every possible way, the means to be adopted for the protection
of the King, the constitution, and the religion of the country.

Upon this, on the 2nd of November, Lord Shaftesbury in
the Upper House opened the great attack. He said that it
ought. no longer to be concealed that there was only one
means of saving the King and the kingdom, and this was, to
ask the King to dismiss the Duke of York from his council.
This attack was aided by those lords who were in the compact, namely Halifax and Essex, as well as by Barlow, Bishop
of London : it was said that soon no one would know who
was actually King in England, nor whether there were two of
them or only one. The Lord Treasurer opposed the motion,
but with less zeal and energy than had been expected. The
Duke was present at the debate but did not speak a word.

This was on Saturday; on Monday, the 4th, Lord Russell
moved in the Lower House an address, that the Duke of
York be removed from the King's presence and councils.
The two secretaries of state, Henry Coventry and Williamson,
remarked that this would drive the heir to the throne to join
the side of the French and the Catholics, from whom they
desired to separate him ; and, even without this, the impending
danger might be avoided by obliging the magistrates, on pain
of punishment, to carry out the laws against the Catholics,
and generally by taking precautions to prevent the heir to
the throne from endangering the religion and government of
the country. But against this it was urged that the further
participation of the Duke in the King's council would make it
as good as impossible for such laws to exist. As yet in the
debates, the Duke of York was not refused the respect due
to his high rank. But no one allowed himself to be misled
by this. On the one side stood religion, the constitution
of the country, the life of the King ; on the other, nothing
more than consideration for an exalted personage ; who
could be undecided in such a case?

The King and his ministers measured the full bearing of

this movement: they felt the coming storm, but they did not despair of still allaying it. To escape being forced out of their path by anti-Catholic zeal, they decided to avoid its outburst by friendly concessions. The King prevailed so far on his brother that he, of his own accord, for the present ceased to attend the sittings of the Privy Council. Then Charles II turned with fresh assurances to the two Houses. He said 'he was ready to join with them in all the ways and means that might establish a firm security for the Protestant religion,' not only for his lifetime but also for the future; he promised his ready assent to the bills which should be laid before him for this purpose, so long as they did not tend to impeach the right of succession, or the descent of the crown in the right line, and did not restrain his power, or the just rights of any Protestant successor[1]. We see that he took up his point of view with considerable decision. His declaration, which seemed to announce even more than the actual words expressed, calmed men's minds; it was welcomed in the capital with demonstrations of joy. Not without hopes of attaining their end, men again took into consideration the conditions by which a king who did not belong to the Protestant religion, might be prevented from doing it any harm. In accordance with this, the King and the minister discovered a way, in a similar question, to satisfy in general the Protestant demands, and yet to maintain the Duke's position. The Commons' bill for procuring the exclusion of the Catholics even from the Upper House was introduced into the Lords, and, under the impression of the prevailing religious terror, was passed, much as it ran contrary to their claim to an hereditary right, which could not be forfeited, and to their feeling of dignity. But as to the intention to exclude the Duke of York, the Lord Treasurer succeeded, even at the last moment, by uniting for that purpose all his friends and adherents, in carrying (by a small majority it is true) an exception for him from this resolution. In the bitter antagonism of religion, a certain

---

[1] His Majesty's speech, Nov. 9, 1678. Journal of Lords xiii. 345.

recognition was still always paid to dynastic privilege, however much it might be attacked and diminished.

In his perplexities the Duke occasionally visited the French ambassador, and spoke with him about a renewal of his old understanding with France ; but Barrillon rejected all positive approaches, and would do nothing which might displease his Parliamentary allies [1]. Even the King himself made overtures to the Ambassador for the establishment of the old relationship, but only on condition that he should be released from the obligation agreed to in the last treaty, of disbanding his troops. What could it signify to Louis XIV whether he maintained 10,000 soldiers or not? He had absolute need of them for his own security. Barrillon made him a short and cutting answer, that Charles must seek his security only in his union with France. This was the point on which the Ambassador was inexorable ; it was precisely the point upon which from the first he had agreed with the opposition in Parliament.

Already the debates were concerned with military affairs. As any day a rising of the Catholics might be feared, against which it was necessary to be prepared, the Lower House resolved that a part of the militia should be put under arms, and be kept in arms for a fixed time : forty-two days was agreed upon [2]. But the King was far from giving his sanction to this resolution. He saw in it the intention of establishing a military force [3] of some 60,000 men, independent of his will, whom he might not disband under a month : he let it be understood that he would not bind himself to this for half-an-hour.

The news of this refusal again put Parliament into a state of irritation ; it was said that this also was the Duke

---

[1] 'Je ne ferai aucun pas de conséquence à l'égard du Duc d'York, que je ne concerte avec les principaux du parlement. Leur interest s'accorde si bien avec celui de V. Mé pour le licentiement de l'armée, que je n'ai pas de peine à les en faire convenir' (Nov. 14).

[2] 'Act for preserving the peace of the kingdom by raising the militia and continuing them for two and forty days.' In North's Examen 'seventy-two days' is without doubt erroneous.

[3] In the debate (Grey vi. 214) Bennett only remarks that by exercising the militia the guards should be made unnecessary.

of York's doing, because he did not wish that any vigorous step should be taken towards the suppression of the Catholics : the great question about disbanding the troops was resumed. Barrillon thought that now was the time to be generous, and so caused money to be distributed amongst those who were willing to receive it. He assured those who refused it that Louis XIV wanted nothing but parliamentary freedom in England. He desired the disbanding of the troops only to prevent Charles from being in a position to put a bridle on the English. It was then particularly that Algernon Sydney negotiated the connexion between the ambassador and the heads of the opposition, and did Barrillon good service. This influence was now stronger than the intrigues of the King and Danby. In the decisive debate the old resolution that the troops should be disbanded was affirmed and repeated. The country party, which was forming itself in opposition to the court, was on this point at one with the lords of the opposition. At the same time another question was decided, which had been often raised in opposition to the court. Attention was called to the fact that the money granted for the disbandment of the troops had, when paid into the Treasury, been employed instead in keeping the troops together. In vain Downing exerted his powers of persuasion in behalf of the government. This time the resolution was actually passed to set aside the Treasury, and intrust the Exchequer of London with the payment of the money (December 1626, 1678).

By these resolutions the position of the Lord Treasurer, against whom personally the last had been directed, was seriously shaken : already he tottered, but still maintained himself ; the French ambassador, however, had prepared a new engine by which to achieve his complete fall.

Ralph Montague, recently English ambassador in France, had quarrelled with the Treasurer because he had refused his request to be advanced to the post of Secretary of State. In politics also they had ceased to be friends, since the minister had gone against the French alliance. Montague, on his side, was one of the foremost adherents of this alliance ; of his own accord he returned to London with the determina-

tion openly to attack and overthrow Danby, for which purpose he had, as he told Barrillon, an infallible means in his
power. This was some letters sent by the minister, during
the last negotiations, to the Ambassador, in which in very
plain terms the payment of those six millions was treated as
the price of the dissolution of Parliament. Danby, for his
own part, had disapproved of this undertaking, and had only
written the letters at the King's wish: Montague had possession of them and brought them with him. There could
be no doubt that their communication to Parliament must be
fatal to the Treasurer. As English affairs stood, however,
it was necessary to set to work with some care. Montague
had first to procure his election to Parliament, not without
communicating some part of his project to those who assisted
in advancing him; these were also the friends of the French
ambassador, who had promised him besides the protection
and favour of Louis XIV in case the undertaking should fail.

The moment was only awaited when a decisive effect
might be expected from this disclosure. Danby himself gave
the desired opportunity. He had heard that Montague intended to accuse him, and knowing well on what he meant
to ground his accusation, he thought it wise to get possession
of his papers. To be able to proceed to this step, he contrived
that there should be sent him from Nimuegen information of
a correspondence between Montague and the Papal Nuntio.
Under pretext of this communication he ordered the seizure
of Montague's papers [1].

But the Lower House insisted upon its right of bringing its
members first before its own tribunal; the papers were put
in their portfolio upon the table of the House. Montague
remarked that amongst them there were some which would
show a great minister of the King's in a different light than

---

[1] Barrillon's despatches about this affair have already been printed by Dalrymple. Lord Russell, in the first edition of his work, expresses a doubt as to
their trustworthiness. He gives them up in the second edition of his work about
his ancestors. In these random extracts not only the decisive influences, which
make the matter comprehensible, were overlooked, but the whole has a party colour
which is unhistorical.

was expected, and drew out those letters in which the acceptance of the peace of Nimuegen was made dependent on a payment of six millions, and at the same time the desire to be independent of parliamentary grants was expressly alluded to. The communication produced, as could not but be expected, an overwhelming impression. Already in the last debate there had been talk of the arbitrariness of Danby's financial administration, and of the possibility of founding an impeachment upon it; this now became at once the universal demand; all clamoured for it.

The next day Danby produced some letters of Montague's from which the true state of things might certainly have been perceived, if any one had had sense left for it. But the commotion about the conspiracy had already produced the habit of seeing treasonable plots everywhere. In many respects Danby must be regarded as in himself an ally of this Parliament; he was one of the most zealous champions of Anglicanism, and with his whole heart an opponent of Popery and almost equally of France. But at the same time he strove to maintain the prerogative and to preserve the hereditary succession; he intended in all sincerity to avoid by legal restrictions the encroachments of a Catholic successor; his idea was, to unite sovereignty and hereditary succession with a parliamentary constitution and the support of Protestantism on the Continent. Whilst, however, by holding fast to the sovereignty he lost the sympathies of Parliament, it happened also through these false disclosures that he was regarded as a partisan of France and at the same time of the Papacy. Two different parties, who both had no other object than the dissolution of Parliament, combined for this purpose. The Lower House had no suspicion; easily deceived in its tumultuous excitement, it lent its own hand to the scheme. It raised an accusation of high treason against the chief minister, who in the most important matter was its ally.

The Upper House did not consider the impeachment sufficiently well grounded. Danby still had an opportunity of clearing himself from most of the accusations brought against him, and this he did in a very telling speech, but he did not answer them all; for had he wished to divert them from himself, some would have fallen upon the King, and he felt scruples about doing this. But as these accusations were the heaviest in the balance, and as the violence of the Lower House was doubled by the opposition of the Lords, who in such cases had already often yielded, he had no hopes of saving himself, unless the King decided to dissolve Parliament. We know how often this had been already talked of, and then rejected on account of the dangerous consequences it might have. But now Charles II decided to do it, not only out of consideration for his minister, but also for his brother's sake, who had just been threatened with a new attack. At the end of December 1678 he prorogued the Parliament once more, and on January 24, 1678/9, he declared it to be dissolved.

Of all the Parliaments that ever existed in England none have filled so many years with more uninterrupted energy than did the Parliament whose eighteenth session was then concluded : it sat from 1661 to 1678. It has imprinted upon the English constitution the deepest traces of its activity, and that in two different directions.

During the first years, in opposition to the Commonwealth, it restored the repute of the royal prerogative; in the later years it not only defended parliamentary rights against monarchical and ministerial deviations, but extended them materially in some of the most important points, such as the superintendence of finance and the responsibility of the minister; it established for all times the parliamentary and Protestant character of the English constitution; it is its doing that the Catholics were excluded from both Houses.

But on the opposition that hence arose it was at last wrecked. The unconditional hereditary right could no longer be combined with exclusive Protestantism, nor the right of granting money and the independence of the ministry with the free exercise of the prerogative. The King dissolved the Parliament, which, he was told, wished to convert him into a kind of Venetian Doge.

CHAPTER VI.

THE PARLIAMENT OF 1679.

FOR eighteen years there had been no general election in England. All the greater was the excitement and the tumult with which the new writs filled the kingdom. Everywhere in the towns and boroughs those who possessed votes met together, eating and drinking, talking and smoking at the fireside: conscious of their importance, they enjoyed themselves together for some days; they were in no hurry, for the candidate had to pay for everything. Foreigners are astonished at the sum to which the costs of an election amounted [1].

When the King determined on a dissolution, which he did most reluctantly, and which without doubt he ought to have done much sooner, he still did not mean to go over from one party to another. He wished, as it were, to punish the encroachments of the existing members of Parliament, who, under the influence of one another's society, ever lost more and more of their old submissiveness, so that he could no longer produce any impression on them. He hoped to procure from the same stratum of the population, the gentry, more trustworthy adherents, for in the country there were many faithful men devoted to the monarchy, who were not affected by the intrigues at court and the animosity against the ministers; these might be won by marks of favour and would hesitate

---

[1] Sarotti: 'Mi vien detto che ad alcuni dé pretendenti nei luochi piu conspicui e popolati costera 5m sc. per cadauno.'

before causing another dissolution, which would render useless all the expenses they had incurred. He thought he would be able to protect his prime minister and his brother against a new Parliament; he feared the Presbyterians less than before, as he was determined to follow a Protestant and anti-French policy.

But the very first names which were returned showed him his error. Once more, it is true, they were for the most part members of the gentry belonging to the Church of England upon whom the choice fell; but many eloquent and persuasive pamphlets, which were everywhere read, had propagated in the counties the dread of the misuse of the prerogative, and of the influence of the Duke of York. The temper of the Lower House which had been dissolved was the temper of the country; precisely those of the old members were re-elected who had expressed themselves most strongly in this sense; with them were associated those who most entirely sympathised on these points; the adherents of the court were designedly set aside. The result was utterly opposite to what had been expected. Whilst the King hitherto had been able, at least in urgent cases, to reckon upon 150 votes, he was now only sure of some 25, or at most 30.

In sight of the gravity of this situation, in which the Anglican Church was also endangered by the increase of the Presbyterians, the Church made one more attempt to bring back the Duke to the religion of the country, since in his departure from their communion they saw, not without good reason, the chief cause of the general confusion. 'Or shall we,' exclaims Sancroft, Archbishop of Canterbury, who above all others took the matter in hand, 'shall we let our ship be driven back into the high seas by a fresh tide? We now row very hard, the wind is against us.' In the midst of the danger which threatened Anglicanism and the system of the Restoration from both the Catholic and the Presbyterian side, the chief means of safety seemed to lie in the success of the attempt to win back the Duke to the religion of the country. Immediately after the elections, on February 21, the Arch-bishop, accompanied by Morley, Bishop of Winchester, whose spiritual dignity was increased by his great age—he was

eighty-two—proceeded with this purpose to the Duke[1]· He
reminded him of the happy time when, at the side of the
throne, as the eldest son of the Anglican Church, he had
filled her with hope that she would flourish under his care;
now he turned his back upon her. By those to whom he
had intrusted the guidance of his conscience, he was bound
to a blind faith; but God had endowed him with the power
of putting everything to the proof; to make use of this he
was bound by his duty to his own soul; if he would listen
to them they would lay before him the texts of Scripture
and some facts from which he might derive the conviction that
he must return to his true mother the Church of England.
These were well-considered and well-meant words; but the
Duke was for ever chained by his confessor and by his Italian
wife, who was Catholic in all her ideas and thoughts: he
refused even to consent to a further discussion. The Duke
had expected that even before the re-opening of Parliament
the groundlessness of the Popish plot would be brought to
light, and was irritated that concessions were again made to
the anti-Catholic tendencies, and that he was molested in his
religious convictions. But if he remained firm he must make
up his mind, at his brother's wish, to leave the court and even
the country. The King's motive was, that he wished once for
all to put an end to the opinion that the Duke's influence
determined his resolutions. The Duke betook himself to
Brussels.

The King also attempted to remove beforehand the widely-
spread anxiety that the freedom of Parliament would be
threatened by the maintenance of the army. He began
really to disband the troops, and acquainted the Lord Mayor
and Aldermen of London of the fact with a certain solemnity.
This produced a very disagreeable impression upon the Prince
of Orange.

The evening before the re-opening of Parliament, he
determined upon a still nearer advance towards reconciliation.
He declared that Earl Danby, who at the same time was

---

[1] The Archbishop's of Canterbury and Bishop's of Winchester speech to the
Duke of York to reclaim him from popery. Correspondence ii. 467.

raised to a marquisate, should only administer the office of
Treasurer until the next quarter, so as to wind up all current
business.   For it was against the existing administration that
the most violent animosity was directed ; Danby himself had
favoured it ; indeed he had originated all these measures, as
his authority was as yet undiminished.   Neither the King nor
the minister gave up the hope of leading by careful management the assembly, as it was now constituted, to the end they
desired.   Danby himself, or one of his friends, published a
pamphlet, which was largely read[1], ascribing all the outcry
against the arbitrariness and the Popish inclinations of the
government to the machinations of the Jesuits and the French
party.   In the two speeches with which the King and the
Lord Chancellor Finch opened the session, March 6/16,
nothing is more strongly put forward than the anti-Popish
attitude of the government ; they demanded subsidies especially for the purpose of enabling them to maintain it by
naval equipments.   Finch sought to excite the ambition of
Parliament in this direction by proving how entirely it
was in its power to unite the whole Protestant interest in
Europe.   Since the opinion prevailed in foreign nations that
a King of England in harmony with his Parliament would be
one of the most dreaded potentates in the world, they should
be shown the spectacle which they feared.   He did not name
France, but there is no doubt that he meant it.   Barrillon
expresses the opinion that Danby still thought he would be
able to excite Parliament against France ; in opposition to
France the English government saw the safety of its internal
position[2].

Who could doubt that this inducement to take up the
defence of the universal cause of Protestantism might make
a great impression upon the members of Parliament?   But they
had still closer at heart their own religious interest ; above all
they wished to save the liberties and the laws of the country,

---

[1] Letter from a Jesuit to his correspondent at London, showing the mo
ways to ruin the government and Protestant religion.

[2] 'De montrer un entier éloignement de la France et une véritabl
d'être dans les interêts opposés.'

which were most intimately allied with English Protestantism ;
to secure themselves from the King's successor was at that
moment more urgent in their eyes than to protect the
equilibrium of Europe against Louis XIV.

Moreover the whole turn which affairs had taken was the
work of the French ambassador and his royal master. The
dissolution of the old and the election of the new Parliament
was the result of the alliance concluded between Louis XIV
and the lords of the opposition, who had gained in consequence great advantage. For the first time, the party out
of which the Whigs originated saw itself in possession of
the chief influence in the state. They had not only broken
up the old majority, but destroyed it by the dissolution and
the new elections. For the most part these had taken place
under their influence; Russell had been elected for two
separate counties, a fact almost unprecedented in parliamentary
history. The opposition was master in both Houses and could
not possibly lend its hand to resolutions by which its opponents
hoped to regain the influence they had lost.

The first encounter showed at once the real position of
affairs; the allied Lords appeared with the proudest bearing.

It is not of much importance that the re-election of Seymour,
the former Speaker in the House of Commons, was rejected
by the court. He had quarrelled personally with Danby, and
to this might perhaps be added that there was no desire, by
the re-election of the old Speaker, to make the new Parliament seem as though it were a continuation of the former one.
The question whether the government had the right of
rejecting a Speaker chosen by the House was not settled in
this way; to put a stop to the discussion a short prorogation took place; on its expiration, Lord Russell himself
proposed and carried the election of another Speaker, Gregory,
since the most important thing for the dominant party was to
begin proceedings without further delay [1].

An incident, which occurred at the confirmation of this
election in the House of Lords, seems of more importance.

---

[1] 'I hope the occasion of the late unhappy difference about the speaker is
removed by the prorogation.' Sitting of 15/25 March, Grey's Debate vii. 2.

When the Chancellor granted in the King's name the usual
demands, of freedom of speech, access to the King, and so on,
he added that the King always supported by his favour the
creatures of his power.

No sooner had the Commons, though not the King, departed, than Lord Shaftesbury rose to attack the expression,
which offended the dignity of Parliament : ' My Lords, I think
we are all agreed that in this kingdom there are none but .
creatures of the Divine Power ; the power of the King does not
extend further than the laws determine.' The Chancellor
made excuses for his words, and the resolution was carried
not to enter them in the Minutes of the House[1].

Soon after the King had to listen to another cutting speech.
The question turned upon the elevation of rank granted to
the Earl of Danby, when he had been deprived of the office
of Treasurer.   Halifax exclaimed that he could not believe it,
for it was too abominable that a traitor to his country should
still be rewarded ; but if it were so, it must not be endured.
The King, nominally incognito, but recognised by every one,
was standing by the fireside ; Halifax fixed his eye upon him
whilst he spoke. ' My God,' exclaimed the King, ' how I am
ill-treated ; and I must bear it, and keep silence[2].'

It was to Danby, and the impeachment that hung over him,
that universal attention was now in general directed. The
King had granted him a general pardon, which was so carefully and comprehensively drawn up, that Danby thought
himself sufficiently secure.   But the Lower House would not
hear of a pardon for one who had been already accused : it
rejected even the modified amendment proposed by the Lords
to its bill ; that Danby attended to neither summons nor trial,
could not protect him from condemnation.   After some resistance and more than one useless conference, the Upper
House agreed on the 14th of April to the bill of attainder

---

[1] In the Journal of the Lords, March **17**, xiii. **47**, the Chancellor's speech is,
on this account, missed out, as well as the whole incident. I take it from the
despatches of the Venetian, P. Sarotti, 21/31 March, which are of great value for
this time.

[2] From the same despatch of Sarotti's.

against the Earl of Danby [1], and the King was called on to give it his consent.

Hardly ever had King Charles II been in greater personal perplexity. He had before him the alarming example of the result produced by his father's compliance in a like case; moreover, he was subject to the affront of a refusal to recognise his pardon; but still worse were the consequences which might be expected from a decided rejection of the bill; the Lower House had threatened that till this matter were despatched they would proceed to nothing else.

Still his easy temper helped him even over this difficulty. The expedient was devised that Danby should present himself only before the Upper House, and allow his trial to proceed. He had the assurance of eminent jurists, that according to the law he could not be condemned. At first he was taken to the Tower, where he remained five years. We shall come across him again; later on, in critical times, he again played a great part.

But all these circumstances, and especially the dismissal of Danby himself, made the continuance of the existing administration impossible. Charles II prevailed upon himself to form a new ministry of a quite different character. Anyhow, the Privy Council was of no importance to him, as he had not even consulted it about the last dissolution of Parliament, for he regarded it as consisting not so much of his friends as of secret adherents of Parliament. It was not very difficult to persuade him to reconstitute it, in such a way that a number of members of both Houses gained a seat and a vote in it.

The scheme originated with Temple, the diplomatist, who at that time had come over from Holland. A doctrinaire by nature, he intended at the same time to carry out the idea of Harrington, according to which authority is dependent upon the amount of landed property. The property of those summoned to the Privy Council was to be placed in the balance as a counterpoise to the property of the members of the Commons. One half were to be the highest officials in the state, the other half, fifteen in number, were to be the most con-

---

[1] Journals of Lords 516.

siderable members of the Houses of Lords and Commons; these were to give a popular weight to the government, without at the same time ever being able to divert it from its course[1]. In the embarrassment of the moment, the King consented to this proposal, which in itself offered the prospect of a successful progress of affairs. It also seemed advisable to him to gain over the leaders of parties, from whom he must expect a new attack upon himself and the prerogative of the crown, by giving them some share in the administration[2]. He promised solemnly to do nothing without their advice. Already it seemed to him to be a gain, that in that case the suspicion of an influence opposed to the popular wishes must die out. He summoned his principal opponents from the Lower House, men like Russell, Cavendish, and Powle, who was in the pay of Barrillon : when he had once made up his mind, he did not shrink even from the men who had recently attacked him in person; he received Halifax, and named Shaftesbury President of this Privy Council. The party which in Parliamentary affairs had gained the preponderance, entered in this way into the government itself.

But this did not give that party the possession of power. To entrust the most important affairs, the treatment of which demands secrecy, to a council of thirty members, was in any case an impossibility. For this a special committee was appointed, in which we find Sunderland, Temple, and Essex, after some time Halifax also, whom it was well worth while to gain over. But this committee was always regulated by the King's word, and the King would never consent to change according to their views the higher provincial authorities as well. He wished to calm parties and to make use of them, but not to fall into their hands.

Of all the pending questions, none was so important as that which concerned the future succession to the throne. Very changeable in his means, but always firm in his object, the

---

[1] Temple, Memoirs from the peace in 1679. Works ii. 494.

[2] 'Sperando che sodisfatta la loro ambitione di governare e con ammetterli al maneggio degli affari si plachino.' Sarotti.

King hoped even now to settle this according to his views, and
that with the help of the Parliamentary party.

King Charles had but few principles in political as well as
in moral matters ; but to one he held firmly, namely, the principle of hereditary right to which he himself owed his crown.
Now, in the great question which had arisen between his
brother's right of succession and the religion of the country,
he was unconditionally in favour of the former ; in this matter
he allowed no diverging proposal to lead him astray. But he
also comprehended the necessity of securing the Established
Church ; he did not mean to break with Protestantism. He
still thought he would be able to find means to attain both
these objects, and that in a way which would be agreeable to
the feelings of the majority. In a meeting of the two Houses
(30th April), in which he himself reverted to the necessity of
a naval equipment, he caused the Lord Chancellor to propose
some resolutions, by which, even under a Catholic successor, the
Protestant religion might be for ever secured. They provided
the following four points. All ecclesiastical benefices and
promotions were to be conferred in such a manner, that the
incumbents should always be the most pious and learned Protestants, and that a Popish successor should have no power to
control such presentations. In the next place, matters were so
to remain, that no Papist could sit in either House of Parliament ; the Parliament existing at the time of the King's death
was not to be dissolved for a fixed time, and if no Parliament
were in being, that which had last existed was to reassemble
without new elections or summons. For it was the general wish
to do away with even the influence of a Catholic prince upon
the formation of the Parliament. But further, no Papist might
hold any place of trust ; no post in the Privy Council, the
Chancery, or the courts of justice, was to be filled up without
the approval of Parliament. And finally, even the Lord
Lieutenants and their deputies, as well as the officers of the
navy, were to be appointed or dismissed either by Parliament
or by a commission nominated by it. These are concessions
which call to mind the conditions which were once proposed to
Charles I, and which he rejected. Charles II was ready to
promise them, if by that means the regular succession in the

kingdom could be preserved. One point might be wanting,—
the independence of the officers of the army from Parliamentary nomination. But as the army was, anyhow, to be
disbanded, this was not of such importance, and it seems as if
there was a desire to hold a conference about this point. The
Chancellor said that if there was any wish to add anything
more, the King was inclined to grant it: as if there could
be no doubt about the acceptance of the proposals, he concluded with the exclamation, 'God Almighty long continue
this blessed union between the King and his Parliament and
people [1].'

Indeed it might have been thought that Parliament would
accept these proposals, for they ensured to it for a long while
the decisive authority over the administration and judicature,
to a great extent over the military force, and above all over
the Church. A government entirely in the hands of the
estates, such as existed in Sweden or Hungary, seemed likely
by this means to be introduced into England also. Clear heads
like Temple objected in warning tones, that Parliament would
never give up what had been once granted to it; that this
would put the crown into chains. The French ambassador,
accustomed to an exclusively monarchical system, breaks out
into the exclamation, that the Chancellor's speech introduced
a Republic into England.

The English Lower House however was far from holding
any such view. It could not be prevailed upon even to thank
the King for his overtures. Was this from obstinacy, ill will, or
zeal against the Stuarts? I think not. Above everything
else there emerged the parliamentary idea itself, which presupposed an understanding between the existing King and
the Parliament; such could no longer be conceived, should a
Papist succeed to the throne. Sacheverell, the first speaker
who expressed himself at length, remarked that to all this the
future king would not be pledged, unless he himself confirmed
it; as soon as a Popish king ascended the throne, it would
all be worth nothing; with such things only those would be
deceived who chose to be deceived. It would not even be

---

[1] Chancellor's speech, Journal of Lords xiii. 547.

possible to resist a Popish king who should disregard these
resolutions. For even to say 'the King is a Papist' was penal;
the oath of uniformity and the militia oath forbade taking
up arms against those who held the King's commission. The
King was mistaken, if he thought that there was any wish to
ruin him or his family; no one wished to attack his right,
but they desired to keep steadfast to the principles which had
been laid down at the time of the Restoration, and not to
depart, from them even towards the popular side. 'If the
crown,' added Vaughan, 'injures our liberties it harms itself,
but if it is too bountiful with its concessions, that very bounty
may be harmful to the people.'

To these considerations, the sum of which is that no
parliamentary compact could give security against a Catholic
king, was now added the old antipathy of the leaders to the
Duke of York. Lord Shaftesbury thought that nothing
could give security from his revenge were he once king.
Shaftesbury was as little moved to change his opinions by his
presidentship as Lord Russell by being raised to the Privy
Council. Russell intimated in Parliament, that if the Duke
ascended the throne, men must make up their minds either
to become Papists or to be burnt. To meet this danger, for
it seemed as if the times of bloody Mary might return, he
called upon the Parliament to do more than its predecessor,
not to allow itself to be misled by fine words, but to promote
with zeal the Protestant cause; this crisis would decide
between the religions. He was supported by the adherents
of the principles of 1641. Hampden, the son, exclaimed,
that to restrain a Popish king by decrees in favour of Protestantism was like binding Samson with withes; he would
break them when he awoke. None could deny that there was
some truth in these anxieties and objections; there lay in
them at bottom even a recognition of the power of the
monarch, and many did not think it advisable to weaken
its constitutional importance. But, on the other side, hereditary right was a main principle for the security of the
throne and of the constitution itself; popular leaders of long
repute, Cavendish, Littleton and Sir William Coventry, spoke
in favour of the government scheme. They remarked that it

was unprecedented to exclude by laws the rightful heir;
but the religion and the constitution of the country might
well be secured by stringent decrees; an accommodation
should not, from the very beginning, be made impossible.
How much better it would have been if, in former days,
the negotiations with Charles I had been carried to a conclusion; then so much blood would not have been shed in
vain; 'we must not do evil,' said Clarges, 'that good may come.'
But in the Lower House the anti-Papist tendencies of the
day kept the upper hand. At first a resolution was carried
which by its very violence terrified all who were impartial:
the King and the religion of the country were to be protected
from all dangers; 'If His Majesty shall come by any violent
death, it shall be revenged to the utmost upon all Papists[1].'
Then a bill was introduced for the exclusion of the Duke of
York from the imperial crown of England: on the 15th of
May it passed the first reading, and as early as the 22nd
the second. There was no lack of warning voices, that they
would drive the Duke of York to throw himself entirely into
the hands of the King of France; the consent of the Lords
would not be gained, the indignation of the King would be
aroused, and incalculable confusion would be caused. But the
majority had once for all made up their minds; they answered
the last warning by passionate cries for the bill, and there
remained no doubt that it would be carried.

This moment may be looked upon as the culminating point
of the authority of the Earl of Shaftesbury, who on his side
had formed the intention of raising to the throne of England
the natural son of Charles II, the Duke of Monmouth, hoping
by his means to bring his own constitutional and religious
ideas into force. Shaftesbury was universally popular, and held
a high post in the government. At that time he succeeded in
introducing his protégé into the Privy Council. They entered
together into the secret committee, which prepared and conducted political business. When it was then proposed there
to determine a fixed time for the Duke of York to absent

---

[1] Journals of Commons ix. 620. Even Ralph is horrified at the way in which
innocent persons are threatened in it.

himself, Sunderland, Essex and Halifax seemed inclined to agree; only Temple resisted, out of anxiety lest Shaftesbury should then obtain complete possession of the chief power. For he already led the great party which formed the majority in the Lower House, and possessed an overwhelming reputation in the capital, in which an address was now being circulated expressing perfect agreement with the Lower House, and promising the most vigorous assistance against all attempts made by the enemies of public freedom. This address had been already signed by some aldermen and several wardens of the guilds. If things continued in this way, an authority might be centred in Shaftesbury's hands before which the King himself would have to bow[1]. To make the adherents of the old system quite harmless, an examination into the employment of the secret service money was instituted, and that too under Shaftesbury's direction, to whom it could matter little if even members of Parliament were implicated, as upon such he would never have been able to count. There were sanguine anticipations that the King, partly from affection for his natural son, partly from want of money, would at last consent to everything.

But the resolution taken by the King was of an entirely different nature.

One day the usual circle of courtiers was assembled round the Queen, when the King entered. 'I have just,' he said, 'freed myself from the burden which weighed upon me. How they have deceived themselves, if they imagined that want of money would force me to extremities! But I shall find means to pay the fleet, and to manage economically; it will be difficult and uncomfortable for me, but I will rather submit to anything than endure the gentlemen of the Commons any longer[2].'

---

[1] Temple's Memoirs (Works ii. 503): 'They began to find the Duke of Monmouth and Lord Shaftesbury unreasonable, and like to prevail upon the House of Commons to endeavour bringing the King into necessities of yielding all points to them, and thereby leaving the Duke of Monmouth and Lord Shaftesbury absolutely at the head of all affairs.'

[2] 'Farò tutto quello che potiò piu tosto che soffrire davantaggio li Signori communi; che furono le precise parole di Sua Maestà.' Sarotti, July 9th.

This was on the 27th of May. The Lower House was just occupied with naming the men who had drawn money from separate items of revenue, when the Black Rod knocked at the door, and the House was immediately declared to be prorogued.

The day is remarkable in English history for another reason also; from it dates the Habeas Corpus Act.

In spite of all the precautions that had hitherto been taken against arbitrary arrests, they still continued to occur repeatedly. Amongst the accusations against Danby, that which related to this point was one of the best founded. In opposition to him, the two Houses joined in an act restricting the time for which imprisonment could last before trial to the shortest possible amount, namely, twenty-four hours; and also in other respects the security of the individual, as opposed to the holder of state power, was increased and established by most wisely weighed resolutions. The act was presented to the King immediately before the prorogation; he pronounced his 'Roi le veult' which made it law; since then it has always been considered as the chief bulwark of the personal liberty of Englishmen.

It was thought that the King himself wished to prevent imprisonments, to which his friends might be subjected by ministers who were not entirely devoted to him[1]. Another motive was that the measure was popular, and might contribute to calm the general excitement which the sudden adjournment of Parliament must necessarily cause. On that day, to avoid any danger from a sudden attack, the guards at Whitehall were doubled.

London and Westminster remained perfectly quiet, even the signatures of the address made no real advance; the King, without any dread of an immediate disturbance, might think of dissolving this Parliament also. He summoned the Privy Council to Hampton Court; the majority were against it, only those were in favour of it who felt themselves injured by the increasing greatness of Shaftesbury. 'Gentle-

---

[1] Barrillon, June 6: 'L'acte est conçu en termes, desquels les Srs catholiques et le Cte. Danby voudroient inferer, qu'ils doivent être mis en liberté.'

men,' said the King at last, 'it is enough.'   In spite of the decided majority, he ordered the Chancellor to issue the writs for a new election.

His principal motive was that a newly elected assembly would not be bound by the precedents of its predecessor[1]; but on the whole he did not give up the hope of attaining, by means of new elections, the aim which he was pursuing.

---

[1] 'Parceque la chambre basse étoit comme engagée à ce qu'elle avoit proposé pour l'exclusion de la succession.'   A reflection which Barrillon ascribes to the Duke of York (24 July).

CHAPTER VII.

THE terror of conspiracy still possessed the minds of all men ; all still considered themselves seriously threatened with a rising of the Papists. The streets were closed with chains at important places, and the militia was kept in readiness to quell at once any rising disturbance. In the transactions of the law-courts, which conducted such trials as did not concern members of Parliament, no less interest was shown by the people than in the Parliamentary debates. Again and again Oates and his associates, above all Bedlow, appeared at the trials to re-peat old statements or to add new ones of increased force ; the judges and the juries always had an overwhelming in-clination to condemn. Coleman and three Jesuits had already perished on the scaffold. In June 1679 five other Jesuits, in spite of their protestations of innocence, were condemned and hanged at Tyburn. They were followed by Langhorne, a barrister of repute, who had been tempted in vain to save his life by consenting to denounce his fellow conspirators. Some impression however was made in these trials by the method of defence, which consisted in proving the contradictions and general untrustworthiness of the accusers. Even Chief Justice Scroggs, who till now, whilst most of the other judges had kept quiet, had conducted the proceedings with the zeal of a violent opponent of Catholicism, was confounded by the fact that great improbabilities, if not impossibilities, appeared in Bedlow's statement. To this another influence was added. In the accusations made against the Queen's physician, George Wakeman, old statements which had been already refuted were repeated, tending to implicate the

Queen in the attempt on her husband's life. But she was
too well known for any one to believe this; it was regarded
as the doing of a party which sought to separate the Queen
from the King and so make room for another dynastic
combination. Wakeman was treated by Scroggs with a
mildness not usual to him at other times, and was at last acquitted. Still that as yet produced no influence on the general
temper, but rather served to excite it. The Chief Justice had
even to endure the disapproval of many. He complained
loudly of the dependence into which the courts of justice
were brought, by the fact that public opinion assumed the
position of censor of their decisions and only tolerated those
which were agreeable to it[1]. Of this the judges were not a
little guilty; they thought it impossible, as one of their
number says, to resist the stream, and allowed themselves,
even when unconvinced, to be carried along with it.

Even if greater moderation could have been expected, it
was destroyed by an unfortunate attempt to produce a reaction. Lady Powis, the wife of one of the Catholic lords
imprisoned in the Tower, thought that she would be doing
them and the Catholic cause good service, if she caused
accusations to be made against the leaders of the Nonconformists similar to those which had been circulated
against the Catholics. But Dangerfield, the man whom she
employed for this purpose, was not at all to be trusted.
When he found himself unmasked, he did not scruple to turn
his denunciations against those who had originally hired him;
it was judged that any one who lent himself to such deceptions
must be capable of all others[2]. Lady Powis was an energetic

---

[1] 'If once causes come to be tried with complacency to popular opinions and
shall be insolently censured, if they goe otherwise, all public causes shall receive
the doom as the multitude happen to be possessed.' State Trials vii. 704.

[2] It is the meal-tub plot which in Lingard's opinion has never been quite
cleared up. Barrillon, who in other cases is very Catholic, expresses himself about
it with the utmost decision: 'Ce n'est autre chose, qu'un dessein, que quelque gens
zélés pour le Duc de York et pour la cour ont eu, de repousser les artifices, dont on
s'est servi contre les catholiques, par d'autres. Le comte de Peterborough et Mme.
de Puez ont cru rendre un grand service d'avoir trouvé un homme, qui voulust
deposer contre Mylord Shaftesbury et les autres chefs de cette faction. Dangerfield est un scelerat, qui n'a songé qu'à gagner de l'argent et si tost qu'il s'est

woman, who was in her element when she held the threads of a great party intrigue in her hands; but the means she adopted in this case, being in themselves unjustifiable, produced the contrary effect to that which she intended.

When, under these circumstances, new elections came on, what results could they have? The government, which still sought for unconditional adherents, had some success in the boroughs; in the large towns and even in the counties their exertions, which were often made in a scandalous manner, remained fruitless. The choice did not everywhere fall upon the same men as at the last election, but the general result was the same [1]; perhaps the only difference was that the Presbyterians obtained a still greater preponderance. They were looked on as the irreconcileable opponents of Popery, against which popular impulse was directed.

By a very unexpected complication of circumstances the same party just then rose into prominence in Scotland.

The system of the Restoration had there been greeted with delight, and was at first fully carried out; but the severities inflicted had awakened in the persecuted party the deepest and most violent passions, which again broke out in a horrible crime.

The Archbishop of St. Andrew's, James Sharp, who had formerly been a Presbyterian, drew upon himself, by the relentless energy with which he carried out the Act of Uniformity, the hatred of the zealous Covenanters, which bordered on frenzy. At last he fell in with a number of these fanatics as he was on his way from Edinburgh to his see: they thought it a good deed to take revenge on the Judas of the Scottish Church, who had dipped his hand in the blood of the saints. Sharp recognised an acquaintance amongst them, and begged his protection. 'My Lord,' he

---

vu arresté a pris le parti de dire tout ce, que luy est inspiré, pour ceux contre qui il voulut deposer d'abord.'

[1] Letters of Algernon Sidney to Henry Savile 144: 'The party that is most averse to the court seems to prevail in the counties and great corporations, as the other doth in many of the small boroughs, and upon the whole matter, many believe, the house will be composed as the last was, or as some think of a more harsh humour, the same men being something sharpened.'

replied, ' I will not lay hands on you '—but he looked on whilst the others carried out the murderous work.

When, in consequence of this act, measures of sanguinary severity were taken against the party to which the murderers belonged, they proceeded to open rebellion. In Rutherglen near Glasgow, the acts abolishing the Covenant and re-introducing episcopacy and the supremacy were burnt, for testimony must be borne against the wickedness of the time. The number of those assembled was so great that they were able to hold their own against the government troops; they might be numbered by thousands[1].

Not so much the outrage itself as the fact that the move-ment could assert itself and find support, may have been connected with the last change in the government of England. Lauderdale's authority, which till now had ruled Scotland, was not a little shattered by this, even though the King did not abandon him. He always ascribed the renewal of dis-turbances to the insubordination to the Scottish lords.

It was impossible, in the condition in which England was, to re-establish the old system by force; least of all could Lauderdale himself have been sent to Scotland for this purpose. Under the influence of certain Scots who were present, and who asserted with one voice that the refractory temper might be allayed by some slight concessions, the King determined to entrust the mission to his legitimatised son Monmouth, Shaftesbury's friend, who himself shared the tendencies of the day. Every one knew his position and his instructions; when he arrived he received the support of the country. Without difficulty he dispersed the Covenanters and re-established universal obedience. The regulations which he then made, although he still forbade the field-conventicles, because disguised Jesuits found admittance to them, otherwise breathed mildness and indulgence, and were favourable to the Presbyterians; he appeared as the benefactor and friend of Scotland, and wished to appear so.

---

[1] Extracts from the contemporary declarations and publications of both parties, in Wodrow iii. 44.

Anglicanism, as it had been founded by the Restoration, remained completely unaltered only in Ireland. Many an attempt had been made to transplant thither also the movement caused by the trials relating to the Popish plot. What might not have been the results there, where two different nationalities and religions, disputing the possession of the country, stood opposed to one another? But Ormond still held the rudder with a steady hand. Moderate and firm by nature, and experienced in the government of the country, he knew how to avoid the agitating influences by which even he was affected; still no one could say how long that would last.

For in the two other kingdoms, Presbyterianism had at this moment gained the upper hand; in the one by the success of arms, in the other by the elections. There was no doubt that Shaftesbury must become just as powerful in the next Parliament as he had been in the last. He was regarded as the champion of tolerance, and as the most active opponent of the strict laws of uniformity. He still held the high post of President of the Privy Council. He was the adviser of Monmouth, who, as Captain-General of the forces, enjoyed likewise a high position, and who, thanks to his success in Scotland, had greater renown than ever. He was greeted by the title of Highness, received by the King with fatherly satisfaction, and by the court with great consideration; the future seemed to be his.

He has been represented by Dryden almost a youth, as he must have been at this time, whose manly beauty seemed to promise him the possession of power: graceful and easy in all that he did, with no mean capacities for the exercises of war; doubtless not without faults, which were, however, excused on account of his fiery blood. Dryden represents him as persuaded by his Achitophel, Shaftesbury, to form the ambitious idea of elevating himself above the rank to which his illegitimate birth entitled him; for the desire of greatness is a god-like crime: he will put himself forward as the champion of religion, of freedom, and of the public good; he will draw his title from the people itself; he hopes at last to win over to his design even his father, who resists, but loves him.

Long ago the assertion had been circulated that Charles II had been secretly married to Monmouth's mother, Lucy Walters; and that she was as respectable by birth as Edward IV's wife; in Paris her son had once been greeted as Prince of Wales. If the King disputed the fact, he only did so under the influence of the Catholic faction and the Duke of York, who had once had the face to deny his own marriage [1].

It is impossible to say what might have resulted if King Charles II had actually died of a violent attack of illness which seized him in August 1679. Would the magistrates of the city of London really have carried out their intention of causing the Duke of York to be proclaimed in such a case? Monmouth had also a party in the Privy Council. Many were convinced that he would himself have assumed the crown. The multitude would have declared for him with enthusiastic affection; he would, in the universal confusion, at least have obtained an increased importance.

But it was precisely this great prospect which awakened dissatisfaction and resistance. The members of the managing committee, rivals of Shaftesbury and Monmouth, for whom they had only unwillingly made room in their own number, would not allow as yet a greater authority to fall into their hands, not only because their gain would be their own loss, but because they feared to be made responsible for their share in the dissolution of Parliament [2]. It was not primarily from legitimist sentiments, but with the especial view of opposing their rivals, that Sunderland and Halifax, agreeing in this with the Duchess of Portsmouth, caused the Duke of York to be invited to break his exile, and apparently of his own accord, but only in the deepest secrecy, to return to court. The sick King was spoken to about it, and approved. Without delay the Duke set out; he reached London unrecognised; there already he learnt that the King was better. On arriving early one morning at Windsor, he was able to announce to Charles his

---

[1] Letter concerning the black book in Somers viii. 187. The story of a contract of a somewhat later date and of its being kept secret is described as an invention made on purpose to be able to upset it; but the fact of the marriage is held to.

[2] Sidney's Diary, ed. Blencowe, i. 176.

own arrival. He said he was come to inquire in person after the health of his King and brother; they both behaved as if his arrival was unexpected. They played the part which public opinion rendered necessary.

As yet the Duke could not have been allowed to remain for a longer space of time. He flattered himself that he would be able to stay, but the men at the head of affairs proved to him, even the very next day, that it would be impossible. Only one thing was conceded to him, that Monmouth should depart at the same time, and be deprived of his position as Captain-General of the troops. But was not this the wish rather of the ministers themselves? It was they who suggested it. For their own interest it was important to be freed from all these immediate machinations.

Monmouth and his friends had heard nothing of the invitation sent to the Duke, but had even been assured to the contrary[1]. When, on the day of the Duke's arrival, Monmouth returned from hunting, he had to bear the news that his rival was at the castle. He refused an attempted reconciliation; but then he could no longer count on his father's favour. The worst possible construction was put upon the alliance which he had formed with the Presbyterians, and even with the fanatics. Monmouth struggled for a moment against the loss of his post as commander-in-chief, but at last submitted. He told his friends that he was persecuted because he wished Parliament to be summoned, and because he was a Protestant; he attached himself all the more closely to Shaftesbury and Montague. At first he went to Arnhem, where he took up his abode in the house which belonged to Prince Rupert. His wife, who had been chosen for him on account of her wealth, and his children, remained in London.

With incomparably more consideration was the Duke of York treated. Although he went back to the continent, he did so only to bring back his family from Brussels; for he had received permission to take up his abode in Scotland, because, as was said, it was not seemly to let the King's

---

[1] 'Essex knew of it, and approved of it, but none of the Duke of Monmouth's cabal.' Macpherson, Extracts 95.

brother live out of the country. On his return he again spent
a few weeks at court.

The higher and lower aristocracy, and every one who had
any position in the country, showed him then the reverence
due to the heir-apparent. The fête provided for him by the
Artillery Company, of which he was captain, on the 21st
October, in the Merchant Taylors' hall, is worth noticing.
The cavalcade of carriages with six horses, which escorted him
there, was greeted, on one spot at least, by the cry, 'No
Popery.' At the banquet, at which the Lord Mayor and
aldermen were present, the Duke replied to their toast of his
health, by proposing the welfare of the city. He had, he said
in his speech, at all times risked his life for the good of the
country and of the capital; in like manner he would not suffer
it to be disquieted on account of the Protestant religion (by
which expression, at that time, episcopacy was meant), or that
any one should suffer the least harm because of it[1]. A few
days afterwards he set out for Scotland. Those who were at
the head of affairs hoped that his influence would contribute
to destroy the party which Monmouth had gained for himself
during his late residence there.

For against Monmouth and his friends the antipathies of
the government were now directed. When Shaftesbury, in
October, returned from the country to his town house in
Aldersgate Street, he was received by the people with the old
enthusiasm; but on the other hand, the King, with the
approval of the ministers, declared at the next meeting of the
Privy Council, that he did not find it advantageous for his
service that the Earl of Shaftesbury should act any longer as
president. Shaftesbury scoffed at the precautions taken by
the government to secure for themselves the newly-elected
Lower House, but they still thought it wise to adjourn the
opening of Parliament till January 1679-80.

Upon this the Earl of Shaftesbury turned once more to the
King himself. He caused him to be informed that if he sum-

---

[1] 'Ne mai andarebbe ad apportare il minimo disturbo alla religione protestante
ne a far dispiacere ad alcuno per cagione di essa, onde ricevo gli applausi di tutti e
lascio di si grande sodisfattione.' Sarotti, Nov. 3.

moned Parliament without delay, and gave way in the matter
of the succession, he might still become the mightiest and
happiest king in Christendom ; he ought only to listen to him,
to his reasons, his ideas, his schemes ; he would give him all
the securities which he might demand. After a preliminary
overture, for which Shaftesbury made advances, the King
remarked that this plan included something which did not
concern the Duke alone, but also the Queen ; he could not
possibly consent to anything which would be injurious to that
worthy lady, his wife, or his brother, who deserved well from
him. He refused the desired audience. This aroused in
Shaftesbury the indignant consciousness of the power he
possessed by virtue of his personal popularity. He answered
that, if he was not believed and trusted, there would be no
longer in England peace between king and people[1] His
health was more wretched than ever, he could not put one foot
before the other ; he looked like a dying man, almost a corpse :
but his ideas were as fiery as ever ; they were a strange com-
pound of political principle and ambition ; he intended to
carry them out either in concert with the King, or in opposition to the King. He placed himself with decision at the
head of the opposition.

Charles II did not exactly fear him. He even said that he
would dine once more in Shaftesbury's country house,—that
is to say, the Earl's proceedings would justify the confiscation
of his goods. But, at the beginning, it was not so certain who
would be the strongest.

One of Shaftesbury's principal weapons was Monmouth's
claim. For the idea of the legal relationship between his
mother and the King would not be readily given up again
by the populace. But a still more active motive in his
favour was by the condition of the country. What mis-
fortunes would begin were the King to die ? The most sanguinary intentions of the Papists would then be carried out.
The one man who could save the nation was he whose
banishment had filled the whole people with alarm. The

---

[1] This information also I find in Sarotti, He tells us that he has it from a
'principal regio ministro, che l'ha havuto della bocca della M.S.' (Dec. 1.)

Duke of Monmouth had courage and conduct ; the inde-
feasible character of his right did not so much matter : he
made the best king who had the worst title to the crown ;
for the motto of such a king was not ' God and my right,' but
' God and my people [1].'

The Duke of York had hardly departed for Scotland when
Monmouth appeared again in London at the end of November,
and even went at once to Whitehall itself. It was at rather
a late hour, on the very same evening, that he entreated the
King most urgently for an audience ; he came in his service,
he only wished to say one word to him. The next day this
entreaty was renewed many times, both in writing and
verbally ; Monmouth's wife also interceded for it ; the King
remained immoveable. He called upon his son to obey him
and to leave Whitehall, London, even England, or he would
never see his face again [2]. Monmouth was still captain of the
guard ; Charles II declared him dismissed from this and from
his other posts. Monmouth left London, but not England,
and with that the King was content. However strongly he
expressed himself, those who knew him still thought he was
not displeased to see his son have the people on his side, no
doubt from a fatherly satisfaction at his reputation, and not
only from that, but also because he seemed to count on him
should his present policy not succeed. Monmouth pleaded as
the cause of his return, that his name also had been mentioned
at Dangerfield's trial ; but he had not only come, he said, to
justify himself, but to defend his father or even to avenge him
should any harm befall him ; he spoke with as great assurance
as if he had the whole nation at his back ; with it and with
Parliament he would reconcile his father, and would seek to
provide the security necessary for religion [3].

A widespread agitation was on foot to induce the King to
summon Parliament in the following January ; that is to say,
to keep to the date last appointed for its meeting.

---

[1] Appeal from the county to the city.　State Tracts ii. 491.

[2] Detailed information may be found in Macpherson's Extracts.

[3] ' Qu'il ne prétend que de voir le roi d'Angleterre d'accord avec son peuple et
prendre avec le parlement les précautions pour la seureté de la religion protestante.'
Barrillon, Dec. 1/11, 1679.

' The Earl of Shaftesbury prevailed upon a number of lords
to entreat the King, at the beginning of December 1679, to
make a decided declaration on this point; he himself accompanied them.   Lord Huntingdon was the spokesman.
The petition was that the King would listen to his Great
Council, the Parliament, and so relieve the anxieties of the
nation in the midst of its pressing dangers and ensure
peace.   The King answered that he would take it into consideration, as indeed he was already doing; he only wished
that every one had as much care for the peace of the nation
as he had himself.

Similar petitions were prepared in the capital and in the
country as well, amongst the gentry; they called particular
attention to the greater necessity, now that the Catholic
party had the prospect of placing one of their own confession
on the throne, of tracking out still further the conspiracy, that
is, of completing in a new session of Parliament the trials
of the Catholic lords, who had been arrested.   The King
should be assured of all possible support, provided only he
would secure religion, punish the conspiracy, and dismiss some
unpopular men from around him: there were hopes of
prevailing on him to consent to biennial Parliaments [1].

The agitation had its centre in one of the London clubs,
which spread its emissaries over the country; signatures were
collected without much regard to the character or position of
those who signed; quantity alone was important [2].

The King caused the Lord Mayor and the aldermen to be
warned against these demonstrations, and threatened punishment on account of them; but what could that avail?   To
avoid this universal pressure of stormy petitions, and the
necessity of either being carried away by them or of resisting
the expression of the popular wish [3] he thought it advisable to

---

[1] So Barrillon sums up the demands: ' Que le parlement s'assemblast au moins
tous les deux ans une fois.' December 29.

[2] Sarrotti: 'Si erano vedute lettere, nelle quali veniva scritto, che non importa
che fossero le petitioni segnate dalle mani dei gentilhuomini ed altri civili e
benestanti, ma solo che si procurassero quante sottoscrittioni che potessero aversi
da differenti mani di persone di ogni stato e conditione.'

[3] Barrillon : 'Il auroit été très perilleux de les attendre pour les refuser.'

publish, as early as December, the declaration that he prorogued Parliament from January until the following November
(Nov. 11). In fixing this remote time he might not be quite
serious, as at a later time he inserted shorter prorogations,
but he intended by such a distant adjournment to nip in the
bud the movement just beginning. The power of the prerogative now centred in the right to summon Parliament or not ;
Charles II wished to make this power once more felt in its full
importance.

The foreign ambassadors do not know how to paint strongly
enough the consternation which this news spread through the
town, especially among the party-leaders ; no one had credited
the King with so much determination.

It is true that petitions in favour of summoning Parliament
had been already presented ; but now the King, by reference to the declaration which had been issued, could more
easily set them aside. And at the same time care was taken
to renew the old laws against meetings, to put the public
places under supervision, and to curb the press. In this the
judges lent the government their support. The publisher of
the pamphlet, already mentioned, in favour of Monmouth was
condemned to pay a very considerable fine. The government
still had influence enough to call forth contrary addresses
which disclaimed these petitions : there was a distinction made
between ' petitioners ' and ' abhorrers.'

Under these circumstances the connexion of the government
with the members of the old Parliamentary opposition was
entirely dissolved. At Shaftesbury's advice his old friends
Russell, Cavendish, Capell, Powle, even Lord Essex himself,
petitioned the King to be dismissed from the Privy Council.
The motive of the leader was that, if they stayed any longer,
they would never again be considered by the people as good
Englishmen, they would even be charged with the unparliamentary conduct of the government ; at present everything
might still be excused and they would be received with open
arms[1]. The King granted their request, as he officially said,
' with his whole heart.'

_____

[1] Shaftesbury's letter, 30th Jan. 1679-80, in Cooke's History of Parties i. 134.

Hereupon affairs were concentrated in the hands of Sunderland, Godolphin, and Lawrence Hyde, who came forward as the first commissioner of the Treasury; they appear in the journals and reports as the triumvirate which conducts the government. They also met with support from a portion of the well-to-do middle class, who were anxious lest the differences should lead to a renewal of the civil war, and who were not exactly in favour of a deviation from the legitimate succession. When the Duke of York came with his family for a time to London, in March 1680, he was very well received; this time also banquets were arranged in his honour.

At the same time Monmouth passed through the western counties. He enjoyed the hospitality of the country nobility who were not connected with the court; the country people streamed in from all sides to see 'the Protestant Duke.'

In Parliament, which was adjourned for constantly decreasing periods, and without doubt might shortly be expected to meet, the two parties would again have to measure themselves with one another.

But in so doing they were to decide not only about internal concerns, but also about the most important questions of external politics.

It is quite true that immediately after the prorogation of the last Parliament, there was a question of the renewal of the old compacts between the two Kings. Charles II was inclined, in return for a considerable grant of money, to postpone an immediate summons of Parliament. Louis XIV would have been glad of this, but as he had a party in Parliament, he would not pay for its temporary suspension so large a sum as was demanded in England. And what he desired, namely that Parliament should remain adjourned for three years, the English ministers could on no account consent to; they said, it might cost the King his crown and them their lives. These negotiations, which could lead to no results, fell to the ground.

However now again, as before, one of the principal objects of the English government was to prevent by all means an understanding between France and the United Netherlands; it held fast to the policy which Danby had introduced, and

Temple, with whom indeed it had originated, had continued, that of keeping on good terms with the neighbouring Resent public. In the instructions of Henry Sidney, who was there as ambassador in the autumn of 1679, it was said expressly, 'all good Protestants here do agree in this, that a firm conjuncture between England and the States-General is the only expedient now left to preserve both.' A renewal of this alliance was also held to be urgent, that it might not be regarded as dissolved in consequence of the subsequent peace with France. The French opposed this: for a considerable time something like a contest might be seen at the Hague between the French and English plenipotentiaries, D'Avaux and Sidney, and their respective offers. Sidney had the advantage that the bearing of the French had now awakened jealousy in the towns also, even in Amsterdam. The Dutch had only one anxiety: they thought that, owing to his alienation from Parliament, the King of England would not at all be in a position even to support them in a moment of danger. The King promised that if they were attacked by France, he would without delay summon his Parliament, whose help in that case would not be wanting. Upon this all scruples were appeased[1]. The States-General declared themselves steadfastly determined not to enter into any alliance which could not co-exist with their friendship towards the King of Great Britain. The Prince of Orange could venture to advance a new scheme for a great alliance. When he proposed that both the King and the Republic should together conclude similar treaties with the other powers, England was very ready to agree with regard to Denmark and Brandenburg; the conclusion of a commercial treaty with Sweden was to become the foundation of a defensive alliance; on the other hand it was still thought possible to put off an agreement with Spain and Austria, because that might lead to too remote relationships. But, in the meanwhile, on this very point a pressing danger appeared; Louis *X*IV had erected his Chambres de Réunion; their action, both on the Upper Rhine and in the Netherlands, developed to such an extent as to affect the state of Europe. Hereupon Sunderland

---

[1] Sunderland to Sidney; in Blencowe. Sidney's Diary i. 220.

informed the Prince that in England it was thought necessary to secure the maintenance of the Spanish Netherlands, and to make by degrees all the proposed alliances[1]. In the spring of 1680 an ambassador was sent to the Elector of Brandenburg, who was commissioned first to communicate on his way his instructions to the Prince of Orange, and afterwards to make overtures to the courts of Brunswick-Lüneburg, which then, after the death of the Duke of Hanover, began to occupy a more important position. In the same way treaties of similar import, for resistance to France, were to be concluded with Austria and Spain. Impatience was caused because the ambassadors of these countries had to wait a long while for their full powers. In May the imperial ambassador, Burgemaine, went from London to Vienna to acquaint his court with the sentiments prevailing in England : Don Pedro Ronquillo came back to London to represent Spain ; he took the matter in hand with such zeal that as early as June a treaty was prepared, the signature of which only depended upon a formality to be completed in the Netherlands. But at the same time he urged that the King should assure himself of Parliamentary assistance. On account of external rather than of internal relations the actual summoning of Parliament was determined on and fixed for October, 1680.

These negotiations were not kept very secret ; Charles II did not conceal from the King of France that he disapproved of his encroachments. He made serious representations against the Réunions in which Louis XIV, one of the parties, made himself judge in his own cause, and by one-sided verdicts had everything which he desired granted him : he was wronging neighbour princes in possessions which had been theirs for many centuries ; he was breaking the peace which had hardly been concluded ; the English nation, he continued, would not look on at this quietly ; it would drive him on to make war against France ; he indeed desired no war, but he could no longer be the martyr of France. Louis XIV

---

[1] Prince William's letters to Temple on this subject from Jan. 16 to Jan. 23, N.S., are amongst those papers the loss of which we most especially regret for the universal history of this period.

had however made up his mind, and had no idea of withdrawing from his undertaking out of consideration for England;
he felt himself almost offended that Charles II, on whose
services he on his side thought he had claims, assumed an
appearance of wishing to set himself in opposition to him.
One day there was a conversation between Barrillon and
Sunderland which characterises the position. Barrillon called
to mind the offers which he had formerly made to the
English court for a renewal of the alliance. But these very
offers by their insignificance insulted the English. 'Fine
offers!' interrupted Sunderland, 'just such as are made to
beggars[1]. You have despised us as if we were of no consequence, but you see we have become of more importance
than you imagined. A war cannot be agreeable to us, least
of all to those who have any share in the government, but if
we are forced to it we must venture upon it.'

And thus appeared a project, from which a direction to the
world's history might have been expected quite different from
that which it ultimately took,—the project of a European
alliance to oppose the preponderance for which Louis XIV
strove, even before the actual accomplishment of the Réunions, before the revocation of the Edict of Nantes, for
which war, had it broken out, would have left no opportunity.

But for this an understanding between King Charles and
his Parliament was an indispensable condition. The King did
not disguise his fear that Parliament by means of the war
might force him into a position of dependence on its grants;
still he hoped, by deciding for war, to win over the majority,
and then to settle the question of the succession according
to his own views. In spite of previous secret approaches to
Louis XIV, the Duke of York was at this moment at one with
his brother, and even in favour of summoning Parliament
immediately to see what could be done. The government
regarded a reconciliation of his claims with the interests of
the Anglican Church as still possible.

Through this very connexion of the prerogative and the
Church the antipathies of their opponents were now united.

_____

[1] 'Voilà des belles offres: vous nous avez meprisé.' Barrillon, March 17, 1630.

Even the moderate Presbyterians feared that Anglicanism would become too strong for them, and would then agree to no concession in their favour; but how much less had the remaining Protestant Nonconformists to hope? The twofold opposition, ecclesiastical and political, became so powerful that Louis XIV thought himself free from all necessity of considering Charles II. He would hear no more of any further negotiations with him; in the first place, because, as he said, it was impossible to count on an alliance with him, as Parliament then was. 'Whatever he may promise me,' he says, in a letter to Barrillon, 'he will break everything to get a regular income from his Parliament[1]; he only treats with me to derive an advantage for his future negotiations with his subjects[2]; he thinks that the further he withdraws from my interest the more easily will he bring the English nation over to his side: so now he allies himself with my opponents in Parliament, but when he has got what he wants, when he is once well armed, he will turn against his own subjects to re-establish his authority; then he will again seek my alliance and I should pay dearly for it[3].' What Charles II hardly himself liked to confess, Louis XIV lays plainly to his charge, and communicates by means of his ambassador to the Parliamentary factions with which he is connected. Barrillon was to nourish their mistrust[4] and lead them to recognise that Charles II was seeking to deceive them when he professed a desire to break with France, for his object only was to gain large subsidies: on this pretence he was to add that however

---

[1] 'Il est persuadé, qu'il n'y a pas de meilleur parti pour lui, que de rompre toutes mesures avec moi.' April 30, 1680.

[2] 'Il ne traite avec moy que pour traiter ensuite plus avantageusement avec ses sujets.' March 25.

[3] 'Sans vous arrester aux belles paroles il faut, que vous vous attachez uniquement à former dans le parlement un parti assez considérable pour pouvoir s'opposer avec succès à tout ce, que ce prince voudra obtenir; et que vous fassiez entendre adroitement par ceux dont vous vous servez à tous les chefs des cabales, que le vrai moyen, de m'empescher de faire une nouvelle alliance avec le roi d'Angleterre, seroit qu'ils ne se reconciliassent point avec lui; mais que du moment que vous les verrez disposez à accorder, il vous sera facile de rompre leurs mesures.' April 30.

[4] 'D'augmenter la défiance et le soupçon, que la plus grande partie des membres du parlement ont déja des desseins, etc.'

much Parliament might grant the King on the ground of the war, it lay at any moment in the power of the French court to draw him over to their side by giving him more money.

As it would have opened out the most extensive prospect if England had at that moment opposed the French Réunions, so on the other hand it was of the greatest importance that France, by her influence in the English Parliament, succeeded in hindering such an undertaking. Who could lift up entirely the veil of the future? Who could have had a suspicion that the proceedings in England would one day act as a precedent for France?

In France it had been taken into consideration, whether it were better to support Monmouth or the Duke of York. At first Louis XIV was in favour of the latter, for it was not fitting for him to oppose an hereditary prince: Barrillon provided him with another motive besides; he said that if the Duke should ascend the throne, he could not and would not be a formidable King, for his nation would never, on account of his religion, entrust him with any considerable armed force[1]. Still for the moment it was thought that the Duke was much too closely allied with the Prince of Orange, and hesitation was felt about declaring directly in his favour. But then, should a declaration be therefore made in Monmouth's favour? There was reason to fear that he, if he won the upper hand, would encourage a declaration of war against France. Barrillon was in favour of supporting Monmouth and his adherents, but on condition that they should allow no grant of money to be made in Parliament for war against France. This coincided exactly with his master's views, for whom it was all-important to avoid any interference of the English power in opposition to his policy.

Barrillon sometimes gives minute details about his connexions in Parliament. The Lords, with whom he kept up an old understanding, refused for the most part his offers of money; Hollis refused even a portrait of Louis XIV set with

---

[1] 'Il ne peut jamais être autorisé en Angleterre, pour porter ses forces au dehors; la nation se défiera trop de lui, pour lui confier des armées et des forces considérables.'

diamonds; only Buckingham took money, which he then at once spent open-handed; still the money may have been even in his case a slight cement. Amongst the receivers of money we find names which occur perhaps the most frequently in the debates of the Lower House, such as Powle, Bennet, Sacheverell. Algernon Sidney devoted himself out of political zeal, without however despising the money, to carry on Barrillon's intercourse with the leaders of the Parliamentary factions. But the ambassador enlisted adherents even outside this circle, city-merchants of repute, active preachers.in the capital and in the country; their part was especially to counteract the attempts of the other party to dispose the people against France.

A grotesque figure is this ambassador, whom perhaps we may be permitted to describe. The air of England agreed well with him, and he seemed to enjoy his increasing circumference; he slapped his hands upon his thighs and exulted in their firmness: he had no objection to performing little personal functions in society; sometimes he pared his nails, or plucked out inconvenient hairs: but all this did not prevent him from being well received by Lady Portsmouth. Here he saw the King, who was sometimes very disagreeably impressed by his indiscretions, but soon again reconciled to him by the Duchess. The connexion between the ambassador and the mistress, who was thought to have her price, awakened a feeling of political virtue in the ladies of the high aristocracy, which finds utterance in their correspondence in expressions of contempt. Barrillon's strength consisted in his connexion with all parties, and in the employment of every kind of means; he informed his court of it with the candour of a man who thinks he is acting rightly, and who is aware of the services which he renders. In the wide reach of his activity he might be compared to Don Bernardino Mendoza, the Spanish ambassador in France at the time of the League, but Mendoza had more style and dash; Barrillon is perhaps more sharp-sighted, but at the same time more cynical; he gives his Prince counsels which, though cold-blooded, calculated and refined in their egoism, still hit the mark unerringly.

CHAPTER VIII.

THE appointed opening of the session, in which once more the most important questions were to be decided, was preceded by a decree of the government, which was likewise of great importance.

To resist the party of Monmouth and Shaftesbury, the leading statesmen had thought it advisable to summon the Duke of York from Scotland; his personal influence over the King and the idea of legitimate succession, which he embodied, formed a counterpoise to the popular tendencies of the other party. His presence however was now regarded as a national grievance. It was asserted that it was in open contradiction to the former declarations of the King and to the laws themselves that so notorious a Papist as the Duke should be allowed influence over affairs; already an accusation against him on the ground of Popery had been presented to the Grand Jury of Middlesex by Lord Shaftesbury and a number of his friends amongst the nobility and gentry, and formal proceedings had only been avoided because the court of King's Bench had succeeded in procuring the discharge of the jury before the case came on. Every one watched eagerly whether the Duke would venture to remain, now that Parliament was sitting. The leading men, who wished to calm Parliament, not to excite it, did not consider it advisable. But this time the Duke very energetically opposed the proposal that he should go away. He would, he said, for his brother's good make up his mind to anything which seemed in any way necessary; for his sake he would allow himself to be sold into slavery; but then the gain must be correspondingly great; he only foresaw evil results from the concessions of the government; he himself desired nothing so much as personally to confront his opponents [1]. He would obey nothing but his brother's express command. But even the King declared against him. His reason was that the impeachment of the Duke by the House of Commons must without doubt be expected; he could not possibly consent to his arrest; but, if he opposed it, he would have to fear a popular tumult, for which everything was already prepared. The Duke did not hide his anxiety lest the King should be induced, if he absented himself, to summon him by proclamation to present himself for trial; if then he did not obey he would be declared a traitor, then even his children would only be able to be re-established in their rights by Act of Parliament. The King promised him to publish no such proclamation; he would, he said, certainly give his support to laws by which Protestantism might be secured, but he would not go further. He would not allow his brother's rights to be impaired, still less his own rights to maintain an armed force or to dissolve Parliament at will.

So they parted,—the Duke this time full of anxious apprehension lest his opponents might, after all, carry the King away with them,—the King in the hope of gaining over Parliament by a change of bearing in foreign concerns, and by favouring the universal Protestant impulse, while, at the same time, he protected his brother's right of succession.

On the 21st of October he opened the new Parliament, as was his custom, in royal pomp, with the crown on his head; moreover he excused himself for reading the speech on this occasion. In it he laid the greatest emphasis on the new treaties for the security of England and the pacification of Christendom, which he had agreed to with Spain and the United Netherlands; and without doubt, he said, they would attain their object, if the consideration in which England was held were not diminished by domestic discord. Whilst he, to obviate this, had already sent his brother away, he now added

---

[1] These words were communicated to Sarotti the Venetian by a confidant of the Duke's.

positive assurances. He even urged the continuation of the investigations into the Popish plot, especially against the lords still confined in the Tower, and declared himself ready to accept any measure for the greater security of the Protestant religion, which was compatible with the maintenance of the regular succession. Upon union depended all the power and all the prestige of the country ; the eyes of the world were fixed on this assembly, as though on it depended the welfare of Europe, as well as of England herself.

And so, without doubt, it was ; every one was conscious of the fact ; but that, under present circumstances, this thought would induce Parliament to consent to the establishment of the Duke of York's right of succession, was hopeless from the beginning. A member of the Dutch embassy, who wished for nothing more than for a union between King and Parliament, remarked on the first day that it was impossible ; no persuasions, arguments nor precedents, neither promises nor threats, would bring it about. It was generally affirmed that no arrangement of any kind would afford the security which was required ; for, according to the principles of the Catholic Church, he would be allowed to break his promise, if it were to her interest. Were the Duke to call to his aid the Pope, or the King of France, or whoever he would, none of these would be so dangerous as the recognition of his succession by Parliament[1].

To this temper the tone and substance of the first debates corresponded. The horizon was again filled with the dangers of the Popish plot, which, since Dangerfield's disclosures, again found credence. Lord Russell, who now reached the zenith of his influence, drew attention to the dismissal of the jury, and the encouragement given to petitions opposed to the popular interest ; if that was done by men of rank and power, with the object of paying court to the Popish successor, what must not be expected if he became King ' This Parliament,' he exclaimed, ' must destroy Popery, or they will destroy us[2].'

---

[1] Particuliere Brieven van den Heer van Munnikhuysen aen den Heer Raedt Pensionaris 22 Oct. 1 Nov. Archives at the Hague.

[2] I follow the text in Grey's debates, which not only is the fullest, but also is most to be depended upon.

He moved in plain terms the decided rejection of the Popish succession, and in this he met with the most active support. Francis Winnington commented on the restriction of the right of petition as an infringement of the liberties of Englishmen, and the suppression of anti-Popish writings as an act of animosity against Protestantism. Complaints were made about the influence which the Duke of York had exercised, and the occupation of the most important posts by his friends. Parliament renewed its resolution to suppress Popery, and allow no Popish successor; it then declared that there existed an undoubted right to petition the King with regard to Parliamentary sessions, and the grievances of the country; to call the exercise of this right a violation of their duty was neither more nor less than an attack upon the freedom of the subject. Temple tried to direct attention to external affairs and their connexion with the great Protestant cause; but it was hardly possible to hear his words in the uproar that was raised. Sacheverell and Powle, the friends of the French ambassador, raised their voices against him, alleging that his only object was to get a money grant; this done, the House would be dismissed. It was at last determined to assure the King, by an address, that it was their intention to maintain his person and his government, as well as the Protestant religion, at home and abroad. Only with difficulty was the word 'abroad' introduced. The French ambassador laughed at the Spaniards and Dutch, who still founded some hope upon it. The King was little edified by this, and gave a very cool answer. The very thing he had wished to avoid happened before his eyes. External considerations, on which he laid the most stress, fell into the background before the complications of internal affairs, and every day resolutions relating to these took a direction adverse to him.

On the 2nd of November there was once more a lengthy debate, whether, following the example of the last Parliament, an Exclusion Bill should be brought forward, or whether once more, in a committee of the whole House, the means for securing Protestantism under a Catholic king should be discussed. The friends of the government urged the latter course, for it could be done very easily; the general need only be robbed of his army,—it was indeed strange and incomprehensible if, under a Protestant king, no means could be found to secure the religion so that it would have nothing to fear from a Popish successor. With great emphasis they added, that dissent from the religion was no legal ground for annulling the claim to the crown ; the King would agree to any other expedient except the exclusion ; if this were insisted upon it would cause a civil war. To all this were opposed by the other side the present and future dangers of the succession : as long as the Duke had a claim to the crown, the King was not sure of his life, as little as Queen Elizabeth had formerly been in the lifetime of the Queen of Scots. Lord Russell's remark was repeated ; there were already many who shouted ' Huzza for the Duke,' and drank his health, without troubling themselves about the King ; what would happen if he even ascended the throne ? On all sides Papists and Jesuits would be seen to gather ; the King would be surrounded by a Popish council and by Popish bishops. No one could then count on moderation ; souls would be damned, bodies burnt, goods confiscated. The most frightful events of former times were called to remembrance—the executions of bloody Mary, St. Bartholomew's Day, the Irish massacre. It was determined to introduce a bill, by which the Duke of York should be declared incapable of inheriting the crown of England [1].

At the same time two other important designs were formed, founded upon precedents in the past, to be applied to the future ; the one to organise, as in the days of Elizabeth, an association for the security of the King and of Protestantism, and the other to grant King Charles the right of naming his successor, as Henry VIII had done. It was thought certain that he would then declare himself in Monmouth's favour. Monmouth was again in the town ; shortly before the opening of Parliament he had been present, with great pomp, at a banquet given by the Lord Mayor, and had then been driven through the town amidst the acclamations of an innumerable crowd. It was desired to put him at the head of the association, so that he might oppose the Duke of York, if necessary,

---

[1] Barrillon's reports (Nov. 4) and the notes of the Duke of York agree on this point.

with force.   Shaftesbury would have returned to his old post as Lord Chancellor, his friends would also have acquired high positions, the administration of the state would have been remodelled according to the views of the Nonconformists, and to the King, on his assent to this, ample supplies would be granted for all contingencies at home and abroad.

But so far as this, Barrillon, even although these were the schemes of his principal friends, would not and could not go with them, chiefly, as we have shown, because Monmouth, in that case, must necessarily have pledged himself to war against France.   Barrillon expressed to King Louis his views, that the hereditary right should not be allowed to fall entirely ; for if retained it would enable the Duke of York to raise himself again ; he was consequently directed to remain in communication with both parties, and to play off the one against the other [1].

In the meanwhile a third claim had also arisen between the two.   In the committee which was to draw up the Exclusion Bill, it was remarked that the bill could only be directed against the Duke himself and not against his heirs ; there was no ground for excluding them also.   Often already the Prince of Orange had been called upon to come in person to England and to affirm the right of next succession to the throne which he possessed through his wife.   A wording of the resolution was demanded in which this should be definitely asserted.

But this was exactly what the adherents of Monmouth opposed.   They proposed a resolution that, if the King were to die during the lifetime of the Duke of York, the crown should pass to him on whom it would have devolved had the Duke himself already been dead.   In this way the claim ascribed to Monmouth remained unimpaired.   They opposed even the expression, accepted in the preamble of the bill, according to which the Duke was described as the presumptive heir to the crown, and succeeded in having it struck out.   As against the Duke of York, so also against the Prince of Orange did the adherents of Monmouth prevail.   In the

---

[1] Du roi a Barrillon, 15th Nov.: ' Empescher que ces deux factions ne se réunissent.   Tachez de combattre une faction par l'autre.'

form which they approved the bill was read a third time on November 11/21 ; once more it was then energetically. opposed. The Duke, it was said, might be brought before a court of justice, and if he deserved it, his head might be cut off, but no one could do away with the fact that he was heir-apparent to the throne ; the oath of allegiance did not concern only the King but his heirs also. With still closer adherence to constitutional principle, it was argued that, if the crown were bestowed by the people, it would be deprived of the reverence necessary to it. It was not customary in England for Parliament to make a king. On the other side, the Wars of the Roses in the fifteenth century were recalled : how often had Parliament in those days disposed of the crown ; there ex-isted statutory decisions on the point ; Parliament must affirm this right, as it was fully competent to exercise it. The bill passed the House as it had been drawn up ; it was its popular tendency which won for it universal approval. The Common Council of London advised the King to follow the counsels of Parliament, and assured him that in all dangers, in which he might consequently be involved, he would have the support of his capital. When Lord Russell brought the bill, on the 15th November, into the Upper House, he was accompanied not only by a number of members of the Lower House, but by the Lord Mayor and other dignitaries of the city. Whilst he read the title of the bill, as that by which the Duke of York was to be declared incapable of inheriting the imperial crown of England, inarticulate sounds were heard among his com-panions, which testified their sense of the high importance of the motion introduced.

In the Upper House also there was a party which wished for the exclusion ; with Shaftesbury and Essex even Sunder-land was agreed, probably because the Duchess of Portsmouth, to whom he prefered to adhere, was likewise inclined to this expedient. She may have had motives for it, above all the wish by a union with the most powerful Parliamentary leaders, to avoid an indictment in Parliament, with which she was threat-ened. But more than this, the Duchess of York had not vouchsafed her the same intimacy as of old ; she seemed to have almost more consideration for Mme. de Mazarin ;

and this time the French ambassador left her full liberty.
At the court itself a cabal was formed against the Duke
of York; the bishops were told that the King wished that a
dispute between the two Houses should be avoided [1].

It was like the King, who never drew the reins tight, to let
this tendency have free course; he would not blame the
Duchess if she secured herself against possible emergencies.
But otherwise it cannot be doubted that he opposed the
exclusion with all his heart. He adhered firmly on principle
to hereditary right; he even feared that, if the Duke were put
aside, the whole force of the opposition would be directed
against himself. But more than this, for the maintenance of
the exclusion extensive arrangements would have been necessary, which would have thrown the exercise of power into
the hands of the opposition. Amongst the statesmen who
surrounded him, he found at least one who attached himself zealously to him, and just for this last-mentioned reason.
Lord Halifax was an old antagonist of the Duke of York, an
opponent of Papacy on principle; but yet he would not suffer
Shaftesbury and Monmouth to come into power; he always
turned his natural vehemence against those who for the moment
stood most in his way, or actually threatened him. Whether or
not he belonged to the Trimmers, who formed a middle party
between the two great parties, I leave undecided; at least
he appears at the same time as an independent character,
full of egoism and ambition. As early as the 15th November
(for every delay seemed hazardous for the powerful popular
influence), the bill which had been introduced was taken into
consideration. The Upper House resolved itself into a
Committee; Shaftesbury and Essex spoke in favour of the
bill; Halifax opposed it. Presence of mind, wit, and a happy
gift of expression peculiar to him — he is one of the best
pamphleteers that has ever lived — made him capable of
coping with both antagonists; the whole debate was a combat
between them. Halifax spoke some sixteen times. It is a
pity that no detailed report of this debate exists [2]. It was

---

[1] From a letter of Hyde's to the Duke of York. Extracts 107.

[2] The best account of it is in the papers of James II, who was informed by his
friends in the ministry and amongst the Lords.

advantageous to the defenders of hereditary right that, in the circle in which he spoke, a natural sympathy in its favour prevailed. After a debate of six hours, the bill was rejected by a majority of sixty-three to thirty, consisting of forty-nine lords and fourteen bishops.

Such had been the King's wish. The bill was to be rejected at once without amendments; not till afterwards was there to be any talk of restrictive decrees. When the Upper House passed on to these, there was no longer any question of sparing the Duke. The House withdrew the Act by which he had been absolved from taking the appointed oath, and declared him incapable of filling any public office; it then proceeded to consider the restrictions to which he must be subjected, if he actually ascended the throne, and circumscribed his power in a manner which would have lessened the influence of the crown itself. All that, however, produced no impression upon the Commons. They were offended that their bill had been rejected by the Lords without a conference, and they were well enough informed to know that the King had been privy to this.

Their temper became apparent when, two days afterwards, a new reminder was received from the King of his demands, especially for the sake of saving Tangiers, which without speedy assistance must be entirely lost. However low the importance of the place might be rated, no one could deny that there lay a danger in letting it fall into the hands of France, who through it would rule the corsairs of Algiers. Still that also met with little consideration, for how could it be discussed at a moment when everything was at stake? 'Who would speak of a cabin, if the ship were sinking? of the preservation of a house, if the enemy were landing on the coast? The danger lay in the Popish successor and his adherents. They would grant money if they had security, but not otherwise.' 'I speak,' said one of the members for London, 'in the name of the greatest part of the burgesses of the city; it will give half of all its possessions, it will give all to save its religion and freedom, but it will not pay a penny either for Tangiers or for any other purpose till it knows it is secure. The city of London is the great bulwark of Protestantism, upon it the

first attack will fall. The Duke rules over Scotland ; the Irish
and the English Papists will follow him ; he will be obeyed
by the officials of high and low rank whom the King has
appointed ; he will be just such a King as he thinks good.
Even the members of this House will then be obliged to
make their peace with him as well as they can. I for my
part will not do so. I move that we entreat the King that he
should not, for the sake of one man, destroy three kingdoms[1].

In this sense ran the answer which the Commons gave the
King ; no resolutions would be taken with regard to Tangiers
at a time when a cloud, which had so long threatened the
land, was ready to discharge itself on their heads. They
first turned all the heat of their indignation against Lord
Halifax, who, contrary to all expectation, had stepped forward
as the champion of the Duke of York's right of succession,
though he had formerly been considered his opponent ; they
called upon the King in an address to dismiss Lord Halifax
from his presence and from his council.

We can now better understand the position which Halifax
took up. He was, as we have mentioned, an opponent
both of absolute government and of the Papacy ; when he
took up the part of the Duke of York, who inclined towards
both, he did so because he still did not think that Parliament
might take upon itself to interfere in the succession, especially
as their decision in the existing state of parties would undoubtedly be given in Monmouth's favour. When the Prince
of Orange had it suggested to him, that the restrictions, to
which the next heir to the throne was to be subjected because
he was a Papist, would be injurious to the crown for all times,
Halifax assured him that these were to apply only to the
person of the Duke. He for his part did not believe that the
Duke would ever ascend the throne ; it would only be to his,
the Prince of Orange's, advantage that the protection of the
hereditary right would redound[2] ; otherwise the next Parliament

---

[1] Sir Thomas Player's speech. Grey's Debates viii. 11.

[2] Mr. van Leeuwen au Prince d'Orange, 7/17 Dec. 1680 : 'Qu'il vous avoit
toujours consideré comme le seul Prince sur lequel le party protestant pourroit
faire fondement—qu'il savoit bien luy que Mr. le Duc de York ne pouvoit pas
régner en Angleterre, qu'il n'y régneroit pas, que luy seroit le premier à s'y opposer,

would likewise exclude him because he was a foreigner, or on some other pretext, and would prefer the Duke of Monmouth; for that was the aim of all the machinations. Halifax at the same time caused the Prince to be assured of his deep reverence, and of his conviction that he was the only man who could save Protestantism. Away above all the confusions of the moment he directed his eyes with clear decision to the Prince of Orange, as indeed his personal position impelled him to do. At first his successful defence of the hereditary right gained him the entire confidence of Charles II. To the address of the Commons he replied that he would dismiss neither Lord Halifax nor any other minister from his council, unless their misdemeanours were proved to him. The bishops above all were agreed with the King and the minister, for Monmouth's rise threatened their downfall, and with them was also a somewhat considerable party in the country. Occasionally the outbreak of disturbances was feared, and for such a case the available forces were counted up, a number of influential men were noted, who would declare themselves against the exclusion and in favour of the government [1].

In the midst of these extensive movements, the trials relating to the Popish plots were resumed. All that had gone before seemed almost to be only preliminary. The chief designs were directed against the Popish lords in the Tower, who were accused of having conspired against the King's life, so as to make way for the Popish successor, who was to re-introduce Catholicism. Of this, above all, Thomas Howard, Viscount Stafford, was accused: he was already advanced in years; on the day on which he entered upon his sixty-ninth year (Nov. 30, 1680) proceedings against him were commenced before the House of Lords, in Westminster Hall, in the same form as was before used at the trial of Lord Strafford. The

---

mais que V. A. se voulût bien garder des personnes, qui le tromperoient,—quils ne vouloient présentement faire passer l'acte de l'exclusion, que pour mettre hors de dispute, qu'il étoit dans le pouvoir du parlement de faire une séclusion—que cette brigue dans 2 ou 3 ans d'icy travaillera de faire d'autres séclusions et à y établir le Duc de Monmouth, à quoi toute cette machine tend.' Groen 454.

[1] Conversation between Halifax and Reresby, in Reresby.

Commissioners of the Commons attempted to prove two things—the reality of the conspiracy, which, at that time, no one seriously disputed ; and the participation of the accused in the designs directed against the King's life. Besides Oates, who stated this in general, the two principal witnesses against him were Dugdale and Turberville, who both of them affirmed that the Viscount had wished to hire them to murder the King. Stafford denied everything and, on his side, endeavoured to prove the untrustworthiness of the witnesses ; but this was not done with sufficient clearness to save him : he especially took his stand upon the fact, that not one of the actions of which he was accused was affirmed by more than one witness, whereas the English law required two. But the judges who were consulted on this point, answered that twofold witness was not required for the proof of separate occurrences, but only for the fact, which in this case lay in the attempt to hire men to murder the King, and for this at all events there were two witnesses. The King was present in his gallery ; he took notice of what was said, and how the votes went ; he was not convinced, but a considerable majority expressed themselves in favour of condemnation : astonishment was felt at finding that it included four members of the Howard family. The King and his government would have had reason to fear immediate danger had they opposed the vehemence of the current. On the 29th December Stafford was executed, still protesting his innocence.

We will not discuss the various motives which brought about this condemnation. In the minds of many, their conviction of the reality of the conspiracy was connected with their dread of an impending Catholic reaction ; upon individuals the proceedings produced the impression that an innocent man had been convicted, but the general opinion was that the reality of the plot had now, once for all, been unconditionally confirmed [1]. But what could be expected in consequence,

---

[1] Sarotti thinks: ' Possessori de beni ecclesiastici, quelli che vivono nel regno ai loro beni senza impieghi di corte ma impressi della congiura per le stampe disseminatesi et altri zelanti della religione protestante e politici essendone stati, i quali liberamente hanno detto convenire, che il Conte muora, per reputatione del parlamento et per contentare la plebe.' The trial is in State Trials ix.

especially considering the legal ground which had been adopted? It was thought that the charge would not be restricted to the lords already imprisoned ; it would again be aimed at the Queen, of whose divorce there was still always a talk, but would especially be levelled at the Duke of York, who was implicated by Coleman's letters, and might possibly even reach the King if he resisted.

In a renewed debate about the supplies, the Lower House at first repeated its resolution with regard to the Exclusion Bill[1]. For, as Lord Russell said, in his dry tone, so well calculated to inspire confidence and awaken conviction, 'from a man whose religion made him the nation's enemy she could never expect either security for her faith, or protection for life and liberty.' The King could reject the repeated demand by referring them for decision to the Lords. In the Commons, hereupon an inclination was shown to accept this view, but on the understanding that the path of impeachment and condemnation should then be entered ; this would have concerned not only the Duke, but also the government at the same time. For to carry out the verdict, as well as to maintain the exclusion, an association would have been demanded, and in this the King saw the intention of making the militia independent of his command. Against this he would have been unable to appeal to the Upper House ; there, on the contrary, the proposal was made in plain terms, that the posts of command in the Tower, at Hull, Plymouth, and Portsmouth, should only be filled up with the approval of Parliament: of the Duke's friends those were singled out for attack who were most attached to the King. Lord Shaftesbury declared that, if the outcry which resounded from the heights,—that is to say, the proposal in the Upper House,—found no hearing, 'the echo would reverberate in the valley; the House of Commons would obtain a hearing for itself. There then appeared, in reality, in the address of the House of Commons, the demand that from henceforth all the posts in the administration, the courts of justice, and the army, should be filled only by men of whose

---

[1] The address in Parliamentary History iv. 1225. From Grey viii. 200, it is to be seen that it was already proposed and accepted on 20th December.

devotion to the Protestant cause there was full conviction. Upon this understanding the Lower House declared itself in general to be inclined to support the King in carrying out his alliances, so far as these tended to the advantage of Protestantism; a restriction which highly displeased him, because by it the Lower House reserved for itself a means of testing his administration of external affairs. In fact, he saw himself threatened in every point of his royal privileges. And besides, the Lower House had hinted at other bills for the good of the nation, upon the acceptance of which it counted. What could these be? Once it was openly said that annual Parliaments were indispensable; next, a Comprehension Bill in favour of the Presbyterians had already advanced far, and had even reached its second reading. It was introduced into the Upper House. Its object was to absolve all Dissenters, who would sign the Test Oath, from all other oaths, even from the Oath of Allegiance, by the wording of which all sectaries were excluded from public posts. Matters seemed to be taking a course similar to that taken in the year 1641. A petition was brought into the Upper House, in which the lords spiritual were not named [1]. The Lower House, to cut off the King from all resources independent of its grants, passed a resolution to call some day to account any one who should advance money to the government on any branch of the revenues [2].

Who would not have thought that King Charles II, in the midst of all these hindrances, demands, and aggressions, would have felt personally also very much oppressed? But he remained always the same. Old acquaintances, who visited him occasionally in the evenings, found him, to their astonishment, not only composed, but even cheerful. This was doubtless the result of his temperament, but still there was an especial reason: he had a means ready for freeing himself from these difficulties. He need only change his foreign policy. Whilst the allies, to whom he, till now, had always

---

[1] Barrillon, 16th Dec.: 'Le but principal de la chambre basse est d'établir des fréquens parlemens,—le parlement gouvernera, quand il ne sera même assemblé.'

[2] Extracts from James II's correspondence, in Macpherson's Extracts. State Papers i. 112.

adhered, urged him to give way to his Parliament, the King of France, whom he opposed, once more offered him support against it.

Louis XIV observed that the anti-French disposition of Parliament could be alleviated by no machinations, but rather increased daily. In what a situation would he have been placed, had the King been not only obliged to give way to it now, but been bound to it by annual sessions[1]! This anxiety gave him uneasy thoughts. Just as he wished to restrict the King of England by the Parliament, he wished to restrict the Parliament by the King. Unanimous action on the part of England he regarded as a danger for France.

Already, in November, when that intention was first expressed, Louis XIV had commissioned his ambassador to strengthen King Charles in his resistance to it, and to assure him of his support, or, as he says straight out, his protection against it.

Upon this the former secret negotiations recommenced, through the old channel, the Duke of St. Albans. France made offers, on the supposition that King Charles would dissolve the Parliament: in his eyes these offers were still too insignificant to be accepted; he neither concluded a treaty, nor came to an agreement, but he became convinced that he would find support with France if he freed himself from the Parliament.

The Lower House, which feared a sudden interruption, was just occupied in carrying its resolution in favour of the Dissenters, when Black Rod knocked at the door on the 10/20th January, 1680/81. The King at once, by a prorogation, brought the session to an end.

---

[1] Du roi à Barrillon, Nov. 23: 'Comme vous jugez que la perte du Roi d'Angleterre est infallible, s'il consent une fois, que le parlement s'assemble tous les ans, sans qu'il le puisse empescher, ny abreger ny interrompre le temps, qui sera fixé par sa séance, il sera bon que vous le fortifiez sous main à s'y opposer.'

CHAPTER IX.

THE PARLIAMENT AT OXFORD, MARCH 1680/81.

IN the midst of these commotions the party names of Whig and Tory arose in England.

The former had been heard in Scotland since the rising in Edinburgh in 1648, which bears the name of the Whiggamore raid. It is worth while to notice the party to which this name was originally applied. It was the party which rejected the agreement that had been made between the moderate Presbyterians and Charles I,—a party of zealous Covenanting views, but in no way of republican tendency. It had contributed sensibly to the victory of Cromwell and the Commonwealth, but did not, on that account, approve in any way of their conduct towards the King. It adhered to the old Scottish combination of the idea of national sovereignty with that of hereditary monarchy. Doubtless, in Scotland also, the republican tendencies appeared; for instance, in October 1680, the King and the Duke were excommunicated with due form; a manifesto was issued, which rejected all authority not proceeding from election, which refused to recognise church law, feudal law, or even the Parliament, and revived the idea that men were bound to live according to the law of the people of Israel, which God himself had given[1]. These were, however, rather Anabaptist than Presbyterian views; their adherents were indeed called Whigs, but 'wild Whigs.'

In the same way there was great talk of 'the wild Irish' in the north of Ireland, who had always been called Tories, amongst whom at that time an Irish Scanderbeg, by name

---

[1] Proclamation of Terwood. Wodrow iii.

O'Hanlon, was prominent on account of his rash, courageous, and fortunate enterprises: he was shot in April 1681. The Tories were outcasts, who opposed the ordinances of the Church and State like the Heyducs elsewhere, and were supported by the clan-feeling of the natives, and, at least according to a proclamation of the Lord Lieutenant's, by the Catholic priests [1].

The wild Whigs and the Tories alike, while taking up a position of hostility to the constitution which emerged from the Restoration, founded as it was upon union between Episcopalians and Presbyterians, had yet a certain internal relationship with the conflicting tendencies which it contained: in them appeared, as it were, the extreme points of this struggle; and the application of these names to the strife of English parties is not without significance.

This happened first with the word Tory. It was used to denote the opponents of the exclusion, because the Duke of York was regarded as the secret protector of the Irish rebels, so that the maintenance of his hereditary right might appear to be one of their demands. They were not a little confounded, that men should wish to identify their loyal and zealously episcopal sentiments with the doings of bands of Irish robbers. The indefatigable persecutor of the Tories in Ireland, Ormond, appeared in England as himself a Tory. It was quite in accordance with the spirit of the trials about the plot, to make the champions of prerogative and of hereditary right appear as the allies of Catholicism. For a time these insulted men sought in vain for a corresponding name for the champions of the exclusion, till they seized on the name of Whigs, which once more arose at the time of the excommunication of the King and his brother. True, the exclusionists had no more in common with the 'wild Whigs' than the opponents of the exclusion with the 'wild Irish,' the Tories; but still they, after all, were very near that Whiggamore party from which this name had in reality been derived. Both were equally far from being republicans; but both were labouring to limit the prerogative, as far as

---

[1] Carte, Ormond iv. 482.

seemed in any way compatible with the maintenance of the monarchy [1].

The contrast between the theories which began to be formed by the two parties in opposition to one another, may be learnt from Algernon Sidney's 'Discourses concerning Government.' In it Sidney derives all power from the people, and defends republicanism against those who rejected altogether this form of state organisation: he himself would give it the preference over monarchy; but still his idea is not to introduce it into England, nor, on the basis of its principle, like the Agitators and Levellers, to alter the constitution of the country: he recognises the King, the Lords, and the existing Lower House, although its character was so little representative. His idea is first of all to restrain the monarchy within the narrowest limits. For as the King receives his right from the people, so must the people determine also his privileges, watch over their exercise, direct him, and provide for the succession. Sidney disputes the King's right to summon Parliament, to adjourn or dissolve it. That was one of the immediately pending questions: he decides it against the crown. The work, more discursive than systematic in its character, contains the result of many varied studies, as far as the existing learning made them in any way possible; it offers wide prospects and general points of view, but bears at the same time the character of the moment, and is founded on the disputes of the time. Great attention was just then awakened by a theological and political theory, which appeared in Filmer's Patriarcha, and was regarded as a manifesto of the High Church party. Filmer describes the liberties of the people as the outcome of royal favour, and demands the unconditional obedience of the subject: he takes his stand upon the Norman Conquest and the right it gave, which he however extends so far as to destroy all national freedom. Sidney, who opposes him in every point, does not enter much into his theological arguments; with reference to the constitution he goes back to the Anglo-Saxon times; the liberties of the people he declares to be

---

[1] North's Examen 3⸱6; Life of Lord Guildford 111.

their original possession, inherited as their birthright; he combats the popular idea of rebellion.

Filmer and Sidney indicate approximately the fundamental views of the two parties, although these parties had not entirely apprehended all the whole consequences of the ideas and doctrines which they expressed. Contrasts like these cannot be expressed by books, manifestoes, and formulae; they spring from the fermenting and divided depths of society; they are mighty movements, without appointed limits or a fixed aim; they are in a state of continual change.

In truth the Whigs consisted of the men of the exclusion, the defenders of the reality of the Popish plot, the Nonconformists and their friends, and those who petitioned for free parliaments; the Tories consisted of the opponents of the Catholic prosecution and the excessive use of petitions, of the adherents of ecclesiastical uniformity and the regular succession, above all of the champions of the prerogative, against which just then opponents were advancing with ever-growing claims [1].

Excited by the unexpected prorogation, the Lord Mayor and aldermen,—for the Whigs were in a strong majority in the Common Council and magistracy of the city, as well as in the clubs and coffee-houses,—turned to the King with the entreaty that he would not only re-open Parliament on the appointed day, but would allow it to continue sitting until it had finished its important duty of securing the preservation of religion and of the King himself, especially its procedure against the Catholic lords. But the very intercession of the city produced an effect adverse to the fulfilment of their entreaty. Charles II began to be afraid lest perhaps, if he again prorogued Parliament, the House, with the concurrence of the capital, might make an attempt to continue its sittings all the same. He announced the dissolution of the Lower House, and whilst he then fixed the re-opening of the new Parliament as soon as possible, the 21st of March, he further appointed that it should be held not in London but in Oxford,

---

[1] North, in the Life of Dudley North, gives as the views of the one party, 'to destroy the then present government,' and of the other, 'to sustain the credit and authority of it.'

for he wished by all means to detach the Parliament from its connexion with the population of the capital, which shared its views[1]. As to the new elections, he thought he could rather gain than lose by them, both because the new members would not consider themselves bound by the former resolutions, and also—for in cases of this kind a man catches at everything which may further the hopes he cherishes—because the Dissenters would endeavour to conciliate him, so as to obtain his sanction for the change of law proposed in their favour.

That there was still a hope of obtaining some solution, appears from the repetition of the almost desperate attempt to bring back the Duke of York to the Anglican Church. It was represented to him that the whole attack on the government originated in the demand for exclusion, and that this would lose all meaning the moment he again attached himself to the Protestant faith. Seymour, who at that time took great part in the government, introduced into a letter to him a significant intimation about the dangers of the future. He told him that it was easier to conquer three kingdoms than to save them from destruction.

But that produced no impression upon the Duke, whose intentions had a quite different nature and aim; he had already reverted, and this time of his own accord, to the idea of seeking his safety in an alliance with France.

When he had been again obliged to go away before the last session, he expressed his most sincere anxiety lest the proceedings should turn out to his disadvantage. In a conversation with the French ambassador, under the irritation caused by a very distasteful journey, he expressed, even to the surprise of his auditor, the unexpected intention, if the worst came to the worst, of standing on the defensive in Scotland against the English Parliament; he hoped that then all Ireland would rise in his favour, and even in England a strong party declare for him. For such a case, in which his cause would have become pre-eminently a Catholic one, he laid claim to the help of the most Christian King.

---

[1] As Barrillon says: 'Où il ne craindra pas, que la séance se continuera malgré lui.'

Not prevented by his existing connexion with the English Parliament Louis XIV gave him promise of assistance, to be given as soon as he had once gained a sure footing in Scotland [1].

One of the first acts of John Churchill was the arrangement of this connexion : he had in his hands the cipher for the correspondence with the French ambassador.

But, instead of the result originally expected, the contrary occurred ; instead of being carried away by Parliament, King Charles fell into the bitterest strife with it, so that, as we saw, at his court even the old connexion with France again seemed desirable. Just at this moment the Duke of York sent his confidant to his brother ; Churchill was to warn him most urgently against the conclusion of an alliance with the opponents of France, and was to represent to him that only by being on good terms with Louis XIV, would he be able to resist the attacks of Parliament ; he was to call on the Ambassador to lay before the King proposals for a new union [2]. At the English court Lawrence Hyde, the son of the Chancellor and brother-in-law of the Duke, enjoyed the greatest consideration ; he was at the head of the financial administration, and possessed at the same time the full confidence of both King and Duke. The King commissioned him to examine the state of the Treasury, and to tell him how far, if the next Parliament also denied the requisite grants, he would be able to proceed with only the regular revenues ; whether, if he introduced some economies, he would be able to meet the expenses of the state and the court. Hyde judged that this was not possible, but that some help, if only a little, was indispensable to make ends meet. Such assistance was precisely what the French ambassador could offer. Three different influences were at work in this matter : the dynastic interest, which was represented by the Duke ; the King's old idea of obtaining perfect independence from Parliament at any price ; and the policy of France. Barrillon represented to his King,

---

[1] Barillon, Oct. 28 and 31. Answer of November 9, in Dalrymple ii. 331.

[2] ' J'espère,' so we read in James' letter to Barrillon, in which he refers him to Churchill for further particulars, ' qu'il n'y aura aucun obstacle n'y aucune cause de différer de faire vos propositions à S. M.'

that Charles II must submit to Parliament, and so make
common cause with it against France, if France did not grant
him some assistance[1]; of such he must be assured before
Parliament was again assembled, so that he might from the
beginning adopt a confident bearing.

The dissolution of Parliament in spite of all entreaties, and
the transfer of the new assembly to Oxford, could not but
double the discontent and ferment in the capital. Once more
a petition, signed by sixteen peers, against the transfer of
Parliament was presented to the King : he rejected it, not
without a show of ill-temper. On the other hand the city
expressed its gratitude to them. Never had the connexion
between the lords of the opposition and the Common Council
been more close : there was a scheme on foot to secure direct
influence to Shaftesbury and Buckingham by conferring on
them municipal appointments. Wherever Monmouth showed
himself he was greeted with rejoicing and hope ; in neighbouring towns deputations came to meet and escort him. The
enthusiasm which he awoke is expressed among other ways
by the belief in manifestations of the spiritual world in his
favour. Forms veiled from head to foot were said to have
appeared to ladies, who felt sympathy with him and his fate,
and to have comforted them as to his future and inspired him
through them with courage : he was only to try the battle
with the lion ; the old Charles would do nothing to him ; his
star would rise again on the 21st of March ;—and more of
the same kind. Occasionally there were gatherings in the city
which required the interference of the soldiers ; but already
it was questioned whether the troops had any right to appear
in the city, and whether the King had any authority for
marching them through the streets to the Tower. In the
midst of this excitement the new elections took place. In
London itself the old members were re-elected and greeted
with an address of thanks for their conduct during the former
session. So also all the exertions of the court at Westminster

---

[1] 'Il faut que ce prince soit appuyé à V. M. et se soustienne par la protection, et
le secours qu'il entirera, ou qu'il se soumette en tièrement au parlement. Il est apparent, que le party du peuple prévaudra sur celuy du roi.'

proved vain; one of the two members was William Walker, who had acquired for himself, by his vigorous prosecutions of the Catholics, the name of priest-hunter. Others who had been re-elected in neighbouring places might be observed assembling in triumph before Whitehall, so that the King should see them. But the same feelings did not prevail every-where; some hundred new members may have been elected, but it was extremely doubtful from the very first whether by this means the disposition of the majority would be changed. The general opinion was, that not a penny should be granted to the King if he did not accept the exclusion of the Duke of York[1].

It happened at this moment that Barrillon, in consequence of his own exertions, and mainly of the negotiations of the Duke of York, was once more empowered definitely to assure the King of England of the support of Louis XIV in case he could not come to an agreement with his Parliament. In London the outbreak of disturbances must obviously be dreaded, if there was the slightest rumour of an understanding between the two Kings. Only in the deepest secrecy in the Queen's apartments could Barrillon hastily speak with King Charles; the actual negotiations he carried on with Lawrence Hyde, the sole confidant of all parties concerned. The annual subsidy from France was fixed at 2,000,000 livres Tournois, a small sum, which just sufficed to cover the deficit in the reduced expenditure of the court; the minister in return held out expectations of a peaceful attitude in politics in accordance with the interests of France.

As yet however nothing was definitely determined; not even a written protocol about the matter had been accepted. Barrillon had even at this moment once more received orders

---

[1] Vignola (secretario Veneto): 'Nelle loro persuasioni al popolo mai tra-lasciano d'andar insinuando—che per modo ne cause alcuna delibrar debbano denaro al re, dovendo piu tosto azzardare le loro fortune e le vote' (6 Marzo). Or, as Barrillon states it: 'La volonté de S. M. n'est pas, que je fasse aucun usage des facilités, qu'elle apporte à la conclusion du traité, si je ne vois les affaires reduites icy en tel état que j'ai sujet d'appréhendre que le roi se soumette au Parlement.' Despatch of Feb. 1681, printed in Dalrymple; but this passage and the explanation following on it is omitted.

not to break off his connexion with the Parliamentary leaders. For as yet there was no question of confidence on any side. We do the King of England wrong, if we imagine that he had determined beforehand not to allow the Parliament, which he had summoned, to proceed to any active work; on the contrary he wished in all seriousness to see how far he could get on with it; he hoped to do so by means of a proposal which ran counter to the French interest. But at the same time he had also determined beforehand that, if Parliament rejected his expedient and refused the supplies he demanded, he would at once grasp again the hand of Louis XIV and give up all resistance to his policy.

The journey to Oxford presented a tumultuous and threatening appearance. The King sent his guards there, and caused some places on the way to be occupied by troops. Similarly the opposition lords rode into Oxford with an armed train, as the German princes in former days used to go to the Diet. The members arrived in companies of from forty to fifty, escorted by their townsmen, especially the Londoners. These wore blue bows and ribands, on which might be read the words 'No Popery,' 'No slavery.' For Protestantism and Parliamentary freedom were now ideas which coincided. The citizens wished to relieve guard in protecting their representatives from any possible act of violence.

On Monday, the 21st of March, the King opened the new session in the Public Schools at Oxford, not without complaining of the conduct of the last House of Commons, and with a repetition of his former declarations with regard to home and foreign affairs. He said also that he could not change his views about the succession, mainly because, without the maintenance of the safety and dignity of the monarchy, neither religion nor property could be preserved; but also he was inclined to remove the anxiety which sprang from the possibility that a Popish successor might come to the throne: if means could be found by which, in such a case, the administration of the government would remain in Protestant hands [1], he was ready to accept it; but it must be an

---

[1] 'That in such a case the administration of the government may remain in Protestant hands.'

expedient by which religion should be preserved without the destruction of monarchy. 'Religion and government depend upon one another, support one another. Let us be united at home, that we may recover the esteem and consideration we used to have abroad.'

But what did the King and his ministers aim at? We can judge approximately when, in the papers of the Duke of York, we stumble upon the complaint that he was treated as a minor; the Prince and Princess of Orange were to be declared Protectors of the kingdom for his whole lifetime. It appears still more clearly from a letter of Temple's to Sidney, who was at that time living at the Hague: the Duke, says he, after Charles II's death is to be king only in name, and the kingdom is to be administered by a Protector and the Privy Council; the Prince of Orange is to be Protector. This had already been thought of during the last session; the measure that had formerly been kept back was now to be brought forward so as to strike the decisive blow [1].

The first occurrences in the session showed that the King this time also would meet with great difficulties from his Parliament. In his speech he had described the behaviour of the former Parliament as unjustifiable, illegal, and arbitrary. As a reply the new Parliament re-elected the former Speaker, and he in his address let drop the words that the new House wished for no change. Without hesitation the impending question was taken up in the Upper House. One morning when the King had come into the House, even before the sitting began, Lord Shaftesbury approached and handed him a memoir, which contained the only possible expedient for smoothing over the quarrel. The King glanced through the paper; it contained the advice that he should recognise the Duke of Monmouth as his successor. Charles thought it advisable to explain himself upon this point: he would wish for nothing more, he said, than to have legitimate children, one of whom might occupy the throne after him, instead of the Duke of York and his children; but nothing in the

---

[1] Sir William Temple to Mr. Sidney. Sheen, Feb. 20, Blencowe. Sidney's diary ii. 177.

world could induce him to do a thing contrary to all law. Shaftesbury rejoined, with bold assurance, that laws could be put aside ; he need only leave it to them, that is, to Parliament. The King rejected this with emphasis : 'the older I grow, the more steadfast I become ; I have wisdom and law in my favour ; well-minded people are on my side ; and there is the Church '—he pointed to the bishops present—'which will remain united to me. My Lord, she and I will not be separated[1].'

Many heard this conversation, Monmouth amongst others, who made a face as if he scoffed at the proposal ; the friends of the Prince of Orange however were for the first time impressed with the feeling that Monmouth's claim was no mere chimera, as they had hitherto thought.

This occurred on Thursday the 24th of March ; on the same day, in the sitting of the Lower House, the debate turned on the expedient which had been announced. The proposal was made to bring in again the Exclusion Bill, but to many such a course seemed opposed to the respect due to the King, as he had spoken of another expedient. A member of the name of Whorwood remarked that this new plan could not be of much consequence, and that to listen to it would rather be disadvantageous to the King's advisers ; a little delay in the matter could do no harm, it would rather contribute to satisfy people. Upon his motion the following Saturday was fixed for the discussion.

This sitting on the 26th of March must be decisive. From the first there was difficulty even in advancing so far as to refer the matter to free discussion in a committee of the whole House, the usual process in such cases, and the one now again demanded by the King's friends. One of these, John Ernly, who held a high position in the administration, determined, though not without a certain amount of hesitation, to come forward with the projected plan, even under the forms of the ordinary business. His view was to separate the succession to the throne from the succession to the administration, and to allow the former to pass to the Duke,

---

[1] The account in North's Examen, from a pamphlet of the time, bears a party colour : I take my account from Barrillon.

the latter to his children, in the first place to the Princess
of Orange. Whether this had been arranged beforehand
with the Prince of Orange has not been as yet ascertained
with certainty, nor even what share Halifax had in it, though
we are aware of the extent of his inclinations in this direction. He preferred at that time to keep at a distance. The
French ambassador indicates Seymour as the originator of
the proposal, and this has every probability in its favour.
As regards the King, it is certain that he was in favour of it ;
he called on all his friends to promote it to the utmost of their
power[1]. The representatives of the allied powers recommended
it with zeal, because they saw in it the only means by which
the English could be put into a position to join with them. In
a still more detailed manner than Ernly, Thomas Littleton,
a man of old Parliamentary reputation, expressed himself
in the matter. Were it a change in the constitution of the
government he would be against it ; it was a different thing to
put a regent in the place of a king. The Exclusion Bill went
too far, and yet left the actual succession to the throne undetermined : if however the regency were accepted, it would
only be necessary to send into the Netherlands ; the Prince
and Princess of Orange would take the necessary oaths, and
there would be a secured future in prospect. If the Princess
died without heirs, her sister Anne would succeed ; should
the Duke still have a son, he would be brought up in the
Protestant faith, and when of age would himself succeed.
The Duke was already exiled ; his exile must be maintained
and enforced by the threat of the confiscation of his goods,
with the value of which he was well acquainted. This was an
expedient which, in its main ideas, may be said to have been
confirmed by history, and even then seemed well adapted to
unite the two parties ; but it cannot be denied that many
objections might be made to it. It was impossible, as was
stated with reason, to separate the person from the power ;

---

[1] Hyde to the Prince of Orange, 29th of March: 'The King on Saturday last
commanded all his servants in the House of Commons to promote them (the
expedients) the most that was in their power, and particularly one, that was the
provide case, the crown should descend to the duke, Your Highness and the
princesse were to have been regents.' Groen 490.

the title of King contained a right, and the possession of it
removed, according to the old statute, all disabilities ; it was
an error to believe that the regency would be more easily
maintained without war than the exclusion : if religion and
conscience were to be secured, the Duke must not be recognised
in any way ; for the regency would not be capable of keeping
him at a distance from the throne ; England would still have
to become Popish.

If in this matter any consideration was paid to continental
relations, it was done with views very different from those of
the government. The impulse given by the thought of danger
to their religion far overbalanced in Parliament any consideration for the legal succession to the throne. Even the danger
of Europe retreated before it. The Spanish ambassador was
unwearied in reminding men that the preservation of the
balance of power in Europe depended upon an alliance of
England with the opponents of France ; and of this such
a regency as was proposed would constitute the connecting
link : but this carried no conviction ; for what would occur
if the rights of the Catholic succession were to be made valid
in spite of the regency? No precautions would then be of
use ; all that had been done would only favour the Catholic
reaction. Everything that was learnt from France, as well as
from the Austrian dominions, tended to show that Catholicism
had made most mighty progress. It was said of the Elector
Palatine, who had just died, and who was very well known in
England, that his heart had been broken by what had happened
in Bohemia. On that day the exclamation was heard, that it
would decide whether Protestantism should exist in the
world.

After the House had once more solemnly taken into consideration the means for saving the religion and the King,
it passed to a resolution that a bill should be introduced to
exclude the Duke of York from the succession to the imperial
crown of England. After this, there could be as little idea as
before of any agreement, or even of a grant of supplies.

Again another dispute between Commons and Lords arose
at this moment.

The King had transferred to the Court of King's Be

trial of an Irishman, Fitzharris, which had reference to the Popish plot, and which threatened to lead to disagreeable disclosures about persons in high positions: the Commons laid their complaint before the Lords, who however sided with the King, and rejected the complaint. The Commons declared this to be an infringement of their right of indictment; they declared that any civil law court which should dare to deal with the matter, should be answerable to them for it.

They took up a decided position, both against the King and against the Lords. 'We stand facing one another,' said a voice of the time, 'like two hostile armies upon two opposite heights.'

At this moment the King determined on the resolution for which he had already made every preparation. With the French ambassador he had had no special talk about the matter; he only saw him once in Oxford, and then in the company of many others, and barely found an opportunity to whisper in his ear, that he was aware of everything, Hyde had told him all. Still on Sunday he was to all appearance employed in looking for a more fitting meeting-place for the Commons, who complained of the discomfort of the place at present assigned to them; he went himself to the very spot to order the necessary arrangements. That evening he spoke about it in his own circle, saying how much more comfortable they would be: but he was a man who did not scruple to say with his tongue what he did not think in his heart, if by that means he could conceal the purpose he actually entertained. Now steps must be taken to prevent the passing, even in the last sitting, of adverse resolutions. On Monday morning he drove to the place of meeting of the Upper House; his carriage was followed by another which was supposed to contain a peer, but really brought only the royal apparel usually worn on occasion of some great official act. One of the lords, who seemed to have his suspicions, and to be thinking of going to acquaint the Commons, was detained by the King in conversation until everything was ready. In the Lower House, one of the legal members was just speaking on the question of jurisdiction, and was demonstrating that the law of the land, according to Magna Charta, meant a procedure in

Parliament, when Black Rod appeared to summon the assembly to the Lords. They expected another communication from the King, perhaps a compliant one; for the former compliances, which had followed after long hesitations, had not been forgotten. The King sat on the throne; he said that after such great divisions occurring in the beginning, no good end could be expected from their deliberations: at his command the Chancellor added, that it was the King's will that Parliament should be dissolved, and it was hereby dissolved. Upon this the King mounted his carriage and set off for Windsor. Shaftesbury, so it is generally affirmed [1], still made an attempt to keep the Lords together, and even to induce the Commons to resume their sittings. It would have been the beginning of open rebellion, as had been the case in Scotland before, and afterwards in France. But in England men's minds, even in the midst of agitation, felt themselves chained by the idea of law. Those present were astonished to see how strongly, in the members of the Lower House, the transition from the opinion that they could do everything to the feeling that at that moment they had no longer any existence, was expressed; for the King had not even spoken of again summoning a Parliament, and there was nothing in the laws to oblige him to do so within three years. Every one hurried to procure a carriage for his departure; it was as if a gust of wind had suddenly scattered all the leaves from a tree.

Now the agreement between the two Kings was carried out. To the French ambassador Hyde said, that Charles II had been determined under all circumstances to hold fast to his legitimate authority; by the offers of the King of France he was strengthened in his determination. It was agreed that, in the next three years, 5000,000 French livres in all should be paid to England [2]. This was only an insignificant sum, but it seemed sufficient to carry on the administration. Whilst in former cases the most confidential ministers had

---

[1] Campbell, Lives of the Chancellors iii. 354.

[2] Barrillon later on calculates once how much was still wanting: 'pour le parfait payement de cinq millions qui composent les trois ans du subside, et qui finissent au 1 Avril 1684.' The payments began on April 1, 1681.

been taken into the secret, and, later, assurances were only interchanged under personal signature and the King's privy seal, this time verbal assurances were thought sufficient ; the agreement is described as a verbal alliance. Charles II did not wish that the Duchess of Portsmouth, who had hitherto mediated his alliances with France, should know anything of the present one. The sole confidant of the secret was Lawrence Hyde. Although at first the French made no demands in return, he knew very well, that even in the very acceptance of money there lay an obligation. He consented to the stipulated agreement that Charles II should by degrees withdraw from his alliance with Spain, and should not allow Parliament to lead him into any hostility against France [1]. The French understood this to mean, that the King of England pledged himself to stand on their side in the continental differences generally, and not to summon Parliament again. These two constructions are very closely allied. The agreement had not been even definitely put into form, it was more an understanding than a treaty, but it was to be decisive both for the affairs of England and for those of the world in general.

---

[1] ' De ne point assembler son parlement et favoriser mes intentions dans toutes les occasions qui se présenteroient, et principalement au sujet des différences, que j'avois alors avec l'Espagne.' Du roi à Barrillon, 1685, 6th April. What Hume relates, ch. lxix. (viii. 207), he only learnt third hand, and is probably not more than an extract from Barrillon's correspondence : on the whole it is correct.

CHAPTER X.

As long as Charles II, in concert with the Prince of Orange, had shown an intention of taking up the cause of the continental powers against the French encroachments, Louis XIV had sought to ally himself with the Parliamentary opposition, and with their aid had put an end at once to every warlike project directed against himself. When however the opposition, now that it had won the upper hand, showed the same tendencies, Louis XIV took up the interest of the Crown and the King of England, and provided him with support against the most hated claims of his opponents; by this means he gained an influence over him, which necessarily paralysed the English power in its relation to the great affairs of Europe.

But at no moment could this have been more important to him than at the present, when he once more set himself to accomplish the great schemes of his life. Or may one not rather suppose that it was the attitude of England which gave him courage to do so?

Just while he was laying the foundation of his new agreement with England, he caused his troops to enter the County of Chiny, and advanced claims to Luxemburg; his Réunion policy similarly extended itself at that time on the Upper Rhine; he raised a pretension to Strasburg. At the same time he proceeded to carry out at home the most severe decrees against the Protestants. For this was the aim of his whole policy, to make France unassailable towards the east, and at the same time to lead it back entirely to the old Catholic uniformity, a policy which then opened the way to the acquisition of the Spanish succession and supremacy in Europe.

Nowhere could the coincidence of these French encroachments produce a deeper and, at the same time, more unfavourable impression than in the United Netherlands, where men looked upon the Protestant cause as their own, where the French edicts were translated and distributed among the people, and where the opinion prevailed that France would in the next winter gain entire possession of Flanders. But if in this double danger they looked out for rescue, it was from England alone that any help could perhaps still be expected.

It would have struck into the very centre of European relationships, had Charles II's intention succeeded of placing the administration, in case of his death, in the hands of the Prince of Orange. After the dissolution of Parliament, Lawrence Hyde wrote to the Prince, that the regency would have been accepted, if the proposal had been made to invest the Duke of Monmouth with it ; Parliament had only rejected it because with it was united a reservation of the hereditary right : but the King of England could not possibly give this up ; it was impossible for him to accept measures, for the sake of the preservation of the balance of power in Europe, which would bring with them the destruction of the monarchical system in England. Still, even from henceforth, so Hyde graciously added, the King of England would do all he could to support his allies [1].

No one could know at this moment how little this expression meant. No thought of a new treaty having been formed with France however entered into the Prince's mind, beyond one of those vague suppositions which suddenly rise into sight and then again disappear. It seemed, however, to indicate an estrangement on the King's side, that he not only refused to transfer the command of some English regiments that had been in Holland since 1678, to Henry Sidney, who still conducted the embassy there and was on the most confidential terms with

---

[1] 'I find his Majesty in the same disposition as to his allies that he hath been of late; and will doe all he can to support them.' Letter of March 29, O. S., in Groen 491.

the Prince of Orange, but he recalled him from his embassy, and replaced him by Skelton, who was not very welcome at the Hague. There were however personal reasons for this, and it was not decisive. As moreover their personal relations did not assume an unfriendly shape, and as everything seemed to depend upon gaining over the King to support Spain and the Spanish Netherlands [1], the Prince formed the idea of going to England himself to try his luck in the matter.

His English friends, of whom he caused inquiries to be made through Sidney, who had returned to England in consequence of his recall, strengthened him in his intention; Godolphin especially was most pressing, reminding him only that he must assure the King of zeal for his greatness and his service. Godolphin did not deny that otherwise a breach between the two might certainly be feared. Much had been told the King about the connexion of the Prince with those parties which he now most hated; his letters also had sometimes held a high tone and had been too sharp. But it seemed as if his presence in person, if he behaved with address, might still succeed in removing all ill-feeling, and restore a good understanding. On the 24th of July, Prince William arrived at Windsor.

Public relations assume, in those who are to direct them, almost a personal form; from the conflict between what is universal and what is individual, or from their union, arises the active movement of the world.

William of Orange might have had, in the interest of his own possessions, many temptations to put himself on good terms with the King of France. With a conscious rejection of these temptations, which gave him a certain advantage, he took up a position opposed to Louis XIV, and made the maintenance of the balance of power in Europe the object of his life. For this cause especially he now sought to win over his uncle in England; but the internal relations of England closely affected him personally, and to these the great cause also

---

[1] Sidney's Diary ii. 192. Fuenmajor told him that he had conferred with Fagel about it, 'how they should make the King [Charles II] propose to these people [in Holland] to make some kind of defense to the low countries [the Spanish Netherlands].'

directed him. The reconciliation of the King of England with his Parliament must unavoidably precede any share he might take in European affairs.

Not only the King, but also his ministers, were at this moment in a disposition hostile to Parliament,—even Halifax and Seymour, who in no way belonged to the Duke of York's faction. Halifax was very much inclined towards the Prince and his plans for their own sake ; he had let him know, that he regarded him as the only man on whom it was possible to build for the future ; still the attacks which he met with from Parliament made it necessary for him to oppose it, otherwise he must expect the most rigorous treatment at its hand [1]. Seymour, who at that time enjoyed great consideration, was not, at least as regards the question about the troops, on the Prince's side ; he thought it would be better to disband them, rather than let him attain his purpose by their means ; he was also offended by Parliament, and helped to keep up the King's alienation from it. How much less would any favourable disposition towards Parliament be expected from Hyde, seeing that by the secret treaty he had provided himself with the means of doing without it.

Soon after the Prince's arrival a conference was arranged, in which he explained his view, that it would be equally impossible to maintain either the United or the Spanish Netherlands without securing the support of England—by the agreement of King and Parliament ; he expressed a doubt whether it had been right to dissolve Parliament twice in such quick succession. He was asked in return whether he would have approved of its demands, for instance, the exclusion ? He expressed his aversion to it. Or the limitation of the royal power ? He had always rejected it. Or even the restriction to which it had been proposed to subject the crown in the appointments to legal, administrative, and even military posts ? The Prince evinced surprise that Parliament should have made this demand. At the same time he held to his opinion, that it would be possible to come to an understanding with regard to external affairs. The King reminded him

---

[1] Sidney to the Prince of Orange, June 28. In Blencowe ii. 217.

how closely in these matters he had at one time approached
the Dutch, but even these negotiations had been used to
awaken suspicion against him ; against distrust and jealousy
there was no defence [1].

Prince William did not disdain to speak about the matter
even with the Duchess of Portsmouth. She told him that
she herself had been of his opinion, and had put herself into
communication, not without the King's knowledge, with the
party leaders ; but she had become convinced that their only
object was to get the King into their power, but not to take
up his cause ; on this account she had withdrawn from them.

The Prince insisted that an understanding might still be
managed by concessions on both sides ; if the Duke prevented it, he would overthrow at the same time both himself
and the King. Charles II did not conceal his opinion that
the Duke's resistance was a security to him rather than otherwise ; for were he first overthrown, the attack would turn against
himself, and to make a lasting agreement would be after all
impossible. When both he and the Duke were dead, and the
Prince had mounted the throne of England, he would learn
how difficult it was to maintain himself there.

As far as he was himself concerned, the Prince would not
have been disinclined to be present at a banquet, to which the
Lord Mayor invited him ; but the ministers feared that compromising declarations might be made there, and on their
entreaties the King forbade it. Privately the Prince saw
many of the Parliamentary leaders, and tried to bring about
an understanding with them. They did not quite reject his
endeavours ; if he would only procure for them a new Parliament, they would engage themselves to provide for the support of the Netherlands, and, while so doing would neither
insist upon the Exclusion Bill nor make an attack on the ministers. This was the temper of some, but not of Lord Russell,
who did not give way a hair's-breadth. He said that if Lord
Shaftesbury, for example, did not insist upon the exclusion, the

---

[1] Conway gives information to the Duke of York about this conference ; and a
passage from his letter is given in Macpherson's Extracts, p. 125. Again, Hyde
gave the French ambassador an account of it, which he relates in his despatches.
The two agree in the main points and have been united here.

only reason was that he was an old man, who did not expect to live to see the Duke ascend the throne; for himself he thought he would live to see it, but to the bloody persecution, which would then certainly follow, he would not expose himself.

If a promise had been given by all sides, Charles II would not have trusted it. He even took amiss an intimation, which the Prince once let fall in conversation, that the King should send English troops to the Netherlands to testify to the world that he would not suffer French encroachments; for he had the most pressing need of the small body of troops which were left him, to avoid being surprised by a sudden rising of the people. He reproached the Prince with only keeping before his eyes his own particular aim, without sufficiently considering the difficult position of the royal house and of the crown; for his own part he would first set his own affairs in order before he thought of foreign affairs.

Open variance on this point did not occur between them: the King only accused the Prince of hereditary obstinacy: they parted on tolerably good terms. Still it was apparent that their paths lay henceforth in different directions. Whilst the Prince wished to regulate the internal affairs of England according to the requirements of European relations, Charles II, by the very resistance which he found at home, had been induced to promise the King of France that he would not oppose his continental interests, nor give his enemies any hope that he would join them. This article of agreement in the treaty, so far as the Prince of Orange was concerned, had been carried out literally; he was under the disadvantage of striving against agreements of whose existence he knew nothing.

Without doubt King Charles and his ministers made representations to Louis XIV against his encroachments on the frontier of Germany and the Netherlands; but how could they do anything to resist him? The very agreement he had made with them was based on his determination to carry out his projected plans. With regard to Strasburg, Louis declared plainly that he could not hold his hand, as his proceedings there rested on an understanding with the inhabitants; by them the justice of his claims was recognised, while he promised them all the advantages which they could reasonably demand; it was a matter of reciprocal advantage. It was necessary to paralyse the English power, so as to make this great acquisition possible for the King of France. When it took effect (October 30, 1681) it still made a great impression; many rejoiced at it, because Charles II would now be obliged to summon Parliament. But neither the occurrence at Strasburg nor the seizure of Casale, which followed soon after, could disturb the English government in their indifference to continental relations. Halifax said, with great coolness, that she must leave it to those who were immediately touched by these occurrences to take the measures which seemed to them necessary. So Charles II himself remarked: the matter was too distant; he could not break with France about it[1].

That he was unable to do so under existing circumstances is clear enough.

Occasionally it was discussed between the King and the First Commissioner of the Treasury, Lawrence Hyde, whether it was advisable to accept the money, which would fetter the political action of England. But the Treasury, as well as the King's privy purse, was in a state of the utmost exhaustion. When an ambassador complains that his salary is not paid, Hyde represents to him, that this is the fate of all who are occupied in the King's service abroad or even at home; the servants must simply have patience with their master; he intimated that even the Duchess of Portsmouth was a sufferer. Deprived of all Parliamentary grants for a long while, the administration was embarrassed how to collect the interest of a loan which the goldsmiths had once more agreed to provide. To fall into arrears with it would, however, have shattered the King's credit in every way. Bitter necessity compelled the First Commissioner of the Treasury to stretch out his hand for the money of which the payment was his secret. On exchange it amounted to 50,000 livres; Hyde was not even obliged to give a receipt for it, for at Versailles a quittance of Barrillon's sufficed; the business was carried through like a private

---

[1] Barrillon, October 5, 12, 28, 1681.

affair between confidential friends. Still the Ambassador never lost sight of the political object. He remarks with malicious satisfaction, that the resistance of Charles II and Lawrence Hyde to the policy of France became visibly less as soon as the bills of exchange reached their hands.

This was perhaps the deepest abasement to which any government of proud and wealthy England has ever been condemned; it hid itself, ashamed, in impenetrable secrecy even from those statesmen who were working with it in the highest positions.

These always kept in view the summoning of a new Parliament as their aim. Halifax and Seymour were at that time opposed to an immediate summons, because it would only have again awakened passions already excited, but at the same time they still held in general parliamentary views; they could not have entertained the conception of permanent unparliamentary government. The wish or the intention arose so to prepare matters as to procure again a Parliament, like the Long Parliament of the Restoration. It was a very natural idea, if it be remembered that the dissolution of that Parliament had had, as its consequence, all the late storms. The charges which had been made against it were disputed; only to a very small extent had bribery taken place in it; it had always maintained the true royalist principles, and had only erred in expressing itself too strongly for the Anglican Church[1]. And how great injury had that Church suffered since its dissolution! It was hoped that its prelates and clergy would use all their influence to exclude their opponents, the opponents of the King, from the future Parliament. A change of this kind was desired by no one more than by the thoroughly Anglican Lawrence Hyde; in that way there would have been a return to the system founded by his father.

---

[1] Lettre de Munnikhuysen au Grandpensionnair, April 26 / May 5, 1681 : 'Ceux gens n'ont jamais été accusés d'autre chose que d'avoir temoigné par leur votes leur attachement aux interests du roi et à des principes qui les ont fait agir un peu vertement pour l'église anglicane.——Toutes ces personnes qui ont été négligées depuis le long parlement, s'employèrent avec (autant) plus de succès pour se faire rechoisir, qu'ils y seront soutenus par tous les prélats et le clergé conformant.'

And the attitude of things was not unfavourable to it.

The dissolution was at first followed by a commotion which awoke some fear of the outbreak of a rebellion, but after a time a change of public opinion came about in favour of the crown. For on many the Parliamentary proceedings had after all produced the impression that the Exclusion Bill, as there was no law which prohibited a Catholic Prince, had no legal foundation, and that the intention had been to take the King by storm. Very efficacious was a declaration made by the King, in which he on his side complained of Parliament, and accused it of arbitrary conduct, for example, in having wished in a one-sided manner to annul all the existing laws against the Dissenters; in general it had endeavoured to make government simply impossible. He, on the other hand, protested that he wished to observe the laws, even to summon Parliament frequently and to root out Popery. The ecclesiastical authorities gladly agreed that this declaration, which was directed at once against Papists and Dissenters, should be read from the pulpits, and supported it with their religious authority. Against the political theories of the Whigs, the authority of recognised learning came to the aid of the King. The university of Cambridge expressed itself against them and in favour of royalist principles. In a detailed address it declared for the doctrine, that the royal authority did not spring from the people but from a fundamental hereditary right, which could not be annulled either by religion or by any legal decree. The Parliament, by attacking the hereditary right, upon which after all the whole existing state of things and the Restoration itself depended, awoke a feeling of opposition in the nation, which greedily believed the tale, that an active and already powerful faction sought to restore the disorder of republican times, which had become unbearable to every one. The official gazette was filled, as the year advanced, with addresses of loyalty from different parts of the country, which expressed, often in impassioned words, gratitude to the King for his behaviour in face of such an attempt. In this there may have been much that was fictitious, but there was still something real and true.

The expectation that this disposition would once more

prevail in England, was confirmed by the transactions which
just then took place in the Scottish Parliament. In July
1681 it was opened by the Duke of York, who acted as the
King's commissioner, and soon it became evident that monarchical sentiments prevailed in the assembly. On the 14th
of August an act was passed, in which the doctrine of divine
right and regular succession was stated; it affirmed that it
could be altered by no statute, and interfered with by no
difference in religion. It was quite in harmony with this, that
on the other hand, the strongest assurances in favour of the
Protestant Church, of course with reservation of the episcopal
form, were also interwoven into it. An oath was imposed
on public officials which neither Covenanters nor Catholics
could take, and which contained the distinct engagement not
to strive after any change in the government of the country.
There was no want of resistance, which however was not
quite unwelcome, in so far as it gave occasion for attacking
opposition lords, like the Duke of Argyle. The Tories
considered it a great honour for the Duke of York that these
resolutions had been passed under his guidance. He had
known how to awaken the natural sympathies for the
established royal house, and avoid any offence that his
religious opinions might give. He even prevailed on himself
to be present at the prayers with which the sittings were
opened. In England the hope of drawing him over to Protestantism was then again immediately revived, for this would
have at once removed the chief difficulties with which the
government was struggling. Halifax, who at times appeared
as his opponent, and then again inclined towards him,
represented to him that no mortal power would be able to
calm the storm, which would arise against him, if he did not
snatch from his enemies the arms which he himself had put
into their hands; his friends' hope that he would do so was
their most powerful motive in defending his cause; if they
saw themselves deceived they would desert him, just as men
leave a fortress which can no longer be held[1]. Lawrence
Hyde himself went, towards the end of August 1681, to

---

[1] Extract from the letter in James II's Life i. 700.

Edinburgh, to bring him the King's answer to his repeated
entreaty to be allowed to return to England. It was, that it
could not be so unless the Duke would conform to the
Anglican Church; if he did not do that, he could no longer
enjoy in any way the King's protection; otherwise he would
ruin himself and the King[1]. ·Hyde took every pains to
strengthen this exhortation by representing the highly dangerous position in which the government was placed. But the
Duke had now once for all irretrievably taken his part. If in
Scotland he had adopted a less strict bearing, he explained it
by the fact that he was acting as the King's commissioner;
in England on the contrary he would appear for himself;
there he could not and would not give way. When all
representations proved unavailing, Hyde produced a written
promise of Charles II, in which the King no longer insisted
upon complete uniformity, but gave permission to the Duke
to return if he would promise to come to church—nothing
more. What might not have been avoided, what might
not have been done at this moment to maintain the crown,
and to bring back affairs into a regular course, if the Duke
could have been prevailed on to make this concession! But
he remained unmoved and obstinate, as he was, and rejected
everything. His spiritual adviser had once for all told him
that every approach to Protestantism was contrary to the
duty of a Catholic Christian.

But then the Tories, now clustering round the government,
and holding fast to Protestantism, could make no further
advance. If disapproval of the conduct of the Commons provided the King and the government with numbers of adherents,
the dread of the Duke's Catholic zeal in its turn caused many
others to hold by the position of the last Parliament. That a
feeling opposed to the Whigs arose and found expression, made
them keep together and strengthen their position. The summer and autumn of the year 1681 were filled with the struggles
of the two parties in the courts of justice and in the press.

In June 1681 the Middlesex jury was composed of friends

---

[1] 'That I should ruin myself and him.' From his own notes in the Extract
129: more trustwórthy than in the account of his life·

of the government, so that in opposition to the resolutions of
the Commons, but confirmed by an expression of the judges,
it took in hand the affair of Fitzharris, and condemned him
for his pamphlet directed against the King. Divided with
regard to the Protestants, the Whigs and Tories were still of
one mind against the Catholics. On the same day the jury
condemned also the Catholic bishop of Armagh, Plunket,
who was accused of having prepared a Popish plot in Ireland.
Lord Essex had remarked to the King that this had been
proved only by the testimony of very unsatisfactory witnesses,
and called on him not to confirm the judgment. The King
reproached him with not having come forward with his opinion
during the course of the trial, for that might still have saved
the accused. 'I however,' he added, 'durst pardon nobody;
his blood be upon your head, not upon mine [1].' Never had
men been further from seeing in the verdict of the jurors
the decision of justice than at that time.

In July, two of those who had gone to Oxford in arms were
accused of an attempt upon the King's liberty. The proofs
against both were identical. But whilst a London jury
acquitted the one, the other was condemned to death by
the jury in Oxford.

How must all passions now have been aroused when the
government decided to prosecute the great leader of their
opponents, Lord Shaftesbury, for an attempt against the
King's liberty and a plan to introduce a republic into
England! They would gladly have transferred the trial to
another place, but the judges considered that illegal; he
must come before the Middlesex jury. It was composed of
twenty-one respectable citizens of London; it was remarked
however from the first that most of them had taken part in
the recent commotions in the city; it must be important to
themselves that manifestations of political tendencies should
not be considered as criminal misdemeanours. The jury
refused to bring in a true bill; they wrote, as was the custom
at that time, their 'ignoramus' on the back of the bill—a
declaration which was received with rejoicings by the people;

---

[1] Echard maintains that he had this 'from an unquestionable hand.'

here and there bonfires were lighted : the government let it drop quietly, out of anxiety lest otherwise greater disturbances should ensue.

But in spite of this result it gained by the matter itself. For during the proceedings came to light the regulations of the association, about which there had been so much talk ; these contained a pledge to show obedience to the Parliament and those commissioned by it, and, if it should be dissolved, to those of its members who should have enrolled themselves in this association : it seemed as though the intention were entertained of setting up against the King's government another government presided over by the most influential Parliamentary leaders. The publication of this scheme of association did not fail to produce a strong impression. The King's adherents rose against it with loyal indignation. A new series of addresses began, in which horror was expressed at an association which, as the lawyers of the Middle Temple said, aimed at producing a tyrannical dominion, not only over the country but also over the King. But Shaftesbury's friends denied the authenticity of the paper, which must have been brought forward by the opposite party only to provoke addresses against it [1], and that these, if carefully examined, were in contradiction with themselves and incomprehensible after what had gone before. Thus how could it be explained, that in the addresses the gentry thanked the King both for the dissolution of one Parliament and for the promise of another, when they had before them the examples of repeated dissolutions? The two parties took up everywhere positions opposed to one another. In the Common Council of London antagonistic addresses were brought forward ; the Tories were in a minority, yet it was thought surprising that this minority was so considerable. If till this time Parliamentary tendencies had prevailed in the literature of the day, pamphlets with opposite views now gained much approval, such as the Heraclitus Ridens, remarkable for its wit, and the Observator of Lestrange, remarkable for its combativeness. A curious product of the times are the political poems, which in Scotland still

---

[1] A letter about abhorrers and adressers in Somers viii. 319.

caught the old ballad spirit, but in England represent the disputes of clubs and parties. Even Dryden let himself be carried, by the rejoicings of the Whigs over the acquittal of Shaftesbury, which they celebrated with a medal, beyond the bounds of satire, which he had observed in the Achitophel, to the most violent personal invectives; yet the lines in which he treats of the great questions at issue are always happy and appropriate. He drew upon himself answers, in which he was dragged through the mire: no one reads them now, but at that time they in their turn met with approval; the 'poetical dissenters,' who did not trouble themselves about rules [1], were regarded as equal or superior to the master of versification and diction. For what men in any way feel and think they like to read, even in the most imperfect form. Whoever studied the parties could not be mistaken about the fact that the Whigs had by far the upper hand, and at the new elections, when these should occur, would undoubtedly maintain the preponderance and would seize their former power again in the ensuing Parliament.

Just then however European affairs took a turn which seemed to make the summoning of an English Parliament inevitable. In November 1681, Louis XIV advanced without disguise his pretensions upon Luxemburg, and ordered, as was his custom, the immediate blockade of that fortress. Every one realised what this project included; how through its execution France would become, from a military point of view, the master of both the Netherlands. And it could not be said that this did not concern England; on the contrary, this is the very point on which English politics have at all times been most sensitive. This time also the old machinations were tried to move Charles II to consent. Considerable grants of money were offered him; the Duchess of Portsmouth told him he would anyhow not be able to prevent it; why would he not gain for himself the credit with Louis XIV of having facilitated the accomplishment of his schemes? But the King fancied that he foresaw a storm which he would not be able to resist, all the more

---

[1] 'Dissenters in poetry, form, sense, and English.' Preface to The Medal.

because, urged by the allies, he had expressly promised in this case to summon his Parliament[1]: he said that if this were to be carried out everything which he had hitherto undertaken would be undone.

We see here the immediate connexion the siege of Luxemburg had with the internal affairs of England. The idea suggested itself, that to avoid extremities the Spaniards might perhaps even be prevailed on to cede the town, which anyhow they would not be able to defend. Louis XIV promised to raze the fortress if it came into his hands, for to him the only matter of importance was, to dismantle entirely the place from which a dangerous attack upon France might be undertaken; to use it as a point whence to attack others was no part of his plans. Charles II seems really to have hoped to bring this matter about; he undertook the negotiation, and only desired that Louis XIV should give him time for it and should not within four months, by a stricter blockade, force the place to surrender. On this understanding the French promised even to allow the introduction into the town of a certain quantity of grain from Namur.

As usual, this time also everything depended on the promise or refusal of the United Netherlands to assist the Spaniards. In the States-General a party was actually found which sought to preserve peace at any price, not only from cowardice, but because it was opposed to the Prince, whose position would be raised by the war: it inclined to approve of the cession of the fortress, on condition that it should be razed. But all the more eagerly did the Prince of Orange exert all his powers against it. His chief interest lay in the preservation of the balance of power in Europe by means of English intervention; what his two uncles, the King and the Duke of York, sought to avoid, the summoning of Parliament, he necessarily desired with his whole heart[2],

---

[1] Extracts **124**: 'The King promised to call a Parliament if France proceeded par voye de fait.'

[2] Barrillon, December 22, 1681 mentions 'le dessein de plusieurs des plus considérables d'inspirer une conduite moderée à la chambre, et de ne dire pas un

particularly as during his presence in England the best assurances had been given him for such a case. The Spaniards supported him very steadfastly. They hesitated even to make use of the permission to reprovision, which did not seem absolutely necessary; they declared repeatedly that they were determined not to give up a foot of land. As however the injury and danger which the Netherlands themselves would incur by a French possession of Luxemburg must at last become evident to every one, the Prince got the better of his opponents. The resolution was formed to keep a small military force in readiness, which could advance, in case of need, to the relief of Luxemburg [1].

The manifold encroachments of the French disposed other places also to lend a favourable ear to the negotiations of the Prince. Any moment a breach might occur at Luxemburg which must lead to a European war. The plan was cherished of reminding the King of England, in the sight of Europe, of his promise to summon Parliament, and, if he did not fulfil it, of appealing to the nation itself.

Charles II, by his connexion with France, was after all again reduced to a very disagreeable position. If we ask how the old politician disentangled himself from it, it is at first sight hardly intelligible how it could have helped him just then to give way to his brother's entreaty and allow him to come back to court; yet such is the case.

There was for this a very personal motive, connected with the affairs of the Duchess of Portsmouth. As the King could not ensure her a fixed income after his death, she conceived the idea that this might be remedied, if the Duke would assure to her a certain sum; she named £5000 out of the receipts of the Post Office, which were granted him for life. The King wished it and the Duke consented, although he did not believe that his consent would remove all difficulties. To put the agreement into proper form, even the ministers thought it advisable to allow the Duke to return to court.

---

mot de la succession ny des ministres, et de faire des offres considérables au roi d'Angleterre pour l'obliger à entrer en guerre contre la France.'

[1] Compare Avaux i. 106; where indeed it is only possible with difficulty to follow the thread of affairs, as he only gives the contents of his own despatches.

With the personal motive there was however bound up that·
other motive, which lay in the general condition of affairs.
The return of the Duke was intended also to serve the purpose
of disposing the King of France to compliance in the great
question of the Netherlands.

For Louis XIV was much more closely connected with the
Duke, who had attached himself to him with all his heart,
than with the King and his ministers, in whom he never again
placed entire confidence. He thought he could only be sure
of the alliance with England when the Duke of York was
again at his brother's side. Ceaselessly he had urged the
Duke's return ; it was now granted to him, to move him in
return to moderation in his conduct in the Netherlands [1].

The fact that the King of France also did not at all wish to
see an English Parliament summoned, also helped towards
this end. He could not deceive himself about the fact, that it
would go over with all its power and influence to the side of
the allies, that it would be the faithful ally of the Prince of
Orange.

Louis XIV possessed acuteness of observation, decision, and
a grand manner. He declared unexpectedly that the blockade
of Luxemburg was raised, without however allowing any of the
motives above mentioned to appear. But just then, Hungary,
Austria, and Germany were threatened with a great attack from
the Turks. Louis XIV declared that, to avoid hindering the
Princes, who would be first exposed to it, from using all their
forces to resist this mighty enemy, he withdrew his troops
from Luxemburg, and confided the decision of all his claims
in the Netherlands exclusively to the King of England.

It was at Newmarket, where the Duke of York had just
arrived, that the French ambassador presented to the King of
England the letter containing this declaration. At the first
words which conveyed its meaning, the King embraced the
messenger, and called his brother to let him know the news
which announced his deliverance from the greatest perplexity

---

[1] Barrillon to Louis XIV, March 2/12 : ' Mr. Jolyde s'est servi du retour du Duc
d' York comme d'un motif pour engage V. Mé à apporter encore plus de facilité
à l'accommodement.'

of his life. Then the declaration, with its pompous wording, was read through.   Hereupon the King exclaimed that the generous decision of Louis XIV would aid all Christendom against its foreign foe, and him against his enemies at home. The Duke of York remarked how important it was for himself; if a breach had come about in the Netherlands, Parliament would, without doubt, have been summoned, and then his succession would again have been attacked; his enemies would have redoubled their exertions against him; he owed all, all to the King of France.

Shortly afterwards arrived a letter from Louis XIV, in which he expressed to the Duke the warmest sympathy on his return, and the confidence that he would maintain unimpaired the friendship of his brother with himself, in the establishment of which he had so largely assisted.

CHAPTER XI.

ENGLISH history in this epoch, as in many others, is French history as well : we learn to know rightly the policy of Louis XIV from his intrigues at the English court. He stopped short at that time in his European undertakings, only to return to them when England should have been entirely withdrawn from the influence of the Prince of Orange, and when the opposing influence of the Duke of York, which was friendly to himself, should have been established there. For these two men were now divided by the great European interest. The Prince opposed the King of France in all his schemes; the Duke was most closely united with him by policy and religion.

In England itself, however, the Duke had another enemy, who was more immediately dangerous; this was his nephew Monmouth, who enjoyed a boundless popularity. We learn that the two ministers, Seymour and Halifax, who at heart shared the Protestant antipathies against the Duke of York, made an attempt in the beginning of 1682, to gain over Monmouth to themselves; he however preferred to hold by his old friends, Shaftesbury, Montague, and Russell. Otherwise the return of the Duke and his continuance at court would without doubt have been made still more difficult. Now however the ministers thought that they would find in him a support against rivals who were both hateful and dangerous.

Very characteristic of the Whigs was their proposal to meet, by a great party-demonstration the first reappearance of the Duke of York, which was made at a banquet which the Artillery Company again wished to give him. They distributed

invitations to a thanksgiving festival for the wonderful protection 'which God had granted the King, the Protestant
religion, and the liberties of England against the hellish
attacks of their enemies;' there was first to be a sermon,
and then a dinner [1]. Eight hundred invitations were issued,
but any one was admitted on payment of a guinea.
Toasts of the most comprehensive character had been prepared, which were expected to produce considerable effect
upon the people. The most popular names of the nobility headed the list. But the government did not think it
wise to permit a noisy meeting of their opponents, which
might have further consequences. As the Lord Mayor, who
was consulted on the point, either lacked the power or the
courage to hinder it, the Privy Council decided to issue a
formal prohibition, on the ground that its only result would be
the promotion of pernicious party connexions between the
King's subjects. This happened on the 19th of April, 1682.
On the 20th the banquet to the Duke of York took place,
which was likewise opened by a sermon, preached by the
well-known Tory, Sprat. After the sermon, the Duke who did
not like to be present at it, made his entry into the city
attended by a large number of Scottish and English noblemen; the banquet passed off without disturbance. On the
21st, the day fixed for the Whig banquet, the constables
were at their posts, and even the militia under arms, to give
due force to the prohibition.

Sometimes there were still consultations about the reconciliation of Monmouth, both with his father and with the
Duke of York. Monmouth however insisted that he was
guilty of no offence against the Duke; he would not submit
to him, but only to the King; if he were called on to break
with any one of his acquaintances, he refused to do so; for
none of them had anything more at heart than the welfare of
England. The disfavour with which he was treated, and
which he principally attributed to Lord Halifax, made him call
that nobleman, with whom he otherwise was most closely connected, to account one day, on coming out from church. It is

---

[1] 'You are desired to meet many of the loyall protestant nobility, gentry,
clergy, and citizens, Friday the 21 of this instant April.' Ticket, in Luttrell 179.

strange that a duel between them did not occur. The only consequence was, that the collective members of the court were forbidden to remain any longer in connexion with Monmouth.

In the summer of 1682 the court and the administration took a still more decided line against the Whigs, combined with closer approaches, on the part of the most influential men, to France. This was caused principally by the continued presence of the Duke of York, who now also summoned his wife. He was on the best possible terms with the Duchess of Portsmouth, who seemed, by a short journey to France, to have gained new charms for the King, and enjoyed as much influence as ever. She had also seen Louis XIV on her journey, and had been treated by him with much considera-tion ; she was considered, even more than she actually was, to be the connecting link between France and the King. Through the Duchess of Portsmouth, who knew how to dispose the Duke of York in his favour, Sunderland was now recalled to office. It is worth while noticing, that he had other means by which he knew how to prepare the way for his return. First of all, he went to the French ambassador, to tell him that he could thwart his plans if he disapproved of them ; at the same time he assured him, that if he came again into office, there would be no more zealous cham-pion than himself of the alliance between the Kings of England and France ; he now saw that a reconciliation between Charles II and the Parliament was a matter of impossibility, and that the union with France was his only right policy ; from his relationship with the Prince of Orange he had completely freed himself. This was enough for Bar-rillon. When the Duchess of Portsmouth herself called upon him to support her with the King, who, under the influence of Halifax, raised difficulties, he answered, with French polite-ness, that it was only fitting that her opinion should be followed in the internal affairs of the court, as his King placed an unlimited confidence in her. It was precisely the French and Catholic interest which united them all. To the French in-terest Lord Hyde also belonged, the sole confidant of the last alliance ; but he did not belong to the Catholic interest from which he was always separated by an unalterably Protestant and Anglican conviction, as well as by his father's example. Only on the last point was the Duke of Ormond at one with him; for being at that time summoned home from Ireland, he had, by the marriage of his grandson with the granddaughter of the Chancellor, renewed his old connexion with the Hydes. Ormond still always possessed the confidence of the King, who could nowhere dispense with his society, whether at Westminster, Windsor, or Newmarket. The people also considered him to be wise, experienced, and moderate[1]; it was thought that he would make no opposition if the Duke of York were again obliged to betake himself to Scotland. An equally zealous Anglican was the Secretary of State, Jenkins, an old lawyer, versed in diplomatic business, a man of a quiet, modest, tenacious, unalterable nature. Without any religious faith, Halifax, for political reasons, still held to this side; he said incessantly, and caused it to be expressly proclaimed in the upper circles by his brother, who just then came back from Paris, that he laboured for a Parliament, and the reconciliation of the King with his people; whoever denied that misunderstood him.

About the parliamentary and religious question the two factions of the court might have different opinions; in this, however, they were perfectly agreed, that the popular movement, now spread through the town and the country, and its leaders must be met with energy. Ormond thought that they would deserve to be laughed at if they could not avoid the rocks on which Charles I had formerly been wrecked; whoever opposed the King and his government must be treated as a rebel[2].

We may regard this as the first decidedly Tory government

---

[1] Falaisan, the Brandenburg Resident, who cherished sympathies for the Whig party, says of him, Sept. 19/29, 1682: ' Sa première maxime est, que sans un parlement les affaires du roi ne peuvent pas aller bien.' The Venetian Secretary, who was connected with the Duke of York, and this Brandenburg Resident, who really himself belonged to the Whig party, give the two opposite representations of these events, and correct one another respectively. Of the essential points, however, Barrillon gives by far the best account.

[2] Letter of the Duke of York, in Carte, Ormond v.

which ever existed. It formed the intention of attacking the main bulwarks of the Whigs, the municipal liberties and the formation of juries, which depended upon the dominant party. Above everything else, the latter seemed indispensable.

Lord Anglesey, himself an opponent of the government, still remarked that the old civil war had now, as it were, transformed itself into a judicial war; men fought with one another in judicial battle—for what was right troubled neither grand nor petty juries, the judgments depended always on the respective strength of parties in any place. Everywhere the one party measured itself against the other. This was peculiarly evident in London, where Lord Shaftesbury had become a citizen, had had himself inscribed in a guild, took part in commerce, stood in close connexion with the most influential men, especially with the sheriffs, and so exercised great influence on the formation of the juries. Sometimes he accused his enemies of the crime designated by law as 'scandalum magnatum'; they then refused to submit to trial before a Middlesex and London jury, for such a jury would take the part of the accuser; the King's Bench had allowed their refusal; but Shaftesbury could never be prevailed upon to entrust his cause to another jury.

To this state of things the government now wished to put an end, not only because it was in itself unbearable, but also because the ministers did not give up the idea of establishing with another jury the accusation against Shaftesbury, which had been rejected by the 'ignoramus' of the jury then impanneled.

Moreover the capital rejoiced in an accumulation of privileges which had gradually grown up and yet were closely connected with one another, and which gave it, with regard to internal administration and jurisdiction, a high degree of independence. Its magistrates required no royal confirmation; the sheriffs, who appointed the jurymen, and in consequence also, the jurymen themselves, were the expression of the ruling temper in the city, as it formed itself in the free movement of men's minds. It seemed to foreigners that the city was, as it were, a republic by the King's side. It ought to have been remembered that the independent spirit of the city, and its religious

and political temper, as opposed to an Anabaptist and republican government, had given one of the most important
impulses to the Restoration. Now it was only felt that the
agitation in the capital became very inconvenient to the
King's government also, and it was thought necessary to take
measures against it. The crown-lawyers questioned the
legality of municipal privileges in general. Before, however, they could open any proceedings against them, another
expedient offered itself for gaining the all-important matter
—influence over the formation of the juries.

The Lord Mayor for the year, John Moore, a good-natured,
quiet, modest man, who, however, when he had once formed a
resolution held to it unalterably, convinced himself in the
administration of his office that a change in the constitution
of the city was required, and was prevailed upon by a word
from the King to lend a hand to it himself. According to an
old, and certainly long obsolete, custom, the mayor had the
right of naming one of the two sheriffs for the next year by
drinking at a solemn banquet a glass of wine with one of the
guests. In this way Moore appointed a merchant who had
shortly returned from abroad, and who had taken little part
in the city movements,.Dudley North, the brother of Chief-
Justice Francis North, and, like him, a Tory in his opinions.
When he invited the citizens to elect their sheriffs, as was
always done on Midsummer's Day, June 24, he observed at
once that the one whom he had already appointed needed
only to be confirmed [1].

Already, two years before, a like attempt had been made
but had failed; it seemed likely to do so again this time.
The introductory words of Moore at the election in the
Guildhall were answered by the most violent outcry against
the procedure in general, and especially against North.
In vain he called upon the assembly to disperse; it was still
continued by the sheriffs. Not on this day, for it would have
been impossible in the general tumult, but on another, which

---

[1] In Ralph there are the most detailed and comprehensive accounts of this. But
the best part of what he says is from Roger North's Examen and Biography, to
which we must refer.

the Lord Mayor had granted for the purpose, but again later
had refused, and which was held to in spite of him, the 5th of
July, did they proceed to an election : it resulted in a large
majority in favour of two men who had had an important
share in the 'ignoramus' verdict, Papillon and Dubois. But
the Lord Mayor did not give way before this result. He
affirmed that the conduct of the elections was his affair,
not the sheriffs'. At a new election, which the government
ordered, he also took votes as well as the sheriffs. By far
the greater number gave their names to the sheriffs, and
now also a very large majority showed itself for Papillon
and Dubois: they were once more proclaimed as sheriffs for
the ensuing year. But a part of the citizens gave their votes
to the Lord Mayor also ; and of these—by far the smaller
number in themselves—a considerable majority declared itself
for Box, the Tory candidate, whose election the Lord Mayor,
who had been expressly commissioned to protect the old
rights, now declared to be the only valid one. He proclaimed
Box and North as the sheriffs for the ensuing year.

This was as yet a very undecided success, and one which
had only been obtained by the immediate interference of
government and court. Moore was kept to his project by
Jenkins, and especially by Ormond, who saw him at his house
several times a week. Ormond's secretary, Gascoigne, directed
the municipal intrigues, which were necessary to gain votes,
with indefatigable zeal and great skill. But still it was a
successful step, which seemed to open the way to the comprehensive undertakings projected against the independence
of London, especially as lawyers of high position took a
decided part against the popular movements. Francis North,
who was soon after promoted to be Lord Keeper, and even
at that time appeared as Vice-Chancellor, declared that the
King's guard was his defensive arm, the offensive one was the
arrangement of the laws, with which he could overpower his
opponents. In this direction worked Chief-Justice Saunders,
who was commissioned to examine the municipal liberties.
He was a corpulent man, who otherwise troubled himself little
about the questions of the day, and knew how to avoid a conversation about them by turning it off with a joke : he had

worked his way from the lowest rank, only as it seemed to
enjoy good days: he conducted his business also with a good
humour which won him the attachment of the members of the
Inns of Court; but as it was always his ambition to fight out
a cause which he had once undertaken, so now he made it
his most earnest endeavour to prove the frailty of the municipal
privileges.   The monarchical import of the old laws was once
more brought forward in all its strictness.

On these steps of the government, at what it did and what
it was expected to do, the ferment of the Presbyterian population in town and country redoubled.   The Whig leaders
were at that time not discontented at the presence of the
Duke of York, because it animated the zeal of the people for
religion and law[1].

In the country this temper found its most vigorous expression when, in September 1682, the Duke of Monmouth again
undertook a journey through some of the counties.   It was an
event in Cheshire that he won the prize at a horse-race ; his
adherents celebrated his victory with bonfires.   No doubt
there were opponents even there who tried to extinguish the
fires; still, in the disturbances which ensued in the streets
of Chester, his adherents had by far the best of it.   The
well-to-do nobility looked upon it as an honour to entertain
him in their country seats; the assembled crowd greeted
him on his arrival at various places with acclamations of joy,
which seemed to be all but a proclamation of him as king.
Monmouth allowed children to be brought to him to be healed
of the king's evil; he touched them, just as if he had the
power of healing attributed to kings, with the words 'God
bless you[2].'   This was truly a curious mixture of superstitious
loyalty extended to an illegitimate son, and of a temper of
strongly-expressed opposition.   Monmouth, men thought,
would decide disputed points in accordance with the popular
ideas: annual parliaments with the right to a session which

---

[1] Falaisan: 'La religion, dont il est, reveille les peuples et renouvelle leur
ardeur pour la religion protestante et pour leur liberté.'

[2] Compare the extracts from the reports received in Roberts: Monmouth i. 136.
Dalrymple's representation is not exactly confirmed by them, although it is repeated
there.

was not to be dissolved within two months; free election of
magistrates in the towns and boroughs ; and, as far as I can
discover, the right of the counties to dispose of their militia,
and even appoint its commanders.   So, at least later, was the
modification of the constitution described to which Monmouth
had pledged himself in case he came to the throne.

We cannot doubt that Shaftesbury's influence was especially
active in this, and that a definite object prevailed in it.

A short while before, Shaftesbury had made yet one more
attempt at reconciliation, and had declared himself ready, if
the King would summon Parliament, to procure for him not
only ample subsidies, but even the recognition of the hereditary succession, provided that a limitation of the authority
of a Papist successor were conceded [1]·   As his proposals were
rejected—for they ran exactly counter to the direction which
matters had just then taken—there remained nothing by which
he could maintain his importance but a great popular demonstration.   According to his views it was to be quite universal.
He counted upon some large towns, like Bristol; upon influential men in the counties, like Courteney in the West, and
Hotham in the North ; upon the support of active preachers,
like Owen and Mead ; similar connexions were formed with
Scotland.   Shaftesbury's idea was, that Monmouth, in the heat
of the excitement, surrounded by his adherents, should express
the demand for a Parliament, and that this, at once repeated
in other parts, should lead to a general manifestation of like
views from the country.   This would then have exercised the
greatest influence on the pending differences in the capital.

But after the approaches of Shaftesbury to the court,
which were no secret, it is easily to be understood that he
was no longer so entirely master of the .party which had
gathered around him.   Amongst the Whigs a separate
society was formed, which appears under the name of 'the
Southamptons,' from Russell's country house where it met,
in the opinion of which Shaftesbury first went too far, and
then not far enough.   It held to the exclusion, but wished

---

[1] James's notes on this subject are confirmed and exemplified in a statement
made by Barrillon.

for no rebellion. To this party Monmouth adhered. Ford
of Grey, Russell and Essex were more his friends than
Shaftesbury. When Monmouth was arrested in September,
whilst taking part in a banquet, he made no resistance,
though it would perhaps have been possible at the moment,
and Shaftesbury would have wished it: he, as little as his
friends, desired to put himself outside the pale of the law.

During this difference of opinion, not to say division,
amongst the leaders, the municipal agitation could lead to no
result; in the great contest about the election of the sheriffs,
the government kept at last the upper hand. On the 19/29th
of September there had been a very stormy municipal meeting.
In the place of Box, who resigned, the Lord Mayor proposed
another Tory, Peter Rich: his name aroused a violent
outburst of dissatisfaction. Some however held up their
hands for him; and as the largest number were opposed to
any election at all, and at first abstained altogether, only those
were counted who had held up their hands; the Lord Mayor
was accordingly able to appear on the hustings, and declare
Rich to be legally elected sheriff, together with North;
with this he dismissed the assembly. That the sheriffs still
thought good to continue the meeting and held another
election in which Papillon and Dubois once more obtained
the majority, could only prejudice their cause: for there
was no doubt that the Lord Mayor had the right to dissolve
a municipal meeting; and in civil agitations of this kind
nothing is more ruinous than to commit any manifest illegality.
An accusation was laid against the old sheriffs; on the
day on which the swearing in of the new sheriffs took place
every year, Papillon and Dubois also appeared to be admitted
to the oath, but the Lord Mayor commanded them in the
King's name not to disturb the peace, whereupon they withdrew. Some companies of city militia kept order in his
interest; Dudley North, and Peter Rich, whom he solemnly
proclaimed as sheriff[1] took the oath, received the badges

---

[1] Barrillon: 'N'y ayant point de concurrent il ne se trouva pas de difficulté de
declarer le Sr. Riche legitimement éleu.' For the particulars of the case Luttrell

of their dignity, and entered on their office. The retiring sheriffs made no difficulty in giving up to them, as was customary, the keys of the prisons.

All this had shown what influence a Lord Mayor was capable of exercising, and it was therefore of double importance that about the same time the government succeeded in securing a submissive man for this office for the next year. The choice wavered between two aldermen, a Whig of the name of Gould, and a Tory, Pritchard. The former had a majority, which indeed was not very considerable, and it was said at once that a number of disqualified persons had voted for him, men who had not taken the requisite oath, especially Quakers. After the exclusion of the disqualified electors—an operation against which the Whigs raised vain objections—Pritchard had a majority ; on the 22nd of October he was declared by the Recorder to be Lord Mayor for the ensuing year.

In this way the public authority in the capital passed into the hands of the Tories, and so was under the influence of the government. None doubted that the new sheriffs or, as Shaftesbury .said, the pseudo-sheriffs forced upon the city, would appoint juries according to their views, and that now in the capital also the Whigs would have adverse verdicts brought home to them.

The first who justly felt himself threatened by this was Shaftesbury. To escape a sudden arrest he went to his friends in the city ; even here only a few trusted persons knew where he abode. In his hiding-place he still cherished the wildest plans. He thought himself able to organise a revolution in the capital ; he had but to say the word and 10,000 steadfast men would rise ; in the neighbourhood some troops of armed cavalry were hidden, which would then enter immediately. Many meetings were held in which an attack upon Whitehall was quite seriously discussed. For this we need not refer to statements made in the trials, which perhaps cannot be depended upon ; we have the testimony of Russell, who

is the best authority. According to him many lifted up their hands by mistake, because in the general confusion it was impossible to hear what the question was.

indeed thought it permissible to be silent on some points, but never would have been capable of affirming any-thing untrue. Once in presence of him and of Monmouth, who had been released on bail, it was proposed to overpower the guards at Whitehall, which, according to information received, might be easily accomplished. Russell declared himself against it, for if the guards were once overpowered they would be destroyed in cold blood, and what an atrocious act that would be [1] ! At these words Monmouth seized his hand and said he saw that they were of the same opinion. Without doubt the only object was to gain possession of the King's person and then compel him to such measures as were thought advisable [2]. But how easily that might go further! Monmouth was horrified to perceive that even his father's life might be endangered. In Shaftesbury's confidence there were not only discreet lords but also men of the lower orders, ready to fight, and full of the wildest passions. More than once the day for a rising was fixed, but always when it came, the matter proved impracticable. Shaftesbury said at last that he had too few confederates to be able to carry it out, and yet so many that it could not remain concealed. He thought himself no longer safe even in the city, and decided to flee to the United Netherlands, which he had formerly described as the Carthage which must be destroyed.

In English history Shaftesbury will remain at all times memorable, because he opposed the establishment of an Anglican and royalist organisation with decisive success. He started from the conception of tolerance, as Locke had done : Locke's principles are those of Shaftesbury ; their friendship rested, like all true friendships in men of mature years, upon a community of ideas. However much the phases vary in which Shaftesbury appears, through all there runs, if we may so say, one single liberal principle logically pursued. For he was only parliamentary in so far as the Dissenters exercised a determining influence on the resolutions of the

---

[1] Paper delivered to the sheriffs. ʃ. Russell's Life of Lord Russell 350.
[2] It is to this time that that confession of Monmouth's must relate which the Duke of York has incorporated in his notes. Extracts 140.

Lower House. He may be regarded as the principal founder of that great party which, in opposition to the prerogative and to uniformity, has inscribed upon its banner political freedom and religious tolerance. Around him gathered first the allied lords, Danby's opponents, and later all the Nonconformists, as well as all the boroughs of the kingdom. Thus supported, Shaftesbury dared as it were to challenge the King to combat. If we consider how he conducted this contest, we may count it his greatest mistake that he regarded external relations only as means for his party efforts at home[1]. He made use of the French ambassador to bring about the dissolution of the Parliament, which he hated, and the disbanding of the army, which he feared : on the other hand, he prevented his friends from declaring themselves against France in the European combinations, which they would otherwise indisputably have done. Whilst he defended the Protestant movement in England in its widest bearings, he helped, on the other hand, to secure the predominance on the Continent of the Catholic movement in its connexion with the French power. And how easy it was for Charles II again to find support from it. When Shaftesbury, who saw the greatest danger in placing money and troops at the disposal of the government, hindered every parliamentary grant, he drove the King to seek French assistance, which Charles II procured precisely by again energetically opposing Parliament, with which Louis XIV could after all not remain long allied. So the reaction became possible, before the growing prevalence of which Shaftesbury now took flight. Whether he was altogether determined to quit the field is still by no means certain. At the time it was believed that his idea was to bring about a reconciliation between Orange and Monmouth, in the interest of his party. But the disagreeables of a long stormy passage, the change of abode and manner of life just at the severest time of the year, perhaps

---

[1] 'If this alliance,' he says in a letter dated Jan. 30th, 1680, speaking of the alliance with Spain and Holland, 'serves to raise money, men and ships for our mutual defence under the conduct of H. R. Highness, it had been much better never made.'

also the effects of the last unsuccessful exertions, and the
feeling that he had suffered a defeat, brought in a few months
his old infirm body, long worn out, to the grave.

In London his loss was not even very much felt; his old
friends thought that at the last he had injured rather than
helped them. Just that Nonconformist tendency which he
nourished, and in which there had been no question of a
difference between the Protestant sects, came at that time
to the aid of the government.

A memoir written at this time by the Secretary of State,
Jenkins, has been preserved, in which he demonstrates that
Anglicanism alone was compatible with monarchy, and
speaks in warning tones against all concessions to the Nonconformists, principally because the points of dispute were
not concerned with doctrine, but only with the form of
government. And who has ever been satisfied by forced
concessions? Step by step they would after all come to a
republic, that is to say to the rule of many instead of the
rule of one; moderate and wise laws would be exchanged for
the innovations of inexperienced dreamers [1].

When the government returned to the strict execution of
the Act of Uniformity, and, in accordance with it, renewed the
sternest regulations of Elizabethan times, it had, in so doing,
at least one immediate object. For the transformation of
municipal institutions it would be of incalculable advantage,
that for future elections the proof of church attendance, and of
the previous taking of the Oath of Supremacy should be
demanded. Many might submit to all this without thereby
becoming Anglicans; but still the systematic opponents of
Church and State would be by this means excluded—the
Quakers, anyhow, as they would, in no case take an oath [2].

· [1] What is amiss in the present state of affairs? In Wynne's Life of Sir Leoline
Jenkins i. xlv.

[2] Unfortunately in Luttrell, who otherwise contributes so much, the election
itself is passed over. Barrillon refers to the preparations for it already on the 23rd of
November: 'Le parti des mécontens paraist affribli et diminué': on the 4th of
January he mentions the method 'd'exclure beaucoup des presbytériens et
autres nonconformistes, qu'on oblige à se déclarer, en les contraignant d'aller à
l'église et de conformer à la liturgie anglicane.'

After this exclusion, however, and especially as the government had no objection to making use of one-sided machinations, the new elections led to quite different results. At the election of aldermen, in some parishes even decided Tories carried the day; in Farringdon ward, for instance, the sheriff Dudley North himself was elected. Jenkins took especial care to influence in this direction the formation of the Common Council, which from all times had interfered powerfully in all political movements. At the new elections on St. Thomas' Day, December 21, 1682, there resulted also a decisive change. It was not that all Whigs were excluded, but some of the most esteemed and influential members of the party, such as Thomas Player, and also the decided adherents of Shaftesbury in general, were not re-elected; the government might once more reckon on a majority in the Common Council at least, except perhaps in quite extraordinary cases.

The extensive character of the transformation was seen soon after the opening of the new council. It expressed to John Moore its gratitude for his administration, recognised expressly the right of the Lord Mayor to nominate one sheriff, and re-established the veto of the Lord Mayor and aldermen on the resolutions of the town council, of which they had been deprived in the times of the last civil wars.

In this way the moment had now come, in which the government, not without hope of attaining the aim which it chiefly kept in sight, might continue the judicial proceedings which it had instituted against the validity of the municipal privileges. The city had been called upon to give an account of its liberties: the question was ' Quo warranto?' the answer was, 'Eo warranto'; and nothing of any importance could be alleged against the validity of the charters. But the doctrine was established that they could be forfeited by abuse, and that such a forfeiture had here really occurred; once, by a duty imposed in an illegal manner, but especially by a petition of the Common Council for the revocation of the prorogation of Parliament pronounced by the King at the end of the year 1680. Expressions were found in the petition which were opposed to the respect due to the King, especially to the principle of the constitution, that the King could do no

wrong [1]. The city objected that the offensive words related
not to the King, but to his ministers; but the lawyers decided
that this should have been said expressly. Equally little
would they, as was desired, distinguish between the city and
the Common Council, so that the guilt should only fall upon
the latter: they maintained that the Common Council represented the municipality.

The matter was twice discussed in the year 1683 before
the King's Bench; in June judgment was given, that all the
liberties of the city had been forfeited and had reverted into
the King's hands [2].

It could not possibly be intended to abolish peremptorily
the liberties of the city, in which were included the most
indispensable rights, such as that of the market; there could
be no intention of governing the great metropolis like a
village. The object only was to put an end to the independence of the municipal magistrates; the King caused the
unconditional restoration of its charters to be offered to the
city, if it would accept the regulations which he proposed [3].
The drift of this was, that henceforth the election of the Lord
Mayor and the remaining municipal officials, the recorder,
coroner, and some others, including the sheriffs, should require
royal confirmation; should the King reject the elections made,
and should those held in their stead produce likewise no
acceptable results, he should be empowered himself to name
the Lord Mayor and sheriffs. For hitherto, so said Lord
Keeper North, a faction in the city had sought to obtain
support for all its insolence and disorderly conduct by only
electing the most decided opponents of the government to
the municipal offices, and that with a heat and violence which
had been the terror of good and peaceful citizens; this faction
must be deprived of the hope of setting up magistrates of its
choice, and so procuring immunity from punishment. What

---

[1] 'That the petition was scandalous and libellous, and the making and publishing
it a forfeiture.' Sentence against the Charter.

[2] Already in March 1683, Barrillon gives notice of this intention: 'Le plan des
ministres seroit, que la ville de Londres remist volontairement la chartre de ses
privilèges pour en retrancher ce qui est abusif.'

[3] Proceedings in State Trials viii.

was the Common Council to do? The loss of its ancient rights seemed to it so unbearable that, however hard it might be, it agreed to accept the regulations; this was decided by a majority of eighteen, 101 votes against 83. On the 21st of June the Lord Mayor and sheriffs went to the King to acquaint him with this result and their submission to his will. Charles II was rejoiced; he thought he had at last really become King of his capital.

Altogether he only now seemed to attain to the fulness of his power. For he had, so it was said, the right of appointing the officers of the militia and of dismissing the judges, according as it seemed good to him : by influence exercised upon the sheriffs, he could determine the jury-lists ; now a veto on the appointment of the magistrates, and, if necessary, their actual appointment fell into his hands; in all other towns things would take the same course as in London ; none would in future venture to resist him ; in time he would succeed in obtaining a Parliament according to his wishes [1].

This affected most sensibly the Nonconformists, who in the last Parliament had had the upper hand, and who now not only saw their position in the towns threatened, but were visited with the strictest execution of the Act of Uniformity. There were amongst them many rich merchants, who withdrew their capital, so that a number of bankruptcies occurred, and money became scarce in London. This was ascribed to government, which desired in general to make the people poor, so as to rule them more easily. What remained when even such moderate men, who had done so much for religion as Baxter, were apprehended? He was accused of having infringed the Five-mile Act : only on the most urgent representations by his physician was he allowed to return to his house, as was said, to die there. The prisons were full to overflowing with Dissenting ministers. Many conventicles were dispersed in the various parishes; even the laity were punished.

---

[1] Gachon, then the correspondent of Brandenburg, asserts on the 19/29 June, 'Le roi viendra à bout à la fin, d'avoir un parlement favorable.' But he adds, 'Les persécutions, qu'on fait aux nonconformistes, produisent beaucoup de mécontentement.'

It is at the time of this powerful advance of the Tory government in temporal and spiritual affairs, that the conspiracy known as the Rye House Plot occurs. It was suddenly learnt that the King had escaped only by accident an attempt upon his life : there had been a plan to lie in wait for him at a lonely house on the way from Newmarket to London, and to kill him and his brother, or at least deprive them of liberty; only through having hastened his journey by a couple of days, on account of a fire which broke out at Newmarket, and reached his house there, had he been saved. Nothing suspicious had occurred to the King himself on the way, but the information which he then received sounded very definite, and the statements of those, who on that charge were first arrested, agreed so well together, that he himself felt no further doubt about the reality of the project. He maintained that the cart which was to be used to obstruct the narrow road, by which he must pass, and the gun that had been kept in readiness, had been found on the very spot.

It would easily be understood, if, amongst the ill-used and threatened sects, a desperate plot had been formed : the Duke attributed the guilt to the old Cromwellians, the Fifth-monarchy men, and the fanatics. From the various statements, which are indeed for the most part guarded, but sometimes very positive, this much at least may be learnt, that everything fits in with the preparations made by Shaftesbury for an insurrection. The very men with whom he had entered into connexion—old soldiers like Colonel Rumsey, Captain Walcot, Rumbold, Wildman, and some civilians highly esteemed by his party, the barrister Robert West, who was looked upon as a freethinker, the old under-sheriff Goodenough,—were the principal persons implicated. In their meetings before and after his departure, they had often discussed the possibility of possessing themselves of the King's person, which would be the decisive stroke for the undertaking ; amongst others, Rumbold had there drawn attention to his own house, where he lived as a maltster, at the Rye, in Hogsdown [1], which the King passed on the way to or from

---

[1] 'At his own house at the rye in Hogsdown in the county of Hertford, where he had married a maltster's relict, and so was designed the maltster.' Lord Fountainhall in Fox, App. iv.

Newmarket, sometimes without an armed escort. He had often thought, he said, that if he put some impediment, so as to stop the carriage, he might shoot the King, and be able to save himself in the neighbouring marshes, where he knew intimately every road and path. Now that the undertaking against the charters in London was successful this proposal reappeared. It was thought to be the easiest way of preventing the destruction of the freedom of the country, to seize the King and the Duke of York. Rumbold, who in former days had been present amongst Cromwell's troops at Charles I's execution, still never avowed the intention of killing Charles II; others also had scruples about staining their hands with the blood of their King; but they would have had no hesitation in attacking his guards, and getting him into their power. How far their preparations were successful, and their plans mature, will always remain doubtful. Perhaps they would have proclaimed Monmouth king; in any case, they wished to separate the Duke of York from Charles II. They counted, should the deed be successful, on a corresponding movement in the towns, especially in London, where Goodenough thought of establishing an organisation of men, holding like opinions, which would have recalled the times of the League in Paris. Of those of this class who were accused, Captain Walcot, against whom his own letters bore witness, was first tried and executed; some others followed[1], without exactly attracting great attention.

But, as from the first it was thought incredible that a few soldiers and lawyers should have intended to change the constitution of the state, without the support of more powerful people, so the statements of those who had been arrested, pointed, with more or less certainty, to the best known of Shaftesbury's friends amongst the ranks of the nobility, and the members of Parliament.

After Shaftesbury's death, Monmouth, Essex, Howard of Escrick, the leaders of the opposition among the Lords, Russell and Hampden, its leaders amongst the Commons, and

---

[1] Copies of the informations and original papers, relating to the proof of the horrid conspiracy. State Trials ix. 366.

Colonel Sidney, who was introduced by Howard, sometimes met together, and debated how to keep alive the
agitation which Shaftesbury had kindled. From the information, which however is only fragmentary, about their
proceedings, we learn that they intended only to act upon
legal ground. At the opening of one meeting, Hampden
reminded them that all personal objects should be put aside,
and only the common good be kept in view; the important
matter now was to see that the property and liberties of the
people should not be easily invaded by those in whose hands
public authority was placed[1]. In so doing, however, they
proceeded on the principle, that the English constitution
granted the right of resistance, which no ecclesiastical
decree could abolish. As far as can be judged, it was
their intention, by means of a general association, to call
for a free Parliament, which should discuss the grievances of
the nation and decide about the succession. As in former
cases, they would not hear of the employment of any force,
which, on the contrary, they detested. Russell flattered
himself that, even without it, he would be able to attain his
object of uniting freedom and loyalty.

In the first trials facts were brought forward which proved
the connexion existing between the two parts of Shaftesbury's combination; those determined to attack the King had
always boasted of support from some great men in the nation.
These also were now arrested; namely, Essex, Russell,
Hampden, Sidney; Lord Grey, who was no less implicated,
succeeded in escaping; Monmouth kept himself concealed;
Howard thought only of his own safety, and even became the
accuser of his friends.

That they had been seriously implicated in the attempt
against the King's life or liberty, Charles II himself did not

---

[1] 'We should resolve into such principles as should put the properties and
liberties of the people into such hands, as it should not be easily invaded by any
that were trusted with the supreme authority of the land; and it was mentioned, to
resolve all into the authority of the Parliament.' Statement made by Lord Howard
of Escrick, in Sidney's trial; the plainest of his statements. State Trials ix.
423, 853. Compare Wiffen, Memorials of the House of Russell, by Natorp and
Grey 266.

believe ; but that did not dispose him to greater leniency ; he let it be understood that he saw no great difference between an attempt to provoke a rebellion in the country, and an attack upon his person [1].

The judicial proceedings assumed, from the first, a threatening aspect ; they led at once to a tragic occurrence. Amongst the accused was Arthur, Lord Essex, the son of Arthur Capell, who formerly, as the accomplice of his King, had followed Charles I to death. He himself had served Charles II in the most secret and important state affairs, had, for a time, conducted the administration of finance, but at last, on account of political principles, had separated from him ; according to the King's account, because he thought that the popular party would win the victory. The reverse, however, had now come to pass ; and the first trials showed that all that had been done for the organisation of resistance had become known. Essex charged himself with the blame of this disclosure : in spite of a warning from Lord Russell, he had introduced Howard, who had betrayed them, amongst his friends ; he took it very much to heart that this should occasion the ruin of them all. We might perhaps imagine that this deviation from the absolute and unconditional personal fidelity which his father had shown had tended to confuse the wits of the son ; but there exists no decided evidence of this ; on the contrary, we find him taking up another and a very strange way of looking at the matter. Essex did not disguise from himself the fact that he would be condemned and executed. But what would then become of his children ? They would lose their estates, possessions, and rank. The idea occurred to him that he could only avoid all this by suicide ; his rank and estate would then, at least, not be forfeited. He had with him a page, a servant, and a warder in the room in the Tower that had been assigned to him as his prison. One morning they saw him pace up and down

---

[1] ' Qu'il ne met pas grande différence entre vouloir soulever ses sujets et conspirer contre sa personne.' Barrillon. The Duke of York's first letters to the Prince of Orange are worth notice ; for this reason amongst others, that he avoids mentioning Russell in them.

for a long while, without saying a word, in deep thought ; he then retired into his dressing-room ; half an hour afterwards he was found dead ; he had cut his throat with a razor [1].

Lord Howard was just going to repeat, at Lord William Russell's trial, his statements about the preparations for a rebellion, when the news of this occurrence came to his ears. Had not his statements caused it ? He began with a choked voice, hardly audible, which he excused on the plea of the impression made upon him by the terrible death of an old friend ; then he continued. He told them of the meetings of the six, at which he had himself been present, and in which Russell had taken part. Colonel Rumsey testified that Russell had been there when news was brought that a movement, planned by the confederates in the West, that is to say, at Taunton, had failed, and affirmed that Russell had declared his approval of the project. Lord Russell denied this, but not the fact of the meetings themselves, which he only represented as being all of them accidental. But he did not commit himself to a minute discussion of the facts; he took up the formal, legal position, that the acts of which he was accused were not proven, and even if they were so, they would not make out, according to the act of Edward III, the crime of high treason, of which he was accused. But he himself scarcely entertained any hope of escaping by this means. For the two most important facts, only one witness had, it is true, been brought forward ; but at Stafford's trial the proof had not been better ; there the doctrine had been established, that that was enough in cases of this kind. And if the act of Edward III had been explained in Coke's Institutes to mean, that only a rising against the King constituted the crime of high treason, this was now declared to be a mistake of Coke's, who thereby had contradicted himself ; for, according to the concordant judgments of other lawyers and of the courts of justice themselves, this crime had been actually committed, when men joined together for a rising

---

[1] Barrillon gives on this point the particular circumstances. The suspicion that the court had caused the murder of the Earl should not be repeated after what Hallam has said on the subject.

against the King, and made preparations for it; on no other
ground had Plunkett been recently condemned [1]. It had
been the curse of the Popish trials, that the crime of high
treason had been stretched as far as possible ; this proceeding,
approved of at the time by the Whigs, now reacted on their
own leaders.   Lord Russell insisted, with convincing vehemence, on his horror at the thought of murdering the King,
for whom on the contrary he had prayed, or even of exciting
a rebellion, which he considered to be hurtful and even impossible.   'I have always been averse to all irregularities
and innovations, and in favour of the maintenance of the
government upon its old rightful basis and the parliamentary
way.'   Such was doubtless the case ; but he had considered
it to be compatible with the laws, to provoke the summoning
of Parliament by resistance to the commands of the highest
power ; to overtures, which had this as their object, he had
lent his ear ; what he thought to be lawful resistance, was
declared to be a project of rebellion [2].   The jurymen accepted
the evidence against him, as well as the explanation of the
statute of high treason which the Solicitor-General put forward ; the testimony borne by some of the friends of his house
to the loyal disposition of the accused produced no impression.
The trial had begun at nine o'clock ; at four o'clock the jury
pronounced a verdict of guilty against him.

Lord Russell was prevailed on by his family to sue the
King for pardon, and to beg the Duke of York to intercede
for him.   To the King he confessed that he had done wrong
in taking part in those meetings; but it was not through
evil intentions against him, but rather through carelessness.
He was convinced that, of the crime of misprision, that is to
say, of neglect of duty, he might be found guilty ; and to
escape such a verdict, he had, at his trial, avoided entering
on a discussion of facts.   To his King he confessed this
crime, and entreated for pardon ; he assured him that in

---

[1] The Solicitor-General's speech.   State Trials ix. 630.
[2] Ormond believed as little as any one else in Russell's intention to murder the
King. But he remarks : ' It should be a warning for ever to all who detest such a par-
ricide, how to enter into consultations to reform the government by force, when such
underplots may be carried on against their mind.'   Letter to Arran, Carte iv. 658.

return he would never again take part in public affairs, unless
the King desired it, and would live wherever the King commanded. To the Duke he promised that, if through his
intercession, he obtained pardon, he would never again in any
way enter into opposition to him ; he would always be under
the deepest obligations towards him. Still, even as a suppliant,
he held fast to his principles. It did not seem to him fitting
that in his letter to the King he should describe himself as a
loyal subject, because this was the quality which was denied
him ; to the Duke he said that, in all that he had done, his
object had been to maintain the religion established by law ;
he hardly admitted that in so doing he had been mistaken.
The greatest offence was given by his view, that the nation
could defend its liberties, even when attacked under the
semblance of the laws. Two clergymen of the most moderate
views, Tillotson, then Dean of Canterbury, and Burnet, endeavoured to convince him that his idea of the right of
resistance was opposed to religion, which ordained submission
to the powers that be. The argument which Russell brought
forward against them is worthy of notice ; it is almost the
same as that which the Scots laid down against Queen Mary,
—namely, that this doctrine only related to the first ages of
Christianity under the Emperor, but had no application to
England, where the religion had been determined by law.
However good an evangelical Christian Russell might be, yet
he would not deviate from the ground which he considered
to be legal. The two clergymen once thought that they had
shaken him in his opinion, and began to hope that he might
win his pardon, if he publicly renounced it ; they informed
Halifax of it, who soon after let them know that it had produced great impression upon the King, to whom he had
mentioned it. The declaration, however, which Russell drew
up on the subject, seemed, even to them, unsatisfactory, and
Russell would consent to no other. He took once more into
long and quiet consideration a letter, which Tillotson sent
him on the subject, but at last declared that, if he said more
than he had said, he would no longer be upright, and would
make himself guilty of a lie [1].

---

[1] Lord John Russell's Life of Lord William Russell.

In this lies the peculiar mark of this century, that in the
clash of political and religious opinions, which struggle for
supremacy, unalterable convictions are formed which lend
the character a firm inward bearing, which again raises it
above the strife of party struggles. As the die falls, so men
either obtain power and gain scope for their ideas, or they
must offer their neck to the avenging axe.

Whether Russell, by retracting his opinion, would really
have obtained pardon from Charles II is indeed very doubtful.

About the disposition and motives of the King much that
is uncertain has been told. The most trustworthy information we get from Barrillon, who here also played a part. He
was commissioned to announce to the King, with recommendations from Louis XIV, the arrival of Ruvigny; it
was again Ruvigny, the father, who was connected with the
house of Russell. Charles II answered that he had no
objection to Ruvigny's coming, but that before he arrived
Russell would be beheaded. ' I know that the King my
brother would not advise me to pardon a man who would
not spare me if I fell into his hands. I owe this example to
my own security and to the good of my kingdom [1].' How
much better he would have done had he let mercy prevail !
The house of Bedford, around which an extensive and distinguished connexion was grouped, entreated for it ; in his
own court voices were raised for pardon ; Russell had the
feeling of the aristocracy in his favour, and how could the
King refuse to rely on the word of so honourable a man ?
He would never again have had to fear anything from him.
But the animosities had already become too personal ; offensive sayings had been carried backwards and forwards ; even
now the King was informed that Russell had described his
trial as a continuation of the Popish plot, just as though he
were suffering from a cabal which aimed at the re-establishment of Popery ; this increased Charles II's displeasure.

---

[1] ' Je ne veux pas empêcher, que Mr. de Ruvigny ne vient pas ici, mais Mr. Russel
aura le cou coupé avant qu'il arrive. Le roi mon frère ne me conseillera pas de
pardonner à un homme, qui ne m'auroit pas fait de quartier. Je dois cet exemple
à ma propre sureté et au bien de mon état.' Barrillon, July 29. He also told the
Earl of Dartmouth, ' If I do not take his life, he will soon have mine.'

The Duke of York thought that the time was come when the King might once for all confirm his authority by severity [1].

It was the opposition between the doctrines of the rightfulness or wrongfulness of resistance to the supreme power which here came into play. Russell regarded as permissible resistance against a limited monarch, who transgressed the laws : in the preparation of such resistance he had taken a share, though but a distant and limited one ; what he had done he considered to be a small offence : the bench and the jury declared it to be a serious political crime. The King suffered the proceedings to take their course, for he thought that this theory would ruin him and his state, and that by a court of justice, which admitted the principle of resistance, he might even himself be condemned to death. The family of Russell made one more attempt to gain, by a considerable promise, the influence of the Duchess of Portsmouth in their favour ; but even towards her the King remained unalterable [2].

On the 21st of July, William Lord Russell drove in his own carriage to the scaffold, which was erected in Lincoln's Inn Fields. His soul was quite tranquil, for God would pardon him the sins of his youth ; if he had erred in public affairs, it had been not from an evil will, or a desire for his own advantage, but from mistaken views. But that his doctrine was wrong, he was not yet convinced. And death by beheading, he continued, was only a moment, which could not even be very painful ; he thought his death would be of more use to the country than his life could have been.

When, conducted by two hundred musketeers and deep in prayer, he arrived at the place of execution, his mind was still only occupied by the thought of the other world which he was about to enter. At the sight of the assembled crowd,

---

[1] From Monmouth's notes, the authenticity of which is undoubted.

[2] Barrillon, August 2 : ' Le roi d'Angleterre a reconnu l'importance de se relascher en une affaire de cette nature.' That which Luttrell, p. 269, tells us, that the King had refused £50,000, with the words, ' he would not purchase his own and his subject's blood at so easy a rate,' is weakened by the fact that ' as is said,' is added, and was probably made by hearsay out of the words which have just been quoted.

he said that he expected in a little while to be in far better company. For he was a believer in God and Christ: he was heard, even at the last, praying for the continued maintenance of the Protestant faith. Only once he had felt the bitterness of death, in taking leave of his wife, but now even that was conquered; his further behaviour, says Burnet, seemed like a triumph over death. The crowd was amazed to see how calmly he mounted the scaffold, with what composure he walked four or five times up and down the black-draped boards[1]. He put his head under the axe as though he were exalted above the horror of the act. He handed to the sheriffs a paper in which he represented with perfect straightforwardness his political and religious position. From it we see that he died for the doctrine of the right of resistance, which to him had become almost a religion.

---

[1] Gachon: 'Jamais homme n'est mort avec plus de courage, n'ayant pas fait paroître le moindre désordre ny dans la prison ny sur l'échafaud ; . . . des gens croyent qu'on auroit fait prudemment, d'accorder la vie à Mr. Russel, et que cet acte de clémence auroit gagné beaucoup de gens à Mr. le Duc, qui lui seront irréconciliables.'

CHAPTER XII.

ON the very day on which Russell was beheaded in London, the doctors and masters of the university assembled at Oxford, and pronounced, in old ecclesiastical form, their solemn condemnation of a series of opinions, which were the foundation of attempts like the last. They were the doctrines of Hobbes and of Baxter, of the Quakers and of the Fifth-monarchy men, above all the political views of the Whigs, such as Russell also avowed,—that all power originates with the people ; that the subject is only bound so long as the Prince fulfils his duty ; that hereditary right contains in itself no unconditional claim to the crown ; and that it is permissible to enter into defensive associations, even in opposition to the will of the highest powers. Against this, it was inculcated, as a peculiarly characteristic command of the English Church, that men should be obedient to authority for God's sake, and that unconditionally, without reserve or exception.

In the same sense public thanksgivings were ordained for the preservation of the King and his loyal subjects from the fury of the fanatics and the godless. The Whigs were preached at as much as the Dissenters. From all parts of the country and from all classes the King received addresses, expressing hatred of their opinions and tendencies. That the doctrine of the lawfulness of resistance threatened the country with disorders which might lead to civil war, procured for the doctrine of passive obedience a momentary supremacy in social life. A number of noblemen, who till now had remained at a distance from the court, returned to it to show the King their devotion ; they were most graciously received.

Just at this moment, when sympathy for the King was awakened in a great part of the nation, and the opposition with which the ministry had so long been obliged to struggle was broken up and as good as annihilated, Halifax would have thought it advisable to summon Parliament. For that would give the King the opportunity of re-uniting the nation around him; he might convince them that his actions hitherto had been necessary for the preservation of the country, and that his intention was to keep within the law[1]; anyhow, he said, the time would soon come when in consequence of the triennial act a new Parliament must be summoned. It was commonly thought that Charles II was inclined for it; he disapproved in his heart of much that had been done; he was desirous of being popular again; he would once more be able to be united with the Parliament, at least from one evening to the following morning. Only a little while before, a society had been formed in the town, which made ample offers to him for such a case. Ormond was counted on, as well aware that England could not be governed without a Parliament, and as wishing that it should be summoned. Many thought that the dislike of the population for the Nonconformists, and the fear of the noblemen, would work together to produce a good Parliament.

But this was opposed by, Sunderland, for whom Conway had again made room as Secretary of State, as well as by the Duke of York. They represented to the King that men's minds were not nearly sufficiently prepared to give grounds for hoping that successful progress might be made with the deliberations; he would certainly be compelled to do what he did not wish to do.

And that a Parliament, composed in such a manner as to answer to their wishes could not as yet be expected, can be gathered from the transactions of the Privy Council, which even retired a step from its former concessions, the definite enactment of which had been neglected. Before the election

---

[1] ' Que c'est un moyen pour réunir tous ses sujets avec lui. Il devroit leur dire que son dessein n'est autre que de conserver sa personne et le gouvernement, sans rien faire contre les loix.' Barrillon, Aug. 2, 1683.

of a new Lord Mayor took place, all parties thought it necessary to give the regulations once more a thorough consideration. In a sitting of the Common Council, which took
place on the 2nd of October, Recorder Treby spoke against
them. His reasons were, that the restrictions to the charters,
which had been ordained, made them altogether doubtful,
and that the members of the Council would break their oath
if they accepted them. He spoke so convincingly, that a
majority, although only a small one (105 to 83), declared itself
for his motion ; what might have been attained in June could
no longer be attained in October; the regulations were this
time rejected. The consequence was that the lawfully expressed abolition of the charters obtained legal force ; the
government was consequently in the position of having simply
to appoint the magistrates of the city, whose freedom it
had only wished to restrict. It considered it the most advisable course, to reappoint for another year those who were
already in office. The Lord Mayor Pritchard laid down
the sword with which he was girded in the name of the
city, and then received it again in the name of the King ; of
the remainder only those were excluded who were known to
be of the the the opposite party, like Treby [1]

It is very remarkable that the government was still in a
minority in a Council, which had been elected under its influence and under the renewed enforcement of the ecclesiastical laws. But those very men who had conducted the
elections were against the repeal of the charters. There
exists on the subject a letter of Jenkins to the Duke of York,
in which he states forcibly the reasons against it, and foretells
that all other corporations would be thrown into agitation by
it ; that the discontent in the nation would increase ; that
disagreeable suspicions would find in it a kind of confirmation[2].
What the government had looked on as in itself only a means
to an end, the abolition of the charters, it must now, quite

---

[1] The proceeding upon the debates relating to the charters of the city of London,
Somers viii. 394. Vignola mentions some circumstances which are not to be found
elsewhere.

[2] Lionel Jenkins to the Duke of York; unfortunately without a date. Wynne
ii. 685.

contrary to the wish of the moderate Tories, carry out as an
end in itself: it was in this way forced into a very one-sided
position, from which its general reputation could not but
suffer.

The alternations in the decisions of the Common Council
may be regarded as the oscillations of the tongue of a balance,
which shows the preponderance now of one, now of the other
side. How far however the fluctuation of the public temper
extended we shall see at once from another occurrence.

The Duke of Monmouth, who was looked on as one of the
ringleaders of the late conspiracy and as its appointed head,
again emerged out of the concealment, in which he had
remained for a time and in which he had made the acquaintance of Henrietta Wentworth, and showed himself in public.
One day, in November 1683, he was seen driving in his own
carriage to Whitehall, with the escort by which he had always
been accompanied before. On the following Sunday he appeared in the midst of the numerous company which then
used to assemble at court; he went up to the Duke of York,
who received him in the presence of many others. Monmouth
here solemnly declared that he would recognise the Duke
as the true heir to the crown, and would support him as such;
he then entreated him to restore him again to the King's
favour. The Duke accompanied him to the King's apartments; there Monmouth threw himself on his knees before
his father, accused himself of acts which he could not
justify, and pleaded for his grace, through the intercession of
the Duke. It struck every one that this was not so much a
supplication as the fulfilment of Charles II's warmest wishes;
he joyfully gave his repentant son his hand to kiss, and led
him into the Queen's rooms; Monmouth was also presented
to the Duchesses of York and Portsmouth, and was again
received into the court circle.

Many secret negotiations had preceded this; Monmouth
had made a confession of his guilt, but had made a proviso
that he should not be obliged to appear against his former
friends: the Duke of York and the Duchess of Portsmouth
had only unwillingly given their consent; but after the first
overtures, which Halifax negotiated, the King could no longer

be restrained [1]. For deep natural inclinations are rather increased than weakened by differences and disagreements. Monmouth had never actually quarrelled with his father; his share in the conspiracy had perhaps even been useful to Charles II, in so far as it had averted the extremest hostility. Charles now wished to keep him near himself; to remove him from court would still, he said, be a punishment; a pardon given him on those conditions would only be a half pardon.

In the country the pardon of Monmouth, who was and must ever be an opponent of the Duke of York, was looked upon as a great event. The oppressed party again took courage. For it showed, after all, that the conspiracy was not looked on as so criminal as had hitherto appeared; there was a flattering hope of opposing a Monmouth faction to the York faction, and of still winning a triumph.

This again caused a ferment amongst the Royalist and Tory party; not that they had made the Duke of York's cause unreservedly their own, but they thought that the system of government was shaken by this proceeding; it was impossible to allow the conspiracy, the investigation of which was still going on, to be declared a vain invention. In the Privy Council a statement from Monmouth was demanded, which should leave no doubt remaining as to the reality of that conspiracy.

Monmouth was also prevailed on to sign a declaration in this sense, which was submitted to him in the form of a letter to his father; but after he had done it, his friends with whom he was dining one evening, first showed him, that it would after all serve as evidence against those accused, and this he had received a promise that he should not be compelled to give [2]: they told him that he compromised himself by this for ever with his contemporaries and with posterity.

---

[1] So the Duchess of Portsmouth told the French ambassador: the matter had been arranged in less than twenty-four hours. Barrillon, 5th Dec. 1683. Compare Monmouth's notes in Wellwood's App. They are without doubt genuine, though not entirely comprehensible. Some notices I take from Vignola.

[2] The words are: 'Though I was not conscious of a design against your Majesty's life, yet I lament having had so great a share in the other part of the said conspiracy.'

Monmouth had in reality imagined that he might be in favour with the King, and at the same time remain in connexion with his old party: he now saw that this was impossible; he decided definitely to demand back from the King the declaration he had made. .Whether Charles II in reality flew into such a violent passion at this, as he is said to have done, or whether he also perceived that the position of his son was not tenable, anyhow he returned his paper to him, but at the same time actually forbade him the court (7th of December, 1683).

Monmouth was already in possession of a comprehensive general pardon, drawn up under the Great Seal; he had nothing more to fear. Still he had so much consideration for his father, as not to wish to remain in his neighbourhood. When he was called upon by public authority to give evidence at a trial, he preferred leaving the country; but even in this he acted, without doubt, in agreement with King Charles, who had recommended him most pressingly to the Prince of Orange; for Monmouth went first to Flanders, then to Holland. The claim to appear as rival to the Duke of York he maintained in both Netherlands, and indeed in Europe.

In England, on the other hand, the Duke of York had the advantage for the present. Monmouth's appearance at the court, and the favour that he enjoyed for a time, far from benefiting his friends, had on the contrary become ruinous to them. Amongst other things it had drawn down the sentence of death upon Algernon Sidney.

It may be doubted whether Sidney was less guilty than Russell, but the proofs against him were still more unsatisfactory[1]. In proof of the principal act which was alleged against him as high treason, a negotiation with disaffected Scots, only one witness was produced. To prove against him, according to the legal custom then prevailing, a second criminal action, in default of a second witness, the manuscript of his work on government, found in his study, was produced. It doubtless contains principles hostile to monarchy, if not actually republican; the most compromising

---

[1] Meadly, Memoirs of Algernon Sidney 261.

was a declaration, which was looked upon as unequivocal, that King Charles deserved his father's fate. The objection might easily be made that it could not possibly be looked upon as a crime for a man to write down his thoughts; it would be different if Sidney had had his pamphlet printed. But the answer was, that even to indulge in thoughts like these was high treason in England, how much more to put them down in writing. And the King was more sensitive to such a statement than to anything else, as he thought that it had for its basis a distinct purpose. He said that Algernon Sidney had, on his return to England, promised him to behave blamelessly towards him; how was he to spare men who would not have spared him had he fallen into their hands? Still, after a great sacrifice had been made of Russell, Sidney's pardon would not have been beyond hope, had there not been a fear that it might specially confirm the assertion that the whole conspiracy had no foundation[1]. Sidney himself still appealed to Monmouth's case, on the ground that he had done nothing in which Monmouth also had not taken part; but the judges remarked, that that would involve a renewal of the proceedings, which could not take place. Sidney invoked the vengeance of heaven upon those through whom his blood—the blood of an innocent man—was shed.

It was in this trial that George Jeffreys, now Chief Judge of the King's Bench, first gave full play in a public position to his wild temper. Jeffreys, a Welshman by birth, had in his youth joined the burgesses of London in opposition to the Lord Mayor and aldermen; later he had gone over to the party of authority, and had entered the personal service of the Duke of York; from that time he became one of the most reckless champions of the prerogative. He had accustomed himself to spend amongst the wits of the coffee-houses long hours in drinking, laughing, and noisy talk: in the administration of justice, which in other respects he understood, he still was deficient in all decency of behaviour; he

---

[1] Ormond, writing to Arran, 13th of Dec. 1683, describes the situation as a 'conjuncture perhaps fatal to Mr. Algernon Sidney, whose life could then not be spared.'

could be heard scolding for a quarter of an hour together, and that in Billingsgate language; it gave him a wild satisfaction to insult his opponent whilst passing judgment on him. But what is more terrible than power and mockery combined?

Amongst the prominent characters of that time we can distinguish three parties:—the men of the absolute reaction, who shrank from none of its consequences; the legal friends of the prerogative, holding Anglican opinions, who only wished to maintain the monarchy, and desired moderation in other things; and lastly the old adherents of the exclusion and the theory of resistance, the friends of the Nonconformists. The leaders of the last party had perished, but the party existed and was looked on as dangerous; in sight of every new movement made by it, all moderation seemed insufficient; the absolute reaction gained in this way increased powers.

One of the principal consequences of the Rye-house Plot was that Charles II considered his brother, who had been threatened with the same danger as himself, as most closely united to him. That there had been an intention of seizing both at the same time convinced him still more that their cause was one and the same; he gave him influence, in order that they might take common precautions against common enemies.

It is a well-known saying that the attempt to exclude the Duke of York from the succession to the throne after his brother's death, with which also the conspiracy was connected, had the effect of making him begin to reign even during his brother's lifetime. Things had not as yet gone quite so far, but he became more powerful every day, and it is true that the personal interference of the King in the events which happened around him steadily diminished.

The most important affairs had till now been prepared by Jenkins, North, Halifax, and Hyde, now Earl of Rochester, for the King's decision, or at least for deliberation in the Privy Council; this ceased when, in the spring of 1684, Jenkins was compelled to resign his office. Godolphin, who succeeded him, did not, it is true, himself belong to the reactionary party; but he was not thought even by Hyde, Earl of Rochester, to be quite qualified, as he did not possess the firmness necessary at this moment. He was thought to be a political artist, who lived much in court cabals, and looked upon steady men of business as beasts of burden. What recommended him was an unusual clearness of perception even in the most complicated matters, yet it was not so much by this quality that he rose, as by his connexion with the Duchess of Portsmouth, who wished to have another man whom she could trust in the cabinet.

Sometimes both parties were united in their interests. The Duke wished that his friends the Catholic lords should at last be delivered from the Tower. The King was still more anxious for the deliverance of Danby, who was imprisoned because he had spared Charles himself; he told the judges that he could not look upon any one as a friend, who did not agree with him on this point[1]. What stood in the way of both was an old resolution of the Upper House, that no one could be released who had been impeached upon a motion of the Commons; but the judges took into consideration, that the prisoners had already been detained so long to no purpose, and that even at present there was little prospect of a speedy summons of Parliament; they ordered their release. With regard to Danby, it was not even agreeable to the friends of the Duke of York that he should be set at liberty; they feared, not without reason, his influence over the King and his connexion with Halifax.

But more frequently, and in fact on every question that actually touched on great affairs, the antagonism of the two parties displayed itself.

In the spring of the year 1684, when nearly three years had passed since the last dissolution of Parliament, Halifax and Danby were in favour of proceeding to summon a new one, urging that the King had then promised even frequent Parliaments. But the band of confidential friends set up, in opposition to the obligation imposed by the triennial act, the most high-flown royalist doctrine. They said that the prerogative of the crown consisted above all in the right to

---

[1] Barrillon makes him say : 'Que c'est une injure de son gouvernement de ne le pouvoir mettre hors de prison.'

summon Parliament or not, the very right that was most
violently disputed by their opponents: it had been practised
to its full extent by the King's predecessors; for how many
years under the first Tudors and under James I had there
been no Parliament? They went so far as to tell the King
that he had had no right to impose such an obligation upon
the crown and upon himself [1]. But if then the question was
raised, whether it would not be advisable to state this argument in a public proclamation, it was considered that such
a course might give occasion for disagreeable discussions
in the country; it was thought better to treat as a state
secret the resolution which had been arrived at, and to carry
it out without a word.

But external, as much as internal, affairs were affected by
the dissensions of the leading men. If only for the sake
of understanding the one, we must turn our attention to the
other, though it also deserves attention for its own sake.

The great European question of the day related to the
offer made by France to King Charles of the office of
arbitrator in the disputes with Spain. The Spaniards hesitated
to agree to it on their side also; they would have wished
to associate the States-General with the King in this matter.
But in the deliberations at the Hague, the States had conceived a different idea. A one-sided settlement of the Spanish
and French disputes was not thought by the Prince of Orange
and the Pensionary Fagel to be even advisable, because
France would thereby have her hands free to turn against
the other allies, and would acquire full supremacy. They
proposed a congress to arrange all questions at issue in
Europe. For some time the city of Amsterdam resisted this,
because an accommodation of the differences with Spain
would be enough to ensure peace, which after all was the
main point: even the two ambassadors of the Netherlands in
England were of different opinions about this matter; Van
Beuningen was in favour of the view held at Amsterdam, Van
Citers in favour of that of the Prince. But in December 1682
the Prince and the Pensionary drew over to their side the

---

[1] 'Que lui-méme n'avoit pu s'imposer la necessité.'

States of Holland, after a feeble opposition from Amsterdam; their opinion was also accepted in the States-General. Upon this it was proposed to the King of England to bring about a congress of ambassadors in London, at which, to be sure, he would only appear as mediator, not as arbitrator; the question of the Spanish Netherlands should not be regarded as settled, even if agreed upon, before unanimity had been reached in the German question also. The desire was, to prevent the German empire from being in any way obliged to cede Strasburg to Louis *XIV*; still less would they expose it to any risk of the King of England, as arbitrator, awarding Luxemburg to him.

In England, two opinions were formed on the subject; the friends of Barrillon, the Duchess of Portsmouth, who interfered everywhere, the Duke of York, and Sunderland, thought that Charles's office of arbitrator could not extend beyond the differences with Spain; Halifax, on the other hand, agreed with the proposal of the Prince and of the States-General, and the Spaniards also assented to them; at least he thought it advisable that both negotiations should go on together.

As yet it was by no means clear which side the King would adopt. Neither the mediation nor the invitation to a congress did he decidedly reject; at least he deferred giving an answer. With the Prince of Orange indeed he stood on no confidential, but still on tolerably good terms. The Prince had declared himself in favour of the proceedings against the capital, as far as they had then been successful, and probably was intending to come again to England. On the discovery of the Rye House Plot, he sent his most confidential servant, Bentinck, to England, to congratulate the King and the Duke of York upon their deliverance; Bentinck was very well received, more especially as he represented the Prince to be a devoted member of the House of Stuart. But this concord ceased when conversation turned to external relations. The Duke of York remarked that he could recognise no difference between external and internal relations; a glance would show the intimate connexion between the two; the Prince must attach himself entirely, in external affairs also, to the family.

This was all the more significant now that the Duke, who since his return to the court had been entirely attached to France, also got a footing in the secret committee by which external affairs were managed. The entire party, which grouped itself around him, worked together with him in this sense. When there was again a question of summoning Parliament, and the assurance was heard that the King might then count on considerable grants, for which either rich Nonconformists or wealthy lords would give security in advance, the Duke of York and his friends could only see in this the intention of forcing the King out of his quiet and secure position : just as before he had been enticed into hostilities against France, to oblige him to summon Parliament, so now the intention was to urge him to summon Parliament, so as to entangle him in complications with France. The last secret alliance with France had been entered upon because Parliament refused every grant ; the pecuniary support, which France supplied, now prevented any mention of a Parliament, which might lead to complications with France.

Barrillon, in April 1684, enumerates his payments with considerable care : he had handed over four of his bills of exchange (each worth 50,000 francs) in October, and two in November 1683, four in January, and four in February 1684 ; but this had not nearly covered the third year's payments ; of the stipulated five millions, 1,300,000 were still unpaid ; he remarked of what great importance it was to continue the payments at the present juncture. These insignificant and not even regular payments had, as we have seen, if not actually produced, at all events contributed to produce, the adhesion of Charles II to the French side in the affairs of the time. When, in December 1683, the Spaniards nerved themselves so far as to make a declaration of war against France, he remarked to them with astonishment and irony, that they would nowhere be able to maintain themselves ; the position of Europe was probably unknown to them. The bombardment of Genoa, which was considered to be an act of hostility directed against Spain, he regarded as only a natural consequence of that declaration. That Luxemburg was now seriously besieged, no longer produced any impression upon him; to the exhortation to take part in the war he replied with a declaration, that by so doing he would expose the royal authority to the greatest danger: when the fortress was taken (in the beginning of June 1684), he even sent the King of France his congratulations. He warned the Dutch to offer no opposition, for by so doing they would only provoke new encroachments. To the question of the Dutch ambassador, whether the King would perhaps allow Ostend also to fall into the hands of France, he answered coldly and ironically, that he knew Ostend; it was a poor harbour. The Prince of Orange had formerly said that the continuation of these seizures might turn out to be dangerous for England herself; after the Netherlands it might be her own turn: he was answered, that England was sufficiently secured by the sea. The Prince replied that England had more than once been overpowered by invasions, and might be conquered again [1]. Ever memorable words;— they indicate a view which might one day have great consequences. But at that time the States-General also were not inclined to allow themselves to be hurried into a war with France. They accepted first the twenty years' truce, under which Luxemburg for the present remained in French hands, and withdrew the troops which the Prince had pushed forward into the Spanish territory. In August the diet at Ratisbonne also decided to accept a truce with regard to all Réunions that had taken place in the territory of the Empire. Charles II looked on all this with selfish indifference. To the remark that the truce would be disagreeably felt in Turkey, against which the German empire consequently acquired free power of action, he replied that it would not be less disagreeable to his factious opponents in England, whose only hope lay in kindling a great European war.

It had been often represented to him how ruinous it might become for England should France entirely overpower Genoa, for that would throw the Mediterranean trade entirely into her hands, and exclude England from it. Already pro-

---

[1] Barrillon, 26th March: 'Que l'Angleterre avoit été conquise plusieurs fois et qu'elle le peut être encore.'

clamations appeared which threatened ships sailing to Genoa, English as well as others, with examination—a measure which did not fail to produce a movement of opposition in the English commercial world. The King however remained very quiet in the matter: though the English ships might be named, such measures would never be carried out against them; in reality they would only affect the Dutch ships. He had no objection to the Doge of Genoa being obliged to ask pardon from the King of France; for if the King demanded it on account of his honour, and Genoa felt her honour wounded by it, the Republic must of course give way to the King on a point of honour. He expressed himself intentionally as strongly as possible on this subject; for the Prince of Orange grounded his desire for war simply upon the hope of enticing England into it, which would be disastrous for the royal power[1]. He wished to deprive him of this hope.

Looked at from without, this policy, the internal connexion of which no one suspected, even met with some approbation; for England appeared rich and tranquil, all revolutionary movements were stifled, trade was extremely flourishing. Upon a statue which the English merchants who carried on business in Hamburg erected to King Charles in the Exchange of London, he is extolled as the British Emperor, father of his country, conqueror in good and ill fortune, arbitrator of Europe, lord and protector of the sea. He was commended by the Elector of Brandenburg as having, in a moment of need and danger for all Christendom, raised his kingdom to the highest pitch of prosperity, and re-established internal tranquillity. Charles II accepted in good faith what the Ambassador said about his external relations; but when he came to speak of the order re-established at home, he was seen to shrug his shoulders: Halifax pushed his wig back from his ears so as to hear whether the matter was indeed so regarded abroad. The audience was conducted without much

---

[1] His words were, 'Le fondement de son opiniastreté pour la guerre est l'opinion d'y pouvoir entrainer l'Angleterre, ce qui ne se peut pas qu'en mettant l'autorité royale en un extrême péril.'

formality ; whilst the Ambassador spoke, a boy pushed himself between him and the King : it was young Richmond, the son of the Duchess of Portsmouth.

The violent and contradictory nature of the position showed itself once more in the execution of a friend of Monmouth, which took place in June 1684. A rising of Monmouth's adherents was still dreaded at any moment ; on one occasion, through fear of an attack which they might attempt, the guards at Whitehall were strengthened. Every one knew of the association of English and Scottish exiles in Holland ; not only was a simultaneous movement in Scotland expected, but it was also thought that it would be supported by the Protestant princes, especially in Germany. It then happened that one of Monmouth's principal advisers, Thomas Armstrong, was seized at Leyden and brought in chains to England, in accordance with a permission granted by the States-General for such cases.. The King declared him to be the greatest rogue under the sun ; even Monmouth had described him as such, though he still allowed himself to be led away by 'him : he had invented the tales on which Monmouth based the assertion of his legitimacy. A letter to the Elector of Brandenburg was found on Armstrong, in which he thanked him for the protection granted him during a sojourn in Cleves, where he had found refuge for a time with Lord Grey. He at the same time asked permission to go to Berlin[1]. King Charles concluded from this, that the opposite party sought to connect itself with foreign princes, under the pretext that his government threatened Protestantism. He tried to convince the Brandenburg Resident of the contrary, whom, in spite of the letter, he did not cease to treat in the most friendly manner. Towards Armstrong he felt no mercy. As he had already been outlawed, it was not thought necessary to take him before a jury to investigate the facts. Chief

---

[1] 'Qu'en cas, que la paix ou la trève se fasse, il puisse aller à Berlin remercier M. l'Electeur des faveurs qu'il en a reçu.' It is put more clearly in Barrillon, June 22, 1684, than in the reports of the Brandenburg Resident, Von Besser. But we see from these that his Prince stood in no further connexion with Armstrong or Monmouth than that he offered them a shelter.

Justice Jeffreys rejected the proposal to do so, because the prisoner had not brought himself under the statute, to which he appealed, by a voluntary surrender of himself. Amidst the outcries of his daughter, that her father was being murdered, he was condemned to death by the King's Bench as guilty of high treason ; he went to meet his fate with unexpected religious elevation [1]. But what a marked contrast was here! Hand in hand with the most extreme severity towards a friend of the Duke of Monmouth there went new approaches to the Duke himself [2]. From his notes it appears without doubt that his reconciliation with the King, and his return to England, were once more being arranged. As yet the moment for establishing this once for all was not come ; the intention was to wait till the Duke of York had departed to suppress the disturbance in Scotland. In the meanwhile Monmouth was in unbroken communication with Halifax, and through him with the King.

If we still try to sketch the internal antagonism which kept the court of Charles II in suspense, we shall be especially struck by seeing that Halifax, without hiding his views, not only maintained himself in Charles II's favour, but even once more gained a considerable success over his opponents.

Often already he had attacked the financial administration of Rochester, who, although only one of three commissioners of the Treasury, possessed as much power in it as any Lord Treasurer ever had, because he always gained over one of the two others to the measures which he desired. Halifax reproached him with conniving at frauds ; this charge was not altogether without foundation, for Rochester did not keep very strict accounts with men who had earned the gratitude of the government. Now, in connexion with Lord Keeper North, he got the old constitution of the Treasury re-established, according to which there were five commissioners.

---

[1] On the way to Tyburn he read ' The Whole Duty of Man.' State Trials ix. 118.

[2] Barrillon only hints, but Vignola states decidedly, that Monmouth had been in London : ' Dopo esser stato in questa citta si dice partito (Dec. 22). La grand tenerezza che conserva il padre verso questo torbido figlivolo, fa sospendere le misure a molti.'

The representations in Rochester's favour, which proceeded
from those who indeed did not love him, but who hated and
feared Halifax, produced no impression upon the King,
as it now seemed after all that Rochester preferred the
interest of his own adherents to the King's interest, to the
detriment of the royal revenues, the increase of which was
very much to be desired. Two new commissioners were
appointed, one of whom was a cousin of Halifax, the other
the brother of the Lord Keeper, Dudley North, who had
shown in the administration of the customs peculiar zeal in
the detection of frauds. Rochester was very much displeased
by this, because associates were given him by whom he
was to be controlled, and he decided, after some hesitation,
to resign his seat on the commission. His place was filled
by Godolphin at the proposal of the Duchess of Portsmouth,
and Godolphin's place was filled by Middleton, a Scot, whose
wife was a Catholic, at the instigation of the Duke of York,
who overcame the difficulties which these relations caused.
As Secretary of State engaged in the most important affairs,
Middleton attached himself unconditionally to the Duke of
York through good and evil fortune. Rochester was appointed President of the Council. But he felt that he no
longer possessed the King's confidence in anything; that he
might retire with honour, he wished to be appointed Lord
Lieutenant of Ireland.

As Rochester and Halifax were opposed in financial questions, so were the Lord Keeper North and Jeffreys in judicial
questions.

In October 1684, Jeffreys returned from his judicial circuit
in the North, and expressed his astonishment at having found
in the prisons many Catholics, who, after all, were the King's
best friends, and most trustworthy subjects. He brought the
matter forward in the Privy Council, in the King's presence,
urging how unjust it was that men, many of whom had even
served under Charles I, and others who had in various ways
done service to the crown, should be left to languish under persecution, the sole reason for which had been the Popish conspiracy, now acknowledged to be entirely fictitious. Amongst
the ministers, Sunderland was on his side; Rochester remained

silent ; Halifax spoke against him [1]. He demanded that every single case should be investigated, and that release should only be granted when either the deserts or the innocence of the prisoners were without doubt. For only in this way could the law be observed. To this the Lord Keeper added that a large number of fanatics and Dissenters were also kept in prison, or were threatened with it ; should they, as would then be inevitable, be restored to liberty, or be allowed to expect release from punishment, many elements hostile to the crown would be again let loose. The King broke up the sitting without any result having been arrived at.

Upon this, at the Duke's instigation, several Catholic priests were released, and even this made bad blood enough ; but to authorise these favours by formal resolutions of the Privy Council was not the King's intention. He did not wish to fall into open opposition to the laws. Jeffreys had been admitted into the Privy Council to demand the execution of the old royalist laws as they were now interpreted [2] ; but beyond this, into the doubtful paths which he, partisan as he was, advised the King to enter, Charles II would never have followed him : the moderate counsels of North, an ultra-Tory, but still no Catholic, ever had great weight with him.

The dominant combination at that time was formed by Sunderland and Godolphin, who, together with the Duchess of Portsmouth, discussed confidentially in her rooms the most important and secret business. She needed neither the Duke of York, who was no longer entirely her friend, nor even Rochester, who now again attached himself closely to his brother-in-law [3] ; she only drew around her her own personal confidants. It was the régime of a most peculiarly constituted

---

[1] In North's Life of Francis North Baron Guildford 237, the Lord Keeper is named as the sole opponent. Barrillon is silent on that point, and gives the information about Halifax quoted in the text.

[2] Barrillon, October 5 : ' Le véritable dessein en cela est, de fortifier par les avis d'un homme fort savant dans les lois d'Angleterre les resolutions rigoureuses, qu'on a dessein de prendre pour les affaires de dedans.'

[3] Barrillon, February 18 : ' M. le duc de York souffroit avec peine la diminution du crédit de Mylord Rochester, croyant que cela retournoit sur lui ; j'ai été souvent employé, d'adoucir ce qui se passoit.'

Camarilla, a mistress who enjoyed unlimited confidence, and two acute, experienced, pliant statesmen, who at that time were entirely devoted to her. But her authority was not, on that account, absolute; in opposition to ˙ her, Halifax still knew how to hold his own.

On one occasion when, in the Privy Council, discussion arose about the American colonies, the charters of which were being treated like those of the city, he was heard to defend their cause with great energy, and on the ground of general principles. He demonstrated that a monarchy limited by laws was happier and more secure than an unlimited monarchy. His opponents and the Duchess drew the King's attention to the undesirableness of a man with such principles taking part in affairs. Charles II even gave them hopes of his dismissal, but took no serious measures towards it. On the contrary, Halifax conducted the secret negotiations with Monmouth, to whom, as early as January 1685, a letter was sent under the King's signature, promising him a speedy return. An entire change in the politics of England did not by this means come into prospect; the King would then have had to break also with France, which was hardly possible : but he always loved to give scope in his immediate surroundings to various tendencies ; it was intolerable for him to perceive that he was dependent on the opinion of foreigners : it just suited him that one of his ministers should keep alive the hope of a speedy summoning of Parliament, while the other opposed it. In the oppositions of parties, to which he allowed free play, he still always maintained, though affected by them, a certain independence ; with quiet tact he attracted, or else he repelled ; even now he did not allow his brother to gain complete supremacy.

In this state of things, the result of what had gone before rather than a secure basis for the future, Charles II was overtaken by the common fate of mortals. His death was in perfect accordance with his life.

In spite of some symptoms which seemed to indicate gout, he still appeared in possession of unbroken strength, and it was even· thought that he might survive his brother, which would change everything. On the 1/11th February, he had supped in his usual good spirits, and then read the letters that had arrived by the French mail : on the following morning, Monday, his attendants observed an incoherence which they had not at other times seen in him ; he addressed in French people who did not understand that language. On sitting down, he lost consciousness suddenly ; he had been seized with an apoplectic stroke [1]. His state appeared from the first moment desperate, so that the Duke of York immediately ordered the harbours to be closed, to prevent Monmouth and his adherents from coming to England to oppose his accession to the throne ; all who saw the King were terrified by his altered appearance. By means however of bleeding and strong blisters, he so far recovered consciousness on the evening of the following day, that his head was relieved, and conversation could be held with him, though even then there were moments of darkness. In this condition he was spoken to about religion. A Protestant bishop had already, on his declaration that he repented of his sins, given him absolution, when the Duke was reminded by Lady Portsmouth herself, and Barrillon, of his brother's leaning to Catholicism, and was called upon by his confessor [2], with the authority which he derived from his office, to see that the King died in the fellowship of the Catholic Church. He acceded with joy : the way and means by which it was carried out were as follows.

---

[1] Vignola, February 23 : 'Essendo stato aperto il corpo fu ritrovato che l'abondanza dal sangue concuso nella testa particolarmente le ha impossibilitato il vivere, anzi si sino meravigliati i medici, che dopo la caduta possa havere ricuperato il sano sentimento, con cui ha potuto regolarmente discorrere.'

[2] True relation of the late King's death, in Somers viii. 429 ; the same document which contains the cipher P.M.A.C.F., which Macaulay has declared inexplicable.' The person so described is named as having first instigated the Duke. But who was it ? From an account which has appeared since then in Notes and Queries (1860) 470, and which came from the English Benedictine convent, established in 1643 at Lammspring in Westphalia, it was a missionary, by name Gibson, who reminded the Duke's confessor to urge upon this Prince his brother's conversion. With certainty we can learn from this, that the first exhortation came from the confessor. With this the words of The True Relation agree ; for it is said there that the person indicated by those letters declared to the Duke that it was his duty to admonish him : 'with this admonition,' the Duke then went to the King. Now the confessor, whose exhortation he obeyed, was a Capucin, who appears in the reports as Père Mansuète. The supposition is probable that the cipher indicates this. It might mean 'Pater Mansuetus Anglicae congregationis frater.'

In Whitehall there lived an old Scottish priest, John Huddleston, to whom Charles II was mainly indebted for his escape after the battle of Worcester, and the dying man was easily persuaded that the man, who once had saved his life, had now a commission to save his soul also. Only a few devoted confidants, who however were Protestants, were present when Huddleston entered ; the Duke himself kept watch at the door, to prevent any interruption. The King declared to his old friend, who knelt by the bedside, that he wished to die in the faith and communion of the Holy Roman Church, and that he counted above all other sins of which he had to repent, the sin of having so long deferred his reconciliation with it. There was here no question of a confession of faith. The King made a general confession, uttered a form of contrition and repentance with a distinct voice, once more received absolution, then supreme unction, and the eucharist, as his viaticum on the way out of life ; all was done according to the Catholic ritual, though emphasis was laid on the common Christian ideas of submission to the Divine will, and of comfort in the passage to another world. Later on, the Protestant Bishop of Bath and Wells, Dr. Kenn, advanced once more to his bedside[1], and reminded him of heavenly things, or else prayed with him. But he was more occupied with this world. He said he felt that he must die : he was sorry in so doing to give his good friends so much trouble. He closed his part in life with a courteous apology. On Friday, February 6th towards noon, he died[2].

By the two great forms of religion, which still struggled for supremacy in the world, he was surrounded and influenced in death as he had been in life.

It was immediately after the flight from Worcester, in the house of a Mr. Whitgreave, at Moseley, where he found refuge with John Huddleston, who gave him a controversial writing[3]

[1] So Barrillon definitely states : when James II disputes it later on, in Chaillot, it must be that in his religious zeal he has forgotten it ; the Queen remembers that formerly he used to give a different account of the matter.

[2] John Huddleston, Brief account of particulars, in State Tracts ii. 280.

[3] Richard Huddleston, Short and plain view to the faith and church, published by John Huddleston 1688, with a dedication to the Queen Catherine, in which he

by his brother Richard to read, that Charles II, impressed by the fidelity which the Catholics especially had shown him, felt the first serious inclination to go over to Catholicism: twice he was on the point of actually going over, once in agreement with Spain during his exile, the second time when he was on the throne, in agreement with France; he would have been quite capable, like his grandfather, Henry IV, of going to mass, if it had been his interest to do so, but the contrary was the case with him; the political position in which he stood forbade it; for the sake of his crown he did not go to mass. In the change of political relations, he even maintained, for a number of years, a decidedly Protestant bearing: now and then he even tried to stop, by his influence, the oppression of the Protestants in France; his official authority as head of the Church, although in his own heart he had the most serious doubts about its justification, he always exercised in the Anglican sense. Yet it agreed with an old sentiment in him, when, in the agonies of death, he received the Catholic sacraments. But it is obvious that the way in which this happened afforded no satisfaction to the Roman See itself. The King, in good health, would never have so far followed an external religious motive without the most decided political aim [1].

For he was a thoroughgoing politician. All that he did in his government was founded on the fact, that he could not bring himself to submit to the necessity of being simply a Parliamentary king. Not that he imagined he would be able to govern without Parliament, to which he owed his restoration, but he strove incessantly to procure for hereditary right, on the strength of 'which he had been restored, an independent importance, as equal, or even superior to Parliament. This was the aim both of his external alliances

---

describes the King's conversion as the happiest moment of her life, 'had it not been so near his end.' He refers once more to his resolution (to join the Roman Church) 'through frailty too late.' The book starts from the principle that Christ cannot have left the believers without the true Church, which is to be found in the Catholic Church.

[1] Barrillon and Burnet say, it is true, that he promised if he recovered openly to profess Catholicism; as however neither Huddleston nor the confessor allude to this, and they alone could know it and were interested both in mentioning it, I do not think that it is possible to accept it.

and of his religious vacillations: the former were to procure
him independent resources, the latter a party dependent solely
on the crown.   The character of his government was determined by the fact, that he let the means he adopted appear as
though they were really the end he aimed at.   In his heart
of hearts he cared equally little for France and the Spanish
coalition which struggled for supremacy on the Continent.
He inclined most towards France, because from it he hoped
to obtain assistance against his Parliament; but for a succession of years he also inclined towards the Spanish coalition,
because he hoped by so doing to beguile Parliament into
making grants, which might procure for him a military power
such as the continental kings possessed.   He thought that
by first making approaches to Catholicism, then by assisting
Protestantism, he would gain a great European support.   As
these interests had in themselves an universal meaning, which
he either concealed or put forward as it suited his purpose,
there entered into his policy a certain falseness, which gave
occasion to his opponents, who saw through him, to meet
him with combinations similar to those he made himself,
only of an opposite tendency.   The relations, upon which the
weal or woe of the continent of Europe depended, were in
England solely regarded from the point of view of home
parties. Around Charles II had grouped themselves a number
of considerable men, each of whom stood in a peculiar relation
to the great questions and interests: he attaches them to
himself or lets them fall as circumstances require; they are
almost his allies or his opponents rather than his servants.
Amidst all their changes, and in spite of the most active
exertions to the contrary, he knows how to maintain himself
in the possession of his prerogative; he asserts the right
of appointing his ministers at pleasure, and of administering
foreign affairs according to his own opinions; he sets himself from the very first above the necessity of summoning
a Parliament; but with all this he is far from gaining a firm
foundation for his state: although he has the government in
his hands, he is not even able to give it a steady direction;
he feels himself every moment surrounded by an opposition
so widely spread and so easily excited that he cannot venture

to summon Parliament, a course to which in itself he would. have been inclined. A monarch in such a position produces results in two ways—by what he consciously achieves and what he unconsciously brings about. As Charles I did not' let the Church fall, so Charles II maintained the hereditary right, even under temptations of a very alluring nature, in such a way that, after a great deviation, it still after some time once more reasserted its position in England. But at the same time, not exactly against his will, but still not in accordance with it, the Protestant character of the constitution was developing itself. After he had resisted for a time the Episcopal Church, he still at the last found her again his chief support. But this Church did not nearly include the whole Protestant population, amongst which on the contrary the old parties which the King looked on as his irreconcileable opponents were most powerfully active. Even the Church was not quite at one with the King. As generally happens, men despaired of coming to a rational decision on the great question involved in the relation between the hereditary right, which devolved upon a Catholic prince, and the Protestant constitution of the country; its solution was left to circumstances.

We are reminded of Goethe when we see how Charles II took life and enjoyed it. He was a man both capable of cultivation and cultivated; full of interest for everything new in nature, science and art; equally at home in his laboratory and on the race-course; a great patron of the theatre, of architecture, and of music; admirably fitted to be the leader of the fashionable, literary, cultivated but corrupt society of the capital: he was himself involved in varied love affairs, each of which bore a different colour and no one of which excluded another. The most important matter for him was his social comfort; he felt most contented amongst his ladies, whilst some French singer amused the company, and the cavaliers of the court stood round the table heaped with gold, where the bank was kept for bold players. We know however that enjoyment and distraction do not prevent intelligent men from taking the most active part in public affairs. It was a curious combination; on the one hand this Prince, whom nature seemed to have intended for an oriental throne in the middle ages, where he would have played a brilliant part, on the other hand the land of old Germanic freedom, and independent ecclesiastical movement, which had called him back from his exile and then had tried to subject him to the conditions of its old historic life. Against Charles II there arose elements like those to which his father had succumbed: he struggled with them during his whole life, however little it might appear, with skilful energy which grew in stormy times. Well might he often wish to shut out disagreeable things from his mind: but what he put away from him in the evening pursued him at night; by the side of his mistress, in his dreams, he called out the names of his opponents. He easily forgot old friends; upon his enemies he bestowed an irreconcileable hatred. Towards men such as Henry Vane and William Russell indeed, he knew no mercy; he thought he could destroy them and their theories as well; for they and his kingdom could not exist together. Still, as a rule he allowed gentleness to prevail—it was thought, because he did not know whether he would not have to call the opponents of to-day to his assistance to-morrow. For who would have ventured to assert, in the continual rivalry of parties, which would next gain the upper hand? Still he was inclined by nature to forgive and to forget. Perhaps it was even advantageous to him that he held so closely to his pleasures: his careless, affable, obliging manners gave occasion for no violent animosities. For elevation of soul, for moral conscience in him we look in vain; his great desire was to assert himself; he lived entirely in the passing moment; he even said that he could not trouble himself about what might come after he was gone.

BOOK XVII.

REIGN OF JAMES II, FEBRUARY 1685 TO
SEPTEMBER 1688.

IN the latter years of Charles II only one, strictly speaking, of the great constitutional questions then under discussion had been decided; and that had itself been decided more by the course of events than by legislation. Hereditary right had prevailed in spite of the antipathies aroused by the creed of the heir to the throne. It was thought that any departure from hereditary succession must give an opportunity for the assertion of principles at once republican and fanatical. The Church of England and the aristocracy allied with it, both the nobles and the gentry, and at least some of the towns, had accordingly ventured, in spite of their Protestant sentiments, to recognise the Catholic successor. No one within the British empire could have ventured to oppose the accession of the king who had hereditary right on his side.

In foreign affairs the last years of Charles had decided another important question. France, if not exactly supported, at least not opposed, by England, was obtaining at that time a position of incontestable preponderance in continental Europe. And the aspect of that kingdom in itself was grand in all respects. Louis XIV had not overthrown the old feudal institutions, but had given them a thoroughly monarchical form; he enjoyed more than any earlier king had done the unconditional devotion of the Gallican clergy. The Protestants had long formed the principal support of his grandfather; but in spite of all promises made to them, Louis suppressed their worship or expelled them from France, and so founded the ecclesiastical uniformity which has, ever since its re-establishment by him, maintained itself in that country. He called into life a new power, uniform in its nationality and ecclesiastical system, with well-defined frontiers, admirabl armed for offence and defence both by land and by sea; and this power knew no law but that of its own interests. Every one knew what objects the ambition of Louis XIV was likely to pursue on the approaching extinction of the Spanish line of the house of Austria, and on the expiration or breach of the armistice concluded with Germany. The old independence of the states of Europe could not be maintained any longer unless this prince found somewhere or other an energetic resistance.

To offer such resistance seemed the natural vocation of England; its old hereditary opposition to France, its position as a maritime power, and the preponderance of the Protestant religion in the country, pointed this out as its duty to Europe. But if it was to fulfil this task, it must not again be crippled by internal disorders. All depended upon the question whether the combination which had just been established, between a Catholic king and a political community essentially Protestant, would prove capable of maintaining itself; if it had proved so, a vigorous policy towards foreign states would have been also possible. But what if it failed to maintain itself? In that case, with the fresh outbreak of religious dissension all other constitutional disputes must revive also, and must bring on a struggle which could not be otherwise than advantageous to the ambitious views of France. It might be doubted which was of the greater importance for the life of Europe, the decision of the internal English, or of the external Continental, questions. The new reign must be decisive for both.

CHAPTER I.

JAMES II was in his fifty-second year; he enjoyed vigorous health, which continued to gain strength as he advanced in years, owing to the bodily exercise which he took every day without exception. He had served under Turenne in his youth; in his naval career also he had acquired good professional knowledge, and had gained as admiral the respect of the seamen; there was nothing of which he spoke with more pleasure than of his services by land and sea. There was nothing in him of the genial and conciliatory nature of his brother; he thought more of outward dignity and ceremonial; he was deficient in the delicacy and discrimination which had always determined his brother's policy. On the other hand, he had a more military vein, was in general steadier and more trustworthy, a far better administrator, and more persevering in work. He could not, any more than Charles, be praised for fidelity as a husband and for moral conduct in this relation. He did not indeed parade his excesses with as little concealment as his predecessor had thought sufficient; and in his case they led to a curious reaction, which made him seek to regain the affection of his injured wife by extraordinary indulgences. He was throughout his life very dependent upon priests and women [1]. But that did not, strictly speaking, impair his energy; he was always occupied with great plans; he wished

---

[1] Bonrepaus, December 1685: 'Le roi n'est pas si maistre de lui-même ny si grand homme que l'on a cru d'abord, il a tous les défauts du roi son frère; il n'a pas tant d'esprit que lui, et est plus opiniâtre et plus glorieux dans les choses

to gain distinction by military exploits like Turenne, or to
found a powerfully organised and compact state like Louis XIV.
He never lost courage. Lightning struck near his horse as
he was hunting without terrifying him. It was natural to him
to go to extremities in every direction; he sought the way to
his end even between abysses.

He was not at all disposed to employ himself, on ascending
the throne, in considering and thoroughly studying his position as king in its various bearings; he belonged to the
number of those rulers who take up a distinct position as
princes of the blood, and maintain it unaltered after their
accession to power.

James II was from the beginning of his career far more
closely attached to France than Charles II had been. He
had served, as has been mentioned, under the French colours,
and would have wished to remain there even when the French
formed an alliance with Cromwell; he would gladly have then
accepted a command in Italy which Mazarin offered to him,
and his acceptance of which Cromwell would not have opposed.
The express command of Charles—and James never ventured
to resist such an order—hindered him from carrying out this
plan, and he betook himself to his brother's court and shared
his exile, but not without taking into account how far more
advantageous the continuance of his earlier relations would
have been for him.

After the Restoration he would have been disposed to
follow the suggestions of his mother, and to marry according
to her wish; but his union with the daughter of the Chancellor corresponded to the Portuguese marriage of his brother;
both these marriages implied a fresh estrangement from
French interests and from the wishes of the Queen-Mother.
And the Duke of York adhered steadily to the party formed
by the Chancellor, even after his brother had deserted it; he
assumed for some time the character of head of the Church of
England party. He did not, moreover, renounce his opposition

---

extérieures.' Diest ('Relationes' from the Hague, Dec. 1686), finds danger ' in the
unruliness of the English nation and in the conceit of this king, who has taken
pleasure from his youth up in risking much for the sake of his designs, as his late
Majesty of England always judged of him.'

to France so soon and so decidedly as has been supposed. He prevailed upon himself, when political relations required it, to enter into the closest family connexion with the Prince of Orange, the outspoken enemy of King Louis; he enjoyed the notion of leading a great army into the field on the Continent against the French.

By degrees however his change of religion brought consequences in its train which led him back to France. By that change of religion he had dared to enter into open opposition to English legislation. Thereupon the Parliament, after a dissolution, conceived the project of excluding him from the succession: even the government seemed for a moment capable of accepting such a proposal. In this danger James sought succour from the great King, at first in opposition to the government of his brother, until he gained over the latter also for his cause. The alliance of 1681 was prepared by the Duke of York on both sides; and, as has been mentioned, in France far more trust was reposed in him than in the King. We know what a great personal interest Louis XIV took in bringing the Duke back to the English court.

Now these events established that connexion of interests and of persons which in the two last years of Charles II both determined, though not without a domestic struggle, the main features of English policy for the present, and also prepared its future.

Sunderland and Jeffreys then first took a leading part in public business; the destruction of the charters of London was carried out on a comprehensive scale; preparations were made for raising a strong standing army. The voyage of Lord Dartmouth to destroy the fortifications erected at Tangier was thoroughly in accordance with the Duke's views; he desired that the troops which were in garrison there should be at the disposal of the government for every possible contingency in England, and that the money which they cost should be employed at home. Without regard to the oaths prescribed by law, which stood in his way, he took into his own hands the administration of the Admiralty even without the title of High Admiral. The repeal of the penal laws against the Catholics was most seriously discussed.

The foundations of a new system were already laid; the principal impediments to its establishment were the support which Charles II gave to the moderate Tories, and his disinclination to follow any undertaking to its extreme consequences. The death of the King freed the Duke of York from this hindrance. His accession did not create a new power; it strengthened one which was already founded, and opened for it the way to a full and free development.

It is worth while to follow his first steps; for the embarrassments of reigns which form important periods in a nation's history are usually prepared at the very beginning of such reigns.

As soon as Charles II had closed his eyes, the members of the Privy Council went to offer their homage to James II, who had gone to the sitting-room which he had previously occupied. A quarter of an hour afterwards he appeared in the chamber where the Privy Council had assembled to arrange for the proclamation of the new king. The keeper of the seals placed the great seal of the realm at his disposal, as did the other high officials their seals of office; he restored them and declared the previous holders confirmed in their offices. Then he spoke, with the view of doing something to remove the apprehensions which had been spread abroad about him. He said, that he was considered revengeful; but that he would be just as gracious as his brother. He mentioned of his own accord that he was held for a friend of arbitrary measures; but he denied the justice of this opinion, and expressed his resolution of maintaining both in State and Church the system of government established by law. 'For he recognised the members of the English Church as loyal subjects; he knew that the laws of England were sufficient to make a king a great monarch; he would maintain the rights and prerogatives of the crown, but would not invade any man's property.' So at least we read in the declaration, in the form in which, by Rochester's wish, it was made known in the London gazette to all the world[1]. It is not placed

---

[1] 'I shall make it my endeavour to preserve this government both in Church and State as it is now by law established.' Ralph, from the Gazette, No. 2006.

beyond all doubt that the declaration originally ran thus word for word. According to the report of the French ambassador, the King had added in express terms that he would only employ the power granted him by God for the maintenance of the laws of England, and would do nothing against the safety and preservation of the Protestant religion[1]. The Brandenburg resident expresses in still more definite terms the language which the King was supposed to have used: 'he had said "as regarded his private opinions no one should perceive that he entertained them"'; the envoy professes to know that James II had struck out these words when his speech was drawn up for printing[2]. But it was maintained on the other side that the speech as actually delivered had been less decided in its terms than the form in which it was taken down by one of those present—Heneage Finch— and then approved by the King. And in this later form the speech is almost too measured and, with all its good assurances, too reserved to have been the first outpouring of the speaker's thoughts. It may suffice, however, to say that in this later form it was published and received with joy; it passed for the Magna Charta of the new government; for a Magna Charta which gave security to the country.

No one who kept his eyes open could remain in doubt that the future of this government depended on its treatment of the difference of religion between king and people. Men considered at that time what prospect of success James would have if he wished to release himself by force from the restraints of law in Church and State, and to establish an absolute government. The answer was, that he would provoke a civil war, in which he would have the Catholics for him but the aristocracy and the people in general against him, and must necessarily succumb[3]. It was thought that if he would spare

---

[1] 'Qu'il ne se serviroit du pouvoir, que dieu lui avoit donné, que pour le maintien des loix d'Angleterre, et qu'il ne feroit rien contre la sureté et la conservation de la religion protestante.' Barrillon, Feb. 18.

[2] Gachon: 'Quand on a imprimé son harangue au conseil, il en a fait retrancher, qu'à l'égard de ses opinions particulières on ne s'en appercevroit pas.'

[3] In a memorial—probably of an exile—placed in the hands of the Elector of Brandenburg, it is said: 'Le gros du peuple et tous les protestants et presque tous

the Church and come to an understanding with it, he would
be able to maintain his position and to become a powerful
king; and that it depended entirely upon this how much
obedience he would find.   This state of feeling had shown
itself when the attempt, already mentioned, was made to proclaim toleration for the Catholics, as well as on other occasions.
The opposition had almost treated it as a crime in Halifax
that he had prevented such a proclamation; 'for there was
nothing which they would have more desired than that a
decided step should be taken in this direction, which would
have thrown the whole nation into agitation.   For though the
Church had contributed its help to restore the authority of
the Crown by a renewal of their old alliance, the Church had
only done this because it had been presumed that the Crown
would in its turn protect the Church, and generally maintain
the legal state of affairs.   To injure the Church was, considering the identity of the political and ecclesiastical constitution in England, doubly dangerous: favour arbitrarily shown
to Catholicism seemed likely to lead to a violation of the
laws in general.

James II would have insured himself a peaceful and perhaps a glorious reign if he could have prevailed on himself to
treat his religion as a private matter.

Before his accession he had so treated it.   As heir to the
throne, though every one knew his sentiments, he had
contented himself with attending mass in the small chapel
which had been allowed to his wife, and with closed doors.
The ministers whom he consulted in his first measures,
Rochester, Godolphin, and even Sunderland, advised him to
persevere in this course, at least until he should have secured
his government[1].

But against such a line of conduct the self-confidence which
James derived from the possession of the crown, and also
his religious view, rebelled.   'To conceal his religion,' he
said, 'was contrary to his nature, and would seem to his

---

les Seigneurs riches suivront le parti du prince d'Orange, du duc de Monmouth, ou
de la république.'

[1] So Barrillon repoits on February 22, in a despatch overlooked by Fox and
others.

enemies a display of cowardice which would encourage them in their opposition to him; but his conscience also forbade it him; for after God had once raised him to this crown he could not hope for the blessing of God if he did not venture to confess his religion openly [1]: if he incurred danger on that account, God could protect him.' From the first moment, however, he looked out for human help also against such a contingency. He told the French ambassador that he reckoned on the support of the King of France if such a danger arose. Louis XIV approved altogether of his design; he let James understand that it was not fitting for a great king to conceal his convictions on so important a matter [2]. James did not even wait till this declaration actually reached him; he could take its nature for granted; the approbation of the great King was one of the considerations which guided him even in the first step which he took in relation to his creed.

On the second Sunday after the accession, February 15/25 1684/5, about midday, when the palace was thronged, not only by the members of the household but by a crowd of other persons who wished to pay their homage to the King, the doors of the chapel near the great hall were opened before every one's eyes; the King and Queen entered and received the sacrament publicly; the doors remained open: at the elevation of the Host the Catholics knelt; the Protestants, who were altogether excluded from the chapel, withdrew.

Hitherto Catholic Englishmen had been forbidden by law the public exercise of their religion: how their hearts beat when the King himself gathered courage to step over the obstacle! They saw therein a disposition of God designed to reopen a way for the 'light of the true faith.' 'Good subjects and believers,' says the Venetian envoy, 'say nothing on the subject for joy; malcontents and Protestants are silent from fear; my heart is consoled.'

---

[1] Vignola, March 2: 'Essendosi espresso, che destinato dal cielo a questa corona non v'era strada di mezzo a sperare le divine benedittioni.' Vignola himself greeted the decision with joy: 'Va permettendo l'esercitio della vera fede, havendosi dato coraggio a questo re, di non temere li malcontenti.'

[2] 'Qu'il ne fust convenable à un grand roi de dissimuler sur une chose si importante.' Barrillon, March 5.

The King's object, as he expressed himself to his confidant
Barrillon, was to procure for the Catholics not only freedom
of conscience but the free exercise of their religion ; he hoped
to obtain this by degrees, and that too in connexion with the
episcopal, which he designated as the royalist, party, and
without at the same time allowing the Nonconformists,
whom he still regarded as mere republicans, to obtain any
relief by his measures [1].

Such were the intentions with which he began his administration; such the sense in which he wished his declaration
to be understood : he was of opinion that the royalist feeling
of the Episcopal Church would go so far as to allow its king
to improve the position of the religion which he professed.

This thought was a legacy from the associations of earlier
times, in which the bishops, threatened by the rise of an over-
powerful Presbyterian agitation, sought their safety in an
alliance with the crown ; but it had lost all its appropriateness
ever since the episcopal system had assumed an exclusively
Protestant form, had cast off Catholicism, and had for a series
of years been dominant in Parliament. Episcopalianism could
only strive to regain this position ; it could only incline to
a royalist policy which respected the laws, not to one which
transgressed them; it had preferred the succession of the
Catholic heir to every other combination, but did not close
its eyes for a moment to the danger thence arising. The
pulpits resounded at once with warnings against Popery ; 'for
a time,' it was said, 'had now come when special watchfulness
against its seductions was necessary.' King James spoke on
the subject, even in the first days after his accession, with
Sancroft, Archbishop of Canterbury, and with Henry Compton, Bishop of London. He even expressed a wish that their
churches might be full, and exhorted them to take measures
to that end: but he made one single condition, that there
should be no preaching against his religion, Catholicism. But
how was that to have been attained ? The first step of the
Catholic King, the public celebration of the sacrifice of the
mass in contradiction to the laws, aroused antipathies which

---

[1] 'D'établir les catholiques dans une entière liberté de conscience et d'exercice
de la religion—en conduisant les affaires peu à peu à ce but.'

could not be kept down. The reports which came in caused
the King shortly afterwards to summon the two prelates again
before him, and to deliver an address to them which announced the coming storm. 'My lords,' he said, 'I will keep
my word, and will undertake nothing against the religion
established by law, assuming that you do your duty towards
me; if you fail therein, you must not expect that I shall
protect you. I shall readily find the means of attaining my
ends without your help[1].' The King seemed to regard the
matter as a personal one, as an affair of honour. The two
prelates were much struck by the vivacity of his expressions,
which resembled threats. They concealed their fears; but,
in the feeling that the misunderstanding would go further,
they were even then considering what steps should be taken
to enable them to resist in the Parliament which was shortly
to assemble every attempt at innovation. The King had
already, we shall presently see for what reasons, ordered a
Parliament to be summoned[2].

The coming dissension was being prepared below the
surface of the political and religious relations of the time.

At first the King avoided everything which might have
caused an outbreak of it. In the first touching for the king's
evil, which he practised according to ancient custom, he
allowed the religious service to be performed by Protestants,
especially as nothing specifically Protestant was found in it.
He would not be debarred from ordering Catholic sermons
to be preached in his chapel, nor from attending them; but
they were delivered in the French language, and he did not
wish controversial matter to enter into them any more than
into those of the Anglican clergy. The most significant
incident was, that when Lord Powis prepared, after his

---

[1] 'Si vous ne faites votre devoir à mon égard, n'attendez pas, que je vous
protège, et croyez, que je trouverai bien les moyens, de faire mes affaires sans
vous.' March 12: a despatch contained in the supplement to the great collection
of these letters of Barrillon. It has not been touched by any hand till now.
[Lingard x. 411, ed. 1849, gives an extract.—Tr.]

[2] Vignola, March 16: 'Li vescovi dubitando di qualche alteratione nel prossimo
parlamento vanno oramai sotto mano lavorando, à formare buon partito per
sostenere che non sia admessa novità di sorte.'

example, to open a Catholic chapel, James did not suffer
it; 'for that was forbidden,' he said, 'by the law: to transgress the law was, no doubt, proper for him, the King, for
he was above the law, but for no one else.' Consciousness
of his dignity as King was blended with his views as a
Catholic; but he wished to see the existing laws observed
by every one else.

And even on the performance of those ecclesiastical ceremonies which he held that his royal prerogative justified him
in ordering, he still at that time showed regard for the convictions of others. He wished, in accordance with the usage
at Catholic courts, to go to worship on high festivals in a
great procession, and required the attendance of the chief
officers of the crown on such occasions. Others yielded; but
the King's nearest relation and most confidential friend,
Lawrence Hyde, Earl of Rochester, whom he had just promoted to the dignity of Lord High Treasurer, raised difficulties on the ground of religious scruples: he declared that
if the King expressly commanded it he would follow him
into the chapel, but that he would not do so of his own free
will. The King hesitated to give the order, for he professed
not to wish to constrain any one to do what was repugnant
to him. Lord Rochester went into the country for the following holy days; for it was important for him to avoid all
observation, as well as for the King to avoid anything that
could give occasion for criticism.

In this spirit the questions which concerned the coronation
were considered. James II wished to be crowned as soon
as possible, for according to the English principle, that the
possession of the crown annulled all incapacities, no one
would subsequently be able to say that his religion hindered
his being king; he wished to appear even at the opening
of Parliament with his crown on his head. He took offence,
no doubt, at being required to receive the Church's sanction
from the hands of Protestant bishops; but it was remarked
to him that the coronation ceremonies were in the main the
same which had formerly been used at the coronation of
Edward the Confessor. And as for the oath by which the
King bound himself to govern according to the laws, statutes,

and usages of England, and to maintain the legal privileges
of the Church of England, this was nothing more than he
had already promised by his declaration. It was the interest of the bishops of the Church of England to keep him
to his promise. They had, to be sure, to agree on their part
also to a great concession; they could not demand of the
Catholic King that he should receive the communion according to the rite of the Church of England; they decided to
allow this part of the ceremony to be dropped altogether.
Such a decision, indeed, was necessitated by the existing
conjuncture, for a Catholic King was now to wear the crown
of a Protestant kingdom. In the late dissensions the Church
of England had decided for the Catholic succession; it could
not retire from that position[1]. A feeling of this kind extended even to the population in general; it remarked the
deviation from usage, but accommodated itself to what could
not be altered.

But would this combination of contrary elements stand the
test of a Parliamentary discussion? Would the Catholic
King, more penetrated than any other prince had been by
a sense of the prerogative which he inherited, co-operate with
a Protestant Parliament, jealous for its ancient privileges?

No one had so decidedly opposed the summoning of a
Parliament as this prince himself while still Duke of York:
one of the conditions of the alliance mediated by him with
France was that an English Parliament, from which Louis
XIV expected opposition to his European policy, should not
be summoned; and who did not remember the old bitter
quarrel of James with these assemblies? The world was
astonished that the same man, as soon as he had succeeded to
the crown, summoned a new Parliament for the month of May
1685. 'Did he not remember that the summoning of a Parliament in 1640, had led his father step by step to destruction? His brother had in his latter days no longer had the
courage to summon one.'

---

[1] According to D'Oyly, Life of Sancroft i. 211, it was assumed that such was
the meaning of Parliament. 'Parliament, by refusing to exclude him from the
succession, although he was an avowed Papist, might be said to have indirectly
consented that the coronation ceremony should be performed in such a manner as
a Papist could conscientiously comply with.'

James II adopted with all his heart the opinion that the
summoning or not summoning of the Parliament depended
entirely on the King's good pleasure; he would not on general
grounds have considered himself to be under any obligation
to summon it; but a moment was at hand which absolutely
required such a measure and admitted of no delay. Of the
revenues of the crown, which were then reckoned at £1,400,000,
only the smaller portion was annexed to it in perpetuity;
the larger, about £900,000, arose from customs (tonnage and
poundage), excise, and other imposts which were granted by
the Parliament only for the life of the King. It was not to
be expected that they should be collected for any length of
time, and regularly, without a new grant. Payment would
be refused some day or other, and the refusal treated as legal
by the courts of justice. And yet another immediate difficulty appeared in this matter. According to the letter of
the law no collection ought to have taken place between the
death of Charles and a fresh Parliamentary grant. But on
the one hand, the continued collection of the usual customs was acceptable to the wealthy merchants of the city
themselves [1]. They would otherwise have had to fear,
their wares being already stored and having paid duty, the
competition of those which would have come in without
paying duty. On the other hand, the government could not
and would not dispense with these revenues for a moment;
it seemed that without them the whole administration would
come to a stand-still. So it came to pass that the proposal
which was made in the Privy Council, out of respect for the
letter of the law, to leave them lying untouched in the Exchequer till they had been granted by Parliament, was decisively rejected. On that occasion however we hear of another
motive as well. King James wished to continue to raise the
taxes for this further reason [2], that it was most important for
him to put himself in possession; afterwards he could easily,

---

[1] 'The unfair traders will undersell us, as they well may, paying no custom.'
North, Guildford 254.

[2] 'Tout de même comme du vivant de notre très cher frère,' as his order is
worded in the French London Gazette. He describes them as 'entièrement nécessaires pour le soustien du gouvernement.'

he thought, find means of maintaining himself in that position. He thought that he did enough when he issued the
order to continue the levy of customs and excise simultaneously with the announcement of a new Parliament, which
without doubt would grant them afresh.

Even at the time some opposition to that course showed
itself, but it was not very strong. For the quiet continuation
of the state's life, which cannot be thought of without an
unbroken payment of taxes, had now become an absolute
necessity for society; constitutional feelings were contented
by the combination with the demand for payment of a proclamation for a Parliament to assemble shortly. Discontent
and impatience had been felt by the nation at having to do
without a Parliament for so long.

About the King, that party amongst his ministers which
had hitherto been opposed to a Parliament, was induced to
drop its opposition, because otherwise its adversaries, who
had always advocated and urged the summoning of a Parliament, would very likely have carried their point and have
gained credit with the people for their success. The rest,
and especially the King, wished to gain credit for it themselves: what James did he wished to do thoroughly.

But he took the most careful precautions against putting
his relations with France on a worse footing by this conduct;
for this reason, without considering others, that he was
uncertain of the issue and by no means disposed to submit to
an unfavourable decision of the Parliament. James II, like
others of his family, was not at all willing to be a Parliamentary king. In case Parliament should cut off the necessary
supplies, he reserved to himself the expedient of having
recourse to France, ' in order,' so runs the expression, ' to make
himself independent of his Parliament.' He assured Barrillon
'that he would never break off his alliance with France, for
that he knew what serious disadvantages had, in his brother's
case, resulted from such conduct [1].' On the first report of
the death of Charles II, Louis XIV had sent unasked a sum

---

[1] 'Que le roi son frère s'est mis fort près d'estre entièrement ruiné, pour s'être
laissé detacher de la liaison, qu'il avoit formé avec V. M.' Barrillon, Feb. 22.

of money to London to form a resource for the King in case
there should be any seditious movement against him. A
far-sighted offer, which no doubt was seriously meant, but
which was also very well calculated! James II was most
deeply touched by it; tears came into his eyes when he
spoke of this proof of a care which anticipated his wishes;
he promised King Louis an inviolable and lifelong attachment in return for this service.

But into what embarrassments must this government fall
.if the new Parliament, like all its predecessors, took part
against France in regard to the conflicts prevailing on the
continent! Among the opponents of France almost the first
place belonged to the Prince of Orange, who had himself
been brought a step nearer to the English throne by the
death of Charles II. He lost no time in sending friendly
messages and letters to the new King; he made offers to
him, in regard to the prevailing differences, which showed a
very conciliatory spirit, for instance as to filling the officers'
places among the English troops in Dutch pay: we cannot
be mistaken in supposing that he expected a change in foreign
relations on the accession of James. Accordingly, in a letter
of the Governor of the Spanish Netherlands, in which the
Prince and the Parliament are both spoken of, a hope can
be traced beneath the surface that the earlier feelings of the
Parliament in favour of Spain would awake again. Barrillon
was alarmed when under these circumstances there was talk
of a journey of the Prince of Orange to England. He set
before the King the consideration how unpleasant might be
the presence of the presumptive heir to the throne who, in
contrast to its actual occupant adhered to the religion of
the country. He presumed to make representations to the
King about an expression, suspicious in his eyes, which James
had allowed to find a place in a letter to the princess his
daughter. Louis XIV declared without reserve that the
alliance which the King of England sought with him was not
consistent with the intentions which the Prince of Orange
betrayed and wished to carry out. King James made a
distinction. The Prince of Orange's drawing near to him was
altogether welcome to him in respect of English affairs; for

he thought that otherwise his irreconcileable enemies might
readily seek for a chief in the Prince; and James found a
sufficient reason for avoiding any direct opposition to the
latter in the reflection that the outbreak of a misunderstanding
would thoroughly arouse his own enemies: for these reasons
he showed the Prince respect and indulgence[1]. But the
affairs of Europe in general were also involved in the matter;
and, considering the hostile attitude of the Prince of Orange
towards French policy, the question might arise to which
side King James inclined. The answer to that question must
needs be, that he felt himself bound to France by former
treaties, by his own antecedents, and by the state of affairs at
the moment. From a consideration, however, of these two
aspects of James' position a new demand of England upon
France arose. The new Treasurer, who was regarded as first
minister, and still reckoned upon French supplies, said to the
French ambassador that the English government had been
well satisfied with its former relations to France, and wished
to continue them; James II himself declared that the King of
France might prescribe to him the attitude which he should
assume; yet both added the warning that there must not in
the first instance be any open breach between France and
Spain, as, if there were, the Parliament would take part for
the latter power. Sunderland said outright that there was
such a close connexion of interests between Spain, the Prince
of Orange, and the English Parliament, that it would be impossible to divide them; the government would at first only
avoid entering into the combination; when the time was come
it would throw off the mask and openly and plainly—he used
the expression 'with éclat'—tear itself away from them[2].

And this alliance with France was now more firmly cemented

---

[1] He explains to Barrillon the reasons 'qui l'obligent à garder présentement
les apparences avec le prince d'Orange pour ne le pas jetter ouvertement dans le
party de ses ennemis et leur donner un chef qu'ils n'ont pas.' The envoy confirmed
him in the 'soupçons que peut lui donner un héritier présomtif qui est de la religion
du pays.' Barrillon, March 18.

[2] 'Il faut non seulement s'abstenir de toute liaison avec eux, mais même s'en
séparer avec éclat et lever le masque, quand il en sera tems c. a. d. après que le parlement aura accordé les revenus.' April 16, already printed in Fox, Appendix lx.

than it had ever been before; the cause which most actively promoted it lay in the design respecting religion
which James II avowed without any concealment. He was
influenced not only by that resolution of restoring a free
scope to his religion with which the consciousness of his
kingly dignity inspired him, but also by his opinion that he
could completely count upon his Catholic subjects only.
When Louis XIV remarked in a letter to his envoy, that the
confirmation of the kingly authority and the restoration of
the free exercise of the Catholic religion in England were two
things indissolubly united; that one could not be carried out
without the other, he quite expressed James' own view : James
said to the French ambassador, to whom he disclosed his
thoughts more freely than to his own ministers on this subject,
that he saw his safety in such an establishment of the Catholic
religion as should make its subsequent destruction impossible,
and for that very reason in his alliance with France also;
for in all probability he would get into difficulties with his
Parliament on the subject and would require support against
it.   Louis XIV was heartily ready to grant him such support.
'If Parliament does not do its duty, he will find in my friendship all the resources which he can expect ; the confirmation of
his authority and the establishment of religion are our common
interest[1] ; a special stipulation on that subject is not required.'
The Ambassador was empowered to pay the promised supply
if King James saw himself obliged to dissolve the Parliament,
or if he should meet with serious opposition to the establishment of a free exercise of the Catholic religion[2].

It is characteristic of James II that he first secured in case
of failure a support which he considered to be beyond the
risk of overthrow, before he proceeded to the execution of his
purpose. That did not prevent him from cherishing at the
same time a hope of attaining his end in agreement with

---

[1] Le roi à Barrillon, April 6.   He will support King James 'tant pour
l'affermissement de son autorité, que pour l'establissement du libre exercice de la
religion catholique, que je considère comme deux choses inséparables et qui
auroient peine dorénavant de subsister et se maintenir, si l'une n'estoit pas étroite-
ment unie à l'autre.'

[2] April 24. Already published in Fox, Appendix lxiii.

the Parliament, which would have been by far the most agreeable course for him.

When it was being considered how a permanent relief could be best secured for the Catholics, whether by a general indulgence, which would have embraced the Protestant Dissenters also, or by a special statute in their favour to be carried through Parliament, most of the Catholics would have wished to see the first method followed ; for it was the only one from which a result could be expected. But James had long regarded the Nonconformists of the Protestant confession as his bitterest enemies; he could not at once make up his mind to appear as their protector[1]. On the other hand, he held strongly that a close relation existed between Episcopalianism and Catholicism ; he thought that he knew Anglicans who were unconscious Catholics; favour shown to the Catholics would find no invincible obstacle with them ; he intended only to try the other way if he could not reach his end by this.

For this purpose, however, it seemed all the more necessary to avoid everything which might arouse men's antipathies in regard to internal and external affairs.

The close alliance which had been formed with France was kept in the background with the deepest secrecy; an extraordinary envoy from that power who arrived in England at this time was received coldly, and with a remarkable display of ceremonial; on the other hand, the Spanish ambassador thought that he had ground for hoping that he should succeed better with the new King than he had succeeded with the old in accomplishing his ends.

Lord Halifax, who was regarded as taking the most eminent part in promoting the interests of parliamentary government, of Spain, and of the Prince of Orange, was named President of the Council. Arlington, who had previously shown himself an opponent of the Duke of York, had still a place at court ; the Catholics would have wished to replace him and other by men whose behaviour inspired more

---

[1] Barrillon, March 12 : 'C'est un party que le roi d'Angleterre ne veut prendre qu'après avoir eprouvé, s'il peut establir ses affaires par le moyen du parti episcopal et en sorte, qu'il n'ait plus à craindre des autres' (if they obtained perfect freedom).

confidence. But the King judged that if he made a complete change at the court it would be believed that a similar change was at hand in every other department—an opinion which he must absolutely prevent from arising. Rather would it be advantageous for him that members of the one party should on account of their previous conduct be apprehensive of losing their places, while those of the other were supported in their hope of obtaining the same ; that would inspire both with regard for him.

The new King showed himself inflexible in one thing alone; he required from Parliament a grant of the whole income which his predecessor had received. No members of Parliament had yet assembled ; the elections had not yet taken place. But negotiations were already beginning with the leading men in the nation, who it was supposed would be the leading men in the Parliament also. The King expressed his demand with emphasis and in plain terms. The judges, who were just then going on circuit into the counties, received a commission to warn people everywhere in the country districts against a resistance which certainly could lead to nothing, and could only have the most unpleasant consequences.

These consequences would ensue because if a wish were shown to withdraw from the King any of the taxes granted to his brother, he would see himself compelled to maintain himself in possession of them by force ; he would even run the risk of a civil war, which, supporting himself on the necessity of the case, he would fight out with his own resources and with the help of France. No one wished to allow matters to come to this extremity; no one thought of making the continuance of the public administration impossible by refusing the necessary supplies. But anxiety was felt lest the King, when his position had been secured by these grants, should feel himself independent, undertake everything which pleased him, and never again summon the Parliament. The expedient was suggested of making him the necessary grants not for his whole life but only for some three years: the necessity of summoning Parliament again would, it was thought, hinder him from undertaking the introduction of those religious innovations to which he was so much inclined.

The King let it be known that he would never acquiesce in
such a limitation : he would dissolve the Parliament which
should attempt to impose anything of the kind upon him, and
would summon another without troubling himself to exercise
any control over the elections, consulting only the feelings
and free choice of the whole population ; he would then propose to it freedom of conscience both for the Nonconformists
and for the Catholics ; such a Parliament would grant him his
revenues for life [1].

How often has wonder been expressed at the confident
devotion with which James II was received on his accession !
And it is true that the addresses which came in from all parts
of the country vied with each other in expressions of submissiveness. The feeling that the project of exclusion had
been unjustifiable was in reality universal. Some exclusionists
were insulted by the crowd in various places when they presented themselves at the elections. And yet for all that
people did not for a moment become unconscious of the great
political and religious opposition which existed between the
crown and the country. The King spared the members of
the Church of England because he hoped to reach his end in
concert with them ; the members of the Church of England
yielded to the King because they had no inclination to provoke him into putting his prerogative in force against themselves as sweepingly as Charles II had lately done as their
ally. A greater danger would have arisen for the Church,
if the King had decided to forget his hatred against the
Protestant Nonconformists and to allow a Parliament to be
elected freely, even if, as was often suggested, an exception
were made of the decided exclusionists, whom it was desired
now to keep out as they had desired to keep out James.
After such a Parliament had met, universal religious liberty
would be proclaimed, and the privileges of the Episcopalians
would be destroyed.

This conflict of religious and financial interests gave em-

---

[1] Barrillon, March 12 : 'Appeller un autre parlement, dont les membres soient
tels, que chaque province les voudra choisir c. a. d. que la cour en prenne aucun
soin et alors le roi d'Angleterre offrira la liberté entière de conscience tant pour les
catholiques que pour les nonconformistes et demandera son revenu pour sa vie.'

ployment to all those minds in the nation which occupied themselves with public affairs. So far as a decision was possible before the deliberations of Parliament began, the opinion prevailed that no opposition ought to be offered to the King with regard to revenue and taxes. The aristocracy and the Episcopalians, including such Protestants as were about the King, considered it quite necessary to uphold the crown and to allow it a certain degree of power, without however permitting it to become strong enough to interfere with the laws and with religion. A refusal of James' demands for money would have thrown everything into confusion, but the members of the Church of England combined with their compliance in this respect a conscious resolve to oppose the King in his designs as to religion. They thought moreover that James, being little younger than his brother, would not long survive him ; and that then the Prince of Orange, a thoroughly Protestant prince, would mount the throne and restore a religious union between the crown and the country [1].

How truly are the outlines of coming complications thus drawn at the beginning of this reign ! In the first instance everything depended on the result of the elections.

Since the first moment when the possibility of a misunderstanding showed itself, the clergy had employed their influence on behalf of men who passed for unyielding Church of England men. Two considerations prevailed at the elections. It was wished in the first place to prevent the old declared enemies of the King from getting into Parliament. James himself required the lords who were about him to prevent it in the districts where they lived, and their exertions were very successful ; even in counties like Cheshire, where Monmouth had seemed peculiarly powerful, royalist members were chosen. In Bedfordshire on this occasion no Russell was elected. The magistrates appointed by the government in the towns worked with equal success. But, in the second place, as the change in the representation of

---

[1] Barrillon, March 12: 'La pluspart des seigneurs protestants qui étoit du parti de la cour regardent Mr. le prince d'Orange comme l'héritier présomtif;—ils veulent que la royauté subsiste, mais ils ne désirent pas que l'autorité royale ait trop de forces.'

the towns depended principally on the enforcement in all places of the exclusive laws relating to the Church, Episcopalians were elected there even on the present occasion. And the Lords declared themselves in this sense with even more zeal than the Commons. A Parliament was chosen at this election nearly resembling the Restoration Parliament of the year 1661 : of royalist sentiments—people professed to be able to count 180 members in it who were dependent on the crown—but at the same time very friendly to Episcopacy ; its demeanour could only become doubtful in case a divergence between these two tendencies showed itself.

In order to appreciate the impressions under the influence of which the English Parliament assembled, we must not neglect to glance at the deliberations of the Scottish Parliament, which on this occasion, as in 1661, met before that of England.

The royalist feelings of the Scots had been already aroused by the mere accession of a native King, the hundred and twelfth of the fabulous series which had reigned during the two thousand years' existence of the monarchy. Such an event had always been advantageous to them ; but, besides this, the new King had during his last residence in Scotland known how to win the personal attachment of the nobility and gentry in spite of the difference of religion, which he treated as a private affair. In the same spirit he now declared to the Scots that he had nothing in view but the confirmation of their religion as it was established by the laws, and the security of their property. The state of affairs in Scotland was such that both Church and State welcomed a strong government. The wild Whigs had completely separated themselves from the Presbyterian Church, and had united in a society which in November 1684 not only renewed a renunciation of the Crown and of the King by a public declaration, but proclaimed all those who should take part in the persecution exercised against them to be enemies of God [1], and announced to such persons their intention of punishing them according to

---

[1] 'Society people's declaration against informers and intelligencers,' in Wodrow's History of the Church of Scotland iv. 148.

their power, and to the degree of the offence.   As shortly
afterwards murderous outrages were perpetrated upon those
very men who had been especially active in the persecution
complained of, an universal terror pervaded the ranks of the adherents of the government: timid parish priests forsook their
villages; the persecutors on the other hand doubled their
severity and ruthlessness.   For instance, two persons were found
one day among the hills and mosses of Douglas, who refused
to take the oath which bound people to disown the declaration
just referred to and the principles asserted by it.   One of them
—he was named John Brown—in whose house ammunition
of all kinds was found, while hidden pistols and bullets were
discovered in the neighbourhood, declared outright that he
knew no King.   For this he was shot upon the spot[1].   And yet
conventicles continued to assemble in which sometimes a few
hundred men met together, all in arms, in the use of which
they are said to have been trained.   Against these 'wild
fanatics and inhuman assassins' King James invoked the
assistance of the Scottish Parliament.   As news came at the
same time of the movements of the refugees assembled in
Holland, who were making preparations for a landing in
Scotland, the whole country was invited to place itself in
a state of defence against internal and external enemies[2].
It is only these circumstances which make us understand how
the Parliament adopted a resolution which condemned to
death and confiscation of goods the preachers in fanatical
conventicles, whether held in houses or in the fields, and, in
the case of the field conventicles, all who attended them also.
There was a feeling that a civil and religious war had begun.
Resolutions of such unheard-of severity were held necessary
for the maintenance of public order and peace.   Under the

---

[1] See the pathetic description of Macaulay i. ch. iv.   The impression made by
it has occasioned further research.   And certainly a better account than that of
Wodrow, on which Macaulay relied, is found in the report of Graham of Claver-
house who inflicted the punishment.   Claverhouse's report is given by Mark
Napier, Memorials of the Viscount of Dundee i. 141.   Cp. Cunningham, Church
History of Scotland ii. 238–242.

[2] The proclamation of April 28 requires information from the inhabitants of the
coast 'so soon as they hear or get notice of any vessels arriving at any place from
abroad.'

combined influence of enthusiasm and of fear the Scottish
Parliament now attached itself most closely to the King.   It
declared its abhorrence not only of all rebellion but also of all
principles and assertions which contravened the supreme sovereign and absolute power of the King.   Moreover, it did
not content itself with renewing in favour of the new King
the grant of the excise and customs which it had made to
his predecessor; it promised them to the lawful successors to
the imperial crown of Scotland for all future time.   Then
there also followed a special grant for immediate needs.   This
however was not made without reserve.   At the same time
all acts and statutes which had ever been passed for the
security and freedom of the Protestant religion—except those
relating to the Covenant, which on the contrary was condemned afresh—were sanctioned by the King and Parliament
in their whole contents, as fully as if they had been re-enacted
word for word.   Without regard to the fact that the King
was a Catholic, the royalist and episcopalian constitution
in Church and State was re-established in all its rigour in
Scotland, with zeal exaggerated into cruelty, in order to crush
the internal elements of resistance before they received a new
life from the attack which was to be expected on the part of
the refugees.

The news of the Scottish resolutions reached England
simultaneously with a report that Argyll had already arrived
among the Orkneys, and that a similar design to that which he
was seeking to execute in Scotland was contemplated by Monmouth with regard to England.   These events, and the expectations which they aroused; the arrangements for resistance
which the King, without an over-strict regard to the legal
restraints on his authority, was making or preparing to make,
filled the horizon of the English Parliament when, after an
interval of four years, it again assembled at Westminster.

The Speaker whom the government recommended was
accepted unanimously; but on the other hand the swearing
in of members had already been effected in the usual manner,
under the form of test which excluded the Catholics, before
the solemn opening took place on the 22nd of May.

King James II, who entered with the crown upon his head,

was not received with the acclamations with which a new
sovereign is generally greeted by the assembled estates.   His
demeanour, indeed, had up to this time been of a doubtful
nature ; the appointment of Catholic officers had been noticed
with some astonishment.   People waited with eager attention
to hear what the speech from the throne, which he was preparing to read, would contain, and how he would express
himself therein about the national Church.   He repeated
word for word what he had said in his first declaration, that
he was determined to maintain the government both in Church
and State as it was then established by law.   He expressed in
still stronger terms than before his recognition of the lawfulness
of the principles of the English Church.   The great satisfaction
which this declaration gave to the assembly could be noticed
upon the spot.   When he now added to his promise a demand
that the income received by his brother should be granted to
himself also, and that for life, the loud murmur which signifies
assent could be heard.   King James did not say, like his
predecessors, 'our religion,' but 'your religion'; he spoke of
the revenue which had not yet been granted as 'his revenue[1],'
as though it belonged to him, and he warned the Parliament
against entertaining any thought of occasioning him to summon Parliaments frequently by a merely temporary grant 'for
that was not the way to obtain anything with him'—words
which certainly contain the doctrine that it depended on his
pleasure whether he would summon the Parliament again
on other occasions : 'the best means to induce him to do so
would be to use him well'—all intimations which at other
times might well have aroused the spirit of constitutional
opposition so easily excited.   But on this occasion that result
did not follow ; every period of the speech was greeted with
applause[2].   Finally the King mentioned Argyll and the proclamation issued by him in Holland, which accused him, the
King, of usurpation, but which far rather proved the treason of
Argyll and of his adherents ; that these might meet with their

---

[1] 'You will give me my revenue.'
[2] Besser. 'Whenever the king finished a period of his speech, the estates showed
by loud cries the satisfaction which they felt at it.' So, word for word, Evelyn.

proper reward he required an immediate grant of his revenue. In the royalist and episcopalian assembly no sympathy could be called forth for an attack like Argyll's, which was aimed directly against its own principles. Amid loud cries of 'Vive le Roi'—for in affairs of this kind the French forms were still used—James II left the chamber, and the two Houses proceeded at once to their deliberations.

On the questions which first came before them, no opposition was to be expected. The Lower House promised the King to support him with their lives and fortunes, not only against Argyll but against all rebels and traitors; a vote which the King praised as the true expression of the monarchical feelings of English churchmen. The House did not hesitate to grant the revenues which Charles II had possessed for life, to his successor also for the same period[1]. The grant of the tax upon wines, which had been voted to the late King for a term of years only, was made almost in the same form to James for eight years, on his first mention of the subject.

The same feeling also induced the Upper House to revoke by a retrospective vote the enactments which had long hindered the release of the Catholic lords and of Lord Danby[2], and thereby to sanction their release. Oates had been already punished as a calumniator. Under the rule of a Catholic king there could no longer be any mention of the Popish plot.

This close understanding, which developed itself before the eyes of all, could not, however, prevent the utterance in the debates of remarks of a contrary tendency, which gave expression to discontent at the domestic and foreign policy lately followed, and to lively anxiety about the future.

Edward Seymour brought before the House the abrogation of the charters of towns and the arbitrary proceedings which had in consequence taken place at the elections. Among the new members of the Lower House there were seen many who

---

[1] The considerations for and against this grant given in Hume belong more to his own time than to that of the events. We gather from the German reporter that the grants were made 'without any deliberation thereon.'

[2] I refer to the resolution [of March 19, 1678–79] that proceedings which had begun on an impeachment by the Lower House were not to be annulled by ·a dissolution.

had no suitable position in the world, and sometimes men who stood in no connexion with their constituents ; they had been elected under the immediate influence of the government. Seymour had left the cabinet of Charles II when the counsels of the Duke of York prevailed in it, because he saw in them a danger for the constitution and for the religion of the country. But what would happen if, under the influence of the Catholic King, a Parliament were to assemble which lent itself to him as a tool? Would not the country have then to expect an abrogation of all the laws which protected religion and personal freedom? Seymour gave to these apprehensions an expression of which the effect was heightened by his personal authority and experience. But he could not produce any practical result by his speech. He could not well expect that a revision of the procedure at elections would be undertaken in an assembly of which no small part had been returned by elections on which his maxims cast a doubt. Seymour found approval in many quarters, but no one was disposed to declare himself for him[1]. It was enough that the danger resulting from the proceedings of the government was brought into prominence with eloquence and emphasis.

Another string was touched a few days later by Sir John Lowther, a friend of Lord Halifax[2]. He wished to know what precautions England was taking against the growing predominance of the great man beyond the sea. This remark, like Seymour's, met with no support, but Barrillon was surprised by the equal absence of any opposition to it : he complained that the King of France did not take any members of the Parliament into his pay as dependents.

A third opposition movement attained much larger proportions and attracted much more attention. A committee for religion which had been appointed made a proposal to invite the King 'to publish his royal proclamation for putting

---

[1] Barrillon : ' Il eut l'approbation secrète de beaucoup de gens, mais personne ne se leva pour l'approuver.' The speech is mainly known through Barrillon. Evelyn adds some arguments which Fox, who first used Barrillon, cannot have been acquainted with when he wrote.

[2] Barrillon, June 10 : ' Le chevalier Louder, gentilhomme du nord, proche parent de Halifax.'

the laws in execution against all Dissenters whatsoever from the Church of England.' Then first the opposition between the creed of the King and the religion of the country appeared in full clearness. For these laws affected the Catholics as well as other Dissenters; how could the Catholic King be required to put in execution the bloody statutes enacted against his fellow-believers? He was embarrassed, moreover, because he did not wish to refuse outright the first petition laid before him by a House which had shown him the greatest devotion. The King staked all his influence to hinder the acceptance of the proposal in the assembly. He spoke himself with the most influential bishops, and with the most distinguished leaders of the House itself; he threatened all who should vote for the proposal with his personal displeasure. He succeeded in causing the motion to be dropped for the present through the adoption of the previous question. A resolution was substituted in which it was said that 'the House doth rest wholly satisfied in His Majesty's gracious word . . . . to support and defend the religion of the Church of England as now by law established.' It seemed good to express at the same time inviolable attachment to this religion. Under the influence, so far as we know, of the bishops, the Commons added the words 'which is dearer to us than our lives.' In this way an open quarrel was avoided, but even the resolution which passed allows us to discern what difficulty the King would find in carrying out his religious project. The resolution was adopted unanimously.

All these transactions, however, whether they led to agreement or to dissensions, were thrown into the background now that the invasions with which the refugees threatened England under Monmouth, and Scotland under Argyll, were effected soon after each other.

CHAPTER II.

MONMOUTH was still cherishing the hope of a speedy return, and enjoying to the full the hospitality which the Prince and Princess of Orange vouchsafed to him in this expectation at the Hague, when the news of the death of Charles II arrived there. In his memoirs he adds to the mention of the letter of Halifax in which that event was announced to him the exclamation 'O cruel fate!' an expression of anguish of which he felt the whole bitterness; for he had lost the most loving and indulgent of fathers; one who amid all the changes of their public relations had at heart been his friend; to whose secret directions he owed it, that he was well treated, and who just then allowed him to expect a change for the better in his fortunes. Nowhere was Charles II more heartily and deeply mourned for than there in the Hague by Monmouth; for what every one laments in the death of another is merely his own loss. What hopes could Monmouth still cherish for his career? There was no lack of entreaties preferred on the part of his old friends in England and of both the English and the Scottish refugees who lived in Holland, that he would put himself at their head. He listened to them, readily affected as he had always been by the persuasions of others; but his feeling nevertheless was, that considering the state of affairs which presented itself at the moment in England there was no reasonable prospect for himself and his friends of effecting anything. 'To tell you my thoughts without disguise' he says in one of his letters[1], 'I am now so much in

---

[1] To Mr. Spence. Welwood, Mem. 378.

love with a quiet life, that I am ne'er like to be fond of making
a bustle in the world again.'

Of quite a different temper was Archibald Campbell, Earl
of Argyll, who had been living for some years in exile in
Holland. He was the son of that great party chief who had
lived and died for the maintenance of the Covenant in Scotland. The younger Archibald had been restored not to his
father's title as Marquess, but to the honours of his forefathers
(he was the ninth earl) and to their great position in the
Highlands, of which he after his father's fall appeared the
natural ruler. But after some time he too, like his father,
drew upon himself the displeasure and persecution of the
Scottish government, especially by the limiting clause with
which he accompanied the oath against the Covenant taken,
as prescribed by the Scottish Parliament, in the year 1681.
He was accused of wishing to maintain the anti-royalist
doctrines expressed in the Covenant, and was convicted of
treason. The principal object of these proceedings was to
wrest from him the local privileges which no longer seemed
consistent with the King's prerogatives, and to prove to him
that he was a subject [1]. The Earl succeeded however in
escaping from prison by the help of his daughter. We have
noticed how much he and his dependants in Scotland were
counted on in the agreements which were entered into
previously to the Rye House Plot. He himself had not for a
moment desisted from preparing for an enterprise on his own
account. And the religious zeal which he displayed procured
him the support of rich private persons in Amsterdam who
considered him an appropriate instrument for counteracting
the spread of Catholicism. In fine, · he found means of
acquiring possession of a frigate and of equipping it; he
bought a great quantity of arms for cavalry and infantry;
his old adherents expected him in Scotland with high hopes.
His friends interpreted of him the saying of an astrologer,
who after the changes in the fortunes of Scotland under

---

[1] Life of James, i. 771. From a letter of Charles II. He requires an opinion,
'how to dispose of those superiorities and offices, which he thought too much for
any one subject.'

Cromwell, Charles II, and James II, had announced the
coming of 'a little Highlandman brandishing his sword over
a field of dead bodies [1].'

But almost more depended upon the refugees in general
than upon the two leaders; especially upon the Scottish
refugees who were then, assembled in great numbers in
Rotterdam, at times in Amsterdam, but principally in Utrecht,
and formed a party of their own. They were zealous Covenanters, who had either taken part in the last risings, or
had incurred suspicion of taking part in the combinations
connected with the Rye House Plot, and had withdrawn themselves from persecution by flight;—Cochrane of Ochiltree,
Patrick Hume of Polwarth, Pringle of Torwoodlee, Denholm
of Westshiels, Fletcher of Saltoun, and James Stewart, for a
long time King's Advocate at Edinburgh, who had defended
the right of resistance even in official papers. In the recent
party movements some of them, as Hume and Stewart, had
owed their preservation to Monmouth; others, as Cochrane,
attached themselves to Argyll. All were sworn enemies of
the Duke of York, now King, whom they held for the head
of the Papist conspiracy, in the complete reality of which
they believed. They would gladly have taken part in the
rising which was contemplated in the year 1683 with the
object of separating King Charles from the Duke his brother,
of subsequently instituting proceedings against the latter,
and of introducing a new constitution in accordance with the
political and religious principles of the Covenant. Affairs
had taken a completely different course. Their opponent,
whom they held for a tyrant of equal craftiness and violence,
had ascended the throne; they did not doubt that the death
of Charles II had been brought about by treacherous means [2],
nor that it had enabled the Papist conspirators to acquire
an immediate prospect of attaining all their ends; not only in

---

[1] Sir Patrick Hume's Narrative, in G. Rose, Observations on the historical
work of C. J. Fox, 18: 'All pointing at some great action to be done by him,
especially some horagliphicks by an English astrologer representing many events.'

[2] Sir Patrick Hume's Narrative mentions the 'Newes of King Charles his death,
with great grounds, and to me convincing, of base and treacherous means of
bringing him to it.'

Scotland, and in Ireland, but in England also the Papists
would know how to secure a Parliament devoted to them,
and would then set on foot strong armies with the intention
of introducing Popery and tyranny, and of extirpating from
the three kingdoms true Christianity, freedom and law—the
greatest blessing of human society.   They thought, however,
that considering the ill-will which the Duke—for they did not
call him King—had everywhere incurred, it was still possible
to resist him ; they declared it to be their evident duty as
Scotsmen and as Christians to attempt it.   When Argyll, soon
after the succession of James to the English throne, informed
them of his preparations and invited them to join him, he
found a ready hearing among them.   They attached, however,
one condition to their consent.

They were of opinion that the undertaking had no chance
of success unless it were attempted simultaneously in Scotland
and in England, and unless measures were adopted in Ireland
to prevent any counter movement taking place from that
side.   They therefore frankly told Argyll that they would
have no share in his enterprise against Scotland unless the
business were taken in hand according to a methodical and
comprehensive plan ; 'if well carried out it might lead to the
preservation, if badly directed it would lead to the ruin, of the
common interest of the three kingdoms.'

All depended on their persuading Monmouth to engage
in an undertaking against England ; and to effect this the
English combined with the Scottish refugees.   It was represented to him 'that the western counties, whose devotion he
had learned on his travels there, would rise for him like one
man as soon as he appeared on the coast ; that as London
would certainly move also, the King would be prevented from
opposing a strong force to him, and that those who were employed on such a service would not fight against him, the Duke.'
Lord Grey remarked to him that in former days Henry VII
had landed with no greater force than his own and yet had
carried England with him.   And a great impression must
have been made upon him by the consideration that without
an attempt upon England nothing could be attempted against
Scotland either.   So many invitations and offers arrived from

his friends in England that even the methodical Scots felt satisfied with them, and were all the more encouraged to combine with Argyll.   An intimation that it would show want of spirit if he delayed longer set Monmouth on fire; he was unwilling to allow a reproach of this kind to attach to him.

Between Monmouth and Argyll there was not naturally any good understanding; they belonged to different factions in Scotland, the first to the opponents, the second to the adherents of Lauderdale.   And Argyll would never have consented to allow Monmouth to share in his Scottish expedition; but they might well come to an understanding for two distinct undertakings, which should only coincide as far as possible in point of time.

The Scots did not neglect to summon together in the first instance the preachers who had emigrated with them, and to secure their approval.   The declaration which they then published—as they held it necessary to prepare the population for their undertaking—still bears the stamp of the old Covenanting character in all its bitterness.   They describe it as their purpose to suppress not only idolatrous Popery, but also its 'bitter root and offspring' prelacy and the supremacy; a restoration of all who had suffered violence, and the erection of a government giving equal security to the liberty and property of all, should go hand in hand with the destruction of the episcopal constitution.   They do not speak of a Parliament, but of a free and sovereign representation of all those who should take part with them [1].   They speak of James II as an apostate and usurper, to whom, according to the laws of the land, not the smallest authority belonged; they make him in fact a professed enemy and rebel.   They did not associate themselves outright with the wild Whigs and their Torwood declaration; but yet they displayed republican tendencies. These exiles even represented themselves as being the true Scottish state; they constituted themselves as the supreme council which was to form the core of a new organisation.

---

[1] 'A fiee, full, just, and sovereign representative of all the present undertakers, and such as shall hereafter sinceiely concur and take part with us.'   In Wodrow iv. 289.

The Scots once asked the Duke of Monmouth in what character he thought of acting. He answered, 'as a Protestant and Englishman.' They asked him further, 'whether he held himself for the lawful son of Charles II?' He answered that he was convinced of it, and had valid proofs of the fact. Thereupon they did not fail to remark that the apprehension that he was striving to obtain royal power, with which so many abuses were connected, estranged many Englishmen from him. Monmouth replied that he would neither make any claim to the power, nor use the title, except on the advice and request of those whose minds were set upon the deliverance of the nation; and that even in such a case, he thought of replacing his power after victory in the hands of the people, or of its representatives, in order that such a government might be established as should seem best to them; he would be contented with any station in the commonwealth. The Scots assured him that he would obtain for himself and his family a more honourable and better established station than any king on earth enjoyed.

In agreement with this language, Monmouth, in his manifesto, leaves the decision about his rights to the vote of a free Parliament. He assumes at the same time the position of a parliamentary reformer. He requires that, as had often been suggested, Parliament should be annually chosen and held, and that with a provision that it should not be prorogued, dissolved, or discontinued within the year; all its rights and privileges should be maintained[1]. Monmouth condemned the abrogation of the charters of towns, and executions on insufficient evidence, such as those of Russell and Sidney; he demands an independent position for the judicial order. He believes that he can solve the problem how the government is to be in a position to do all the good which can be expected of it, without injuring anybody's rights. He does not express

---

[1] The declaration of James, Duke of Monmouth, and the noblemen, gentlemen, and others now in arms for the defence and vindication of the Protestant religion and laws, rights, and privileges of England from the invasion made upon them, and for delivering the kingdom from the usurpation and tyranny of James Duke of York. See Roberts i. 235.

R 2

himself with anything like the same rigour against the Catholics as the Scots do ; he declares that they shall have nothing to fear from him if they quit the camp of his enemies ; but he certainly lays most emphasis on the repeal of the penal laws, so far as they affected Protestants ; the Dissenters were to have equal freedom with the dominant Protestants.

This manifesto has much significance in the constitutional conflict of the time. It embodies the intentions which had prevailed in the last two Parliaments of Charles II, but expresses them in a still more decided form than that in which they had been there declared : the system of Shaftesbury can be recognised in it, and, indeed, Shaftesbury's friend Ferguson is said to have been its penman. What it had been proposed, under Shaftesbury's guidance, and after his death, to effect by a general movement in the country, was now to be carried out by invasion. The undertakings of Argyll and Monmouth are, as it were, an execution of the plans then conceived.

There is yet, however, a difference between the two declarations. The Scottish declaration is Covenanting and republican ; it passes over the Parliament, and wishes to put a new representative body in its place ; the English is parliamentary and whiggish. They resemble each other in both attacking the Episcopal Church ; but Monmouth wishes principally to deprive it of its penal jurisdiction ; Argyll would like to destroy it altogether. He counted on the old Scottish antipathy to this form of church government, which must have been doubled by the accession of a Catholic king who, in spite of his religion, took Episcopalianism under his protection.

The aim of one of the earlier projects had been, that on the first news of an insurrection in England, a rising should also take place in the southern and western counties of Scotland. Agreements had been made for that purpose, and signs and words arranged by which the insurgents were to recognise each other [1]. No doubt was now entertained that a similar feeling still prevailed in the Lowlands. Patrick Hume and his friends wished therefore to make their attempt in that

---

[1] Trial of Tarras. Wodrow iv. 224.

quarter; it would, as had been previously intended, have coincided with movements which were being prepared in the north of England.

But Argyll expected still more from his hereditary tribal authority in the Highlands; he thought that he could there gather around himself a force of at least 5000 men, and take up a position in the mountains at their head, in which he could resist the Duke of York, for so he continued to call the King, a whole year. His son Charles had arrived a little while before, and had brought him from his vassals in Argyllshire assurances of devotion and invitations to return; he thought that he had trustworthy connexions farther to the north also, in the Orkneys. The more precise disclosures which Argyll made on the subject to a commissioner of the other party, induced the latter to follow him, under the reservation that the combined forces should advance as soon as possible into the inner country. Monmouth said to the confederate Scots, that unless he were convinced that they would bring the Earl to that course he would not move a foot[1]. In this thought may be seen the central difficulty of the whole enterprise.

With three vessels, one of thirty, one of twelve, and one of six guns, the Scots put to sea on May 2, after a slight examination by the Dutch authorities. They had a small number of volunteers—not more than 300 men; they relied especially on an excellent supply of arms and ammunition, for it was their main object to excite and maintain an insurrection.

But by this time the government had armed also to resist them. It put in force the severe Parliamentary resolutions before referred to. Moreover the manifestations of the wild Whigs had at that time excited the feeling of the nation against the republicans.

The refugees had a favourable passage; on the 6th of May they anchored off the extreme point of the Orkneys. But

---

[1] P. Hume. 'He told us that he found that Argyle was fond of the western isles of Scotland, and that wee thought it unfit to make stay there, but to haist to the inlands; that he was altogether of our opinion, and entreated us that wee might hinder his stay and get us quickly to the Lowlands; for, said he, if I did not know you are able to overrule his inclination in this and to effectuate it, I should not stir a foot.' Rose 37.

thus early they were to learn that preparations had been made for their coming. The two who first landed to seek friends and collect information in Kirkwall were arrested, that they might be sent to Edinburgh. Argyll, favoured by wind and weather, continued his course to the Western Isles. In Islay he hoped to find a considerable force of adherents assembled : some of them had indeed tried to assemble, but had been already dispersed by the troops of the government. The Earl's son landed to summon the followers of his house. But the government had already anticipated him by a very sweeping measure. It had summoned the vassals and under-tenants of Argyll to Edinburgh ; 160 of them. had appeared, of whom sixteen of the greatest name had been arrested, the others set free on bail ; they did not venture to move. Of all the Highland gentry only one, Duncan Camp-bell, dared to join the head of his clan ; the insurgents with his support mustered 1800 strong at Tarbet castle. But how could they think with this small force of attacking the govern-ment, or even of merely maintaining themselves in the High-lands? It was in vain that the declaration was printed afresh and spread abroad in the country. The Highlanders hardly understood what was in question ; even of those who one by one appeared, very few showed any real heartiness in the cause. Many took the excellent arms that were offered them, and then made off.

Argyll was a strong Covenanter, well grounded in his belief, and well versed in Scripture ; of fiery zeal in the observances of religion—he was said never to have allowed a jest on sacred things—as well as blameless in his behaviour; but he was jealous about his rights, unyielding, vehement, self-willed. The peculiarity of his position was, that he sought to combine his learned Protestantism, which was not without a tincture of republicanism, with the hereditary authority of the chief of a clan, which assuredly rests on quite a different principle. He could not carry his Highlanders with him at all in such a course ; moreover, he could not come to an understanding with those who accompanied him on his expe-dition. He avoided listening to them as far as he could ; whereas they thought that they had equal rights with him, and would have wished to direct everything according to their own views. It is not worth while to enquire who was in the right in each case : the defect lay in the combination of two different interests which could never be thoroughly fused. The Covenanters of the Lowlands sympathised as little with the position of the chief of a clan in the Highlands as the Highlanders did with the liberties of the Covenanters, and with Protestant and republican ideas generally [1]. Argyll was ruined because he attempted to combine Teutons, at the stage of national development which they had then reached in Scotland, with the Gael who knew no law but that of their native impulses.

Under the circumstances described, nothing remained for the insurgents but to seek their way to the southern counties, in spite of the troops of the government encamped near them under the command of the Earl of Dumbarton and of the Marquess of Athole. Their stores of arms and ammunition were taken from their ships to Eilan Ghierig Castle, which was situated between steep cliffs, and seemed to offer a safe refuge. It was intended to return for them subsequently. But two English frigates which arrived in the meantime found their way thither in spite of the nature of the place ; they succeeded in occupying the castle without delay, and gained possession of the stores, which consisted of the cannon of Argyll's ships, of 5000 muskets, and 500 barrels of powder. And when the insurgents fell in with Athole upon their march, he showed himself three times as strong as they were. Under the impression of these disadvantages every one lost courage ; the troops began to disband : on one morning only a hundred of them remained together, and these took different ways in order to save themselves. The larger body, with which were Hume and Cochrane, was completely dispersed at Muirdyke. Argyll attempted to return to his native Highlands. He had defended himself with the utmost courage against the enemies who pursued him, and threw himself into one of the

---

[1] The two principal reports, one in Wodrow, which in part is traced back to Argyll himself, the other in Patrick Hume's narrative, maintain the opposite points of view.

lochs that intersect the country there : he hoped that on the other side he would be in safety[1] ; but midway, according to the statement of a report sent to London, he was overtaken, stunned by two blows on the head, and brought to land half drowned. So he was sent to Edinburgh : there was no inclination to begin new and tedious proceedings against him ; and the government ordered his execution without further enquiry, on the ground of the condemnation which had been already passed upon him. On the 30th of June, 1685, the second Archibald, Lord Argyll, was beheaded, as the first had been. He died with the remarkable prayer on his lips that there might always be living one of the royal family who should be devoted to and defend the old true faith, which he described as at once Catholic, Apostolic, and Protestant.

At the time of the catastrophe in Scotland, the Duke of Monmouth, who had reached England not long before, could still flatter himself with the proudest hopes of a great success.

His preparations were still more insufficient than those of the Scots had been. Mrs. Smith, the rich widow who out of religious zeal had spent £8000 for Argyll, had hardly £1000 left for Monmouth. With much trouble he was enabled, by means of the contributions of private persons, and of a sum which was lent him on the security of some valuables, not to purchase, but to hire a frigate of thirty-two guns, with two smaller vessels ; he could only procure an insignificant supply of arms—and those not suitably chosen—and of ammunition. Not more than eighty-two companions in all joined him ; among them was a Brandenburg captain named Buyse, who had been stationed at Minden and had been enlisted by Lord Grey. Buyse was struck off the list of his regiment by his sovereign in consequence.

We are not, indeed, to suppose that these undertakings had been favoured by foreign powers. Neither the Elector of Brandenburg nor the Prince of Orange had any share in them.

---

[1] In Arran's report it is stated that 'ayant sceu ses vaisseaux pris Myl. Argyle s'était avancé pour combattre ou le duc de Gordon on le Cte. de Dunbarton, mais ayant connu que ses gens commençoient à le quitter, il avoit lui même pris le parti de se déguiser pour se retirer dans les montagnes.'

Only the town of Amsterdam, in reality out of opposition to the Prince of Orange, who at that time was on good terms with King James [1], regarded them with favour and allowed them to take place, if it did not actually support them.

Monmouth hesitated at first whether he should land in Cheshire or in Dorset. They were the two districts in which he had found an enthusiastic reception on his journeys. As in Cheshire some noblemen of influence, especially Lord Delamere, the son of George Booth, were in a position to begin the movement by themselves, Monmouth preferred to land in Dorset, where a great number of his adherents lived, but where his personal presence would be needed to induce them to rise [2]. Once, during the ferments of the year 1682, the friends of Shaftesbury in that quarter had promised him to take up arms for him as soon as they should be called upon to do so. The family of most reputation among them was perhaps that of the Spekes, of Whitelackington House near Ilminster; it was a family of the gentry, and the Spekes had once, like the Booths, fought for the Stuarts; but subsequently Protestant zeal and anxiety about the purposes of James II had led them to support the Exclusion, in combination with the freeholders in the country, and especially with the citizens of the manufacturing towns of Somerset and Dorset, among whom Nonconformist views prevailed. John Trenchard, the son-in-law of the elder Speke, passed for the most effective agitator. He had been examined as an accomplice in the Rye House Plot, and his declarations had contributed to the condemnation of William Russell: he himself had been once more acquitted; but the tumultuous joy which the members of his sect displayed on his return home made him again an object of suspicion. Subsequently it was desired to arrest him, but he had succeeded in escaping. The ladies of the family were not less zealous than the men. Mrs.

---

[1] This is shown from the negotiations of Diest, the Brandenburg envoy at the Hague, who in the name of the Elector congratulated the Prince of Orange on 'a good understanding and friendship having been so well rest)red with his now ruling Majesty in England.'

[2] Trial of Henry Lord Delamere, State Trials xi. 540.

Speke was considered to be, among the women of the West, the most formidable to the government [1].

After a long and stormy passage Monmouth arrived in Lyme Regis bay early in the morning of the 11th of June: he caused three of his companions to land in a boat at about two English miles from the place. Two of them went immediately to Lackington House to announce their arrival, the third returned to the frigate to impart the information which he had obtained where he landed. After his return Monmouth held a council of war, and it was decided to put in without delay.

This decision was taken because, although the preachers and some heads of the Nonconformists had been thrown into prison at Lyme, that party from its numbers was still practically master there. Monmouth landed towards evening, and not only met with no opposition, but was greeted with enthusiastic applause; he first uttered a short prayer, and then drew his sword and took the way to the town at the head of his companions, who arrayed themselves in rank and file. A little revolution had taken place there at this moment; the mayor, who had previously administered the Acts of Uniformity most rigorously, took to flight; his adherents were now thrown into prison in their turn. A custom-house officer who had drawn near to the forces, which were marching upon the town, but had no understanding with them, asked what their purpose was. One of the body answered that they came to fight the Papists. The officer said that there were no Papists to fight. The other asked 'if the Duke of York were not a Papist.' The officer replied that there was no Duke of York; for he would not understand the application of this title to his King. One or two persons might hold this language, but the majority attached themselves as joyful adherents to the banners on which the words 'For religion and freedom' could be read. When Monmouth and his followers reached the market-place, the declaration was read. It explained at length, and in

---

[1] Roberts, Monmouth 213; whom, however, I only use when he refers to the authentic papers which lay before him. Would that he had at least given them in an authentic form.

accordance with popular feeling, how the motto was to be understood.

The English government, foreseeing that the attack of Monmouth might be directed against these districts had sent the Duke of Albemarle, son of Monk, to Exeter, that he might oppose it at the head of the militia of the neighbouring counties; and many really thought that the movement would be confined to the small place where it began, and might be stifled there. That was impossible, however, because the militia shared the universal feeling of the district. After two days Monmouth could march out from Lyme with forces considerably increased; people only wondered that he did not throw himself upon the militia whom he would have dispersed and deprived of their arms without trouble, if indeed they did not go over to him; Albemarle did not venture to place himself in his way. Monmouth advanced without opposition to Taunton.

Taunton was a place where in the last civil wars the Cavaliers had failed in a siege, and the day of deliverance had since been kept there every year as a high festival: in the late movements most reliance had been placed on a rising at Taunton. But in opposition to this feeling the general reaction had taken an extreme form there, especially in ecclesiastical affairs; the pulpits and benches of the Nonconformist meeting-houses had been destroyed, the conventicles abolished, the population disarmed and constrained to attend the Episcopalian churches. But such compliance was no sign of an intention to submit to this coercion for ever. On the news of Monmouth's approach the population rose in all its strength and secured possession of the arms which had been taken from it, and of the town. The flourishing state of its manufactures and the profit which they yielded gave the inhabitance a certain feeling of self-importance. One of the wealthiest manufacturers mounted his horse, and at the head of a considerable retinue attended the Duke to Taunton, where the latter lodged in his house. Who has not heard of the Maids of Taunton? Twenty-seven of them brought to the Duke twenty-seven flags which they had worked with materials provided by the town. They were led to him by their teachers, one of whom with eccentric taste ·carried a sword in one hand, while in the other she held a neat little Bible. The Duke took the hint which lay in this combination ; he said that he was resolved to shed his blood for the contents of that book. That was not what the young ladies meant to suggest by their gift ; they hoped to greet as their King the handsome man whose power consisted in part in the impression which he everywhere made upon women. On one of their flags appeared a crown with the cipher J. R. (Jacobus Rex), Monmouth, like his uncle, being named James. He mounted his horse at this moment ; a male companion then stepped to the side of each of the maids, and so they followed him with their flags [1].

We know Monmouth and his romantic ambition ; how could it be that the reception which he met with, this meeting itself, the crown on the flag, should not make an irresistible impression upon him ? He had promised his Scottish friends that he would leave his claim to the crown to the decision of a free Parliament ; but did not the enthusiasm which met him rest precisely upon this claim ? What was he, if he was not a king's son ? To this consideration another was added : if the gentry of the country who had previously received him with such joy now kept quiet and neutral, he ascribed this to their disinclination to a republic, and especially to their wish that he would proclaim himself King ; for to have followed a king would, according to old English usage, have secured them, he thought, even in case of failure, from becoming amenable to the laws of high treason [2]. The arguments on both sides were considered by his advisers ; finally even those yielded who had before been opposed to his assumption of the title. So it came to pass that on the 20th of June the Duke of Monmouth was proclaimed upon the market-place of Taunton, where the town authorities attended in their robes of office, as the lawful King of England, Scotland, France and Ireland, Defender of the Faith, and was greeted thereupon with the title of Majesty. That did not however

---

[1] Their names may be found in Roberts i. 304.

[2] Reflections of Ferguson, in his notes, printed in Echard's work.

prevent many old Cromwellians from joining him, as well as other supporters: his power grew from day to day; in Taunton he counted already 5,000 men. He could proceed with confidence to a greater undertaking. And without doubt he must make himself master of a larger and better situated town, so as to secure greater resources. Now in the movements of an earlier date a remarkably numerous and devoted party had begun an agitation in his behalf at Bristol; and some of his companions who were natives of Bristol assured him that he need only draw near to that place in order to be received with joy by its population. The success which he had or might have depended altogether upon his placing himself at the head of the party, which had some years before been formed at the time of the Exclusion debates, against the succession of the Duke of York. It seemed to Monmouth that he needed only a strong position to animate the adherents of his cause in all quarters. They consisted of the friends in Cheshire already referred to, of many others in all the counties, but above all of the inhabitants of the towns who had been or were to be deprived of their municipal self-government and of the free exercise of their religion. The Nonconformists, the trading class of the population, the old and still unreconciled opponents of the Restoration, made common cause with the pretender. Everywhere in the places through which he passed the magistrates assembled in their robes of office to greet him and to hear his proclamation.

But on the other hand the understanding between the Crown and the Church, which formed the twofold object of Monmouth's attack, had been drawn still closer in spite of the difference between the creed of the King and that of the Church. The Parliament, in which the union of monarchical and ecclesiastical interests was represented, had not yet separated. The first information which the King gave to the Commons about the landing of Monmouth was met by them with a declaration that they were resolved to support him with their lives and fortunes both against all other rebels and especially against Monmouth and his adherents; they decided to bring in a bill of attainder for high treason against the Duke, which was read a third time as early as the 15th of June.

On the day on which Monmouth marched into Taunton, the 18th of ʼJune, the Parliament voted the King a subsidy of £400,000 for his extraordinary necessities. The first consequence which the undertakings of Argyll and Monmouth had, and could not but have, was to strengthen the alliance between the two elements of public life against which they were directed.

It will be a subject for subsequent discussion how King James even at that time conceived the purpose of availing himself of the state of affairs to strengthen his power; without now considering this point, it cannot be denied that he took the most appropriate measures for crushing the insurrection.

It was his order that Albemarle should not engage with his militia in a struggle which, if unsuccessful, might be followed by a very dangerous counter-stroke. He thought that he could only depend upon the obedience of regular troops. But he could not dispose even of these in great numbers, as the adherents of Monmouth only waited till the capital should be stripped of troops to rise there in his favour. It was of service to the King that the garrison of Tangier, before referred to, had now arrived in England: it furnished the first troops which he sent into the field against Monmouth, under the command of Churchill. They were mounted on horses that they might reach the scene of action the sooner. At first the communication between Churchill and Albemarle was interrupted; they left their adversary a free space for his movements. But while the latter moved slowly with his forces against Bristol, one of the royalist grandees had already entered that city, Henry Somerset, Duke of Beaufort, who belonged to the family of Worcester, which had supported the royalist cause with its wealth in all vicissitudes of fortune. The present Duke held the sentiments of his house with all his heart; Bath was confided to hands equally trustworthy; and meanwhile a body of troops was assembling, though in no great force, at Chippenham, under Duras Lord Feversham, to whom the command in chief was assigned [1].

---

[1] The Gazette de Londres, No. 1946, describes the state of affairs at that moment and the plan of the government.

In face of these preparations Monmouth reached the neighbourhood of Bristol on the 24th of June. He received offers
to conduct him along byways into the city, where he was told
that he would be recognised by the populace as soón as he
appeared, and would be greeted with joy ; and that the county
militia would go over to him at once. That, however, was
not so certain as people said ; for Beaufort kept the leaders of
the Dissenters in prison, to the number of seventy, and had
threatened that, if such a movement broke out, he would level
the town to the ground by a cannonade from the castle.
Monmouth let it be understood that he would not be the
cause of the ruin of his friends,—a humane and reasonable decision, perhaps also the wisest that he could adopt ; but only
unconditional self-confidence could have led him to his end :
he must have unexpected successes if he was to keep alive and
to spread over the country the enthusiasm which his enterprise required. To retire before the first important obstacle
which he encountered was a confession of the superiority of
his opponents. And if he did not penetrate into the town he
could not maintain himself any longer in its neighbourhood.
He might have marched further up the country, as far as
Gloucester for instance, in order that he might thence join his
friends in Shropshire and Cheshire, but he received news that
the bridges which he must have crossed had been broken
down ; and a surprise which he suffered at Keynsham gave
him sufficient proof how little his cavalry would be capable
of protecting his march against a pursuing enemy : nothing
remained for him but to retrace his steps. The way by which
he had come was at any rate left open to him : and it seemed
advisable to return by it, especially as he might hope for some
reinforcements in Wiltshire. We find him during the next days
at Phillips Norton, where he succeeded in repulsing an attack
of his half-brother Grafton ; then at Frome, where the work-
men in the factories were altogether devoted to him ; finally, in
Bridgewater, where a number of clubmen did actually join him.
But his undertaking no longer offered any prospect of success.
No one declared for him in the existing state of things ; no
town, no great nobleman, no county. Lyme, and the vessels
in the roads there which had brought him over, had fallen into

the hands of Albemarle, who now again kept the whole district in alarm, in spite of his previous check. A deputation from the townsmen of Taunton visited Monmouth and entreated him not to return to them, for that that would be their ruin. On the march Monmouth had received news of the failure of Argyll, and could not conceal from himself that he was about to meet a similar fate. He fell into a deep melancholy when he thought what hopes had been held out to him, and how little they had been fulfilled [1]; might not one of the men whom he admitted indiscriminately among his troops hit upon the thought of earning the reward which was set upon his head? Amid these apprehensions it seemed to many the best course for him, attended by his original companions, of whom only two were wanting, to try to penetrate to some seaport and to embark there. It was open to the rest to accept the pardon which the King offered to all who should voluntarily return to their allegiance. After some consideration Monmouth rejected that advice as cowardly and disgraceful. But when a proposal was made to advance even now to Gloucester or to Exeter, in order to obtain a tenable position somewhere, he found neither course more practicable than his previous attempts had proved. Feversham had already posted himself at Somerton and Sedgmoor, and that in such a way that he could prevent any movement to the one side or to the other. If Monmouth did not wish to fall disgracefully, nothing remained for him but to try the fortune of a battle. And the superiority of the enemy was certainly not so great as to compel him to despair of a good result, while a victory in battle might still give a different turn to the whole affair. From the tower at Bridgewater Monmouth surveyed the enemy's camp, and resolved to attack it by a night surprise, for all reports announced that it was only carelessly watched. In the night between the 5th and 6th of July, 1685, he proceeded to carry out his design. The civil strife of England came to a battle in the field once more.

At the head of the English loyalists there stood on this occasion a foreigner. Lewis Duras, Lord Feversham, a nephew

---

[1] Wade's Information, in the Hardwick Papers ii. 326.

of Turenne, had pitched· his camp, after the French fashion, in the open field : it was only protected by a ditch ; he had not considered entrenchments necessary. Hence it followed that the first onset of Monmouth at about an hour after midnight had a great result ; the royal troops suffered serious loss, and the whole camp fell into confusion. Strangely enough, the first to offer an energetic resistance was a bishop, who, as one of his predecessors had formerly done in the struggle against Wat Tyler, had arisen to defend Church and State in arms: I mean Dr. Peter Mew, not long before made Bishop of Winchester. He had hastened from the Parliament, which James prorogued on the 2nd of July, to the field of battle. Here he noticed that the royal artillery was at a great distance from the decisive spot ; he brought up two cannon with his own horses, and these offered the first check to the advance of the enemy. Contemporaries are, however, of opinion that Monmouth would have obtained the victory if his cavalry, which Grey commanded, had held their ground better. But the horses, which had been taken from working in the fields, became unruly when the fire of the artillery and small arms began ; their riders, who were still untrained, could not control them : the whole of this cavalry was driven headlong from the field. Feversham had the judgment, instead of ordering a pursuit, to turn with his cavalry against Monmouth's infantry. This, however, fought most obstinately. It consisted, like the cavalry, of untrained men who had flocked together, and had not the appearance of soldiers ; but if they did not know for what, they knew at least against what they were fighting. They were fighting against the union of Church and State, which they did not doubt would lead to Popery, and against the execution of the Acts of Uniformity by which they felt themselves most seriously threatened. They had procured two iron cannon, but did not know how to use them, and pointed them far too high ; they were for the most part armed with muskets, but their ammunition was soon exhausted, so that they could only fight with the butt ends ; in this plight, however, they stood by the others, who from the beginning had nothing but sharp scythes fixed on long poles ; yet they maintained themselves, though attacked in front and flank, against the cavalry and infantry, till the royal artillery appeared, consisting of eighteen good field-pieces, which were admirably served: here, as often, rebels armed with simpler weapons gave way before cannon balls; and when once broken, the insurgent forces were completely cut to pieces [1].

Monmouth at the beginning of the action had been seen advancing at the head of his men against the enemy. When the battle was lost he took to flight: for he did not even now despair of his cause. In company with Grey and Buyse he hoped to reach Lymington in Hampshire, and with the help of the adherents whom he had there, to get safe over the sea, with a view to returning under favourable circumstances. They thought of getting to the sea-coast, disguised and unarmed, through Holt Forest and New Forest. But meanwhile every one in those parts had already got in motion to arrest all suspicious strangers. First Grey was seized with his guide on the open public road near Horton, on the borders of Dorset and Hampshire, and was recognised. Monmouth and Buyse took refuge in an enclosure overgrown with fern and with all manner of bushes, where they hoped to remain concealed till the pursuers who were on the look out for them should have passed. The latter, however, had pledged themselves to each other to earn in common the reward of £5,000 which had been promised to the man who should deliver up Monmouth, living or dead; they separated into troops for a thorough search of the different enclosures. On the morning of the 8th of July the fugitives were discovered—first Buyse, then Monmouth also, who lay under a bush in a ditch covered with fern; he had fallen half asleep in his exhaustion. He was recognised by the George which he kept with him even in this disguise.

He had thought that he would enter London as a king; many thousands had expected this; they saw him now arrive

---

[1] Barrillon, July 19: 'Ils combattirent avec la crosse des mousquets et les scies, qu'ils avoient au bout de grands batons au lieu des piques.' According to the report of Besser, James II expressed in his own circle his surprise at their resistance; 'it had been impossible to break them till a fire had been directed upon them from eighteen pieces, which had been served so well that no other nation could have done it better.'

as a prisoner, already by attainder condemned to death : they were perplexed and confounded, but dumb at the sight.

On the urgent entreaty of Monmouth, James II granted him a last audience. Monmouth thought that his position at the head of a great party, and his acquaintance with its leaders, would induce the King to pardon him. He apologised for what had happened as the result of the influence of others and of ignorance ; he fell at his uncle's feet and besought him not, by ordering his death, to shed the blood of the Stuarts —his own blood. The King felt no touch of pity nor of any other emotion ; he warned his nephew to take care for the welfare of his soul. 'Then, sire,' said Monmouth, 'there is no hope for me?' James did not answer him. Some consciousness of his own dignity awoke once more in Monmouth : he. had come trembling ; he left the place with steady steps.

An audience without a parallel! Yet it did not convince Monmouth, who loved life, that he was hopelessly lost : he prayed the King at least to grant a delay that he might be able to attend in earnest to the welfare of his soul ; he sued for every kind of intercession. James II remained immoveable.

Monmouth had been allowed to choose the form of religion which should supply clergymen to attend him. Many thought that he was without any religion, as so many others were at this time ; he declared himself a Protestant of the Anglican confession. But the clergymen who attended him had a difficult task in dealing with him. He told them that he was no atheist, but believed in a Supreme Being and in a future life ; that he thought that he was reconciled with his God [1]. He was reminded of the offence which he had given by his way of life : he had for many years kept separate from his wife, and had lived in company with Henrietta Wentworth. He complained 'that his wife had never been willing to support him with her money, which Henrietta had done with gladness ; he had been too young when he married ; the marriage was lawful in the sight of the Church, but not in the

---

[1] Barrillon. 'Il parla toujours de sa paix avec dieu et le bon état de sa conscience ; c'est la religion des peuples du ouest, où Monmouth est abordé.'

sight of God; he allowed it only an outward, not an inward legitimacy; his second connexion on the contrary had been favoured by God, and had converted him to a regular life.'

Yet he did not refuse to the Duchess his testimony that she had always dissuaded him from his undertakings against the present King. And in order to protect his children from all persecution that might have threatened them on account of his former pretensions he declared that Charles II had never told him that he had been married to his mother.

And yet he had from the first based all his actions on the supposition that such a marriage had taken place. He repented of his last undertaking and of the blood which had been shed in its prosecution; but he would never acknowledge the doctrine that resistance to a king was unlawful, nor the fact that he had been engaged in a rebellion. The ministers of the Church had refused him absolution and the sacrament; he affirmed that an inner voice told him that he was going to God.

In his religion there was a vein of enthusiasm; he did not absolutely reject the mediation of the Church in his relations to God, but he was also very far from completely acknowledging its necessity.

Monmouth may be counted among representative men. They are not always great men, but rather men in whom society and the age exhibit themselves in their contradictions. The dearly loved son of a king, of whom no one knew whether he had not really been married to Monmouth's mother; in the fresh beauty of his childhood eagerly flattered and spoiled by the ladies who were then most closely attached to the King by lawful or unlawful ties; as he grew up, entangled in the sensual life of the court, which however offered intellectual excitements also; married early to a rich young lady without having any attachment to her at heart, or being more faithful to her than his father and even his uncle were to their wives; not free from complicity in the rude insults by which an affront offered to the King in Parliament was avenged; then taking part, body and soul, in the military enterprise which was intended to hinder or undo the peace of Nimuegen, and in which the Stuart family, of which he felt himself a mem-

ber of equal birth to the others, acted together for the last
time;—he was thus in the first epoch of his life an image of
the nobility of the courts of the time, which was brilliant in
outward cultivation, immoral, active, and arrogant. But when
the great quarrel about his uncle's change of creed broke out,
and the Exclusion question divided men's minds, Monmouth
was induced by the great Whigs to oppose his uncle, and
assumed this position in its whole significance; he adopted
the fundamental principles of the Whigs, and drew near to the
Nonconformists. At the same time Shaftesbury's doctrines
set his deepest ambition in motion : if the Exclusion had
been carried he would have gained the position of heir to the
throne. Monmouth cannot be compared, even at a distance,
with William Russell as to morality of conduct, nor with
Algernon Sidney as to intellectual cultivation; but he belonged to their party and school : in the year 1682 he only
escaped their fate because he was the King's son. He would
have been absolutely incapable of aiming at the death of
the King, his father; he loved him as he was loved by him,
from nature and habit. But Monmouth would have readily
co-operated in inducing the King to separate himself from the
Duke of York, and to throw himself altogether into the arms
of the other party, so far as that could be effected without
personal violence; just as his father, on account of possible
contingencies, was not sorry to see Monmouth in the ranks of
his opponents. In these relations Monmouth lived for a
second series of years, supple, compliant, yet at last full of
resolution to resist : always under the influence of others, to
which, however, he gave effect by decisions of his own ; driven
hither and thither in many directions, yet not given up by
any side; and more truly at peace with himself than he had
been before, because the kind of marriage of conscience in
which he lived saved him from other excesses, and kept alive
higher tendencies in his soul. Finally the death of his father
summoned him to assert in person the claim which he preferred,
and to defend it in arms; he adopted this course unwillingly
and yet willingly ; not without a sense of the danger into which
he was rushing, but without measuring its full extent. We dwell
on his character all the more, because he was a thorough Stuart;

ever full of hope and spirit in the midst of his difficulties ; more
carried away by impulse, than guided in his course by well-
considered resolutions ; his soul always swelling at once with
ambition and with ideas, though the latter took with him
a direction different from those of his family. The cause
entrusted to his guidance was indeed of no small consequence :
it was the cause of the Nonconformists as against uniformity,
and of political freedom as against the rising arbitrary
power of the sovereign. Monmouth stood in opposition
to the Parliament of that time as well as to the King ;
his peculiar position was that he attempted to combine a
hereditary right, which however in his person was very doubtful, with the wishes and will of the people, and thereby to
give effect to both. He was not moulded of as strong metal
as Argyll, yet he possessed qualities which were wanting to
the latter : he knew how to gain and to keep friendships ;
men marvelled at his understanding so well how to treat the
people, to keep together his undisciplined forces even without
money, and to obviate the unfavourable impressions which
might be feared from the defeat of Argyll, and from the
King's offers of amnesty. James II himself was astonished
at the ability with which Monmouth had made his arrangements for the surprise of Sedgemoor ; but the battle was
a type of his whole undertaking ; the power which he attacked was at once too strong and too well disciplined for
him ; he succumbed with all his plans to its superior force ;
and like so many other eminent Englishmen he died on the
scaffold, where he showed a brave spirit and met with cruel
sufferings. When he had already knelt down he raised his
head once more, leaning upon his elbow, and asked the
executioner to let him feel his axe ; he found it not sufficiently
sharp : the man maintained that it was sharp and heavy
enough ; but he had to strike five times before life left the
body of the victim [1].

The Bloody Assizes then followed in the districts which
had been the theatre of the insurrection and of the struggle.

---

[1] Official report of the clergy who were present and of the sheriffs. State Trials
xi. 1072.

Chief Justice Jeffreys put the criminal law in execution with all the rigour of the Norman period. More than 300 of those who had been convicted were executed; more than 800 transported to the colonies. And the same measures were taken in Scotland as in England. In Dunottar Castle the vault is still shown where the wild Whigs were kept in unendurable captivity till they were transported to America: not till they reached New Jersey were they again treated as freemen. On the other side of the ocean they could take breath again.

Still, the violence of the moment could not destroy the Nonconformists; they held their meetings in small congregations and in deep concealment—but they had still a future.

CHAPTER III.

LATER SITTINGS OF THE PARLIAMENT.

THAT the agitation aroused by the exiles did not spread further at this time was due in part to the withdrawal of the motion made, as before mentioned, for the rigorous enforcement of the Acts of Uniformity. That withdrawal had been partly prompted by consideration for the King, who saw in the motion a menace for his Catholic fellow-believers; but, in the case of many, consideration for the Protestant Dissenters, the moderate Presbyterians, whom it was not wished to irritate, had co-operated with this feeling; the rigour of the law would have struck both classes with equal force. King James felt little anxiety that the Presbyterians should be spared; he had only the Catholics in view, whom he had now quite decided not only to protect from continued oppression but to place on an equality with the adherents of the Episcopal Church. The submissiveness which the Parliament showed towards him, and the close connexion of interests on both sides which late events had brought to light, strengthened him in his hope of attaining his end with the help of the Parliament, especially as French support was at his disposal for this object. He said, 'that to carry such laws in the Parliament as would authorise the course of conduct which he thought of following was just the object for which he needed French subsidies[1].' Barrillon

---

[1] 'Les subsides (qu'il demande) ne sont pas pour contraindre par force ses sujets à luy obéir, mais pour se maintenir par les loix (according to his construction) et faire prendre des resolutions dans le parlement, qui autorisent la conduite qu'il a le dessein de tenir à l'avenir.'

paid the rest of the funds which had been deposited in his hands for James' service; he was also placed in a position to make fresh payments, but his court reminded him to keep them back till the expenditure should be of service to religion, for that it would not be necessary for the maintenance of the King. Louis XIV still drew a distinction between the interest of the English crown and that of the Catholic religion; . for King James they were one and the same.

Nothing could have happened which agreed better with his wishes than the invasion of Monmouth. For both during his brother's lifetime and after his death James saw the best means of strengthening his authority in the creation of a· standing army, and this attack gave him a welcome occasion for proceeding with his project. 'So far as I see,' says Barrillon, just after the arrival of the first report, 'the King of England is very well satisfied to have a pretext for the enlistment of troops; he believes that the undertaking of Monmouth will give him an opportunity for making himself master of his own country.' The Parliament's grant of money placed him in a position to attempt it. But he combined with this project a resolution to appoint Catholic officers without regard to the Test Oath, or to the provisions of other statutes. Three regiments of cavalry, one regiment of infantry, and one of dragoons were formed; among those to whom the recruiting was entrusted we find Catholic lords of reputation, such as Lord Dover[1]. But as needs must happen, even the enlistment itself, and still more the Catholic colour which it bore, attracted a great deal of notice; anxiety about the consequences was aroused even among those who generally held with the King. A serious warning was given by those ministers who under Charles II had supported the regular succession, without approving on that account of Catholicising tendencies in the court or of a French alliance. Lord Keeper North told the King that he would not gain but lose by his policy; he would not draw anybody over to his side, but would arouse discontent which might increase by degrees;

---

[1] 'La resolution est prise de lever un nombre considérable de regimens de cavallerie et d'infanterie: la plus grande partie sera donnée aux catholiques.'

such discontent would prove mischievous, especially in the administration of the finances, and might perhaps subsequently force its way into the army; 'he had got rid of Monmouth, but he had another far more dangerous opponent living beyond the sea.'

Lord Halifax, President of the Privy Council, joined the Lord Keeper. The King, at one sitting, expressed a hope of seeing the Catholic lords again in the Upper House; Halifax reminded the council of the statutes by which they were excluded, and brought before it the decided contradiction to those statutes involved in the King's having taken Catholic officers into his army and wishing to maintain them there. The King answered thereupon, according to his own narrative, 'that in the moment of danger and of need he had not found Protestant officers enough to be able to dispense with the Catholics; now that he had once taken them into his service, he was resolved to keep them; he did not expect opposition from his ministers but good advice, such as would enable him to discover the necessary means and forms for carrying out his plans [1].'

The King had not in view an admission of Catholic officers into his army merely by connivance and tacit toleration; he wished to propose that Parliament, when it reassembled, should expressly sanction their admission, yet he was determined beforehand to retain them whatever the Parliament might say; a course nearly resembling that which he had intended to pursue on demanding his income. It was his general intention to get all the anti-Catholic laws which had been passed during the agitations of the last few years in his brother's reign repealed without exception, as inconsistent with the dignity of a King professing the Catholic religion.

And perhaps this might have been possible in other times; not so in those of James II, in which the persecutions inflicted by Louis XIV on the Protestants of France—it was just

---

[1] 'Que sa résolution étoit prise de les employer et qu'il les soustiendroit, que c'étoit à eux, qui lui parloient, chercher les expédients et les formes compatibles avec les loix.' Barrillon, Aug 2.

towards the close of 1685 that Louis proceeded to revoke the Edict of Nantes—had the effect of bringing the religious question into the foreground, and of giving it the foremost place among all the affairs of Europe.

Charles II had assumed an attitude for a long time of resistance, and afterwards at least of neutrality, towards all such undertakings on the part of his neighbour ; King James had the scheme of the revocation imparted to him before it was issued ; he expressed the greatest delight at it. The rapid progress of the conversions in France revived the hearts of the Catholics at the English court ; in the circle of the King's confidants an universal voice of approval was heard.

But on the other hand the refugees, the Reformed, of whom many sought their safety in England, found among Protestants of all parties that sympathetic and even hearty reception which is so gladly given to fellow-believers who have been persecuted, oppressed, and hunted from their homes. In the Church of England a consciousness of its Protestant character was awakened most vividly by these events. The exiles stood far nearer to the Nonconformists in creed and ritual than to the High Church party, but no regard was paid to this. Henry Compton, Bishop of London, devoted to the unhappy strangers an attention which they could ordinarily only have expected from one who was in complete agreement with them.

A remarkable proof of the change of feeling which had taken place in the circles of the Episcopal Church lies before us in a pamphlet by Lestrange, who in his Observator continued to identify the interests of Church and State under the new government as he had done under the old. But his inculcation of the doctrine of obedience in connexion with High Church ideas no longer gained any acceptance. He suddenly found himself regarded as a promoter of Popery and an opponent of the Protestant clergy, and an object of ill-will on that account. He now turns to the reverend father in God his diocesan, Henry Lord Bishop of London, to appeal to his justice against calumny, 'for he certainly stood on the same ground and maintained the same principles as he had done hitherto [1], only the enemies of the government were now diligent in blackening the characters of its friends; what had been invented in the interest of the last rebellion was now to be employed for the defence of the Church established by law; the Protestant religion was to be the trump card in their hand.'

The position of the Episcopal Church has naturally two fronts; on the one side it is opposed to the various kinds of religious dissent which threaten its predominance founded on the maintenance of ancient forms; on the other to Catholicism, to which its creed stands in contradiction. The feelings of the moment live even in this dignified and serious society. After the danger of a rising of the Nonconformist elements had been removed, the danger from the Catholic side assumed a threatening aspect. If the King of France held himself justified first in depriving the edicts which protected the Reformed of their force by odious partisan interpretations, and then in revoking them altogether, a similar transgression of the laws of England might well be expected from King James. Much attention was attracted by an address which the Bishop of Valence had made at that time to King Louis XIV in the name of the French clergy. While he compared the achievements performed by this King in favour of the Catholic Church with the deeds of a Caesar and of an Alexander, he added that the King's power had been given him that he might effect similar results in England also, and that nothing was more ardently desired there. People saw in these words an announcement of what England had to expect with or without the intervention of the King of France; they contained as it were a threat of the Catholic clergy of France against the Protestant-Episcopal clergy in England. The religious feelings of England received an additional stimulus from patriotism.

As Lord Halifax could not be induced to support the King's undertakings, James II, in order that he might not experience open or secret opposition at the hands of his ministers them-

---

[1] The Observator defended, in a full answer to severall scandals cast upon him.

selves, held it good to remove that nobleman, not only from the presidency of the Privy Council and from his other offices, but also from the Privy Council altogether. When James stated this fact at a meeting of that body he also declared that he would allow no one to meddle with his affairs, and would give his confidence to no one, who did not completely agree with him in feelings and principles [1]. He was reminded that Halifax would exercise an influence hostile to the crown in Parliament. James II remarked that nothing could be so injurious as his remaining in the Cabinet. The affair had however another side also.

Halifax was the man whose opposition had once brought about the failure of the Exclusion Bill. It excited surprise that this service was so soon forgotten. The Duke of Albemarle too, when he asked for his discharge, because he was unwilling to be placed under Feversham, had it granted him without hesitation. The vacant post was given to Churchill. It had been expected that the King would show greater consideration for the son of a man whom more than any one else the Stuarts had to thank for their restoration.

The King seemed to wish to govern with the aid of those only who concurred with him in his plans. He took advice especially from those Catholics who stood closest to him. No one who loved his place might dare to oppose him. Lord Keeper North had died a short time before; he had for a successor the most fiery champion of the prerogative who could be found, Chief Justice Jeffreys, who was raised at the same time to the dignity of Lord Chancellor.

Such had been the action of the government and the resistance offered to it; under these auspices the second session of the Parliament opened on the 9th of November, 1685. In the speech from the throne King James announced his purposes without further reserve. From the experience of the late disorders he drew the conclusion 'that the national militia' was ineffective against attacks of this kind, and that a well-disciplined standing military force was indispensable to guard against all disturbances from without and from within: he

---

[1] Barrillon: 'Qu'il ne vouloit point admettre dans ses affaires et dans sa confiance ceux, qui auroient des sentiments et des principes opposés aux siens.'

had formed such a force; but it required twice as large an outlay as that which had been sufficient for his army up to that time, and therefore a grant of corresponding amount from the Parliament would be necessary.' He was well aware that offence had been taken in Parliamentary circles both at the increase in the army and at the admission of Catholic officers into it: he held it good to bring this matter directly under discussion. 'Let no man,' such are his words, 'take exception that there are some officers in the army not qualified according to the late provisions as to tests for their employments. The gentlemen, I must tell you, are most of them well known to me, and have formerly served with me on several occasions, and always approved the loyalty of their principles by their practice. . . .. . And I will deal plainly with you, that after having had the benefit of their services in such a time of need and danger, I will neither expose them to disgrace nor myself to the want of them if there should be another rebellion to make them necessary to me.' In conclusion, he expressed his confidence that no division, no coldness even, would arise between him and the two Houses of Parliament on this point: he himself was, and remained, determined to venture his life for the true interest of the kingdom.

The speech made almost as great an impression by what it omitted as it did by what it contained. It has always been thought that the King had better not have mentioned the Catholic officers at all: for that he would have been tacitly permitted to keep them in his service. On the other hand, a new assurance had been expected that the religion and laws of the country should be maintained and defended; such an assurance as had been contained in his first declaration to the Privy Council, and in his previous speech from the throne. Such a declaration seemed more urgently necessary now than then; but the King never thought of making it. That the one point was brought prominently forward and the other passed over confirmed the general apprehension that a scheme opposed to the laws was being carried out. The expression, 'the true interest,' suggested the thought that the King understood that interest differently from the country.

And no doubt these impressions of the King's meaning were correct. He did not wish to bind his hands by repeating assurances which were expounded in a more comprehensive sense than that in which he understood them; he wished to bring the question of the necessity of the test oaths to a Parliamentary decision, and thereby to prepare his way for that removal of all restrictions imposed on the Catholics which he had in view. He feared some resistance in the House of Lords, but he hoped to bring the Commons over to his side, considering the nature of the composition of that house.

And there certainly sat in the Lower House a very numerous party which was devoted to the crown without reserve; but by its side there was growing up another, consisting partly of old Tories who, with all their devotion to the crown, could not reconcile themselves to innovations in religion, partly of the few Whigs who had, in spite of all difficulties, been successful at the elections. This party was supported by the influence of those members of earlier Parliaments who had come to the capital.

Thus in the compact majority of a Lower House there appeared tokens of a disposition contrary to that which it had previously shown—an incident which seldom happens. One of the best-known Tories, Edmund Jennings, who had hitherto taken the lead in showing zeal for the crown, said at the very beginning of the session that he must now be also the first to declare against its demands, so completely altered were the relations of the two parties in his opinion.

A proposal to thank the King for his speech from the throne without further discussion was rejected; it was resolved to discuss it in due form. And though the House originally consented to deal first with the article on subsidies, yet a definite resolution on that point was delayed by the interposition of another debate of still greater significance as affecting constitutional principles. This debate arose on the King's expressions concerning the relation of the militia to the standing army. It could not be denied that the militia would be ill-suited to resist a serious hostile attack; but even the Tories were not inclined to seek the safety of the empire solely in the establishment of a strong standing army. For such an army consisted, it was said, of people whom nobody knew and nobody could trust ; it was equally oppressive to the private citizen and dangerous to public freedom, especially as the national religion was left out of sight in its composition. To this effect Edward Seymour raised his voice once more. He saw the party which had caused him to retire from the council of Charles II advancing to full possession of power. Sir Thomas Clarges, the uncle of Albemarle by the mother's side, undertook the defence of the militia, which he said would have done still better service if that nobleman had been better supported ; at the same time he reckoned up the revenues of the King, and stated the surplus amount at that time, to show that a new grant would not be needed. There was an unanimous agreement that, above all things, something must be done for the improvement of the militia : but the indispensableness of a strong standing army was nevertheless not seriously disputed. Such a force was thought to be required, not only for raising the consideration of the English power in Europe, but also for maintaining the internal relations of the country in a satisfactory state. 'If we had it not,' said Ashton, 'a new rebellion would break out in a few days [1].' The proposal had been made to grant the King a subsidy 'for the maintenance of his increased forces,' and this statement of the object was no doubt rejected at once ; but the adherents of the crown did not attach any great value to it, as the King would have been bound by it afresh. The grant itself proved more liberal than had been expected ; it was fixed, not, according to the tenor of one proposal, at £400,000, but at £700,000. In the establishment of a strong standing army, which did not, to be sure, exclude the improvement of the militia, the King would have met with no opposition from this House, assuming that an agreement could be secured upon the great point in dispute with reference to the admission of the Catholic officers ; for this must be settled if the grant which had been made was to acquire the force of law by the close of the Parliament.

---

[1] 'Were not those forces standing to prevent a rebellion, you would have one in a few days.'

In this quustion the whole weight of the debate was concentrated; as early as on the 14th of November it was
considered at length in a grand committee. Many declared
it quite unimportant of what creed the officers of an army
were; 'only a few years ago they had seen Catholic Portugal
tear itself away from Spain under a Protestant general, and
that general, Marshal Schomberg, was still in the service of
the King of France.' Others saw a political danger in the
introduction of Catholic officers. 'The clearest argument of
the champions of Exclusion had been that a Popish successor,
like the present King, would introduce a Popish army also;
and there was evidence already that the creation of such a
force had begun.' Sir Thomas Clarges intimated that such
officers might be tempted at some future time to resist the
Protestant succession, that of the eldest daughter of the King
and of her husband. The apprehensions of the majority did
not, perhaps, go so far as this, but it was unanimously of
opinion that the arbitrary disregard of the test oaths could
not pass unnoticed. John Maynard reminded the House of
old occurrences in English history, for instance how Henry IV
had yielded to the wish of Parliament even with regard to
his confessor: 'so, no doubt, the King then reigning, who
surpassed Henry in all respects, would grant the request
which should be delivered to him in a respectful remonstrance;
he would not break with his Parliament for the sake of
twenty or thirty officers whose services could be discharged
equally well by others.' The motion to draw up an address
to the King still however met with opposition, principally
because the House ought not, it was said, to do an injury
to the deserving Catholic officers: an objection which was
removed by the remark that the penalties which they had
incurred might easily be remitted to them by a resolution
of the Parliament. An address was accordingly resolved
upon; but when the draft of it was brought before the House
it was thought necessary to soften much of its language. Its
proposal 'that the King should be requested in plain terms
to remove the officers from their posts' appeared to the
majority too abrupt a demand, and one irreconcilable with
the reverence due to the majesty of the crown. The address

assumed the form of an expression of thanks for the speech from the throne; the disputed question as to the standing army and the militia was not mentioned in it. The King was only reminded of the statutes according to which Catholics were incapable of serving in the English army, and of the principle that these disabilities could only be removed by Parliamentary resolutions. The House declared itself ready to remit the penalties which the officers had already incurred: 'but because,' so it went on, 'the continuing of them in their employments may be taken to be a dispensing with that law without Act of Parliament, (the consequence of which is of the greatest concern to the rights of all your Majesty's subjects and to all the laws made for security of their religion,) we therefore . . . . . do most humbly beseech your Majesty that you would be graciously pleased to give such directions therein that no apprehensions or jealousies may remain in the hearts of your Majesty's good and faithful subjects.' It was of set purpose that the expressions of devotion were multiplied and that the demand made was not expressed in plain terms; but it might be gathered from the way in which the propositions were combined, and the constitutional importance of the question, owing to which it attracted so much attention in the nation, assumed the greatest prominence in the address.

It is said to have been the purpose of the leaders in this matter to give greater emphasis to the address by having it laid before the House of Lords and made into a joint address of both Houses; but the adherents of the court were against this course, and as there was also a formal objection to it in the fact that the Lords had already returned thanks for the speech from the throne, the proposal was rejected. In the afternoon of the 17th of November the Commons repaired to Whitehall to present their address without the Lords[1]. Not all, but most of the members were there.

---

[1] The doubts of Macaulay as to the position of parties on this question are removed by the report of the Brandenburg correspondent Bonnet: 'La chambre se partagea et 136 furent d'avis de demander la concurrence, et 212 furent d'avis qu'elle présentoit seule cette adresse; ainsi ces derniers, qui étoient pour la cour, l'emportèrent.' In general the simple reports of Bonnet contain the best information about this session which has come before me.

A brilliant company of the king's military attendants, a kind of noble guard, bearing their partisans, escorted them to a chamber where a throne had been set up for the King. The Speaker read the address; the King heard it without emotion; he answered in a remarkably loud voice and with a more serious air than was usual with him. He chiefly expressed surprise at the distrust shown him after what he had last said to them and in spite of the reputation which he had acquired in the world for trustworthiness. He added, nevertheless, that however they might behave themselves, he would keep the promises which he had made them, and would be very just to his word in this and all his other speeches[1]. These words produced a favourable effect in general; they were greeted by most of those present with a murmur of applause; for they appeared to contain that renewal of the King's old promises which had been missed in the speech from the throne. There were, however, also many who did not share this expectation. They were of opinion that the King had used different expressions on different occasions, and that he would not be able to reconcile them; they thought that in the harsh tone of his censure they had noticed something of the demeanour of an absolute sovereign. This discontent first found an expression on the following day when the royal answer was read at the sitting of Parliament. It was proposed to consider the speech once again: this course was most zealously recommended by John Coke, a member of the Queen Dowager's household, and known besides for a very loyal subject; 'we are all Englishmen' he exclaimed; 'and are not to be frighted out of our duty by a few high words.' This Parliament was not yet accustomed to such expressions; amidst a violent tumult, which Coke attempted in vain to quiet by an excuse, he was sent to the Tower as a punishment, for he was thought to have offended against both King and Parliament. After this the proposal above

---

[1] His words were 'but however you proceed on your part, I will be steady in all my promises I have made to you.' I hold them for genuine, yet it is strange that they are not found in the Journals, ix. 759, where there is a gap—especially as the Speaker assures the House that he has procured a copy of the answer to avoid mistakes.

referred to could not pass. The prevailing feeling was, on the contrary, that the House must content itself with the King's words, which certainly did not embody a decision opposed to its wishes. The King also would have been satisfied with this result.

At this moment, however, the Upper House took a step preparatory to dealing itself with the question. An active spirit of opposition to the court had already been shown among the Lords on various subjects, especially on the limits of the jurisdiction belonging to them. Without consideration of the fact that the House had already returned its thanks to the King, a proposal was made to reopen the question by a retrospective debate on the speech from the throne. Lord Devonshire, who had grown up under the eyes of Hobbes, and was considered at the court a decided adversary; Viscount Halifax, who had been obliged to leave the ministry on this question; Lord Mordaunt, a young freethinker, who spoke then for the first time in Parliament, recommended the proposal in elaborate speeches. On the other hand, the objections of the Chancellor to this proposal found the less consideration because some members of the Privy Council, Lords Bridgewater and Nottingham, opposed him. They expressed their astonishment that a number of officers had ventured to accept their posts in indisputable contradiction to the laws of England, and at the same time stated their suspicion that a trustworthy support had been promised them. The greatest impression, however, was made by Henry Compton, Bishop of London. He was the youngest son of that Spencer Compton who in the civil wars had fought most bravely for Charles I, and had been slain in a skirmish, refusing quarter from the rebels; the Bishop himself had the advantage of having spent some time upon the Continent, where he had made himself acquainted with the affairs of Europe and had gained a conception of their connexion with those of England. He had originally entered upon a military career, but had passed over to an ecclesiastical one early enough to fulfil all its conditions. No bishop was thought to have shown more zeal in the management of his diocese. In the dissensions of former years we find him most closely connected with

Danby; after that statesman's fall he continued in his position as bishop to resist every tendency to Catholicism; he was especially famous as the Protestant bishop. Compton considered the appointment of the Catholic officers less from a jurist's point of view than from that of a Protestant ecclesiastic, as an attempt to prepare the way by such a measure for a general transformation. If it were acquiesced in, all the higher posts would very soon be filled with Catholics, and the whole administration would assume a Catholic character. He said that the case resembled that of the dykes which protected the land in Holland; if they were broken through on one point, a general inundation followed. English Protestantism appeared to him a district embanked by the laws, and the power of universal Catholicism the great flood which it alone kept back. These words were heard at a moment when two great powers usually opposed to each other, France and Austria, were exerting themselves to the utmost for the promotion of Catholicism; they were corroborated by the sight of the French exiles who filled the streets of London. When Compton added that he spoke in the name of all the English bishops, it was objected that he certainly had not been commissioned to say so; but it cannot be doubted that by far the greater number of them were at the bottom of their hearts of his opinion. Compton's speech, unhappily handed down to us in a very incomplete form, is in a historical point of view one of the most remarkable speeches ever made in Parliament; it set forth in full distinctness the breach between the Episcopal system and the crown, which had previously been allied together.

The proposal to fix a day for the discussion of the King's speech from the throne was accepted. What was to be expected when the day came?

The Lords would have resolved on an address which would have taken a stronger form than that of the Commons, and to which no evasive and ambiguous answer would have been possible [1]. And the King had another cause for anxiety.

---

[1] Bonnet: 'Il ne faut pas douter, que le but de ces seigneurs ne fut qu'on proposoit une adresse à S. M. à peu près de la même teneur que celle de la chambre

The purpose of a part of the Commons to invite the Lords to accede to their address had failed to secure a majority for this among other reasons—that a declaration of the Lords had a legal as well as a parliamentary character. It was now heard that the Lords themselves were disposed to put themselves in communication with the judges in due form, and to invite them to express an official opinion on the admissibility of the proceeding of James II. The decision of the judges could be safely predicted, considering the known disposition of the persons who then held high judicial positions, and the influence which the Lords would have exercised upon them; they would have declared against the King, and would thereby have made it almost impossible for him to carry out the intentions which he had once formed.

However, even the Lords did not aim at an open quarrel with the King; notwithstanding their difference with him, they contemplated a settlement which might have been acceptable to both parties. They were willing to grant by Act of Parliament the necessary dispensation to those Catholic officers whom the King was not inclined to dismiss. Halifax said that the King would have been allowed to appoint other Catholic officers also, if he had wished it, but under the same condition. And this settlement would have been acceptable even to the moderate Catholics; for they saw no good for themselves in a quarrel between the King and the Tory Parliament.

All the more might it be expected that the King would enter into such an arrangement, as only so could he secure a peaceable conclusion of the session, and without such a conclusion he would be unable to get possession of the subsidies granted.

But such were not the guiding considerations with the King. The sum of money voted was not absolutely necessary to him; he attached far more importance to the right of dispensation, and that on other grounds; it agreed with his idea of the prerogative, and offered the best means of carrying out his Catholic projects. If he had allowed the matter to go

basse.' In describing it as stronger I rest on the fact that the address of the Commons was attacked as insufficient.

further, he would have been declared not to possess this right by a combination of the two Houses with the judges; he would not have been able to put it in force. He resolved to anticipate the creation of such an obstacle, and to prorogue the Parliament without delay.

He appeared unexpectedly, as his brother had done so often, in the House of Lords on the eleventh day of this session, the 20th of November; he took his seat on the throne in his royal robes, and had the Commons summoned before him. When they had appeared, with their Speaker at their head, the Lord Chancellor knelt before the King and received his orders. 'My lords,' he then said, 'and you knights, burgesses and citizens of the House of Commons, the King commands me to let you know that it is his royal pleasure, that this Parliament, for many weighty reasons, be prorogued to the tenth day of February next, and the Parliament is prorogued to the tenth day of February next.'

No breach with the Parliament, properly speaking, was as yet announced in these words; still less could there be discerned in them any intention to overthrow the parliamentary constitution. In proroguing the Parliament James II only wished to prevent a formal declaration on its part against himself; he thought of first exercising and taking complete possession of the right in question, which he considered to be well founded, and hoped that in another session of the same Parliament he would get it recognised.

But for all this it is clear that he was putting himself in opposition to the Tory, but also Protestant, element which he had to thank for his peaceable accession; and no one could say how far that opposition would lead him. For what would happen if the Parliament held fast to the sentiments which it had expressed?

King James did not shut his eyes to the difficulties which he would meet with; but he was resolved to encounter them at any cost. He told Adda, the Pope's plenipotentiary, who had arrived at that time, that he knew he could be a great and prosperous king if he were willing to leave things on their old footing as regarded religion; but that he thought that such behaviour would be contrary to his religious duty.

To certain members of Parliament w
and made him secret offers, which did
his ideas, he gave the answer, that h
three crowns for the sake of his reli
given him power he would employ it
advancement of his religion [1].

---

[1] 'Après avoir hazaidé trois couionnes en se déc
de ne se pas démentir.' Barrillon, Maich 25.

CHAPTER IV.

DECLARATION OF THE RIGHT OF DISPENSATION.
THE ECCLESIASTICAL COMMISSION.

LOUIS XIV did not fail to express to the King of England approval of the attitude assumed by him, and represented that his authority must gain strength if he did not suffer the religion which he professed to be subject to the oppression of the old laws. James II answered by a declaration that he held fast to his purposes in relation to the Catholic religion, and hoped to carry them out by a close alliance with France [1]. Both princes were agreed that the Parliament had better not be reassembled at once ; the King of France because he continued to fear that it might make approaches to Spain, the King of England because he could not at first expect any result corresponding to his views. When, as early as January 1686, he again prorogued Parliament to the following May, he allowed it to be understood that he did not pledge himself thereby to convoke it at the latter date : 'he wished to show the members that he could carry on the public administration without their grants ; when they saw that, they would be less refractory.' Lord Rochester too held it possible to call out .a more accommodating disposition ; perhaps by presents— for Louis XIV, on his side, placed some resources at the disposal of his envoy for this purpose—and by moderating the Catholic zeal of the government [2]. James II did not

---

[1] Barrillon, Jan. 17 : ' Que sa principale espérance est, d'en venir à bout par une union étroite et une entière liaison avec V.M.'

[2] 'Le trésorier essaye à persuader au roi, que les esprits seront plus traitables, si on fait avant la séance du parlement les choses nécessaires pour leur imprimer des sentiments modérés.'

promise himself much from bribes ; he was not at all disposed
to spend his money in buying uncertain services. But he
yielded thus far, that he put off some promotions of Catholic
friends which he had in view, and instructed the preachers in
the chapels which had been opened not to discuss the questions
in dispute between the two confessions : moral sermons were
generally heard from them. On his side the King demanded
that the same, or almost the same, rule should be observed in
the Protestant pulpits also, especially as it was unseemly, he
said, that the King's religion should be attacked and reviled
in the churches. But we have already mentioned the event
which rendered such abstinence impossible. The revocation
of the Edict of Nantes might even be regarded as an act of
hostility to England to some extent ; for the English crown
had always endeavoured to protect the Reformed in France,
and had even undertaken obligations towards them. As the
thought had often been entertained of employing this relation
for the renewal of the earlier connexion of the French coast-
districts with England, and Charles II himself had not entirely
lost sight of his political duty, so now it was said that matters
would not have gone so far if there had been a Protestant
king in England. Thus the affair fell in exactly with the
quarrel which had broken out between the crown and the
nation.

We know that James II approved at bottom of the proceedings of Louis XIV, in support of which Barrillon placed
in his hands the most effective of the pamphlets written in its
defence—that of Durand. Among the people, on the other
hand, the complaints of the Reformed, especially a paper by
Claude, were read with general approval. On the one side
stood the Catholic and monarchical, on the other the popular
interest and that of general Protestantism. Of all the events
which aroused a feeling of its community with continental
Protestantism in the Church of England, the persecution of
the French Reformed was no doubt the most effective. From
all pulpits the sympathy of the hearers was aroused for their
persecuted fellow-believers. We can learn from the journals
of the time what an impression was made by the fact that
the bishops, especially the Bishop of Bath and Wells, Dr. Ken,

who had previously been considered to be half a Catholic, the Bishop of Gloucester, above all the Bishop of London, took the lead of the other clergy in this matter. Under the influence of their exhortations a collection which was ordered in favour of the exiles proved most abundant.

The King had prevailed on himself to give his permission for the collection, though in his heart he rather hated than loved these exiles, to whom he ascribed republican senti-ments; he only made it a condition that in the public pro-clamations there should be nothing said of a regular perse-cution in France; he demanded this consideration for the King his ally. And as for the gifts themselves, he required that only those should have a share in them who would con-form to the Church of England. This compliance, though limited and half extorted, had still a great value. It was the work of the Tories, who sought to hold back the King from all steps which might draw upon him the thoroughgoing religious hostility of the Protestants.

Less anxiety on the last point was felt by that society of zealous Catholics which had formed itself around the King since the beginning of his reign, in the first instance only for confidential conversation, but conversation in which the most important affairs, especially of a religious nature, were dis-cussed. It consisted of the old friends whom he had known since the time of the alleged Popish plot, Arundel, Powis, Castlemaine, Dover, and the Jesuit, Edward Petre, who was the most intelligent of all, and gained the greatest in-fluence over the King, both because he possessed the support of the powerful order which at that time played a great part in Europe, and because he belonged to a noble English family, and combined the points of view of English with those of European Catholicism. Sunderland associated him-self with this party, without any preference for one religion or the other: in reality only hoping to gain the King's con-fidence by following his inclinations as closely as possible, and so to get the guiding influence into his own hands exclusively. His accession to this party first gave it any real importance in public affairs.

While the antagonism between the two parties was thus

increasing, an event happened at court which aroused once more the expectations of the one and the apprehensions of the other in the most lively manner.

A lady who had stood in the closest relation to the Duke of York, in spite of his marriage, but who' had for some time been kept apart from him, Miss Catherine Sedley, found access to him again. It was heard that he had promised to receive her at court and to grant her a position such as the Duchess of Portsmouth had held; she was in fact created Countess of Dorchester. Every one knew that she was an opponent of the Catholic faction. She could no longer be called beautiful, but she shone in conversation, and it was just the Catholics who were the targets for the lively sallies of her wit [1]. What, said she, would or could the society of bigots do in England? Its project was impracticable and ridiculous: it would only serve to hurl the King to destruction.

A renewed intercourse with Catherine Sedley would have formed a counterpoise to the influence exercised by the Catholic party over the King. It was assumed that those of his friends who still adhered to Protestantism, Lords Rochester, Dartmouth, and Preston, favoured the reception of the lady into the palace, that they might preserve a support near the King [2]. Whether that was really the case cannot now be made out for certain, nor can it be discovered who had a hand in the business. But there is no doubt that this affair, which was of a most private nature, played a part in the great strife of factions.

The Catholics fell into no small agitation; but they had in this instance the better cause, and, as may be supposed, the Queen was on their side. Mary of Este was not exactly beloved in England; she always appeared not much less of a foreigner than her Portuguese predecessor upon the throne, without having the latter's talent or inclination for acquiring friends: even during the reign of James the court of the

---

[1] Barrillon, Feb. 18, 1686: it had been intended 'tourner en ridicule ceux qui ont le plus part aux resolutions qui se prennent, à quoi cette dame étoit fort propre.'

[2] Bonnet, Feb. 11/21, names these names. At a later period too the Queen considered Preston to be an adherent of the Countess.

Queen Dowager was more frequented than her own. Mary of Este showed a haughtiness which gave offence to the English ladies ; she did not at all know how to control herself. It was related of her that she had once in the excitement of con- versation struck her mistress of the household ; so violent were the outbreaks of her passion at times. How then must the King's design have made her proud blood boil ! That he wished to receive a rival into the palace exceeded the measure of what she could endure, at any rate, by ignoring it. She declared to the King with emphasis that she would never tolerate such treatment, and would rather leave the court ; that he had received her as it were from the cloister, and that she was determined to return thither [1]. And as has been mentioned, her influence increased when she had ground for complaint. On this occasion she had the support of the King's confessor, who showed double inflexibility as there was a question of thwarting an anti-Catholic influence. The bad effect which scandalous behaviour in this point must needs have was represented to the King, and he was thus induced to give up his wishes. After some resistance the new countess had to leave the court and take up her residence in Ireland.

It can hardly be believed that Rochester had taken part in the intrigue, especially as the serious religious sentiments which then actuated him may be noticed in his journals : his friends too deny the charge. Others however have accepted it as true, and have founded a bitter moral accusation on this very combination of high religious professions with un- scrupulousness as to means. Sunderland did not delay to employ against him the suspicion, which was very general [2]. He caused the Queen to be informed, through Madame de Mazarin, the only woman who possessed her confidence—and a second French plenipotentiary in England, named Bonrepaus,

---

[1] Barrillon, Feb. 7, 1686 : 'Je crois que sous main on l'a fortifié.'

[2] Bonrepaus, March 28, 1686: 'Moi qui ay veu Mylord Sunderland conduire cette intrigue par Mme. Mazarin, par le jeune Villars et autres personnes de cette capacité, desquels j'ai été confident malgré moi.' Lord Macaulay has, I think, placed too much confidence in the reports of Barrillon and Bonrepaus, who say expressly that they have their information from Sunderland.

condescended to bear the messages to and fro—that Rochester's object was to estrange her from the King, and if possible to prevent her marriage from being still blessed with male off-spring, lest Rochester's niece, the King's daughter by his first marriage, should be excluded from all prospect of the throne. The Queen believed this, and exerted all her influence to drive Rochester himself from his position near the King, as she held him for her principal enemy : she became with all the more zeal the patroness of the Catholics, whose cause she regarded as her own.

But now the Catholics also on their side, in order to obtain security for the future, without which they could not be secure of the present, hit upon a thought which opened wide prospects, and could hardly be justified.

Nothing was more repulsive to them in relation both to politics and to religion than the prospect which the Princess of Orange and her husband had of ascending the throne of Eng-land at some future time. To this claim was attached the hope entertained by the opponents of France, by the adherents of the Parliamentary constitution, and by all Protestants, that after a short time they would recover freedom of action. In reality this opposition of interests had already led to the marriage of Anne, James' second daughter, with Prince George of Den-mark,—for Denmark then belonged to the French alliance,— and that marriage effected this if nothing more, that there was now in the family a prince of ancient royal descent, who could on that account claim precedence over the Prince of Orange. On one previous occasion the thought had been entertained of granting the Princess Anne, if she went over to Catholicism, a claim prior to her sister's. The second French ambassador, before referred to, Bonrepaus, who had only received full powers for commercial transactions, but who liked to have a hand in all things, thought it his vocation to set the affair in motion. One day he laid before the Danish ambassador the question whether Prince George was the man to bring forward his wife's claim to the throne of England, even to the exclusion of her elder sister, the Princess of Orange : that claim might perhaps be recognised if he became a Catholic. The Danish ambassador then spoke on the subject to the

Prince, as though the thought had arisen in his own mind;
and, as he said, became convinced that the Prince was capable
of taking this view; that he would get himself instructed, in
order that he might at some future time declare himself a
Catholic when a favourable moment appeared [1]. Bonrepaus
remarks that the Princess was timid and said little, but that she
passed among those who enjoyed her confidence for a lady of
intelligence and ambition; that she too wished to be instructed
about religion, and that he knew how to get controversial
writings into her hands; that the Prince of Denmark was dull,
but possessed sound good sense. Thus for a moment the
hope was entertained in Catholic circles of securing the future of
Catholicism in England, by employing another combination
to hinder the succession of the Prince and Princess of Orange.
The apprehension which Clarges had expressed in the last
session was not altogether chimerical. But when Bonrepaus
adds to his reports about the Princess that she hated the
reigning Queen,—for that the latter had repelled her like
others by her pride,—and spoke ill of her, his own words
contain an intimation of the hindrances which such a plan
must meet with in the personal relations of the court; for the
whole Catholic party grouped itself round the Queen, and if Bonrepaus thought the two kings inclined to support his machinations he did not know them well. They were both too strongly
attached to hereditary right, by virtue of which the one possessed his throne, and the other maintained that the Spanish
monarchy must fall to his son: they would have renounced
their own principle if they had entered into Bonrepaus' projects. King Louis remarked to his ambassador that he did
not approve of the plan of altering the succession. There
was nothing which James II would have seen with greater
pleasure than the conversion of his second daughter and her

---

[1] The proposal runs: 'S'il croyoit que le Prince George fut homme à songer à
faire succéder la princesse sa femme à cette couronne au préjudice de la princesse
d'Orange, ce que je croyais practicable s'il se faisoit catholique.' The answer, after
a conversation held with the Prince: 'Qu'il croyoit qu'il prendroit cette vue, et qu'il
se feroit instruire pour se mettre en état de prendre son parti en cas qu'il trouvoit
quelque jour à faire réussir ce projet.—Je sais aussi certainement, que la princesse
sa femme veut être instruite.'

husband ; but any wish to constrain them to such a step by his authority, or to persuade them to it by holding out a prospect of the succession, lay outside his horizon.

His purpose was far rather to secure the rights of the Catholics, for the present and for ever, in a parliamentary way without so violent an interposition as that above mentioned, which would have brought him into contradiction with himself. He prorogued the Parliament again in May, and that till November 1686 ; but the usual forms were observed on the occasion, and the use of such forms implies the maintenance of a parliamentary system. The King's notion was to carry matters so far in the interval that people might get accustomed to see the Catholics in possession of certain rights, and then to establish those rights so firmly that no one should be able to reverse them [1]. He wished to assert his prerogative in opposition to the last resolutions of the Parliament, and to maintain it as the supreme source and support of the arrangements which he employed it to effect. He expected that Parliament would approve his conduct, and supposed that it would not wish him to take further steps, and those in favour of the Nonconformists ; but if Parliament refused its support he would rely on his army and on his alliance with France. He purposed in carrying out this policy to have recourse to the right of dispensation which his brother had claimed twenty-four years before ; he thought that he would in his way attain to an end which his brother had failed to reach.

The right of dispensing with existing laws had been formerly exercised by the Tudors, especially by Henry VII, to a great extent, and that with the sanction of the judges ; even under the Stuarts it had been recognised by the greatest jurists, although with the necessary limitations. It was agreed that this prerogative did not apply to the common law, nor to questions of property and possession, nor in any case to things

---

[1] 'Etablir ses affaires de sorte qu'il ne sera pas au pouvoir des factieux de rien entreprendre contre lui ny de traverser l'exécution des choses faites—il voudra, si je ne me trompe, tenter encore, si la fermeté ne surmonte pas leur faux zèle et s'il ne pourra point les accoutumer à souffrir la religion catholique plustost que de voir toutes les sectes différentes s'établir.'

wrong in themselves, but only to the provisions of statutes :
there was a difference of opinion, however, on the question
how wide its scope was when thus applied, and whether it
extended to absolute or only to limited ordinances. Coke had
defined the frontiers of the prerogative and of statutes as
follows :—that Parliament had not the right of depriving the
King of the service of his subjects, which every one was bound
to render[1]—a point which came in question more strongly
than ever after the profession of Protestantism had been made
by Act of Parliament a condition for admission to the civil
and military service. There were still lawyers who held that
the King had a right to dispense with the statutes which imposed this restriction. Thus, during the life of Charles II,
when there was a discussion on the restoration of the Duke of
York to the dignity of Lord High Admiral, which he had
given up on account of his religion, Herbert, Chief Justice of
Chester, had declared that a dispensation by the King would
be quite sufficient to legalise it. The Parliament declared its
abhorrence of this opinion. It insisted that only the power
which had enacted the laws could dispense with them—namely,
the King and Parliament, not the King by himself. This
view had been expressed by the Lower House in its last
address ; it preponderated among the Lords and even among
the majority of the judges, in spite of some divergences of
opinion : we have seen that an apprehension of a decision of
the judges in this sense, which the Lords thought of procuring,
was the real ground of the last prorogation.

King James not only wished to anticipate such a decision,
but entertained the purpose of calling forth from the judges
a declaration of a contrary nature. The question was of
high political significance; it concerned the limits of the
monarchical power in its conflict with the power of a Parliament; it would have demanded the freest and most tranquil
consideration. The King however resolved, under the influence of his friends, to employ his prerogative of appointing

---

[1] Coke justifies the King's dispensation on the principle of its being beyond the
power of Parliament to take away his right to the service of his subjects.
Compare a note in Hargrave in the State Trials xi. 1189.

and dismissing the judges, so as to secure a decision favourable to himself. Lord Chancellor Jeffreys, who had previously raised legal objections against Herbert's view, was nevertheless now heartily ready to aid in carrying out the changes of persons indispensable to secure such a result [1].

In Easter Term, 1686, on the 21st of April, the four most inflexible among the higher judges, Thomas Jones and Charlton of the Common Pleas, Montague and Neville of the Exchequer, received their provisional discharge—their quietus as people said ; they were replaced by more devoted men. Two days afterwards there occurred a great promotion in the class which stood next to the judges, that of the serjeants-at-law ; at the banquet which they gave to the Lord Chancellor they bore on their rings the words ' God, the King, and the law' (Deus, lex, et rex) ; some of them were at once promoted to higher places. Christopher Milton, for instance, brother of the poet, was raised to that of a baron of the exchequer.

No one deceived himself as to the ground and object of these alterations. ' They might have kept their places,' says Barrillon of the old judges, ' if they had been willing to declare that the King of England has the right of dispensing with the laws.' And their resistance was not, strictly speaking, attributed to their conscientiousness, but to their apprehension of being called to account for compliance by Parliament at some future time [2] ; it made a certain impression that there were men of penetration found who held it safer to adhere to the declarations of the two Houses than to support the King. Those who attached themselves to the latter were supposed to be of opinion that he would keep the upper hand. And the way in which their subserviency was to be made use of had already been considered with much precision. ' Now that once,' says a letter written by Monsignor Adda at the beginning of May, ' the refractory judges have been replaced

---

[1] ' The judges goe upon these grounds.' State Trials xi. 1198. On the main question, however, even Hallam says ' it is by no means evident that the decision in this particular case of Hales was against law.' (ii. 227, ed. 1846.)

[2] ' Ils ont cru trop s'exposer aux peines portées par les actes du parlement contre ceux, qui sont convaincus d'en avoir violé les actes.'

by persons who have credit for sound judgment, an accusation is to be brought before them against Sir Edward Hales, lately named governor of Dover, for being in the King's service without having taken the Test Oath ; he will lay the King's dispensation before them in his defence, and the judges will acquit him ; when then the right of dispensation has been recognised by the expounders of the law, people will form the conviction that the King does not wish to introduce an arbitrary government, but only to maintain the prerogatives legally belonging to the crown ; it was expected that this decision would produce a favourable impression in Parliament also.' ' On the first assembling of Parliament,' adds the Venetian Vignola, ' it will be shown to that body that the King has the laws for him on the point which gave occasion to the prorogation : for what has been declared legal by the judges, that, by virtue of the statutes, passes for law in England[1].'

The issue of the affair was not however yet completely certain ; when it was to be brought to a decision in Trinity Term (June 1686), Herbert, who had now been raised to the post of Lord Chief Justice, held it necessary to assure himself beforehand of the opinion of each one of the twelve judges. He summoned them together on a certain day at Serjeant's Inn in Fleet-street, and laid before them, in due form, the question whether the King had the right of granting a dispensation from the statute, and of appointing officers in the army on the ground of such a dispensation. Some would have preferred to put off their answer ; one was disposed to deny the legality of dispensation in cases concerning the Church ; another declared himself even now against the claim ; but the result was that Herbert could say, when the case was being tried, that of the twelve judges ten were decidedly in favour of the right of dispensation[2].

---

[1] ' Nella prima sessione del parlamento S. M. farà vedere che tutto quello si è operato nel tempo del suo regno, è stato con fundamento delle leggi, e particolarmente nell punto dell' introduttione de officiali cattolici nelle truppe per il qual è stata interrotta l'assemblea.' A better issue is hoped from the next : ' S.M. nel mentre dando sesto agli affari.'

[2] No protocol was drawn up. The account was furnished by Justice Powell before the House of Commons, June 18, 1689. Grey, Debates ix. 337.

On the 16th of June, 1686, the case was tried in the Court
of King's Bench.   Sir Edward Hales was accused of having
been for many years colonel of infantry without having taken
the oaths prescribed by law: 'by this neglect he had even
disregarded his duty as a subject, for that his conduct had
disqualified him for being in the King's service'—a turn of
the argument no doubt adopted on purpose, in order to
prepare for the conclusion at which the promoters of the
suit desired to arrive.   The plaintiff maintained 'that the
King's dispensation was the King's affair, and did not touch
subjects, who were bound by the statute.'   The counsel for
the defence directed his argument to this very point.   He
argued 'that the service of the Prince was a duty on which no
Parliamentary statute could have any effect; when it was
said that it was open to anybody to qualify himself for the
King's service by submission to the Act, that would mean
that any one might also withdraw himself from that service
by non-submission, a principle which, if extended far enough,
would destroy the King's service.'   With much forethought
any mention of religion was avoided in this argument; the
lawyer's point of view only was maintained; but the court,
in deciding for the defendant, decided also the political question connected with the legal one, and decided it in the
interest of the prerogative against the Parliamentary statute.
And the court was not content with pronouncing this indirect
decision.   Chief Justice Herbert proclaimed at the same time
some general propositions which he said were recognised by
the judges as the law of the land.   The sum of them is 'that
it is a privilege inseparably connected with the sovereignty of
the King to dispense with the penal laws and that according
to his own judgment; the right had not been given him,'
continues the statement, 'by the people, but was the ancient
remains of the sovereign power and prerogative of the kings
of England, which never had been and never could be taken
from him.'

However the posts of the highest judges might be occupied,
the decision which proceeded from them still possessed, as
such, a great authority in the country.   It appeared a gain of
great importance for the King that he could, in opposition to

the declarations of the House of Commons, appeal to the
sentence of the judges, and so maintain his assertion of the
legality of his measures. Nothing prevented him from receiving still more Catholic officers into his service, a step
which he held almost necessary to make him completely
secure of the army. But in every other department also he
could promote his friends without regard to the Test Oath.
He appeared, as a Venetian says, to be the master of the laws.

But another scheme, not less comprehensive and thoroughgoing, had been already conceived.

King James, provoked by the conduct of the Bishop of
London in Parliament, to which he chiefly ascribed it that he
met with so much opposition, had immediately after the prorogation · declared in his Privy Council that it did not seem to
him expedient that the Bishop should have a seat and voice
in that body any longer. Compton was at once Clerk of the
Closet and Dean of the Protestant Chapel Royal, which still
continued to exist after the death of Charles II : the King
deprived him of these two places also. It was not doubted
that if it were in his power, James would deprive him of his
bishopric too : chronicles and collections of records were
searched through to see if a precedent could not be found for
such a step.

This however does not seem to have been thought practicable ; the Bishop remained in his office, and did not allow
the royal displeasure to disturb him in administering it according to his Protestant principles.

James II demanded, as we mentioned, that no sermons
should be preached in the national church against the religion
which he, the King, professed ; he was especially annoyed by
the lectures given on the catechism on Sunday afternoons, in
which the points in dispute between the two confessions were
discussed. He had the Archbishops of Canterbury and York
summoned, that he might desire them to discontinue this
arrangement, which he said had no foundation in the regulations of Edward VI and of Elizabeth, for that then homilies
prescribed by authority had been read to the people. The
archbishops took counsel with other bishops, but declared
after some days that it was impossible for them to comply

with his request; for that there were many who could only
come to church in the afternoon, and that it was contrary to
their episcopal duty to deprive such persons of the explanation of the catechism, or even of the instruction given about
points of controversy; all that was practicable was that such
points should be discussed with discretion; that they had
warned the preachers never to forget that their King professed
Catholicism, and to avoid all invidious expressions[1]. But such
restrictions could not be imposed without a complete suppression of the practice complained of. The episcopal clergy did
not think that their position required them to submit to constraint, for they maintained that their Church was the dominant
one in England, and that even the Reformed Church in France,
though under Catholic supremacy, had never allowed itself to
be forbidden controversy. The King thought fit to renew an
ordinance of his brother which warned the clergy against controversial preaching; but it was remarked that what might in
the first instance have been honestly meant was now only
intended to suppress the anti-Catholic zeal of the preachers[2].
It became, as it were, a point of honour for the latter not to
be silent, just as it was a point of honour for the King to
confine freedom of speech within certain limits in reference to
the religion which he professed. That he did not attain his
end, and in his capital least of all, he thought was chiefly the
fault of the Bishop of London, whom he suspected of conniving at transgressions of his orders.

Irritable and sensitive by nature, and under a feeling of
having been injured, the King on his side now proceeded to a

[1] Bonnet, who is well informed about ecclesiastical affairs, Feb. 23, 1686:
'Empescher l'explication du catéchisme ce seroit renverser la plus considérable
partie de leur liturgie et priver le peuple du fruit qui leur en revient, qui est d'estre
instruits dans la verité de leur religion, ce qui ne se peut faire sans expliquer les
dogmes de celle qui luy est opposée: mais qu'ils avoient ordonné à tous les pre-
dicateurs de la faire avec toute la modestie imaginable, de s'abstenir de tout terme
odieux et de bien considérei de quelle façon ils parleroient de la religion de leur
souverain, pour lequel ils ne sauroient avoir trop d'égard.'

[2] 'Il vescovo di Londra, ammonito piu volte della bontà del re a voler imporre
qualche freno alla licenza di predicanti contro la religione cattolica qual S. M
professava—il re avisato che l'invettive andavano aumentando si è risoluto dis-
graciarlo.' (Amb. extraordinari, 1686.)

striking demonstration. He ordered the paper of Claude, before referred to, to be burned at the Exchange by the hand of the hangman. It contained a justification of the good reception which the French refugees received under the influence of the Bishop of London. The reason assigned by James for this step was that his great ally was abused in it. Louis XIV did not at all approve of James' conduct; for he thought that such a proceeding for the first time decidedly attracted men's attention to writings of this kind. But James thought it important to show what his sentiments were.

Public affrays soon followed. Philip William, of the Catholic line (that of Neuburg), had lately succeeded to the dignity of Elector Palatine. His resident in England, an English Catholic, was, by virtue of his privileges as ambassador, fitting up a chapel, and that in the middle of the capital, while the Catholic places of worship hitherto established were situated near the court at Westminster: we are assured that the resident acted not only with the consent, but at the instigation, of the King[1]. The Protestant population became agitated at this, and the Lord Mayor thought it necessary to forbid the building of the chapel, which was intended to be a public one, to go on. The King maintained that this had been brought about by no one else than the Bishop of London, but that he would no longer endure opposition to a just cause; if the faction threw off the mask, that would be only an occasion for him to promote the interests of Catholicism all the more[2]. In vain did the Elector inform him that he attached no importance to the erection of the chapel; the King insisted upon it, especially as he was told that sermons preached in the very middle of the city might be expected to have a result beneficial to the religion which he professed. At the opening of the chapel disorderly scenes were witnessed; they were stopped, however, as on other occasions, by the train-bands; for no one

---

[1] Vignola : ' Nel corpo della città, ove non ven' è alcuna altra—con il consenso del re, anzi col motivo che si hebbe di S. M.' 13 Maggio.

[2] Barrillon : ' Que le maire ayant été suscité par l'évesque de Londres, à s'opposer à l'établissement de cette chapelle.'

desired to give the King an opportunity for ordering his regular troops to interfere, as he threatened to do [1].

In the beginning of May the dispute assumed a still more personal colour, and at the same time fastened on a definite object.

The rector of St. Giles', in London, Dr. Sharp, had drawn up one of the first congratulatory addresses with which the King had been greeted on his accession; it had been composed under the influence of James' first declaration, and had expressed devotion both to the crown and to the Episcopal Church. Its author, a worthy man in his whole conduct, and one whose sermons were heard with pleasure, had in one of them dwelt at length, not so much upon single controverted points, as upon the question how far the Church of England was a true church. The occasion for doing so had been furnished him by a member of his congregation, who after the preceding service, as the worshippers were leaving church, had pressed into his hand a paper in which the claim of the Catholic Church to be the only true one was mentioned. Its arguments seem to have coincided with the reflections which Charles II had left behind him in his papers. Dr. Sharp contested the claim, and expounded the idea that the Protestant, and especially the English, Church must be regarded as the truly universal Church. He took care not to introduce anything personally offensive, and neither touched upon affairs of state nor upon questions of theological controversy, other than that which formed his immediate subject; but the notion of catholicity which he set forth, and the reference to the religion of Charles II which his exposition voluntarily or involuntarily recalled to his hearers' minds, were the topics best suited to arouse the King's sensitiveness—for James attached the highest importance to this part of the subject. After the Chancellor had had a conference with Sharp, which held out no prospect of any violent step being taken, there was issued unexpectedly an order of the King to the Bishop of London directing him to suspend the rector from his

---

[1] Barrillon: 'Les gens sages craignent, que, s'il arrive quelque désordre au sujet de cette chapelle, le roi ne prenne le prétexte à mettre des troupes en differents endroits de Londres.' May 6.

office for a breach of the ordinance against controversial preaching already referred to. The government wished to make an example, and at the same time to test the Bishop's disposition to obey.

The Bishop replied that he was ready to comply with the King's orders in all cases in which his conscience allowed it, but that in this matter he must, as judge, proceed according to law, and that he could not condemn Dr. Sharp before he had heard him and examined the case. But a judicial investigation, or even a public hearing, would have been thoroughly disagreeable to the King. The very essence of his claim may be thus stated :—that the Bishop was under an obligation to obey him on his order without further examination ; for was not James the head of the Church of England, its supreme bishop? Had not the Papacy's highest rights of supervision been transferred to him by law ? What was the meaning of his supremacy if he could not by a mere command procure the suspension of a parish priest who was disagreeable to him ; and must see the bishop of his capital city oppose him in this, as in everything which he had at heart, with influence superior to his own?

The great historical question whether a Catholic could fulfil the duties of an English king and exercise his prerogatives was here brought to a focus. The Whigs and Dissenters had denied, the Tories and Episcopalians had affirmed, the possibility ; but the latter came themselves to feel still more than their adversaries the inconsistencies which arose from such a combination. For the English crown had been to a peculiar extent endowed with the spoils of the Papacy ; as much so as any crown in the world : what a contradiction that a zealous Catholic prince wished to exercise the rights transferred to him by the revolt from the Papacy! But the dominant party conceived in all seriousness the project not only of doing this but of employing these very rights to the advantage of the Church from which England had then departed.

The plan first thought of was to employ the authority of the metropolitan, and to invite the Archbishop of Canterbury to suspend the Bishop of London, as the latter had been invited to suspend the rector of St. Giles'; but Archbishop Sancroft could never have been induced to take such a step, as might be inferred from the resistance which had been already met with on his part[1]. It was needful to set the authority of the royal supremacy in its full extent against that of the bishops. The first thought was to appoint a vicar-general of the King for his spiritual prerogatives, such as Thomas Cromwell had been under Henry VIII; and Sunderland, who only longed for power, seemed ready to accept such a position. But the King was not disposed to concentrate too much power in the hands of any one man; he decided on having the powers of the supremacy exercised by an ecclesiastical commission[2], a system of which he approved in general.

The objection was obvious that an earlier ecclesiastical commission had been abolished by Parliament, and the creation of a new one with similar authority forbidden. It was not the case that the government was resolved to transgress a Parliamentary statute openly, for the King did not wish to assume a position altogether outside the laws; but it was thought to be sufficient if the powers on account of which the old commission had been abolished were omitted from the authority granted to the new; it was further said that the government's intention was only to exercise a regular jurisdiction, not to create an extraordinary one such as that of the earlier commission had been. The legality of this act was doubtful even to the Lord Chancellor. He held it advisable to collect the opinions of other judges afresh before he signed the proclamation by which the new commission was called into life. Its wording is partly no doubt taken from the instructions to the old commission, but partly also from the document which gave full powers to Cromwell[3]. A

---

[1] Barrillon, July 8: 'Le roi d'Angleterre cherche présentement comme il pourra selon les loix interdire l'évesque de Londres lui-même et commettre son autorité à un autre'

[2] I take the account from the despatch of Citters, July 6/16.

[3] The commission was not empowered, like that of Queen Elizabeth, 'to require by all wayes you can devise, of all offenses,' nor, 'to enquire of all and singular hereticall, erroneous, and offensive opinions,' nor, as may be well understood, directed to enforce uniformity, but 'to enquire, search out, and call before you all and every ecclesiastical person or persons as shall offend, and them and every one

difference of intention may be easily detected. The object of
the new commission was rather the exercise of disciplinary
powers, like those of the Vicar-General, than the exercise of a
criminal jurisdiction like that of the old commission. It was
not intended to search after departures from ecclesiastical
uniformity, but to keep the clergy under strict supervision.
The earlier commission was the representative of royalty combined with episcopacy; the later, of the highest authority in
opposition to the Episcopal Church itself.

On this commission the most important functions were
assigned to Lord Chancellor Jeffreys, a man absolutely reckless in the administration of his office. Nothing was to be
done without him; the quorum, that is the number of members sufficient to give a valid decision (three), was not to be
complete without him. The Lord Chancellor was assigned
a position similar to that formerly held by the vicar-general,
so far as such a position could be reconciled with the existence
of a commission: and this arrangement harmonised with the
notion entertained by the government of restoring Catholicism
by the same means by which it had formerly been abolished.
The task of Jeffreys however, though similar in form, was
in substance precisely opposite, to that of Cromwell. Thomas
Cromwell had by his Injunctions laid the foundation on which
the Protestantism of later times was erected; Jeffreys was
to put in force orders calculated to open a free path for the
return of Catholicism.

Besides Jeffreys, Sunderland, Lawrence Hyde, Earl of
Rochester, and Herbert, the Archbishop of Canterbury, and
the Bishops of Durham and Rochester were also to sit on
the commission: the aged Archbishop Sancroft hesitated

---

of them to correct and punish . . . . by suspending and depriving them from all
promotions ecclesiastical,' &c. On the other hand, this bears some resemblance
to the commission of the Vicar-General, Thomas Cromwell (Wilkins, Concilia
Magnae Britanniae iii. 785): 'De vita moribus et conversatione tam praesidentium
sive praelatorum . . . . (in locis ecclesiasticis) quam aliarum personarum . . . .
inquirendum et inquiri faciendum; ac illos (illi) quos . . . culpabiles fore com-
pereritis pro modo culpae corrigendi, puniendi et coercendi et, si delicti qualitas
poposcerit, officiis sive beneficiis suis pro tempore vel in perpetuum privandi et
amovendi vel ad tempus ab eisdem suspendendi.'

about taking his seat upon it; in the first place because, as he said, his health did not allow him to cross the Thames so often as these new functions would require;—whereon the King, in one of the ebullitions in which his displeasure was so ready to show itself, had him told that that would also hinder him from coming again to his court at Whitehall. Sancroft however also remarked that he could not take part in a spiritual commission in which a layman, the Lord Chancellor, was to preside [1].

The objections made to the commission referred generally to ecclesiastical law. The contradiction implied in the wish of a Catholic king to act as head of the Anglican Church was not much dwelt upon; for if the King had been declared not to possess the rights which had been transferred to him at the state's emancipation from the Papacy, those rights would have reverted to the Pope. On the contrary, the notion of a transference of rights from the Papacy to the crown was firmly maintained; the King possessed just these rights and none greater; but not even the Pope had ever possessed, either over the legislative power of Convocation or in reference to the official conduct and jurisdiction of the bishops, any such right as that now claimed by the King [2].

On the 4th of August the commission opened its proceedings by an examination of the Bishop in the apartments of the Privy Council. The trial offers no features of peculiar interest, especially as no discussion of the legality of the commission was allowed. The Chancellor reminded the Bishop that the members were completely convinced of its legality, and that they would otherwise not have been worthy of the honour of sitting upon it; the Bishop's counsel restricted themselves to prove the blamelessness of his conduct up to that time. Compton had required the rector not to mount the pulpit again in his diocese till he had given satisfaction to the King; and

---

[1] 'Qu'il ne peut, étant le chef du clergé d'Angleterre, faire partie d'une commission dont la principale autorité réside en la personne d'un laique.'

[2] Robert Atkyns, Discourse concerning the ecclesiastical jurisdiction in the realme of England: ' The exclusion of the Pope in the time of King Henry VIII made no diminution of the power or jurisdiction of the clergy, as to determining of ecclesiastical causes.' State Trials xi. 1148-1154.

this the rector had in vain tried to give. The Bishop refused
however to proceed to a formal suspension, because in that
case there must first be a trial. The members of the commission were divided in their opinions. Lord Rochester, who
had already disapproved of the removal of the Bishop from
the Privy Council, judged in this case that he must be allowed
time for the bringing of a formal process against Dr. Sharp
to an end; even the Lord Chancellor inclined to this view.
Sunderland opposed them[1]. He never in any case which
occurred lost sight of his principal object, which was to set
Rochester at variance with the King. He himself expressed
his opinion in favour of the suspension of the Bishop of London; Bishop Crewe of Durham went with him. In presence
of this difference of opinion among the commissioners, Sunderland declared it advisable to have recourse to the King
himself. The commission, in which no Catholic sat, because
it was entrusted with the exercise of the rights of the
supremacy, requested the King, who had become a Catholic
and was under the direction of a zealous spiritual adviser,
to declare his own personal will in a case which had an
intimate connexion with religious differences. Rochester was
persuaded to declare, in presence of the King, his readiness
to submit beforehand to whatever opinion his Majesty should
hold. Thereon the King declared himself in favour of the
suspension of the Bishop. The motive which influenced him
and the Catholics about him was that the opposite party
would triumph if this result were not arrived at. And certainly the object of the plan originally formed was to withdraw
the ecclesiastical administration of the capital from the hands
of the refractory Compton; and to place it in those of men
in whom more confidence was reposed: two members of
the commission itself, the Bishops of Durham and Rochester
were entrusted with this office together with the Bishop of

---

[1] Barrillon: 'Mylord trésorier n'était pas d'avis d'interdire l'évesque à Londres,
croyant qu'il est juste de luy donner le tems pour exécuter les ordres qui luy
étoient envoyés (namely a suspension after regular proceedings). Le chancelier
penchoit aussi à l'avis de Mylord trésorier, et peut-être que les autres commissaires
s'y seroient conformés; mais Mylord Sunderland représenta, qu'il étoit d'une
nécessité absolue de savoir les intentions du roi.'

Peterborough. Henry Compton retired to his episcopal country house at Fulham, and the visitor is still vividly reminded of him there. He was acquainted with and fond of botany, and planted the exotic trees which are seen adorning the garden of the palace in the fulness of their rich foliage.

King James had laid hands on two powerful instruments of authority; one to give him freedom in the appointment of officers and civil functionaries, and even in granting ecclesiastical benefices, in spite of all the resolutions of Parliament; the other to enable him to stifle in its origin any resistance to such appointments which might be aroused in the Church of England or among Protestants in general. The prerogative, because now possessed by a king who did not adhere to the Established Church, became stricter and more precise in its pretensions than it had ever been before. Any feeling that the state of affairs was still in accordance with law was only kept up by the fact that the King himself still regarded his measures as simply provisional.

CHAPTER V.

JAMES II adhered to his purpose of effecting in a parliamentary way the repeal of the statutes by which the Catholics
were oppressed, and of so making the measure legally valid.
But in this case, as in more than one previously, Scotland was
to set an example to the English Parliament.

On the 29th of April, 1686, the Parliament of Edinburgh was opened by the reading of a letter, in place of a
speech from the throne, in which the King reminded that
body of his exertions to promote the material prosperity of
the country, especially in relation to trade, and announced a
general pardon for all offences and crimes committed against
the crown, but on the other hand recommended to the care
of Parliament his subjects of the Roman Catholic religion,
'who had given so many proofs of their loyalty and love of
peace': he begged that they might be granted the full
protection of the laws, and might be relieved of obligations
with which their religion could not be reconciled.

It was the same Parliament which, at its last session, had
made the King a declaration of the most zealous devotion to
his interest; he hoped that it would also grant him the
repeal of the penal laws against his fellow-believers, and the
abolition of the oaths which prevented their holding appointments in the public service.

But the sympathies which James II had won in Scotland
did not certainly reach far enough to procure him satisfaction
in this matter. Episcopalianism had attached itself to the crown
in a struggle in which both were threatened, but could not

be inclined to join it in a cause odious to the Episcopal Church itself. For the anti-Catholic spirit was still more vehement in Scotland than in England ; Popery was still regarded there as idolatry. If the bishops had been willing to consent to the King's proposals they would have become suspected of apostasy from the Protestant religion, and would have confirmed the charges made against them in this respect. The nobles would have feared that their own positions might be impaired by the intruding Catholics, who in many cases were their old adversaries. They saw in the oaths a bulwark even against the court, especially as it was then constituted ; a bulwark which they ought not themselves to overthrow.

Even the Parliament's first answer, in which conscientious obligations were mentioned, gave promise of resistance. The Lords of Articles then laid a bill before the estates which promised the Catholics—(they were described as 'members of the Roman communion,' for even the expression 'Roman Catholic' went too far for the Scots who would have been best pleased to have spoken outright of Papists, in the style of the old laws)—freedom for their private but not for their public worship ; the Lords held fast to the other statutes against Popery. The committee of the estates amended this bill by a still more emphatic expression of Protestant zeal, and by an express confirmation of the oaths as imperative upon all persons in the public, even in the military service. And it was by no means certain whether the first concession would pass in the assembly of estates ; the government held it good not to allow the bill in its actual form to be put to the vote, especially as it would have contravened the King's intentions. The court for some weeks flattered itself with a hope of producing a different disposition, but then decided to prorogue the Assembly which remained stubborn, as it had previously prorogued that of England [1].

But the King thought that in Scotland the national constitution subjected him to less restraint than in England. Provoked at

---

[1] Barrillon, June 13: 'On ne mettra pas les choses au hazard d'un refus, si on ne voit quelque certitude d'obtenir ce qui est demandé, le parlement sera prorogé avant qu'il puisse former une résolution contraire.'

the unexpected contradiction which he met with, he ordered that a public Catholic service should be set up in the chapel of his palace, Holyrood House,—an order which rested upon the same claim to personal exemption from the laws which had prompted the opening of the chapel at St. James', but which was still more significant, as King James was not himself present at Holyrood. At the same time, moreover, he said plainly that the Scottish Catholics should be allowed to have private worship in their houses, and that he took them under his royal protection against the rigour of the laws. He did not think that he required in Scotland a special judicial recognition of the dispensing power; his resolution was to have the arrangements which he thought needful adopted by the Privy Council of that country; afterwards they would be sanctioned by Parliament, either by the present or by a future one [1].

His purpose was similar in England also, on which the events in Scotland had an immediate retroactive effect, as might be expected.

For in spite of their renewed legislative separation the two countries were still most closely connected in their inner movements. They had been brought together not so much by the existence of a common sovereign as by resistance to him; the personal union of the crowns called forth a national union of the peoples also. There can accordingly be no doubt that the refractoriness of the Scots was connected with the resistance which the King experienced in England. James II regarded the affair principally from a personal point of view; he said that he had now learned to know his enemies: 'so much the worse for them,' he exclaimed; 'he would chastise them for such behaviour.'

The highest places in the three kingdoms were in the possession of the same party which had first obtained the upper hand at the time of the Restoration and had subsequently recovered it in the last years of Charles II. The

---

[1] Barrillon: 'Qu'après avoir établi par les ordres de son conseil d'Ecosse la liberté qu'il prétendoit donner aux catholiques, il la feroit confirmer par le même parlement ou par un autre, si celuy-ci ne veut pas s'y commettre.'

post of Lord High Treasurer, which was esteemed the most honourable in England, was occupied by Lord Rochester; his brother, Henry Earl of Clarendon, was Lord Lieutenant of Ireland; the man who had hitherto been most powerful in Scotland, William Douglas, first Duke of Queensberry, was connected with the two brothers by the marriage of his son to one of their nieces. The system which they pursued in common was that of maintaining the Episcopal Church against all serious attacks from the one side or from the other, and of taking it under their protection so effectually, even against the Catholic King, that it might remain unshaken even at the next change of sovereigns. King James ascribed the failure of his Scottish attempt principally to Queensberry, who, he thought, was already in alliance with the presumptive successor to the throne, the Prince of Orange. The great turn which both political and religious affairs had taken appeared in full clearness in both kingdoms. Episcopalianism, which had seemed inseparably connected with the royal authority, and which accordingly had submitted even to a Catholic King, was now estranged from, and fell into open opposition to, that authority. The Episcopalians of England greeted what had happened in Scotland as a victory of their own. What the King undertook and instituted appeared transitory so long as it was not confirmed by the two Parliaments.

As the time of the prorogation in England was drawing to its close, no one could imagine that the new session would produce a better result than the earlier one had produced. Neither the King nor his Catholic advisers wished to expose themselves to a defeat. If the end they had set before themselves could not be attained under the influence of the Tories attached to Lord Clarendon, they were of opinion that that influence must as a first measure be broken down.

It had been found easy to deprive Queensberry of his offices; the Lord Lieutenant of Ireland had already had a zealous Catholic, Tyrconnel, placed at his side, who crippled and checked him; but would the King also decide to remove Rochester from the public service, a man to whom he was under the greatest obligations? Personal considerations had never much influence with James; he was induced to believe that he could never attain his end so long as Rochester was in office, and that he could only govern by the help of ministers with whom he agreed completely.

This was one of the fundamental ideas of Sunderland, who at a later epoch became the principal founder of the system of united ministries: in the present instance, no doubt, he followed his own interest; for Rochester was the very man who stood in the way of his getting the direction of the administration into his own hands.

It was no doubt only as a means for getting rid of Rochester that it was decided to offer him the alternative, that he must either become a Catholic or part with his high office. Some one objected that it would be a misfortune if he decided to go to mass; for that he would even then remain · an enemy of Catholicism. The King, who knew him best, replied that that was not to be feared, and that nothing was risked by leaving him the choice [1]

Barrillon first made overtures to the Lord High Treasurer on this point, then the King himself told him what had been determined. Rochester replied that the danger of losing his office on a question which touched his conscience could not have any effect upon him; but at this crisis he consented that a formal discussion should be held in his presence on the points in dispute between the two confessions; it took place at Whitehall, and ended with a declaration by Rochester that it had confirmed him in his Protestant convictions. The King remarked that his dear brother-in-law had no feeling whatever for the truth; that he had only attended the debate to show his party that in order to maintain himself in office he need. only have gone over. After Rochester had declared himself, the King stated in council in the January of 1687 that he had no reason to be dissatisfied with the Treasurer's administration, but that Rochester might not remain in the high position which he occupied, and on which all England had fixed its eyes, since every one knew that he disapproved of all that was done for the benefit of Catholicism: the general good must with the King claim

---

[1] 'Qu'on ne bazardera rien, en le lui proposant.'

precedence over his personal friendship. He adopted at
the same time the monarchical idea of not allowing the
high offices of the old feudal state, which united excessive
powers in one hand, to exist any longer. The place of the
Lord High Treasurer was occupied by a commission, among the
members of which, moreover, a Catholic, Lord Bellasis, was
admitted, in accordance with the fundamental principle which
now prevailed.

Lawrence Hyde, Earl of Rochester, must be regarded as
one of the principal founders of the High Church Tory party.
At the moment when Charles II got into a position in which
it seemed that he must yield to the pressure of the Exclusionists and Whigs, Hyde, by negotiating the new French
treaty, procured him secretly and adroitly the means of escaping from this necessity. He afterwards did more than any
one else to re-establish that connexion between the King
and the elements of the long Parliament of the Restoration,
which had been broken off since the fall of Danby, and to
strengthen the crown by a rigorous execution of the statutes
beneficial to the prerogative, and by a financial administration
adequate to the public need. He paved the way for Charles'
successor, but did not gain control over him, for James had
his own independent connexion with France, which moreover
embodied the views of a religious party. Rochester adhered
strictly to the exclusive Protestantism, and to the High Church
character, of the constitution ; in James II the Catholic idea
combined with his conception of royalty to make him esteem it
his duty and his right to change that character. His principal
motive for the removal of Rochester sprang from the representations made to him that with such a first minister he
would never get the approaching Parliament to go so far as
to grant the Catholics the alleviations of their position which
he had in view. But if he now dismissed, for this reason
only, his near relation and partisan of many years' standing, to
whom he was under the greatest obligations, such a dismissal
was also an unmistakeable threat for all others who should not
comply with his will. He fixed, however, so early a day as
the 29th of April, 1687, for the end of the new prorogation
of Parliament, for he thought that would give him time

enough to convince himself by personal enquiry who would join him and who would not. The purpose had been formed and was plainly expressed not to tolerate any one in any office dependent upon the crown who did not agree with the King on the two questions which were to be decided by the next Parliament, that of the repeal of the penal laws and that of the abolition of the oaths, and who did not declare himself ready to support the King upon them. A preliminary enquiry on these matters seemed to many to be contrary to the constitution: James II, however, did not hesitate to make in person, without delay, the experiment on which everything depended for him [1].

At this time the word 'closeting' came into existence. It describes the negotiations of the King in his cabinet or 'closet' with the personages whose support he wished to gain for his object. So far as is known the chief objection made to his proposals was that the abolition of the need of taking the oaths would exercise a controlling influence on the composition of Parliament; for that the Catholics when once admitted would only allow laws to pass in which they saw something advantageous for themselves, and would repeal the old laws by which the established religion was secured. In vain did the King remind the objectors that there were too few Catholics in the country to have a decisive influence in Parliament; his representations had no effect, for no one doubted that under the influence of state authority conversions in crowds would ensue, as was being shown at that very time in Scotland. And how easy would it be for the Catholics to combine at some time with the Protestant Nonconformists in order then to transfer to other hands the authority which naturally belongs to the majority of a parliamentary assembly. The question was not so much of the limits of kingly and parliamentary power as of constituting

---

[1] 'Le roi d'Angleterre est résolu de faire expliquer positivement tous ceux, qui ont des employs dépendants de lui, et de scavoir ce qu'il en peut attendre pour les choses, qu'il désire d'eux, avant que le parlement se rassemble ; cette nécessité de s'expliquer et de promettre nettement de consentir à la révocation des loix pénales et du test paroit à bien de gens une nouveauté, qui blesse leurs libertés et leurs privilèges.'

the elements of the latter in such a way that the measure might be decisive for all future times. People shared the thought expressed by the Bishop of London, that they ought not to grant an entrance to the Catholic religion, thinking that supported by the influence of the crown it would gradually get the upper hand, and bring Protestantism to ruin[1]. Against these popular conceptions no assurances of the King, neither the promises which he did not spare nor his threats could effect anything[2]. It was striking, but under these circumstances very intelligible, that James met with opposition among those very men who had previously associated themselves with the tendencies of the government. When he required among others John Moore, who as Lord Mayor had laid the foundation for the restoration of the royal authority in the city, to support the crown in its present project, as he had supported it in its earlier projects, Moore answered him roundly and plainly that he was told that his Majesty wished to introduce Popery, and that he could not lend a hand to such work. The King lost no time in removing him from his place—he was then an alderman; in like manner, and for a similar reason, Rich the chamberlain lost his office: both were in political matters zealous royalists, but both were also men who did not wish to support the extension of the royal authority to the province of religion. Similar measures were taken in all branches of the public service. The Treasurer of the royal household, Newport, and its controller, Maynard, who had borne their staves of office for many years with great honour, were, on account of their resistance, and without regard to their merits, removed from their offices and replaced by men of more accommodating character. This rigour ex-

---

[1] Barrillon : ' Ce seroit ouvrir la porte à la religion catholique, qui étant appuyée de la faveur et de l'autorité royale deviendroit la plus forte et opprimeroit avec le tems la religion protestante.'

[2] Sarotti : ' I piu veri motivi della proroga sono, che non vi é stato tempo sufficiente per poterse del re o suoi amorevoli andare negotiando con tutti quelli' che si desiderava e si credeva necessario.' He mentions then further : ' Le diligenze di S.M. e le applicationi pin fisse e continue con tutti i mezzi possibili per guadagnaie quel numero maggiore che puo con le ragioni, con le preghiere, con le offerte di cariche honorifiche e lucrose e di grosse summe di danaro ancora.'

tended even to the military service. Both Lord Shrewsbury,
who under these circumstances had taken a step contrary
to that expected, and had passed over to Protestantism, and
Lord Lumley, lost their places as colonels in the cavalry : even
the subaltern officers who should declare against the King's
purposes were threatened with dismissal from the service.

There was at that time in London an extraordinary ambassador representing at once the States-General and the
Prince of Orange, Eberhard Weede, lord of Dijkvelt. From
the first he held a commission to assure the members of the
Parliament which was then still expected to assemble, that
the Republic was penetrated by sentiments of devotion to the
nation and crown of England[1]; from the second he brought
with him friendly letters to the leaders of the Parliamentary
party, which he delivered to them. And it could not be
without influence that the presumptive successor, to whom all
expectations for the future attached themselves, was diligent
in renewing his connexion with those statesmen. In other
respects Dijkvelt seems to have been rather passive than
active. He had long audiences with the King ; he negotiated
even with Catholics and Nonconformists ; but he did not
take up a decided position.

The dislike which the King met with from the English
arose in them spontaneously for the most part. It was
doubled by the assignment to Catholics of the places wrested
from the Protestants, if not always, at least in most cases.
The personal negotiations referred to above rather provoked
than softened opposition.

It made an extraordinary impression on King James that
even Vice-Admiral Herbert, who was under the greatest
personal obligations to him—for James had made provision
for his education, had promoted him step by step in his career,
and had created for him the post which he then occupied—
opposed him. James reminded him of the favour which he
had shown him, and requested him, in return for all that he
had done for him, to oblige him in this one matter only, and

---

[1] 'To convince the nation of the *deference* of the States to the crown of
England,' as Diest expresses it (January 11/21, 1688).

to support him in the abolition of the requirement to take
the oaths ; Herbert answered that he should wound his honour
and his conscience by such compliance. The King was amazed
and perplexed. He saw that he would not attain his end by
this way [1], and expressed his intention (on March 24) of not
reassembling the Parliament even in April.

But it was inconsistent with his character and with his
principles to renounce his purpose on account of such difficulties. What he blamed most in his father and in his
brother was that they had not been steadfast enough. Far
from giving up his purpose, he intended, on the contrary, to
carry it out in a more comprehensive form. The time seemed
to him to have now come for putting in practice what he had
said at the beginning of his reign—that if the Episcopal Church
did not comply with his wishes he would turn to the Nonconformists. It had been even remarked to him by one or two
of the great nobles of Scotland that he would obtain nothing
for the Catholics unless he at the same time did something
for the Protestant Nonconformists. The powerful elements
which at the time of the Rebellion had overthrown the Episcopal Church and the constitution of the realm which was
connected with it still existed ; conquered but not extirpated,
they bore with murmuring and reluctance the ecclesiastical
yoke imposed upon them. The restored King could not
think of reanimating their hostility in all its keenness ; he
rather thought of making them his allies in his strife with the
Episcopal Church by rescinding the laws which oppressed
them. He took up the idea of toleration which had once
already, though in a different sense, been introduced into
the state in Cromwell's time, and which it had never since
been possible to put down again.

The man who conceived it in the deepest and most far-
reaching sense was William Penn the Quaker.

William Penn, the father, had already, without joining any
particular party, favoured the Dissenting sects even in his

---

[1] Barrillon : ' Que les gens qui devroient être les plus attachés à ses interêts et
à sa personne, sont capables de lui manquer et de se faire un point d'honneur et de
conscience s'opposer directement à ses desseins.' The anecdotes connected with
this audience may be left unnoticed.

position as admiral.   Yet it was much against his wish that
his son went over to one of them.   The young Penn felt himself neither satisfied by the external ecclesiastical system
which presented itself to him in Oxford, nor yet attracted by
the life of courts and of the world which he saw in France ;
but from his earliest youth he was very deeply touched by the
words of the 'Friends'—so the Quakers called themselves—
who moved about the country in different directions ; as soon
as he could perform his first independent act, in his twenty-
fourth year, he attached himself openly and irrevocably to that
sect.   He professed their views about the Trinity and Justification, and adopted their external peculiarities.   He, like
others of his sect, refused to take off his hat even before the
highest personage, for he said that there must be a difference
between the honour shown to God and that shown to men.
His resistance to the Acts of Uniformity involved him in
a quarrel with the Church, but not directly with King Charles
II, or with his ministers, who on the contrary showed favour
from time to time to Dissent.   'I beseech thee,' writes Penn,
in the summer of 1669, to Arlington, 'to entreat the King
not to believe every man to be his enemy that cannot shape
his conscience by the narrow forms and prescripts of men's
inventions . . . nor do we own one principle that will not at
all times in our stations fit us to dispute with any . . . the
first place of obedience to his commands[1].'   His resistance
was only directed against the legislative power, to which
he, like his fellow-believers generally, would not allow the
right of making regulations about religion.   In short papers,
which he issued from time to time, he argues that religious
compulsion is repugnant to the essence of the English constitution ; for such compulsion, he said, 'was an attack upon
the rights guaranteed by the fundamental laws, which rights
ought to suffer no injury except in the cases provided for by
the laws ; civil society had existed before Protestantism, and
even before Christianity : was it wished to deny any man the
right of breathing freely and of following his trade or pro-

---

[1] Letter to Lord Arlington, 1st of the 6th month, 1669.   Life prefixed to the
Select Works of W. Penn, xii.

fession because he did not profess Christianity in a certain
form? If the legislative power inflicted imprisonment, or
even merely took away a small book, in the interest of uniformity, it was guilty of an outrage against the rights of freedom and property, which belonged to every one originally,
and had been guaranteed by all together.' He regarded the
part taken by the English in legislation as a further original
right which belonged to them : ' their participation formed
the basis of the representation created by the people ; but the
essential being of the people was not imparted to the representatives, who were still bound to respect the fundamental
laws, the original rights to freedom and property spoken of
above [1].' A statement made in Parliament that religion formed
' a part of our laws, and a part, and a necessary part, of
our government,' aroused him to offer the most zealous contradiction. ' For if,' he said, ' the original rights were given up
for religion's sake, that amounted to a disarming of the civil
magistracy, and to a subjection of the prince to the prelates.'

If we consider the depth and extent of these ideas, and also
the difficulty, bordering on impossibility, of procuring a field
for their growth in England, we shall understand how William
Penn came to have recourse to an attempt at their realisation
beyond the ocean in a new foundation. How many of his
fellow-believers had found a refuge there in the colonies! But
his object was not merely to extend and secure these settle-
ments, but at the same time to put in execution his political
principles, to establish a just government which might serve
as a model to other peoples. ' There alone may there be
space,' he exclaims, ' for such a holy experiment [2].' In Penn-
sylvania, which Charles II, in repayment of a debt due to
Penn's father, assigned to him as hereditary property with
unlimited powers for its internal organisation, he undertook
the task of giving life and embodiment to his ideas, which had
their source partly, indeed, in the original aspirations of his

---

[1] England's present interest considered, Select Works iii. 220. ' Here is no
transessentiating or transsubstantiating of being, from people to representatives, no
more than there is an absolute transferring of a title in a letter of attorney.'
[2] To Harrison. See Janney, Life of Penn 175.

sect, but still more in philosophical abstractions, and recollection of the old Anglo-Saxon times: the three fundamental rights with which he started,—that of voting the laws, that of raising the money necessary for the common good, and that of administering justice,—he deposited in the hands of the free settlers; no one who should engage to live peaceably, and should profess belief in Almighty God, was to be molested on account of his religious worship and belief.

Penn never, however, lost sight of England, where the old personal relations which he had derived from his father, and had maintained, procured him admission at court and a certain influence over the royal brothers. Without their protection he would probably have succumbed to the persecutions of his enemies. When he returned to Windsor, in October 1684, an epoch at which the Dissenters, on account of the previous disorders, were as good as proscribed, he yet recalled their case to the mind of Charles II: 'let him forget the past, think not as a man but as a king, and be just to all parties; then would he be truly king, and have the people for him.' In the Catholics he only saw allies against the domination of the Episcopal Church: after the accession of James II, to whom he had always stood particularly near, and whom he had to thank for a suitable definition of the frontiers of the new colony as well as for other favours, Penn expressed to him his approval of his open profession of Catholicism, and his expectation that even the Protestant Dissenters would benefit by that step, that is, by the King's being in opposition to the dominant Church. James II replied that it was not his will that people who lived peaceably should be molested on account of their religion. Penn thereupon warned his friends and adherents not to provoke the King by attacks upon the Catholic religion. His compliance went so far that he was himself held for a Catholic; he was often obliged to protest that he was not. Such protests however were hardly needed, for nothing could have been more opposed to all his ideas than the restoration of the sovereignty of the Catholic Church. He never shared James' notion of bringing about an union between Catholics and Episcopalians, but expressly declared it impossible: for the obvious reason that the Catholies would infallibly claim the Church property of which the Episcopalians were in possession. He advised the English Church not to oppress the Protestant Dissenters[1], as it needed a counterpoise against the Catholics, who were no doubt few in number, but still powerful, especially through their foreign connexions. He completely approved, not exactly of the dispensing power, but of the reception of Catholic believers into the King's service. For the King must have a free scope for his appointments; he must be able to take every one into his service who was qualified for it, without being hindered by his opinions: had the objectors forgotten what harm had been caused in the last Dutch war by the fact that so many brave Nonconformist seamen had remained excluded from the service, or even if they were admitted to it, had not been zealously attached to it? The monarchy must support itself not on ecclesiastical but on civil obedience. He set forth to the King that if civil rights were altogether independent of religious opinions, no one would be able to think of making the profession of a particular creed a qualification for succession to the throne; all parties would combine into one whole around a civil head; the King would be master of his whole people.

The man who on the other side of the ocean had laid the foundations of a future republic, appeared on this side as the champion of monarchical ideas. His fundamental thought is that civil life is independent of positive creeds; a thought which implies an equal independence for religion from any restriction produced by the connexion of Church and State. He goes back from the Parliament, which identified itself with the existing Church, to the simplest fundamental lines of civil organisation which, according to him, had been already laid down in times anterior to the Christian era.

William Penn possessed in full measure the culture of his century, and was himself a zealous writer, always full of his object. His abstractions remind one sometimes of Hobbes:

---

[1] A persuasive to moderation to church dissenters in prudence and conscience; humbly submitted to the king and his great council; published in the y. 1686 (and therefore in expectation of the Parliament's meeting). Select Works iv. 319

his arguments of Sidney and Sidney's historical learning; like Harrington, he loves to analyse and weigh the interests on which states appear to rest. But all acquires a special character and vigour from the special end which he pursues, namely, the emancipation of his sect from all oppression. We can form a vivid representation of him,—a stately, tall, and somewhat corpulent man, as he walked up and down his room and dictated to his amanuensis, with the stick in his hand which he always used to carry; he struck smartly upon the floor with it when he came to expressions which seemed especially important to him, as though to give them emphasis. His writings are flowing and impressive, like his speeches and his sermons. With all his seriousness he was amiable in intercourse, witty and agreeable in conversation, and always a thorough gentleman. For his doctrine was that a strict piety could be reconciled with the good manners of the world; the operation of his influence depended upon the combination of the one with the other. He had the gift of being able to satisfy the prince and the peasant by his words. Among the sons of the wilderness, the Indian tribes, his dignified and affable bearing, his simple address, which bore the stamp of truth, gained him a confidence such as no other European has ever enjoyed; he became the hero of their traditions. For he was a man still more than he was an Englishman : he had wide sympathies; his religion extended beyond any sectarian notion; the connexion in which he stood with the world filled him with great views. No one who adhered to the Episcopal Church and to the English constitution as it then was could be pleased with him, as people let him feel at the Hague. For him as for others it was necessary, if he was to exercise persuasion, that his hearer should be to some extent on the same ground with him; but then he was irresistible. He obtained the greatest influence over James II. It is an exaggeration when he is described even by his own adherents as almost a favourite of that King; but it is true that he saw him as often as ever he wished, and held the most confidential conversations with him for hours together, at Whitehall, or even at Windsor, where he took a house in the neighbourhood of the Castle. Penn ought not to be made responsible for the individual measures on which the King decided : for he held no official position, and there were many other influences at work with which he had nothing in common. But he exercised the influence of a confidant, whose convictions agreed with the direction which his prince had already taken independently of him. He confirmed James II no doubt in his alienation from the Episcopal Church, and must have contributed most to his conceiving the idea of freedom of conscience more and more comprehensively, and bringing it into prominence with continually increasing energy.

As early as February 1687 an edict was read in the Scottish Privy Council by which James II granted his royal toleration to the moderate Presbyterians, to the Catholics, and to the Quakers ; they were to be allowed, not only to exercise their religion, but to administer the offices conferred upon them [1] and to enjoy benefices : he declares this by virtue of his sovereign authority, royal prerogative, and absolute power. Some reserve and circumspection may be remarked in the answer of the Privy Council, if carefully studied ; on the whole, however, it approves the declaration and believes that there are adequate reasons for it.

In England the King was still seeking at this time to gain admission for his ideas by the employment of his personal influence. But even those who showed themselves most accessible would yet only recognise the right of dispensation for certain definite cases ; the majority, comprising the men of most importance, opposed even this limited concession. While James II again prorogued the Parliament he expressed at the same time in the Privy Council his resolution to accept the principle of religious freedom, for that in his opinion to constrain men's consciences was now certainly impossible, and to attempt it would be ruinous for the country. So far as we hear, one member ventured to speak against the measure : the

---

[1] 'Not by law, as he had proposed. The offices which the King empowers members of nonconforming bodies to hold are designated [by the Privy Council] as " military " and " civil," by which expression spiritual offices were supposed to be excluded.' Documents cited by Wodrow.

others received the announcement in silence. After a report on the sitting published in the newspapers had prepared the way, there appeared on the 4th of April a detailed declaration, in which the King assured, indeed, to the Church of England its possessions and the liberties which it enjoyed, but at the same time suspended all penal laws relating to ecclesiastical affairs: for every one of his subjects was to be at liberty to worship God after his own way and manner. He ordered that neither the oaths of supremacy and allegiance, nor the newly-imposed test oaths, should be in future imposed. All this was ordered on the strength of the royal prerogative, but a confident expectation was expressed that it would be approved by the two Houses of Parliament when the King should hold it good to reassemble them.

All the kings of the house of Stuart made it one of their principal objects to bring their Catholic subjects into harmony with the Protestant constitution. James I employed himself throughout his life in attempts to restore the old unity of the Church as it existed before the rise of the papacy; Charles I worked hard to compose a form of oath which should express the obedience due from subjects in language acceptable to Catholics. Charles II contemplated a reconciliation and fusion of the Roman and Anglican Churches, or at least, as that showed itself to be impracticable, a general indulgence by which even the Catholics should profit. It was not, however, in his nature to expose himself to the danger of a serious estrangement on this question from the Parliament which opposed him. But James II by no means recoiled from such a dispute: he thought that by this very Indulgence he would inspire the monarchical authority with fresh vigour. In the English document he declared the oaths objectionable because they hindered the king from making use of the services of his subjects, which belonged to him by the law of nature. In the Scottish, which brought the monarchical element into still stronger relief throughout, we read that no law, no difference in religion, or other impediment whatsoever, can release subjects from the duty of obedience which connects them with the crown; and that oaths which have such an effect are adverse to religion and loyalty. The King thus adopts the

thought which Penn had expressed ; he takes his stand on the
existence of rights and duties independent of legal definitions.
The Stuart dynasty seemed to be turning into a new path,
almost the same as that upon which the most vigorous princes
of the eighteenth century entered, both in the Protestant and
still more in the Catholic world—princes who have acquired a
great name precisely by their struggle against the hierarchical
and representative institutions which restricted them in their
operations.

The governing power had hitherto been formed by an
alliance of the King with the Church of England ; the Nonconformists had been oppressed and harassed by this alliance,
which, moreover, had brought about the failure of Monmouth's
movement ; what an impression must it have made upon
those Nonconformists, that the King now regarded them as
the allies of the monarchical power against the Church ! They
joyfully accepted this alliance [1]. In the addresses in which
they express their thanks they assure the King at the same
time that they will so conduct themselves that he shall never
have to repent of his conduct. Those who thus spoke were the
Anabaptists, who showed themselves more numerous than had
been believed—principally men of low rank, but yet with many
among them who belonged to a higher ; the Independents,
who now called themselves Congregationalists ; the Quakers
of the capital ; the Presbyterians were least zealous, but
they were not unrepresented. The Roman Catholics, whose
deputation was composed of men of the highest nobility,
declared themselves peculiarly gratified that it was a prince
of their religion who introduced the general Indulgence : and
said that he strengthened thereby the foundations of all
government. In the addresses the King is compared at one
time with Moses, ' who redeemed the people of Israel from
the land of Egypt,' at another with the great Cyrus, ' who
redeemed it from the Babylonian captivity.' On one day a
number of persons were seen to enter Hampton Court headed
by a leader who bore a parchment roll in his hands ; they

· [1] Vignola : 'Con infinito giubilo si radunano nelle loro assemblei dove huomini
e donne predicano gli uni e gli altri la fede et le buone opere secundo la lorò
inspiratione.'

formed the deputation from Coventry, and delivered to the
King an address of thanks in the name of the various religious
parties of their city: 'Presbyterians, Independents, Anabaptists, and even Church of England men, they were now all
united in Christian love'; they expressed their expectation
that trade would be thereby advanced, and the power of the
King strengthened. Deputations from other towns, from the
grand juries of several counties, and from the legal corporations followed. The fact that the declaration had been issued
in contradiction to the existing laws did not cause the learned
Inns of Court in London to feel much hesitation. The barristers of the Middle Temple declared the prerogative to be
the true life of the law; their motto was 'God gives the king
and the king gives the law [1].' But in the whole affair nothing
perhaps attracted more attention than the speech with which
William Penn presented an address of the general assembly
of the Quakers. About twelve hundred 'Friends' had been
at once delivered from prison; in their deliverance they
saw also the confirmation of their religious principles. Penn
named the King, not Majesty, because this designation,
he thought, was due to God only; nor yet 'thou,' from
social consideration : he spoke of him in the third person.
'The King while he was a subject gave Cæsar his tribute,
and now he is a Cæsar he gives God his due, viz. the
sovereignty over consciences. . . . he is now upon a principle that has good nature, Christianity, and the good of civil
society on its side; a security to him beyond the little arts of
government.' The address expresses a hope that Parliament
would be induced by the good results which might be expected from this declaration for internal peace, trade, and the
prosperity of the country, to confirm the concession for ever [2]
The King in his reply referred to Penn himself 'who would
bear him witness that his principle had always been that conscience ought not to be forced. . . . What I have promised in

---

[1] 'A deo rex, a rege lex.' Extracts from the addresses. Ralph i. 947 (ed. 1744)
[2] The address is dated 'from their usual yearly meeting in London, the nine-
teenth day of the third month, vulgarly called May, 1687.' Life prefixed to the
Select Works, xcix.

my declaration I will continue to perform as long as I-live; and I.hope before I die to settle it so that after ages shall have no reason to alter it.' So he said shortly afterwards to the deputation from Coventry: he thought of securing the religious freedom of which he approved by a law—without doubt by an Act of Parliament—in such a way that it should never be possible for his successors to withdraw it.

CHAPTER VI.

THE government then still clung to its purpose of persuading, if possible, the Church of England Parliament to approve
the Indulgence, and it even cherished decided hopes of success.
'Were the Indulgence only practically carried out, people
would get used to it: after the King had once irrevocably
expressed his will, they would not wish to estrange him completely, nor to provoke him by fruitless resistance into becoming a decided enemy.' To this effect spoke William Penn. He
reminded the Episcopal Church 'that its connexion with the
crown formed the principal basis of its authority at that time ;
it had made the prince great in order itself to secure greatness
by his aid. There was a king on the throne whose interests
it had once zealously defended, and who wished to remain its
ally except in the one point which concerned the persecution
of those who held other creeds ; would it separate from him
on this ground ? It would certainly not be able to hinder the
relief of the Papists during his lifetime ; but if it assented to
the General Indulgence it would at once satisfy the instinct of
the Protestant Dissenters for self-preservation and attract
them to itself; none, certainly, of their different sects wished
that the Catholic Church should become the national Church ;
even after toleration had been granted the Episcopal Church
would remain the dominant one, maintained no longer by
force but by the approval of all parties, which would be won
by its compliance, and would seek to support it.' A certain
prospect of success was held out by the fact that some Church

of England corporations declared themselves in favour of the King's views, as did even a bishop, Crewe of Durham.

But by far the greater number of the Episcopalians were obstinately adverse to them, especially the members of the Parliament. At the ceremony of the prorogation those who were present had been heard to say, with the anger of men who felt injured, that the King need not hope that they would ever abolish the requirement to take the oaths; if it had been necessary a few years ago to impose them it was doubly necessary to maintain them now, considering the increasing preponderance of Popery[1]. The intrusion of Catholics was not so much feared in the Lower House, where the majority was beginning again to count on the Presbyterians, as in the Upper House, where the majority could be shaken by a numerous creation of peers[2]. And it was certainly from the Upper House that the principal opposition had lately proceeded. But the Episcopalians could not yet convince themselves that the King would decidedly separate from them: for they thought that the Anglican system formed the principal support of his power. It seemed incredible that the King would appeal to those elements which had caused the rebellion and the ruin of his father: he would thereby, it was said, endanger the monarchy[3].

In the opposition of ecclesiastical systems, and of general ideas which embraced the future, there was also involved a struggle for power at the moment and for authority in the state. James II wished to carry out the purpose which he had once declared for the following reason amongst others: that he might get a new version of the prerogative accepted, and secure it a broader field; the leaders of the Parliament, the influential men of the country, wished to retain him within the limits that had been drawn, and not to agree to an alteration which might perhaps have their destruction for its issue.

---

[1] Sarotti: 'Si sono udite le memorationi di diversi—sostenendo che le apprensioni dei pericoli del aumento del papato, i queli gia diedero occasioni per li testi sono adesso maggiori d'allora.' (17 Maggio)

[2] Good advice to the Church of England, &c. Select Works iv. 421 [or 423?].

[3] 'Qu'il seroit périlleux pour l'autorité royale de convoquer un autre.' Barrillon, May 16.

Here one question before all others came into prominence. Even if, as Penn said, the King's regulations must be respected during his lifetime, it was yet assumed that they would lose their force at his death. The question which predominated over everything else was, how the presumptive successor, the Prince of Orange, would behave with regard to the purposes of his father-in-law. His representative in England, Dijkvelt, gave no trustworthy guarantee on the subject at the moment; but seemed to wish to stand well with all parties; it even appeared as though he could be won by the party opposed to the majority of the Parliament.

Under these circumstances the prevailing agitation about the rights of the Episcopal Church and of Parliament led those who were influenced by it to make friendly advances to the Prince of Orange; a step which deserves especial notice. It originated with Anne Countess of Sunderland, the wife of the first minister, who, however, had often to apologize for the fact that his Countess pursued a policy divergent from his own. Henry Sidney was the friend of her heart and the confidant of her political thoughts; her letters to him breathe at times very anti-Catholic feelings. But she also stood in connexion with every one else who was powerful and noble in England.

Nothing was more feared in these circles than that the Prince might be won over by the good words and promises of the court, and accede to its plans; the Countess undertook to warn him against such a course. She explained 'that whatever promises might be made him, they would not afterwards be considered binding: moreover he must not believe that his consent, if he gave it, would do much in the business in hand; the exaction of the oaths would certainly not be discontinued; he would only arouse jealousy and hostile feelings against himself[1].' She enclosed this paper in a letter to the Princess of Orange, and that again in a letter to Bentinck, to whom

---

[1] Given by Dalrymple, Memoirs ii., Appendix i. 188, 2nd ed. 1773: 'It will create jealousies of your Highness here, which may be of very ill consequence to you, and even your joining in it would never do their business, I mean the repealing the laws.'

she sent it by a messenger of her own—a necessary precaution, for no suspicion of this communication must reach any human being except the Princess. But what could have made a deeper impression upon the Prince and Princess than such a warning coming from the midst of the powerful aristocracy whose support only remained assured to them for the future in case they did not join the King in this matter?

King James however now demanded their concurrence with imperious earnestness. When he gave Dijkvelt his farewell audience towards the end of May 1687, he repeated the wish which he had already often expressed, that the Prince should declare himself favourable to the abolition of the penal laws and of the Test Oaths. Dijkvelt, who had recently had most intercourse with the other party, remarked hereupon, that all that could be required of the Prince was that he should assume a neutral attitude in this matter, and that this would be advantageous for the King himself in so far as it would nourish in the enemies of his system a hope of seeing it withdrawn after his death, which would hinder them from proceeding to open resistance during his lifetime. Apparently a very prudent remark; but the King could not be content with the course recommended, as he wished to establish his Indulgence for all future times. He answered 'that it was the interest of royalty not to allow the Catholics, the most faithful subjects, to be oppressed. Everything which had been done against them under the pretext of religion had only been done in order to weaken the royal authority: the Test Oaths had been first imposed on the ground of a fictitious conspiracy only in order to exclude him from the succession.' He described the exaction of these oaths as intolerable for himself. 'For it was impossible to be loyal to a King whose religion was at the same time maintained to be of an idolatrous nature: the oath had been first imposed and was now maintained by a faction; it was impossible for the same man to be his friend and at the same time to wish to maintain a provision which had been invented to injure him [1]. And he declared himself with no less

---

[1] Barrillon, June 9-12, 1687: ' Que ce serment contient des choses atroces, qui blessent mêsme la conscience de la plupart des protestants,—qu'il est incompatible

zeal against the penal laws. ' I cannot do less for my true friends than effect the abolition of laws the execution of which would ruin them : conscience, honour, and good policy bind me to procure safety for the Catholics : what will be after me I must leave to the providence of God, which directs the hearts of kings ; but I am responsible for that which I do myself : I cannot leave those who have remained faithful to the old and true religion subject to the oppression under which the laws place them. I do not think of an alteration of the succession,' which had been spoken of ; ' I love my children, especially the Princess of Orange ; but the Prince and Princess must know that they cannot set themselves against my purposes without arousing my displeasure ; their duty is to submit to my will and to earn the continuance of my friendship by good conduct.'

King James held it to be the duty of his son-in-law to stand by him in a project which seemed to him to tend to the advantage of the crown. He attached all the more value to the Prince's support as he still thought of attaining his end by the aid of the existing Parliament, which would, by the union of the royal family, be deprived of all hope of a future change of policy.

But together with these demands Dijkvelt took over a number of letters from English noblemen which struck an opposite strain. Some content themselves with assuring the Prince of their personal friendship and reverence, as did the two Hydes, although even they were then members of the opposition ; the old Earl of Bedford thanks him most warmly for the sympathy which the Prince has shown him on the death of his son. Devonshire goes even further : he expresses the wish that things might so stand in England that the Prince could be content with their state. Lord Nottingham assures him that the eyes of all Protestants are directed to him ; Lord Shrewsbury, that their only consolation in their misfortune lay in the Prince's allowing them to know his opinion that

---

d'estre fidèle sujet de son roi et de déclarer, que la religion qu'il professe est remplie d'idolatrie,—qu'il n'est pas possible d'èstre dans ses interèsts et de vouloir faire subsister, ce qui a été inventé pour le ruiner.'

they were in the right. Churchill announces in the name of
the Princess Anne and for himself a resolution to hold fast to
Protestantism under all circumstances. Danby goes to the
greatest lengths : he proposes a meeting that he may make
disclosures to the Prince which may tend to his advantage ;
adding that he had not found it advisable to tell Dijkvelt
everything which he wished the Prince to learn.

And yet he had already told Dijkvelt a great deal. For
instance, 'that the King would grant the Catholics so many
privileges that they would not be inclined to accept the Protestant succession at his death ; that he inclined to an arbitrary
course, and was supported by a strong standing army ; that
he would, if he gained control over the Parliament, get all
the laws he pleased voted.'

The Prince could not long hesitate between these contrary
demands. The letters which Dijkvelt brought with him,
though far from causing us to admit that an agreement had
already been concluded, yet comprise the germ of such an
agreement. They rest on the presumption of an inward
harmony, and agree with the religious and political attitude
which the Prince had up to that time maintained. On the
other hand, to attach himself to the King would have been to
place himself in absolute contradiction to that attitude, would
perhaps not even have brought him to the end desired, and
would have estranged his friends from him for ever. The
Bishop of London had intimated to the Prince that the King
in the moment of danger would have to rest on him for support ; as though an insurrection might be looked for in which
the Protestant sentiments and political position of the Prince
might make him the saviour of the crown [1]. There are cases
in which, though opposite courses appear possible, they yet do
not allow of any choice ; and such a case was the one before
us. The Prince answered the King as early as June 7
(O.S.) : 'There could be no one who loathed religious persecution more than he did ; but he could not for all that decide

---

[1] Dalrymple ii. App. i. 199. The words are purposely obscure. 'If the King
should have any trouble come upon him, which God forbid, we do not know any
sure friend he has to rely upon abroad besides yourself.'

himself to do anything contrary to the welfare of the religion which he professed.' The letter contains some softening words, but amounts in the main to a complete refusal. ' I cannot,' it says, ' concur in that which your Majesty desires of me[1].'

The King had by no means, so far as we know, expected a zealous consent ; but neither had he expected such a cold and sharp refusal[2]. His rejoinder betrays a much-irritated state of feeling. He remarks therein that the Prince contradicted himself when after affirming that he hated religious persecution, he opposed the repeal of laws which bore so heavily upon all who dissented from the English Church. He ascribes the Prince's conduct to the influence, brought to bear through Dijkvelt, of people who were not well disposed towards him, the King, nor towards the monarchy. For although James was not informed of the special relations of the Prince to leading personages in England, he yet did not doubt that such relations existed.

But it was just his perception of this, and the keen opposition offered to him by a far-ramifying and closely-connected party that caused him to take a definite step with regard to the Parliament. Had James allowed the old Parliament to reassemble under such circumstances he would have had to expect decided opposition, and even vehement attacks.

In the last negotiation with Dijkvelt, however, he had not only declined all mediation, but had expressed in the strongest terms his intention to dissolve the Parliament as soon as he should see that he could effect nothing in concert with it : that he would in like manner again dissolve any other Parliament which should be elected if it refused him its co-operation, and would so proceed until he had attained his object[3]. He held it almost a point of honour to make good his threat, but

---

[1] ' Ainsi je ne puis concourir en ce que V. M. désire de moi.' June 7/17, 1687. Dalrymple ii. App. i 184.

[2] Remark the difference of the signatures. Usually ' as kind as you can desire ' —on this occasion (June 16, O. S.) ' as kind as you can expect.' Dalrymple ii. App. i. 185.

[3] Sarotti : ' Ne fara elegger un altro, il quello pur disunira, se mostro renitenze alle sue sodisfattioni ; al fine trovera modo di spuntare al suo intento.'

he held it at the same time for an absolute necessity also; for he thought that as he had quite lost the Church of England party, he must destroy it and protect its adversaries [1].

It may be regarded as a sign of this irritation against the Church of England that on one of these very days an audience was granted with all ceremony to the Papal Nuncio on his entering upon his functions.

Ferdinand, Count of Adda, had already been in London ever since November 1685 as Papal plenipotentiary. He had come over at the express wish of the King, without any expectation of remaining, and still less with any expectation of being recognised as Nuncio; the English court made greater advances to him in all such matters than he had ever hoped for. For among the anti-Catholic laws which James II wished to repeal, was one forbidding diplomatic relations with Rome: that seemed to become quite absurd when the King belonged to the Catholic Church: James thought that he might at once show disregard for it. He on his side also sent an envoy to Rome in the early part of the year 1686—Lord Castlemaine. The two embassies had very different success. Castlemaine, who had a commission unacceptable to the Pope, and who behaved with haughty arrogance—we shall return to him once more—had soon to be recalled. Monsignor Adda, a well-bred man, of pleasing appearance and good demeanour, knew how to acquire the full confidence of the King and of the first minister. He has become of importance for the historian through the detailed reports which he sent to Rome about his negotiations with them [2]. He did not by any means agree with James as to all his undertakings; but he represented Catholic ideas and a connexion with the centre of the Catholic world, just as the King wished, and was treated with the most respectful regard. It formed a subject of complaint for English churchmen that a man who ought not, according to the laws, to be in England at all, was received at the court and even in the city—as, for instance, on one

---

[1] 'Considerava che dopo esser perso il partito Anglicano conveniva distruggerlo.'

[2] 'Ex literis autographis nuncii apostolici.'

occasion he attended an official banquet of the Lord Mayor. His consecration as archbishop, 'in partibus,' took place at St. James' Chapel ; the King was present at the ceremony. But that did not satisfy the King ; it formed a part of his ambition as a Catholic to receive the representative of the Holy Father solemnly at Whitehall, and that with the cere- monies usual at the French court. In accordance with French practice the chamberlain of highest rank who bore the title of duke was to introduce the Nuncio. That position was held by the young Charles, Duke of Somerset, of the old Protestant house of the Seymours. The King was much annoyed when he met with a refusal from the Duke to perform this service on the ground that by rendering it he would do an illegal act, and might incur the penalties of a premunire. James asked whether he, as King, did not stand above the law. He saw in the refusal an affront, dismissed Somerset from his service, and had his place supplied by the Duke of Grafton, a natural son of Charles II. In pushing on the affair itself he only became all the more zealous. It gave him a kind of satisfac- tion that at the very moment at which he was experiencing such an offensive Protestant opposition he was able, early in July 1687, to arrange a splendid procession to Whitehall for the Nuncio. The envoy drove to his audience with a long line of six-horse carriages ; the King and Queen awaited him in the great hall and rose when he made his second-bow in the middle of the apartment ; the Nuncio during his address re- mained covered, just like the King himself. The population of London had flocked to the spot, all windows were filled with spectators ; even then high prices were paid for them ; but every one kept quiet ; the remark most frequently made was that it was a spectacle which London had not seen for a century and a half.

About the same time the dissolution of Parliament was pronounced, on July 2, 1687. The reason stated even to the Nuncio for resorting to this measure was that it would not otherwise be possible to frustrate the intrigues of the Prince of Orange, and to rend asunder the bond which had been formed between him and the members of the Church of Eng- land. But the thought was not therefore renounced of confirming in a Parliamentary way the liberties granted to the Roman Catholics and to the Dissenters. The Nuncio himself was continually calling attention to the absolute necessity of such a step; 'the Catholics would otherwise find themselves in the worst position on the King's death.' But if such was the case it was indispensable to reconstitute the Parliament in such a way that it might possibly consent to the King's proposal.

It was agreed that in order to prepare for a Parliament from which favourable resolutions might be expected, two things were necessary; a transformation of the corporations, in order to influence the elections through the magistrates, and the removal from the administration of the counties of persons who proved refractory [1].

We have seen how great exertions it had cost to bring civic offices a few years before this time into the hands of members of the Church of England, and that the process had been one of rather doubtful legality. Now the magistrates who had then been put in office held fast to their own opinions even when those of the government changed. They formed as it were the links in the chain of opposition which extended over the country. But, if they had been put in office by an exercise of the King's sovereign power, there was nothing to hinder their being deprived of it again by virtue of the same power. One of the principal internal reasons for the existence of corporate rights might be sought for precisely in the doctrine that the whole life of the state ought not to depend on the tendencies of the sovereign power which are fluctuating by their very nature; there must be somewhere a limit to their momentary influences beyond which a free development of municipalities and, under their protection, of individuals remains possible. At the time under consideration everything was drawn into the great currents and countercurrents of controversy. James II did not hesitate to remove, without delay,

---

[1] Barrillon, July 4/14: 'Le dessein du roi est de prendre ses mesures pour avoir un parlement mieux disposé en faveur des catholiques. Il faut pour cela faire beaucoup de changements dans les communautés pour nommer le parlement; il faut aussi changer la pluspart des sheriffs dans les provinces et quelqu'uns même des lieutenants et gouverneurs.'

from their offices six members of the court of aldermen of
London, who had opposed an address brought before them
in favour of freedom of conscience. In their places he
appointed not Catholics, whose nomination would have
given fresh nourishment to the suspicion already aroused, that
he had only had in view the advantage of those of his own
creed, but Dissenters of good repute, Independents, Anabaptists, Quakers: one of the most zealous Presbyterians
was raised to the office of Lord Mayor. And James thought
that he must carry out an encroachment far more serious
still. The Tories were excluded from the administration of
the guilds also ; it is said that nine hundred of them could be
counted who were visited by this fate. The King entertained
the purpose of creating a new foundation altogether for the
constitution of the city. All foreigners, and among them
especially the French immigrants, were to obtain the rights
of citizenship by a comprehensive act of naturalisation. At
the next civic elections James recommended the exclusion of
all who would not declare themselves in favour of the act of
naturalisation and of freedom of conscience.

In August of 1687 the King undertook a journey into the
western counties, and attended his queen, whose health had
been shaken, to Bath : he did so mainly with the object of preparing for the next Parliamentary elections, and of showing
men that he was in earnest with respect to freedom of conscience. At Chester it was remarked that the country people
hesitated to come into the city on market-day while the King
was there, as they feared being compelled to accept Catholicism.
It was hardly an accident that the leaders of the Quakers, Penn
and Barclay, entered Chester just at that time, and preached
on freedom of conscience to a great concourse. The King's
presence during the delivery of these addresses made a great
impression on people in general. He took pains everywhere to
treat every one well, and became to a certain degree popular.
The journey led him to some extent into the same counties of
which Monmouth's insurrection had shortly before taken hold ;
the remarkable spectacle now presented itself that the nobility
and gentry who had not been willing to take part in the
rebellion, now also in presence of the King kept quiet, and

showed themselves sullen : while the people, on the contrary, displayed their good-will as unequivocally as they had formerly shown it to the Protestant duke[1]. Parts were as it were exchanged. Previously the King had been connected with the Episcopal party, to which the nobility and gentry for the most part adhered; now he was estranged from it. As Monmouth formerly, so now the King sought the support of the Nonconformists, and knew how to procure it. In more than one town people promised him only to send such representatives to Parliament as would vote for the abolition of the requirement to take the oaths[2]. At Bristol, which a short time before had only been held in check by force of arms and threats of destruction, the King and Queen, who made a visit to the place, were received with enthusiastic devotion[3].

With the increased self-confidence which arises from a belief that the ground under one's feet is sure, the King made on his return to Windsor a short stay at Oxford, in order to bring an affair to a close there which was very well calculated to let the Church of England feel his displeasure.

He had already been making constant attempts to exercise influence on the elections in the colleges of the two Universities : in the conviction, as he said, that there were many secret Catholics there, for whom it was only necessary to make an opening in order to call out in the great places of education an opposition to the Episcopalian doctrine, which then had the sole supremacy.

. One of the first in whose favour the dispensing power was applied was Obadiah Walker, Master of University College, in reality a secret Catholic already, but who now first gained courage to come forward with a confession of his belief[4]; he

---

[1] Sarotti, Oct. 3 : 'Non si sono veduti se non pochissimi di quei molti nobili e benestanti del regno, che hanno da mantenersi delli loro entrate e possono vivere independente della corte—ottimo effetto pero ha fatto nella plebe la presenza del re non prima veduto.'

[2] Barrillon, Sept. 20 : 'Quelques communautés promettent de faire élire des deputés, qui soient disposés à abolir les loix pénales et le test.'

[3] Sarotti. 'Con le possibili demonstrationi d'ossequio gli diedero un lautissimo disnare come pure a tutto il regio seguito con abondanza e profusione.'

[4] Bonnet relates that he would have declared himself sooner if he had not hoped to become Bishop of Oxford.

was released from the obligation of attending the Anglican service, and established a printing press from which Catholic treatises issued ; he seemed well qualified to found a Catholic school in Oxford.

After some time there followed the nomination of John Massey, Fellow of Merton College, as Dean of Christ Church, with a very extensive dispensation from all oaths and from all declarations prescribed by the statutes of the University and of the college, and with the right of living at the courts of the King and of the two Queens, in spite of this omission.

The King went yet a step further when, in February 1687, he commanded the University of Cambridge to grant its academical degrees to a Benedictine monk ' of whom he heard much good,'—for such a grant required not only passive but active obedience. The Vice-Chancellor resisted, but was on that account deprived not only of his office but even of his place in a college, by the ecclesiastical commission, which summoned him before its bar. The King did not continue to press for the execution of his order : it was enough for him that disobedience to him was punished[1].

But the most important step which he took in relation to this matter was, without doubt, his undertaking to give a president after his own mind to the wealthiest and most famous college in Oxford, on occasion of a vacancy which occurred in March 1687. So many well-grounded objections, however, were made against his nominee, that he let him drop, and commanded the governing body to accept another in his place, Samuel Parker, Bishop of Oxford. Parker was acceptable to him because he had, even in contradiction to his earlier writings, declared himself for the Indulgence, and opposed the treatment of Popery as idolatry. But meanwhile, the college not without some haste, had already made another choice, and would not give it up again. The King found therein a renunciation of the old loyalty of the Church of England, and even a personal affront ; he now demanded, with violent threats, the acceptance of his candidate. Penn, who accompanied the King, and condescended to recommend

---

[2] So Barrillon assures us, who spoke on the question with the King.

compliance to the fellows, made an observation during the discussion, which throws a certain light on the prevailing ideas. To the remark of the fellows that they were engaged in the defence not only of their rights but of religion, he replied that he could not see that the profession of a particular creed must be made the necessary condition for receiving a learned education[1]. He made a distinction between ecclesiastical offices and places in colleges: the first were to be reserved for men who held the Episcopalian creed, but not the second. He thought that three colleges, University, Christ Church, and Magdalen would suffice for the Catholics. So Penn might think, who was always full of new plans; so perhaps might the King think also: but even this demand went much too far for men who felt that they had a right of possession confirmed by the laws; and, moreover, who would absolutely engage that the encroachments which had begun would find a limit at that point? Neither the arguments of William Penn nor the threats of the King made any impression upon the fellows: they would not even admit that they had been guilty of disobedience; for they maintained that whoever obeyed the ecclesiastical and civil laws confirmed by kings, he was obedient to the king[2]. This was no doubt the first occasion on which zealous members of the English Church defined obedience to the King in the same way in which his enemies also defined it. But King James II was not minded to accept such a definition. The Ecclesiastical Commission put in operation again, and that in the greatest extent, the procedure to which it had once already resorted; it decreed the removal from the college of all its fellows (Dec. 1687/ Jan. 1688). For people were to learn that the King's resolution to maintain his prerogative yielded to no opposition, not even to one based upon law and custom.

It was just at the time when this violence was being practised

---

[1] Hough's letter, Windsor, Oct. 9, in Janney 327: 'I hope you would not have the two Universities such invincible bulwarks for the Church of England that none but they (the Episcopalians) must be capable of giving their children a learned education.'

[2] 'Our statutes are agreeable to the King's laws both ecclesiastical and civil; and so long as we live up to them we obey the King.' State Trials xii. 47.

that the most serious measures were taken in order to remove from posts in the public service all those who would have acted in opposition to the King's purposes at the next Parliamentary elections.

In the counties the King had the question laid before the officials and justices of the peace, whether they would conduct themselves generally in accordance with the Indulgence which had been published, whether at the approaching elections they would only vote for such candidates as were in favour of it, and whether, finally, if the choice fell upon themselves they would vote for the repeal of the penal laws and for the abolition of the oaths[1]? James announced plainly that he was engaged in a revision of the lists, and would only retain those from whom he might expect support in the wholesome work of conferring equal rights in respect to religion upon all his subjects ; all others he would strike off the lists.

The state of the case, however, was not such as to enable him to effect much by promises or by threats. Among the adherents of the Church of England, who still for the most part occupied the posts in question, it had become almost a point of honour to hold fast to the form of religion established by law. The answer was easily found, and in most cases given, that they could not bind their hands until the arguments on both sides had been considered in Parliament itself. In some cases, however, the matter was entered into more fully, and those addressed declared that they approved of the Indulgence and were much inclined to repeal the penal laws, it being well understood that this repeal should operate just as much for the benefit of the Protestant Dissenters as for that of the Catholics ; but the general voice was against the abolition of the oaths, as it was thought likely to serve the interests of the Catholics only ; 'if the Catholics were merely allowed access to offices they would, considering the King's predilection for them, get in a short time most of such offices into their hands ; but that if the Parliament were

---

[1] 'Whether in case they chose a neutrality, they would live in fellowship with those who differed from them in religion, agreeable to the principle contained in the Declaration of Indulgence.' Ralph, 967. This means that they would not place any hindrance in the way of the execution of this Declaration.

opened to them without restriction, there would be cause for anxiety lest resolutions should be taken in it with the support of the royal authority by which the position of the country in respect of law and religion would be endangered[1]; that every man was bound in conscience rather to decline an advantage offered than to draw down so great a danger on the country.'

This was substantially the same opinion which had been expressed already in the last Parliament, especially by the Bishop of London : it was the opinion of the Episcopal Church, and of the upper strata of society connected with it. The King had made it his task to break the force of this very opinion, to carry out in spite of it that system of religious equality which he contemplated, and to establish such equality as a permanent part of the law of the land. Without a moment's delay he deprived the refractory under-officials and justices of the peace of their places. But the lords lieutenants themselves had announced their attachment to Episcopalianism, some of them in a very emphatic way : it was to them principally that the failure of the King's measure was ascribed[2]. In their case also the King did not allow himself to be deterred by their high rank and their reputation in the country from depriving of their offices those who offered a decided resistance ; there were sixteen of them. Their deposition interrupted the existing local relations in those counties in which their families possessed an authority to which people had long been accustomed : it even produced administrative difficulties in so far as those who replaced them were Catholics whose nomination seemed illegal to many : but all that formed no obstacle to the King, who always pursued his own object and nothing else. He hoped to attain it by the influence of the new officials and of the new justices of the peace. At the beginning of the year he altered the lists

---

[1] Sarotti, 13/23 January, 1687/8 : ' Mostrandogli la dovuta gratitudine per la concessa liberta di conscienza, la quale pero si attendeva meglio confirmata e stabilita da un parlamento, ma aggiungono, che universale et constante sia l'avversione al revocarsi ed alterarsi quelle leggi, nelle quali si crede che principalmente consista la sicurezza della religione.'

[2] Barrillon expresses himself as though nothing else had been expected : ' Il falloit faire cette tentative pour avoir un prétexte de les changer.'

of the sheriffs also, whose behaviour might have a most important influence on jurisdiction and administration. One third of those whom he appointed were Catholics, another third were Nonconformists : only one third consisted of members of the Church of England, and that too of men from whom no contradiction need be feared.

It might be doubtful how much he would effect in the counties by all this ; but far more depended on the elections in the towns, and for the towns he had ordained still more thoroughgoing measures.

As early as November 1687, he established a special authority for the regulation of the municipalities, and gave it the power of deciding on the qualification of the electors and of effecting a change among the holders of the magistracies. It was a board consisting of six members, Catholics and Protestants, among whom Sunderland, Jeffreys, and Butler possessed the chief authority. Sir Nicholas Butler was one of James II's personal friends and confidential advisers, an Irishman and Catholic by birth ; he had taken a leading part in bringing about the fall of Rochester, and had been admitted to the Privy Council. He now appears as one of the triumvirs of the Regulation.

The principal object was to drive the Tories and Episcopalians from the places which would have given them influence upon the elections. But how could they possibly offer resistance, since they owed the possession which they held to a measure similar to that now promulgated against themselves? The principle of an effectual influence of the sovereign power upon the municipalities, which had once been advantageous to the Tories, was now employed against them. What had first happened in London was accordingly repeated in most of the other corporations ; Dissenters and decided adherents of the Indulgence in its full extent succeeded to the Tories. The municipalities which made a show of opposing the new Regulation were intimidated by a threat which made them fear the loss of their corporate rights. The agents of the board were furnished with lists of the persons whose advancement was desired.

All these measures produced a kind of revolution in the

public service. And who would have ventured to say whether they could not and would not lead to their end? How often had the government in earlier times succeeded in bringing into existence Parliaments after its own mind! Even the episcopal and parliamentary system as it then existed had had a similar origin, in so far as it might still be considered as a continuation of the Parliament of 1685, which had itself been the offspring of that revolution in feeling which attended the Restoration. Now the government seemed to aim at a re-establishment of that state of things which had been over-thrown in 1660. Its measures seemed to be devised with the object of restoring preponderance to the Protestant sects—as was said, of bringing a fanatical Parliament into existence [1]· The times were recalled to mind in which religion had been altered by similar measures.

Even as early as February, 1688, many held that the time had come for ordering new elections. They thought that for a new and special reason they might assume by anticipation a good result. The Queen's pregnancy, which had been spoken of in private ever since the journey to Bath before mentioned, could now no longer be doubted, and it was thought that the expectation that the Queen would be delivered of a prince, who would then be Prince of Wales, would have an influence on the disposition of Parliament favourable to the King's interest. The leading minister, the Earl of Sunderland, who in other respects agreed with his colleagues, did not, how-ever, think that sufficient preparations had been made for the business. A preliminary agreement with the future members of the Parliament was, he thought, that on which the success of the whole undertaking depended ; the govern-ment must, before it proceeded to new elections, have a moral certainty that it would carry the affair through. The regula-tion of the constituencies must first be completed [2], and the

---

[1] ' The whole machine was fanatic; and the design was declared to compass a fanatic Parliament.' North's Examen 627.

[2] The Dutch ambassador Citters, February 3/13, remarks this motive: the ministers of the King were against the summons ' so lange de corporatien waermede men nu nog dagelyk besig is niet alle naer S. M. sinnelyckheyt syn gereguliert en verandert, waertoe deser dagen maereerst an somige nog quo warranto syn toe gesanden.'

new sheriffs allowed time for the development of their influence; it must be the business of the judges on their next
circuits to refute the opinion that the King's views were
opposed to public liberty.   A resolution was taken in
accordance with these counsels.   The summoning of a Parliament was put off till November.   Meanwhile a Declaration of
Indulgence was to be promulgated afresh, in order to recall
these points of view into lively recollection by an act issuing
from the highest place, and to show men that the King would
not allow any contradiction to disturb him in carrying out
the purposes which he had once formed.

CHAPTER VII.

MANY had expected that the King, moved by the manifestations which had made themselves heard on all sides, would be content with the repeal of the penal laws, which was offered him, and would give up his demand for the abolition of the oaths, which seemed universally unpopular. The new promulgation of the Declaration of Indulgence which took place towards the end of April, 1688, undeceived people on this point. It not only comprised the earlier Declaration in its full extent, but was provided with a postscript in which special emphasis was laid on the intolerable nature of the oaths. The King says in this postscript 'that a government had never yet maintained itself by limitations of this kind; offices and dignities ought to be distributed according to merit; his resolution was to establish universal liberty of conscience in England for all future generations; in next November at latest he would summon a new Parliament; and that he hoped to carry out his plan then. He demanded beforehand that the electors should then only choose such members as would be able to bring to an end that which he had begun for the advantage of the monarchy[1].'

We are assured by those who enjoyed the confidence of the court, that in this publication, as in his previous deliberations, the King was partly influenced by the prospect that an heir to the crown would soon be born. As he expected from that event an effect in the nation which would promote his ends,

---

[1] For the very words see Ralph i. 982.

so, on the other hand, its approach caused an apprehension for the future to arise in his mind. For what would be the child's fate if James left it a minor at his death? What else could be expected but that in such a case the powerful party at the head of which the Prince of Orange stood would get possession of the heir to the crown, have him educated in the Protestant religion, and restore the unconditional supremacy of Episcopalianism? James thought it necessary to bring about such a state of things during his lifetime that his wife and son might be secured against the possibility of oppression by the Prince of Orange and his adherents[1]. For success in this purpose two things seemed to him to be necessary; the closest connexion with Louis XIV, or, as Barrillon expresses it, the protection of that King, and especially the carrying out of the arrangements which he had taken in hand—particularly the abolition of the oaths—with a view to the formation of a strong and trustworthy party for the heir to the throne. For if the oaths remained in force, the Catholics, to whom he would have of course to look principally for aid, would be forced to retire again from the posts which had been granted them. It was not only his predilection for those who held his own creed which induced the King to persevere with his projects, but the party position which he had assumed and in which those about him held him fast. We have already mentioned this Catholic camarilla; it was in itself a combination of insignificant men. Dover and Arundel were passionate gamblers; the last, moreover, far advanced in years and of little use; Powis and Castlemaine had no natural talent. But the King judged men not, as he gave out, according to their real gifts or services—he had certainly rejected those who had been in reality useful to him—but according to the zeal with which they joined in the views which prevailed with him at the moment; he wished only to hear his own thoughts from them, perhaps grounded on better arguments or more strongly expressed. That was what gave Father Petre such

---

[1] Barrillon, March 11: 'De mettre pendant la vie du roi d'Angleterre les affaires en état que la reine sa femme et le prince de Galles, s'il y en a un, ne soient pas opprimés d'abord par la faction du prince d'Orange.'

influence with him : a. man of intelligence, as has been mentioned, but one whose intelligence was not free from mis-
directed subtlety, and who did not get beyond a point of
view which he had once taken up.   The position of his order
in the world, especially that of the fraction of it to which he
belonged and which was dominant in France, made him incapable of being the adviser of a king of England in that
king's own interest.   The man of business, and one fully
furnished with the talent and versatility required for its
management, was Sunderland.   He, however, was destitute of
firm and lasting convictions, and of all political morality.
At play, which he, like some of his colleagues, passionately
loved, he usually lost ; in the embarrassments into which he
then fell he took money from France.   Another reason for his
attaching himself to Louis XIV was that, in case the system
under which he served should some day be overthrown, he
might find a personal support in him.   He only cared for
gaining possession of authority, and remaining in possession
when he had attained it ; to which end the factions of the
court—as formerly Lady Portsmouth, so now the Catholic
party—must serve him.   He had given that party a pledge by
secretly making a profession of the Catholic faith to Father
Petre.   The maintenance of the concessions guaranteed to the
Catholics, and the formation of a solid Catholic party in the
state,—such were the ideas which the King, his friends, and
his ministers alike entertained.   James II had no eye for the
selfish objects which those about him might have in view;
if he conceived a suspicion against them it was only after the
event ; in the first instance, the more their counsels coincided
with his own antipathies, with the less hesitation did he follow
them.

Now these antipathies were being directed more and more
decidedly against the English Church, in which the men whom
he regarded as his principal enemies enjoyed the highest consideration.   Like the establishment of the High Commission
and the application of the dispensing power, the Declaration
of Indulgence also contained a hostile demonstration against
· the privileged position of that church in the state.   On
occasion of the new proclamation of Indulgence a further

step was taken on this path. The King commanded the clergy of the Church of England to read the Declaration in the churches. This order was, as it were, double-edged; indeed it was intended to be so. If the clergy complied, they themselves recognised the legality of the step which was directed against them, and gave up their own cause; if they resisted they fell into contradiction with their doctrine of obedience, and seemed likely to estrange the Nonconformists by their conduct.

Crises of this kind must come, in which a great institution has to develop its own inner vital force, and to assest its position in the world to the utmost.

It was not certain beforehand whether the English Church would not obey the commands which it had received. Similar occurrences had certainly taken place before : edicts of kings —for example, Charles the Second's justification, already mentioned, for the dissolution of Parliament which he had ordered— had been read in the churches. And might resistance be offered to a King who was still recognised as head of the Church? If, moreover, the clergy ventured upon such a step, what would they not have to apprehend from the recklessness and self-confidence of James II! The lower clergy could not come to any regular understanding on the subject : and no one could foresee whether the Bishops would not yield for fear of something worse—especially considering how doubtful had hitherto been the demeanour of the primate, Sancroft Archbishop of Canterbury.

In civil conflicts those alone as a rule are rewarded by admiration who do not yield a step to the pressure of hostile elements, and are always ready to plunge into open combat with them ; they are the heroes of the theatre who fill the stage with the din of their actions : but there are others of less energetic temper who appear undecided, pliant, weak, and yield as long as it is at all possible, until a moment arrives when their convictions absolutely forbid a continuance of such conduct ; then, however, they rise and sometimes interpose with even more effect than the other class. Sancroft's nature was pure, deep, poetical, and religious. A letter of his has been preserved, written at college, which breathes a

strain of youthful friendship such as only the noblest dispo-
sitions are capable of [1].

In the subsequent ecclesiastical controversies and crises he
appears as an enthusiast for the Church of England, which he
judges to possess a more complete liturgy than any other
ecclesiastical society; he had to suffer much from the Parliament of the Rebellion on this account, and for this Charles II
after his restoration recompensed him by advancement to high
offices. With all his absence of pretension he showed himself
energetic and active : it was not to be forgotten how large a
share he as Dean of St. Paul's had had in bringing about the
erection of a cathedral worthy of the Church and of the
country. As moreover his idea of the Church required that
it should be connected with the crown, he belonged to the
number of those who submitted even to a Catholic King as
being the legitimate heir; he did not, to be sure, attend the
sittings of the ecclesiastical commission, but neither did he
speak against it, any more than he did against the Declaration
of Indulgence. But we know the distinction which was made
between passive and active obedience. There is a difference
between allowing a thing to be done and actually helping in
the doing of it. Sancroft deliberated long with himself how
he should proceed in the case before him; whether he should
allow the Declaration of Indulgence to be read in the churches
or not; he represented to himself what his most celebrated
predecessors in office had done in similar cases, and arrived at
the conclusion that it would be unjustifiable in him to carry
out this order, for that he would thereby co-operate in the
work of destroying his own Church and Protestantism in
general [2].

Characters of this kind require support and something to
fall back upon; and these could not be wanting to the Archbishop. The two Hydes were of the same way of thinking
as himself; both the younger, Rochester, and the elder,

---

[1] I mean the letter given by D'Oyly, Life of Sancroft, on the death of a fellow-
student whose love for him had been 'wonderful, passing the love of women.'

[2] Cp. Minutes for H. G. of Canterbury, prepared by Mr. Hanse, to have been
spoken at the trial. State Trials xii. 466.

Henry Earl of Clarendon, who had already been intimately
associated in the policy of his father the Chancellor, and regarded the alliance with Anglican episcopacy as a kind of hereditary charge. All the displeasure and neglect which he had for
some time experienced from James II did not prevent him from
appearing occasionally at court at a levee ; he did not wish to
break with his King, but repudiated with his whole heart that
King's tendency to favour the Catholics and Nonconformists.
He had had in Ireland to feel for the first time how the
Catholics were forcing their way upwards with all their
energy. His influence in some quarters had been immediately
affected by the regulation of the corporations. Clarendon
might even then be considered the head of the party whose
power, or rather whose very existence, presupposed the unbroken credit of the episcopal system ; he could not see any
security for the general interests of the state and for his own
except in the resistance of the Church, which he thought had
now a right to offer such resistance. The affair was maturely
discussed between him and certain Bishops, among whom
Compton is named, at Lambeth Palace in presence of the
Archbishop, after a dinner. Their decision was, that the
order should not be carried out, that the Declaration of
Indulgence should not be read in the churches, but that a
petition against it should be presented [1] ; for that to appeal
to the prince himself against one of his orders was a proceeding sanctioned by custom and by law.

But for such a course the participation of a larger number,
and a formal consideration, was necessary.

On the 18th of May, in Lambeth Palace, as before, a
great ecclesiastical conference was held. Besides Sancroft,
Compton, and Bishops Turner of Ely, and White of Peter-
borough, there had also been summoned Lloyd of St. Asaph,
Ken of Bath and Wells, Trelawney of Bristol, and Lake of
Chichester—all of whom appeared. Compton and Ken

---

[1] Clarendon's Diary (Correspondence of Clarendon and Rochester ii. 176): 'I
confess I do not understand his lordship's (Halifax) notions. I am sure when the
reading the Declaration was under consideration, and the petition for which the
bishops now suffer, he was so very cautious that he would give no advice at all.'

passed for the best champions of Protestantism as a whole.
The admittance of the first named as equally qualified with
his brethren, was a proof that ecclesiastical authority was
rated higher in the assembly than the King's orders which
encroached upon it. Ken had by his sermons—one preached
shortly before at Westminster, in which he spoke of the Babylonian captivity and the unexpected deliverance from it—
powerfully confirmed the confidence of his Anglican congregation in their cause ; they heard in every word a hint at their
own condition ; among the hearers were the most eminent
men of the realm ; the Princess Anne, too, had attended. By
the side of the Bishops there were seen some of the deans,
who had won a name by the opposition they had offered in
the pulpit and in literature to the progress of conversion to
Catholicism ; such were Tillotson dean of Canterbury, Stillingfleet of St. Paul's, London, Patrick of Peterborough, and two
other brave champions in the strife of the two Confessions,
the elder Sherlock and Tenison. They began their deliberation with prayer.

They very soon came to an agreement upon one point, that
it would not be possible for them to allow the Declaration to
be read without exposing themselves to be called to account.
' For the dispensing power,' it was said, ' had been designated
in many Parliaments as illegal, and really was so, especially
in the extension given to it, whereby it became equivalent to a
right of repealing the laws.' They thus expressly adopted
the doctrines of the last Parliament. The doubt arose
whether they would not, by declaring against the Indulgence,
estrange the Dissenters from them again ; they judged that
the Dissenters would on the contrary see in their conduct
a proof of their Protestant sentiments, and would be reconciled to them—of which, moreover, they said they had received
the best assurances. The question how their. refusal would
agree with the obedience due to the King weighed far more
heavily in the balance. And in deciding this they returned to
the principle which Orlando Bridgeman, who sat as judge at
the trial of the regicides, had once proclaimed as the bulwark
of freedom, that the King could do no wrong, that is, that
every illegal act which took place under his authority did not

proceed from himself but from his officers : but that to resist them could not be considered as disobedience, for that it contained no illegal refusal [1].

The import of their decision was then that they no longer considered the will of the Sovereign to be law, but regarded the law as the only true expression of the Sovereign's will—a view which the English Church had hitherto contested. Like the fellows of Magdalen College, the theologians and high ecclesiastics assembled at Lambeth declared themselves for the doctrine that true loyalty consisted in the observance of the laws.

A further objection made against the contemplated refusal was that the King would proceed to the severest measures, perhaps to the deposition of the Bishops, and would thereby bring the Church itself into danger ; they answered that that would be a less misfortune than an illegal compliance on so important and fundamental an article. Their view was, as is said in an ecclesiastical pamphlet, that they should certainly be lost if the King declared the step they took an act of illegal disobedience, but that they would be lost quite as certainly if they did not take it : while in the last case no man upon earth would pity them ; they would be cursed by the nation, and would never be able to lift up their heads again.

The deliberation expresses the spirit which had formed itself in the clergy and in the episcopate of the Church of England under the Catholicising influences of the King. In earlier disputes between the crown and Parliament the Church had for the most part stood on the side of the crown : a position which it had resumed very decidedly on the Exclusion question. The importance of the transaction of the 18th of May, 1688, was that the leading Bishops placed themselves openly on the side of those Parliamentary rights in the maintenance of which they saw the best support of their own existence.

This feeling also animates the address which was drawn up

---

[1] ' For the King can do no illegal thing, and if his officers do it, they do it not by the King's authority, and therefoie the refusing of it is no disobedience, being no illegal refusal.' Echard iii. 858.

at the sitting, and delivered to the King without delay. James is assured therein, no doubt, of the old undoubted loyalty of the English Church, which he had himself recognised, and even of its consideration for the Dissenters whom he had taken under his protection, but at the same time an earnest petition is laid before him that he will be pleased to desist from enforcing his command to read the Declaration in the churches, for that it founded itself upon a right which had often been declared illegal in Parliament, especially as late as the beginning of his own reign [1]; by publishing it they would take a side in the dispute, which prudence, honour, and conscience forbade them to do. Compton, who was suspended by the King, could not add his signature to the address if it was to be received ; Sancroft, too, could not take part in its delivery, as he had been forbidden to appear at court; but the other six Bishops took it without delay to Whitehall, for they had no time to lose ; the reading of the Declaration was appointed for the 20th of May. The King, who saw the names of some of his most devoted friends among those of the Bishops who were announced, appears to have expected a qualified assent or some other tolerable issue; he gave them audience at once, had the address handed to him, and read it through. Its contents filled him with the utmost astonishment. ' He had not expected,' he said, 'such words from them, least of all from some of them ; the address was a standard of rebellion.' By declaring that they could not take part for him, the Bishops had taken part against him. What they quoted from the Parliament's votes he held for mere expressions of one or the other House which had no binding force; what he had wished to avoid on occasion of the last prorogation, namely, a declaration under valid Parliamentary forms, that they treated as having been already made: they put themselves directly in his way, and denied the doctrine on which he based his administration. 'God has given me this dispensing power, and I will maintain it.' The Bishops on their side had

---

[1] 'That declaration is founded upon such a dispensing power as hath often been declared illegal in Parliament, and particularly in the years 1662 and 1672, and in the beginning of your Majesty's reign.' Life of Sancroft i. 263.

not expected such a strong ebullition on the King's part. No one was more deeply struck by it than the Bishop of Bristol, Sir Jonathan Trelawney, who was descended from an old aristocratic family. He declared it impossible that any member of his family, or he himself, should take part in a rebellion; he did not, however, allow the charge to disturb his consciousness of his ecclesiastical duty; he added, that the duty of obeying the King only extended so far as it did not contradict the duty of obeying God[1]. The doctrine 'that we must obey God rather than men' now entered even into this ecclesiastical organisation, which rested on the closest union between the King and the Church. The Bishops left the King with the words ' God's will be done.'

The foreign ambassadors who were present report to us what was said in the circles in which they lived against the Bishops. 'The King's command contained nothing contrary to morality, faith, or Christian love; in the liturgy a moment was reserved for imparting the King's orders to the congregations; and so long as the practice had been serviceable to the Church of England it had always been adopted; then the clergy had gladly spoken of the prerogative; but that now it fell away from the principles of obedience which the former generation of Bishops, an Usher and a Sanderson, had professed; and it did this only in order to prevent the Catholics from attaining to the enjoyment of their civil rights.' They ought long ago, says a pamphlet of these days, to have invited the King to issue a Declaration of Indulgence, or at least to have now received it with joy; but this glorious act had only produced murmuring. Had the King on the contrary enforced the laws against Dissenters anew, with what satisfaction would the parish clergy have held his order up above their desks, have read it with a keen look round, and have explained it at length another day, instead of their text. In an article of the Gazette of May 22 the resistance of the Bishops to the abolition of the oaths is violently attacked. In the contest about

---

[1] 'We will do our duty to the utmost which does not interfere with our duty to God.' In the printed copy of Sancroft's Life I do not find this; the copy in Clarendon's Diary ii. 480, is more trustworthy.

the Exclusion they had maintained that no one could lose
a natural right in civil society on account of his religion : this
indisputable truth must have equal force against the Test
oaths ; if any one was excluded from Parliament by them, his
birthright to a participation in the civil government was taken
from him on account of his religion.

In all this there was much truth ; but it did not meet the
fears and questions which occupied the moment; it glanced
off from those who heard it.   The petition of the Bishops on
the contrary, which was forthwith published in all quarters, it
is not precisely known how, produced with its brief, striking,
and yet moderate terms, the deepest and at the same time
the most general impression.   No consistency is required of
those who side with public opinion.   That the Bishops gave
their voice against the elevation of the Catholics to equal
rights, in which every one saw a danger for religion and for
the laws, aroused general satisfaction, especially as they at the
same time drew near to the Nonconformists.   And the step
they had taken was, in reality, of world-wide importance ; of
still more importance, it may almost be said, than they themselves thought.   Their alliance with the crown was the cement
which held the building of the English state together.   When
they broke away from the crown the continued existence of
the building became doubtful.

The first result of the Bishops' protest was that the publication of the royal order was hardly anywhere carried out,
either on the 20th or on the following Sundays appointed for
the purpose.   At the very few places where it was obeyed in
spite of the Bishops' decision, the congregation went away
when the reading began.

This was, properly speaking, the first open resistance which
the government had met with in its course; it fell into great
embarrassment.   Even Sunderland and Father Petre were perplexed ; at the first moment they are said to have advised James
to give the Bishops a serious reprimand and to do no more.   On
further consideration, however, that course was not thought
advisable, as it seemed likely to foster an opinion that the
government had not courage to prosecute the Bishops, and
likely therefore to double the agitation which prevailed, and the

zeal of the opposition [1]. It would have looked as if the King mistrusted his own cause and despaired of maintaining the legality of his dispensing power: which would have shaken his whole state. For this very reason, to bring the case before the Ecclesiastical Commission would not attain the end desired; for the punishment of the Bishops through the action of that body for their disobedience, would not remove the impression just referred to. After some lawyers had been asked their opinion it was decided to call the Bishops to account, not so much for their disobedience as for the offensive contents of their address, and that before the same court by which the right of dispensation had formerly been recognised [2]. If the Court of King's Bench adhered to its principle, it must also condemn the petition of the Bishops, which denied the legality of that right. But this would impose silence on the outcry of opponents; the charge of illegal conduct brought against the government would rather tend to its advantage.

In the first place the Bishops were summoned to a preliminary hearing before the Privy Council, where the Lord Chancellor made known to them that it was intended to bring them before the Court of King's Bench, in order to get a decision upon the question whether or not their address could be reconciled with the reverence due to the King. As they refused to give security by bail—in this case their own recognizances—for their appearance before the court, saying that as peers of the realm they were under no obligation to do so, they were taken to the Tower, under the authority of the Privy Council.

Even at this early stage of the proceedings unparalleled marks of sympathy were shown to the Bishops. As they

---

[1] Citters: 'Dat so ongemerkt te laten passeren is byna onmogelyk, omdat sy des Coninx doen veer illegael oft on wettig opentlyck verclaeren en alsoo hem voor injusticie mede betichtigen en van wat consequentie dat soude syn te lyden.'

[2] Adda, 4 Giugno (about a council of June 2): 'Vi furono chiamati alcuni giudici ed altri della legge perche considerato minutamente il fatto con le sue circostanze esaminassero siu dove legalmente possa arrivare il castige e il regio potere nel medesimo.' Barrillon, June 17: 'Il y a des gens fort habiles dans les loix d'Angleterre, qui croyent que les évêques ont fait une faute, qui peut dans les règles être punie fort severement.'

stepped on board the barge on which they were to be taken
to the Tower, during the passage, and on their landing they
were greeted by the assembled throng with acclamations in
which religious reverence and political sympathy were combined. It was the moment at which Episcopacy concluded,
as it were, its alliance with the population of London. The
Bishops were popular because they maintained the cause
of all.

The same scenes were repeated when they were brought
back to Westminster Hall, on the 15th of June, to read the
information laid against them, and to fix a time for the actual
trial. They now paid their recognizances, the Archbishop
£200, each Bishop £100, and then returned to their homes.
The people, though wrongly, thought that this meant that
they were already at liberty, and greeted them with the
loudest shouts of joy.

At this time the King might have taken advantage of the
happy delivery of his wife, who in fact gladdened him by
bringing forth the wished-for son, to suspend further proceedings, and to declare to the Bishops his forgiveness for
the injury they had done him. The universal sympathy
for them made this in itself advisable, considering the popular
nature of English judicial procedure, especially as the government on this occasion could not count even upon the judges.
The King was, moreover, invited to take this course. But
anxiety for the future of his son was, as before mentioned, one
of the principal motives of his whole conduct. And he was
by nature fond of political danger; he felt at home in the
midst of it. Whether he was really convinced that he was
completely in the right in the case may be left undecided:
but he flattered himself with the hope of getting the better at
law on this occasion as he had on others.

The 29th of June was the day of that great political and
legal trial of which all parties eagerly expected the result.
The noblemen of parliamentary sentiments who had visited
the Bishops in their confinement in the Tower, and had greeted
them on their first return thence in Westminster Hall, **had**
appeared on this occasion also in great numbers; **not only**
Clarendon, but also Halifax, who had hitherto taken **little**

interest in their cause ; and in general Tories and Whigs acted together, Danby, Nottingham, Bedford, Shrewsbury, Lumley. Differences of view disappear when the system to which both parties are attached is endangered. The general feeling of devotion to Protestantism and Parliamentary government prevailed throughout the assembly which had met in Westminster Hall ; and in proceedings of this kind, the expressed or even unexpressed agreement of men's minds contains in itself a power, sometimes an irresistible power.

The Bishops were accused of having, in the form of a petition, delivered to the King, and then published, unlawfully and maliciously, a false and seditious libel, to the dishonour of the King, against the laws of the land and the public peace.

Many hours were occupied with the proof that the petition· had been really written by the Archbishop, signed by the Bishops and delivered to the King ; the Lord President Sunderland had himself to appear before the court—in his wheel chair, for he was tormented by gout—to give his evidence ; even so, the fact was not thoroughly proved according to law. We will not however dwell upon the particulars which were then discussed ; they have more importance for the forms of English procedure than for the case itself. Let us only consider the speeches on both sides which concerned its substance.

Sir Robert Sawyer, one of the most eminent barristers in the Tory ranks, spoke first on behalf of the Bishops. He sought, in the first place, to prove that there was nothing in the form of their petition which could justify the severe expressions of the indictment ; then he brought forward the indispensableness of permanent ecclesiastical rules for the state and for civil life ; otherwise the Sabbath would no longer be observed ; the distinction between heathens and Christians would cease : he argued at length that the Bishops, who by a statute of Queen Elizabeth were charged with the care of the uniform execution of the ecclesiastical laws, not only had a right, but were under an obligation to remind the King of them.

This display of an intention to pass from the more ecclesiastical ground to that which properly belonged to political jurisprudence, aroused in the first.moment some hesitation in the court ; yet even among the four judges one spoke in favour·

of the course pursued. Heneage Finch, the second advocate
of the Bishops, was able to enter without interruption upon the
great question which occupied all minds, the dispensing power.
To the charge made against the Bishops of having curtailed
the royal authority and prerogative by the denial of this right,
he opposed the assertion that this right was not included at
all in the King's prerogative.   He had never heard or learned
otherwise than that the legislative power rested in the King
and the two Houses of Parliament ; but that the suspension of
the laws formed a part of the legislative power ; that the
Bishops had said, quite rightly, that the power claimed for the
King had never been recognised by Parliaments : as bishops
and peers they had been under an obligation to make representations to the King against a declaration, by which all
the laws enacted for the protection of the established Church
and for the maintenance of religion were suspended at
once. Finch justified on this occasion, as on others, the
reputation which his family enjoyed of possessing, as it
were by inheritance, the best qualities required for success in
the legal profession. He was a Tory like Sawyer ; they had
both promoted the Tory reaction of the last years of Charles
II, and had only renounced James II when he began to
exercise the dispensing power on his own authority ; in opposing him now they contended for their own cause. They
were supported by the young Somers, a representative of the
sentiments of the moderate Whigs, who concluded the defence
with the happy saying that the petition of the Bishops did not
deserve a single one of the charges made against it, that it
was neither false, nor malicious, nor seditious, nor even a libel.

But let us hear also what was said on the King's side in
support of the charge. Parts were singularly changed. The
King's cause was pleaded by an old champion of the
advanced, almost democratic, Whigs, Sir William Williams,
formerly speaker of the Lower House and one of the leaders
of the Exclusion party ; but he had some time ago made his
peace with James II and appeared as solicitor general. He
drew many formal arguments from the mode of procedure
which his two principal opponents had with doubtful legality
adopted when formerly pleading for the government. On

the substance of the case Williams argued that addresses and resolutions could not be regarded as declarations of the Parliament, otherwise the Exclusion bill, which had formerly been defended by him and objected to by his opponents must also have passed for such a declaration. He made it a charge against the Bishops that they had quoted expressions which possessed no binding force as if they were a declaration of the illegality of the dispensing power—an act which certainly implied a diminishing of the King's authority. The King maintained that the dispensing power belonged to him, the Bishops denied it,—who was to be the judge between them? At least they ought to have waited for the meeting of Parliament, which the King had announced for the next November; for that was the right place in which to decide the question[1]. It was without doubt an offence that the Bishops had absolutely denied a right which the King claimed, and had accused the King of illegality before the King.

And this argument made so great an impression that the Archbishop for a moment gave himself up for lost[2]. For the judges also declared that there was something seditious in an interference of anybody with affairs of government in an improper place—as of the Bishops out of Parliament. The right reverend prelates, it was urged, had certainly done something which lay outside their powers. It was not, however, possible that this impression should prevail. No one could be convinced by a reference to the Parliament, which had been so often announced as about to meet, yet had always been put off, and had not yet re-assembled, although a dissolution had intervened. And when Williams finally declared that the Bishops ought, even if anything was commanded them which went against their conscience, yet to have complied till the next Parliament met, he aroused a loud outbreak of general contradiction. The preponderance of arguments, even without considering the party-position which might affect each man's

---

[1] ' If they were commanded to do anything against their consciences, they should have acquiesced till the meeting of the Parliament.' State Trials xii. 416.

[2] So he said afterwards in an audience of the King.

views, inclined to the side of the Bishops. One of the judges, whose turn now came for stating their opinion, doubtless expressed the general view, when he remarked that the Bishops could not obey for conscience sake, and that when they had once made up their minds on this they could not avoid also stating their motives. The weakness of the accusation consisted in this, that it could not deny the conflict of the royal order with the religious convictions of the Bishops, nor yet could it maintain the legality of the dispensing power. Every one, moreover, feared the danger to religion and to the laws which as most men thought arose from the claim to exercise that power. One of the judges even, Powell, warned the jury in a fiery address not to sanction the crown's claim, which, if enforced as it was then understood, would cause the substance of the legislative power to devolve upon the crown, and would for the future make a parliamentary assembly useless.

There could not well be any serious doubt as to the verdict of the jury : many striking arguments had been used on behalf of the Bishops ; public opinion had taken their side decidedly ; a part of the judges even and the jury were under the influence of the general feeling. The sitting had lasted till late in the evening, and the jurors remained together through the night ; it was only on the following day that they pronounced their verdict of ' Not guilty ' on the indictment. Never had the verdict of a court of law been received with greater and more universal joy. People saw in it a decision of the religious and political questions of the moment. The news spread with electric speed on both sides of the river, through the capital, and over the country, and was passed on everywhere with loud expressions of delight. The Bishops as they left the court were received by the crowd with the reverence shown to ecclesiastical superiors. People kneeled down and asked for their blessing [1].

James II was unwilling to recognise in the result, disagreeable as it was to him, a positive defeat. He said that

---

[1] Lonsdale, Memoir of James II . . . . 'people that upon other occasions had perhaps but little religion, did not fail to fall upon their knees.'

the jury had only decided that the petition of the Bishops could not be regarded as a libel, but nothing more. In the Privy Council he declared his intention of having the disobedience of the Bishops condemned by the ecclesiastical commission, and of having the question about his dispensing power decided by the next Parliament.

The King was confirmed in the unyielding attitude, to which his nature already inclined him, by the fact that a son had been born to him. The reasons have been already given for its producing this effect upon him.

The lying-in had taken place somewhat sooner than had been expected. There had only been time to transfer the Queen's residence from Whitehall to St. James' Palace, which was convenient and remarkably cool. And not all those had been summoned whose presence would have been necessary for a satisfactory attestation of the birth of an heir to the throne. At all epochs cases of this kind occur; the more desirable the result to one party, the more does it arouse among all others the suspicion of a trick being practised. At present there is hardly any one who seriously doubts the legitimacy of the prince.

He was born on the 10th of June. On the very same day the Papal Nuncio offered the King his congratulations. James led him into the chamber in which the child lay, and, in order that the Nuncio might see how well he was formed, drew aside the veil which covered his face; 'with great satisfaction,' says the Nuncio, 'and to my indescribable pleasure.' On the occasion of another visit the King drank the child's health to the Nuncio out of a silver cup; the Nuncio pledged him, as after him did Sunderland and some others who were present. The Pope was to be the godfather of the future King of England. James said to the French ambassador that this child would one day need the aid of France, which assuredly would not fail him; that he for his part would do everything to deserve the friendship of Louis XIV: 'I hope' he said, 'that we shall yet do great things for religion.'

Yet even now conciliatory and moderate counsels were once more offered. But the zealous Catholics saw in the birth of the prince a proof that their prayers were heard,

a pledge which God gave to Catholicism for its future in
England. Father Petre drew from it the conclusion that the
King was now doubly bound to persevere in the work which
he had undertaken.

It was remarked that his zeal rather increased than cooled.
The judges who had made themselves objects of displeasure
were removed from their places; even Jeffreys, who was
considered to some extent responsible for the unwelcome
issue of the trial, found it difficult to maintain his position:
and as the King generally expected more from old enemies
who had been reconciled to him than from men who had
been his friends up to the present time, Williams obtained
a good prospect of being Jeffreys' successor. The judges who
had been kept in office continued upon their circuits to declare
the Bishops to be seditious libellers, and to reproach the
English Church with bloodthirstiness and cruelty [1].

James II did not renounce his intention of having the
Bishops and clergy punished by the ecclesiastical commission;
but in the first instance it was more important for him to get
together a Parliament of which the disposition should be
hostile to the Church. The Regulations of the corporations
were continued recklessly, with the intention of placing
municipal offices in the hands of the sectarian Nonconformists. One day William Penn visited the Nuncio and
represented to him how necessary it was to place the adherents of the sects in a secure position against the time when
Catholicism might again attain to authority. But even before
any interference of the Nuncio, who completely understood
this and spoke on the subject with Sunderland, the government had already thought of it. In order to give a guarantee
to the Nonconformist sects, Colonel Titus and young Vane,
son of the Henry Vane who had been executed, were taken into
the Privy Council. The astonishment and terror of the
Episcopalians shows itself in the words with which Clarendon
accompanies this notice, when inserting it in his journal:
' My God,' he exclaims, ' what will become of us? '

---

[1] The Archbishop upbraided the King, even bitterly, with this somewhat later.
Clarendon's Diary ii. 498.

· About the end of August, accordingly, the resolution was
taken to try in earnest whether an anti-Episcopal Parliament
could not be brought into existence [1]. The King declared in
the Privy Council that the Parliament of England should
re-assemble on the 27th of the next November. He was
convinced, he said, that all reasonable men, all friends of
the true interests of the country, recognised the value of his
projects, which only aimed at the public good, and would
further them; he repeated that he only wished to establish
freedom of conscience for ever in a legal way. One of
those present remarked that it were only to be wished
that the King's opponents had been there: 'his frank way
of expressing himself would have inspired them with full
confidence.' Others of his adherents added that he had the
best assurances from many important quarters; and that with
the zeal which he showed in the cause he would carry out his
design.

And in fact the larger party certainly feared what the
smaller hoped for. For it was thought that 'the changes of
persons which had been produced by the Regulations would
strengthen the influence which the government had in nearly
all cases exercised on the elections up to this time; in cases
where, in spite of this, the elections did not turn out as was
desired, there would be found sheriffs and clerks, willing to
lend themselves to the task of falsifying the result; and if
such a Parliament were once assembled it would behave
itself as the true Parliament and enjoy the authority of such
a body. It was to forward the adoption of resolutions desired
by the King that sectarian party leaders like Vane had
been added to the Privy Council [2]. The King had once, in
his youth, praised Cromwell for having admitted his officers
into Parliament; probably he would follow his example:

---

[1] In the Nuncio's letter of September 3rd, printed in Mackintosh's history, the
words are found, 'resolutione presa di non convocare il parlamento,' after which
there is mention of the ' elettioni di membri che hanno da comporre la camera
bassa.' The ' non ' is a blunder of the copyist or of the compositor.

[2] Bonnet, July 10/20: 'On a consideré qu'on feroit un grand gain dans un
parlement, si par une telle récompense on pourroit gagner trois personnes (Trevor
was the third) qui y ont autant de voix que ceux cy.'

he would create himself a majority in the Upper House by
new nominations. And if resolutions agreeable to the King's
views had once been passed who would dare to resist him?
The standing army was strong enough to put down all
resistance; in case of need, Tyrconnel had forty thousand
Irishmen under arms who might at any moment come over
to England.'

The report was that further measures were to be taken
against any danger that might be apprehended from the
alliance with the sectaries; that it was intended to impose a
new oath upon officials, an oath of obedience, not only to the
King, but also to the new-born Prince of Wales, and to the
Queen herself, in case there should be a minority. The
government seemed to wish to secure the future, both by
Parliamentary and by dynastic measures, in order to carry
out the plan of a thorough reform favourable at once to the
monarchy and to the Nonconformists.

To this point had James II been led, step by step, by his
idea of procuring for the Catholics political equality with the
Protestants. His forefathers had cherished similar projects
before him. They thought that by relieving their Catholic
subjects from disabilities they would establish their authority
over them, exclude the action of hostile influences from the
Continent, and would so, for the first time, really establish the
unity of the realm of Great Britain. King James II however went much further. He had himself become a Catholic,
and saw in his project in some sense the fulfilment of a
religious duty; he wished rather to introduce than to repel
foreign influences.

If we consider the import of this policy in the light of
history, we shall find that it ran directly counter to the
whole current of affairs. For since the oldest times the
national opposition to the Papacy had been the sphere in
which Parliament had risen; with its help the crown had
carried out the Reformation, and had assumed and defended
its European position as a Protestant power; since the Restoration the Parliament had fused itself with the Anglican
Church, and had repelled all attempts to impair that combination by assuming an attitude which was constantly becoming

more and more exclusive. The nation saw in the Protestantism which had been fortified by the legislation of a century and a half the guarantee of its freedom and of its rights.

James II attempted to undo all this, and that at a time when the renewed outbreak of religious strife, and the oppression of fellow-believers abroad, had aroused Protestant feeling and inspired it with the most active life.

His weapon was the authority properly inherent in the King, the prerogative. He still possessed it; for Charles II had not allowed it to be wrested from him; after the storms of the Rebellion it seemed necessary for the commonwealth. James II, however, did it the worst service by employing it for one-sided religious ends. The crown's power of summoning the Parliament, its share in the composition of the courts of justice and in the appointment of magistrates, its military and administrative authority, were all made to serve this one object. The right of dispensing with the laws, which could not be doubted as to particular cases, became a mockery of the legislative power by the way in which the King applied it; and who could endure the employment of his ecclesiastical supremacy to further a policy opposed to the Church? To these faults was added the administration of foreign affairs in subserviency to the predominant European power; a subserviency odious to the nation and ruinous to the balance of power in Europe.

And in considering the special position of James, we must remember that he had been enabled to mount the throne by the Episcopalians having combined with him in his struggle against the Presbyterians and Whigs. What would be the consequences now that he attacked those very men on whose support his kingly power was founded, and drove them to the side of his enemies, who had hitherto been theirs also? Never has a prince so wilfully undermined the ground upon which he stood.

He undertook an attack upon everything in his kingdom which had usage and right for it, and appealed for support in his enterprise to the elements which were, like him, directly opposed to the existing state of things and to the constitution. What could be the result if he succeeded in bringing into existence such a Parliament as he proposed to assemble? The alliance of the prerogative with the Catholics, for whom James wished to procure a share in that public life from which they were altogether excluded by law, and with the members of the Protestant sects, threatened the country with a revolution.

James II did not find himself in a position entirely resembling his father's. Perhaps he may be best compared with Richard II, who, supported by the judges, quarrelled with his Parliament, showed leanings towards the Lollards, and formed an alliance with France which was odious to his people. And, in fact, the events of 1399 often hovered before his eyes and before those of his adversaries; the precedent did not terrify him, though it inspired his adversaries with courage.

We do not consider ourselves authorised to adopt the tone which English historians have borrowed from the proceedings of criminal courts; we have only to do with the contemplation of the historical event. What an extraordinary spectacle does that present! On the one side stands the old England formed by the labour and the strife of centuries, lately shaken, but finally restored in the old forms, and on the other a prince who, from a one-sided point of view, although not without the support of general tendencies, and on the plea of removing mischievous restrictions, sets himself with rash hardiness in opposition to the state of things which is the result of past history. He does not intend, strictly speaking, to violate the laws, nor yet to evade them ; but he has so high a conception of his prerogative that he thinks himself exalted above them ; and, when he finds it impossible to alter them in any other way, he thinks himself able to transform so as to suit his own views that very legislative power on which everything depends. Under the impulse of religious zeal, he disregards the limitations of his power, which usage has consecrated, and endangers the foundations of the state and of life. He necessarily thereby provokes an open contest with the Parliamentary and ecclesiastical powers of his realm. Will he overpower them, or they him? Either the previous constitution of the country must perish, or the royal prerogative must succumb.

The Spanish ambassador, Don Pedro Ronquillo, once warned King James not to go too far, nor to venture too much.

'Monsieur Ronquillo,' answered the King, 'I will either win all or lose all[1].'

---

[1] 'Monsieur Ronquillo estoy fixamente ressuelto a conseguir el todo o a arriescarlo todo.'

BOOK XVIII.

THE FALL OF JAMES II IN ITS CONNEXION WITH
THE EUROPEAN CONFLICTS WHICH MARKED
THE CLOSE OF 1688.

THE states and empires of Europe are often held to be more independent of, and more distinct from, each other than they really are. They belong, however, to the general community of peoples of the West, which rests upon common bases, and has grown up from elements near akin to each other; from which community each one has risen to a separate existence, without, however, ever tearing itself away from the whole. Even insular England feels constantly the effect of tendencies general in Europe, and influences them in turn: it is clear, for instance, that the proceedings of James II, which aimed at a re-introduction of Catholicism, do but represent upon a definite stage the general struggle which had arisen between the two confessions.

Sixteen years earlier, on the occasion of the second war against Holland, similar projects entertained by Charles II had led to a great European crisis. The Republic of the Netherlands, which formed the principal bulwark of Protestantism in Western Europe, especially when the crown of England refused its support to the cause, was then very nearly destroyed by the co-operation of that crown with the predominant power of France. At the moment now in question the connexion of events was not so evident. But it was only in consequence of that war, and of the treaty to which it led, that the predominance of Louis XIV had fully established itself, and had at the same time assumed an exclusively Catholic character. The changing tendencies of Charles II's policy had not hindered that result, but had rather promoted it.

And James II now resumed the policy of 1672, and attached

himself unswervingly to the King of France. Nor was this surprising; for what was it on which he principally relied in his religious and political undertaking? The commanding position in which the neighbouring monarchy stood guaranteed him support and a feeling of security, even in case his proceedings should arouse opposition in his own country: he thought that foreign aid was at his disposal at every moment, and that an anticipation of this would deter his foes at home from manifestations to which they would otherwise proceed. The religious impulse was no doubt supported by political calculation; the first would not have led King James as far as he actually went, had he not had confidence that he could support himself on a great foreign power against all opposition. But that power on its side secured in him a trusty ally by the existence of this relation. The strife which awaited its decision in England thus lost its insular character; it entered into connexion with the great religious and political conflict which then in various ways divided Europe, and appears as an essential part of it.

CHAPTER I.

A DOCUMENT, of doubtful origin to be sure, lies before
us, in which there breathes the liveliest feeling of the connexion existing between the religious and political questions
which divided the states of the Continent, and those which
divided English parties; it is a project which is said to
have been laid before the English Privy Council as early as
the summer of the year 1686, in order to persuade the King
again to make war upon the Republic of the United Netherlands, and that a second time in alliance with France. The
starting-point adopted in it is, that King James II would
never be secure upon his throne unless he carried out, in spite
of all resistance, what he had once undertaken in favour of the
Catholic religion; but that no power offered him such an
effective opposition in this work as the Republic of Holland,
to which he had owed the invasion of Monmouth, which gave
the rebels a refuge, and kept up disaffection in England.
Now, as he was evidently by himself too weak to subdue at
once his domestic enemies and the Republic, he was advised
in plain terms to put himself in a position to do so by a close
alliance with France. 'For the King of France was his friend,
and certainly ready and willing to aid him in this work; he
had placed his whole power at James' disposal from the
beginning. And never had there been a more favourable
moment than the present, in which all the powers from which
Holland could expect support were fully employed in the war

against the Turks. By a military undertaking, resolutely carried out, he not only might gain distinction, but would become lord and master in his own country. Let him only require from his Parliament—it was still the Episcopalian Parliament—the money necessary for his undertaking, and if it was denied him, accept the support of France. If that power should become troublesome to him in consequence, he might at some later time employ the help of Austria against it, as soon as Austria should have its hands free; everything, how-ever, depended on his first overthrowing the Republic. And even dependence upon France,' it was added, 'was not the worst evil; it was in any case better than that his subjects should re-main slaves of the evil spirit by the abuse of their freedom[1].'

The tone and contents of this document, especially these last intimations, show that it cannot possibly have been laid before the Privy Council of England, in which so many Pro-testants still had seats. James II first became acquainted with it through the agency of a foreign ambassador, and gave way to a violent outbreak of passion about it as a composition of his most hated enemies. For only one of them could hold him capable of having recourse to dependence upon France—him, who wished for nothing else but to make his nation great and powerful, if only it would follow him. At that time a step of this kind was still almost inconceivable to King James.

Although some have been disposed to derive this expression of opinion from France, the conjecture has little probability. For the policy of Louis was still at this moment of a peace-able nature: the expressions about his power in the document, though apparently friendly, seem very offensive; and a close alliance of the King of England with the Parliament, to which importance was attached in it, never formed part of the objects of Louis. Still less could it originate, as James II said, with a journalist in Holland: for then it would have first come to light there, and not in England, in the immediate

---

[1] Mackintosh, ii, gives an extract from this paper, sent by Ronquillo to Madrid. The French original accompanies the despatch of Citters of August 1686. Yet the two envoys did not possess the document in a complete form. The whole begin-ning was absent in their copies. A complete communication on the subject is found in the Papal Nuncio's ' Dispacci ' of the year 1686, in the British Museum.

neighbourhood of the Catholic ambassadors; besides, it has too much internal truth to have sprung from such a source. The fundamental idea, that there was an opposition between the policy of Holland and that of the King of England intolerable for the latter; that it was necessary for England to conclude an alliance against Holland with the Catholic powers, especially with France; and that the state of affairs promised well for the success of such a combination—this idea contains a correct view of the case: it is rooted, moreover, in the interests of the party of action which had formed itself round James II. He did not yet consciously cherish these thoughts; but others, if one may say so, had *felt* them out of his soul by anticipation, and held it good to express them.

Nobody, however, could have ground for supposing that this was the intention of the Catholic world in general; quite the contrary. The court of Rome especially did not approve of the proselytising zeal with which the violent English Catholics went to work. As formerly Paul III and Urban VIII in other decisive crises, so now Pope Innocent XI assumed in the crisis of his own days an attitude of opposition to the Catholic zealots. The employment of violent means in affairs of religion was altogether odious to him. In his instructions for a papal plenipotentiary at this time there is, no doubt, expressed a hope of procuring greater freedom for Catholicism in England, but, to adopt a common expression, the evangelical way alone is recommended for the attainment of that object. 'It was necessary,' says this document, 'to appoint good bishops and by their agency to form a clergy of similar sentiments, which would then have to content itself with simple toleration; the past taught that neither violence nor even political influence could in England attain the end desired; that neither the regular nor the secular clergy ought to have much to do with the court, nor to meddle with the affairs of this world, still less to arouse a suspicion that it was capable of violating the constitution of the country [1].'

The authorities at Rome stood in other respects also in

[1] 'Ricordi da darsi ad un ministro pontificio—e da suggerire da parte di sua Santità alla Maestà del re della Gran Bretagna.'

declared opposition to the proceedings of the Jesuits, and
especially to Father Petre.

We have mentioned Petre's ambition, which aimed at the
possession of a high spiritual dignity, perhaps of the archbishopric of York: a position in which he might have employed at once the authority of his ecclesiastical office and his
favour with the King for the restoration of Catholicism in
England. But he was a professed member of the Society of
Jesus; and, according to its statutes, he required the Pope's
dispensation to enable him to accept such a post. The principal object of the mission of Castlemaine to Rome had been
to persuade the Pope to grant such a dispensation. The
statute says that no professed member may accept the position
of an ecclesiastical prelate, unless compelled to do so by the
obedience which he owes to the Roman See; rather, accordingly, in consequence of a distinct command from Rome than
of a mere permission. But Innocent XI could not be induced
to issue such a command. He declared that his conscience
forbade him to do so, for that he should thereby awake the
ambition of other members of the order who were either con-
fessors of persons in the highest positions or otherwise in
favour with them; the same request would be addressed to
him from all sides; he dared not tamper with a statute the
very object of which was to keep the order free from all
worldly ambition. Castlemaine was commissioned, in case he
could not procure for the father the title of bishop, to propose
his elevation to the dignity of a cardinal; for by such an
elevation Petre would have held the highest rank in the King's
council. Probably the example of the great French ministers,
who had also been cardinals, hovered before his eyes. But
Innocent could not be induced to comply with this request
either; he represented that this dignity was still higher than
that of a prelate, and would gratify ambition in a still higher
degree. The King supported the request with the greatest
energy in his negotiations with the Nuncio, saying that the
circumstances were so extraordinary, and Father Petre so
singularly serviceable in dealing with them, that even an
extraordinary display of favour to him seemed justifiable.
Castlemaine, a party-man of much zeal but little sense, be-

haved with impatience [1], and even intimated that the refusal of his request might have the result of making it impossible for the Papal Nuncio to remain any longer in England. The Pope did not attach any very great importance to the presence of his plenipotentiary in England, while the reckless importunity of Castlemaine, and his constant boasting of the services of his King was intolerable ; the Pope demanded his recall, which could not be refused him. The Pope also had Father Petre rebuked by the General of the Jesuits for his ambition.

We remark a singular connexion between the court of Rome and the opposition of English parties. Cardinal Norfolk, Protector of the English nation, was in agreement with the Pope, and there was nothing which the moderate Catholics would have more desired than his presence in England, which would have enabled him to employ his influence with the King in accordance with the Pope's views. The jesuitical faction which surrounded the King not only opposed this suggestion, but wished also to dislodge Norfolk from his dignity as Protector, and to replace him by Cardinal Este, whom they reckoned as one of their party on account of his relationship to Queen Mary.

But enough of these relations, which no doubt concerned high personages, but in themselves were of only subordinate importance. The negotiations of James with the Pope touched upon other questions also, and those such as must exercise a decisive influence upon the Roman court. They arose out of the close connexion existing between the Catholic party of action in England and the King of France, whose intentions were in all respects most adverse to Pope Innocent.

Among Catholic princes and kings not one has ever attempted to establish the ecclesiastical independence of his realm in a more comprehensive sense than Louis XIV. While he thrust out the Protestants from it, he at the same time systematically opposed the influences of the Roman See. He made common cause with the Gallican clergy against

---

[1] Adda derives his zeal 'dalla sua natura calda e violenta e dalla passione che ha di mantenersi l'affezione del padre Peters che gode il favore del re distintamente.' All the information here given is derived from this correspondence.

the Protestants, and the Gallican clergy made common cause
with him against the Pope. The extension of the rights
belonging to the crown on the occurrence of vacancies in
bishoprics—the *regale*—over those provinces of France which
had hitherto been exempt from them, was in opposition to the
declarations of the Pope. Thereupon followed the Four Ar-
tieles of the Gallican clergy, the most important manifesto of
ecclesiastical independence against Roman supremacy which
has ever appeared. Louis XIV wished to enforce his claim to
a peculiar ecclesiastical independence even in the capital of the
Catholic world; he disputed the Pope's full sovereignty in it;
for he said that Rome was not the capital of a country like
other cities, but the common home of all Catholic believers [1].
When Pope Innocent abolished by his own authority the
established liberties of the ambassadorial quarters, which
served as asylums for criminals, in order to check the disorders which sprung from such a state of things, Louis declared that abolition an encroachment upon those rights of
the realm of France which his ancestors had possessed, and
which he could not allow to be wrested from him : the Pope
should at least have had so much consideration for the services
done by the Kings of France to the Church as to have asked
his leave beforehand. The ambassador, whom he sent to
Rome in the November of 1687, made his entry into the
place without renouncing the liberties in question. We may
not see a mere momentary display of self-will in this ; there
was system in it. For this very reason a new and more
violent dispute was kindled on the point. The Pope pronounced his interdict on the ambassador and on the special
French church in Rome, that of St. Louis. The Great Chamber of the Parliament of Paris replied by a lengthy declaration
that the interdict and the bull which preceded it were null
and void ; they required their King, on the basis of the Four
Articles, to summon a national council which might when it
assembled make orders with regard to the vacant bishoprics.;

---

[1] 'La patrie commune,' as Louis XIV says in a letter to James II, 'où les
princes de notre religion sont obligés indispensiblement de tenir leurs ambas-
sadeurs.'

the clergy and the Sorbonne assented to this suggestion ; the affair began to assume the aspect of a schism.

In what embarrassments must the King of England now become involved owing to this, occupied as he was at the very moment in an attempt to undo the effects which had followed in England from an attempt similar to that of Louis! He saw himself placed in an unpleasant dilemma by the rival claims of the two potentates of that Catholic community to which he thought of attaching himself. He abstained from giving any judgment about the *regale ;* in the affair of the freedom of the ambassador's quarter, he not only declared the Pope in the right, but expressed his astonishment at the claim of Louis XIV [1]. But he was so closely attached to that prince that he could not part from him,—still less enter upon an opposition to him. James at last decided to offer himself as mediator between Innocent XI and Louis XIV. The French Ambassador made no objection, provided that the mediator did not confirm the Pope in his obstinacy. But the Nuncio remarked from the first that the offer would lead to nothing, as the Pope could not admit of any negotiations whatever in these affairs under existing circumstances. The English, however, persevered in their project, especially as in their view negotiation did not prejudice a right. And on this occasion they took care not again to send to Rome an adherent of the Jesuitical faction ; the nephew of the Cardinal Norfolk, Thomas Howard, who had already given proofs of skill and energy, and was a Catholic, was entrusted with this commission (June 1688). Howard was very well received personally, but he effected nothing in the matter in hand. Pope Innocent said to him that if his own affairs were in question, there was no one to whom he would entrust their settlement more gladly than to the King of England ; but that the dispute concerned his sacred dignity and the rights of the Apostolic See ; he could not, accordingly, accede to any negotiation by a mediator, as though the King of France had even the shadow of a right to insult, injure, and maltreat him as he did [2].

---

[1] He said ' che tali quartieri erano un ridetto di tristi.' Adda, April 18, 1687.

[2] ' Che il re chmo. abbia avuta nessuna benché minima apparenza di ragione in

Pope Innocent XI saw in everything which was done in France and in England contrary to his wish and will the work—not indeed of the whole order of the Jesuits, for their General in Rome stood rather on the side of the Pope—but of a section of it, which had attached itself to the policy of Louis XIV, and on its side did not recoil with horror from a breach with the Pope.

But the quarrel with this party and with the King of France, in which Innocent XI became involved, forms only one element in the great political disputes which then set Europe in a ferment; these disputes arose altogether from the development of French predominance, which went on gradually indeed, but all the more surely, and in which the crown of the lilies seemed to aim at an universal ecclesiastical and secular authority over all other powers.

For more than twenty years the acquisition of the Spanish monarchy had been in view; Louis XIV never lost sight of it. And as on most other questions, so on this also, James II attached himself to France, as he could hardly help doing, considering his conception of unconditional hereditary right. At the moment, however, other projects lay still nearer, which were of the greatest importance for the consolidation of the power of France in reference to its immediate frontiers, and which especially concerned the German empire.

The twenty years' truce had granted to King Louis the provisional possession of those districts in Germany and in the Low Countries which had been adjudged to him by his 'Courts of Reunion,' and which he had occupied [1]. His purpose was to unite them for ever with his kingdom. Everywhere the districts were filled with troops, the strong places fortified, the internal organisation transformed after the French pattern. Moreover, the claims which the King deduced from the rights of his brother's wife caused an attack upon the ter-

---

fare alla Santità sua et alla sede apostolica strapazzi ingiustitie e violenze cosi strane, che hanno mosso un infinito scandalo ed orrore sino alle nationi piu barbare.'

. [1] I may here be allowed to refer to the third part of my French history, in which I have sought to explain these negotiations with the aid of original materials.

ritories of the Palatinate to be expected. The first result of
this apprehension was a defensive alliance between the Emperor and the more westerly circles of the empire, which
was concluded at Augsburg in the year 1686; it was the
universal opinion that preparations must be made against
possible contingencies; under the circumstances which then
existed this union obtained an European no less than a German character. But this very fact gave Louis XIV also an
occasion or a pretext for going further; he required the immediate transformation of the truce into a peace : ' for he saw,'
he said, ' the hostile object of the union, and could not doubt
that he should be attacked as soon as the war with the Turks
had been brought to an end.' Even the military skill and
military honour which the German forces acquired in that war
caused him anxiety. The words ' transformation of the truce
into a peace' sound very harmless, but they included a demand
of immense extent ; all those territories which at a moment of
distress had been provisionally left in his hands were now to be
definitely ceded to him. The Emperor answered by an offer
to pledge himself to keep the truce for the full time for which
it had been concluded, and thought it suitable that England
should give a formal guarantee to that effect. The English
government, too, was inclined to comply, if only for the reason
that such a course would prove its high position in Europe,
and must be of service to it in its contest with the English
opposition. But Louis XIV did not intend to content himself
with a simple guarantee ; he reserved to himself as a recognised right that mode of treating the territories referred to
which had been urged against him in Germany as an unauthorised extension of his provisional occupation—especially
the fortification of the towns [1]. In England it was thought
necessary at least to investigate whether the words of the
document admitted of such an interpretation or not. Lord
Sunderland insisted on this ; representing that the guarantee

---

[1] According to Barrillon, July 3, 1687, James declared beforehand that the
French were justified in doing as they did: ' Le roi dit qu'aux termes de la trève
V. M. est en droit de fortifier les lieux dont elle est en une possession, qui n'est
pas contestée.'

of an act of which the interpretation was doubtful would involve the English government in complications of which no
one could see the end. But the imperial ambassador would
not hear of this: for he did not doubt that the English
ministers would declare the explanation proposed by France
well grounded; in which case the guarantee would no longer
possess any value for Germany; it would have formed a
'præjudicium' in favour of France. And without doubt this
opinion was correct. James II had already expressed himself
to this effect: he made it no secret that he thoroughly
desired the transformation of the truce into a peace as
demanded by Louis XIV [1]; he stood unconditionally on the
side of that prince in this matter, and declared it to be a
piece of folly in the house of Austria that it would not consent to such a measure.

We have yet another question of more remote interest to
mention on which the French crown, in combination with that
of England, took part against Germany; it affected the North
of Europe; I refer to the affair of Sleswick-Holstein, which
first came to the surface at this time.

By the peace of Roeskilde the younger line of the house of
Oldenburg had acquired sovereignty over certain districts of
Sleswick, which had been considerably extended while in
its possession, and it had retained them, in spite of all hostile
attacks, as the ally of France and Sweden, in consequence of
the treaty of Nimeguen. Subsequently, however, political
relations changed. Denmark entered into alliance with
France, and, now in its turn depending on the protection of
that power, revoked its previous concessions; Christian V
declared himself sole sovereign of Sleswick, and compelled the
knightly order of that duchy to profess itself a member of the
Danish state. On the other hand, however, King Charles
XI of Sweden took up the cause of Holstein-Gottorp; he
threatened to throw twenty thousand men into Denmark, and
as he was at that time in close alliance with the German

. [1] As early as January 6, 1687, James said this expressly to the French ambassador. He did nothing afterwards on which he had not previously consulted
with the same person.

Emperor, and with the Republic of the Netherlands, it seemed possible that this affair might bring on a general war. In this quarrel Louis XIV now took the side of Denmark and sought to win England for it also. As far as the immediate question was concerned, the English government was not disposed to comply; Sunderland drily characterised the proceedings of Christian V as an usurpation. Barrillon replied that it did not signify who was in the right in the quarrel, especially as Denmark offered an equivalent; but that it was important to be able to check the machinations of a great opposition party in Europe [1]. Or would England permit that Holland should combine with Sweden and arm on this pretext? that might possibly become very dangerous for England.

Things certainly now began to look as though an understanding would be effected between the two Kings, though not primarily with a religious object. They co-operated already on some occasions. When, for instance, in January 1688, the King of England recalled from the Dutch service the English and Scottish regiments which had remained in it since the year 1678, he was no doubt partly influenced by increasing antipathy to the Prince of Orange: the first and principal incitement, however, proceeded from Louis XIV, who had not forgotten that the employment of those regiments dated from the time when England and the Prince of Orange were seeking in common to prevent the ratification of the peace of Nimeguen, so that he saw a kind of threat in their presence in Holland. Sunderland stooped so low as to receive a present from Louis for his services in bringing the matter to a conclusion. The States-General were reluctant to comply with the demand, and only carried out their compliance very imperfectly; the incident, however, made the impression on them that they had nothing good to expect from the two powers, and must put themselves in a state of preparation against any attack from them, in order to avoid experiencing a similar disaster to that of the summer of 1672.

---

[1] Sunderland is at first opposed to the equipping of a fleet 'pour soutenir l'usurpation du roi de Danemark.'—Barrillon: 'Que les puissances qui veulent le maintien de la paix soient bien fondées à traverser les desseins de ceux qui la veulent rompre.'

Some believed then, and have believed subsequently, in the
existence of an alliance concluded between France and
England ; but it results most distinctly from the ambassadors'
correspondence that no such treaty ever existed.   A general
understanding existed, no doubt, but without being reduced
to a definite form ; separate agreements had to be made for
each separate case.

In the spring of 1688 the two powers agreed that it would
be advantageous, with a view both to the disputes in the
North, and to their own relations to Holland, for an English
fleet to appear in the Channel.   Even for this purpose
James II claimed the support of France, and Louis XIV
declared himself ready to grant it, under the condition, however, that the fleet should have for its first object the preven-
tion of a combination between the Dutch and the Swedes
for an attack upon Denmark[1].   He used the expression
'to prevent effectively'; Sunderland asked what that might
mean?   For surely it would not be required that England
should attack the Dutch fleet if it sailed for the Sound ;
that would be a beginning of war, an undertaking which
opened very wide prospects, and which England certainly had
not in view.   Barrillon withdrew the expression when thus
construed.   The two ministers came to an agreement that an
English fleet of twenty-five to thirty ships of war should put
to sea in the spring, and make the demonstrations necessary
for preventing the Dutch from supporting the Swedes against
Denmark, without, however, being required to proceed to an
actual attack.   Louis XIV promised for that purpose subsidies
of half a million livres Tournois.

King James was still most urgently desirous of keeping the
peace : but it can yet be seen that he had already at that time
come to an understanding with France for operations against
Holland and the German empire.

At this very moment an event occurred which brought this
twofold direction of his policy into the clearest light.

The kind of joint sovereignty which France had exercised

---

[1] 'À effectivement empêcher que les Hollandois ne donnent la main à la Suède
pour attaquer le Danemarc.'

in the German empire since the peace of Westphalia rested, in great measure, on the ecclesiastical electors having fallen into dependence on the French crown. Thus Maximilian Henry, Elector of Cologne, who also held the bishoprics of Liége, Münster, and Hildesheim, had for a long time been politically almost a vassal of France, and one of the principal supports of its authority in Germany. He himself in January 1688 furthered the appointment by postulation of Cardinal William Fürstenberg, under whose influence he had entered into that relation to France, as his coadjutor in the archbishopric. As Maximilian Henry died in this very year, it now formed an important object for France to gain the succession in this great ecclesiastical district for the coadjutor. Fürstenberg was the warmest and most active of all the dependents whom France still had in Germany. The French power would have become dominant in North Germany by his establishment at Cologne.

But for that very reason this project must needs meet with the opposition of all the independent neighbouring states. In the three other chapters it failed completely; even in Cologne it could not be carried out as its authors wished. The election of Fürstenberg was carried, no doubt, by a majority of votes; but a majority was not sufficient in this case. The Emperor and the empire thought themselves justified in giving the preference to the candidate of the minority, Prince Joseph Clement of Bavaria; and in this, as in other cases, the Pope agreed with them.

But the King of France was determined to maintain his client; and he had the English government on his side in this as much as in any other case, principally from that government's hostility to the Dutch, who would be immediately affected, and, to adopt the expression used, mortified, by its conduct[1]. Thomas Howard received a supplementary commission to employ his influence at Rome in securing the recognition of Fürstenberg.

Such was the state of European politics in the summer of

---

[1] Barrillon, September 2: 'Sunderland me parut fort aise que V. Mé. soit resolue de soustenir le Cl. de Furstenberg.'

1688. Louis XIV still appears as the man of the epoch.
Favoured by the continuance of the Turkish war, which employed the forces of his antagonists, he was resolved to establish
on a permanent footing before that war should be concluded,
the preponderance which he already possessed. The affair of
the newly-elected archbishop at Cologne, an agreement just
then concluded with Hanover, and his alliance with Denmark
against Holstein, seemed to lay Germany defenceless at his
feet. We must not forget the importance of the two objects
which he made it his business to carry out. If he succeeded
in uniting for ever with his kingdom those districts of which
the temporary occupation had been allowed him, that kingdom
would thereby acquire complete military preponderance in
central Europe, both for defence and offence, especially with
regard to the German empire. Louis at the same time intended to drive the Roman See to adopt a policy of concession which would have confirmed the ecclesiastical independence of France, and would have procured it the primacy
of the Catholic world. On ecclesiastical questions James II
remained as neutral as he could ; on all others he placed
himself without hesitation on the side of Louis XIV. No
prince has ever had less thought for the balance of power
in Europe than James II. It was needful for him, as has
been mentioned, that the predominance of France should be
assured, in order to enable him to carry out in his kingdom
the undertaking which he had once set on foot. But this
undertaking again itself contained something of interest for
the King of France ; for Catholic action in Western Europe
was then concentrated in it. The path on which the two
Kings had entered in common would have led to the suppression of the political independence of states and of the religious
independence of confessions.

But one of the causes which enable the European commonwealth to maintain itself as a living whole is, that there are
active forces latent within it which have always hitherto restored the balance of power when disturbed.

On the present occasion, as in earlier and later times, those
forces came into play unexpectedly, suddenly, and decisively.

CHAPTER II.

THE PRINCE OF ORANGE AND THE PROTESTANT
EPISCOPALIAN PARTY IN ENGLAND.

THERE was one man in the world whom the foreign policy of France and the domestic policy of England, though they did not yet completely coincide, affected from different sides with equal force.

William Henry, Prince of Orange, was considered by Louis XIV to be his principal antagonist. Not as though he could with his own forces only have measured himself against the King in any way. What great enterprise could the captain-general of a commonwealth, which in anxiety for its freedom watched every independent step that he took with jealousy, undertake and carry out? But the effect which a man can produce on the world often depends, not so much on the power which he possesses, as on the attitude which he assumes and is able to maintain towards those forces which contend with one another for the control of the general life of which they form a part. Prince William rose to the position of representative and acting champion of the idea of the balance of power, which is necessary to the existence of the states of Europe. Around him the resistance which Louis XIV still encountered grouped itself. The persecutions of the Reformed Church in France secured him lively sympathy in the Protestant, as did the autocratic demeanour of the King of France towards the Roman See even in the Catholic world; every violent act of that prince turned to the advantage of his rival. Louis XIV made the man great whom he feared; his own conduct made the attitude assumed by the other an European necessity.

Now with this position of the Prince his relation to the affairs of England is connected. That relation has been already often mentioned in connexion with the course of events, but now deserves to be considered as a whole.

It had arisen altogether from the resistance which had been aroused in the English nation by the policy adopted by Charles II in league with Louis—a policy aiming both at a restoration of Catholic ascendancy in the government and at an extension of its prerogatives. Even at that time the English reposed their hopes for the future on the Prince, who, moreover, was connected with the house of Stuart through his mother; the various sections of the English opposition sought to ally themselves with him.

These relations were altered no doubt when, on the invitation of Charles II, the Prince married that King's niece, the Duke of York's daughter. The King had then given up his Catholicising ideas, and had resolved to make common cause with his Parliament and with the Prince against Louis XIV. It was not the fault of Charles and William that the peace of Nimeguen was concluded upon terms which founded the preponderance of Louis XIV in Europe. That result was owing far rather to the fact that France gained over the domestic adversaries of Charles and William, the members of the opposition in the States-General and in the English Parliament. It was impossible for Prince William then to retain the favour of the leaders of the English Lower House, those old Whigs who had been the founders of their party. Lord Danby, whom they overthrew, was one of his best friends and had promoted his marriage. The Prince was regarded as an adherent of the King, and of the Duke his father-in-law.

When the great agitation began, which arose out of the belief that no Catholic could perform the duties of an English king, and which was meant to lead to the exclusion of the Duke of York, it was not the Prince of Orange, but the Duke of Monmouth who was brought forward against the Duke of York. Shaftesbury, his Whig friends, and the Presbyterians saw in Monmouth a representative of their ideas; the Prince of Orange had too strong a claim of his own to suit them, and showed a predilection for the prerogative.

The man who first suggested that if the future Catholic King should be excluded from the administration it should be entrusted to the Prince of Orange, was Charles II himself, who thought that he thereby maintained the idea of hereditary right. The principal defender of hereditary right against the Exclusionists, Lord Halifax, made it no secret that he thought that he had thereby maintained the cause of the Prince of Orange more than that of the Duke, who in his opinion would certainly never be able to reign. The Prince was still on good terms with the King: he adhered to the royalist party.

But he could not, assuredly, approve of the policy adopted at and after the dissolution of Parliament in 1681; he had thought that a reconciliation might still be arrived at, and for this reason he made approaches to some of the eminent members of the opposition. But with them also he could not come to any real understanding, as they continued to declare Monmouth their future king; their idea of the Parliament and of the constitution was not his. Standing thus between the two parties he did not join either. He believed in the reality of the Rye House Plot; but at the bottom of his heart he disapproved of the condemnations of Russell and Sidney, if only on account of the doubtful and tyrannical construction of the law which was then applied. He disapproved of the system of government which under the influence of the Duke of York was adopted during the last years of Charles II; especially as it was connected with an approximation to Louis XIV which was ruinous to the European commonwealth. He then even kept up a good understanding with Monmouth; for a change of system might still have been expected from Monmouth's return to England, of which Charles II allowed hopes to be entertained.

The existing system, however, first received its full development from the sudden death of Charles II and from the accession of James II. What under these circumstances was the position of the Prince of Orange?

That he supported the undertaking of Monmouth, as many supposed, is incredible in itself; for Monmouth's claims were directly adverse to his own. And besides, how could he have thought of overthrowing the King in favour of a third competitor? He gained consideration even in the Netherlands from the fact that he was the son-in-law of the reigning King of England : there was nothing which troubled his opponents so much as the prospect which their Stadholder had of the English throne. We learn that the ruin of Monmouth was considered an advantage for the Prince; his authority in the Netherlands was increased by it and that of his adversaries impaired.

But although the Prince had thus done nothing either for Monmouth or for Argyll he still had not a good understanding with James II.

No confidential relations existed between the two courts. Prince William once conceived a suspicion that the correspondence of the members of his wife's household with certain personages who were not agreeable to him at Whitehall, or even with the English ambassador at the Hague, might have an injurious effect, and that perhaps even his wife might be estranged from him thereby. He did not hesitate to have the chamber of the English chaplain, whom he regarded as the go-between, opened, and his letters taken away and deciphered so far as they were in cipher. As the result of this investigation was to show that the gossiping letters of the ladies of the court were certainly calculated to arouse distrust, he decided at once to remove them all from his court, the chaplain and the ladies: his wife supported him thoroughly in this step; she herself announced to the ladies the day and the hour by which they must have left the country[1]. Personal quarrels of this kind never fail to have some consequences; yet on the other hand too much importance should not be assigned to them; in this case at least the main point lay in the important political and religious relations existing between the two parties.

---

[1] According to Diest (October 27, 1685) the Prince remarked that 'all manner of gossip was going on and all kinds of jealousy showing themselves among the ladies in attendance on his wife; that they were reported to England in order to cause distrust:' that from the letters which had been taken away and deciphered he had discovered all the 'accomplices who had dabbled in this correspondence.' The principal one is 'Mrs. Langfort, nurse of the princess;' she is removed with the others, but has a pension assigned her.

Between James and William a good understanding as to general policy could only exist so long as the King showed consideration for English Protestantism. For, while the Episcopalians supported his accession in spite of his creed, which differed from theirs, they assumed nevertheless that the Princess of Orange, as to whose Anglican sentiments there could be no doubt, and her husband, one of the most zealous Protestants in the world, would step into the King's place by succession before he should have been able to carry out any important encroachment upon the Protestant constitution. Even the first attempts of James to retain the Catholic officers in the army without the consent of Parliament left no doubt that this was the position of affairs.

Now at first the hope was entertained at Whitehall that as the Prince, if only from dislike of the persecution of the Reformed in France, was an adherent of the idea of toleration, he might from this point of view be found open to the kindred ideas of the King. In the summer of 1686 William Penn arrived at the Hague, in order if possible to gain him over to the notion of general toleration, but of a toleration which should be in opposition to the sole supremacy of the Episcopal Church. Although Penn did not say so outright, his demeanour allowed it to be seen that he had been commissioned by the King to make his overtures. He employed himself in making certain positive proposals, of which the object was to establish a balance between the different confessions. According to these proposals one third of the public offices was to be reserved for the Episcopalians, another to be assigned to the Catholics, and another to the Protestant Dissenters; it was desired to publish a kind of Magna Charta of freedom of conscience; universal toleration was to be imposed on future kings as an unalterable law[1]. With the ideas which Penn expounded most impressively were combined promises which he was allowed to make. But provision had already been made, owing to a peculiar accident, for his

---

[1] That such was the tendency of his ideas results from Mackintosh 1, 341. Apart from that, we have to refer on this point, as on what follows, to Burnet's communications. Own Times 441.

meeting with a very effective opposition at the Prince's court.
Dr. Gilbert Burnet, who by his history of the Reformation
had essentially helped to revive the anti-Papist spirit in
England, but who had thereby incurred the displeasure
of King James to such a degree that he thought it advisable to leave that country, was then at the Hague;
he enjoyed the confidence of the Prince and Princess, and
combated the counsels of Penn with the greatest energy.
The opposition in which the two men stood to each other
is of universal interest : Penn took up his position outside the
strife of the two confessions, Burnet in the midst of it; the
first denied the right of the legislative power to enact laws
ecclesiastically binding, and therefore demanded universal
toleration ; the second ascribed such a right to a legislative
power in which the Church itself took part, and only required
consideration for Dissenters and a partial toleration. Penn
had an ideal of human freedom in his head ; Burnet contented
himself with a definite measure of it corresponding to the
principles of the constitution. In depth and originality of
point of view Burnet cannot be compared with Penn ; in
a sense of the position of things at the present moment, of
the attainable and the necessary he was without doubt
superior to him. A reply was made to the Quaker at the
Hague which did not go very deep, but was striking. When
he spoke of irrevocable laws which were to secure freedom
of conscience, he was asked whether the Edict of Nantes
had not also been a law solemnly confirmed and declared
irrevocable ? Yet it had been annulled by a zealous
Catholic prince who had been conscious of his power so
to annul it.

As Penn pleaded the cause of the King, Burnet pleaded the
cause of the Episcopalian party. Yet he, too, had some difficulties to get rid of in his negotiation.

The Prince was a zealous Calvinist, like his forefathers;
he was strongly attached to the doctrine of unconditional decrees, and disapproved of the ceremonial service of the English
Church. He had not moreover acquired in Holland the reputation of being a lover of free constitutions. Who could
guarantee that if he came to England he would not work in

opposition to the Episcopalian and Parliamentary party in more than one relation?

Burnet did not hesitate to bring these questions formally under discussion. And he soon convinced himself that the Prince completely understood the necessity of the Parliamentary constitution in England. For the Prince allowed, in the first place, that religion could not dispense with the protection of the laws, and, what was most important, that without a Parliament the means of offering resistance to an over-powerful enemy could not be found. But if this was once granted, the Episcopal system ought not to be injured, for it alone .enjoyed the protection of the laws ; Prince William promised expressly not to show any one-sided favour for Presbyterianism. It had long been the object of Burnet's own doctrinal exertions to reconcile this party with the Anglican form ; he lived and acted with a view to comprehension ; on the basis of this idea he came to an understanding with the Prince.

But even so the most delicate question remained behind. What was in future to be the relation between the Princess, to whom the right of succession belonged, and her husband who had to vindicate her right? Which of the two was to be the future sovereign of England? That was a difficulty which the Prince had often had in his mind, but which during the nine years of his married life he had never been able to bring himself to mention. Dr. Burnet was notorious for not always having kept within proper limits in conversation, and for having allowed too much scope to his natural vivacity ; but nevertheless he certainly possessed the gifts necessary for exercising a deep religious influence, and a great position raises a man above himself. He felt himself enabled to discuss even this question by the confidence which the Princess showed him. After recalling various points in English history—for instance, the relations of Henry VII and his wife, a daughter of the house of York—he added the question whether the Princess, if she succeeded to the throne by hereditary right, would keep the authority in her own hands, or be willing to leave it to her husband? She answered, in the words of the Catechism, that she would adhere to God's law, of which the purport was that the woman must be obedient to the man, not the man to the woman; that if her husband kept the one commandment, 'Husbands love your wives,' she would on her side observe the other, 'Wives be obedient to your husbands in all things.' A declaration which announces a resolution matured in the heart, and on which it may be said that the future history of England depended; she herself informed her husband of it. The cold, reserved, and laconic William did not utter one word of thanks to Burnet; but from that hour he entered into a confidential and cordial relation to him which was only interrupted by death.

These conversations form a kind of negotiation. In their result there can be almost seen the programme of a future government; the Prince, not the Princess, to have authority; Parliamentary forms and privileges to be confirmed; Episcopacy to be maintained as the dominant form of religion; the Catholics to remain excluded from offices; the resources of the country to be employed in attaining that object of national and European interest which demanded immediate attention.

For all this a regular succession, one brought about in the course of nature, was presupposed; but at the same time an understanding was effected as to the points of view which should be maintained in common till such a succession occurred. We ought not to forget that it was one of the moderate clergy, one of those of latitudinarian sentiments as they were called, who brought about this understanding by his mediation; another would have hardly found the task feasible. The Bishop of London, who followed a similar path, expresses shortly afterwards his thanks to the Prince for the friendly sentiments which he cherished towards the English Church: 'he would reap the fruits of this wise conduct as soon as King James should be no longer among them.'

The Prince's refusal to assent to the abolition of the oaths taken as a qualification for office contained a guarantee of the Anglican and Episcopalian system for all future time : only with this refusal he must needs combine some consideration for the element second in power in the state, the Presbyterians.

For that body had, in subsequent years, risen decidedly

from the oppressed position in which it had been placed by
the Act of Uniformity, and by the later laws which supplied
what were thought the omissions of that Act. The Presbyterians
had become influential in the long Parliament of the Restoration
by means of the elections held to fill seats vacated from time
to time ; the right of resistance expressed in the Covenant,
and maintained by them, formed the basis of the political
theory of the Whigs : in the two last Parliaments of Charles II
they had been the stronger party. More than once it had
been owing to their estrangement from the sects which went
further that new disorders did not break out ; the undertaking
of Monmouth, for instance, might have had quite a different
result if they had joined in it. When the King dissolved the
Parliament it might be considered as the most important
question whether or not he would, by his Declaration of Indulgence, gain over and carry with him the most numerous
Nonconformists, the Presbyterians. He reckoned on the
antipathies which he supposed that the harshness and im-
periousness of the Established Church must have produced
among them.

The first writer who warned the Nonconformists against
attaching themselves to the King on this question was Lord
Halifax. In a pamphlet issued at a happy moment he represented to them the danger to themselves which would arise from
such a course, and assured them that the disposition of the
English Church was changed : if it had hitherto opposed every
kind of indulgence, and rejected very reasonable arguments for
it, this obstinacy had now been overcome ; the danger of all
Protestants had opened its eyes ; it now only desired peace
and agreement ; the universal conviction of thinking men now
pointed to the necessity of an union with the Protestants of the
continent, and of enlarging the foundations of their common
defence. They must only, he added, not allow themselves to
be divided, and hold fast to religion, law, and loyalty ; so
would the present danger pass by 'like a shower of hail.'

Without any special engagement the Presbyterians could
have counted on the Prince of Orange, whose personal belief placed him upon their side ; but even they wished very
much for an express declaration on his part. Such a declara-

tion was given them in a flying sheet brought from the Hague to England about the end of 1687. It was an open letter, signed by the Grand Pensionary Fagel, in which he affirmed that he expressed the sentiments of the Prince and Princess of Orange. The letter says that the abolition of the requirement of the oaths seemed impracticable to the Prince and Princess because the English nation and Church would clearly incur danger thereby; but that on the other hand they were ready to give their approval to the repeal of the religious penal laws if the King wished it; with the distinction, however, that the Roman Catholics should only be granted liberty of conscience, the Protestant Dissenters free exercise of their religion also. The Prince and Princess thought that in this way they would combine the idea of toleration with an indispensable care for the state.

In this letter there is combined with a defence of the Episcopal Church not only an assurance for the Protestant Dissenters, but also a promise for the Catholics. The Prince thus precisely hit the feeling of the nation as it then was.

'I could not express,' says Sarotti, 'what a thoroughly injurious effect for the King's purposes this declaration produces, especially as it agrees with everything which has here been maintained by the Protestants with much decision.' At the English court it was denied that such a declaration could have issued from the daughter and from the son-in-law of the King. But it was just this origin which formed the most important point in the paper; for the Prince and Princess still passed for undoubted successors to the crown; care was taken at the Hague to remove all doubt on the subject.

A fact previously noticed, that the attempt of various kings to combine the Anglicans and the Catholics had had the opposite result of awakening among the Anglicans a consciousness of belonging to the general Protestant body, and of bringing about an approximation between them and the Presbyterians, repeated itself now in a higher degree, as James II allowed the Anglicans to feel his displeasure so decidedly. In his opposition to the King, the Prince had the two greatest religious parties, the Church of England and the Presbyterians, on his side. These were the same parties by the

combination of which the Restoration had formerly been
effected. As they even at that time excluded the Catholics
from any real share of political power, they now also opposed
their intrusion among the elements which formed the state.

It is a marked feature in the history of the time that the
Episcopal Church, the Parliamentary party, the Prince of
Orange, and the Pope of Rome himself, shared an opinion
that the Catholics should remain excluded from political
rights, on the ground that the grant of those rights seemed
likely to shake the edifice of the English constitution, while
King James, on the other hand, in his Indulgence aimed
principally at procuring for his Catholic fellow-believers a
complete political equality.

The Church of England men and the Presbyterians had
certainly not arrived at a mutual agreement; but nevertheless
they held together on the whole against their common antagonist : and that not more against the Catholics than against
the Anabaptists and Quakers whom the King strove to unite
with the Catholics. Principally in order to quiet the apprehensions of the Presbyterians, the bishops of the Church of
England declared themselves ready to consider the rights of
the Protestant Dissenters. This was expressed even in that
first petition which led to their trial, and with still more
emphasis in a pastoral letter of the Archbishop of Canterbury
to his clergy which appeared in the autumn of the year 1688[1].

The King was disturbed when he noticed this daily growing
combination of his subjects with each other and with his
hostile son-in-law. One of the grounds on which he again in
the spring of 1688 put off the summoning of the Parliament,
was his fear that the Prince might then appear on the coast
with the Dutch fleet, and either procure for the Episcopalians
a preponderance in that assembly or cause them to make a
demonstration against him in some other way. His ambassador in Holland went still further in his fears on this subject.
He did not hesitate to assure the King that if a son was born
to him the Prince of Orange would come with an armed force
to England, in order to oppose the recognition of that son.

---

[1] Some heads of things to be more fully insisted on. D'Oyly i. 324.

As is always the case in controversies which affect the general course of affairs, an impulse given from one side provoked one fròm the other. James II intended by his demand addressed to the bishops, and by the proceedings taken against them, to humiliate the members of the Church of England, or at least to separate them from the Nonconformists: but the contrary happened; under the influence of public opinion, and of anxiety as to his objects, the judicial authority on which he counted in this undertaking refused him the support which it had hitherto given. The birth of a Prince of Wales awoke in him, and in those about him, a redoubled confidence in their cause, as it seemed to bring with it a guarantee that God willed the success of their project; but the coincidence of the event with the purposes of the Catholic camarilla was just what made the other side see in it a sort of coup-d'état of that very camarilla, executed in order to enable it to go to work with a full justification. On the first report of the Queen's pregnancy the opinion began to circulate in England and Holland that a trick would be practised in the matter[1]. Accordingly, when, at the time of the lying-in itself, all the usual forms were not accurately observed, the suspicion that a child had been introduced from without acquired a certain plausibility. A plan of St. James' Palace still exists on which the way is marked by which the spurious child was said to have been brought from room to room to the Queen's bed-chamber. And yet it was not doubted that such a Parliament as the government aimed at getting together would recognise the child as Prince of Wales, confirm the prevailing system in all points, and assume a hostile attitude towards the opposing party, which might become dangerous to the latter in the highest degree. 'Blows given by a Parliament are deadly ones;' so says a letter which Lord Mordaunt addressed to the Prince of Orange. It was considered quite possible that a majority of fiery sectaries, with whom aversion to the English Church prevailed, might be procured, and thereby apparent legality be obtained for the King's projects.

---

[1] Diest, January 16/26, 1618. It was said, 'that all was only feigned in order at the proper time to palm off a son with the more plausibility, and to confirm the Catholic religion in the realm': there were 'wagers that it will be a prince.'

In the conflict of these tendencies and expectations, of
hopes on the one side and apprehensions on the other, which
embraced the religious and political future of the realm, it
came to pass that some of the most eminent leaders of the
Protestant and Parliamentary party, allies of the Prince of
Orange, held it necessary that he should come himself with
an armed force to England, in order to make an open resistance
to the faction which oppressed them possible. They were
resolved now to put in practice the right of resistance of
which so much had been said.

'We have great reason to believe,' they say, 'that we shall
be every day in a worse condition than we are, and less able
to defend ourselves, and therefore we do earnestly wish we
might be so happy as to find a remedy before it be too late
for us to contribute to our own deliverance.' They thought that
they could foresee three things :—a new thoroughgoing change
of persons, both in the civil administration and among the
officers of the army ; further, the resolutions of a Parliament
brought together by the means which the government had
already begun to employ—resolutions which would be aimed
at those very persons whom the Parliament might regard as
its opponents ; finally, if the objects desired could not be
carried out in the Parliament, the adoption in some other
way of arbitrary measures which would make it possible for
the authors of those measures to save themselves. To this
gloomy prospect, which might be realised, they said, very soon,
even before the lapse of a year, they opposed the hopes
which might be drawn at the actual moment from the disposition of the country. The evils that people had already
experienced, or still apprehended, had brought it to pass
that nineteen-twentieths of the nation were eager for change,
and ready to rise if it were only possible for them to do so
without having to fear that they would be struck down
at the first moment ; the greater part of the higher nobility
and of the gentry shared these feelings. But all depended on
the Prince's landing with a force strong enough to defend
itself ; it would then become possible for the lords who were
in the understanding to arm their people and to lead them to
join him. There was nothing to be feared from the King's

land force, as internal divisions prevailed in it, and still less from his naval force, which assuredly would not fight for him in such a cause as this.

As one sees, this is not a proposal to the Prince to accept the English crown, but a plan for a general rising against the existing government of the King, to be undertaken with the support of the forces which the Prince should bring over. What was to happen afterwards was not at first discussed. William had decided to congratulate the King on the birth of the Prince of Wales; but at the same time he caused an assurance to be conveyed by the same ambassador, Zuylestin, to the friends with whom he had an understanding, that his intention of supporting them was not altered by that event. Theirs of invoking his help was first brought to maturity by it. One of the principal grounds of their decision was furnished, no doubt, by the Queen's lying-in : their deliberations were held on the following days under the impression produced by it, and their letter is dated on June 30, the tenth day after it. As all previous hopes had rested on the expectation of a Protestant succession, they became null and void on the appearance of an heir to the throne, who would, without doubt, be educated in the Catholic religion. The lords who were in the secret let the Prince know that his recognition of the child was injuring him in England, for that there was not one man in a thousand who was not convinced that it was a supposititious child ; the Prince must, if he came over, make this opinion the ground of his undertaking ; but, they added, if he wished to attempt such an undertaking, it must be done in the current year. Only on this condition did they promise to keep themselves ready to join him. That he should refuse to recognise the new-born child, and seize the present moment for action, were as it were the conditions of their invitation[1]. A letter from Shrewsbury to the Prince deserves notice, in which he tells him that he still entertains the same sentiments towards him as he had entertained on the 9th of June—that is, before the Queen's lying-in.

---

[1] 'The association inviting the Prince of Orange over,' and the documents connected with it, in Dalrymple, Memoirs, App. i. 228.

We cannot concern ourselves with all the petty expedients
by which the connexion of English magnates with the Prince
was kept up; it was maintained especially by the personal
interposition of Edward Russell and Henry Sidney, whom we
find at one time at the Hague, at another at Westminster,
and by the communications of Vice-Admiral Herbert, who then
betook himself to the Hague to stay there.

Those who signed the document above referred to with
their ciphers were seven : Edward Russell and Henry Sidney,
the cousin and the brother of the two great sufferers, who
represented the antipathy of the English nobility to the tyrannical treatment of their kinsmen; Shrewsbury and Lumley,
whose signatures attested the newly-awakened zeal in the
nation for that Protestantism to which they had been converted; the Bishop of London, who had persuaded them to
take that step, and in whose garden at Fulham the threads of
the combination had their principal centre. The most important
names were those of Danby and Devonshire. The first was one
of the principal founders of the combination of the aristocracy
and of Episcopalianism with the King's government under
Charles II, and was one of the oldest Tories, one of the
founders of that party; the other was one of the oldest and
most celebrated Whigs. Previously warm antagonists, they
had now combined in their hatred for the Catholicising tendencies of James II. Their names implied the support of
the two parties, which for the moment laid aside their old
quarrels in order to save Protestantism and the constitution
of the country. Halifax and Nottingham had been drawn
into the negotiations, and had only recoiled when the last
step had to be taken. Nottingham said indeed that, according to the Italian practice, he should deserve to be murdered
for not joining after having gone so far; but he promised to
take upon himself the guilt which lay in privity to the design,
and there was no reason for distrusting him. But there were
also many others who, though they had taken no part in the
last negotiations, had yet long shared in the understanding,
men of the highest rank, and of a zeal which staked everything on the cause : we find individuals who contributed
£30,000 towards the preparations for the undertaking. For the

Prince the invitation of the seven was invaluable, principally as containing a definite personal obligation and an assurance of well-informed and trustworthy men as to the feeling of the nation; its peculiar contents made it necessarily the standard which he was to judge by.

He inferred from it that the outbreak of an insurrection in England was inevitable, even if he did not take part in it. But in that case the result must in any event be injurious to him; if the King got the upper hand it might easily be foreseen what he had to expect from him; but if the King's opponents obtained the victory they would probably proclaim the Commonwealth and deprive him of all that he claimed for the very reason that he had refused them his help. But besides this, they were his friends and allies; he resolved to risk the undertaking which they proposed to him if his position in other respects made it at all possible for him.

CHAPTER III.

PREPARATIONS AND GERMAN ALLIANCES OF THE PRINCE OF ORANGE.

IN these preparations by no means all, but yet by far the most important part, depended on the United Netherlands themselves.

At the beginning of the year 1688 no one had any ground for thinking that the States-General would aid the Prince in an undertaking against England. The first hint of such a project, which Fagel uttered in the assembly of the councillors-plenipotentiary, was answered by an ironical remark, recalling the undertaking and ruin of Monmouth ; even the best friends of the Prince avoided further disclosures as far as possible, as they feared that they might be involved in a dilemma between the conflicting claims of his interest and the Republic's.

In a short time, however, people perceived that these interests touched one another very closely.

We have already mentioned the apprehension of a new alliance between England and France which arose out of the recall of the English regiments from the Dutch service. It was France which incited James to give the order, and a religious motive was urged in support of it ; for Albeville constantly represented that those regiments were a nursery of Protestantism which might be expected to exercise a most disagreeable influence in England. This side of the question, its relation to the strife of creeds, was taken into consideration in the Netherlands also. When the affair came before the rulers of Amsterdam for discussion, the remark of one of the burgomasters, who reminded his colleagues that

King James intended to employ the troops, on their return
to England, for the suppression of Protestantism, made
so great an impression that a resolution was carried to persist
in refusing their discharge. The friends of the Prince remarked that the King could have done him no greater
kindness than he did by making this demand ; for that thereby an understanding would be effected between him and his
previous opponents. The city of Amsterdam now also took
under its protection his friend Burnet, whose surrender was
demanded by the King of England : it gave him its citizenship in order to secure him against party persecutions.
Religious feeling was supported by a consideration drawn
from public law, which we ought not to pass over. In
favour of the King's right to recall the troops the English
ambassador pleaded the obligation which binds subjects to
their sovereign, in his opinion an indissoluble one. The republicans replied that every freeborn man had a right to
take military service where he would. The fundamental
position itself, that men were born free, did not fail to give
offence on the other side : it formed an element in the great
conflict of ideas which agitated the time. It did not much
affect the nature of the transaction, that a number of officers,
who were not so convinced of the truth of the Dutch position
as to be willing, on the strength of their conviction, to expose
themselves to the punishment prescribed by the English laws,
returned to England[1]: that was rather advantageous than
otherwise to the Prince of Orange ; he replaced those who
had departed by others who were completely devoted to him ;
and thereby became for the first time completely master of
the regiments. But this affair, as well as some disputes
of maritime origin, for instance about Bantam in Java, where
at that time the English company had been dislodged and
the sovereignty of the Dutch company founded, had already
interrupted the good understanding between England and
Holland, when James II took the side of the King of France

---

[1] Barrillon, April 1 : 'Les Anglois ne veulent point être exposés aux procédures
de justice.'—He noticed in the declaration of the Dutch 'le faux principe, que les
hommes sont naturellement libres.' March 22.

in the quarrel between Denmark and Holstein. While the States-General saw in this a reason for putting their naval force into a state of readiness for war, their doing so naturally provoked opposing demonstrations on the other side from James and Louis. In June 1688 the English fleet of twenty men-of-war appeared in the Downs. It is certain that in ordering this measure James II had only his domestic affairs in view. He wished to deprive his domestic opponents of the hopes which they entertained of help from Holland. But an eventual combination of the English fleet with a French one was certainly discussed. The King of France, who was then engaged in an undertaking against Algiers, let it be known in England that he would cause his armed fleet then employed off Algiers to sail subsequently to Brest in order that it might unite itself in case of need with the English Channel fleet. James II accepted the offer with thanks, although he thought that in that year no such step would be needed. Barrillon assured him that the offer of Louis XIV implied also an engagement on the part of the same monarch to support him against all domestic and foreign enemies. He was empowered, he said, to accept proposals made in reference to this subject. The government at the Hague, without being instructed as to all details, did yet receive information as to the intention of uniting the fleets.

This change in the general position of things proved a powerful support to the Prince. It coincided with the invitation from England, and strengthened him in his resolution to accept it; but, besides this, he might now count on the aid of the States in his enterprise. He had the first overtures made by Dijkvelt to the burgomasters Hudde and Witsen at Amsterdam. The worthy men were terrified when they learned that there was a question not only of defence against impending dangers, the existence of which they could not deny, but of the necessity of anticipating them. They did not certainly regard the danger as so urgent; they thought, and from their point of view not without grounds, that they had nothing more to fear in the current year. The Prince shared this impression; but he was convinced that both the affairs of England and those of the world in general

would in the coming year have taken a turn which would make
it impossible to carry out his undertaking. In this feeling he
uttered the exclamation 'Now or Never!' (Nunc aut nunquam).
He felt that everything on earth has its time. To one of the
burgomasters, whom he summoned to the Hague, he represented that the business might be effected in a fortnight,
and that even if it were to take more time that would
be no injury for the Republic, it would have no attack to
fear meanwhile. The principal point in the new overtures
was that he distinguished the undertaking itself and the
co-operation of the Republic in it : he asked—for Witsen
refused to give any advice—whether he might reckon on his
support if he entered on the undertaking without his advice.
After Witsen had conferred once more with two of his
colleagues at Amsterdam he repeated in their names and in
his own that they were not in a position to give him their
advice in this important business, but that if he undertook
it without their advice they would personally speak in favour
of supporting him in it, although without much hope of
prevailing. They expressed themselves with extreme caution ;
but the Prince saw nevertheless that the leading men in that
city, which in its turn exercised the greatest influence upon
the state, would not when the case arose be against him but
for him. This was enough for him in the first instance ;
he declared that he would prepare everything which was
necessary for the undertaking, but would only inform the
States-General of it when he was about to proceed to its
execution [1].

In his character of admiral and captain-general Prince
William could make military arrangements so long as he did
not exceed the limits of the means usually at his disposal.
But he employed even extraordinary means, and that not
without the complicity of the burgomasters,—he made use,
for instance, of a fund of four millions assigned for the im-

---

[1] Narrative of Witsen, in the extract in Wagenaar, xv. 530. I have not been
able to procure the original ; Grovestins, v. 429, seems to have had it in his hands,
but does not contribute anything from it which the more trustworthy Wagenaar had not already quoted.

provement of the fortresses. The admiralties of Rotterdam and of Amsterdam, of Zealand and of Friesland, received notice from him to put a number of ships of war in readiness for service: under the impression which the events of those days had produced, a levy of 9000 seamen, which had long been under discussion, was carried out in July; in the beginning of August a small squadron went to meet the fleet which was returning from the East Indies, for it was almost feared that without such a precaution it might experience the fate of the Smyrna fleet; a larger squadron sailed to the Dogger-bank in order to observe the movements of Strickland and his vessels. Meanwhile new ships were got ready, manned, and furnished with guns and ammunition from the great arsenals. At first the quarrel of Denmark and Holstein and the alliance of Holland with Sweden, afterwards the appre-hension of an union of the French and English fleets in the Channel, served as an explanation and justification of these armaments without any trustworthy information being circu-lated in the country as to the Prince's object.

All this, however, would certainly not have sufficed to put the Prince of Orange in a position to undertake his expe-dition.

Among the objections which the burgomasters urged to him against it, one of the most important was that it would strip the territory of the Netherlands of troops, and place it in danger of having to succumb without resistance to a French attack: the States would thus expose themselves to a defeat like that which they had suffered in the year 1672, and would also bring upon themselves a disaster at home like that which had then ensued. That an attack made upon the King of England from the Netherlands would arouse the hostility of France against the latter was evident.

But these very relations, which looked so threatening, aroused on the other hand an universal interest in the undertaking.

For in the combination of the two great western powers, which, whenever it has been effected, has controlled Europe, there then lay an oppressive force which was everywhere most seriously felt. The balance of power in Europe was prin-

cipally endangered by the alliance of James II with the over-
powerful King of France ; the principal danger of the Protestant confession lay in the support given by Louis XIV to
the attempted re-conversion of England to Catholicism. At
all times great impressions made by one side produce great
counter movements from the other. It was not very important
whether an alliance had been formally concluded between
France and England or not; it was impossible to know how
far Sunderland had come to an agreement with Barrillon, or
upon what points they were still at variance. Moreover,
agreements which are only about to be made are almost more
effective than those which have been already concluded. In
a word, a faction which had its support in France was seen to
be dominant at the English court also, and to determine the
measures of the King. A conviction prevailed that it had
in view the suppression of the complete independence of all
other powers and the ruin of Protestantism.

Nowhere in the world could this conviction make a
deeper impression than among the Protestant princes of
northern Germany, whose whole position rested upon the
territorial and religious freedom guaranteed them by the
laws of the Empire. They saw both the one and the
other threatened and endangered by the alliance of France
and England. But among them, again, there was not one
who had been more deeply touched by the combination
which became prominent in the beginning of the year 1688
than Frederick William, Elector of Brandenburg. For while
this prince had, even since the peace of Nimeguen, entered
into very close relations with Louis XIV, it was yet intolerable to him to think that the territories and the power of
the German empire were to be curtailed by France. And
he had at all times made the maintenance of the Protestant
religion, to which he adhered with all his heart, the guiding-
star of his policy. He almost regarded it as an affront to
himself that Louis XIV persecuted the Reformed in France ;
but the fact that the existence of Protestantism was endangered by the alliance above referred to aroused in
his soul, advanced as he was in years, an ebullition of its
deepest feelings. He returned to the ideas which he had

cherished before the conclusion of the peace of Nimeguen,
that other states must man themselves for a general struggle
against the rising predominance of France. He held the
task all the more practicable because the power of that
realm had been much weakened by the flight of the Reformed ; Germany must only wait till peace should have been
concluded with the Turks, and then press upon France with
the whole forces of the Empire, which could bring 150,000
men into the field ; while an attack upon the territories on
the Upper Rhine, Burgundy and Lorraine, should be reserved for the Imperial army, he himself thought of taking
the road to the French capital with his Brandenburgers,
other north Germans, and the Netherlanders. From what
the refugees, whom he had received into his country, told
him, he derived a hope that the great nobles of France, and
even the parliaments, would take his side, and that generally
the power of resistance which had indeed been crushed in
France, but lay dormant in its representative constitution,
would awake once more. He thought of restoring that constitution, and of setting a limit both in France and in Europe
to the arbitrary power of Louis XIV. It was in connexion
with this project that he took into his service by far the most
important personage among the French refugees in a military
point of view. That personage was a Marshal of France,
Frederick of Schomberg, the man who had once by his
defence of Portugal given effect to the European opposition to
the predominance of the Spanish monarchy. His conduct on
that occasion had been dictated mainly by his Protestant antipathies, but he had since seen the same system against
which he had contended in the Spanish peninsula become
dominant in France ; he could not remain there, as he was
unwilling to deny his religion ; even in Portugal, to which he
retired, he found no security against the attacks of the Inquisition ; considering the state of feeling at the time, nothing
remained for him but to seek an asylum among the Protestants ; the Great Elector not only offered him such an
asylum in his dominions, but confided to him the highest
post in his military establishment, the improvement of which
according to the pattern of the service then most thoroughly

developed and tested, that of France, formed his most pressing
task [1]. For how should any one have hoped at that time to
effect anything against the King of France without opposing
to him military forces as well trained as his own! Now the
English business had from its very beginning opened a prospect of the carrying out of these ideas, which no doubt were
rather projects framed for the future than plans matured for
execution. The thought that the Prince of Orange would
be obliged to make himself master of the crown of England
was, I think, not perhaps first conceived, but certainly first
expressed at Potsdam by the Great Elector, and that many
years before it was carried out. What indeed gave the mind
of that Prince its peculiar character was his power of
appreciating the transformations which occurred in affairs of
European interest, and the possibilities which such affairs contained. His first thoughts were equally comprehensive and
enthusiastic: the practical difficulties which he encountered
then made him cooler and more inclined to yield. He always
held fast the practical point of view.—At that time then the one
alliance of the predominant power of France with the English
crown was confronted by the other of the Protestant and
Parliamentary party in England with the European opposition to Louis XIV. But Marshal Schomberg was just the
right man for this alliance, as he had been for others. Of
English descent on the mother's side, and already once employed in England in the service of Charles II, he enjoyed
among the leaders of the party referred to that high consideration which European celebrity usually obtains in England for
its possessor; he knew the Prince of Orange, who had inspired
him with much esteem; his wife enjoyed the confidence of
the Princess in a high degree; he stood in a friendly relation
to Henry Sidney, to whom, perhaps, sooner than to any one
else, he had announced his wish to leave the French service [2].

---

[1] The story, found in Puffendorf and repeated countless times after him, of a
participation of Schomberg in the meeting of the Elector and the Prince at
Cleves (in the year 1686) must be given up, as Schomberg only left Portugal in
April, 1687. Cp. Kazner, Leben Schomberg's i. 274. This being so, the further
narrative on that topic loses all credit.

[2] Diary of Sidney ii. 265–268.

One example may suffice to illustrate the connexion between these points. At the court of Brandenburg we find the young Lord Leven, great grandson of Alexander Lesley on the mother's side. He was the son of that Lord Melville who had been compromised by the investigation as to the Rye House Plot, and had taken refuge in Holland ; he had accompanied his father, and was employed by the Prince in keeping up his communications with the Elector during the very transactions now under consideration [1]. While thus engaged he was also for some time employed in the military service at Berlin. When he returned to his father, in September 1687, Schomberg also gave him a letter to Sidney, from which we are able to learn the Marshal's sentiments. He remarks in it that James II was exerting himself to throw the English Church into confusion, and that the zeal of the Jesuits would lead him further and further; how much better would it be if English Churchmen combined with other Protestants. Sidney should certainly remain with the Prince of Orange, who was doubtless thinking of preventing the evil threatened. Schomberg expresses his wish to see the Prince and Princess once well established in England. 'For that,' he says, 'I would sacrifice everything ; it would give me great satisfaction if we ever found ourselves together on occasions on which we could do them service [2].' Just when the beginning of the crisis was seen to be approaching, the Great Elector died ; the last words which he uttered, 'London, Amsterdam,' betray the thoughts with which his soul was then occupied. (April 29, 1688.)

His son and successor Frederick III rivalled him in lively sympathy for the general interests of Europe, though not altogether in other qualities. He had been initiated into his father's plans, and approved them. He certainly stood even a step nearer to the House of Orange, to which his mother had belonged, than his father himself had stood; the blood of Admiral Coligny flowed in his veins, and he was considered the heir-presumptive of the Prince of Orange. The new minister whom he introduced into the Privy Council,

---

[1] Leven and Melville Papers, Appendix to Preface.
[2] Lettre de Schomberg à Sidney. Diary of Sidney ii. 268.

Eberhard Dankelmann, was himself, in consequence of the party position which he had hitherto assumed, just as zealous in this cause as the old members of that body.

Almost the first business which engaged the attention of the new government was connected with the great questions which were then important both for Europe and for Germany: I mean the claim of Fürstenberg to the territorial inheritance of Maximilian, Elector of Cologne. It was mainly owing to the exertions of the Brandenburg government that Fürstenberg did not carry his election in Münster and Hildesheim as well as in Cologne; just as the government of the Netherlands hindered his election at Liége; but even his obtaining a plausible claim, at least at Cologne, and his applying himself to make it good with the help of Louis XIV, seemed in itself an imminent danger for the independence of the German empire.

What view the Elector Frederick took of the case is shown by the treaty for joint resistance which he arranged with Charles, Landgrave of Hesse, the brother of his deceased wife, when the Landgrave was on a visit at Berlin. The two Princes say in this treaty that 'they have considered how many splendid and most important portions of its territory have been lost to the empire under the pretext of "reunion," how exceedingly dangerous the present conjuncture is, when the whole course of the Rhine is in danger; that in accordance with their personal friendship and the old connexion of their houses they have combined for a perpetual alliance, intending to direct all their thoughts and endeavours towards maintaining the empire unimpaired, and to the preservation of the towns of Coblentz and Cologne and of the United Netherlands. They will consider with all possible circumspection what can be done for the protection of the Protestant religion, which is being assailed at the instigation of foreign powers[1].'

Now even in this treaty the relations of the Netherlands and England were considered. The two princes wish above all things to deliberate with the Prince of Orange as to the

---

[1] Alliance with Hesse Cassel of July 27, 1688, concluded at Cöln on the Spree, in the Prussian State Archives—unhappily without any appendices as to the previous negotiations.

protection of Protestantism, and to defend the Netherlands in case they should be attacked on account of their interference in the affairs of England.

The Prince of Orange had indisputably already come to a general understanding with the two Princes on these points. The conversation which his confidant, Bentinck, and the Brandenburg privy-councillor, Fuchs, held on the subject in an interview at Celle was very remarkable and characteristic. It took place in the deepest secrecy. Fuchs travelled under another name; he had made a wide circuit and stopped at a retired inn; two hours afterwards, in the evening, Bentinck arrived also. But it might have aroused curiosity if they had chosen to meet at that late hour: it was only on the next morning, but early, at six o'clock, that Bentinck presented himself at the lodging of Fuchs, and they proceeded to a decisive conference. Bentinck described especially, as extremely urgent, the danger which everything would incur if King James brought together a Parliament which should suit his views; such a Parliament would abolish the necessity for taking the oaths, would pass new laws, and would vote the money necessary for the military and naval forces; the English government would, in alliance with France, first establish absolutism and Catholicism in England, and then overthrow Holland and attack Germany; by the spring of the next year all might be almost accomplished. But, he added, it was still possible to resist; they must not allow the rope to be drawn round their necks; conscience and prudence placed them under an obligation to anticipate the attack before it was undertaken. He remarked that the Prince of Orange was determined, and had received permission from the most eminent chiefs of the commonwealth, to assemble as many troops for the undertaking as he could, only the apprehension still prevailed that Holland might succumb before a diversion made by the French; the Elector of Brandenburg could better than any one else prevent such a movement [1]. Fuchs

---

[1] Mission of the Lord Privy Councillor Fuchs to Zelle. Instructions and report; in the State Archives at Berlin. An extract may be found in Puffendorf, but the whole document deserved to be known.

was empowered beforehand to consent to a proposal of this
kind; the two plenipotentiaries agreed that a considerable
division of Brandenburg troops (their number was fixed afterwards at nine thousand men) should enter the territories of
the commonwealth for its service, and should be paid and
provided for by it; the Elector, to whom assurances were
given at the same time in relation to the Orange inheritance,
was to receive recruiting money for new regiments, in order
that he might fill up the vacancies in his army. Brandenburg,
however, was by no means as yet strong enough to undertake
a matter of this importance by itself; the alliance with Hesse,
which Bentinck had just then confirmed at Cassel, was also
insufficient for the object in view; not a moment was lost in
conferring on the subject with Bernstorf, the leading minister
of George William, Duke of Celle. In this case also the
secret was most carefully kept. The meeting took place in a
garden outside the town; the two strangers went thither on
foot, as the driving up of a carriage might have excited
curiosity. Bernstorf showed himself very accessible to their
arguments. The most important one used was always that, if
the contemplated conversion to Catholicism was carried out in
England, the same process would be attempted in Holland,
and, finally, 'as Polyphemus promised Ulysses,' Germany
'would be devoured last.' The affair of Cologne was considered in connexion with it: it was thought that Cardinal
Fürstenberg had had the ruin of Germany in view. But not
only Coblentz and Cologne, but Hamburg also and Lübeck
had to be protected, for the second ally of France, the King
of Denmark, would readily avail himself of the favourable
opportunity for an attack. It was under the influence of a
very lively common feeling for the great interests of their
nations and of Protestantism that these statesmen came to an
agreement in the name of their respective princes. But it
was still a serious question whether they would attain their
end thereby.

William of Orange, who had held a meeting with the
Governor-General of the Spanish Netherlands between Breda
and Antwerp, repaired about the end of August to Minden
for a conference with the Elector of Brandenburg. All these

regions of the Netherlands and of North Germany must be combined before he would be able to undertake his expedition to England. But that combination was not yet nearly complete. Hanover certainly had not been drawn into it; on the contrary, a provisional agreement with France had been concluded there. The Prince was still far from feeling that confidence in a happy issue which Bentinck professed. He expressed to Bentinck himself the apprehension that all would become known before it was matured, and that then the French army would hurl itself upon him and destroy him.

So might a declaration be interpreted which Louis XIV commissioned his ambassador at the Hague to make in the beginning of September. He caused the States-General to be informed that it must necessarily be inferred from their armaments that their purposes were warlike: that probably those armaments would be directed against the King of England; but that, considering the close relation of friendship and alliance in which he stood to that prince, he would consider the first act of hostility to James as a breach with the French crown.

Such was the state of affairs throughout Europe at this moment that a resumption of the general war, which had been adjourned since the Peace of Nimeguen, might be decidedly expected. The Emperor and the Pope rejected with emphatic decision the proposals made by France for the recognition of Fürstenberg, and for the conversion of the twenty years' truce into a peace; at the same time the successful progress of the imperial and German arms against the Turks not only held out no prospect of any concession, but rather allowed an attack upon France to be expected as soon as ever peace should have been concluded in the East. Louis XIV formed the purpose of anticipating such an event by a speedy recourse to arms; but in doing so he did not take the course which his opponents most feared that he would take.

We learn that in the French deliberations as to the measures which should be first adopted, the proposal was made, and that by the principal promoter of warlike resolutions, Louvois, to deal the first blow against the republic of Holland and the Prince of Orange. It was a proposal suggested by a compre-

hensive view of political relations, in which the interests of
the Kings of England and France coincided.   Prince William
might be regarded as the most active and effective opponent
of both of them ; in him the heart of the resistance to
be expected would have been crushed.   But in the King's
council the consideration preponderated that such a movement
would certainly be of more interest to England than to
France apart from England ; that for France it was of far
more importance to assert the rights to the Palatinate succession, which the King's brother had acquired through his wife
on the extinction of the line of Simmern, and at the same
time to compel the Emperor and the empire to a definite
cession of the territories which had been placed in the hands
of France by the truce.   The French troops were already
prepared for war, and were assembled near the frontier ; in the
middle of September, without a previous declaration of war,
they broke into the territories of Upper Germany.   Their first
object was to besiege Philipsburg.   A manifesto appeared in
which, while peace was offered on the terms above mentioned,
Germany was threatened with a continuation of the war for
more extensive objects if those terms should not have been
accepted in the course of the next January.

These resolutions contain a decision important in more than
one respect.   They led to a resumption of offensive operations
on an immense scale by the French along their eastern
frontier ; but all the vehemence of their attack proceeded
from their right wing in the first instance, while with the left
they only made demonstrations, in the hope that these would
suffice to keep up alarm among the enemy.

'The result, however, of this step was different from what
Louis XIV expected.

Hitherto the Dutch had regarded the military power of
France as a storm-cloud by which they must fear to be struck
and cast down at any moment.   The armaments which the
Prince was making were justified in the eyes of patriots as
being destined for the defence of the country.   No one could
yet have heard that they were intended to be employed
against England.   It was only with reserve that the timorous
burgomasters, who had been taken into the secret, accepted

the disclosures which Bentinck made upon the subject after his return from Celle; at a supper at which they met him they took care not to empty their glasses to the success of the undertaking. They took some slight precautions to prevent his presence in Amsterdam from being known, as they might otherwise have incurred the suspicions of the population as adherents of the Prince. This state of things changed completely on the news of the siege of Philipsburg. Every one breathed more freely; the threats of Louis XIV no longer made any impression, as he was occupied elsewhere. On the contrary, those threats had confirmed the Prince's assertions as to the existence of an alliance between France and England; but in that the Dutch saw the greatest danger for their future, and were unanimously of opinion that an end must be put to it by a great blow; the opposition to the Prince's project ceased; he was thought to have done well in having already armed.

The undertaking of the French did him equally good service with the German princes. He had already himself opened a negotiation with Saxony; but it was still far from having arrived at any arrangement, when Frederick, the Elector of Brandenburg, under the impression of the events above referred to, took the affair in hand. About the end of September he sent an extraordinary ambassador, Schmettau, whom the Prince of Anhalt joined, to John George, Elector of Saxony. He had representations made to the latter that the main forces of the Emperor, as well as of the circles of Suabia, Bavaria, and Franconia, were employed in the Turkish war; that it would be hardly yet possible to save Philipsburg; but that at any price Frankfort must be preserved, otherwise the attack would fall at once upon Coblentz, Cologne, and the Netherlands, and the independence of the Empire would be destroyed. And he had no difficulty in gaining attention for these representations. Field-Marshal Flemming, who then possessed the principal influence at the Saxon court, silenced every hesitation of the other ministers. He declared that the Saxon infantry would be ready to march in eight days, the cavalry and artillery soon afterwards; he himself, and his sovereign the Elector, would not be wanting. It was the ambition of Saxony to conduct the war upon the Middle

Rhine, while Austria should have the carrying out of the joint undertaking on the Upper, and Brandenburg upon the Lower Rhine [1].

About the same time Fuchs went for the second time to Celle, where he met Ernest Augustus, Duke of Hanover. The Elector of Brandenburg had the Duke's daughter for his second wife, and had already persuaded him at a personal interview to promise that if France took the offensive against the Empire, he would aid the Empire to maintain the struggle against that power [2]. 'For no defensive alliance with one who was the assailant could be thought of.' But the case contemplated had now come to pass. Ernest Augustus assured the Ambassador that he would keep the promise which he had made to the Elector.

The Dukes of Celle and Wolfenbüttel shared these sentiments; they both held the opinion that, if the line of the Rhine were not maintained, Germany would fall into subjection. The three princes pledged themselves to make contributions for the war to the best of their power; their eyes were in the first instance especially directed to Coblentz and Ehrenbreitstein.

Thus the same princely houses which had formerly carried the Reformation of the Church through its early struggles, now combined to preserve its cause in Europe. Brandenburg, which had by this time become the most powerful among them, took the lead.

The Elector Frederick did not hesitate to give up the great general who was in his service, Marshal Schomberg, to the Prince of Orange for the execution of his plans. Those in England who were in the secret, and knew Schomberg, had made an express proposal to the Prince to that effect; it may have formed one of the subjects of the negotiation at Minden. Schomberg himself wished for nothing better. For it was only now that in his advanced age he could retrieve the misconduct towards his fatherland of which he had been guilty

---

[1] Instructions to Schmettau for his journey to Dresden, September 28. Schmettau's Report, October 12.

[2] '. . . firmly promised, that if France should attack the empire, he would then aid in its defence with all his power.' Instructions to Fuchs, September 28.

while in the French service; he wished to show his value to the King, by whom he felt himself ill-treated. He saved Cologne by throwing troops into that city before the right moment had passed. He then marched to Holland at the head of Brandenburg troops, intending to leave them, or at any rate the majority of them, behind, for the defence of the Dutch Commonwealth; but he himself was determined to take part in the undertaking against James II. The Elector had placed one of his own aides-de-camp by his side.

How all these measures were connected with one thought can be seen from the instructions with which Fuchs was sent in October to the Hague. According to them the Prince was to be reminded, if God should give him success, to procure first of all a declaration of war against France in the English Parliament, for thereby he would completely deprive King James, who could only expect aid from France, of all sup- port[1]. In these instructions there was no mention of a change of kings, but only of the closest union with the Parliament, in opposition to the ruling King, James. To engage the forces of England, in opposition to its King, in the struggle against Louis *XIV*, was the principal object which the government at Berlin had in view. It was to be represented to the Prince that if he effected this he would do the greatest service both to the United Netherlands and to collective Christendom; and that not only to the evangelical Christians, but even to the Catholics; the Emperor, the crown of Spain, the Pope himself would greet him as their preserver.

---

[1] 'It was the only way to assure themselves of England, for it was known that the King of Great Britain could nowhere meet with help and protection but from France, but that he would be at once cut off from all hope of this if the course suggested were taken.' Words of the Instructions for a Mission to the Hague.

CHAPTER IV.

WHILE an offensive and defensive alliance against the combination between France and England was thus being formed, it began to appear possible that the King of England might of his own accord turn away from France.

He had now declared his purpose of summoning a Parliament, and was busied with all sorts of precautions for exercising a favourable influence on the elections, when France resumed the great continental war against allied Europe. Charles II had always made it a condition of his alliances with France that there should be nothing of the sort, as the antipathies of English parliaments to the growth of that power would be aroused by such a step, and must necessarily touch the English crown also. All parliaments were like-minded in relation to this, however different their composition might be in other respects. An alliance with France would just then have had a most unpleasant effect upon the elections.

Just as the government was occupied in preparing for them, Bonrepaus, already well known to us, who then held a high post in the French marine, appeared again in England to propose an agreement as to an union of the two fleets, such agreement to be immediately adopted. In England even then the purposes of the Prince of Orange were not misunderstood; but it was thought that he would find difficulties in carrying the States-General with him in his undertaking. A movement of the French against Holland would have been looked on with pleasure, for it was thought that such a move-

ment would bring the republicans to a consciousness of their
own danger, and would hinder them from making any attack
in another quarter. But the English government did not wish
to take a direct part in any such demonstration. The combination of the fleets would have produced a general ferment
among the English. An alliance with France was not compatible with the summoning of a Parliament. King James
was told at the time that the only object of the offer of
Louis XIV was to make the assembling of a Parliament
impossible.

The proposal was not absolutely and summarily rejected,
for the English government did not wish to offend France.
Some conferences were held between Bonrepaus and Sunderland, in which Barrillon took part. But no understanding was
arrived at either as to the number of ships which should take
part in the combination, nor as to the time of it. Something
also was said as to a general treaty for mutual support in case
of an attack upon the one or the other of the two kings. But
against this proposal also the English had many arguments
to urge. 'An attack upon France,' they said, 'could only
concern the possession of certain districts which had never
been rightfully acquired ; an attack upon England would
be aimed at the King and the crown, and would make it
needful for France to render aid of quite another kind than
that which would be required in the event of an attack upon
itself.'

And when Louis XIV, not indeed quite uninvited, yet only
on the spontaneous request of the English ambassador, who
expressly declared that he was not authorised to prefer such
a request, caused the declaration already mentioned to be
made at the Hague, his conduct was regarded at the English
court as an usurpation and almost as a danger. For it was
thought that Louis assumed therein the air of a protector ; that
he spoke of England as of a Cardinal Fürstenberg, just as
though it could not defend itself without foreign aid. In the
social circle which assembled round the Queen, and in which
the most lively sympathy was generally professed for Louis
XIV, it was now said that he sought to humiliate England.
In a conversation about the behaviour of that prince to the

Pope, James II had himself said that he had been corrupted by flatterers. For the first time since his accession he excluded Barrillon from his political deliberations.

And it must not be believed that Sunderland, who projected and promoted this turn of policy, did not act under the influence of serious conviction. For if a Parliament was at last to be summoned the needs of the case commanded him to desist from any further combination with France. By making advances on the contrary to the Dutch he could hope at least to hinder them making common cause altogether with the Prince of Orange, and at the same time to keep open for himself the means of coming to an understanding with the future Parliament.

A preliminary condition of any approximation to Holland was that the impression should be effaced which the declaration of Louis XIV already mentioned, referring to an alliance existing between France and England, had produced among the Dutch. The English ambassador in Paris, Skelton, who was responsible for it, was recalled, and on his return was sent to the Tower. The King thought it worth while to come to an explanation on the subject in person with the Dutch ambassador, Citters. He would not go so far as the latter proposed and publicly declare the words of the King of France false: but he assured Citters that they had not only been uttered without his knowledge but that an alliance, such as that mentioned in them, did not exist at all. Quite the contrary was the case: his resolution was, not to take any active part at all in foreign affairs, but at some future time to appear as a mediator in them; his armaments only existed for the maintenance of his own security and of the credit of his navy, but were far too insignificant to be able to inspire any apprehensions; he would certainly keep the peace with the Dutch Commonwealth if it were not the first to break it. Citters answered by giving corresponding assurances as to the armaments of the Commonwealth. He had just been in Holland, but he was not, as far as one can judge, one of those who had been admitted into the Prince's secret; he told the King that he had visited the assembly of the States-General and had spoken with eminent members of the government:

he had not heard a word of any intention to attack England ; the armaments were only designed for the protection of trade. James II asked him whether he could say that not only for himself but in the name of the States-General. Citters answered in the affirmative without hesitation : he assured the King in the name of the High and Mighty Lords of their inclination to keep up a confidential friendship and good correspondence with him[1]. And this assurance was now gladly caught up in England; nay, the English government went a step beyond the limits of strict neutrality; Albeville received a commission to offer the States-General a treaty for the maintenance of the peace of Nimeguen and of the twenty years' truce. The French ambassadors at the Hague and in London were dissatisfied at this. They expressed their opinion that this proposal might perhaps be eagerly embraced in Holland in order to hurry England into a struggle with France. Barrillon addressed reproaches to his friends about the King on the subject; they answered that the stream had been too strong and that they had been unable to resist it[2].

At this moment Sunderland and Jeffreys, who had for some time detached themselves from the Catholics, had the control of the Cabinet to a greater extent than the latter. They took advantage of the King's sensitiveness as to the French declaration and of his old tendency to neutrality, to bring him back for a moment to a policy suited to the natural position of England. But they could not stop there. For, even if the States-General were really hindered from uniting with the Prince, the Prince, according to all reports, was making the most serious preparations for his expedition on his own authority; and it could not escape Sunderland and Jeffreys that he, even if he only appeared with a small force, would find among the parties which then prevailed in England sufficient

---

[1] 'Van derselben enixe Geneygtheit en dispositie om met S. Mt. in aller vertroude Vriendschap en mutuelle naburlyke correspondentie te wyllen bleven leben, en van haer vollstandig vornemen in aller occurentie to betoonen.' Despatch of September 12/22, in the collections of Heer van Citters.

[2] 'Qu'ils n'ont pu soutenir le torrent. L'humeur hautaine et fière des Anglais a prévalu dans le premier mouvement.'

support to make him formidable. In their anxiety on this point they thought that safety for the King and for themselves could only be secured by a change, and that a fundamental change, both of foreign and domestic policy. Sunderland said one day to the papal Nuncio that there was no longer any good in defending single transactions as to which the government had not the law on its side; he and his colleagues would only ruin themselves by such a course, and that so thoroughly that they would not even at any future time be able to raise their heads again; the only means of saving themselves lay in an agreement with the Episcopalian party, which they had exasperated; it was an imperative necessity to conciliate it[1]. Sunderland probably applied to the Nuncio because he too had no understanding with the Jesuitical faction and yet was listened to by the King. Adda warned him not to go so far as to endanger religion and the royal authority; the Lord President answered that everything should be most maturely considered[2].

The King also was convinced that the best means for resisting the Prince of Orange lay in depriving him of the support of the Episcopalian party, by doing justice to its demands. James II hoped in doing so still to maintain his position on the whole.

The first public announcement of an altered disposition was a proclamation which appeared on the 21st of September. There is not in it any further mention of the abolition of the requirement to take the oaths; the continued exclusion of the Catholics from the Lower House is conceded. The King still adheres to his wish to procure general freedom of conscience for his subjects; but, he adds, the omission of some oppressive provisions in the Act of Uniformity would suffice for that without its being needful to repeal that act altogether.

Jeffreys, who had drawn up the proclamation, told Lord Clarendon that the King's object was to 'set all things on the

---

[1] 'Che infine non sarebbe che cedere alla necessità, per non avere dove voltarsi.' Adda, October 8, N. S.

[2] 'Indicando che lo stato presente sia all' ultimo grado di pericolo pero che non si lascierà di procedere con ogni maturità nelle resolutioni.'

foot they were at his coming to the crown,' and to that end
to call together the spiritual and temporal peers for a consultation. Such at least was the course recommended by the
most influential members of the government, as Sunderland,
Godolphin, Middleton, Dartmouth ;—they would have had
all the decided Protestants who were still at the court for
them ; but even on the ground which they now took up, they
met with strong opposition ; some limiting clauses were added
to the proclamation, which Jeffreys did not approve ; a summons of the peers in such great numbers was avoided. The
King only spoke with the lords who continued to visit the
court, for instance with Lord Clarendon ; he told him that
there could be no doubt that an attack was imminent, and
that he would see what the Church of England men would do
for him. ' They will,' said Clarendon, ' behave themselves
like honest men, though they have been somewhat severely
used of late.'

The antagonism of parties showed itself on every question.
The old lists of persons qualified to act as deputy-lieutenants
and justices of the peace were restored ; leave was merely given
to the Lords Lieutenants and to the Lord Chancellor to have
recourse to men who were excluded from them. Sunderland
would have wished that the changes among the magistrates
of towns which had been made by means of the Regulation
should be revoked at one blow. But the King could not be
induced to go so far ; he wished first to ascertain by enquiry
from the Lords Lieutenants where that was advisable and
where it was not.

The only point on which there was a general agreement
was that a consultation with the bishops was necessary, in
order to learn from them what would content the English
Church, and then to consider what concessions could be made
to it. The King first saw one or two separately, and then a
number together : those who had formerly delivered to him
the famous address, the Bishops of Ely, Chichester, Bath and
Wells, Peterborough, Bristol, were joined by some others.
He received them with a declaration that he wished to learn
from them what seemed to them necessary in order to secure
religion in the realm : he would grant everything which was

compatible with his prerogative. How their position had
changed for the better! After they had felt the heavy hand
of the King, but had resisted him, they were now summoned
to his aid, and could offer him conditions of reconciliation.
Many demands were discussed in a free conversation—for
example, the restoration of the Bishop of London and of the
charters of London, which the King accordingly ordered
forthwith. In fact he agreed to every demand, except that
he refused to renounce the dispensing power, saying that it
formed so important an ingredient in the prerogative that a
decision upon it could only be arrived at in Parliament[1].

On the 3rd of October there was a second conference, in
which the Archbishop also took part. The bishops showed
themselves very moderate. They did not even suggest the
dismissal of their principal enemy, Father Petre, from the
Privy Council, although that had been much discussed in their
meetings. With reference to the Act of Uniformity they
agreed that, while it should be again put in force, some regard
must also certainly be had for freedom of conscience. They
did not require that the King should renounce his dispensing
power, but only that he should desist from such an exercise of
it as was then practised, and leave the decision on its legality
to Parliament. The election-writs had been revoked in the
agitation of the last days; the bishops required the issue of
new writs without delay for a free and regular Parliament.
Their most immediate and precise demands were, the abolition
of the Ecclesiastical Commission, the immediate filling up of
the vacant episcopal sees, discontinuance of the administration
of so-called vicars-apostolic, the removal of Roman Catholic
schools, and the restoration of the Protestant fellows at Magdalen College[2]; precisely the most important points in dispute,

---

[1] So we gather from the reports of Bonnet, which were written at the time :
' Qu'il étoit prest de leur accorder tout ce qui se trouveroit de raisonnable et qui ne
dérogeroit point à ses prérogatives.' According to the Dutch secretary he added :
' Qu'il étoit prest à redresser les griefs sur les premiers points, mais pour ce qui
regarde ses prérogatives, que c'est un point si délicat, qu'il en faut laisser la
décision à son parlement.'

[2] Account of the late proposals, in Somers, ix (W. Scott's edition Tr). In one
copy of the original the remark is found that the publication had been procured by

and those on which the King's hostility to the Church of England had principally shown itself. The King did not allow people to wait long for the fulfilment of the last demands.

On October 5 he stated in the Privy Council that, in order to prevent all further suspicion, he had resolved to abolish the Ecclesiastical Commission ; on the 6th the Lord Chancellor Jeffreys went to the city, where he was solemnly received at Temple Bar, to restore the charters; on the 10th an order was issued to discontinue the irregularities which had been practised in connexion with the Regulation of the corporations ; on the 12th the Bishop of Winchester received a commission to organise Magdalen College at Oxford in accordance with its statutes. The King had asked the advice of Monsignore Leyburn on this point, who declared that the possession of the Catholics could not be considered as legitimate, and that they could not be upheld in it ; it rested on a robbery of the Protestants, about which the Parliament would raise complaints, and which would then have to be retracted. The King told the Nuncio that, however painful it was to him, he could not refuse this concession, for that what had occurred involved a contradiction to the promise which he had made on his accession. He even prevailed upon himself to order the closing of the Catholic chapel in the city, and of an institution for education managed by the Jesuits.

And if it was the principal object of these measures to regain the sympathies of the nation, and so to put the King in a position to resist the Prince of Orange, that object seemed to have been attained. The address of thanks presented by the restored deputy-lieutenants contained an assurance that they would never suffer the King's peace to be disturbed by his enemies on any pretext. The civic authorities of London, who had newly entered upon office, asserted their willingness to risk life and property, according to the principles of the English Church, for the defence of his Majesty and of the government of the country which had been established. The

---

Sunderland with the object of dissipating the apprehensions of the Nonconformists. The form of the impression in Sancroft's Life is the most trustworthy.

bishops ordered new prayers in the churches, both for the most gracious King, who they prayed might be protected by the angels of God, and for religion and the laws of the land. The old doctrine that episcopacy and royalty were indissolubly connected, on which the original organisation of the sovereignty of the Stuarts had rested, was making way again ; James II seemed to be returning to it. We learn that some of the most eminent noblemen, as Newcastle, Aylesbury, and Lindsay, declared to the King their approval, and promised to give him their aid whether he demanded it or not.

Many thought that what was to have been obtained by the expedition of the Prince of Orange had already been obtained by the threat of it. And the state of affairs really was such that the grievances which had been stated to the Prince as the ground for an armed intervention, and which he adopted as his own, had now to a great extent been removed.

But would this suffice to secure that the undertaking for which preparations had been made should be renounced or should be free from danger to King James? No one concealed from himself that, even after these concessions, the government would have to meet a great crisis.

It was once considered in the Privy Council whether it would be advisable to oppose the Prince if he succeeded in landing. For the King could not, it was said, so thoroughly depend upon his army, which was in great measure composed of Protestants, as to expect from it a decided resistance to the Prince. And if a battle were lost, what a storm would be raised against the poor Catholics! But negotiation seemed to present still more serious grounds for hesitation. For the King would, if he entered upon it, be obliged to sacrifice those very men who were most faithful to him ; he would not find any faithful servants afterwards : a battle was an attempt which might, no doubt, result in ruin ; but negotiation was submission, not perhaps unconditional, but still submission [1].

Sunderland and Jeffreys, between whom and the bishops a good understanding had now been restored, held it, as they did,

---

[1] Citters, October 9/19, who gives this information, erroneously places the deliberation on the last Saturday. That would have been October 6.

most advisable to call Parliament together immediately [1]. It would undoubtedly have been an Episcopalian body ; but yet the sovereign might still have come to an understanding with it on the old terms. No doubt other far-reaching possibilities came also into view. The Parliament might take the negotiation with' the Prince into its own hands, and to a certain extent make common cause with him. The position of foreign affairs seemed to suggest still more decided measures. The Spanish ambassador proposed to the King one day that, as his only chance of safety, he should himself summon the Prince of Orange and give him a great position at the head of his army and of his fleet in the war against France.

But nothing could be more repulsive to James II than this request ; he felt himself wounded by it in his personal honour. He would hear nothing of a Parliament composed of Episcopalians if it was to lead to these results. He decidedly preferred to trust to the fortune of war. He expected that the concessions which he had made in the last few weeks would so far establish a good understanding between him and his people as to enable him to resist his hostile son-in-law, especially as he still thought that the States-General, to which he had given such good assurances, would not range themselves altogether upon the side of the latter.

But in great events there occurs a moment at which no conciliatory step can any longer have any effect ; the events have been irrevocably prepared by the past, and then develop themselves by their own impulses. How seriously did James II deceive himself as to his influence upon the Netherlands ! The feeling there had become decidedly favourable to the Prince's project from two causes—the fresh outbreak of the great war, and the direction which it took.

On September 27 / October 7, Prince William held it good to make a public communication on the subject to the deputed counsellors who had the direction of foreign affairs. He started in it from the French declaration already mentioned,

---

[1] Citters says of them that they ' de sentimenten van de Heern Bischoffen schynen to amplecteren, en alles gerne in den ouden pli souden brengen.'

which, he said, left no doubt as to the existence of an alliance between France and England. The King of England, however, he continued, who in all his acts kept the religious point of view before his eyes, still found opposition among his people on that very ground; if he put down that opposition, he would infallibly direct his power in alliance with France against the Netherlands; it would even be dangerous for the latter if he were to succumb in the struggle which had become inevitable, for then England would declare itself a republic; and the Dutch had been sufficiently taught by experience what they had to expect on their side of the sea from such a form of government; how much better to go in good time to aid the English in their resistance: that would be for the United Netherlands the means of maintaining themselves in their independence, and of procuring security for their religion for ever. He then mentioned his rights as a prince of the blood in England, and above all, the claims of his wife to the English crown; but said that those rights would be forgotten amid the disputes that were breaking out unless he and the Princess went to the support of the nation. 'He was determined,' he said, 'to do this, to take the matter in hand in his own name and in his wife's. In all human probability they might reckon upon a good result. He did not think of thrusting the King from his throne and of putting himself in his place: he would only take care that a Parliament should be summoned, formed of persons who had the qualifications required by the laws for membership; that religion and freedom should be secured, and the nation placed in a position again to support its old allies, especially the Netherlands.'

The deputed counsellors agreed with him in everything. They remarked frankly, and in accordance with his warnings, that if a Popish government were established in England it would exclude the Prince of Orange from his throne, as Henry IV had experienced similar treatment in France at the hands of the League; but that if discontent took the form of a republican movement, the royal house in general would be excluded by it; no one could take it ill of the Prince that he put himself in readiness to prevent either result, and he had every claim to be supported in doing so by his country, in a cause in which justice and equity were on his side.

On the following day the matter came on for consideration in the States-General; there was no display of opposition. The Prince was thanked for applying for aid, and a resolution was passed to support him in the execution of his project with men and ships, by sea and land.

All this still remained a profound secret. The members promised each other, by the oath which they had given to the country, to keep it inviolate. In reality no one heard of it [1].

The first manifestation of the complete understanding between the Prince and the States-General was contained in the answer which the latter caused to be given to King James with reference to his overtures for a mutual approximation. They did not feel themselves bound by the assurances which Citters had given; Fagel remarked that the Ambassador had not spoken in the name of their High Mightinesses, but only for himself. The tenor of the declaration, which the States now really issued, was such that the Prince himself might have dictated it. They took for their starting-point the fact that the King of England refused to deny officially the alliance which, according to the assertion of France, existed between the two powers; while they laid the blame of the estrangement which this conduct indicated upon the influence of those who were ill-disposed towards them, they at the same time made the discord which existed in England the express subject of their statement; they mentioned the discontent which had arisen in the English nation, owing to the irregular conduct of certain persons in reference both to the religion and to the freedom of the country; it would be their principal wish that such discontent should be removed, religion and liberty maintained, the King and the nation brought again into thorough confidence and agreement with each other [2]. While they described it as

---

[1] Secrete Resolutien 1688: 'Syn Hoocheit doet ouverture van syn vornemen jegens de desseinen ende menies van Vranckryk ende Engelland.'

[2] 'De onlusten, die in deselve natie werden (verweckt?) door de irreguliere conduite by eenige gehouden, soo well te regarde van gereformeerde religie, also van vryheit en seekerheit in die natie seifts dat hare Ho. Mo. als noch niets soo seer wenschen dan dat de voors. onlusten in haer grond mogten werden wegh-

their principal object to co-operate with the King for the
maintenance of the peace of Nimeguen, and of the agreements
which had been concluded subsequently, they gave it clearly
to be understood that an internal change in England must
precede any such action on their part.

So ran the Republic's answer to the peaceful approaches
of the King; it refused to come to any agreement with him
till he should have altered the system of government in
the interests of a party which he was carrying out. One
cannot be surprised that the English court regarded this conduct as intolerably arrogant; it appeared very offensive that
the King and the nation were opposed to each other as
though England were another Poland. King James himself
broke into the most violent ebullition of passion. In an
audience which he granted to the Dutch ambassador, he
described the Prince of Orange as 'the worst man whom the
earth had produced; his ambition transgressed the limits of
reason and of nature; he wished to dethrone his father-in-law
and near blood-relation[1].' Citters tried in vain to appease
him. The King tore open the door, went away, and left him
standing where he was.

But while the Republic repelled James II and insulted him,
the French made fresh approaches to him, without even
reproaching him for his alienation from them. They tried
to remove his suspicion that he had suffered want of consideration and neglect at their hands. Barrillon was placed
in a position to offer the King once more, amid his increasing
embarrassments and wants, a supply of money, though not to
a very large amount. He cannot describe how great an impression this offer had made on James[2]. The unexpected

---

genomen, de voors. gereformeede religie gemainteneert en in seekerheit gestellt en
de vryheit en liberteyt van de natie geconserveert.' These words are wanting in
the extract in Wagenaar xv. 468, which is throughout very insufficient.

[1] Report of October 19/29. The expressions are not given in so strong a form
in Wagenaar. They have, however, been already correctly given in Van Wyn's
Byvoegsels en Aanmerkingen to Wagenaar (to Part XV, p. 107). I have to thank
the kindness of the young Herr van Citters at the Hague, for having been able to
see the originals.

[2] Nov. 4: 'Je le vois fort résolu de ne rien faire indigne de lui ny qui le peut
priver du secours de V. M., mais sa résolution a besoin d'estre fortifiée.'

demonstrations of friendship on the part of the French, coin-
ciding with the offensive declarations of Holland, had the
effect of making King James once more take a turn in his
policy. The French and Catholic party, never altogether
abandoned, but yet thrust decidedly into the background,
regained the preponderance. Sunderland, whose policy of
mediation then inclined towards the opponents of France,—it
really failed on account of the resistance of the Netherlands,—
could no longer maintain himself.

While the domestic measures which he had projected were
still continued, his opponents made the objection to him that
he was going much too far in them, and involving the King in
a contradiction with himself which must be ruinous for him.
That he strongly urged the summoning of a Parliament made
him appear to the Catholic party an enemy, and to the King an
untrustworthy friend. Sunderland complained that his greater
discernment was made a reproach to him; he saw clearly in
what position the King was; as it had become so completely
different, different measures must also be taken from those
previously adopted. But his opponents maintained that he
was playing into the hands of the Prince of Orange in thus
advising his king. The suspicion was even entertained that
he had a secret understanding with the Prince, and many
circumstances which seemed to give colour to the suspicion,
but in reality proved nothing, were adduced in support of it.
The suspicion was so widely spread that William of Orange
himself was asked one day by his confidant, Burnet, whether
there was any foundation for it. The Prince assured him with
calm distinctness that he was keeping up no correspondence of
any kind with Sunderland. On the contrary it was remarked
at the Hague how dangerous it might be for the Prince's
undertaking if Sunderland's counsels were adopted and followed [1]. No doubt Sunderland recommended precisely what
the Prince of Orange demanded above all things, the election
of a Parliament according to the forms sanctioned by old
usage; but Sunderland regarded this as the only means of
resisting the Prince. He would himself have taken up a grand

---

[1] Burnet, Own Times iii. 1294.

position if he had succeeded in reconciling the King again
with the Episcopalians, and in mediating between the King
and the Prince, with the support of a Parliament.   But the
King saw in Sunderland's suggestions extreme danger for his
honour and authority; after he had followed his minister on
the new path as far as was possible for him, he parted from
him, and let him fall.   He told him himself that he did not
reproach him with faithlessness but with want of firmness in
conduct and with want of spirit [1].   Considering the turn which
things were taking, he and Sunderland could not go together
any more.

The end which is usually pursued in the dismissal of leading
ministers—namely, the restoration of unity in the counsels
which guide the government, was not attained on this occasion.
James II certainly did not wish to disoblige the Protestants;
he put a Scottish Protestant, Preston, in Sunderland's place.
But would Preston ever agree with the Catholic and French
camarilla?

Towards the end of October Sunderland left Whitehall.   In
the very first transaction which ensued the want of his talent
for mediation was felt.   On the 1st of November the proclamation of the Prince, which had not yet been published, came
accidentally into the hands of the King.   Its contents could not
make any great impression upon him, for they consisted mainly
of a statement of the well-known grievances which, since that
statement was drawn up, he had sought to remove.   He was
more deeply affected by the doubts expressed in it as to the
Prince of Wales being the Queen's child.   In order, however,
to check the adverse reports that were in circulation, he had
already two days before had the statements of the witnesses
who had been present at the Queen's delivery recorded at a
solemn assembly; even the Queen-Dowager, whom he led in
by the hand, had been present at it; he thought that he had
thereby suppressed all doubt for ever.   There yet remained,
however, one assertion of the Prince which might inspire him

---

[1] Adda, Nov. 5: 'Sunderland ha mostrato maggior apprensione d'ognuno e
facilità a disfare quello che s'era fatto col suo consiglio, ma avendo egli nemici
presso dal re, ho riscutir che ne abbino dateti impressioni alla Ma. S. accusandolo
di poco provido—et era di troppo timoroso.'

with some apprehension—the assurance, namely, that he had
been invited to engage in his undertaking by spiritual and
temporal peers. King James was himself inclined rather to
consider this an empty boast than to think it well founded.
He was easily contented with a declaration to the contrary,
especially from the bishops whom he questioned upon it ;
although the Bishop of London, for instance, expressed himself ambiguously enough. But James wished not only to
counteract the impression which the proclamation might
make in the country, but, even more, to produce a contrary
impression. He required the bishops to declare publicly
their abhorrence of the undertaking ; 'to exhort the people,
on the ground of the recognised principles of the English
Church, to resist all invasion and rebellion, which was contrary
to divine and human laws.' Such a declaration would certainly have been in accordance with the system hitherto
pursued by the English Church, and it would have been of
inestimable value to the King ; but, under the circumstances
then existing, the bishops hesitated to issue it. At a fresh
interview many offensive words were exchanged, which are
not worth repeating, especially as no one even then expressed
his full meaning freely. The bishops required that the King
should allow them to proceed to a consultation with the
temporal peers, who desired one most urgently ; and the
bishops were unwilling to risk their authority by making
without their co-operation such a declaration as that desired[1].
But the King felt anxious lest at such a consultation much
that was disagreeable to him might be brought forward, and
lest even a declaration in favour of his rights might be com-
blned with a protest against his acts. His pride was aroused,
and he told the bishops that if they were not inclined to
support him as he requested, he must stand upon his own
feet and rely upon his arms.—An important moment for

---

[1] Clarendon, Diary, Nov. 5 : ' They had no mind to make a declaration under
their hands, except the temporal lords would join with them.' (ii. 201.) We learn
from the Diary the substance of the King's conversation with Clarendon and
Rochester. As there is no mention in it of a declaration of disapproval, and the
King in his answer protests that he has not required one, I abide by the statement
given above, in spite of a contrary account in Citters.

English history! The good understanding between the crown
and the bishops, on which the government of the country
rested, having been once interrupted by the partisan proceedings of James II, could not be restored by his later concessions, which, though considerable, did not go far enough.
He had to meet the invasion which threatened him without
the support of the Church.

If we turn our eyes to the invaders themselves—as the
affair ran its course on both sides simultaneously—we shall
find that among them also, in the camp of the Prince, the
ecclesiastical controversy played a great part.

Among the Englishmen who assembled around the Prince,
in order to take part in his expedition, there were two distinct
parties, which found representatives in the two clergymen
Ferguson and Burnet. Ferguson would have wished to give
the undertaking a tendency towards a thoroughgoing ecclesiastical and political transformation, such as the Duke of
Monmouth had formerly contemplated under his influence.
Even among the lords present there were some who agreed
with him in this, as Lord Mordaunt, and Gerard, Earl of
Macclesfield—strangely enough, for he had once appeared in
the field for Charles I with troops raised by himself; it was
said that he had not thought himself adequately rewarded
and had therefore gone over to the other side. But Burnet
opposed any such turn being given to the enterprise: any
quarrel with the English Church, in which, partly owing to
his own mediation, the Prince of Orange counted his bes
supporters, would have seemed to him senseless and dangerous,
and herein he had both the fiery Shrewsbury, and Russel
and Sidney on his side: they did not, indeed, at all wish
to repel the Dissenters, but they wished above all things to
place the Church of England under an obligation.

It was not, to be sure, the High Church idea as still held
at Lambeth that prevailed in the circle which surrounded the
Prince, but rather the latitudinarian notion, which had in
view a reconciliation with the Presbyterians. Monmouth had
formerly sought to unite such Presbyterians as stood neares
to him with the members of the more violent sects, and ha
made an attack on the High Church party, whose alliance wit

the crown ruined him. William of Orange, on the contrary, identified himself with the opposition of the Church of England to the crown, and strove to engage the moderate Presbyterians in that opposition. He justified his undertaking by the complaints which the Church raised against the King : the refusal to consent to an abolition of the oaths, as to which he agreed with the Church, formed for him, as for it, the ground of all his proceedings. The man whose constancy in relation to this matter had stimulated and inflamed the general opposition, Vice-Admiral Herbert, was of all the exiles the one whose desertion to him caused the greatest surprise. The maintenance of the interest of the Church of England in opposition to the Catholics was the condition of all success ; which does not, however, imply that nearly all those who wished to maintain it were Church of England men at heart. Even Herbert was not that, any more than Russell and Shrewsbury. And many others who were even opponents on principle of the Church of England united in the movement. Common antipathy to Catholicism and to the King who was seeking to pave the way for its revival in Great Britain combined those whose sentiments differed on other questions. In the Scottish and English regiments, which formed the core of the Prince's expeditionary army, this Protestant and English sentiment, as estranged from the royal authority, was distinctly represented ; for those regiments had remained in the Dutch service against the will of their King. But further, European associated itself with English Protestantism in the Prince's army, and that in the most impressive way, by sending as its representatives the French refugees. These were partly old soldiers, who had conformed in France to the externals of Catholicism, but had yet at last taken to flight when they found themselves oppressed in conscience. Many served in the Prince's guard, others were enrolled in other regiments ; and there were distinguished engineers and artillerymen among them. Besides these, however, there appeared a brilliant corps of men who had never yet served : about five hundred French volunteers of this kind could be counted. These Frenchmen might be said to identify the Prince's undertaking with their own cause.

F f 2

They contended against the system which had driven them
from their country, and which now threatened, if it conquered in England, to subjugate the world. Marshal Schomberg, whose surrender of his high position in France had
been quite in accordance with the sentiments of these
refugees, was greeted by them as their born leader. The
cavalry of the Prince consisted principally of Germans[1],
especially of Brandenburgers; and some of the regiments[2] of
Brandenburg infantry lately placed at William's disposal also
took part in the expedition, as did some bodies of Swedes.
In them there was especially represented the policy which
aimed at restoring the balance of power in Europe, at detaching England by force from its alliance with France, and at
saving the German empire from destruction. The Dutch co-
operated heartily with the Germans and Swedes; for they
fought also for their own independence, which was threatened
by France and England. How powerfully did all those
elements which were endangered by French predominance
and thereby aroused to a sense of their duty, co-operate with
the English opposition! They were kept together by the
universal feeling that the preservation of European freedom
and of the Protestant religion depended upon the success
of this undertaking. In all churches prayers were offered
to Almighty God, the Lord of Hosts, that He would protec
this undertaking, to the honour of His Name and to the
welfare of His people.

At this moment the complication of affairs brought it to
pass that even the highest authorities in the Catholic world
which felt themselves threatened by the universal ascendancy
of France, approved of the scheme. We know how much
that was the case even at Rome; no desire was felt there for
the carrying out of the plans of James II. Pope Innocent XI

---

[1] Bonnet: 'Les chevaux et les dragons sont tous allemands.'

[2] On the list of regiments lately placed at William's disposal by Brandenburg,
there appeared the name of Prince Philip of Brandenburg and Old Holstein, and
on the list of those who joined in the expedition, that of the Prince of Brande:
burg, Duke of Holstein. In the spring report of the year 1689, however, the li:
is given in an unintelligible form (p. 88); on the other hand it is clear in th:
remarkable book 'Engelaand's Godsdienst en Fryheit hersteld,' p. 108. 1689.

declared that it promised to be less advantageous to religion than to the ambition of Louis XIV : the result would be that the English crown would finally itself succumb to French predominance. The German ambassadors at Vienna, who had made indirect overtures which at first were coldly received, were astonished that their best support came from Rome[1]. Besides, the invasion of the Palatinate produced a conviction at the imperial court that the connexion which enabled France to defy the whole world, that is its alliance with England, must be destroyed. The Spanish ambassador at Vienna remarked that that would only be possible if the Parliament kept the upper hand in the internal quarrel in England. He said that, according to his experience—and he had been long in England—the house of Austria had nothing to expect from King James but hostility; from the Parliament, on the other hand, it might expect every possible service.

William himself at last held it advisable to make a declaration to the Emperor. He sought thereby to remove the objections which sympathy for legitimacy and for Catholicism might raise against his enterprise at the imperial court. In reference to the first point he expressed himself with much prudence ; he protested that he was far from wishing to do an injury to King James, and to those who had a legal claim to the succession, or from wishing to appropriate the crown himself[2]; he announced his purpose, which he had already declared to the States-General, of sparing the King as far as possible, and of having the question of the succession decided by Parliament. He added, in reference to religion, that he would employ all his influence to procure for the Catholics a repeal of the penal laws : his object was only to take care of the privileges of the Estates with the aid of a

---

[1] Letter of the Hessian ambassador, Görtz, from Vienna, Oct. 4.

[2] The words are: ' Je n'ay pas la moindre intention de faire aucun tort à S. M. Britannique ni à ceux qui ont droit de prétendre à la succession de ses royaumes.' These words were expounded at Vienna in favour of the Prince of Wales ; the ambassador of the Netherlands replied, ' that no recognition of the legitimate birth of the Prince of Wales was in any way implied in them ; the decision had been reserved for Parliament.'

regular Parliament, and to restore a good understanding between King and Parliament, in order that they might be in a position to promote the general good—meaning, no doubt, the welfare of Europe. He thus hit the Emperor's sentiments; his letter was very well received.

Under these auspices, arising out of the general relations of Europe, the Prince of Orange put to sea at Helvoetsluys on November 1/11, 1688, with a favourable and long-wished-for north-east wind. The fleet consisted of three squadrons, each numbering thirteen ships of war of more than thirty guns, and of a considerable number of small vessels; they had fourteen thousand men on board. The first squadron was considered the Prince's own; it was commanded by Herbert and bore the flag of Orange; the two others formed the auxiliary force of the Republic. William himself embarked on board the lightest and safest of the greater frigates, the Brill, Captain Esch. His vessel hoisted a flag with the inscription, 'for the Protestant religion, for a free Parliament,' with the long-proved manly motto of the house of Orange[1]. A deep inward emotion had been noticed in the Prince on occasion of the farewell which he took of the States-General; then there had been so much business to attend to that he himself once complained on the subject; at least he had been obliged to employ blame and threats, contrary to his custom, in order to avoid further delay. Not till the morning of the 2/12th was he informed that everything was embarked; when the despatch yacht announced this he had the topsail hoisted, and steered for the Channel. Dijkvelt, after accompanying him for a distance of some marine leagues, returned to the shore in order to give the Princess information of the actual beginning of the undertaking on which she bestowed the full sympathy of her soul. She wished to see not her father, but his policy, over-thrown; she now only sympathised with her husband.

French and English comrades in the undertaking always retained a lively recollection how the splendid fleet of more than five hundred great and small vessels lay at anchor in

---

[1] 'En caractères grands de trois pieds : pro religione protestante pro libero parlamento; et dessous les armes; je maintiendrai.' (Avaux, November 16.)

mid-channel; while the two coasts of the opposite countries were being crowded with people, the hearts of the troops were inspired with courage and hopefulness by military music. Meanwhile the Prince held a council of war.

Even at the last moment before the departure many expected that there would have to be a battle with the English fleet; Herbert, at least, did not possess popularity and reputation enough to gain it over. There had certainly been a very active agitation among the crews in favour of the Prince; the commander, Lord Dartmouth, however, affirms most distinctly that the fleet would have fought bravely if he had given orders to that effect. But he did not feel himself in a position to do so: he held the enemy to be about twice as strong as he was[1]. The King too hesitated to expose his fleet to ruin. His only orders were that Dartmouth should disturb the Prince's landing, and that only if he believed that he could do it with success[2]. It proved however impracticable, as the wind went round from east to north-west, so that Dartmouth could not even sail in the latter direction along the coast of Sussex. The Prince of Orange arrived without hindrance at the spacious and safe roadstead of Torbay in Devonshire. He, with his frigate, was always in advance of the fleet: he cast anchor in the bay; while the ships of war formed a line some miles to seaward as a protection against interruptions of any kind, the landing of the troops from the transports was effected. It was the 5th of November, the day on which Protestants commemorated the Gunpowder Plot.

No preparations had been made for his reception, but neither had any measures been taken to resist him. On this occasion no Albemarle held the neighbouring city of Exeter under occupation. The magistrates of this city had the gates shut; but on a threat of Lord Mordaunt, who first arrived, to punish further resistance with death, they were opened again. This enabled the Prince to make his entry into the town with

---

[1] The English fleet was reckoned at thirty-three, the Dutch at sixty ships of war. Barrillon, November 25.

[2] According to Barrillon he had been informed, 'que s'il le pouvoit faire avec quelque apparence de succès, il ne doutoit pas, qu'il n'entreprist de troub débarquement du Prince d'Orange.' (October 29.)

a portion of his forces ; the remainder were quartered in the neighbourhood.

King James was not thrown into any great consternation by the news. He had expected that the invasion would take place in the northern provinces ; he now hastened to recall the regiments which had marched in that direction, and to order them to the west. He thought that he had it in his power to cut off the Prince from all communication with the rest of the country, to shut him up in the western counties, and to destroy him with his own forces, which were twice as numerous as those of his son-in-law.

CHAPTER V.

ANY one desirous of describing accurately the point in dispute between the King and the Prince must have made it
refer to the summoning of a Parliament. Of all the grounds
assigned by the Prince and his English friends for their undertaking, none was so urgent as the danger which the internal
peace of England seemed likely to incur from a Nonconformist Parliament. The King had renounced his intention of
summoning such a body, and had declared himself ready to
return to the old forms, but afterwards, at the decisive moment,
he had nevertheless refused to issue the writs : that had been
the real cause of Sunderland's fall. The Prince appeared in
order to extort the summoning of a Parliament consisting of
persons qualified by custom and law for membership ; the
King was still obstinately opposed to such a course.

But further, this one question included most of the others
which concerned the domestic and foreign policy of the
country.

In the Prince's proclamation, which now came into circulation in all the counties and among all classes of the population,
the removal of grievances was not only demanded, but, like
the decision on the relations of the different creeds, reserved
for the Parliament which was to be called. The toleration
for Dissenters and peaceable Catholics, of which he held out
a prospect, did not however at all meet the King's views ;
still less would the latter have ever allowed that Parliament
should decide on the legitimacy of the Prince of Wales, and
on the succession generally, as the Prince of Orange de-

manded : the declared intention of establishing the Protestant
religion and freedom so securely that there should never again
be any ground for fearing a restoration of arbitrary government might lead far beyond all that James held it possible to
accept, especially as the Prince, in a postscript, denied all
value to the concessions last made ; for they left untouched,.
he said, the claim to a despotic power ; no act of grace could
be of any avail in this case, but only a declaration of the
rights of the subject in a lawful Parliament.

What were these rights of the subject, generally stated?
Without directly thinking of doing so, their advocates yet
recurred to that assertion of Parliamentary privileges on the
most extensive scale which had been made good in practice
under the house of Lancaster. The notion of the prerogative as it had prevailed since the time of the Tudors would
no doubt have to be restricted by the new Parliament. The
constitutional question bore, however, at the same time an
ecclesiastical character. By coming with an armed force to
the support of the popular cause, the Prince of Orange
assumed a position like that which the Scots had held in
the year 1640 ; no doubt with the essential difference that
he was connected with the Episcopalians, and not, as they had
been, with the Presbyterians especially ; this did not, however,
matter much as regarded the rights of the King, for discontent had taken hold of the Episcopalians themselves.

The influence of foreign relations upon the dispute was not
less important. From a Parliament, under whatever forms
summoned—but especially if summoned under those which
had been long familiar—there must be expected, as has been
mentioned, energetic opposition to the alliance with France.
The King, however, had already returned from his momentary
departure from it, and was as much disposed as ever to form
a closer connexion with that power ; he declared his opinion
at that time that he would be able to overpower the Dutch
fleet if he had only ten French frigates on his side of the
Channel. The negotiation as to an alliance with France was
resumed, and that not only for the present business but with
a view to the future also : for a limit, it was said, must be set
to the insolence of the Dutch Republic and of the Prince of

Orange, and they must be punished for their unlawful proceedings.

This was the very thing which was most feared in Europe. Parliamentary principles in England had the advantage and the good fortune to enter into alliance with the general interests of Europe. Every power which has ever attained to independent life in Europe has had to win its position while thus participating in the conflict of general interests, and has had to prove itself indispensable to the European commonwealth. It depended on the victory or defeat of parliamentary principle whether there should be a balance of power between states and religions, and consequently whether there should be personal independence of the individual or not.

For some time after the Prince's landing all remained quiet in England. The commercial classes did not wish for a disturbance of trade; no more did the King himself, whose principal revenues were supplied by it: the Exchange of London was frequented by a large crowd as usual. Even in the western counties, which were at other times so agitated, and on which the Prince chiefly reckoned, there was delay in joining him. He himself expressed his astonishment at it; but the often-repeated story that in his indignation he even thought of returning to Holland is hardly credible. For some delay was to be expected. It had been agreed that those of his companions who were most intimate with the party-leaders with whom he had an understanding should go to the different counties and stir up an agitation there. The object originally contemplated when the Prince was invited to engage in his undertaking,—the object, I mean, of giving employment to the King's forces through the appearance of the Prince in England, so that an opportunity for organising a revolt might be gained—was attained at once, as the King summoned his troops away from the north, where the most extensive preparations had been made. The letters of the Prince himself are before us, in which he applied to those from whom he expected support; they differ according to the degree of intimacy of his connexion with those to whom they are addressed. And meanwhile the proclamation must be spread about everywhere in order to produce an impression. In a

short time the impression produced proved equally decided
and universal. It was easy to get over the objection that the
Prince was an invader; for it was thought that he certainly
did not intend to injure the country, by his invasion but on the
contrary to deliver it from oppressive violence and to take
care of its most sacred interests. How much must those have
been excited who had been placed in a disadvantageous position
by the measures of the government, Episcopalians as well as
Nonconformists, the old opponents of Monmouth as well as
his adherents and friends! For regard was had to the interests
of both classes. Even those who had been at any rate contented by the King's last concessions nevertheless thought that
there would be a much better security in their being carried
out by Parliament. The King reckoned that the power which
was as it were inseparably united to hereditary royalty would
save him from desertion; but the feeling on which he relied
had been weakened by the fact that his own daughter and
son-in-law took part against him. From the outset there
could be no doubt that the nation would adhere to the Prince's
cause: it was only needful to find an acceptable form for
its transfer of obedience. The first man who put out such a
form was Edward Seymour, naturally a zealous Episcopalian
and Tory, for some time a member of the ministry of Charles II,
which he left, however, when the counsels of James gained the
preponderance therein; he had been the leader of those who
opposed James II in the Parliament of 1685. He recurred
to the form of association which had been once applied in
the times of Queen Elizabeth for the security of that princess
herself and of Protestantism, and which had also been proposed of late years, by Shaftesbury for example, although
with a somewhat different view. The new Association pledged
all those who signed it to God, to the Prince of Orange and
to each other, to hold together until religion and the laws
and liberties of the country had been securely established in
a free Parliament; if any crime were attempted against the
Prince they would take vengeance for it, and even if it
succeeded would only persevere with all the more vigour in
their purpose. It was a combination for the attainment of the
ends announced in the Prince's proclamation, with him if

possible, but even without him in case any mishap befel him. Seymour was a man of high personal authority, whose words passed for law with the English[1]; he said now that if they did not bind themselves by some such mutual obligation, those who joined the Prince would be like a heap of sand. This association, however, now formed a cement which held them together against all chances. It was signed first at Exeter and then in all the western counties[2]. William of Orange for his part also gave an assurance. He told the nobles and gentry of Somerset and Dorset who came to join him that he might have a bridge of gold built for him if he were willing to go home again; but that his objects were just, and above all price; he wished to deliver the kingdom from Popery and arbitrary power, to re-establish its old rights and liberties, to promote peace and trade; his thoughts were only directed to the welfare of the human race; he would rather die for this good cause than live in a bad one[3].

While this first union was being formed at Exeter, the King on the other hand was being pressed by those about him to make up his mind once more, before the matter went further, to summon a Parliament: 'let him not wait till he was compelled to take such a step by a general insurrection; and what had he so much to fear from a Parliament? If it were to make unfair demands of him, he would be able to dissolve it, and in any case to gain a party for himself; in the last resort he had yet his army at his disposal.' It was especially Preston, Sunderland's successor as secretary of state, who made these representations[4]. And the spiritual and temporal lords, who had come to an agreement at

---

[1] Citters: ' Ein seer wis man geltende syne woorden als wetten.'

[2] An engagement of the noblemen, knights and gentlemen at Exeter. Second collection of papers, No. iv.

[3] The speech of the Prince of Orange to some principal gentlemen of Somersetshire and Dorsetshire. November 15th, 1688. Fourth collection, No iii.

[4] According to Citters, November 16/26; a letter which is printed without his name in Engeland's Fryheit, but which is found among his papers: 'Hebben sommige van het cabinetconseil—den konink oern anraaden, sonder uitstell siin parlament te doen vorgaderen,—dringende darop te meer aan, om dat hy' de adresses doch niet sal konnen verwerpen of anders de gantsche natie in so grooten opstand geraethen, dat hy en alle de catholyken selver sullen gevaar loopen.'

Lambeth Palace, declared themselves most emphatically to the same effect. They told the King that the only chance of safety for himself and for the realm lay in the immediate summoning of a Parliament free in every respect; they conjured him to provide that there should be no bloodshed. James II replied, that he wished as much as they did that he were in a position to summon a Parliament, but that it was impossible to do so while the Prince of Orange was in the country. The Catholic camarilla kept him fast to this resolution. It represented to him that no understanding with the Parliament could be conceived which should not be prejudicial to him, the King; but that if no agreement were arrived at, he would be held responsible for the failure: he would thereby for the first time completely estrange his people: it would be better that he should abide by the resolution which he had once formed: he could still trust his army, and if he proved to it that he did so, it would for its part remain obedient; in which case he would find support from other quarters.

In deciding hereupon to repair to the army, which was stationed near Salisbury, the King did not precisely intend to come to blows; he wished in the first place to withdraw himself out of the way of the storm of addresses asking for a Parliament which threatened him in his capital both from that city itself and from all other quarters, and at the same time to confirm his army in its obedience. Some attempts at revolt had occurred, but had not been fully carried out; corps which had at first followed a deserting leader had yet returned to their standards again; it seemed that the King's présence might put an end to all such attempts. And when the news came that Lord Lovelace, who had wished to join the Prince at the head of an armed force, had been disarmed and detained at Gloucester by the county militia, it seemed that only a firm attitude was needed to suppress the movement everywhere. The French ambassador accompanied the King on his journey; on this very occasion a renewal of the French alliance was continually discussed.

On the 19th of November the King reached his army at Salisbury. That army was not one of those in which a rigorous military discipline and subordination controls the soldiers. Not only did it stand far beneath the French army in reference to organisation, but King James had cherished the spirit of religious party in it, one might almost say on purpose. He had announced without disguise his conviction that he might trust the Catholic more than the Protestant officers. An attempt, which had been lately made to have a number of Irishmen admitted into a regiment stationed at Portsmouth, had given rise to an opinion in the army that he thought of filling its ranks with foreigners and Papists, and that opinion spread widely. But such a suspicion, roused by the bigotry of James, could not fail to excite the religious feelings of the Protestants also; and a man's duty to his Church was in those days rated almost more highly than military obedience. To the defect thus caused by religious dissensions, there was another involved in the peculiar constitution of the armies of the time. The regiments remained constantly in a relation of dependence to those who had provided for their enlistment: and as the latter were chiefs of the factions which held possession of the court and the state, they carried the troops with them into their own contests.

The presence among those who had signed the peers' last address of a man like Grafton, to whom an important command in the army was entrusted, made it improbable that he and his men would draw the sword very zealously against a cause to which he was personally attached. A still more important position was held by Churchill, the King's old confidant in his first connexion with France, but who had been long estranged and driven to the other side by the preference given to the Catholics. He had promised Sunderland to support him if he succeeded in getting a Parliament summoned, but if a Parliament were not summoned no loyalty could be expected from him; he had been for some time in correspondence with the Prince of Orange. These circumstances explain the fact that when the King arrived at Salisbury, expressions were heard in the ranks of the army itself which were opposed to his views[1]. In some corps, especially in the first regiment of

---

[1] The assertion that the army declared to the King that it would not fight against the Prince of Orange was spread abroad even at the time; but no proof of it can be found anywhere.

Guards, the King's policy was loudly and bitterly censured. These unreserved expressions were attributed to the influence of Grafton and Churchill, and the King was advised to have them removed to Portsmouth; he did not take this step, as he feared to raise an insurrection among the soldiers thereby; but he could not place much confidence in those two noblemen. He paid far more attention to the French generals who were about him, to Duras Lord Feversham, and to Roye, than to the English field-officers. He had offered Roye the command-in-chief of his army; but the latter objected that he did not know the language of the country well enough to hold the command; his real reason was, that he feared the jealousy of the English : he had, however, now accompanied the King to support him with his counsels.

This personal opposition came to an outbreak in the camp on the following occasion.

The King's plan had originally been to extend his quarters as far as Axminster and Langport, in order to enclose the Prince in the western corner of the kingdom which he occupied. The Prince, however, had already himself occupied Axminster, and it had become doubtful whether the King's forces would be able to hold their ground at all against him on Salisbury Plain. A purpose of visiting the most advanced post at Warminster was given up, as the King, while preparing to carry it out, was attacked by a most violent bleeding at the nose, which could only be stopped by his being bled in the arm. On the general question, Roye maintained that neither Warminster nor Salisbury could be held, but that as soon as the Prince drew near, those positions would have to be abandoned; he advised the King to retreat of his own accord, and without delay, while it could still be done in good order and without interruption. A council of war was held to consider this question, at which both Grafton and Churchill were present. They declared against the retreat, and showed marks of lively discontent when the King finally took the advice of the French general and ordered a retreat.

It has been made a charge against them that if the King had followed them to Warminster they would have got him into their power there, and would perhaps have delivered him to the Prince, or at least would certainly have compelled him to accept the terms which they thought of prescribing to him.   But would they, it may be objected, if they had contemplated such a decided act of treachery, have spoken as loudly as they did against the King's policy, and have made themselves suspected thereby[1]?

That other reasons as well as such as were purely military helped to suggest the order for retreat there can be no doubt ; it was desired to check the insubordination which was beginning to show itself, to separate the suspected regiments from each other, and perhaps to disband them.   It was thought that by withdrawing beyond the Thames the King would obtain a position which could be more easily defended, and at the same time would keep the capital in check, where, as often in times of general excitement, disorderly movements were now taking place.

But Churchill and Grafton were not disposed to carry out arrangements which were to some extent directed against themselves.   In the next night they rode away from the camp, accompanied by a number of devoted officers, and went over to the Prince of Orange, with whom they had long been in communication.   The King was amazed ; but he remained cool and composed on hearing of it.   He ordered the regiment which Grafton had commanded to assemble on the spot, presented a new commander to it, and as he passed through the ranks addressed words of exhortation to the troops, to which they replied by joyful acclamations.

But at this moment the rising, for which preparations had been made, broke out in all parts of the country.   It seemed as though the King's refusal to summon a Parliament had everywhere given people a signal for helping themselves.   One of the first in arms was Lord Delamere, in Cheshire, who had already been closely allied with Monmouth, but at the time of the latter's insurrection had fortunately been saved from ruin by a verdict of acquittal.   The Earl of Devonshire was

---

[1] Churchill denied it, when spoken to on the subject, ' with many protestations.' Clarendon's Diary 214.   It looks quite like a suggestion of superstition that the King thought he had been preserved by his loss of blood from an extreme disaster.

able at last to give a free course to his discontent; he invited
Derbyshire to declare its approval of the Prince's proclamation, and then set Nottinghamshire in motion.   In
Yorkshire Danby's rising brought about a revolution in the
city and county.   But what made the greatest impression upon
the King was that his nearest relations fell away from him.
His son-in-law, Prince George of Denmark, withdrew from
the camp at Andover; when James arrived in London he
had to learn that his daughter Anne, Prince George's wife,
had also fled: she appeared in a short time in the midst of
the rebels.   Lord Churchill and Prince George stated in letters
which they left behind the reasons for their departure, of which
they quite felt the odious character.   It was the preponderance
of the French and Catholic faction in the affairs of England
and of Europe which drove them over to the opposite side.
On account of the predilection of the King for that faction,
all who were attached to him tore themselves from him,—
his two daughters, his two sons-in-law, his most trusted
favourite, for whom he had long shown a preference, the
prelate who had crowned him, the Cavaliers who had fought
for the restoration of his house, the leaders of the army to
the formation of which he had looked for security.

Hatred of the faction above referred to was the feeling
which prevailed generally in the nation; after being long
suppressed it broke out at once.   The King's Declaration of
Indulgence was now only thought of as having been intended
to pave the way for the execution of his projects in favour
of Catholicism.   Where were the Anabaptists and Quakers
who had expressed their approval of the Declaration with
enthusiasm, or again, the magistrates and noblemen who had
greeted with thankfulness the withdrawal of the measures
which James had taken to the injury of the old constitution?
These opposing sympathies destroyed each other's effect; all
men were silenced or carried away by the zeal felt against the
French.   A new proclamation, which the Prince is said to
have issued at Sherborne, on his march, but which he never
acknowledged, was circulated through the country; by it the
Papists who should be found in arms were as good as proscribed,
and the public officers were invited to secure their arms and even

their persons [1]. Papists were in consequence disarmed and
forcibly arrested throughout the country ; it was thought that
they would rise and join the French, who might, it was said,
be expected to land. In some places the population seized
arms of every kind in consequence of reports that French
vessels with troops on board for landing had appeared in
the neighbouring roads. They were really merchantmen
which had been driven to the coast by the Dutch.

No doubt the case was not as supposed ; French auxiliary forces had not been embarked, and the Catholics in the
country were not just then at all dangerous ; but the suppositions referred to had yet so far a certain basis of truth that
the King was at that time really seeking for and expecting
aid from France, and that his whole policy then as previously
had its source in a desire to promote the interests of Catholicism. In the great conflicts of the world decisions are for the
most part brought to pass by those general antipathies which
take hold of peoples and carry them away ; these are the
inner storms in the life of the community. Popular impulses
secured the victory to the Prince's cause.

At Bristol the Protestant inclinations which had formerly
been kept down, and which the King had hoped to win for
himself, took, under Shrewsbury's influence, a direction decidedly hostile to him. An opposition between the Protestant and Catholic parts of the garrisons, in which the first
were supported by the citizens, caused the two great ports of
Plymouth and Hull to go over to the Prince. What was
peculiar in the counties was the adhesion of the authorities
to the Prince's cause, which took place with some system.
Thus the Earl of Bath assembled the administrative officers,
the justices, and the nobility and gentry of Cornwall at
Saltash, and induced them to sign Seymour's association.
On his entry into Salisbury William was received both by
the mayor and aldermen in their robes of office, and also
by the dean and chapter of the cathedral, amid the applause

---

[1] A member of the Speke family in Dorset, to which Monmouth first applied on
his arrival, boasted afterwards of having composed it : and it may have originated
with fanatical Protestants of that class; at the time it was universally regarded as
genuine.

of the population. The gentry presented themselves in great numbers, and bound themselves to make contributions for the regular payment of the troops. The news arrived there that Herefordshire as well as the Welsh counties of Brecknock, Radnor, and Montgomery, had declared for the Prince. The Act of Association was also, under the influence of Ormond, signed at Oxford, which had suffered in an especial manner from the King's encroachments. The whole North had in a short time organised itself anew after the same fashion. At Nottingham the nobles of the North who appeared, together with their ladies, formed a kind of court around the Princess Anne.

The influence of this general revolt was felt even in the districts in which the King's authority was still recognised—especially in the capital. James at length convinced himself that he must yield to the demand which was put forward on all sides as most important, and announce his intention of summoning a Parliament. As early as the 27th of November, the day after his arrival in London, he assembled a great council of magnates after the old fashion—the spiritual and temporal peers who happened to be just then in London, in order to make the announcement to them. But he had then to hear much that was unacceptable, and that from those very Episcopalian Tories with whom he had at an earlier time had most in common. The announcement of a Parliament did not settle the whole matter; the King was required to proclaim pardon beforehand for all those who had attached themselves to the Prince, as without this no Parliament could possibly be assembled; further, to allow a negotiation to be entered upon with the Prince himself, in order that there might be no collision between the two armies; finally, to remove all Catholics from his council and from the neighbourhood of his person. All these were things which wounded his sense of dignity most deeply; he had to feel that his position in general was suffering a heavy blow; the final decision no longer rested with him; it was forced upon him by an influence which he had hitherto resisted. He did not decide at once. But on the next morning (November 28/December 8) he declared before the Privy Council that he would summon a Parliament for the 15th of the next January, and also proclaim a general pardon. Hitherto he had always declared it to be a personal insult when any one ventured to request him to enter on a negotiation with the Prince of Orange : now he showed himself ready to have the means concerted with him for enabling the Parliament to assemble in tranquillity, and to proceed to definite delibera- tions. He named commissioners who were to visit the Prince in his camp with that object.

The united spiritual and temporal peers believed that they had obtained a great victory. For they believed that in a Parliament summoned according to the forms sanctioned by long usage and under the authority of the King, they would still be able to effect an amicable settlement of the matter in dispute. That was especially the idea of Lord Clarendon, the leader of the high Tories, and the man who had expressed himself most loudly and bitterly in the last assembly. Hav- ing been instructed by the Lord Chancellor that the writs for the Parliament had been already prepared, he held it ad- visable to betake himself without delay to the Prince, in order to secure his consent. He thought that he could still combine both the Prince and the King in the state, by the King's retaining his title, while the Prince took the administration into his hands; a recognition of the Prince of Wales by the Parliament seemed to him quite compatible with this arrange- ment, especially if measures were taken for his education in the Protestant faith. The Prince of Orange gave Lord Clarendon a friendly reception when he visited him in his camp; Clarendon's son, Lord Cornbury, had been one of the first who had gone over to him, for which he seemed to give the father credit ; William asked Clarendon in what light he regarded the present position of affairs. Clarendon answered that if his Highness adhered to the declaration which he had issued it would still be possible to arrive at a happy settlement. Prince William replied that his de- claration should be rigorously observed. Bentinck, whom Clarendon visited next day, repeated the same assurance. 'Many,' added Bentinck, 'said that the Prince was aspiring to the crown ; but that was a malicious calumny ; the prospect

of winning three kingdoms at once might certainly arouse
ambition ; but the Prince preferred to keep his word : he
would adhere to his declaration, and seek to settle everything
on a permanent foundation.' Clarendon replied that if such
were the Prince's sentiments there could be no difficulties in
arriving at an agreement. In forming this hope he reckoned
confidently on the Parliament which was soon to assemble,
the summoning of which busied him more than anything
else. As the country gentry, who kept arriving at Salisbury,
promised him to give his son their votes for a seat in the
Parliament, he introduced them to the Prince, to whom they
expressed their thanks for his expedition undertaken for the
defence of religion and of the laws. Clarendon made no
difficulty about signing the Association of Exeter, as every
one else had done. It was only when there was a talk of
contributing money that he dissuaded those present from
fixing a definite sum, because by so doing they would
encroach upon the rights of Parliament which had to provide for the public needs. All the efforts of his party had
been directed towards bringing together a Parliament of an
Episcopalian character ; from such a Parliament he expected
the restoration of the order of things which the policy of
James II had interrupted, and the placing of the Prince on
an equality with James without any shaking of the old
foundations [1].

If he looked around him he must no doubt have noticed
that many of those about the Prince were not of this
opinion. He saw Ferguson and Wildman frequenting his
presence. It made a great impression on him that during
the church service Burnet arose and went out as soon as the
collect for the King was to be read ; Burnet would not hear
of any treaty, nor even of the Parliament which had been
announced ; it seemed as though he no longer recognised the
King as king.

This, however, would not yet have decided anything, had
not an analogous influence from another side co-operated
with it.

---

[1] On these events I everywhere derive my information from Clarendon's Diary.

In despatching his commissioners to the Prince, King
James had not named men of the Lambeth party, like
Lord Clarendon, whose harsh Protestantism inspired him with
distrust, but certain others whose position was in general
further removed from his own—Halifax, Nottingham, Godolphin. James II never knew how to distinguish men's
sentiments; he had no suspicion that the two first were
even old adherents of the Prince. They had been informed
of the invitation to him; Nottingham had only drawn back
in alarm from the last step, the actual signature. Halifax
stood as it were in a historical relation to this cause. At
the moment at which he had in the Upper House hindered
the exclusion of the Duke of York by the vigour of his
eloquence, he declared to the Prince of Orange his opinion
that the Duke would nevertheless never mount the throne
of England, which, on the contrary, would be reserved for
William. If he then defended hereditary right it was in
opposition to Monmouth and his friends. Now, what Halifax
had then foreseen was at the present time about to be fulfilled.
What a mistake it was that James II at the decisive moment
entrusted the negotiation with the Prince to a man from
whom the latter had received the first hints to adopt the
hostile attitude which he had actually assumed!

Halifax was by no means the most trustworthy or conscientious of the statesmen of that time, but he was perhaps the most intelligent, and the one whose judgment was
least biassed by prejudice; he saw farthest into the distance.
Sunderland, with all his talent and with all his ambition, cast
himself into the ranks first of one party and then of another,
and served both as a tool. Shaftesbury fell in attempting to
found a great party. Rochester and Clarendon placed themselves at the head of factions, beyond the interests of which
their insight did not reach. Halifax, on the contrary, drew
near to the different parties in turn, without allowing any to
get possession of him. He had formerly availed himself of
French influence to secure the interests of Parliamentary
government against Charles II; but he had never placed
himself at the disposal of France for its own objects. He
had frustrated the great projects of Monmouth; but he

maintained the policy which suggested them against the opposing influence of the Duke of York; for he always strove to baffle the endeavours which that prince was making in favour of Catholicism, and in opposition to Parliamentary government. His letters are remarkable for the calmness and solidity of their impartial arguments; we have mentioned how he took part in the movement of the moment by publishing a striking and effective pamphlet, but also how on the other hand he neither joined in a demonstration of the bishops, nor in the invitation to the Prince. On the present occasion it would not have been at all agreeable to him that the object of his mission should have been attained; in that case the Hydes, whom he did not love, and the men of the Lambeth party would have succeeded in carrying out their purposes. While he accepted the commission which was to prepare for a reconciliation according to the wish and proposal of the party last named, he yet either instructed or allowed some of the members of the circles in which he moved to carry a warning to the Prince against listening to the offers which were to be made him. In that warning the Prince was told that it would be a misunderstanding of the state of affairs to expect a reconciliation; difference of religion would make it impossible, as experience taught them, to leave even the name of power where it was at present; the hopes of every one were fixed on a complete change of persons; confidence could be felt no longer; a new building could only be built on a new foundation[1]. The anonymous paper in which these passages occur refers to the approval of Lord Halifax. The Prince is plainly told in it that after he had saved the country from Popery and slavery, the country could not entrust even the name of power to any one but himself.

Such were the views entertained by the commissioners when they met. They were men who stood, not indeed in the first, but in the second degree of proximity to the King and to the Prince. Their first meeting was characteristic. When the King's envoys reached the camp at Hungerford, where

---

[1] Everything must be built upon new foundations He (Halifax) seemed then fully to agree with me. (Dalrymple ii. 1, 337.) But who could speak with Halifax, or write of him to the Prince, in such terms?

the negotiations were to take place, the Prince had forbidden
all about him to hold any private intercourse with them.
Halifax and Burnet found nevertheless an unobserved moment
for the exchange of a few words. Halifax asked if the other
party desired to get the King into their own hands? For
things began to look daily more and more as if this were
possible. Burnet denied it. 'But,' said Halifax, 'what if he
had a mind to go away?' 'Nothing was so much to be wished,'
replied Burnet. So he himself reports in his History of his
Own Times. In spite of the prohibition of private intercourse
he made no secret of the matter to the Prince, and the Prince
showed himself very well satisfied with what had passed.

In the negotiations, to which the Prince invited the lords
and gentlemen who were staying with him, the majority of
them would have been in favour of refusing to recognise the
Parliament announced by the King; the Prince, however,
sided with those who recommended acceptance of the offer:
but, from the conditions which he added, it may yet be seen
that he already felt himself the stronger, and intended to
assure his superiority still further by means of the prelimi-
naries which were to be arranged. He required, amongst
other points, the removal of all Catholics, both from the
military and from the civil service, which the King had not
yet carried out: the surrender of the Tower to the authorities of the capital, and the nomination of a commandant for
Portsmouth whom he as well as the King could approve of;
for he wished to be assured that both he himself and the
future Parliament would be secured against all military
counter-movements.

The King too, on his side, had omitted nothing which might
aid him in arming for his defence. The passages over the
Thames were fortified, cannon conveyed to the Tower,
and even preparations made for new enlistments. The
King thought that, after the announcement of a Parliament,
he would again be able to count on the loyalty of his troops,
and to maintain himself in London. Forces were being
armed on two opposite sides at once, on both under the
pretence of hindering the enemy's action upon the Parliament.

The question, however, certainly arose whether the King,

who had refused to summon a Parliament from a consideration
of the Prince's influence, at a time when the latter was still
far off, was now really in earnest in summoning one after the
Prince had gained over the greatest part of the country?

James told the French ambassador just then that he had
seen no other means of self-preservation than the summoning
of a Parliament, for that he could thereby still gain time enough
for taking measures to avert his complete ruin. But, he added
—as though it were his purpose really to allow the Parliament to assemble—that he would never consent to anything
which ran counter to the interests of the King of France[1].

There were two things of which, even at this moment, the
thought was intolerable to him : that he would have to give
up taking his Catholic fellow-believers under his protection for
the future, and that he would have to renounce his connexion
with the King of France.   Indeed a new alliance with France
was at that very time being discussed, and one to be settled
by word of mouth, as if so settled it could be denied without
difficulty.   The Secretary of State for Scotland, Lord Melfort,
the only minister to whom, as being a Catholic, the King
opened his mind freely, even made a fresh proposal for the
despatch of an auxiliary force without delay.   He required
that at least there should be military preparations at Calais
or Dunkirk, from which ports the passage was, he said, so
easy, and could not be hindered by the Dutch.   Barrillon
objected that Louis XIV could not be required to arm his
fleet if he did not know how he could unite it with the English
fleet.   Melfort replied that, if Louis would only keep himself
prepared, they would soon find means for effecting the union.
It struck Barrillon that no corresponding assurances were
given, and that James only expected to be saved by France;
but he nevertheless entered into the scheme so far as this,
that he even asked on one occasion whether it would not be
well for the King to send over to England one of his ablest
marshals : the state of things was such, he said, that the

---

[1] Barrillon, Nov. 29/Dec. 9: 'Qu'il ne voyoit plus de remède pour lui que de
convoquer un parlement, que cela lui pouvoit donner quelque tems pour prendre
les mesures et se garantir d'une ruine entière—qu'il ne se laisseia aller à rien, qui
fût contraire aux inteiests de V. Majesté.'

ablest would be wanted. But whatever might be wished in England, and whatever the ambassador might think possible, it is certain that the King of France himself would never have entered into the plan. He only allowed further aid in money to be hoped for, and even this could not be very considerable, as he was engaged in war on all sides: he declared it impossible to furnish other help either by sea or land. 'If French troops,' he said, 'were to attempt a landing, all the enemies of King James would immediately turn against them. And how should he be able to direct his ships of war to join the English, seeing that the King of England himself was not sure of the latter?'

In this position, destitute of the assistance on which he had counted in case of the worst happening, and assailed in his own country by a hostility which was stronger than he had ever imagined it could be, James II hit upon the thought of escaping to France.

The idea was first suggested by Father Petre in reference to the Prince of Wales. 'For it would terrify the English,' said Petre, with the false subtlety which characterised him, 'if they saw that, however the question might be decided for the moment, they would yet subsequently have a war of many years with France before them.' Just as though the antipathy to France which already prevailed must not far rather, if such a step were taken, extend to the English royal family also. The Prince of Wales was actually taken to Portsmouth; but the admiral, Lord Dartmouth, refused to carry over the heir to the crown to France, for to do so might, he said, involve him in the most serious responsibility. The child was brought back to Westminster, not without difficulty. If a decided wish was felt to place him in safety, it only remained to make the attempt from London, and to provide for the mother's safety in the same way; for neither mother nor child would have, it was supposed, to expect any favour from the Prince of Orange's hatred. What was the King to do? He was at heart resolved not to submit to the future Parliament on the two great points which had been touched upon—the case of the Catholics and the French alliance. But nothing was more certain than that the Parliament would on both give a decision adverse to his wishes, and on the last more eagerly than on the first.   If he did not wish to suffer constraint he must leave the capital.   He thought at first of escaping to Portsmouth, or to Ireland, or to Scotland, and had taken some steps in preparation for carrying out such a purpose [1] : but as all these projects proved impossible of execution, he finally expressed to the French ambassador his intention of going to France, and of begging Louis XIV to grant him an asylum in his kingdom.

Barrillon was not at bottom altogether favourable to this plan.   For even if the King retained only a shadow of power, that would still be better for France than if the Prince of Orange became altogether lord and master ; Barrillon had been already reminded to take care that France should keep some influence in the Parliament which was about to assemble. Among the English councillors of James also some voices were heard in favour of his remaining : no doubt on the supposition that he made up his mind to give way in reference to religion and the laws.   It was thought that, in that case, he would still find many adherents ; as, in fact, after the declaration that a Parliament would be summoned, some new addresses expressing devotion came in.   It was remarked that an opposition was already in movement among the Nonconformists against the alliance of the Church of England with the Prince, and that there was no good ground for the apprehension that the Parliament would rob the King of his liberty, for that it was a legally recognised condition of the validity of the Parliament's resolutions that the King should be free.   To this the Catholics answered : that to surrender himself into the hands of his enemies would be the height of imprudence ; whither might not the Prince of Orange, who was indisputably aspiring to the crown, allow himself to be hurried by his ambition, and who would be willing to oppose him in anything he might undertake?   There hovered before the eyes of the King the end of his father, and still more the fate of Richard II, to whose position his own had in reality a certain resemblance ; he said more than once during these distresses that he did not mean to expose himself, to a similar

---

[1] Danby has narrated that the King offered him to go to the North.

fate. In the Prince of Orange he saw a new Henry of Boling-
broke. And in contrast to these dark shadows which threatened
him with ruin he might form brilliant hopes if he accepted
what was inevitable and withdrew. He was told 'that he
would thereby save his right, and might assert it on another
occasion'; 'many a King of England before him had fled and
had been restored ; for England returned in time to itself and
renounced its prejudices ; and certainly it would be impossible
for the Prince of Orange to found a stable government which
should find obedience : he would never content all those whose
services he was now accepting.' It was with the object of
increasing the confusion which was expected that the King
induced the Lord Chancellor to take up his abode at Whitehall ; he wished to carry away with him the great seal, which
was considered absolutely necessary for the authorisation of
important acts in England. He did not think of renouncing
the English crown by leaving England, but, on the contrary,
of putting himself in a position to regain it at some future
time, without any limitation of the prerogatives which he had
hitherto exercised ; 'for the time would surely come when
Louis XIV would be able to give him effective aid to that
end.'

One consideration caused the King to hesitate : what,
he thought, would the world say if he retired before his
son-in-law without having drawn the sword in defence of his
throne? Meanwhile it became clear that in spite of his
new precautions it would be impossible to meet the Prince in
arms. As to the English naval force it was proved again
beyond a doubt that the King must not reckon upon it.
When it sent him its congratulations for having decided on
summoning the Parliament, that could only be understood
as showing an inclination towards the Prince who had put
forward a demand to that effect, and indeed a deputation had
gone from the fleet to the Prince himself. And it became
daily less and less probable that the army posted on the
Thames would oppose a serious resistance to the Prince.
How little even those who when left to themselves still stood
by the King, were inspired by any warlike spirit, was seen
on the occasion of an attack made upon the garrison of

Reading by a party of the Prince's cavalry. It consisted of about 250 horsemen whom Colonel Marwitz led up, his true object being only to reconnoitre the place; but the enemy's outposts were overthrown upon the spot. With sword in hand the horsemen pressed forward to the market-place, where some 600 Irishmen and Scotsmen were posted: instead of resisting, these men broke at once into a disorderly flight, for they knew very well that the inhabitants of the place as well as William's troops were their enemies.

This event, and others like it, could not fail to make the greatest impression upon James II. Lord Feversham told him that he could answer for himself but for no one else. The King's last hesitations now disappeared: he said that he was not sure of a single body of troops; that he had no longer the smallest hope of maintaining his kingdom; that no one could reproach him if he left it.

In the night between the 9th and 10th of December, Queen Mary, under the protection of Count Lauzun, to whom the King entrusted her, stepped down a secret staircase at Whitehall; she crossed the Thames with her child and its nurse in a boat kept in readiness: on the other shore they found a carriage which took them to Gravesend. There they embarked on board a yacht which with a favourable wind carried them to Calais on the next day.

It was now that the King first received the reports from Hungerford and the propositions of William of Orange. Had he accepted them he would thereby have declared his determination to submit to the Parliament and its resolutions: if he resisted the latter he would have to fear imprisonment and even death. His father had said that from the prison of a prince it was not far to his grave. James II had only one task remaining for him in England; to revoke the summons of a Parliament which the general movement in the country had as it were compelled him to issue. Had it assembled on the strength of his writs the High Churchmen and Tories must have derived most advantage from the circumstance. But it was against them that he felt the greatest rancour, ever since they had opposed him on the petition of the Bishops, for that opposition had been the beginning of the movement before which he had now to retire. All his concessions had failed to win them to his side; they had pressed most sternly for a Parliament, and had every prospect of obtaining a predominant position in it. The Prince had accepted James' proposal to summon a Parliament because he did not see how one could be assembled otherwise; the Prince's reason for accepting it supplied the King with a motive for making the execution of his proclamation impossible. He did not wish by his own act to give the Tories the power of bringing the mediation between him and the Prince to an end in accordance with their own views as they purposed. Only a small number of election writs had actually been issued; the King destroyed the rest. The nominations of the new sheriffs, whose co-operation was indispensable for the elections, were still in his cabinet: he destroyed these also. He had already some days before had the great seal delivered up by the Lord Chancellor Jeffreys; he wished to prevent the possibility of its being used to authorise in the eyes of the people new writs or any other act which he thought contrary to his interest: in one way or another he caused it to disappear; he said that the Queen had taken it with her in her flight. He intended that when he was no longer in England the royal authority, the key-stone in the state edifice, should also cease to exist there; that the legal continuity of public order should be broken; and that all things should be left to their own chaotic impulse until a revolution of fortune should bring him back to England. That was the object of King James in finally directing the disbandment of his army by a letter to Feversham. He thanked those who still adhered to him for their constancy, and warned them not to attach themselves to the Association for the Prince but to maintain their faith to himself till the feeling of loyalty and honour should awake again in the nation. 'Time presseth so, that I can add no more. James Rex.' It was the last time that he ever signed his name in England.

He intended that after his departure his name should only promote disorganisation. It seemed that the 'war of all against all,' to which political theory traced the origin of sovereign power in all cases, was to be brought on by the deliberate breaking up of that power. What the death of James II could not have effected—for, as it was said, 'the King never dies,'—that his departure was intended to effect.

In the night between the 10th and 11th of December, King James descended the same stairs by which his Queen had previously escaped. He was attended only by Sir Edward Hales, his old confidant in his projects and helper in their execution; at Vauxhall[1] they reached the other bank, where a carriage stood ready which took them to Elmley Ferry; here a custom-house boat which Hales had hired was to take them on board and convey them to France. James had promised, and, as it is said, sworn to his wife to follow her within twenty-four hours. But he did not fare so well as she had done. On account of the fresh wind that was blowing, it was necessary first to provide the small vessel with some ballast. Time was spent in doing so, and meanwhile the general agitation produced by the proclamation against the Catholics before mentioned spread in these districts as in others. On the public roads those who wished to escape were detained; the seamen too, as if this had roused a spirit of rivalry among them, prepared for a thorough search of the coasts; there they found the boat in which their King was. They held him and his companions for fugitives like others, loaded them with terms of abuse such as were then usual, caused their ready money to be given up to themselves, searched their clothes for the valuables which they might be carrying with them, for they wished to divide the booty regularly among themselves, and finally brought the prisoners to land for a hearing. What surprise took possession of them when the King was recognised in the inn at Feversham! It is related that the first man who recognised him fell before him on his knees with a loud cry. James II had fallen into a state which offered a sharp contrast between his dignity and his present position. He once more entertained a hope

---

[1] That the King threw the great seal into the water at Vauxhall is a conclusion from its discovery a few months later in this neighbourhood. The Spanish ambassador mentions the belief that the Queen had taken it away with her: ' El sello que havia dijen lo levo la reyna.'

that he could reckon on the obedience of his subjects. 'Am I not your king,' he exclaimed, 'and sure you will not hurt my life? Will you stand by me? I will reward you; get me a boat and I'll go off.' He sought to convince them that he had only had the best interests of the country in view, that he was unjustly persecuted, and that his throne and his life were aimed at; he begged and conjured them to save him. At times he turned in such suppliant fashion to individuals that he seemed to have forgotten who he was; then suddenly a sense of his rank awoke in him again; he ordered those who were to watch him to keep themselves at a proper distance from his person. But all that he might say no longer made any impression. These people thought that they were doing a service to the nation by detaining the King; they placed themselves closer together, and cried out that they would rather die than let him depart; with wild huzzas they doubled their watches and threatened to shoot every one who should try to force his way through their ranks to the King. From amidst this wild tumult the King was once more brought back to London and there even welcomed with joyful acclamations as he drove through the town to Whitehall: but yet he was no longer treated as King; an order which he had got sent to the Treasury was not received by the officials after what had passed. We shall have to mention the events of these days again in another place: for the establishment of a new government was connected with the destruction of the old at every step. Here it is enough to remark that the King himself even then did not wish to remain in England. Already on the way, at Rochester, he had had one moment in which he thought that he might escape: 'I see well,' said Barrillon, who greeted him at Whitehall, 'he has still this purpose[1];' when a longer stay in London was not allowed him, the very place which he chose among those offered him to remain in was Rochester, whence he thought that he could most easily escape. As late as the evening before his departure he

---

[1] Barrillon, December 17/27: 'Je vois bien, qu'il est encore résolu de chercher les moyens de se sauver, il avoit même hier ce dessein à Rochester.'

expressed this intention[1]. How little did the High Church
Tories know him, who thought that by offers of reconciliation
they could keep him back from carrying it out! For they
could certainly give him no assurances which would have
been able to make him change his mind. We will only
mention what is most important. The Prince of Orange said
that, while as to all other things he found the most different
opinions among the English, they were all of one mind as to
one point alone, that war must be declared against France.
On the other hand, James II even yet told the French ambassador at Whitehall, 'that he was now at ease as his wife
and son had happily reached France': he repeated 'that
whatever might be his fate he would never consent to war
with France.' What the nation demanded with the greatest
unanimity was·to him the most repulsive of all the requirements that could be made of him. And on this occasion no
one hindered him from escaping : on December 25th, Christmas Day, he reached the French coast at Ambleteuse.

That roadstead forms part of the tract of coast on which,
six centuries before, the splendid fleet had been assembled
with which William the Norman accomplished the conquest
of England. The crown of the Conquest, expelled as it
were from the island, returned to the shores from which it
had once come over.

I fear to weary my readers : yet perhaps many, without
distinction of political or religious sympathies, will still follow
me in studying the general combination of historical forces
which here displays itself.

The Norman Conquest in the eleventh century was destined
to attract the old-fashioned Christian and Teutonic commonwealth established in Britain into communion with the hierarchy
and with feudalism, in the form in which they were then·
acquiring sovereignty in the West. That communion was
itself a condition necessary to procure for the Teutons in the·
island a preponderance over the Keltic tribes among which
they had penetrated. A world then arose in the British Isles,
and in the French coast districts, made up by a mixture of

---

[1] Barrillon, December 20/30.

elements belonging to different peoples, yet in itself homogeneous; to that world belonged the knightly castles and the
colleges of the universities, the constitution of the courts of
justice and of the Church, and the old forms of representation
by estates. Royalty was one of the most brilliant and vigorous
growths of the middle ages, and its dominion had a wide
range. But by its nature it stood in two different relations.
It was bound by certain obligations to the subject population,
over which it claimed a hereditary right, and yet at the same
time it was attracted to the general life of the West, from
which it derived its power. And these relations only coincided for a certain time. In the island there developed itself,
on the basis of the old nationality, a new one, of which the
English language is the expression, and which did not allow
its kings to attach themselves to the spiritual head of the
western world in the same fashion as the princes of other
countries; on the contrary, it was precisely in opposition to
this process that there arose the first enduring national opposition which the Papacy met with anywhere: that opposition
finally carried away the kings also; they made common cause
with the reforming movement, which was extending itself over
the world. So far the great Queen forms the most remarkable
contrast to William the Conqueror, whose crown she bore.
William the Conqueror in all his actions had belonged to the
hierarchical community which embraced the West, and had
brought England into subjection to it : Queen Elizabeth, who
renounced, after it had been already lost before her time, the
last continental possession derived from the Plantagenet inheritance, gathered about her, on the contrary, the national
forces, in order to keep off every kind of influence which
sprang from that hierarchical community; her crown itself
was endowed with the privileges of the Papacy.

Under these circumstances the Stuarts assumed the
kingly power in England. They brought it a dowry of
the greatest importance—the personal union with Scotland,
and even a recognition of their hereditary right to Ireland,
which the Roman See did not deny. It was their aim and
their ambition to succeed in this combination, to effect
which the previous centuries had vainly striven, and to

carry out in reality the formation of a realm embracing the
whole of Britain.   But as they would have that result obtained
peaceably, they drew near again to those general forces which
might otherwise have interrupted the work : they sought for a
form which would enable them to secure the loyalty of their
Catholic subjects.   At the same time they thought that in
this way they would strengthen and fortify for ever that royal
authority of which they as foreigners did not feel their grasp
completely sure.   But thereby they fell into contradiction
with the spirit and temper of the state into which they had
entered.   In a short time they roused against themselves that
national opposition which had already contended centuries
before against similar endeavours, but which was now heightened by the vigorous impulse imparted to it through a change
in the national religion—a change which admitted of no reconciliation with those of an antagonistic creed.   That opposition
now assumed a character of the bitterest hostility : it embraced both the spiritual and temporal provinces.   The ecclesiastical reformation had been carried out in Germany by
the princes : in England it was associated with Parliamentary
rights; for it was sanctioned by the laws; and every failure
to enforce them rigorously seemed a crime against the ancient
privileges and liberties of the estates.   The government's luke-
warmness threw all the original vital forces of the country
into a ferment : a time came at which it seemed that everything on which the life of the community rested, royalty and
aristocracy, the property of the Church, the existence of the
law-courts, would be overthrown and destroyed.

Matters did not, however, go so far : in the historica
elements of the state there lived an inherent·power which
could not be stifled by any violence.   Royalty itself could no
be dispensed with : Parliament, when its own authority wa
restored, set up the monarchy again, without the interven
tion of any foreign power, without any written conditio
even, but on the supposition that the old ecclesiastical an
political legislation was to remain in force.   There was n
thought of a reconciliation with the Papacy ; on the contrary
the exclusive sovereignty of Protestantism and of the con
stitutional forms identified with it was assumed.   Only on thi

understanding was the crown stained with the father's blood restored to the sons. The first of them who bore it had a sense of the condition tacitly understood ; he repressed the divergent tendencies which lived even in him. The second sought to assert similar tendencies at any cost. His religious zeal entirely prevented him from understanding his position. He thought that he might once more find support in the Catholic world and in the power of the great neighbouring King: but such a project naturally aroused against him all native elements, the ideas of nationality, of political indepen-dence, of legality in domestic government, of Protestantism : his connexion with the Continent caused the storm which his ally was raising against himself to discharge itself first upon James. Instead of attaching himself to the nation, as his predecessors had often done, he fled to the representative of the system against which that nation was contending. James had steered the authority of the restored kingship between reefs where it could no longer be maintained in the form under which it had hitherto existed ; he quitted the helm which he had guided by a false polestar. The nation remained left to itself—broken up no doubt into various parties, which showed vehement hostility to each other, and among which there was even one in favour of the King who had fled—but determined, and almost unanimously so, to oppose to the last that system to which he had attached himself.

BOOK XIX.

COMPLETION OF THE REVOLUTION IN THE
THREE KINGDOMS, A.D. 1688–1691.

IT has been chiefly during great European conflicts that the English Parliament has obtained its power and importance.

Properly speaking, it owes its formation to such a conflict. When in the year 1265 Queen Eleanor, in alliance with the powers predominant in the West, the Pope and the King of France, was arming a mercenary force in Flanders for an invasion of England, Simon de Montfort, in order to obtain a broader basis for resistance, introduced the lower nobility and the deputies of the towns into the council of the spiritual and temporal magnates in England.

Parliament was formed while England stood on the defensive; it subsequently acquired its most important powers while the undertakings of different kings against Scotland and against France were being carried out. On the chief question in dispute during the fourteenth and fifteenth centuries, that relating to the succession to the French throne, the English Parliament gave the support of popular co-operation to its kings who claimed a right to that throne. There was no parallel to the personal position which kings like Edward III and Henry V, thus supported, attained in the world; but their government assumed at the same time a parliamentary character.

In the sixteenth century ecclesiastical questions came everywhere into the foreground. In England the crown and the Parliament made common cause in order to establish the ecclesiastical independence of the country,—under forms however which departed as little as possible from those previously accepted. The idea of the legislative omnipotence of the national authorities which was carried out in this case became also the supreme principle of the nation's life, more decidedly than in any other realm in the world, and in harmony with the insular separation of Britain from the European continent. When, accordingly, the continental powers, especially that which was then predominant among them, the Spanish monarchy, attempted, in combination with the head of the Catholic Church, to bring England back to its old ecclesiastical dependence, which would have become a political dependence also, the result was that the Parliament and the Crown of England exerted all their powers to resist the attempt, and in doing so bound themselves most closely together for a kind of companionship in arms.

Both rose together, the prerogative of the Crown, which was furnished with new privileges for the suppression of foes at home, and the importance of Parliament, without the assent and cheerful assistance of which no effective step could have been taken against the external enemy. Queen Elizabeth, proud, and jealous both for her rank and for her rights, was yet, by the pressure of the European struggle which endangered her own existence, induced to grant to the Parliament powers of very wide scope, which were indeed necessary for the success of her own policy. The opposition of the claims made on both sides, which certainly showed itself, was thrown into the shade by the necessity for defence against the common enemy, who threatened both with the like destruction.

Under the Stuarts this alliance ceased to exist; on the contrary, the Parliament and the Crown in their mutual relations fell into those discords which have enchained the attention of subsequent generations by their domestic importance and by the vicissitudes of great events to which they led. An external cause of those disputes was furnished by the political relations of the period. Those were the times in which the French monarchy and the allied Spanish and German branches of the house of Austria strove for mastery in Europe. English parties stood in continuous relations to the strife of the two powers, without however being ever altogether absorbed into it. As the strife of parties on the Continent formed by its very existence a guarantee for a balance of power, the interest of the country was not affected by it in any very high degree: there was no need to fear any great disaster.

But things took another shape towards the end of the seventeenth century. There was a new crisis in the history of Europe when the French monarchy, which had gradually gained the preponderance over the Spanish, undertook in the year 1672 to overthrow the commonwealth of Holland, at that time the bulwark of all religious and political independence. Charles II combined with the King of France in the attack, and that with the purpose of overpowering at the same time the resistance which the English Parliament offered to him: but he thereby forced the feelings of antipathy to France and of opposition to himself into an alliance which was very disadvantageous to him in its result. The Parliament at that time enacted statutes which excluded the very men whom he wished to promote from any share in the legislative power, and gave to that power a completely Protestant character. After the lapse of some years, however, the same danger recurred in a still more aggravated form. What had been in the case of Charles II a mere attempt, from the prosecution of which he soon desisted, that was for James the most serious business of his life. The position of Louis XIV had meanwhile become still more threatening to the independence of Europe, and had never been more so than at that moment: James II nevertheless placed himself, if not in every single transaction, yet on the whole upon the side of the French king. He hoped that in alliance with Louis he would get the statutes above referred to repealed, and would secure a free field for his religious and political ideas, without having to pay any regard to Parliament. But what a mistake it was to place himself in opposition to that which the state of Europe demanded as necessary, and to wish to turn this false position to advantage in securing power as the head of a party! The attempt could only result in throwing all who were interested in maintaining the rights of Parliament and the majority of the nation into connexion with the representatives of the balance of power in Europe, and in giving them thereby the support which was indispensable if they were to set themselves against the King in open resistance. In this conflict, which equally concerned the interests of England and of Europe, the English Revolution had its origin.

Its most important feature was that the King left his realm in order that, with foreign help, he might return stronger than before, while the Parliament undertook to settle the country without him, and in opposition to his project.

CHAPTER I.

WHEN James II took the resolution of fleeing to France, he reckoned that the interruption of the exercise of the royal power, which was certainly interwoven with all business and indispensable for the administration, would occasion such confusion as must make people desire his return, and must facilitate it. And in fact the confusion produced in the three kingdoms, first by the tottering of the throne, and then by the news of the King's flight, was indescribable.

In Ireland the idea entertained by the natives and Catholics of emancipating themselves from England, which had never died out, and had been fostered by James II, awoke; the Protestants feared a massacre like that of 1641, and prepared themselves for resistance or for flight. In Scotland, on the other hand, the old feeling in favour of Presbyterianism rose up in energetic self-confidence. It directed itself, no doubt, against the Catholics, yet not less against the Episcopalians, whom the crown had favoured; at Glasgow the effigies of the Pope and of the Protestant archbishop were burned together. It seemed that the fall of James had recalled to life the old national party in both countries: the one and the other sought alike to rid themselves of all subordination imposed from England.

In England the confusion was connected from the beginning with an attempt at a remoulding of public relations, which we now follow step by step, as everything else depended upon it.

The first thought of the ecclesiastical and aristocratical powers which James II had slighted was to go forward even without him on the path upon which they had entered. Immediately after his flight had become known, on the morning of the 11/21 of December, the lords who happened to be in London met at the Guildhall; even Archbishop Sancroft was among them; they drew up a declaration, in which they lamented that the execution of the King's proclamation, according to which a free Parliament was to have been called, was hindered by his withdrawal, but at the same time expressed their expectation that such a Parliament would assemble with the co-operation of the Prince of Orange, in order to place in security the laws, liberties, property, and especially the Church, of England, with all necessary consideration, however, for the freedom of the Protestant Dissenters. The words have an anti-Papal and Protestant tincture, but they are weighed with much consideration. The lords did not confer any power on the Prince; they did not even invite him to come to London: the proposal to sign the Association for him was no doubt made in their assembly, but it was rejected. It seems as though the object if not of all— for there was no want of differences of opinion among them —yet of the lords of most reputation, was to take in hand the direction of affairs while occupying the position they had once assumed; to restore, in alliance with the Prince, but yet, for all that, independently of him, the constitution of the country and of the Church which the King had assailed [1].

But they were not equal to the very first task which they took upon themselves; the precautions which they took for the maintenance of public tranquillity proved insufficient and even pernicious. The order given by them for the disarming of the Catholics, and the arrest of priests and Jesuits, could lead to nothing but to a violent outbreak in London of that passionate anti-Catholic excitement by which all the world

---

[1] Declaration of the Lords spiritual and temporal in and about the city. December 11. I do not find in the text the words ' till His Highness should arrive,' which have been quoted from it, but only, ' in the mean time,' which must refer to the summoning of the Parliament.

had been seized for very intelligible reasons. A wildly excited mob, carrying oranges as badges, assaulted on the evening of that day the Catholic chapels, the houses of Catholics of name, and even the ambassadorial mansions of some Catholic powers. The Spanish ambassador, who had an understanding with William of Orange, could not, for all that, escape from the blind fury of the populace. And yet another outcry was associated with that against Popery. People seemed to think that after the King's flight no one had an indisputable power of maintaining public order; the cry was heard 'no King, no law.' It was said that if there was no King in the country the duty of obedience came to an end[1]. A symptom of this state of things was the so-called Irish night in London. Those Irish troops whom James II had brought over, and who were now, as it were, left to themselves, were not far off, and the fact aroused general anxiety. A report was spread abroad, originating no one knows how, to the effect that the Irish even contemplated a massacre of the Protestants in England, and had already begun the work; that a mass of Irish troops was already approaching the capital itself with this object in view: the report was everywhere believed. The train-bands were called out and marched through the streets, the windows of the houses were lighted up. It was a sudden alarm, such as sometimes occurs, which all share, and of which no one can give himself an account, springing from the feeling that there is no recognised authority to uphold public order.

The eyes of all turned towards the Prince of Orange, who in this struggle, no doubt chiefly of opinions and interests, but yet also of arms, had kept the upper hand and presented himself as conqueror. He felt himself to be in that position, and was of opinion that by the King's attempt at flight the military power had legally passed over to him. Some colonels in London had regarded the matter in that light from the beginning. Even on the 11th of December, a day before referred to, the Marquess of Miremont caused his regiment to assemble in the park near Westminster, and declared that he placed himself and it under the Prince's orders. Lord Northumberland, with some troops of the Life Guards, followed his example. The Prince required the same conduct from every one else. His first act of government, not yet authorised by a Parliament nor by any other civil power, was the issue of an order of the day, in which he required the colonels of the English army to keep their men together, and to make a report to him of the execution of this order. 'It would be unjustifiable to allow them to disperse: the peace of the country would be endangered thereby.' When Lord Feversham came to him once more in the name of King James, he had him arrested without hesitation. It seemed to the Prince a personal injury and an offence against the security of the country that Feversham had proclaimed the disbanding of the troops; for he ought, in the Prince's judgment, to have directed them to obey him, the Prince[1].

The man who was at the head of the armed force held it for his vocation and his duty to maintain public order, even without any authorisation from a higher source. All his power was derived from that position. The lords no doubt had avoided inviting him to the capital, but the capital itself had invited him. The Lord Mayor, the Aldermen, and the Common Council had entreated the Prince, as their only refuge, for his protection, and had begged him to come to the capital, which, they said, would receive him joyfully. That King James had, as previously narrated, been arrested in his flight and brought back to Whitehall, formed no hindrance to the Prince in his present frame of mind. For he did not doubt as to the right of defending religion, when in danger, with the sword, a right in the exercise of which his house had risen: he said that his conscience was at peace while he stood against the King in arms. When he was advised to have James II arrested outright, and to secure him at all hazards, he declined the pro-

---

[1] Bonnet relates that the order for the arrest of Feversham had been already given before, ' parcequ'il congédia l'armée de son chef, après le départ du roi—sans en avoir au moins l'avis des pairs du royaume, s'il ne vouloit attendre l'ordre du prince.' (Archives at Berlin.)

posal[1]; he said that it would displease his wife, the King's daughter; he did not wish to do any violence to the King's person. But military considerations were in themselves sufficient to forbid the King's being allowed to remain at Whitehall. For how easily in that case might there be a collision between the guard which Lord Craven had formed around the King and the troops of the Prince! James II had an unhappy part to play at Whitehall. He had been greeted with tokens of reverence; foreign diplomatists, English Catholics, Scottish loyalists again visited him: but he was no longer obeyed. We have already mentioned that the Treasury would not pay an order for money which he had issued. And meanwhile he saw the control of the army pass over to his rival. His unhappy thought of occasioning confusion in order to draw profit from it, bore the bitterest fruits for himself. Now it was announced to him without any circumlocution that he must withdraw from Whitehall. Personally he did not feel that very seriously, as for other reasons he did not think of remaining there. On his journey back he had already noticed at Rochester that he would be best able to effect a second flight from that town ; of the places that were offered him to reside in he chose Rochester with this very object[2]. The promise which he had given to his wife, and the apprehension that he might be dealt with like Feversham, caused him to give up the thought of making any resistance. He had only returned under compulsion ; the command of another now forced him to withdraw. That this was more to his mind does not deprive the measures taken of any of their rude violence. On the evening of the 17th of December the Prince's guards, under Count Solms, occupied the posts about Whitehall ; the King's guards retired before them. On the morning of the 18th, eight days after his first flight, the King left the palace again, to embark on board the vessel which was to take him to Rochester. The French ambassador saw him embark, but could not speak to him again ; the Spanish ambassador, who succeeded in doing so, was charged once

---

[1] Ronquillo : ' Por ninguno caso se dexo convencer a esto.'
[2] So Barrillon assures us in one of his last letters.

more by James to take care of the Catholics. A few Englishmen also had come up, and showed some regret ; but they
looked on quietly at the sight of their King passing down the
river already under the escort of Dutch troops. This happened
at about eleven o'clock in the morning ; three hours later, at
about two in the afternoon, Prince William arrived in Westminster, attended by the citizens in carriages and on horseback, amid the joyful acclamations of a countless throng.
General Schomberg sat with him in the carriage : he took up
his abode at St. James'.

At first Williàm Prince of Orange appeared as general in
command in the midst of his troops. His head-quarters were
now at St. James'. The Dutch guards, both horse and foot,
were still gathered around him at Westminster ; the most
important points of the capital were occupied by the English
and Scottish infantry regiments which accompanied him ; the F
first lay near the Tower, the others in the neighbourhood of
Lambeth. In the nearest districts round about the capital the
German infantry was quartered—the regiment Birkenfeld at
Kensington, the regiment Brandenburg at Paddington, a few
companies of Holsteiners at Woolwich [1] : somewhat further off
lay the colonels of cavalry who had come over with the Prince,
Germans for the most part, with their squadrons ; Waldeck at
Kingston, Nassau at Richmond, Marwitz at Eltham : the
French refugees were quartered at Edgeworth [? Edge-
ware. Tr.].

In this fashion the victorious invaders took possession of
the capital and of the surrounding districts ; the troops were
at that time seen in London with pleasure, for they observed
discipline and furnished a security against any danger of
mutiny.

The old army of King James, as far as it had come under
the command of the Prince, was distributed in the country
districts. The cavalry lay in Kent, Essex, Cambridgeshire,
Lincolnshire, and Buckinghamshire ; the English infantry at
the sea-ports, at Chichester for instance, and in some inland

---

[1] 'La marche qu'a faite l'armée de son Altesse Royale le Prince depuis Torbay
jusqu'à Londres,' from November 17 to December 28. MS. in the library of Sir
Thomas Phillipps at Cheltenham, 6679.

counties—Oxfordshire and Worcestershire; the Scottish regiments were mainly posted at Woodstock and Abingdon; the Irish in Hertfordshire. The order of the day in which the Prince assigned them their quarters is dated January 20. He was now recognised by all as their commander-in-chief. Some of them had gone over to him; the rest had been induced to submit to him by the King's flight—many, no doubt, much against their will [1]. In a military point of view he was lord and master of England.

The proposal was accordingly made to him at the very first moment to have himself proclaimed King. The Spanish ambassador tells us that the proposal came from two lords of reputation, and was soon afterwards seriously considered at a numerous meeting in the Prince's presence. He was told that the people would in its first zeal be ready to recognise him: no one would venture to resist him; let him only first become, as Henry VII had formerly become, king in fact, and then, like Henry, summon a Parliament, which would procure for him a position established by law [2]. William would then, supported by his arms, have founded, like the first Tudor, a new monarchical power, and would have made it the centre of the state. But that was not the line which he was following. By adopting such a course he would have fallen into contradiction with his own declaration and with his assurances to foreign powers; he would have appeared to the world as a destroyer of the laws which he had professed a wish to restore. To the Spanish ambassador, who visited him at St. James', and who cannot find words to describe the modest fashion in which he found him living—he had at first taken him for a servant— the Prince expressed himself in a way which leaves no doubt that he did not think of stepping beyond the limits of his position. 'They have,' he said of the great English nobles, 'invited me to put a stop to the injury done to religion and to the laws: we shall see what they themselves will do to bring about that end [3].' He gave this to be understood most

---

[1] History of the Desertion, State Tracts of William III i. 94.

[2] Despacho de Ronquillo, January 3, 1689.

[3] ' Que venia llamado de esta gente a evitar una violencia a la religion y a las leyes y que veeria lo, que harian de si mismos.'

distinctly in an audience which he granted to a number of lords on December 21/31. They consisted of those who had come with him and of those who had remained in London, both spiritual and temporal peers, more than sixty in number. He reminded them 'that he had framed his declaration according to their wish, and had come over the sea, not without danger, to carry it out; that he claimed nothing more than the right of directing military affairs according to his own judgment: the civil government he left to them, especially with reference to the Parliament which was to be summoned[1].' The lords, or such of them as had not already done so, signed on their part the Association which had been formed for carrying out the suggestions of the Declaration.

It was the universal conviction that a Parliament must be summoned; the only question was, how this could be legally effected after all that had passed. The High Church Tories entertained the hope that it might even be brought about with the consent of the legitimate King, who was still in the country: he must himself issue the order for it, and the Parliament must meet on the ground of his authorisation. The course of things would, if this plan had been adopted, have adhered very closely to old usage. The King would have co-operated, after the struggle had been finally decided, in a measure which the Lords had wished to extort from him before the decision had taken place. Nothing was more likely than that the authors of this resolution would have obtained a preponderance both at the elections and, in consequence of them, in the deliberations of the Parliament also: they would have taken up a position between the King and the Prince and would have got the decision of the most important questions into their hands.

And there were good grounds for expecting that James II

---

[1] Sarotti: 'Ch'essi sapevano, a qual fine una parte di loro l'haveva chiamato qua, dov'era venuto ad esponer la vita insieme con le genti condotte seco, per conseguire un parlamento libero in ordine di quanto conteneva il suo manifesto corrispondente al loro desiderio; che non pretendeva altro se non disponer egli conforme stimera a proposito del governo in quanto spetta al militare et che lasciava a loro il buon incaminamento e direttione del civile cosi per la radunanza del parlamento come nel resto.' (Archives at Venice.)

would condescend to take this course. Its adoption was certainly the only means open to him for recovering his grasp of that authority which had already been wrested from him, and for forming around himself a powerful party opposed to the Prince. The lords sent a deputation to Rochester to represent to him how important compliance was for his own interest.

But James II could not be persuaded. Religious and personal motives co-operated to influence him, now as always. The religious motive was that he would have had to concede to a Parliament summoned under these circumstances the continuance of the test oaths, which it was his precise object to abolish; he held this to be incompatible with his religious duty. And personally, it was just by the Tories that James II felt himself most bitterly wronged; he was unwilling to procure for them the advantage which would have lain in the summoning of a Parliament in legal fashion and on their urgent request. Moreover he had promised his wife to follow her as soon as possible. Without even hearing the deputies of the lords he carried out his flight from Rochester to France, to which no one any longer offered opposition [1].

This was no doubt the heaviest blow which could have fallen upon the High Church Tories. Their estrangement from the King had been the original source of the agitation in the country; the King had already succumbed to it: but without the King they were not themselves able to resist the coming storm.

They had hoped to maintain their principle on the strength of the King's assent, at a meeting of the peers which was to be held on the 23rd of December, and in which a decision was to be arrived at as to the summoning of a Parliament. Sancroft had promised to appear; it was expected that his words would have a decisive influence. But as the King refused his consent, Sancroft stayed away; he meant only to put some pressure upon his sovereign, not to fall away from him; even those who did attend shewed perplexity in their mien. It had now become impossible to bring about the

---

[1] Diary of Henry Earl of Clarendon. Correspondence of Clarendon ii. 235.

assembling of a Parliament in legal form, by royal writs, and this was what they had wished. A proposal was made to have the elections held even now in the districts to which the last writs of James II had actually gone: the members of the Lower House, thus legally elected, would then have ordered the other writs. But this escape from the difficulty was of doubtful legality and unprecedented; it found no favour in the assembly. On the other hand there was a different remedy for a case like the present, and one already resorted to in the history of the constitution. What is called a Convention is nothing but a parliamentary assembly without a royal writ. We remember the celebrated convention of the year 1643 in Scotland, which was summoned because the King would not grant the convocation of a Parliament: a resolution taken by it led subsequently to the advance into England of that army which caused the defeat of Prince Rupert. In England a convention had assembled at least once, immediately before the Restoration,—in the interest, no doubt, of the hereditary sovereign, while the desire for the meeting of such an assembly was now dictated by hostility to the hereditary sovereign; but that did not prejudice the formal right; the assembly, resting on this precedent, resolved that a convention should be summoned. As it was impossible in the mean time to dispense with recognised government, even for the execution of this resolution, the lords added another of no less importance. The Prince of Orange was to be requested to co-operate in the summoning of a convention and to take in hand the administration of the country until it should meet.

This sitting of the Lords, the born counsellors, and in a certain relation, representatives of the crown, is for ever memorable in English history. In it the Tories, who kept as near as possible to the old forms, and the Whigs, who departed from them without scruple, measured their strength against each other. The position of affairs involved the defeat of the Tories; the resolutions adopted were in accordance with the views of the Whigs: they are the first step on a path which diverges once more from the idea of an inseparable connexion between the crown and the other powers in the state—an idea which had prevailed both formerly, before the civil troubles, and also in the last epoch, after the Restoration.

Another still more important step was then taken at the instigation of the Prince of Orange.

The peers themselves did not think that it belonged to them to decide on their own authority matters of such national importance [1]. Still less could the Prince have been contented with their decision: he thought that if he was to grasp at anything beyond the limits of his military power he needed a broader and more popular authorisation. He decided to call together all those men who had sat in the Parliaments of Charles II, 'whereas the necessity of affairs do need speedy advice.' He purposely avoided summoning the members of the Parliament which had assembled under James II; among them the Catholic King whom they had recognised would even now have found devoted supporters. He invited in addition the Lord Mayor, the Aldermen, and a committee from the Common Council of London. The sympathy of that city with the cause which he maintained was undoubted. When they presented themselves before him at St. James' on the 26th of December there were so many of them that he himself made them the proposal that they should meet in different places. They went to the hall where the Lower House usually sat, which was large enough to hold them all. The Londoners, feeling that that was no proper place for them would have wished to withdraw, but at the general desire of the others they remained.

This assembly faithfully reflected the spirit of the revolution which had come about. The Prince passed over the Parliament of James II and appealed to the members of those earlier Parliaments in which the opposition to any recognition of a Catholic king had been dominant. Powle accordingly, the former Speaker of the Exclusion Parliament, was chosen chairman in the assembly; and in the committee which was

---

[1] Thus Sarotti: 'Hanno considerato non esser conveniente, che si assumino sopra di loro soli, pari del regno, quelle deliberationi che concernono l'interesse commune di tutti, e richiedono un publico consentimento, mentre gia si cominciavano a sentire delle mormorationi.' According to Citters the idea arose in the Prince's own mind

chosen to draw up an address there appeared the opposition names of that period, Hampden, Capel, Maynard, Treby, Wildman. But such a result was implied in the very nature of the event through which that one of the two contending parties which had lately been depressed now at once arose again. Every objection to the legality of the course taken was removed by a consideration of the necessity for finding a way out of the existing difficulty. And the assembly certainly did not consist of mere unconditional adherents of the Prince. Many refused to sign the form of association which was laid upon the table on the ground that, as they said, such a step might be construed as conspiracy. But they were unanimously of opinion that the substance of the Prince's first declaration or proclamation must be put in execution. They agreed to the two resolutions which the lords had adopted. They, as well as the lords, begged the Prince to take into his hands the administration of the country, the civil and financial as well as the military administration, and to issue the letters required for the election of a convention. They laid especial emphasis on the point that the letters should contain a direction for the election of such persons only as should be qualified to sit in Parliament [1].

On the 28th of December the Prince declared, first to the Lords and then to the Commons also, that he accepted the proposals made to him.

What induced the Lords, the Commons, and the city more especially, to form a government without delay was the daily increasing disorder in Ireland. Many of them had themselves possessions in Ireland ; it was their personal interest to maintain them. The Prince promised them to direct his special attention to the subject.

How speedily, in the midst of chaotic confusion, are the foundation stones of a new commonwealth thus being fitted together !

The Prince, who had brought over an army, had by victory

---

[1] The documents were then printed on separate leaves; at the Record Office especially they are found in that form ; they are printed in a collective form in the introduction to the Commons' Journal. Yet there is no detailed report. Bonnet only says ' il y eut quelques questions agitées ; ' but what questions were they ?

attained to the practical possession of an authority of which no one could have deprived him. The Lords and the Commons, who joined him, knew no other means of maintaining public order than to confer on him for a while the civil as well as the military administration. The first did not form an Upper House, the second did not form a House of Commons; he was far from being a King. But even in a sphere outside the laws, and though destitute of legal authorisation of any kind, the different elements which had co-operated to produce the event were nevertheless moving under forms analogous to the old, and were making the great interests of the country their own.

CHAPTER II.

WHILE Prince William was making it his principal endeavour to combine the two elements of the army with each
other, and to give them a common organisation, in which task
Churchill assisted him on the part of the English, the elections
to the Convention were completed. The first had been held
in the capital, for this reason if for no other, that the smaller
places might be encouraged by its example[1]. Wherever
they took place the troops were withdrawn, as has remained
the custom subsequently; nor was any other influence exercised. The old forms, which had lately been called in question, were adhered to all the more rigorously on that account.
As the majority of the nation had taken part in the resistance
to James II, it could not be but that the result of the elections
should harmonise with this feeling.

On the morning of the appointed day—the 22nd of January by the Old Style, the 1st of February by the New—the
members who had been elected assembled in the House of
Commons at Westminster. Henry Powle was now chosen
no longer chairman, as in the preliminary assembly, but
Speaker.

This Convention was not what has been called in later times
a National Assembly. It had itself been elected in accordance
with the old exclusive privileges, in the established parliamentary forms; by its side there appeared the lords spiritual

---

[1] Bonnet: ' Pour empêcher que les chétifs bourgs ne trouvassent de la difficulté,
que la capitale n'en trouvât point.'

and temporal, who also chose their Speaker—Lord Halifax—on the same day, and claimed the exercise of their old
customary privileges in full: the assembly formed a Parliament, only without a king; but from this very omission it
derived an enormous increase of power.

The two elections of Speakers are remarkable in so far as
men were disregarded in them who had exercised a still
greater influence on the revolution in affairs than those who
were chosen: in the Upper House Danby, who had signed
the invitation to the Prince, and had set the whole North in
motion for him; in the Commons Edward Seymour, who had
founded the Association, and had by his words contributed
perhaps more than any one to secure a decision in favour of the
Prince. It was asserted that Seymour had aimed at taking the
place of chief counsellor of the Prince, and had already become
discontented because that position had not been granted him [1].
He had quarrelled with James II, not so much on account of
his ecclesiastical tendencies, like the men of the Lambeth party,
as on account of his political measures: he was an opponent
of his Parliament, but for all that a Tory of the old school.
And Danby too was one of the founders of the Tory party.
But even in the first stage of the new course of things their
policy no longer coincided with the general sentiment. They
were both passed by in the election of Speakers.

The Prince of Orange would have held it an usurpation to
take part in person in the opening of the assembly. He
greeted it in writing as a free representation of the people,
which might be expected to carry out the purposes expressed
in his first Declaration. He urgently reminded it at the same
time of the danger of its allies on the Continent, and of Protestantism generally.

After a short debate the two Houses united in an address,
in which they describe the Prince as the glorious instrument
for freeing the kingdom from Popery and arbitrary power,
and express to him their gratitude both for his undertaking
and also for the care which he had devoted to the adminis-

---

[1] Bonnet: 'Le principal unique conseiller.' He adds, 'Ses intentions ne sont
pas si droites que de l'autre.'

tration. They beg him still to retain it in his hands until the Lords and Commons shall apply to him again. While the Convention made it its first care to confirm the existing arrangement of things, it guarded its rights for the future completely in doing so. The Prince accepted the new commission, without however, it is important to remark, expressing any gratitude on his side. Many even in the assembly thought that the address did not by any means do justice to the Prince's services.

But these provisional arrangements were now followed by decisive debates. Hitherto every assertion had provoked a rejoinder, attack had provoked resistance, resistance more sweeping attacks, and these an universal resistance ; people suddenly found themselves face to face with the great questions on the decision of which the forms of states depend. In the struggle men of opposite tendencies had united, not, as formerly in the Long Parliament, Presbyterians and adherents of the Protestant sects, Republicans and Liberals, but Presbyterians and Episcopalians, the Liberals and Conservatives of those times, Whigs and Tories. Accordingly there could not on this occasion be any question of destructive tendencies such as showed themselves on the previous occasion : the fanatical sects were excluded ; the movement, far from directing itself against Episcopacy, had on the contrary been aroused by it ; and Episcopacy is the most Conservative institution, or at least the most stable among the Conservative institutions, of England. Once already, in the times of the Exclusion Parliament, the two parties had stood opposed to each other ; then there had been no agreement possible between them. But now a great event had changed the position of affairs. The Tories had got into the worse position owing to the conduct of James II ; the Whigs had the advantage in the actual state of affairs : yet the Tories were not therefore either overpowered or set aside, for they had separated their cause from the King's, and the Whigs were accordingly not masters of the field at starting. The debates which took place must needs bring to light the differences as to the constitution and the state which existed between the two parties. We know how deep, how abrupt, how comprehensive those differences were. As the Convention was about to discuss a definite arrangement diverging from that already in force, it was even now still doubtful whether any terms of union would be discovered.

January 28th/February 7th, 1688-9, had been fixed as the day for taking the state of the nation into consideration. It was purposed to bring to a decision under this head those great questions then before the assembly, on which each member had already formed an opinion, and it was hoped that a decision might be arrived at in one sitting of the House. On the suggestion of Sir Edward Seymour a resolution was adopted that the House should proceed to the discussion as a grand committee. The subject was so important that every one must wish to be able to speak more than once and to interpose in the discussion as often as it seemed neces-sary for the refutation of opposite opinions—and this was only allowed in committee.

The discussion was opened, from the point of view then adopted by the Tories, by Gilbert Dolben, a lawyer of reputa-tion, whose descent is traced back to the German painter Holbein. He was of opinion that there was no need, even in the case before the House, to depart from the doctrine of hereditary right to the crown, if only his legal interpretation were accepted. The import of it was that the withdrawal of James II contained a laying down of the government, a demise of it. The word designates the legal passage of an inheritance from one possessor to another, wherein it does not signify whether it be occasioned by death or by cession[1]. From a letter which had become public, and in which James mentioned his promise given to the Queen to follow her as soon as possible to France, Dolben drew the conclusion that his withdrawal had been voluntary, and sought then by appealing to Littleton, a lawyer of the days of Edward IV, whom he described as the oracle of the law, to prove that the with-

---

[1] 'The meaning of that word demize is demissio, laying down, whether actually relinquishing the government, or passively by death, in either of which cases 'tis a demize.' So Dolben himself. From Blackstone (Stephen,.Bk. iv. Pt. i. Chap. vi. p. 512) we see that the application of the word 'demissio' to the change of sovereigns was no novelty in English jurisprudence.

drawal of James II from the country might be considered as
a laying down of the crown, especially as he had made no
provision for the administration of the government in his
absence. He recommended to the House a resolution that
'James II had voluntarily quitted the government and the
kingdom, and that this proceeding was to be considered as
a voluntary demise.

Dolben's argument was too artificial to find much acceptance. It was objected to it that the withdrawal of the King
at the moment of a foreign invasion and of a general revolt
could not possibly be regarded as voluntary. And if some
were disposed to see a kind of laying down of the royal
office in the fact of the King's having taken the Great Seal
with him, it was said on the other side that that implied quite
the contrary. What found least favour was that Dolben
limited the right of the Parliament to that of merely recog-
nising the new prince ; it was not known who that new prince
might be. A formal declaration against the legitimacy of the
Prince of Wales would have been a necessary previous condition for the recognition of the succession of the Princess of
Orange.

Sir Richard Temple, who spoke after Dolben, gave quite a
different turn to the debate. He was nephew of Sir William
Temple, the diplomatist, who many years before had first
gained currency for the thought that William of Orange must
one day mount the throne of England. Richard was not a man
of so much talent as his uncle, but more energetic ; he was a
thorough Whig. He did not hesitate—for every one, he said,
was now at liberty to disclose the inmost thoughts of his
heart—to maintain that King James had attempted to overthrow the constitution of England : he argued that his proceedings against the Parliament and against the Church, and
his treatment of the courts, proved this : such a king, he said,
was no better than a tyrant. He maintained that King
James had himself made his power—to use the speaker's own
words—inconsistent with the government of the country, and
that a vacancy had occurred. 'If King James has left the
government, and there be not a vacancy, what do we do here?'

Every one perceived the range of these statements. They

certainly implied, though the proposition was not expressed in words, that King James had forfeited his crown, and that the Convention might proceed to his deposition. Sir Christopher Musgrave, an old Tory, raised the question whether that was really the object in view; he invited the lawyers present to declare whether Parliament had the right of deposing a king.

There were members enough in the assembly who cherished that opinion. It was expressed with much liveliness, after some other speeches had intervened, by Sir Robert Howard, who returned once more to his original ideas, which had formerly procured him the title of a champion of the liberties of England. He recounted once more all the complaints against James II, and maintained that a king who broke the laws after this fashion was no longer king. 'I have heard,' he continned, 'that the king has his crown by divine right; but we, the people, have a divine right too. The government was grounded upon a compact with the people[1]: the King had broken this compact with the people; he had thereby renounced the government : the government was dissolved, and the right of disposing of it had devolved upon the people.'

The lawyers, when called upon to give their opinion, opposed this theory with the greatest energy. They were the same men who had once successfully defended the cause of the Bishops against King James—Sawyer and Finch. The first denied altogether that any superiority over the king belonged to the people; least of all, he thought, would the Commons of the Convention be authorised to claim such a superiority; 'for in them the freeholders and the class possessed of property are represented, by no means the nation, perhaps not the fourth part of the whole: we are the third estate in the regular course; even in the Prince's Declaration the Parliament, that is, the constitution and the monarchy, are reserved. If the constitution were dissolved the Lords also would have no right to appear as a corporation[2].' Finch dis-

---

[1] 'The constitution of the government is actually founded upon pact and covenant with the people.'

[2] The communications on these debates in Grey, as well as in the Phillipps MS., are derived from rather incomplete copies. If I have departed from them in some places, I have done so on the ground of another record, derived from Lord Somers.

cussed the point of law in yet another connexion. He warned
his hearers against appealing to the state of nature; 'for in
that case where would be the right of property which everybody possessed?' He thought that no one would seriously
wish to go so far as to ascribe to the people the power of disposing of the crown, or to transform the hereditary monarchy
into an elective realm. 'However badly King James might
have administered the government, he yet could not have forfeited more than he had possessed—namely, the personal
exercise of the government; no one could dare to say that a
bad administration involved a forfeiture of the crown itself.'

The fundamental notions on which all political government
rests, are vividly contrasted with each other once more in this
discussion: the sovereignty of the people and the inviolability
of the crown; representation by number of heads, and an
organisation by estates; the connexion of the sovereignty of
the nation with the supposed state of nature where property
ceases, and the connexion of that sovereignty with the condition of a regulated world. It was dangerous on the one side to
put the right of the nation in the foreground, because such a
course threatened to dissolve the whole state; and it was dangerous on the other side to lay too much emphasis on hereditary
right, because if its claims were admitted no escape from the
impending embarrassments could be seen. Sir George Treby
argued very impressively that the question which had been
raised was not in its place there. 'We found,' he said, 'the
throne vacant, and are to supply that defect; we found it so,
we did not make it so.' He did not allow himself to be embarrassed by the objection that the Convention did not represent the whole nation. 'I say,' he exclaimed, 'we represent
the more valuable part, and all those that deserve a share in
the government.' He considered that England had made
the greatest possible mistake in failing to insist on the
Exclusion Bill, and in subsequently accepting the Popish

According to this Sawyer said, 'We are not the people, collectively or represen-
tatively; we are the third estate in the regular course, and the constitution
monarchical. The Prince's Declaration is for a Parliament, which supposes a
constitution. If dissolution, Lords only represent their own vote as individuals,
and ought not to meet as an estate.'

successor, in the expectation that he would never be able to do much harm; but it was now perceived to what such weakness had led. 'I think it was an error to let him into the throne, and I would not do another in not keeping him out.'

The general conviction was that the fact must be accepted as it lay before them; that there was no need for King James to be deposed, as he had deposed himself; that the throne was vacant, and that it was the duty of the Convention to find an occupant for it. As Sir William Williams expressed it, the King had by his withdrawal deprived the kingdom of England of the exercise of kingly dignity. 'We come,' said Pulteney, 'to supply what the King has taken from us.'

Such was the general course which the debate took; the resolution in which it was purposed to embody its result only imperfectly expresses its substance. That resolution assumed that the King had abdicated. So had the Netherlanders formerly expressed themselves when they renounced obedience to Philip II. But they had in so doing referred to the privileges of the provinces secured by oath, and to their treaty with the house of Burgundy, in the breach of which, according to them, the practical abdication lay. In England such a reference could not be made, as the King, in accordance with the conception of his power as originally independent, was entitled to conduct the government before taking the coronation oath. It was fresh in men's recollection how long Charles II had put off his coronation, with the definite purpose of bringing into view the right which he possessed anterior to all promises. The Convention, instead of referring to positive obligations, now referred to the breach of the original contract with the people, which was assumed to have taken place by a violation of the fundamental laws of the realm on the advice of Jesuits and other wicked persons; and we can easily see how little inner connexion the original contract had with the ecclesiastical constitution and the legislative enactments which James II had attacked. The doctrine of the original contract had formerly been rejected by the Tories—by the universities in very express terms: it may be considered as a great victory of the Whigs that it was now described as the motive of revolt from the King. But while the Whigs were thus satisfied, an opinion put forth by the Tories was also adopted in the addition that the King's withdrawal from the government involved in it his abdication as well. The aim was to combine the views which had been expressed on both sides, without, however, assenting to the conclusions which each side drew from its premises. The view of the Whigs would have led to the necessity of declaring the crown forfeited—which would have involved a deposition of the King by the people, not his abdication. According to the views of the Tories the hereditary right of the family would have been asserted. But neither the one result nor the other was desired : for the right of the people would have made the right of the Convention doubtful, the recognition of hereditary right would have restricted its further deliberations. It was not from this weak argument, but from everything else which had been said, and from the general sense of the situation, that the resolution sprang which declared the throne vacant. That was the essential part in it. For to fill up the vacancy was the purpose and the end of the Convention.

The negotiations were conducted under the idea that the withdrawal of James II must be accepted as definitive, and that the country must be settled without him : without, however, allowing this immense departure from the old principle to degenerate into a revolution affecting the whole country. The revolution on the throne was mainly demanded by the Whigs, the avoidance of its consequences by the Tories. The resolution adopted comprises a kind of compromise, in which no doubt the Whiggish tendency obtained the upper hand, but the Tory tendency also asserted itself.

The expressions were again discussed somewhat later between the Lower House and the Lords. The Lords would have preferred the word 'desertion' to the word 'abdication.' But the Commons insisted upon the expression which had been once chosen, because, as they understood it, it described the character of the transactions which had formed a breach of the laws. In opposition to the word 'vacancy,' the Lords reminded them that it contained a hint of an apparent desire on the part of the Commons not to recognise hereditary monarchy any longer. But from the speeches and replies it was seen nevertheless that the Commons cherished sympathies for their royal house ; it was only among its members, and in the present case, that they wished to have freedom of choice. The Lords finally accepted the two expressions, about which the two parties in the Lower House had combined, and which also fell in with the feeling of the Upper House.

The Parliament, holding the position which had thus been taken up, proceeded forthwith to sanction yet another enactment, which, while it originated in the circumstances of that time, has yet remained valid ever afterwards.

Colonel Birch, who in a long life full of the most varied experiences had accustomed himself to look at the events which he witnessed from a religious point of view, spoke, immediately after the vote as to the vacancy had passed, in order to prove that the dangers which the country had endured had arisen, so far as he could remember, from the alliance of its kings with Catholic powers, from their marriages with Catholic princesses, and finally from the Catholic creed of a reigning king, 'who would have led them all like sheep to the slaughter if God had not stopped him.' For these reasons he proposed a declaration, 'that it was inconsistent with a Protestant state to be governed by a Popish prince.'

In the times of the Exclusion Bill this idea had provoked a violent struggle ; now it no longer encountered any opposition as to its substance ; the debate was only concerned with the expression which should be given to it. Sawyer found the form proposed too general. For even a Popish prince,—he did not doubt,—might possibly rule well. But a Protestant government was impossible if the Popish prince entrusted the government to Papists, and allowed himself to be led by such persons. According to his opinion the form should run 'that it was inconsistent with a Protestant government to have a Popish prince [1].'

The assertion, which was put forth with great zeal, that it was contrary to the law of England for a Catholic to sit on the throne, was most decisively rejected by the lawyers them-

---

[1] Grey's Debates ix. 27.

selves; they feared lest it should cast a stain on the edifice of legislation erected under the old Catholic kings, which they wished to maintain untouched. It is remarkable with what foresight the Convention proceeded in the matter of these resolutions. It was not desired to proclaim any universal propositions which would have admitted of one-sided deductions; it was wished not to say one word too much or too little. The declaration, which all agreed to, runs thus: 'that it hath been found by experience to be inconsistent with the safety and welfare of this Protestant kingdom to be governed by a Popish prince.' It was quite designedly that experience was mentioned. The word was to serve as an excuse for those who, before the experiment had been tried, had declared themselves against the exclusion of a Catholic from the throne of England.

The English intellect is as far removed from the keen dialectic of the French as from the world-embracing ideology of the Germans; it has a narrow horizon; but it knows how, to comprehend and to satisfy the requirements of the moment with circumspection and great practical sense.

With all their moderation in expression, the resolutions which passed in the Convention on the 28th and 29th of January were yet a contribution of great importance to the development of the constitution. Some effect must needs follow the admission of the idea of an original contract into the formula by which England severed itself from its legitimate sovereign, however much the passage referring to that contract may seem out of place. And as on this side the Convention allied itself most intimately with ideas politically popular, so by undertaking to limit the succession by a rule affecting religious belief, which lay outside the sphere of natural law, it allied itself most intimately with Protestant ideas. But the main point of the vote lies in the word 'vacancy,' which implies the Parliament's claim not only.to declare the government of King James at an end, but also to declare the regular succession interrupted, and to fill up the throne according to its own judgment. Attempts to assert a similar claim had been made, as formerly by the Witan in Anglo-Saxon times, so also by the Lords and Commons in

the Plantagenet times; and during certain periods the claim
had been established. The principle then adhered to, that,
namely, of always, notwithstanding all the absolute power
of the legislature, having recourse to one of those who had
the nearest right to the crown, prevailed also on the present
occasion. Immediately after the vacancy of the throne had
been declared, the friends of the Prince of Orange made the
proposal to place him and his wife upon it. 'Consider of it
a thousand years,' exclaimed the mover, the younger Wharton,
'and you cannot cast your eyes upon a person so well to fill it
as the Prince and Princess of Orange.' It was a very obvious
course, and agreed with public feeling, but it was impossible
to arrive at a decision upon it as quickly as many thought
might have been the case. Great difficulties were involved in
the thing itself, and in the mode of carrying it out. But the
most important arose from its relation to the constitutional
interests of the Parliament.

CHAPTER III.

ELEVATION OF THE PRINCE OF ORANGE TO THE ENGLISH
THRONE. CONSTITUTIONAL LIMITATIONS OF THE POWER
OF THE CROWN.

IT is not by Parliamentary discussions that great constitutional questions, in which each party thinks itself in the
right, can be decided. Such decisions can only be arrived at
in consequence of events which give one side or the other the
preponderance. An event of this kind had now come to pass
in England. Because James II had overstrained the prerogative to attain an end lying outside its natural province, its
opponents had gained the victory over him: he himself was
excluded from the throne; they were the masters in the
country. Now, however important it was to fill up the vacant
throne, this was by no means the only matter affecting the
general interest which came under discussion. On the contrary, another matter was connected with it which, in the eyes
of many, possessed even more importance, namely, the
decision of the questions pending between the Crown and the
Parliament, as to the extent of the prerogative. The general
desire was not merely to exchange one prince for another,
but, as Lord Falkland said, who spoke after Wharton, to
secure the country against the return of an arbitrary government, and to remove all doubt as to the extent of the royal
power. 'Before you fill the throne I would resolve what
power you will give the King and what not[1].' It was Sir

---

[1] 'We have had a Prince that did dispense with our laws, and I hope we shall
never leave that doubtful . . . Therefore, before you fill the throne, I would resolve
what power you will give the King and what not.'

Richard Temple, who on this occasion, as on the previous one, decided the course which the debate should take. 'Secure your liberties,' he exclaimed; their establishment would, he said, best recommend the government to a successor who had stated in his Declaration the ends which must be followed. This speech of Sir Richard Temple holds a very remarkable place in the history of the English constitution. He touches the most important points which can be discussed in connexion with the opposition between parliamentary rights and tendencies and the power of the crown: the securing Parliament against all encroachments of the crown and of the King's ministers; the responsibility of the ministers to Parliament, irrespectively of any pardon that may be bestowed on them from another quarter; the dependence of the military power on the votes of Parliament; at the same time the emancipation of the bench of judges from the court, and the subordination of Westminster Hall, which ought not, according to Temple, to get the control of all cases, under the higher authority of Parliament. He wished also to see the rules which should be adopted secured by the coronation· oath. 'For, as we are sworn to our kings, so must they also be sworn to protect us [1].'

Temple, as it were, opened the way. Many others gave their opinions after him, and not merely to the same effect; they brought forward also a mass of grievances which must as they thought be removed, and of precautions which must be taken against the arbitrary power of the government. And some of the suggestions made went very far; a general repeal of all the laws passed under the last governments was recommended, and there was even something said of the necessity of a new Magna Charta. The Convention now almost assumed the appearance of.a modern constituent assembly.

But by this very pretension it aroused the opposition of its experienced members, amongst others that of old Maynard himself, whose inclination towards the popular side no one could doubt With his voice no longer loud but still in-

---

[1] Grey's Debates ix. 31.

telligible, which was heard with all the more attention for its feebleness, he warned his hearers against wishing to carry out everything which was pointed out in the coffee-houses—perhaps with intelligence—as desirable: otherwise they would sit for a whole year and produce nothing but confusion: they should not overload the horse. Pollexfen added, they should not let it be heard beyond the sea that laws were made there to bind the Prince: no more ruinous counsel could be given. 'While they quarrelled Popery increased; they talked, without making provision for a government. Something better was hoped from them abroad.'

Edward Seymour interposed, saying that he did not care for foreign countries if they must fall into slavery at home: they must certainly even then try to put an end to the ruinous abuses that were current; or would they do nothing at all because they could not do all at once? 'Though the clock did not strike twelve at once, must it therefore not strike at all?'

The resolution, once taken, was adhered to, that before the throne was filled up the liberties of the nation must be secured. An understanding was however arrived at, to the effect that in the first instance only what was most important and necessary should be embodied in short general heads, and that this work should be made over to a committee.

But while the Commons were employed in establishing the rights of the subject, the lords took the initiative in their own way in reference to the filling up of the throne, even before they had agreed to the vote as to its vacancy.

At first there had been a party amongst them disposed to invite King James to return on the conditions which should be prescribed to him; that was held to be the proper course. But by degrees a conviction was arrived at that this was hopeless and might even be dangerous. In the Convention such a policy was never advocated. On the other hand a different plan, which rested on the basis of the same political view and seemed more practicable, the erection of a regency in the name of James II, was very seriously mentioned; this proposal was made by Lord Nottingham, who had contributed, no doubt tardily, but yet at last decisively, to bring about the Revolution. According to it the Prince of Orange was to conduct the administration as prince-regent, but the nominal possession of the crown was to be reserved to the legitimate king. He had for this suggestion the approval if not of all, yet of nearly all, the bishops, who thought that they could thus consult at once the claims of legitimate right and the requirements of the moment [1]. But the lawyers and politicians made an objection to this proposal, derived from the laws of the land themselves. They remarked that the subjects' security in case of a change of government rested on the fact that according to old usage and statute they might obey the king who was in possession of the crown without examining the legitimacy of his authority. If a prince-regent were now to be appointed in opposition to the nominal king, there would be, as it were, two kings, and obedience to the Prince might one day be treated as a crime. Moreover, it would be impossible to prevent interferences on the part of the nominal king; and such interferences would make it impossible to attain the ends expressed in the declaration. Lord Danby, who combined with the party position which he assumed the most lively feeling for the practical needs of the government, a man less *doctrinaire* and less scrupulous than Nottingham, would not accept this middle course. Even the turn which he succeeded in giving to the form in which the question should be put showed this; the question ran 'whether the administration of the royal authority by a regency in the name of King James was the best and safest means for maintaining the Protestant religion and the laws of the realm? There were only fifteen bishops present, but not even all of them felt able to answer Yes. Two, London and Bristol, said No to the question; and among the temporal peers there were so many against a regency, that when the votes were counted there was a majority of the whole House against this expedient. But it was not large; it only amounted to four

---

[1] So Burnet tells us in the first draft of his history. After the words 'the right of sovereignty should be owned to remain still in the King, and the exercise of it should be vested in the Prince of Orange as Prince-regent,' there follow in the original text the words 'all the Bishops, the Archbishop of Canterbury only excepted, went into this.'

votes ; it was decided by fifty-three votes to forty-nine that the name and the right of James II should not be mentioned in the new organisation of the government.

The complication of motives which existed deserves notice. The acts by which James II thought of producing a general lawlessness and confusion which would facilitate his return not only gave his antagonist from the very beginning a great position, but contributed mainly to bring about the declaration that the throne was vacant. But when that result had once come to pass, the English laws themselves prevented the replacement of James by a substitute bearing another title. The great national party which had forced James to retire from the country must, for the sake of its own security in the eye of the law, have a king at its head.

Even after the rejection of a regency and the admission that there was a vacancy, the Tories thought that they could still maintain their principles. They made a proposal to transfer the crown to the nearest Protestant heiress, the Princess of Orange, who might then leave to the Prince as large a share in the government as should seem good to her. In the eye of the law it was the same thing whether obedience were paid to a king or to a queen. It seemed that a very slight departure from hereditary right might in this way prove not inconsistent with a vigorous administration. This view derived an especial weight from the fact that the Princess Anne, who if it were adopted would be one step nearer to the throne, and her friends, Churchill at least privately, recommended it. But against this plan also the most important considerations forced themselves into notice. Might not King James yet have another son of undoubted legitimacy, whose right would take precedence of that of the Princess of Orange? But the main question was, what would happen in the case supposed if this Princess died before her husband? The Prince of Orange, whom the country had to thank for everything, would in that case lose the position granted him by his wife. It was remarked that with this possibility before him he would only take a half-hearted interest in business ; he must be attached completely to England.

The Prince of Orange had hitherto kept quiet and silent

during these negotiations. He was hard of access; to those who did find admission to him he only listened without saying much in reply to them. Such behaviour was natural to him, and it was perhaps his wisest course not to entangle himself in the windings of the debate of which it was hard to see the end. He only declared himself now and then at the decisive turning points. He said that he left it to the English to dispose of their throne as it might seem good to them: many might think differently on the matter; it was not of much consequence to him to wear a crown; he could go back to Holland and live there as Stadholder as he had done before: that would please him better than if he had to remain in England with the title of king but as the servant of his wife. He loved her and valued her highly; he had all possible confidence in her: but he would not become her subject. He was reminded of Philip II, who also had been only a king-consort in England; he remarked that Philip had nevertheless worn at the same time the crown of Naples and Sicily: he himself on the contrary, if his wife were to die before him, would come into the unpleasant position of having conducted a government and maintained the royal prerogatives and then being obliged to return to the position of a private person[1]. Even in Holland he would then no longer be what he was on that day. These were arguments of a very personal nature, but they had the greatest weight; the Prince could not be dispensed with under any circumstances.

In this controversy, on the contrary, the notion gained ground that the Prince must be raised alone to the throne which had been declared vacant. 'For it was impossible,' it was urged, 'that sovereignty should admit of division: if the Prince would not stand beneath his wife, he must be placed above her; the Princess could then only be queen as the King's wife.' This project agreed with the conceptions of the advanced Whigs; for, had it been carried out, a king

---

[1] 'Enviudando quedava particular y inapto a lo que es oy, haviendo reynado y mantenido las prerogativas reales.' Despacho de Ronquillo—the only man who noted down on the spot what he heard from the Prince himself. Burnet deserves all respect, but here he only repeats what he heard from others, 'many of them, who were there, have told me,' as he says in his first draft.

would have been obtained who could not have referred to
any apparent hereditary right; the idea that the right had
returned to the people, and that the crown could be given
away by it, would have been realised[1]. Among the Whigs
there were many who were esteemed republicans. It was
asserted that they looked forward in thought to the election taking place once or twice more, but not at all afterwards. But on the other hand an energetic and well-grounded
opposition arose against this plan. Men who belonged to no
party took into consideration the probability that the Prince,
if he consented to it, would arouse against himself the clergy
and the great party which adhered to hereditary right under
the limitations which had been determined upon; he would,
they said, even have all the women against him. He had
come to England on the ground of his right acquired by
marriage; was the right of his wife now to be neglected?
He would be ungenerous and unjust if he were minded to
demand it; it would even be doing him an injustice to believe
him capable of it.

Among those who were about the Prince different opinions
prevailed. Bentinck would have been in favour of the Prince's
mounting the throne by himself: he once fell into a lively
dispute with Burnet on the subject. But Bentinck did not
yet enjoy a high reputation among the English; he was considered imperious and covetous, and the desire of a powerful
favourite to raise himself by the side of the sovereign was not
looked upon with pleasure. On the other hand Dijkvelt, who
had formerly conducted the negotiations from which the
whole undertaking had sprung, enjoyed the confidence of
everybody. He knew the conditions on which the undertaking had been originally based better than any one else,
and continued decidedly to assert the Princess' right. The
Dutchmen who were present ascribe it to him that this view
triumphed; they assume that he had been commissioned

---

[1] Reasons humbly offered for placing H. H[ss]. the Prince of Orange singly in
the throne. A single sheet, of which only one side is printed. It is said there
' it will be a clear asserting of the people's rights, when the estates of England declare, that, the King having abdicated the government, and the throne being
vacant, they think to fill it again with one who is not immediate in the line.'

to that effect by the Prince at a secret conference which aroused their suspicion; for in their opinion the Prince loved to make other people work for him, while he himself remained quiet.

Among the population, which wished for haste and decision, there was a feeling at work for the Prince; and Lord Lovelace made preparations for producing a demonstration in his favour, in order to exercise a pressure upon the two Houses [1]; Prince William however, who already held the reins of administration with a steady hand, forbade all unauthorised popular assemblies, even at a moment when their results might have been advantageous for him [2].

How much is he mistaken by those who charge him with an extravagant personal ambition, and who have ascribed his whole undertaking to his wish to wear a crown! The ambition of these princes of the old house of Orange sprang from the conflicts of great ideas in which they took a side; their personality is fused with the cause which they defend, and grows with it; their claims do not grasp at anything beyond the immediate and attainable end.

A most extraordinary resolution had in fact to be adopted : it was wished to raise to the throne a married pair most closely united together, but of which each member should be recognised as separated from the other, and as having distinct rights. When examples were sought for, and yet nothing could be cited except the usages at Muscovite coronations, this only shows that the advocates of the plan felt embarrassed. But it was yet the notion which before all discussion presented itself as the most natural expedient. After long and tedious negotiations, after consideration of the political, religious, and legal points of view, it was still found to be the only practicable one.

In the Upper House a decisive sitting took place on the 6th of February. Lord Halifax arose, the same man who formerly

---

[1] Bonnet speaks of an address which had been set going by Lovelace, and already numerously signed, but that the Prince had prevented its going on.

[2] 'Het gemeen op de been gekommen, door Andringen van den Lord Lovelace vordert by request van het huis, dat men den Prinz Konink maake. S. H. verboet die samenrotting.' So the ' Uittrecksel nit het biizonder verbaal' of Wilsen's embassy, in Scheltema, Mengelwerk, vol iii. The repoits of Wilsen, an earlier one of 1688 and this of 1689 deserve to be sought out and printed in full.

had defended and maintained hereditary right in the debates on the Exclusion Bill: who would not have thought that he would, on the present occasion, also declare himself in favour of the preservation of this right in the person of the Princess Mary? But conviction in regard to political doctrines is certainly but seldom to be found in the men of this time. As Halifax had already, in the days of the Exclusion Bill, fixed his eyes with foreseeing glance on the succession of the Prince of Orange, so did he now also, without regard to the doctrines which he had once defended, declare himself for him exclusively; he would not hear of any divided authority: he demanded the crown for the Prince alone. On the other hand, Clarendon and his brother defended once more the Princess Mary's right to the exclusive possession of the throne. They thought at first that in doing so they would have the Princess Anne and her friends on their side, as the succession would, had they succeeded, have belonged to her after her sister. But Anne had already been satisfied by an increase of her allowance, and by a representation of William's weak state of health, who would hardly, it was said, outlive his wife, and might be expected never to wear the crown alone. What success could the Hydes hope for under these circumstances? As a compromise between these two contrary proposals, the third, to confer the crown on the Prince and Princess together, obtained general approval. Lord Danby, who had opposed a regency to be exercised in the name of King James, and had caused the rejection of that plan, opposed also the recognition of the exclusive right of the Princess Mary; but he spoke in favour of combining her with her husband upon the throne. He found himself in the favourable position of recommending an expedient which the majority had, independently of his arguments, decided to adopt. Burnet affirms that the moderate Whigs, such as Shrewsbury and Sidney, and the moderate Church of England men, had from the beginning been in favour of that course [1]. No division was needed. The resolution that

---

[1] In a passage of the original narrative of Burnet which has been left out subsequently, it is said: 'Danby, Shrewsbury, Sidney, and all the moderate Church of England men were for putting both in the throne.'

the Prince and Princess should thenceforth be King and Queen of England was adopted by the Lords without opposition.

This was natural, and suited to the state of the case, considering the position of affairs in England; but it was also the settlement in which the two parties which had co-operated to produce the Revolution could once more unite.

Their agreement was not more complete than the expedient adopted was logical. When the oath was drawn up which was to be taken to the new royal pair, the expressions ' rightful and lawful,' which had for a series of years been added to the title of king or queen, were omitted on purpose; for they would have raised scruples in the minds of the zealous Tories, which it was desired to avoid.

Thus the Lords decided the personal question, at least among themselves. Let us now turn to the Commons, who had meanwhile made progress in their equally important deliberations referring to the securing of religion and of the laws and liberties of England.

A commission had been named which was to put together the chief articles indisputably required to secure that end. We find in the long list of its members the names of the leaders of all parties, of Temple, Hampden, Wharton, but also of Clarges, Seymour and Musgrave, and of the lawyers Finch, Sawyer, and Pollexfen : the draft, therefore, which the reporter Treby laid before the Commons as early as the 2nd of February, could not be regarded as the one-sided work of a party [1].

The document in the first place declares illegal the proceedings which had set James II at variance with the nation : suspension of laws, dispensation from the same, and even the execution of them by royal prerogative without consent of Parliament, especially the levying of taxes in another manner and for a longer time than the same had been granted by Parliament; further, the establishment of the ecclesiastical commission and of similar commissions, the disarming of Protestant subjects; the raising and keeping a standing army in time of peace without consent of Parliament. All the

---

[1] Commons' Journals x. 17.

questions which had arisen as to the respective extent of the prerogative and of the rights of Parliament were to be decided in favour of Parliament, before the accession of a new sovereign, by an authentic declaration to which he might be bound to consent. But the committee did not intend to be content with this. Resolutions of the widest scope were added, referring to the points which Temple had brought forward for discussion. The existing organisation of the national militia was declared to be oppressive to the people. A freer position was demanded for the judges, and at the same time a series of alterations in judicial procedure, especially on trials for high treason. Parliament was not only to have the customary privileges of its members secured to it, but, as a main point, frequent sittings, and their continuance till the business before it had been settled. Effective provisions for the free exercise of their religion by Protestants, and for their union as far as possible among themselves, were also demanded, and it was proposed that for the future no member of the royal family should be allowed to marry a person who held the Catholic creed. The King and Queen should on entering upon the government bind themselves to maintain the Protestant religion as well as the laws and liberties of the nation, and the coronation oath should be subjected to revision.

At the sitting of the House one or two points were added to the commission's proposals, especially in reference to the constitution of the courts of justice: in other respects they were agreed to as they stood; each article was separately read and accepted.

They do not indeed contain a systematic project of a constitution such as those which have in later times been brought forward in Europe; but yet they embrace all the departments of public life—religion, the army, the courts of justice, and the rights of Parliament; they even here and there touch the administration.

It could not be said, however, that the articles were an assertion of Parliamentary claims in their most extreme form. As we remember it was the Scots who first asserted for their transformed Parliament the right of having a concurrent voice in the nominations to the highest military and civil dignities, of calling the members of the Privy Council to an account, and of limiting the royal jurisdiction. That was in the year 1639. Two years later the adherents of the Scottish system had obtained the upper hand in England. They too on their part put forth the demand that the King should promote those men only who possessed the confidence of Parliament to positions of influence, and should tolerate no others about his person; their attempt to get possession of the military power in the country was the matter on which the civil war then broke out. In the year 1689 these claims were not, expressly at least, renewed; the altered position of parties would not have permitted that at all; but the articles proposed were not on that account less thoroughgoing and comprehensive in their substance. Two points were found in them which seemed to touch the monarchy in a vital part.

There was no claim that the Parliament should be summoned to assemble in every third year, and still less any attempt to repeat the strange provisions which in the year 1641 were added to a law passed to secure that object; but the new regulations proposed would yet have altered the previous relation of constitutional powers in so far as they would have as good as deprived the King of the right of proroguing and dissolving the Parliament when assembled. This right had been under Charles II the principal resource of the government, and remained so still: for how could it otherwise offer resistance to the formation of the supremacy of a party? And not less importance belonged to the resolution by which royal pardons in relation to parliamentary impeachments and sentences were declared invalid beforehand. How if that were adopted could the King have been ever again able to reckon on the devotion of a minister? The claim seemed to be an encroachment on the rights of sovereignty.

We do not find any report of negotiations between William of Orange and the Parliament; we only learn that this was one of the matters on which the silent Prince declared himself, as he had done with regard to his acceptance of the crown.

He said 'that he had come to England to restore its laws and liberties, but not to rob the crown of its rights[1]; he would not accept any limitation which was not prescribed by the existing laws; he would not allow the prerogative to be destroyed.'

And even at this moment the sovereignty of the Parliament was by no means so absolute as to raise it above all need of considering the Prince's wishes. He had no right to this throne: he had no other claim than that which lay in his position; but the circumstances of that position were such that he was not obliged to agree to every condition which was attached to the acceptance of the crown; his position had a certain independence which arose from the course of events. For his coming over to England had certainly brought about the great change which had occurred; and the new settlement could only be maintained at all by his co-operation. Between the Tories and the Whigs, and even in presence of their combined demands the Prince of Orange appears as a third power, as a representative of the highest authority even before it had been transferred to him.

Even apart from this consideration, the greatest difficulties lay in the way of carrying out the Parliament's resolutions. New laws would have been necessary for that purpose; but how much time would their further consideration in the Lower House, and still more the deliberation upon them in the Lords, have demanded; how much opposition would have had to be overcome! This reflection, and respect for the Prince's wishes, co-operated in inducing the committee itself to consider an alteration of the proposals made. It was resolved in the first place to separate the declaratory articles in which the proceedings of James II were declared illegal from the demands which it was desired to put forth in addition; and the latter were themselves subjected to a revision. There was then no further mention of the intolerable burden of the militia regulations, any alteration of which would have been intended to diminish the King's influence in that

---

[1] Ronquillo: 'Ha dicho, que como vino a reintegrar la religion, las leyes y làs libertades del pueblo ingles, no vino a quitar las de la corona.'

department; nor was anything said of the provisions by
which it was desired to emancipate the judges from the
influence of the court, or even of the article before mentioned
referring to the marriages of the royal family; the liberties of
Parliament were mentioned, but there was no further question
as to a limitation of the rights of the prerogative with regard
to dissolutions; the most offensive of the regulations contemplated, that which referred to the right of pardon, was expressly renounced, as the reporter said, 'for important reasons.'
The policy which declared itself in the first draft of the
articles was not on this account given up; it forms a permanent leaven in the late‚ proceedings of Parliament; in the
first instance, however, its advocates acquiesced in its not
finding a place in the Declaration of Rights which was to be
laid before the new Prince—this title was given to the articles
in remembrance of the Prince's declaration.

This Declaration of Rights, adopted under such circumstances, is far from satisfying all popular claims and wishes;
but it ought not therefore to be considered unimportant.
The Parliament's authority was much strengthened by the
mere acceptance of the declaratory articles. The abolition of
the right of dispensation guaranteed to the Parliament the full
possession of the legislative power. The levying of the taxes
was now first placed beyond the reach of arbitrary encroachments on the part of the royal authority. The kingly
power which derived itself from the Conquest was denied the
right of keeping up a standing army without consent of
Parliament. As the ecclesiastical commissions of the supreme
head of the church were also declared illegal, holders of
ecclesiastical dignities acquired an independence which was
all the more important as the bishops had seats and voices
in Parliament.

But while the Commons extended in this way the rights of
Parliament, their further deliberations showed that they were
convinced of the necessity of so constituting the government
that it should possess in itself strength, and above all, unity.
They joined gladly in the transfer of the crown to the Prince
and Princess of Orange; but they took precautions lest the
combination of two persons upon the throne might have for

its result the action of two independent wills. The regulation that the administration must remain exclusively in the hands of the future king originated in the Lower House. The proposal that at least when the King should go to Holland the administration should fall to the Queen by law was rejected by the majority ; for that, it was thought, would have impaired the effect of the resolution just adopted : it was believed necessary to leave the question to the King's own judgment. With wise foresight Serjeant Holt, who undertook the conduct of the debate at this stage, carried a provision that the government should not only belong to the Prince and Princess jointly, but should from the very beginning be conferred by anticipation on that one of the pair who should outlive the other. It was important for the Prince especially that the possession of authority remained assured to him in case of the death of his wife who certainly had a better right than his. Even the chance, in itself improbable, that he might yet marry once more, was considered and the posterity of such a marriage was declared capable of succeeding to the throne of England, but only after the children of the Princess Anne. It was intended thus to give a proof that the legislature would secure the monarchical constitution for ever by providing for a regular succession, and did not at all wish to destroy the royal family, an intention of which the Parliament was accused [1].

The Upper House had only transferred the crown of England to William and Mary. It was the work of the Lower House that the Plantagenet title 'King of France and Ireland' was continued in full. 'Whatever,' said Hampden, 'might be the importance of the first addition it would not certainly, at a moment when England was about to begin a new war with France, be proper to let it drop.' And the mention of Ireland seemed absolutely necessary, if only for the reason that everything there seemed to threaten an attempt at emancipation from England. The title had once been

---

[1] 'So shall you shew your regard and kindness to the royall family and you be vindicated from all aspersions abroad of destroying the royall family.' Speech of Sergeant Holt.

adjudged for ever to the imperial crown of England by a Parliamentary vote: that resolution was to be adhered to. The maintenance of the English and Scottish colony in Ireland, and of the authority of the English Parliament over the Irish was a purpose in carrying out which both parties combined with equal zeal.

Thus were effected the transfer of the crown of England to the Prince and Princess of Orange, and the adoption of the Declaration of Rights. The regulations agreed to are of a similar character in reference to both matters. Popular claims obtain a most extensive recognition, but by no means an absolute supremacy. As the prerogative is restricted but not destroyed, so is the right of birth limited no doubt but yet recognised. It was held good in the Lower House to combine the constitutional definitions and the offer of the crown in one act; this was approved by the Lords, and preparations were made for laying it before the Prince and Princess for acceptance.

Mary, Princess of Orange, by birth Princess Royal of England, returned from Holland to England, for the first time since her marriage, for the occasion. Everything which at the time of her marriage leading men had had in view as possible, had now come to pass. It was to Lord Danby, the minister of Charles II who considered himself the principal author of the marriage, that the definite transfer of the crown to the Prince and Princess together was owing [1]. It seems not to have made the slightest impression upon the Princess herself, that there was a party which ascribed to her an exclusive right to the crown. She adhered to the result of her conferences with Burnet, and did not allow any reference to her personal claim to perplex her as to her principle that she must be subordinate to her husband. She had approved the Prince's undertaking with her whole heart, and had accompanied its success step by step with the liveliest sympathy, although it was directed against her father. She regarded the latter as a misguided

---

[1] The correspondence between Danby and Mary, quoted by Burnet in his second version, does not agree with his original statement in the first, that Danby had been in favour of raising William and Mary jointly to the throne.

man, as an enemy of the true religion and of the freedom of
Europe, who must for the welfare of the world remain excluded from the throne. Religious discord had always in
England had a dissolving influence on the old established
relations of loyal subordination; but it was a new thing for
a daughter to lend her aid in excluding her father from the
throne in the interest of her husband. For the latter Mary felt
not only the affection of a wife but the sympathies of a member
of the same party: she reserved unconditional reverence for
him: what he did was right in her eyes: his will was, as it
were, her conscience. For her father she limited herself to
the wish that no harm should happen to him personally. She
had never ceased to grudge her Italian step-mother a position
beside him. By nature easily excited and free from reserve,
on taking possession of the apartments which had previously
belonged to the Queen and were now hers, she displayed a
satisfaction which gave offence to the court-ladies who received her, instructed as they were to show outward self-
control, and educated in it.

On the 12th of February the Princess Mary arrived in
Whitehall; on the 13th the great ceremony of the transfer of
the crown took place. In the morning the Lords and Commons of the Convention assembled in the Banqueting House.
After the Prince and Princess had appeared together and the
ceremonial greetings had been exchanged, a royal clerk read
the Acts of Settlement and the Declaration, in which the
crown was offered to the princely pair. The words deserve
notice in which the Settlement and Declaration are combined
together. 'We do claim and insist upon the premises,' referring to the concessions described above, 'as our undoubted
rights and liberties; encouraged by the Declaration of His
Highness the Prince, we have confidence that he will perfect
the deliverance which he has begun, and will preserve our
rights against all further injury.' Ever since the times of
Magna Charta there had always been in the English constitution an element which had the character of a compact: and
never had this appeared in a stronger form than that which it
assumed in the Settlement. Definite rights were reserved;
definite expectations expressed: on these conditions the

crown was offered and accepted. To the simple words with which the Prince accepted the crown in his wife's name as well as in his own, he added further that he would protect the rights, privileges, and religion of the country; would often summon the Parliament, and would attach even more importance tò its counsels than to his own opinion; but that he also intended to maintain the lustre of the crown as long as he wore it [1].

Thus the long negotiation ended. A new and durable order of things arose, in spite of the mutual strife of opinions and of parties, from among the perplexities which had seemed interminable. The throne, which had been declared vacant, was occupied afresh. The proclamation of the new King followed without delay by his express wish. After it had first been made, near Whitehall, the procession set itself in motion towards the City. Behind Garter King-at-Arms, there drove, with the insignia of their dignity, Halifax, the Speaker of the Upper House, then the Lords, then the Speaker of the Lower House, Powle, after whom came the Commons. It was the two Houses of the Convention which were conducting the new government to the city. All old ceremonies were carefully observed. The procession knocked at the gate of Temple Bar: the two sheriffs appeared to enquire the reason: then the gate which separates the city from the liberty of Westminster was opened; the Lord Mayor of London and the aldermen placed themselves at the head of the procession; the proclamation was then repeated inside the gates, in Cheapside, and finally at the Exchange, amid the full and hearty sympathy of the people, who thought that they had secured the triumph of their cause now that they heard a king proclaimed who had pledged himself to defend it.

---

[1] According to Bonnet the words ran: 'Que comme il étoit venu icy pour les 'préserver de la violation de leurs droits et pour maintenir la religion protestante, aussi continueroit-il dans cette intention aussi long tems qu'il vivroit, il empescheroit. qu'aucun tort ne leur fût fait en tous leurs privilèges—il préferoit toujours leurs conseils à son avis propre, resolu de leur consulter souvent; qu'il espéroit que la couronne ne perdroit pas son lustre si long tems qu'il la porteroit.' What Halifax communicated to the Upper House seems to be an official and not verbally faithful edition.

The whole government now assumed a permanent form.

On the 20th of February the Convention declared itself a Parliament. In defence of that step it might be said that parliamentary forms had been observed at the elections; it is however equally certain that the elections had not been held for the purpose of returning a Parliament. But the members naturally wished to keep a position which conferred substantial power upon them, and, as often happens in similar cases, they were told that they would serve the best interest of the whole community by doing so. This regard for the general welfare was invoked as the highest law on the present occasion, as on others. The men who had carried out the Revolution and given it its actual form, constituted themselves as a body representing the country: King, Lords, and Commons, made up a single great party.

But was a majority of the people on its side at this moment, and prepared to support its resolutions? That is certainly very doubtful. The Convention avoided having recourse to new elections principally because they might very likely have resulted in favour of views different from those of its own members. The clergy of the Church of England especially were in a state of excitement. They had intended to resist the encroachments of James II, but not by any means to overthrow him, still less to put another king in his place. The Parliament complained that sermons were preached against its resolutions. We are astonished to find that a statesman like Halifax said to a confidential friend at this time, that if it came to a struggle between both parties no one could know which would prove the stronger. That was the conviction even of his rival, Lord Danby. He gave it as his opinion that 'if King James would but give us satisfaction as to our religion, as he easily might, it would be very hard to make head against him[1].'

Under these circumstances, a Scottish regiment, Dumbarton's, which had been destined for the Continent, refused to obey orders, and took the road to Scotland, where everything was still in a very unsettled state. The movement seemed to

---

[1] Memoirs of Sir John Reresby, 398 (334, ed. 1734. Tr.).

create a general danger. It was known that the English regiments also were not disposed to exchange one king for another, according to the Parliament's resolution, and it was feared that they would follow the example of disobedience set them. It was hard to estimate the possible effects of such a mutiny. Jacobite conspirators were already stirring; a loud and violent protest against the acts of the Convention was raised in the press.

But the Commons were resolved to resist such a movement at any cost. On the news of the mutiny of the Scottish regiment, Jack Howe, one of the most zealous Whigs that ever lived, whom we shall often have to mention again, proposed that Dutch troops should be employed to put down the mutineers. 'I say *Dutch* troops, for I know not which else to trust[1].' The House assented. General Ginkel with some Dutch regiments overtook the mutinous troops on their self-authorised march, and defeated them; they were then, notwithstanding what had passed, embarked for Holland.

For the suppression of the conspiracies on the track of which the authorities might come, Parliament granted a temporary suspension of the Habeas Corpus Act: for the government would never, it was thought, be able to get such plots under its control if it must set at liberty, even upon bail, suspicious persons who had been arrested.

Sir Richard Temple, whom we know as one of the greatest champions of popular liberties, did not in spite of his general views hesitate to propose the renewal of the laws of Queen Elizabeth against the Papists; he demanded the punishment of all who expressed themselves whether in words or in writing in favour of James II. A rigorous government could not have wished for a more compliant Parliament in this respect. Every act of hostility which affected their common principle reminded the various powers in the state of the unity of their interests. In the consciousness of a common danger even differences of creed were got over which were otherwise very well calculated to arouse party feelings.

When towards the end of March there was a discussion

---

[1] Grey's Debates ix. 165.

about the oath which the King was to swear at his coronation, the Presbyterians entertained the project of carrying an
alteration in it which might be of use to them, not indeed at
once but at some future time. It was proposed that the
King should bind himself to protect and defend, not the
Established Church but the Protestant religion as it was or
should be established by law. This form of the oath would
have furnished a positive ground for pressing at some future
time for a limitation of the actual privileges of the members
of the established Church. The latter were still the stronger;
the Parliament could not on any consideration venture to
estrange them by a kind of threat. But it could not have
ventured to injure the Presbyterians either; they had done
very good service to the cause of the Revolution; it was impossible to reject their claims altogether; it was said that
they would perhaps be wanted again on another occasion.
An escape was found from this embarrassment in a declaration that the Parliament had always a right to fix and
to alter again the externals of worship which were here
concerned—'for religion,' it was said, 'which rested on
Holy Scripture, was not affected by that right: and as the
King would at all times comply with the Parliament's
resolutions, that special clause was not needed in the
coronation oath and would rather make the Parliament's
right doubtful. The addition was rejected as being useless, and as being assumed in substance in the rest of the
form. In later times the words were insisted on and the
explanation was forgotten, as has happened in the case of
other important acts also—the Religious Peace of 1555 in
Germany for example.

On the 11th of April the coronation was performed in Westminster Abbey. The King and Queen, kneeling before the
altar, swore to govern according to the statutes established
by Parliament and to maintain the religion established by law.

King William was not much edified by the ceremonies;
he found in them too many remnants of Popery, so that in
the circle of his Calvinist friends from Holland he described
them as a comedy. He could, however, swear the oath with
a good conscience, and in the conviction that he was not

hindered by it from making such regulations in favour of the Presbyterians as he contemplated.

The medal which was distributed at the coronation is significant. It represents Phaeton in the chariot of the sun when struck by the avenging lightning to prevent his ruining the earth. This was an appropriate device: for the overthrow of James II was justified by the danger in which his rash and arbitrary mode of government had involved England and Europe, Church and State.

The ecclesiastical element in English history appears at every step. As the relation of Protestantism to Catholicism decided the course of all foreign affairs, so did the relation to each other of the two Protestant confessions, or, to speak more correctly, forms of church government decide the course of all domestic affairs. Their opposition had for more than a century shaken the kingdoms of Great Britain to their foundations. It must needs make its influence felt on occasion of their reconstitution.

It will be our best course to narrate without interruption the progress of the revolution in Scotland also.

In Scotland, Presbyterianism, which had originated there, and was interwoven with all the ideas of its civil law and constitution, naturally obtained on the first disturbance of the existing state of affairs the ascendancy over Episcopalianism, which on the other hand had always been regarded as forced upon the nation.

The success of Presbyterianism was in the first instance due to the demeanour of the Scottish bishops, which was quite different from that of the English bishops, at the moment when the revolutionary troubles began. While the English bishops declined to declare themselves against the undertaking of the Prince of Orange, the Scottish did so without hesitation. The bishops of the Anglican Church in Scotland promised King James at that time to inculcate the duty of obedience and loyalty as a religious one [1]: 'might God clothe the King's enemies with shame.' In Scotland Episcopacy owed its existence to the influence of the crown and

---

[1] 'As an essential part of their religion.' November 24 [qy. 3, Tr.] 1688.

especially to the protection of James II : it adhered to him unconditionally.

That prince was advised at the critical moment to assemble a body of troops consisting of Scottish militia and Highlanders on the borders of England and Scotland ; he was told that the effects of such a measure would be felt in the north of England also : but at that time he looked for preservation to the establishment in the west of England of an army superior to the forces of his adversary ; not only did he not take any further precaution for the defence of Scotland, but he called away the troops which were stationed in Edinburgh and which served even in ordinary times to maintain ecclesiastical and political obedience.   Thereupon the fire of the revolt which had been secretly prepared in Scotland as well as in England broke out in full flame ; people did not, however, content themselves with a struggle against Popery ; an appeal was made to the Prince of Orange to deliver the country from the rule of the prelates which he was told had been laid on it against its will, and to re-establish the Presbyterian Church-government which was said to be of divine right[1].

As the decision of the struggle had been staked upon one cast, and that properly speaking by James himself, the speedy revolution in England determined the course of events in Scotland also.   A Convention was summoned there, as in England, with the co-operation of the Prince, whom the Scots present in London had invited to take that course.   But in Scotland a difference showed itself in the policy of the Prince as well as in the desires of the people.   The sympathies of the Scottish Anglicans for James caused the Prince of Orange to favour the Presbyterians.   The English convention had already declared him king, when a zealous Episcopalian, Rose, Bishop of Edinburgh, presented himself to him. ' I hope,' said William, ' that you will be on my side ; ' ' Sir,' replied Rose, ' so far as law, reason and conscience shall allow me.' William turned away without saying a word ; the answer displeased him.   Burnet, a zealous advocate of the reconciliation of the two parties, made it no secret that the King, if the

---

[1] Balcarras, Memoirs touching the revolution in Scotland.

Anglicans were to forsake him, would side with the Presbyterians. 'Having thrown himself upon the water he must
keep himself swimming with one hand.'

This is the spirit of the instructions which William gave to
Lord Melville, whom he sent as his commissioner to Scotland.
Melville was one of those Scots who, having been suspected
of complicity in the Rye House Plot, had formerly taken
refuge in Holland. William III commissioned him to ascertain above all whether the cause of the Presbyterians was
really the strongest in Scotland, and, if such were its position,
to support it, only without lending himself to the persecution
of the other party.

On the meeting of the Convention, March 14, it could not
be doubtful for a moment to which side the preponderance
would incline. Even in the choice of a president the public
displeasure towards the Episcopalians displayed itself. Their
candidate, the Duke of Athole, had to give way to the Presbyterian candidate, the Duke of Hamilton, who had taken the
chief part in conducting the negotiations with William III
in London. In the committee for trying the elections, which
consisted of fifteen members, there were twelve Presbyterians;
the questions arising out of disputed elections were decided
in accordance with their views.

The resolutions which followed agreed with this beginning.
In Scotland the Presbyterians and Whigs had not to undergo
a serious contest with the Episcopalians and Tories. The
Scots entered but little into the questions about abdication
and desertion, and the competence of the nation to take care
of its own interests—a competence supposed to arise from a
breach of the original contract : it was settled without hesitation that King James, by violation of the liberties and laws of
the kingdom, by the introduction of a despotic and arbitrary
power, and by the employment of that power for the sub-
version of the Protestant religion, had forfeited his right to the
crown [1]. The Scots put forth, after the pattern of the Declaration of Rights, an act which they called Claim of Rights;

---

[1] Claim of Rights, April 11, 1689 : 'He hath forfeited the rights of the cr
and the throne is become vacant.' Burnet : 'they passed the judgment o

most of its provisions went one step further than those of
the English Declaration. They gave their most decided
approval to the exclusion of Catholics from their throne and
to the old Protestant coronation oath. They declared without delay the dependence of the judges upon the crown to
be illegal. They expressed themselves with more precision
than the English as to the summoning of frequent Parliaments[1]. On political questions, however, no extreme obstinacy
was shown even in Scotland; the proposal to put off a
definite arrangement until the most important of all national
objects, the union with England, had been attained, was
ultimately rejected; but in reference to the religious quarrel
no regard was shown for the minority. Presbyterianism
seized the favourable moment to secure, not only its existence,
but its sovereignty, for ever, and to decide according to its
own views the questions which had been in dispute during
the last century. Lord Melville himself was an adherent of
the party; he had been confirmed in his zeal for it during his
exile. It was declared an intolerable grievance that, in contradiction to the historical development of the Church of
Scotland, there was an ecclesiastical power there which stood
above the presbyter, and the removal of the prelates was
demanded as the lawful right of the country. On the assumption that this as well as all their other demands would be
accepted and fulfilled—for the Scottish Claim was to have
validity for ever just as much as the English Declaration—
they begged the new King of England and his wife to accept
the crown of Scotland also. The regulations referring to his
personal rights and to the succession, which had passed in
England, were adopted by the Scots too.

King William did not hesitate to agree to the bargain. It
was at Whitehall, on the 11th of May, 1689, that a Scottish
deputation offered the crown to him and his wife, and laid
before them the obligations into which they were to enter in
return. The King only objected to one point of them. When

---

[1] They did not content themselves with the English regulation, 'Parliaments
ought to be held frequently,' they substituted for it, in order to leave no doubt
'called and allowed to sit.' Printed in Tindal.

the article was read in which was contained the promise that
he would extirpate heretics and enemies of God's truth, William stopped : he said that he only intended to work towards
that end by legal and evangelical means, and that he would
never be a persecutor. The deputies assured him that the
import of the Scottish law also, and the object of the oath
was nothing else. It was only after this explanation that the
King and Queen swore to observe the articles [1].

Under the first Stuarts it had been intended to make Episcopalianism, in the times of the Rebellion it had been intended
to make Presbyterianism, the dominant form of Church government in Great Britain. The two systems had, however, only
maintained themselves in the countries in which they had originated. The later Stuarts rested again upon Episcopalianism : they wished to procure for it an exclusive sovereignty in
England, and an indisputable preponderance in Scotland. The
conduct and the downfall of James II put an end to these
attempts also, with the difference, however, that in England
the episcopal system maintained the upper hand, while in
Scotland Presbyterianism aspired to exclusive sovereignty.
In their letter to William III the Scots declared themselves
ready to enter into the closest union with England in one
political body and one Parliament; but they expressly reserved the maintenance of their Church. Such a close union
was not yet in question, but they insisted all the more upon
their condition. The King, who was to govern the two realms
under forms of church government which differed from each
other, but yet had the closest relation to the state, fell into a
position of the most curious embarrassment. Coronation
oaths implying opposite lines of policy were laid before him.
In the one he swore to defend the constitution established in
England—that is, the Episcopalian ; in the other, to defend
the Presbyterian constitution which had arisen again in Scotland. He would have fallen into an intolerable contradiction
with himself had not his conscience been set at rest by the
English debate on the one side, and by the declaration of the

---

[1] England's Fryheit, &c., ii. 56. According to Bonnet, in whose papers a
copious report of the act is found, his statement ran thus: ‘qu'il ne voulait pas
être persécuteur.’

Scottish deputies on the other. In the English Parliament the advocates of the old form had remarked that the word 'established' did not designate the ecclesiastical constitution as that which was established for ever; the Scottish deputies declared that the practice of religious persecution was not in accordance with the import of the Scottish law. To wear both crowns was only made possible for the King by the notion of toleration, which was worked out from the mutual conflicts of the Protestants as absolutely necessary. Toleration had not yet been declared by law; it was involved however in the idea of the kingship in the new form which it was assuming.

Thus formerly Queen Elizabeth, though the principal foundress of Protestant Episcopalianism, had been unable to refuse her protection to the Presbyterians in Scotland, and had prevailed upon herself to tolerate them even in England; because, without the co-operation of the two parties, the great war against Catholicism could not even then have been fought out to a successful issue.

The position of William III in general may be considered a further development of the position which the Queen had assumed; for even the connexion of England with Holland which now found a full expression in him had been prepared by her in past time. England was now again to become just what it had then been, the bulwark against which all attacks upon religious freedom and the balance of power in Europe broke themselves. In one point alone there was a profound distinction between them. The Queen had been recognised as the lawful heiress to the crown according to divine and human law. No one could have said that of William III. The Queen found a powerful support in her Parliament, but kept it in rigorous subjection to the royal authority. The title of William III was derived from the Parliament and from its claims which were opposed to the hereditary kingship; and it could not be seen from the beginning how he would be able to resist the Parliament. William took upon himself the direction not only of Protestant, but also of parliamentary ideas, and became as it were their condottiere in the European struggle which was beginning.

CHAPTER IV.

AN adverse combination had in the meantime also been formed to encounter William. While he became master in England and Scotland, the cause of James II was maintained in Ireland. The great monarchy which represented the ideas opposed to those of England made the interests of James its own.

The letter is still preserved in which the wife of James II informed King Louis of her arrival upon French soil. 'A poor fugitive queen,' she says therein, 'bathed in tears, has exposed herself to the perils of the sea, in order to seek an asylum from the greatest and most generous monarch in the world.' She represents her decision to him as a matter not only of necessity, but also of choice : surrounded by sorrows, she wished for nothing else but to live under the shadow of his protection ; she entrusted to him the most precious thing that she had on earth, the Prince of Wales [1].

The fugitive Queen, Mary Beatrice, born Princess of Este, daughter of a niece of Mazarin, owed to King Louis himself her position in the world ; he had brought about her marriage ; she had paid him a visit with her mother when she was on her way to England, and had enjoyed a hospitable reception. She knew how to strike the note in which he wished to be addressed.

---

[1] In the documents relating to the history of the Stuarts collected at Windsor Castle.

For all that, it was not only sympathy with the misfortune which had visited her that influenced Louis XIV. The first expressions which we hear from him in this matter show that he formed at once a political purpose in connexion with it.

Those were the days in which the destiny of James II had not yet been completely decided ; on his first return to London it was thought that he might regain possession of his authority. Mary Beatrice had, as a temporary measure, gone to Boulogne, where she waited for further news from England. Louis XIV sent her his first equerry to conduct her to his court. But it is to be remarked that he commissioned the equerry to take that measure even in case King James should require the return of his wife and child to England. The Queen's companion, Lauzun, received the same instructions : he was to bring the Queen and her child to the French court under excuses as good as ever he could invent[1]. A desire not to expose them to the vicissitudes with which the disorders in England still threatened them may have in part suggested this conduct. But it cannot be denied that quite another motive also prevailed. The French court had regard above all to the advantage which lay in getting possession of the heir to the crown, the Prince of Wales; and was resolved to detain him and the Queen even against the wish of the King of England.

Such constraint was not, however, necessary. James II had been obliged to retire again from London, and his second flight might with certainty be expected when Queen Mary Beatrice complied with the invitation of King Louis and entered upon her journey with the escort which had been sent to meet her.

In the neighbourhood of Versailles she was received by Louis XIV, and that with a pomp which could not have been greater if she had been in full possession of the foremost throne in the world : he had driven to meet her with his whole court : it is affirmed that a hundred coaches-and-six were counted there. The first greeting of Louis XIV was addressed to the child ; then he turned to the Queen and

---

[1] See the two letters in Rousset, Louvois iv. 151.

invited her to get into his coach : thus he conducted her to
St. Germains which he had in earlier years fitted up for his
own residence. The Prince of Wales was to be treated as a
short time before the son of the Dauphin had been treated,
the Queen just like a queen of France. Mary Beatrice had
always remained a foreigner in England ; at the French court
she felt herself at home. She possessed its culture ; the ease
and propriety with which she expressed herself was admired ;
she seemed to have risen above her misfortune. She asked
for nothing, but she gave up nothing of her dignity. Louis XIV
judged that she bore herself as a true queen. When James II
appeared he did not make so favourable an impression by a
great deal. He had too much the appearance of a petitioner
for help ; at the first meeting he bowed so low as to seem
desirous of embracing the knees of Louis XIV. It gave
offence even in France that he mixed mostly with priests
and Jesuits. But nevertheless his arrival gave pleasure. His
presence and the reception given to him had a political
significance. Louis XIV appeared even more magnanimous
and unselfish than he really was, and his treatment of James
increased men's disposition to regard him as the principal
support and protection of Catholic and dynastic ideas in the
world. From the connexion of the two kings the royalists
expected the maintenance of the old forms of the state, and
the Catholics the strengthening and extension of their church.
The adherents of James II in England and Scotland took
breath again when they heard of his happy arrival at St.
Germains. Those who could do so put themselves in readiness to follow him as soon as possible and to offer him their
services in promoting his return [1].

But the main point was that in the third of the British
realms the adherents of James II had the upper hand.

The friendly relation of James to the native Irish rested
not only on his Catholicism, but also on common views of
a question of political law. The distribution of land effected
by Cromwell, and confirmed on the whole by Charles II,
which formed the greatest grievance of the Irish, was held

---

[1] From the MS. Journal of a Jacobite.

M m 2

by James as by them to have been an unjust transaction, and he had always announced his wish to mitigate its rigour. And moreover, when an union formed for the emancipation of Ireland strove to get the Catholics placed on an equality with the Protestants in regard to civil and military offices, this agreed with the principle which was most truly James' own, namely, that he must be at liberty to employ whom he would in his service. At the head of the administration he placed, without regard to what had hitherto been usual, a Catholic in his confidence, Richard Talbot, Duke of Tyrconnel, who in the formation of the army gave even a preference to the Catholics.

The Irish Protestants, already long placed in a state of excitement and anxiety by these occurrences and demonstrations, thought, on the first intelligence of the king's flight, of making themselves masters of Dublin Castle, where the arms were kept; and this would have made them masters of the government. Probably, however, they subsequently felt themselves too weak to be able to undertake such a plan with any confidence; and besides this, they did not wish to be the aggressors, they did not wish. to set the example of violating the public peace.

Tyrconnel, who held the highest authority in his hands, then entered into negotiations with the Prince of Orange. It has always been taken for granted, and that on both sides, that he was never in earnest in doing so. But even if he had been in earnest the natives would not have suffered him to carry out his intention. On the first report to that effect they threatened to set on fire the palace in which he lived and to burn him in it [1].

On the other hand, the Protestants, especially such as had anything to lose, fled to England with their property, or sought to secure the strong places of Ulster, or appeared in the field in armed bands which proclaimed the Prince of Orange king after the same step had been taken in England. Tyrconnel declared them rebels; they replied by making the

---

[1] Avaux, April 4. 'Dans le tems que le Viceroi prenoit le parti de vouloir amuser le Prince d'Orange en faisant semblant d'écouter ses propositions, le peuple, qui ne savait pas que c'estoit une adresse, déclaroit hautement, que, s'il songeoit à entrer dans quelque traité, il iroit à le brusler dans son palais et se donner à la France.'

same charge against him, saying that James was no longer
king. But Tyrconnel had a decided superiority. He placed
himself in possession of most of the strong places, and assembled a fine army round him. Occupying this position he
invited King James to return to Ireland, and assured him at
the same time of his unconditional loyalty : he added, that if
he had ever assumed a different bearing he had only done so
to save himself from being constrained to adopt a line of conduct distasteful to him ; he would never adopt it if only he
met with support.

It was a saying of Vauban, that when a man had lost everything else he must enter on the contest in person for what was
still left him, and fight for it. This remark contains something chivalrous, and would have led to James' making common cause unconditionally with Tyrconnel. It is remarkable,
however, that Vauban's suggestion did not furnish the only
nor even the chief motive of the conduct of the French court
and of King James. The considerations which ought to persuade James to go to Ireland were put together, and the
decisive one was that he would there find an army completely
devoted to him, with which he might be able to support his
friends in Scotland, and—a consideration to which most value
was attached—to pass over to England [1]. The discontent of
the officers of the English army was thought to give ground
for hoping that a fresh encounter would lead to quite a different issue from that of the earlier one. The object in view
was the re-establishment of the authority of James over the
three kingdoms, which had from the beginning formed part
of his idea ; Ireland was only to serve as the basis and the
means for setting on foot a great undertaking against England
itself. But from this view a conclusion followed which diverged
widely from the tendencies of Tyrconnel's policy ; namely,
that matters must speedily be settled in Ireland, and that in
a form which might promote the restoration of the royal
authority in the United Kingdom. The world has assumed

---

[1] 'Toute la question est, de passer en Angleterre avec une armée de la fidelité de
laquelle on soit assuré, comme on pourra l'être de celle-la.'—Raisons qui doivent
obliger le roy d'Angleterre de passer en Irlande.

that the leading motive of James was the desire of securing full recognition for the principles of the Catholic and native party in Ireland. Such however was not the case; on the contrary, nothing is more urgently recommended in the considerations above referred to, than a pacification of Ireland by forbearance shown to the Protestants there; it was not intended to expel them, but to gain them, which it was supposed could not be difficult, for that their hostility was not directed against the person of the King[1].

It was a further question whether Louis XIV should take part in this undertaking or not. For war with England had not yet broken out, and it was clear that it must be provoked by such a step. Parisian society was terrified at the prospect of the country's having to encounter a maritime war in addition to the continental war which had begun. But the conviction prevailed that, as things now stood, this could not be avoided any longer. It happened that at this very time the Spanish ambassador was negotiating with William III as to the practicability of a landing on the French coast, and that such a landing was feared in France. No connexion can be proved between the project and the apprehension of it, which sprang up independently of each other. The French set themselves without delay to place their coasts in a state of defence. They hastened to renew and extend the fortifications of Calais and of Rochelle. But what could have been more serviceable to them, in this respect as in others, than a diversion of the military resources of England and Holland to Ireland? They thought that by the presence of James II in Ireland they would employ his adversary after such a fashion that he would not be able to act vigorously in any other quarter[2].

---

[1] ' Beaucoup de Protestans, pour éviter la perte de leurs biens, se réuniront à luy, étant certain, que beaucoup sont opposéz à ses sentiments qui ne le sont pas à la personne et qui ne luy demeureront opposéz, que tant que l'affaire sera douteuse.' Raisons, &c.

[2] The apprehensions of the French appear in the letters of Madame de Sévigné among other places. In the ' Raisons ' it is said, ' C'est l'interêt de la France, qu'il soit, où il peut le plus nuire à l'Angleterre ; ce qu'il sera en Irlande en ruinant le commerce d'Angleterre et obligeant le Prince d'Orange à tenir une armée en Ecosse et une en Angleterre, ce qui le consommera en frais de sorte qu'il ne pourra agir ailleurs.'

And that object seemed attainable at the cost of proportionably small sacrifices. James II required above all things arms and ammunition, to procure which Louvois and Seignelay, the two ministers of war and of marine co-operated, though they did not generally altogether agree with each other.

A number of officers were placed at the disposal of King James to discipline and lead his army: they followed him gladly, for each one of them obtained a higher appointment than corresponded to his rank in the French service. Lieutenant-General Rosen was to act as a full general, the Maréchal-de-camp Maumont as a lieutenant-general: the others received similar promotion. A sum of money also was issued. It was entrusted to the Count of Avaux, who was appointed to attend the expedition as a diplomatic representative of Louis XIV. The sum was not very large; it did not amount to more than 500,000 livres Tournois, and Avaux was instructed to administer it economically, and to save a part of it (200,000) for cases of utmost need.

The directions which Avaux received in two different sets of instructions (that of February 11 and that of March 12) deserve notice throughout [1]. The only mention in them of any selfish purposes of the French is the expression of a wish to facilitate the intercourse between France and Ireland by a removal of the imposts which burdened it. Louis XIV had no thought of acquiring Ireland for himself: in a later set of instructions he declines to entertain such a project even in view of the possibility that James II might perish in his undertaking; if that happened the Prince of Wales was to be proclaimed without delay. The real object of the instructions was, as it is expressed, 'to unite all the good subjects of James II in the country under his sceptre.'

The Ambassador was invited to employ all his dexterity in reconciling the Catholics and Protestants with each other, and to exert his influence to prevent King James from making any

---

[1] .Négociations de M. le Comte d'Avaux, ambassadeur extraordinaire auprès du roi de la Gr. Bretagne. Much of them has been divulged in an extract privately printed, and has been already used; but it was of the greatest value to me to see the whole series of the originals themselves in the archives of the Ministry·of Foreign Affairs.

difference in their treatment [1]. Such is the tenor of the first instructions. In the second this recommendation is repeated and set forth with more precision in connexion with the most important question in dispute. Loyal subjects were to be left in possession of the property which they held; no ground was to be given any one in England or Scotland for apprehending that his property would be endangered by the restoration of the King. We are astonished to find that, according to these instructions, it was not the object of the two Catholic Kings to assert the claims of the Catholic population to a recovery of the possessions which had been taken from them by the confiscations of Cromwell. A note inserted on the margin no doubt diminishes the value of the concession. It is said therein that James might put off the consideration of the just claims of the Catholics till the time when his authority should be restored in his kingdoms [2]. The principle was not to be given up, but it was not in the first instance to be carried out, and even for the future King James was not to enter into any binding engagement. Louis XIV reminded him that he certainly could not promise the Catholics everything which they wished; what he would now attempt in vain would perhaps be possible for him at a later time; God did not require any impossibilities from men.

On March 12/22 James II arrived at Kinsale. He gave oral assurances of a conciliatory nature to the Protestant clergy of that place, and soon afterwards he gave similar assurances to the Bishop of Cork in writing, and they made a good impression. The Protestants had just prepared for flight in these places as in others: they now joyfully accepted the King's letters of protection. In Cork there appeared a deputation from a Protestant congregation which had just been overpowered: their minister begged the King in a solemn address for pardon, which the King then pronounced; the Bishop of Cork was seen at his levée. Everything seemed to be preparing for a reconciliation.

---

[1] 'Sans aucune distinction de religion.' Mémoire du roi pour servir d'instruction · à M. le Comte d'Avaux.

[2] 'Remettant à entrer en connoissance des justes prétentions des Catholiques' lorsqu'il aura rétabli son autorité dans ses états.'

When the King (March 14) had returned to Dublin, amid the enthusiastic joy of the Catholic population, he thought it one of his first tasks to do justice to the Protestants also by a general assurance, and to gain them over.

Melfort was one of those about him and passed for the most zealous champion of Catholicism : but now he shared the views which had been adopted at Versailles. He drew up a form of proclamation in which not only were the refugees to be invited to return to the country under a promise of the King's protection, but the Protestants in general were to be assured that they would be restored to the possession of their estates, and admitted to public offices [1]. It was expected that such a promise would break down their resistance, and would co-operate very essentially in the pacification of the country. And the assurance was absolutely necessary, if it was desired to avoid arousing the apprehensions of the whole Protestant population in England and Scotland against James II.

But even in taking this first step the returned King fell into antagonism with the national feeling of the Irish.

Formerly, during the civil war, the attempts at pacification made by Charles I and Ormond, had failed, owing mainly to their having refused the restoration of the monastic lands which had been confiscated in the times of the Reformation. But how far more ample had been the extent of Cromwell's confiscations, which were now in question! The forfeited lands of the conquest had been distributed by lot among the conquerors, and the greater part of the old Irish property had passed into the hands of the English [2]. The natives lived entirely in the hope that now that things had taken an opposite turn they would regain possession of the soil of their fatherland.

Their army had been formed under the influence of this feeling. The Catholic nobility and gentry had brought it together in accordance with the customary tribal relations,

---

[1] 'Qu'on maintiendroit tous les protestans dans leurs biens, et on leur feroit même des avantages considérables pour les établir dans le gouvernement.'

[2] The acts of injustice committed on this occasion have been recalled vividly to remembrance by Prendergast, The Cromwellian Settlement in Ireland, 1865.

had given it to some extent a military organisation, and had even clothed it. In it the mind of the emancipation associations of the last years displayed itself. The army was, no doubt, as badly armed as it was badly disciplined : but the Irish have always been good soldiers, and its numbers were very considerable : even according to the lowest statements of well-informed persons it amounted to 50,000 men. James II, who understood military affairs, thought that with the help of the officers who accompanied him he should soon bring it into a state of readiness for action. It was this very army upon which he chiefly reckoned for his projected undertaking against England. But could he hope to keep it together and to use it with effect if he placed himself in opposition to the feelings which had prevailed in its formation, and which he was assumed to share?

Immediately after the King's arrival it was represented by the leaders of the Irish to the French ambassador Avaux, and he was convinced by them, that a further advance in this course would undermine everything.

The Count of Avaux had shortly before won the confidence of Louis XIV by his reports from Holland, which, little regarded at first, had been confirmed by the result ; and no one who read them could deny him the possession of acuteness and zeal ; but they also show that he was not the man to fulfil a conciliatory commission ; he was better fitted to stir up dissensions than to allay them. In Ireland, without troubling himself much about his instructions, he sided with the native and Catholic party, which for its part wished to enter into the closest relations with France. He opposed with the whole weight which his position gave him the proclamation suggested by Melfort ; for it would only serve, he said, to estrange the party on which alone reliance could be placed, without thereby securing the other any the more ; he did not recognise the distinction between loyal and disloyal Protestants[1] ; for loyalty could not, in his opinion, be counted on amongst the Protestants at all. The proclamation appeared

---

[1] Avaux, ' on aura peine à faire une distinction entre les protestants fidèles et ceux, qui ne le sont pas.'

without the promises above mentioned relating to the property wrested from the Protestants, and to the share in public offices which was to be granted them ; it appeared in a form in which it could not tranquillise or gain anybody.

On the 20th of May the Irish Parliament assembled at Dublin. In its composition it recalled the English Parliaments of the times of the Roses : it consisted of those who were just then in the ascendant ; the other party was excluded. Of the sixty-nine Protestant peers who usually sat in the Upper House, only five had remained in Ireland ; of the twenty-two spiritual lords, only four took their seats ; on the other hand a number of men appeared who were under .sentences which ought to have kept them away ; fifteen such were counted. Similarly the Lower House had been returned, under the predominant influence of Tyrconnel, by corporations which had only just been constituted in the Catholic interest, and by county meetings in which the Protestant freeholders no longer ventured to appear. Those men especially had been chosen as members who felt themselves most aggrieved by Cromwell's distributions of land, and complained most loudly on the subject.

And this assembly now possessed legislative power in Ireland. It did not delay a moment to recognise James II as its lawful king, but it would hear nothing of any influence of England, either parliamentary or judicial ; it disapproved of the Protestant bishops not having been removed at one blow, and Catholics set in their place. It demanded above all the abrogation of the acts of Cromwell, and the restoration of every man to his fathers' possessions. It was objected that the settlement which had been carried out by the supreme power under all legal forms was the basis on which the actual state of the country rested, its agriculture and its cattle breeding, the rise of its towns, its trade, which had thriven so as to attain a certain degree of prosperity, and its whole civilisation ; that the present possessors, who had risked their money and spent their labour on their property, were ready to give up everything to which it could be proved to them that they had no legal right ; but that to wish to drive them away by an ex post facto law from the property which they had

legally acquired was unheard-of injustice. And the necessary
consequences of such a measure might be seen already. The
town of Dublin had grown to twice its previous size under the
protection of the regulations above mentioned ; now, from an
apprehension of their revocation the shops had been shut ;
there was no longer any trade ; countless numbers had fled
with their property, the country was growing desolate[1]. King
James, whose own inclination was to be just to the claims of
the Irish, but who was nevertheless bound by the agreements
which he had made with Louis XIV, listened to these objections, which were principally raised by the learned judges, and
declared that he agreed with them. But the Irish Lower
House insisted on its demand : for wrong, it was said, could
never become right by any lapse of time ; those who had
acquired the property must have known this from the beginning. The King felt himself not a little mortified by this
opposition ; he was once heard to exclaim, as he recalled the
past discontentedly, that Commons were Commons every
where ; he thought of dissolving the Irish Parliament. But
that was impossible if he wished to maintain himself at all.
The Irish Commons had voted him considerable subsidies for
the war ; but they hesitated to give legal validity to the grant
before their most important demand should have been conceded. They gave it to be understood that if the King did
not help them to their rights they were under no obligation
to serve him in the war ; the soldiers were heard to repeat this
saying in the streets[2]. At the decisive moment, Avaux sought
out James, in order to represent to him the danger of further
resistance ; thereupon James yielded, and the bill passed.

Another notion had been from the beginning connected with
this measure. The Catholic Parliament wished on its side to
pass an act of confiscation against the Protestants,—that is,

---

[1] Judge Keating's address to King James in behalf of the purchasers under the
Act of Settlement.

[2] Avaux, June 3: 'Plusieurs membres à la chambre basse disoient assez pub-
liquement, que si on ne leur faisoit pas justice, ils ne serviroient pas le roi dans la
guerre.' They delayed, 'de consommer entièrement l'affaire des subsides, craignant
que la roi n'auroit pas tant d'égard à ce qu'on lui demande pour la cassation de
l'acte, qu'on appelle du settlement.'

upon the adherents of William III, who were to be punished as rebels against James II.

It was principally with this object in view that the great bill of attainder was framed which has done most to give this Parliament a bad reputation. All those who should not, within a definite and short term, have submitted to King James, were declared in it guilty of high treason. It was not thirst for blood which dictated the ordinance : for how did the Parliament intend ever to get these adversaries into its power? Their lands and possessions were in question, which, it was maintained, had been legally forfeited by their treasonable behaviour, and which were adjudged to King James and his heirs. Without any long enquiry a list of the guilty was put forth,· in which there were comprehended one duke, seventeen earls, twenty-eight viscounts, fifty-nine barons and baronets, besides a great number of other spiritual and temporal adherents of William III; in all about 2,500 names. The mass of property which would thereby have incurred the penalty of confiscation was enormous. The two bills, the revocation of the settlement and the threat of this confiscation, are as it were a declaration of war by the party which had for the moment obtained possession of the state's power against that which was excluded from it ; they gave notice of the treatment destined for the latter in case the Catholic party became completely master of the country and remained so. The King assented to the bills, because he thought that by this confiscation of the property of the rebels he would find means for indemnifying the loyalists, who would suffer injury by the revocation of the settlement.

James did not by any means give way to the Parliament on every point. The idea entertained by the French of placing themselves by a special treaty in possession of the Irish trade, found much approbation among the Commons ; they drew up at once a prohibition of the export of wool to England. The King however procured from the House of Lords a refusal of its consent to the measure. He rejected likewise a proposal by which the naturalisation of the French in Ireland was to have been facilitated ; for he did not wish to seem to attach himself altogether to the French interest. In reference to mercantile affairs he granted nothing which he could not have revoked if he had ever returned to England. The French took careful note of this, and were much discontented at it. From aversion to the English they attached themselves all the more to the interest of the native Irish, especially as it was also the Catholic interest, of which they were thorough adherents.

When the elements of which a state is composed tear themselves asunder, and each of them awakens to a consciousness of its own distinct existence, how utterly fruitless is the endeavour to establish and to maintain peace between them! Both James and Louis were in earnest in trying to give to the government in Ireland a form under which the Protestants could exist, and a reconciliation with England would remain possible; their policy and their hopes of success rested upon their effecting this; but before their eyes the native and anti-English tendencies in Ireland obtained the upper hand. I even find that a threat was held out of excluding the Catholics of English descent, for they, it was said, were the very worst enemies of old Ireland. In times like these, inborn impulses are always stronger than the will of another; they mock the control which it is sought to impose upon them.

But under these circumstances the original design of a pacification, which both James and Louis had entertained, failed at the first moment. James II could subsequently expect his safety only from the full and unbroken action of the elements which were opposed to the change that had taken place in England and were gathering around his standard; as was the case at this moment not only in Ireland, but also in the Scottish Highlands.

CHAPTER V.

DUNDEE IN THE SCOTTISH HIGHLANDS.

IT ought not by any means to be denied that a real feeling of loyalty to James II was at work. His hereditary right had certainly found powerful advocates even in the English Convention, which had owed its existence to the revolt against him. And many did not believe in the existence of the great danger to religion and to the laws which had been the ground of the revolt. They maintained that the nation had allowed itself to be persuaded of the reality of that danger by Pharisaical teachers, and disowned the Parliament's claim to dispose of the throne. In spite of the resolutions of that assembly they held James II to be the true king, and the Prince of Wales to be the rightful heir. In remains which have come down to us from these circles William III is described as the unnatural son-in-law, the nephew, and at the same time the enemy of the legitimate king; the Jacobites spoke of him with abhorrence, and counted it an honour to themselves not to bow the knee to Baal like others [1].

In Scotland legitimist feelings were aided by a peculiar religious and political motive. Episcopalianism had, as we know, been planted, and its interests advanced, by the crown: it had not been able to gain over the nation to itself, but, in spite of the efforts of the extreme Presbyterians, which always retained something of violence, it had nevertheless taken root

---

[1] 'In Exilio memorabilia.' Journal of a Jacobite, which I found in the original MS. in the library of Sir Thomas Phillipps. A remarkable memorial of true-hearted and actively zealous loyalty.

in the country, and counted many even enthusiastic adherents. But all Episcopalians in Scotland were also Jacobites, for a state authority which was not in the hands of the Presbyterians was necessary to them. In the resolutions of the Convention they saw arbitrariness and an usurpation which ran counter to all laws: for the Episcopal constitution, they said, had been legally introduced in Scotland, and the Covenant of the Presbyterians had been everywhere abjured.

The resolutions of the Convention were far indeed from being greeted with universal approval[1]. Among the nobility and gentry, in many town corporations, in the capital itself, sentiments antagonistic to them were noticed which foreboded a speedy outbreak of troubles. Yet matters would hardly have gone so far even in Scotland had there not still existed in the Highlands a population of kindred race to, and homogeneous with, the Irish, almost independent, owing to the clan organisation which existed in living efficacy; and, most of all, had there not been a man living who had the capacity and the resolution to make use of that population in order to unite the forces of resistance in his hand.

John Grahame of Claverhouse[2] was a Scottish laird from Angus (Forfarshire), of middle rank and moderate property, but one who, in spite of that disadvantage, had already long played one of the first parts in the country. He was a soldier by profession, and had acquired the military education of that century under Turenne and William Prince of Orange in the campaigns of the war between France and the Netherlands. He had then, apparently on William's recommendation, entered into the service of the Duke of York, and had gained his absolute confidence. Claverhouse was about his person in Scotland and during his journeys to England, accompanied him on his long walks, or deliberated with him in the retirement of the cabinet as to what was immediately to be desired in reference to persons and affairs, and what advice should accordingly be given to King Charles. He obtained over James the

---

[1] Major-General Hugh Mackay's Memoirs of the War carried on in Scotland and Ireland, p. 7.

[2] John, not James, as he is often called.

incalculable influence of a military coadjutor who adheres completely to the political points of view of his prince. In this position Claverhouse came into manifold relations with the high nobility; he lived with its members, without however abandoning himself to the debaucheries which were then common even in Scotland: he remained always temperate and morally blameless. In reference to Charles II and the Duke of York his principle at least was the correct one: to be at once a subject and a man of honour—that is to say, never to neglect the interest of the crown for the sake of a personal advantage, never to yield to any influence in this matter, not even to the most tender which can sway a man's heart[1], but withal never to do anything exceptionable or debasing in order to gain the favour of the prince. No trace was observed in him of that leaning to Catholicism which many of his friends professed after the accession of James II; yet even he would not suffer the King's religion to be reviled in the pulpits; he held fast to the Episcopalian and royalist system as it was established by the Scottish Parliament amid the opposition of parties in the year 1685; while he did not display any leaning towards Catholicism, he showed a hostility to the Cameronians which went so far as to become cruelty. The laws themselves were cruel. To the rise of a republican and fanatical party, which proclaimed open war against the crown and the King, and revenge and death to their adherents, the government opposed a system of repression which subjected all those who refused to abjure the principles of the party above described to a summary jurisdiction from which even female delinquents were not exempted. Claverhouse did not hesitate, in presence of the hostile banner which the fanatics displayed, to execute the bloody laws and ordinances of the ruling powers. When the invasion of the second Argyll set all recalcitrant elements in a ferment, Claverhouse held districts in subjection which were especially strong in their views. Who can ever say in such a case whether the law is merely carried out or whether personal arbitrariness and even passion intervene? Claverhouse practised

---

[1] 'I will let the world see that it is not in the power of love nor any other folly to alter my loyalty.' Letter to Queensberry.

an inexorable rigour, which was purposely directed against the men of reputation in the country; he said that to get rid of a laird was better than to put to death a hundred common people. A soldiery, not very numerous, but composed of vigorous young men, well trained, and completely devoted to him, posted at the most important points, held Scotland in check when the undertaking of the Prince of Orange against England was being carried out: Claverhouse thought that with these troops he could hinder that undertaking from exercising any influence upon Scotland[1].

The destiny of James II was decided by this among other causes, that he summoned the Scottish troops to England, where, like the English troops, they were seized hold of by the impulse of the general Protestant idea which directed itself against his authority. Even the supreme commander of the Scots, Douglas, associated himself with the Prince of Orange. The second in command, Grahame of Claverhouse, who was then raised to the title of Viscount Dundee, resisted every temptation to such a defection. He never lost sight for a moment of the peculiar connexion of Episcopalianism and royalism in Scotland. He hastened at once back to Scotland in order to maintain the King's interest in the Convention. But we know how little success he had. Before his eyes the party which he had kept down gained the upper hand; loaded more than any one else with its hatred, and threatened with danger to his life, he held it good to repair in the first instance to his property in Angus; sought out and endangered even there, he took his way to the Highlands, in order both to save himself and to collect a party for King James. Some fifty horsemen who had followed him from England—the only loyal subjects in the eyes of James II, rebels in the eyes of William III, formed his escort.

The Scottish mountain districts were the only region in the civilised world in which private wars had not yet been suppressed by a superior judicial authority. Dundee arrived

---

[1] Thus much follows from Balcarras' Memoirs touching the revolution in Scotland, p. 32. It is a report to James II which bears the stamp of truth. The accounts derived from hearsay, which are repeated in Napier iii. 490, cannot well be combined with what is there related; I do not venture to accept them.

at the moment when, in consequence of a quarrel between a Macintosh and his vassal, a Macdonald, the town of Inverness was threatened with plunder by the latter, who thought that he had claims upon it. Dundee induced the town to buy off the danger with a sum of money, in the expectation that King James would repay it on his return. Since the arrival of James II in Ireland, confidence in his cause had been aroused again in such vigour that his name could help in the negotiation of a treaty. When Macdonald's men and Dundee's troopers caught sight of each other they greeted each other with a joyful cry: they were both engaged in a struggle against the Convention.

In the Highlands there was another and a peculiar incitement to take up arms which was extensively felt: I mean the return of the young Argyll, whose father had been ruined there, and against whose grandfather the loyal clans which held fast to Charles I had fought out many a bloody struggle. The recollection of Montrose, who had often in those days stood at their head, of his bravery and of his tragical fate, still lived among them. But in Dundee, who, like Montrose, was a Grahame, Montrose seemed to live again. Friends and foes thought that Dundee was appearing as his avenger: he is reported to have said that he was going whither the spirit of Montrose should guide him. At the moment in which the Convention resumed the policy of the Covenanters, the appearance of Dundee awakened among the clans their hereditary royalist sympathies. It is very true that they apprehended being constrained to restore the possessions of Argyll which had passed to them; but it is equally true that they honoured the general chief of their race in the king of the house of Stuart. Among those who had formerly entered into an alliance with Montrose we find the Macleans, the Macdonalds of Clanranald, Keppoch, and Glengarry, the Camerons of Lochiel, the Stuarts of Appin; all these now listened to the invitations of Dundee[1]. What they had once witnessed, not thirty years ago—the return to the throne of the royal family

---

[1] 'Mackay, the general, wrote to Lochiel several times, but had no answer.' It was thought that he would yet imitate Monk at last. Mackay's Memoirs, 19.

in spite of its having been driven out—confirmed them in the expectation that the same result would happen in the present case also; and they were ambitious of taking part in producing it. Once more the fiery cross, which announced imminent war, was carried over mountains and valleys, with the wild sound of pipes and cymbals. In the latter half of May the tribes assembled on a wild heath in Lochaber.

We have still a description of the muster of them which Dundee then held; it exists in the Grameis, a heroic poem in Latin hexameters, which celebrates the actions of Dundee himself and which we may well follow for a moment as we should follow a rhymed chronicle of the fourteenth or fifteenth century; it is written by an ensign of Dundee, with a claim to complete truthfulness: 'what my eyes saw, what my ears heard, that I relate.'

First appears, with his brother, the proud Glengarry, as he had been also the first to join Dundee, on horseback surrounded by three hundred companions who are all in the flower of their youth; then the stately Glencoe clothed in the untanned skin of a wild beast, with a hundred tall companions, all of whom however he surpasses in height by a head and shoulders; the youthful Sleat follows, and Clanranald, still a boy, accompanied by his tutor as we afterwards learn; but all the people of the islands have gladly come over with them to the war; Keppoch follows them with his brothers and his clansmen, who delight in plunder, bearing various arms, the light javelin, the battle-axe, the club or the musket. These are all Macdonalds separated into many divisions, but all ready to unite into a great body under one banner, and to fight shoulder to shoulder as brothers in arms.

After them the Camerons are seen marching in under old Lochiel; it is remembered that he has even fought against Cromwell and has been allied with the second Marquess of Montrose[1];—the author describes his dark Spanish-looking face shaded by a forked beard: 'his fiery eye might appal the bravest.' The Macleans have come from Mull and Col, men who never yield, but prefer to die on the spot which they

---

[1] [Probably under Middleton, in the year 1654. Tr]

have occupied; they are commanded by two brothers, heroes
alike, Duart and Alexander, whom the learned poet compares
to the Tyndarids. Warlike and fierce appears the chief of
Rasay, who has lived barefoot from childhood among rocks
and caves; he is strong enough to seize the wild bull by the
horns and swift enough to overtake the roe. In some tribes
strife has broken out; many chiefs among them are degenerate, but others hold fast to the right principles; they
come in their warlike attire over the pathless mountains to
fight for their hereditary and dethroned prince.

Dundee greets them in the evening; next morning he
speaks with them in detail. He reminds them that they are
not hirelings but loyal warriors; in order that they may drive
away the intruding tyrant, he invites them to attack at once
the foe who dreads them. His words are followed, first by
deep silence, then by a sudden cry of assent which re-echoes
in the mountains[1].

The Grameis is, to judge from the extracts before us, a
remarkable production even in a literary point of view. It
combines classical forms—the style of Lucan, who is imitated
not without skill—with a tincture of the spirit of Ossian. A
partial gleam of light falls on this Highland world under
which it appears yet once more in its ancient and unaltered
individuality; as it then threw itself boldly and not without
success against the far more powerful and developed military
forces of civilised Europe to which it was destined to succumb.

It was an advantage for Dundee that he did not belong
to any of these Highland tribes. He could check the revengeful feelings of the clans, which even at this moment
broke into a flame on one unexpected occasion or another,
and which once even threatened to set at variance his two
most powerful comrades, Lochiel and Glengarry; he said
plainly to the rapacious Keppoch, who would not renounce
his private feuds, that he would rather be a common soldier

---

[1] 'Ingens post alta silentia clamor Exoritur,' etc. Thus the Grameis of James
Philips of Almericlose, from which Napier (Dundee iii. 501 foll.) has given an
extract. The publication of the whole, so far as it exists, would perhaps be
desirable even for the history of poetry: it would certainly be so for the ethno-
graphy of the clans and for our knowledge of the event.

in a disciplined regiment than the general of an insubordinate force, and induced him to make excuses and to obey. But Dundee combined the rigour which discipline demands with the indulgence which was necessary among these rude forces ; though naturally inclined to parsimony, he gave with a full hand as soon as it seemed advisable ; though inexorable and even cruel to republicans and fanatics [1], he was in the same degree, among the troops who followed him, accessible, familiar, and thoughtful for their comfort. Even when the auxiliaries whom James II at last sent over from Ireland proved far less numerous than had been expected, he still knew how to keep his camp in good spirits. A number of cavaliers had already joined him ; many other members of the nobility and gentry gave hopes of their accession. What kept them back was their apprehension that James was still planning a restoration of Catholicism : they feared Melfort and his friends. Dundee invited Melfort in plain terms to give up his position near the King, on the ground that his name aroused antipathies in Scotland. We know that Melfort himself was at that time in favour of an adjustment and of indulgence to the Protestants ; such was the import of the letters which arrived in Scotland from Dublin. Dundee spread them abroad on all sides. He hoped to combine around himself all the loyalists professing the Anglican or the Catholic creed ; his letters breathe the spirit of chivalrous loyalty and absolute confidence of victory.

William III opposed to the fiery and skilful Episcopalian Jacobite one of the most determined of Presbyterians, a Scot like Dundee, Hugh Mackay. Mackay and Dundee had formerly served together in the wars in the Netherlands, afterwards their paths had parted. Mackay had found a second home in Holland, where he married ; he served among the Scottish troops which were in the service of the republic, and at the proper time he took a chief part in causing them to turn a deaf ear to the invitation of James II to return into his immediate service. As the one general attached himself unconditionally to James II, so did the other to William III.

---

[1] 'Fanatismi et perduellionis terror, malleus, fulmen,' as it is said in his proposed epitaph. The other traits are found in Balcarras, and in Drummond's Memoirs of Lochiel.

Mackay was fully possessed by the conviction, which was general in Holland, that the government of James was opposed to all the political and religious interests of Europe. He was one of the generals who combined military discipline with religious strictness in their camps after the fashion of Gustavus Adolphus. In his personal conduct he passed with those who knew him for one of the most pious and devout men whom they had ever met. This did not however hinder him from treating enemies and rebels with extreme severity. In the field he met with many mishaps: we find then that he afterwards meditates on their causes and seeks to remove them.

The point in dispute between Dundee and Mackay was not whether Catholicism or Protestantism should rule in Scotland; they were both Protestants; the religious question between the leaders themselves and between the parties which joined them was whether Episcopalianism or Presbyterianism should be supreme in the Scottish Church, but this question then comprised in itself the sum of all the rival political principles. For with Episcopalianism was connected the recognition of the legitimate king of the house of Stuart and the continuance of the order of things which had been established since the Restoration; with Presbyterianism the re-establishment of the earlier ecclesiastical constitution of the Scottish reformers and submission to King William. Dundee represented local, Mackay European interests.

The castle of Blair in the earldom of Athole had declared for Dundee, and Mackay sought to wrest it from him; thus their little armies, after various marches to and fro, fell in with each other in that district. They represented two different mental tendencies. Mackay set before his troops the importance of their cause to the world at that moment, and the obligation of self-defence which conscience imposed on them. Dundee, of whom, however, we cannot speak with the same certainty, is said on the other hand to have reminded his Highlanders of the gulf fixed between a king and an usurper, between loyalty and treason, and how much the loyal subject was superior to the traitorous rebel [1].

---

[1] For Mackay we have his own testimony, for Dundee only an apocryphal one.

With Dundee were most of those who had joined him on
the heath in Lochaber, Macdonalds, Camerons, and Macleans,
together with the small force which had come over from
Ireland; they would have wished to meet the advancing
enemy at the entrance of the Highlands, in the pass of
Killiecrankie, which has been well described as the Caledo-
nian Thermopylae. Dundee did not share this view: for
he said that they would thus give Mackay an opportunity
for drawing reinforcements to himself, while he might be
overpowered if he were allowed to pass the defiles before
he had increased his force. Mackay had thereupon marched
unopposed through the pass in order to advance further
towards Blair when he caught sight of the forces of Dundee,
who at that moment was taking up his position upon an
opposite height. Mackay resolved to await him; he drew
up his men, according to all the rules of continental warfare,
in a long line of little depth, broken by intervals through
which the cavalry was to advance; his intention was to attack
the enemy on both flanks when he pressed forward. Mackay's
force might number 4,000 men; Dundee had not more than
2,000; but when he surveyed the long line of the enemy
unsupported by any reserve he told his men that they would
win. He formed them in three divisions separated by
intervals wider still than Mackay's in order to prevent the
possibility of being outflanked; then he gave the signal,—
it was on a long summer's day, July 26th, and already late
in the evening (eight o'clock) when that happened. The
Highlanders, barefoot and half-naked, in ranks by no means
well closed, set themselves in motion; they were received with
a lively platoon fire which had some effect, but could not
prevent their advancing at a pace which grew quicker every
moment. They too discharged their guns, as many as they
had, then threw them away, took their targets in the left,
their broadswords in the right hand, and charged Mackay's line before there had been time for his men to fix the
bayonets upon the muskets. Such were the Highlanders'
tactics. The whole line of Mackay's army was broken to
pieces on the spot. Neither the general nor his men had any
notion of the Highlanders' mode of warfare. The cavalry

drew aside instead of resisting the attack by which, on the contrary, it was appalled; the general found himself once in the middle of a body of the enemy and immediately afterwards was quite alone; fugitives and pursuers had disappeared down the hill. Except a single battalion which still made a stand, Mackay's army had been completely overthrown. The native mode of warfare of the Highlands employed in defence of the hereditary King had gained the victory over the continental tactics of veterans who defended the interests of Europe.

This was not the last occasion on which these distinct forms of national life encountered each other. · Half a century later there was again a pitched battle between them at Culloden, in which the broadsword, which was again brandished for the Jacobite cause, succumbed completely to the firearms of the disciplined English.

Even in the present case, at Killiecrankie, the Highlanders, although the day was theirs, suffered a disaster which outweighed all their successes,—they lost their leader. Dundee had, at the head of a small body of men, captured the enemy's cannon; while he retired, in order to bring up a Highland detachment which was slow in advancing, he was struck by a bullet, and fell from his horse. In the moment of death he had the single consolation that the cause of his King had remained victorious [1].

An indescribable impression was made on the Parliament and government at Edinburgh by the first news of the defeat of its troops. People thought that they saw the enemy already in Stirling or before Edinburgh itself; it was supposed that, had he arrived there, all Episcopalians would have risen for James II. Some have pretended to notice an after-effect of the event even in the English Convention. But all grew calm when it was heard that Dundee had fallen; for there was no one left in the Highland army capable of commanding it. In an attempt to advance it met with obsti-

---

[1] Balcarras has the most trustworthy accounts of the battle and of the death of Dundee. Some others can be gathered from the depositions in courts of justice. A letter is extant, which Dundee is said to have written to the King after the battle, but its genuineness is contested with reason.

nate and successful resistance on the part of the Cameronians. In a short time the chiefs held it good to return to their homes in order, in the first instance, to place their booty in safety and to wait for the time, which they believed to be near, when the King would place himself in person at their head [1].

A complete .change thus came over the state of affairs. Dundee had intended to make Scotland the seat of war, so that William should have been compelled to direct his forces thither in the first instance. James II would then have had his hands free for operating in Ireland and from Ireland. But now William could direct his views to the reduction of Ireland, especially as the undertakings of James II in that quarter had not been altogether favoured by fortune.

---

[1] 'Ils ne trouvent pas à propos de s'assembler, que le roi d'Angleterre Jacques II ne soit prêt.'

CHAPTER VI.

MILITARY EVENTS IN IRELAND IN THE YEAR 1689.

THE contest in Ireland had in itself far greater importance than that in Scotland. In both countries the Keltic population was on the side of the hereditary King, but in Ireland it formed a large majority, in Scotland a small minority of the population. While the Jacobites in Scotland, far from contesting the preponderance of the Teutonic population, or even of the Protestant religion, only opposed a revolution which had taken place suddenly, and strove to maintain the constitution which had been legally established during the last twenty years and more, the object aimed at in Ireland was the complete transformation of the mode of government which had previously existed, and either the destruction, or at least without doubt the subjugation of the Teutonic element. The members of the native party in Ireland persisted in their attachment to the Catholic religion, which procured them a support in Roman Catholic Europe; that attachment was not perhaps necessary in itself, but they had been accustomed to it for a century and a half, and it had become indissoluble. The consequence of this was, that the Teutonic element, so far as it was also kept together by Protestantism, united for resistance without regard to the ecclesiastical differences which prevailed in its bosom. The Protestants of Scottish and English descent formed an association against the Popish and illegal counsellors of King James, and attached themselves expressly to the government of England in the form which it was assuming at the same time under the influence of continental relations. The

great religious and political strife in which Europe was engaged found its fullest expression in Ireland.

King James had, immediately after his arrival, made an
attempt to subject the Protestant association to his authority,
and succeeded in doing so up to a certain point. The troops
of the association, free corps which had been formed on the
outbreak of the troubles, were everywhere defeated ; we find
that in some cases the citizens of considerable towns, discontented at the independent behaviour of the Protestant
troops, preferred to replace themselves under the control of
the legitimate King [1].

Strictly speaking, there were only two places which resisted
the adoption of such a course, Londonderry, situated on the
Foyle, near the spot where it flows into the inlet of the sea,
called Lough Foyle, and Enniskillen, on one of the small
islands in Lough Erne in Fermanagh ; the first the centre of
the Scottish and English colonies formerly planted by James I
in Ulster, and the most important place for the immigrants in
Ireland in a military point of view, the last mainly a colony of
Cromwellian soldiers. Their being able to take up an independent position was a result of a mistake of James II similar
to that by which he had occasioned the revolt of southern Scotland. In order to put himself in a posture of defence against
the invasion contemplated by William III, he drew away from
the districts about those two places the regular troops which
were posted there as garrisons, and were on good terms with
the inhabitants. Since that time there had never been a full
re-establishment of subordination. Londonderry had shut its
gates against a regiment of native Irish, and though it had
afterwards admitted a royal garrison, that had only happened
after all Catholics had been removed from its companies,
and even then upon conditions which secured the citizens an
independent share in the service [2]. The inhabitants were

---

[1] ‘ Le maire et les bourgeois (de Coleraine) murmurèrent contre l’armée et
eurent envie de se mettre sous la protection du roi (Jacques II).’   ‘ Thus ‘l’état
d’Irlande’ (May 1869) by a secretary of Rawdon, to whom the movement is here
principally attributed.   In this little memoir (Paris Archives) there is found
much more which would be useful for a detailed narrative.

[2] Capitulation in Harris, Life of William, 194.

determined to adhere to the Protestant interest under all circumstances. The troops present did not prevent the proclamation of William and Mary, even in Derry, after the English Convention had decided for them ; William III sent over arms and ammunition for the defence. It has been often maintained that even Lundy, the commander of the troops, took the oath to him ; Lundy always denied it ; his inclination at all times was to remain loyal to the old King, from whom he had his appointment, if it should be compatible with his own religion. So, too, were some of the magistrates disposed. Under these circumstances James II, as his troops were advancing upon Londonderry, and investing it, held it advisable to go there in person, in order to support the superiority of his arms by his personal presence ; Lundy and the magistrates of the town entered into negotiations with him from which he might expect a favourable issue [1]. The citizens, however, and the greater part of the common soldiers, were opposed to such a course. Their zeal had fresh life given it by the fugitives who had escaped to the city from all the neighbouring districts, and by the enthusiastic preachers who had accompanied them. James II gave assurances of his willingness to maintain Protestantism, but they failed to make any impression ; strangers and natives alike thought that whatever he might promise in the moment of difficulty would all be forgotten as soon as he again became master in the country. They were not altogether wrong in apprehending this ; in the instructions of Louis XIV to his ambassador, in which he recommends forbearance towards the Protestants, there was certainly, as we know, a reservation inserted for the times in which James II should again rule over the three kingdoms. And opposition based on religion and nationality had obscured or destroyed all feelings of loyalty. At Londonderry, in the bosom of a population ecclesiastically zealous and thoroughly English in its sentiments, the questions on which the destinies of Britain turned were,—one cannot say considered but—brought to a decision according to the inclina-

---

[1] O'Kelly, Macariae excidium 33, and the other authorities brought toge
by O'Callaghan in the notes.

tions which prevailed there. The occasion for that decision was furnished by the appearance in the neighbourhood of a captain named Murray, with a force considerable in number, and praised as heroic. He had made himself a name by re-sisting the Irish troops. Lundy wished to keep him at a distance, but the citizens opened their gates to him; with their help, and after a joyful reception on the part of the common soldiers, Murray put himself in possession of the main guard, and of other important posts in the town, and took the chief command into his hands. Lundy, not precisely a traitor, but weak and vacillating, gave up the place to him, and escaped by flight from the danger of further unpleasant treatment. Hereupon all consideration for King James came to an end; the negotiations with him were most abruptly broken off: the citizens had him told that if he again sent them a trumpeter to invite them to submission [1] they would fire upon him. King James, most painfully undeceived, left the camp. His presence in it had only served to bring out in their keenest form the general antipathies by which he was assailed, and to give them exclusive sovereignty in the town which he was besieging.

The town had about 30,000 inhabitants; as many perhaps as 10,000 of these had quitted it in order not to incur the dis-pleasure of King James; those who remained behind were the most determined adherents of William possible. The military service was discharged by some 7,000 men, divided into eight regiments, according to the eight bastions of the town, and the regiments were again subdivided into 117 companies, each of 60 men, under three officers. It was not Murray who took the supreme direction, for which he did not think himself suited; it was entrusted to a Major Baker, and with him was associated—a most significant fact—a clergyman. This was Walker, the pastor of a country parish, who on the outbreak of the troubles had assembled an armed force for resistance, and had then led it to the town. One day he was seen on horseback directing the execution of a sally; on the next he

---

[1] So Avaux narrates, May 6. He then finds the King 'très mortifié,' and the minister Melfort 'bien souple.'

again mounted the pulpit to keep up the liveliness of religions impulses. As formerly at Leyden and Rochelle, so now
also in Derry, military exertions and religious zeal co-operated
most heartily and effectively. The opposition between Episcopalians and Presbyterians grew dumb at the sight of the
great common danger. The clergy of both were inspired by
the conviction that they were fighting for God's Word and
for the true religion. But at the same time the besieged were
defending the relation of the Teutonic to the old Keltic population, a relation which had now become in Britain a historical
fact, as well as the self-government of the English and Scottish colonies which had become domesticated on the soil of
Ireland. For the course of events in the world's history it
was important whether the fortifications of Londonderry were
maintained against the Irish and French attack or not.

The forces of the besiegers were not in themselves strong
enough to make themselves masters of those defences. They
had but little artillery fit for use, and had to be sparing of
their ammunition: they did not do much harm to the fortifications. They were not, moreover, particularly numerous; the
reinforcements which arrived not seldom merely served to fill
up the vacancies caused by desertions and by epidemic sick-
nesses which swept off many men [1]. In order to put an end
to the business, General Rosen, who had, like Avaux, attached
himself to the native and Catholic party, and combined these
sentiments with the harsh maxims respecting the conduct of
a war which then prevailed in the French army, hit upon the
strange and cruel thought of driving the neighbouring Protestants from the country round—men, women, and children—
under the walls of the city, where it was intended that they
should perish before the eyes of their fellow-believers, or, if
the latter should not discontinue their resistance, perhaps by
their bullets. The besieged, however, continued their fire
without troubling themselves about the poor people. Rosen
saw himself compelled to have them led away again; it is
affirmed that on this occasion many who had nothing more
to live upon in the town took the opportunity of going off

---

[1] I take this from the Jacobite journal, In Exilio Memorabilia.

with them[1]. This must have been a most desirable relief for the besieged, who suffered far less distress from the attacks of the enemy than from the want of provisions, which increased every day. Walker needed all his eloquence to keep up the confidence of his military congregation under the grievous pressure. He succeeded in doing so once more on the 30th of July; but it would have been the last time, for a wild despair was already beginning to seize men's minds. A few hours afterwards, however, two English vessels effected a passage through the obstacles which were opposed to their arrival[2]. The deliverance which their pastor and colonel had announced to his flock reached them in the last hour, when distressed to the point of death. The Irish fired their camp and marched away.

The besiegers had suffered especial injury from the hostilities which they experienced on the part of Enniskillen, from which place the population, in itself hardly numerous, but increased and animated by the accession of those who had escaped the maltreatment of the Catholics, especially of Rosen, made the district of Fermanagh and Donegal insecure.

On their little ponies, in robber guise, often clothed in the spoils of Catholic priests, they ranged through the country and interrupted communications. At last General Macarthy, Viscount Mountcashel, to whom many fortresses had already yielded, was commissioned to subdue them[3]; his forces were numerous, but raw recruits; before the wild onset of the Enniskilleners, who charged them with the cry of 'No Popery,' they scattered, and suffered a complete defeat. Macarthy himself was taken. Even Sarsfield, the bravest and most renowned of all the Irish loyalists, quitted his position near the neighbouring town of Sligo.

The successful defence of the two bulwarks of Protestantism against the attacks of the Irish and of the French generals,

---

[1] Order of the day. Letter from Rosen in Macpherson i. 205.

[2] According to the Jacobite journal they were not very important. 'The mouth of the logh or bay—was not either choked by sinking some vessels in it or secured by a strong boom, but only a chain laid across it, tied at both ends on the shores with some old ropes.'

[3] 'Hos perduelles vi et armis ad obsequium cogere,' as it is said in Macariae excidium.

and still more, the forced retirement of the Catholic army
from the field in a state of disorganization, produced an impression all the deeper because it was heard at the same time
that the long-prepared expedition of the English, who had no
longer anything to fear from Scotland, would put to sea for
Ireland without delay. From what James II wrote at the
time we learn that he deemed his position to be in the highest
degree critical : Tyrconnel declared that he thought of giving
up everything and burying himself in the deepest concealment; the wildest projects suggested themselves to the mind
of the French ambassador Avaux. He told King James
himself that he had two sorts of enemies to resist—the one,
those who would land, and the other, those in the interior who
would rise against him ; to the first he must oppose his army,
while the second, the Protestants, must be left to the Catholic
militia : but in their case it was not enough to contend only
against those who were actually engaged in open insurrection ;
for that there was no doubt that all the rest would do just the
same as soon as it was in their power ; the King was in danger
of being at last crushed by their revolts. He advised King
James, if a landing took place, and the Protestants consequently rose in any quarter, to have them all massacred at
once [1].

It was while the affairs of Ireland were in a position which
gave occasion to such desperate counsels that Schomberg
arrived in the bay of Carrickfergus. The preparations for his
expedition were far from being completed; only some 6000
men embarked with him in the first instance. But William III
pressed for immediate action ; he would only have wished that
the landing should have taken place in the neighbourhood of
Dublin; for things seemed to him to wear such an aspect
that a decisive result might be expected from an immediate
attack. Schomberg chose, however, the roadstead of Bangor,
where the Protestant population would greet the troops as
preservers when they arrived, and where a connexion could

---

[1] 'Qu'ainsi j'étois d'avis, qu'après que la descente étant faite, si on apprenoit que
des Protestans se fussent soulevés en quelque endroit du royaume, on fit main basse
sur tous généralement.' August 10.

be established with Londonderry and Enniskillen : that was
also the advice of the pilots. The landing was effected without opposition. After a short siege Carrickfergus fell into the
hands of Schomberg[1] ; he issued a proclamation there in
which he offered the protection of William III and of his
Queen even to those Catholics who should submit ; for it was
not, he said, the intention of the sovereigns to bring the
population to one belief by fire and sword as had been done
in France. It was expected that he would advance against
Dublin without delay.

James II had at first little hope of preventing him from
doing so. He made it no secret that his only intention in going
to Drogheda with a small party of horse, not more than 200
strong, on the news of Schomberg's landing, was to show his
spirit, that he might be free from blame if the cause went ill
and he gave it up[2]. He had his great standard hoisted on the
tower at Drogheda, in order to try whether his vassals would
assemble with their forces under this ensign, as he had already
invited them to do by a proclamation ; he was anxious lest
it might fare no better with him in such a course than formerly
with his father at Nottingham. His cause however was not
in such a bad position as he himself supposed. In the moment
of danger the Irish nation developed once more a vital force
and energy for which no one any longer gave it credit. From
all sides the regiments which were in the country advanced to
Drogheda ; in a few days twenty-four battalions of infantry
had assembled. A cargo of French arms had just then arrived,
which were distributed among them. In a short time there
were Irish troops to the number of about 30,000 around the
King, who saw himself with astonishment stronger than the
enemy before whom he had been minded to evacuate the
country. In cavalry especially he was incomparably superior
to him. Schomberg, who advanced cautiously, as he did not

---

[1] See a French journal of the Irish campaign in Kazner, Life of Schomberg,
vol. ii. p. 288.

[2] He said subsequently to the ambassador, the Count of Avaux (Despatch of
Oct. 21), 'Qu'après être venu à Drogheda avec 200 chevaux seulement, sans avoir
pu assembler une armée, il ne pouvoit être blasmé, s'il songeoit à sa sûreté.'

know Ireland and its inhabitants, had pitched a camp near Dundalk, where he waited for reinforcements, and intended to accustom his newly raised and by no means altogether trustworthy troops to war. James II had him challenged to battle, and, as he received no answer, was emboldened to advance against his camp. In the journal of a Jacobite who took part in the campaign it is said, 'that the army of James advanced up hill against the enemy in two columns, in order to bring them to an engagement ; that the cavalry advanced to their camp ; but that none of the enemy appeared outside their entrenchments. These, however,' it is said, 'were too strong, too well garrisoned, and too well furnished with artillery, for the Irish to be able to attack them ; that after some time the forces of James retired ; but that it conduced to their general satisfaction that they had challenged the enemy, and that he had not shown the least inclination to fight them.' Schomberg in fact did not on his side feel tempted to march on marshy ground cut up by fences, against an enemy superior in numbers and commanded by generals of reputation, and so, under these circumstances, to hazard the great cause which he represented on the event of one day of battle. He thought that if a disaster befell him Ireland would be lost, Scotland would break out into insurrection, and that even in England the party of the malcontents would rise very much in influence [1].

But now that he neither advanced nor fought, but remained in his camp, which was visited by an epidemic sickness to which half the men succumbed, the impression was produced that James II had evidently had the better in the campaign, and might still hope for complete success.

This impression was deepened by the fact that the French, in their first encounter with the English fleet in Bantry Bay, on the coast of Ireland, had got the advantage. They had been the better led and had surpassed the English even in handling their guns.

Scotland was for the moment neutralised by the balance of parties existing there since the death of Dundee : in Ireland

---

[1] See the justification of the campaign in Kazner ii. 335.

and at sea the cause of James II had even the advantage.
But what afforded him the greatest prospect of success,
especially in his own apprehension, was the ferment of men's
minds in England, and the opposition of parties in Parliament,
which was as strong under the new government as it had ever
been under any earlier one.

CHAPTER VII.

WILLIAM III had formed his court and ministry principally from among those men who had been serviceable to him in the acquisition of the crown, as though it had been his object to let them share in the enjoyment of the power which had been acquired with their co-operation. So, too, did they seem to understand the privileges of office. Mordaunt and Delamere, for example, to whom the principal offices in the Treasury fell, made use of them in order to admit their friends and those who shared their sentiments into the subordinate posts; Delamere not without stipulating for advantages for himself in the process; Mordaunt preferred men of the extreme Whig or even republican shade of opinion to all others. Neither of them had any knowledge of their business nor any fitness for it. How should Mordaunt, who never knew how to keep a hundred pounds together, administer the finances of a great kingdom? The management of them fell into the hands of a third man, who had also claims on the King's gratitude, the versatile and gifted Godolphin, who was acquainted with this very department and qualified for it; it only caused some surprise that Mordaunt and Delamere were zealous Whigs, while Godolphin then belonged to the Tory party. But such was the system of the moment throughout. Thus the two Secretaryships of State, no doubt the most important of the offices of that time, had been assigned one to a Whig and the other to a Tory, and indeed even to men who might be considered as the heads of their parties. One was Shrewsbury, who had gone over from Catholicism to Protestantism in its least positive aspect, so that people doubted whether he were not a mere sceptic in religion ; an amiable quiet character, tormented indeed by ill health, but yet good-humoured ; he had a delicate wit which , never went so far as to give offence, and a patience which no violence in others provoked into passion ; he was trustworthy in his judgments on things and persons, but at the same time not to be shaken in the party-position which he had adopted[1]; he clung to the opinion that it was only on Whig principles that the new government could support itself. The other Secretary of State was Daniel Finch, Earl of Nottingham, the true representative of a family in which attachment to the pre-rogative, legal training, and eloquence might be called here-ditary. His share in bringing about the Revolution perhaps principally lay in the fact that he had not opposed it ; but for the carrying out of that change the accession of an undoubted Church of England man by conviction, such as he was, was of indescribable value; his influence induced those church-men who did not exactly belong to the Lambeth party to recognise the government and to take the oaths prescribed to them. In the first draft of his history Burnet says, that ' he does not think he goes beyond the province of the historian in declaring that the entrance of Nottingham into the govern-ment saved the Church, and by saving it saved the crown[2].' King William liked Shrewsbury more than any other English statesman ; he had a kind of natural aversion to Nottingham, the Episcopalian, almost priestly, man of law ; but he could no more dispense with him than he could dispense with Shrews-bury. The two Secretaries of State were certainly the heads of the two parties, but yet they were in turn dependent upon them : Nottingham, for instance, when entering upon his office, assured the King indeed of his devotion, but declared to him roundly that cases would occur in which he would have to vote against him in Parliament.

---

[1] Burnet says in the first draft: ' He is the worthiest man I know ;' he there praises in him ' a considerable tincture of learning, true exactness of judgment, great integrity and truth.'

[2] ' Nottingham's being in the ministry first preserved the Church and then the crown. . . . He took much pains both by himself and all his friends, to persuade all his friends and the friends of the Church to take the oaths and to come into the interests of the government.'

The course of affairs depended less upon the holders of the great offices, among whom no freedom of view could be expected, than upon the Parliament, and especially upon the Lower House, where the two parties sate together, and could agree with or contend against each other.

On one or two great questions, even of an ecclesiastical character, the men of both parties who sate in the House of Commons then worked together.

The House of Commons though not unanimously, yet by a large majority, required that the oath prescribed should be taken by every one, even by the clergy, a section of which body had scruples about taking it. The Commons fixed a term by which the oath must be taken : refusal was to be punished by suspension, and, if it continued after the expiration of six months more, by deprivation. The King and his ministers were well aware how many unpleasant consequences the carrying out of so precise a regulation would draw after it, especially on account of men's secret relations to James II. The Lords proposed, in agreement with them, to leave it to the King to settle at what time he would hold it good to tender the oath to each person ; but in the Commons this proposal found no favour. The scruple of the clergy was 'that their oath taken to King James, from which he had not released them, must prevent them from taking an oath to another prince.' This very reason displeased the Commons : 'for Parliament,' it was urged, 'had ordained the earlier oaths ; the same power which had ordained them could also abolish them. What was stronger than Parliament? who could venture to resist its resolutions[1]?' And further, 'how could bishops be tolerated in the House of Lords who were of opinion that their obedience was due to King James?' For one who adhered to such a view the Parliament was no Parliament; King William III was for him an usurper. The Commons maintained the omnipotence of the state's authority even in reference to the alteration of the oaths.

At the head of those who would not take the oaths stood

---

[1] Williams, April 19 : ' It is part of your security that the old oaths be abolished : and what can resist an Act of Parliament ? '   Grey's Debates ix. 215.

five of those seven bishops who had once declined to read the
Declaration of Indulgence of James II. They opposed to
the principle of parliamentary omnipotence the principle of
ecclesiastical independence.

In an assembly, which took place at the house of the lawyer
Sawyer [1], the bishops adopted the resolution, that Parliament
had no right whatever to prescribe an oath to the clergy.
The movement which led to the Revolution had mainly
originated in their quarrel with King James on this point.
The bishops were not so inconsistent as has been thought:
they intended to maintain the ecclesiastical principle against
the Parliament just as they had maintained it against the
King. But with all the religious incitements that were at
work the times had long ceased to offer the old field for
the action of hierarchical views. Between King and Parliament where was the Archbishop? And Parliament was still
more powerful by far than the King. The penalty which the
bishops had to pay for their opposition to the omnipotence
of parliamentary legislation forms a stage in the history of
the relations between the spiritual and the temporal power.

But while the two parties of which the Parliament consisted
were agreed in maintaining its power, and had thus a principle
in common, there were yet differences between them as to
the share of each party in that power which they could not
accommodate.

Matters could not go so far in England as they had gone
in Scotland, where the opposition between Episcopalians and
Presbyterians just then brought on civil war. Both parties
had co-operated in the English Revolution; even in the
declarations of the clergy of the Church of England assurances
had been given to the Presbyterians which made impossible
the renewal of the oppression that had hitherto burdened
them. The least which could be granted them for their share
in the great common cause was a release from the penalties
which were annexed by law to dissent from the State

---

[1] The participation of the lawyers, even of the younger Finch and of Pemberton
himself, in the assemblies of the bishops is mentioned in the reports which arrived
in France.

Church. The laws themselves were not abrogated, for that would have benefited the Catholics also, but their application to the Protestant Dissenters, among whom the Presbyterians were by far the most numerous, was suspended. This partial abrogation was called toleration. It is needless to point out how remote it was from the system which James II had intended to introduce mainly for the benefit of the Catholics. The Quakers were, however, admitted into the category of the Protestant Dissenters to whom this toleration was granted, although their heterodoxy as to the doctrine of the Trinity caused some hesitation. It was feared that if they were not admitted they would still adhere to James II, and would perhaps support him with their money; for at that time they were already rich.

But now, for the first time since the Revolution, the great question came under discussion which concerned the personal share of each individual in the rights guaranteed by the constitution; the question as to placing the Presbyterians on an equality with the members of the State Church. The grant of such equality in respect of their admission to state offices was called their Comprehension. Such a project had been often discussed even under the Restoration. Charles II had entered into many negotiations upon the subject; even the House of Commons had once agreed to such a scheme out of opposition to the Catholics. But the Presbyterians thought that they had now acquired a new right to have such a measure passed as had then been allowed to drop; and they found their warmest advocate in King William. As early as the 16th of March, wearing his full royal robes for the first time since his coronation, he made the proposal to the assembled Houses that, as he was just then engaged in filling up the posts that were vacant, they should adopt such regulations as should enable him to take all Protestants who wished it into his service. 'This conjunction in my service,' he said, 'will tend to the better uniting you among yourselves and the strengthening of you against your common adversaries[1].' It was not a clause which he had approved

---

[1] Speech of the King in the Journals of both Houses. The report of Burnet in his first draft is more correct than that in his second.

incidentally on the advice of others, but a proposal which he made in his own person with all the pomp of royalty. It was his principal and most pressing care, and its adoption would have furnished a new basis for his administration.

But his plan encountered decided opposition; public opinion, if we are rightly informed about it, was against him. It was thought objectionable that all Dissenters, from the most credulous enthusiasts down to atheists, were in this way to find access to offices. The King was a Calvinist; it was thought that he therefore wished to transform the English Church in conformity with his personal convictions. A Dutchman who was then in England informs us that this proposal had alienated from the King a great number—he gives it at 80,000—of his adherents in London.

Thus little indeed could be expected beforehand from the proposal which was made a few days later in the House of Lords—as an interpolation in another bill however, and in a modified form. The provision, according to which a certificate of having received the Lord's supper in an Episcopalian Church was necessary for entrance on public office, kept at least conscientious and zealous Presbyterians who could not prevail upon themselves to take part in the Anglican Church ceremonies excluded from the service of the state. It was now proposed that the certificate of any other Protestant congregation should have the same value[1]. But even in this shape the motion did not meet with any approval; it was rejected by a large majority. A comprehension so thorough and sweeping had no prospect of success.

The only way left for attaining the end aimed at was that which had already been taken more than once. An attempt must be made so to modify the ritual of the Church of England as to the points at which the Presbyterians took offence that they could take part in its service without scruple.

The King was advised—so far as we know the then Dean of Canterbury, Tillotson, was the author of this advice[2]—to

---

[1] Lords' Journals, March 22, xiv. 158.
[2] Birch, Life of Tillotson 165. [? 179, ed. 1752. Tr.]

manage the transaction synodically, so that while a theological commission should be appointed the results of their deliberations should afterwards be laid before the Convocation of the clergy.

The Parliament had adjourned from August till October. It was during this recess that the commission was named, and even assembled in the Jerusalem Chamber at Westminster. Conciliatory and moderate views prevailed among its members. It formed the mouthpiece of that school among the clergy of the Church of England which had made a reconciliation with Presbyterianism the end of its endeavours. Stillingfleet, Patrick, Tenison, and Burnet, who had lately become bishop of Salisbury, co-operated with Tillotson. The old negotiations between the two parties were now resumed : the ceremonies and even the words of the liturgy which gave offence to the Presbyterians were considered in detail. A scheme was completed for which its authors promised themselves a good reception. So far more progress was made than had been made in a similar undertaking under Charles II, in which even the preliminary deliberations had led to no result. But when on this as on the former occasion the final decision was left to Convocation, matters again took such a shape at once that but little prospect of an agreement was left. The elections to the Lower House of Convocation returned simply the most zealous Episcopalians. Personal animosities of various kinds seem to have had influence on them ; but some plausible reasons were also brought forward against the scheme of the government. It was said that by the corrections proposed the credit of the liturgy and of the Church of England would be impaired, and the Church divided in itself. The events which had happened in Scotland were recalled to remembrance ; it was said that they showed that the King favoured Presbyterianism [1] ; that he intended to show it the same favour in England also, and that the commission was to prepare the way for the accomplishment of his design ; that

---

[1] Burnet's MS. The clergy say 'that it was very visible from all the proceedings of Scotland that the King was no friend to the church, and it was therefore necessary for them to stand their ground and to stick firm to one another.'

for that very reason churchmen must hold together against it. The universities, Oxford especially, declared against any concession. And the choice of a prolocutor showed at once how decidedly this disposition had the preponderance in Convocation. The candidate of the moderate party, Tillotson, was rejected in spite of his recognised services, and Professor Jane of Oxford was preferred to him, a man who is supposed to have been mainly responsible for the decree of that university by which the Whig views of the state were condemned. The bishops who formed the Upper House of the Convocation, the very authors of the scheme, were too weak to oppose the Lower House, especially as they were still without a metropolitan. After a series of fruitless debates they themselves begged the King to adjourn the assembly. We shall meet them again at a later epoch, in which they resumed the contest thus broken off.

This, for the time, decided in the negative the question which had remained undecided in the discussion on the coronation oath, whether an alteration in the Church of England was to be expected. The Church would not consent to any concession except the revocation of the penal laws against Protestants : for itself it continued to assert that it needed no improvement. It placed itself with a strong feeling of its own dignity in an attitude of resistance to any attempt at placing it on an equality with Protestant churches of a different constitution. It wished to be the Church of England, nothing further; but this to the exclusion of other bodies.

It is evident that jealousy of the King, who was at the same time the supreme governor of the Church, co-operated to an important extent in producing this result. The strict ecclesiastical party feared his Calvinistic and Presbyterian tendencies just as keenly as under Charles II it had resisted that Prince's real or supposed leanings to Catholicism.

And therein it fell in with the temper then prevalent in Parliament. Many Presbyterian Whigs are said to have been pleased, in spite of their opinions, that the Comprehension was not accomplished. An apprehension is said to have been felt that the King would gain too much influence by an union of the Dissenters and Episcopalians brought to pass under his authority. But a powerful king was just what was not desired.

William III had to feel this very bitterly in an affair to which he attached perhaps more importance than to anything else.

The purposes of William, which were not quite systematically expressed, may be described concisely as follows. He wished in the first place to combine all Protestant parties in the service of the state, and then to procure for himself a permanent revenue independent of an annual grant. The adoption of both his recommendations together would have secured him the independence and the personal influence which he thought that he still needed in order to maintain the prerogative of the crown in full efficiency even after the change which had taken place, and at the same time to interpose at pressing moments in foreign politics according to his own judgment. He would have become, had this combination been effected, a very powerful king in accordance with law.—But he was destined to meet with just as obstinate a resistance in his second design as in his first.

He had disclosed that design on his very first entrance upon the government. He considered it natural and fair that the revenue of James II should be transferred to him. For how, he argued, could it be wished to refuse what had been granted to the Catholic King, who threatened religion and the constitution, to him who was honoured in the country as the preserver of both? When his view was at once met by the objection that the abdication of James II had been admitted, and the throne declared vacant, the lawyers who attached themselves to the King maintained that the revenue nevertheless was not affected thereby ; for that it was annexed to the crown, and followed the arrangement of public affairs ; that where the crown was there also must the revenue be ; that James II had possessed it in his political capacity : if he no longer was invested with that capacity, to whom should the revenue fall? Assuredly to no one else than to him to whom the political capacity had passed over. This line of argument, however, aroused the opposition of the zealous Whigs. 'If Parliament,' they said, 'had to dispose of crown, was it not also to have the power of disposing of its revenue? The latter was derived, like the crown, from the people, and had lapsed to the people.' In the discussion on this question the assertion that James II had forfeited the crown appears once more; and the conclusion was drawn from it that Parliament had absolutely no right to dispose in another way of the revenue annexed to the crown. The decision, however, depended less on the strength of the reasons alleged than on the interest of parliamentary government itself. It was precisely in the large grants which had been made to the previous King for his lifetime that the Convention Parliament saw the principal cause of his encroachments. And so many stories came over from Amsterdam about William III's self-will and inclination to a personal government, that they could not fail to arouse an apprehension that Parliament might one day fall into a dissension with him as it had done with other princes, and that the thought might readily occur to him of acting without regard to Parliament. It was thought that he must be bound to it by the need of grants frequently to be renewed. ''Tis our security,' exclaimed Sir William Pulteney, 'to have the revenue in our disposition.' It was quite impossible that while this was the disposition of Parliament the whole revenue of James should be transferred to William. Nothing was urged against the crown being supplied with £1,200,000 a-year, just as it had been under Charles II; as it had to meet the expense of the ordinary civil service, nothing could be deducted from that sum if it was to be able to fulfil its obligations. But the Parliament was not disposed to secure this sum to the new King for life. A design was disclosed of which there had already been some mention even under James II, and which had been revived as soon as ever the change of government took place; a design to secure sessions of Parliament at least once in every three years, by granting the revenue for three years only. In its definitive deliberations, however, the Parliament went still further. The taxes required to produce the necessary revenue were only voted for one year, and that with the express addition 'no longer.' All those who had upheld the idea of the hereditary nature of the government were against this course; for by this settlement, they said, especially by the two last words, the hereditary right of the crown to a definite property was set aside [1]. The learned lawyer, Somers, though a Whig, yet declared this to be an innovation which might have the most dangerous consequences. But he and those who agreed with him produced no effect by their arguments. When the policy of the advanced Whigs parted from the Presbyterian tendencies with which it had hitherto been connected, and coincided with the parliamentary interest, it was always irresistible in Parliament. The resolution, once adopted, was adhered to.

William III was deeply wounded: he felt it as a slight offered to him when compared with the treatment of James II, and almost as a personal insult; but he had no means for resisting.

Even in the sphere of his own power he already experienced very unpleasant attacks.

The House of Commons was no doubt acting as it had a right to do when it brought before its tribunal the cases of peculation which had occurred in the preparations for the expedition against Ireland; Schomberg himself had made a complaint on the subject; the King found reason for dismissing the military commissary Shales from his service. But that was not enough for the Commons. Shales had already occupied a similar post under James II; it was considered scandalous that he had now been taken into the service of the new King also, and men pretended to know that this had been brought about through his personal relations to some of the leading ministers, and even by corruption. They hit upon the notion of asking the King who the man was who had recommended him this commissary-general. In spite of all objections a resolution to lay this question before the King was adopted. He was as it were to become himself the accuser of one or other of his confidential advisers. 'Gentlemen,' answered William with calmness but with decision, 'it is impossible for me to give you an answer to this question.'

---

[1] Sir George Treby: 'The operation of those two words, "no longer," is to take away the inheritance of the crown.'

It was not, however, so much against himself that the majority of the House of Commons wished to proceed in this matter as against his confidential advisers.

As Burnet says, the Whigs occupied the most important posts, but they were discontented at not having them all in their hands[1]. It was very unwillingly that they saw their old adversaries of the Tory party occupying state offices, whether of higher or lower grade; they wished to compel the King to dismiss such officials. It was said in the House of Commons 'that the game which King James had harboured in his park must be driven out from that of King William; the park-keepers too must be changed.'

The combination of the two parties, which had been brought about at the critical moment by the necessity of common action against James II, was dissolved as soon as the new government had been founded. This showed itself in the rudest form in the discussion of a Bill of Indemnity, by which William III hoped to calm men's minds. The Whigs received the proposal with a remark of contrary tendency— that for the good of posterity an example must be made of those by whose agency the laws had been overthrown. They wished to turn the Bill of Indemnity into a bill of retaliation and revenge, as has often happened at seasons of violent reaction. As early as the end of May a series of transgressions was specified in the committee appointed for the purpose as being such that no pardon should be granted for them. The principle was to bring all those to an account who had cooperated in the proceedings of James II which were declared illegal in the Declaration of Rights. 'It is the opinion of this committee,' so its chairman, Sir Thomas Littleton, expressed himself on the first article, 'that the asserting, advising, and promoting of the dispensing power,' and similar proceedings, 'is one of the crimes for which some persons be excepted out of the Bill of Indemnity, for the safety, settlement, and welfare of the whole nation for the future.' This principle was then applied to the other proceedings which were treated

---

[1] First draft: 'The chief places, both in the government and household, were filled with Whigs, but they were highly displeased they had not them all.'

as criminal in King James: the trial of the bishops, the Ecclesiastical Commission, the arbitrary raising of taxes, the unauthorised formation of a standing army, and the like; for it was said to be needful to punish the assistants and tools of this prince in order to justify the resolutions adopted against him. But how far that might lead! Where would a limit be found if such rules were adopted? Even an improper interpretation of the laws, and a share in the collection of the taxes above referred to were declared to be actions for which no one might expect forgiveness. And, as in the year 1660, so also in the year 1689 it was intended to seize the property of those persons who were thought to have been enriched by unjust proceedings, and even that of their families; confiscation found warm advocates in this Parliament. Only the reaction took a different direction from that taken in 1660. After the Restoration the adherents of the Long Parliament, the enemies of royalty—after the Revolution those who had promoted the interests of royalty and had fought for it—were to be punished. The executions of Russell and Sidney were described as judicial murders; the lawyers who had helped to bring them about found themselves treated as criminals. The conception of the state for which the late events had procured acceptance acquired a retrospective force; whoever had disputed it was made personally responsible for having done so.

And the Whigs intended while they overthrew their enemies to secure to themselves full possession of power. A proposal was made to declare that all those who had taken part in the surrender of the charters of towns should be declared to have lost the right of holding any office in the corporations. The Tories, in whose hands those offices were, would have lost them at one blow; the Whigs would not only have stepped into their places there, but would, as the corporations exercised a decisive influence upon the elections, have been sure for ever of the majority in Parliament [1].

---

[1] Bonnet: 'Les Whigs cherchent l'occasion d'avoir la revanche sur l'affaire des corporations.—Une infinité de personnes, la plus part d'entre la noblesse, étoient interessées dans cette clause.'

What a prospect for the King, who would have been absolutely subjected to Whig control; what a prospect above all
for the great Tory party which, in consequence of the Revolution, to which it had itself contributed to the best of its power,
would have been driven from its positions, and threatened in
property and life!

CHAPTER VIII.

DISSOLUTION OF THE CONVENTION PARLIAMENT. FIRST
SITTINGS OF THE PARLIAMENT OF 1690.

WE have the report of an agent of James II as to his
residence in London; it dates from the last months of 1689,
during which the dissensions just mentioned made way and
increased in violence. He received the impression that everything was ripe for the overthrow of the new government; 'the
country was ruined, the nobility discontented, the Church of
England estranged by the treatment of the bishops, William
III suspected of aiming at absolute power, and a combination against his supposed aims was being formed between
Scots and Englishmen; if the government was still standing, the reason was, that it was not attacked speedily and
energetically.' So said William Penn, who was still a friend
of James II, and travelled about the country at his personal
risk, in order to confirm the adherents of that prince in their
devotion to him. We are astonished when we become more
familiar with the Jacobite movements of which Preston and
Dartmouth then formed the centre. Dartmouth offered to
carry over a part of the English fleet to the French. He
had, he said, already gained over a part of the officers and
crews by saying to them that the Dutch were more their
enemies than the French; for that Louis XIV acted from
generosity, while Holland had only its mercantile interest in
view, which it pushed to the injury of the English. Dartmouth sought to arrange good terms beforehand for the
officers and crews, as well as for himself. His advice was
that at the same time a harbour, such as Falmouth, should be

occupied, and a landing carried out; then William of Orange would be ruined; for as soon as he drew his troops together to oppose it, a general insurrection would take place against him in the country [1].

There was much negotiation at that time between James II and Louis XIV as to such an undertaking. They had not, as we know, carried out their original purpose in Ireland, but even under these circumstances affairs seemed to them to be sufficiently promising to justify them in thinking of an attempt upon England, where the whole hostile system might then be overthrown at one blow. Even Louvois approved of this plan.

It is not clear whether William III had received any information, properly speaking, of these projects. But for him, on the other hand, it was clearly necessary to bring the struggle in Ireland to a decision. Schomberg had wished to come to London during the winter; William refused his consent, saying that such a step might endanger everything; the complaints of that general as to the unruliness of his colonels and the want of the materials of war, only led William to the conviction that he must go over himself. 'But the whole world,' so he says in one of his letters, 'is against it [2]'; he did not venture to communicate his purpose to the Privy Council, thinking that it would have met with general opposition. And certainly if any misfortune had befallen him it would have recoiled upon all those men who had attached themselves to him. The Whigs displayed most anxiety for his person. The King mentions their remonstrances with bitter scorn: for he no longer believed in their friendship; he thought that they only wished to use him as their tool. 'They fear to lose me,' he said, 'before they have attained their ends by means of me.'

William had at this time another dispute with old allies which excited him much. The city of Amsterdam hesitated to leave any longer to the absent Stadholder the nomination of the magistrates [3], which had been usually made from

---

[1] A detailed account, anonymous but thoroughly credible, is to be found in the Archives of the Foreign Office at Paris, dated December, 1689.

[2] To Bentinck, Jan. 21 : 'Tout le monde désapprouve mon voyage à Irlande.'

[3] [Germ. Schöppen ; Fr. échevins—nearly = 'aldermen.' Tr.]

a list which the city laid before him: relying upon some previous cases, it demanded that the Court of Holland should be commissioned by the Estates of the Province to make the selection and the nomination. The citizens thought that they were thereby restoring an old privilege, and declared that they would pay no taxes till it had been secured. But William was not disposed to give up a right on the exercise of which depended his influence with the city, which was powerful, jealous of his power, and never trustworthy. He was satisfied that it had been induced to offer opposition by French influence, as both he and his allies would suffer the greatest disadvantages from a quarrel with it[1]; never, he thought, had France laid a mine more skilfully. This danger, however, could not induce him to assent to the proposed diminution of his authority, whatever the consequences of his refusal might be; for he thought that he was innocent in the matter; his opponents would be obliged to give an account of their conduct before God. Even when the estates rejected the city's demand, it remained of the same mind. Bentinck, whom William had sent to Holland to make up the quarrel, intimated that it would be most advisable that he should go over himself. 'Ah,' he exclaims in one of his letters, 'if I could make a journey to Holland! But it is impossible. I would embark to-morrow if I could do so without abandoning everything here[2].'

These transitory thoughts must have suggested the story then told, and often since repeated, that William III had been induced by the resistance which he met with in England, and by the serious position of affairs at the moment, to think of abdicating; that he had wished to leave England to Queen Mary in order to live himself in Holland, in enjoyment of his old dignity. As if such a course had been possible! He would then have been obliged to give up his Irish undertaking, which he nevertheless declared absolutely necessary; he would have

---

[1] Extrait de toutes les lettres du roi touchant les affaires de Hollande. MS. of the British Museum.

[2] 'S'il étoit possible sans vouloir tout abandonner icy, je m'embarquerais demain pour venir vous trouver en Hollande.'

abandoned his own cause in the midst of the most dangerous crisis.

The quarrels with Amsterdam were made up even without William's presence, by Bentinck and Witsen; he remained in possession of his old privilege; the taxes were again paid.

As for English affairs, the question was not whether he would retire from their management, but in conjunction with which of the two parties, seeing that the discord between them had come to an outbreak, he would venture to administer the state, and to go through the struggle which had begun.

He could not forgive the Whigs for wishing to subordinate his authority to that of the Parliament, to confine him altogether within the narrowest bounds[1], to remove from him the men whom he trusted, and to transform his government into that of a dominant party. But on the other hand, how could he make common cause with the Tories, whose principles inclined them to assert the hereditary nature of the sovereign power, and who had only reluctantly consented to his accession? He had, however, now actually mounted the throne: it was impossible for the Tories, after they had once fallen off from King James, to make any effort to restore him, for his restoration would have involved them in the greatest danger; William needed not to fear anything from them if he did not estrange them still further. The attacks of the Whigs at once upon his authority, and upon all of those who had adhered to the earlier governments, had brought about a kind of understanding between him and the Tories. The Tories sought protection against the Corporations Bill from the new King; they were in favour of his prerogative. Halifax, the principal object of the attacks of the Whigs, had quitted office; but we learn that he still exercised a considerable influence secretly[2]. The experienced Danby perhaps possessed still more. William III granted him a similar

---

[1] Similar grounds are mentioned in a Dutch report of April 14, 1690, which was communicated to Berlin.

[2] The Dutch report already mentioned says, 'Den Marq. Halifax outsloegh sich selven van langer des conings raed te willen syn, hoewel he sedert meer heft gedaen, als jemand.'

confidential position to that which he had formerly held under Charles II. It was under the influence of these two statesmen and of Nottingham that William III took his resolution. Unexpectedly, without having given even a hint of his purpose, he pronounced the prorogation, and immediately afterwards the dissolution of the Convention Parliament, in which the Whigs had the upper hand; and he issued the writs for new elections which would, it could hardly be doubted, have a contrary result to the last.

The decisive reason which had in the previous year led to the transformation of the Convention into a Parliament had been, that the influence of the Tories and Episcopalians at new elections was feared. What had happened since had strengthened Tory feeling in the corporations as they were then constituted, and in the counties ; it now manifested itself in the most vigorous way. In some places the parishioners appeared with their clergymen at their head to give their votes unanimously for the Episcopalian candidates[1]. It was surprising that Presbyterian or sectarian candidates did not succeed in London, as had so often been the case. This result was ascribed to the influence of Bishop Compton—a man upon whom William III could still count, even though he now appeared again as a zealous champion of the Episcopalian system—as it is assumed, from dislike of Burnet. The elections could not, to be sure, result exclusively in favour of the Tories. For although the King let it be known on every occasion that he intended for the future to rely mainly upon the interest of the Church of England[2], yet some of the statesmen who surrounded him belonged to another school, and worked in its interest.

In the new Parliament, which was opened on the 20th of March, the altered relation of parties was shown at once on the election of a Speaker. When Trevor, the candidate of

---

[1] Bonnet: 'On vit les curés de paroisses aller donner leurs voix à la teste de leurs paroissiens.'

[2] In a letter of Lord Clarendon on election affairs, dated Feb. 16, 1689/90 (Sir T. Phillipps' Library), we read : 'The King takes all occasions to profess his kindness to our church, and his resolution to support it, and of relying chiefly on that interest.'

the Tories, was named, the Whigs made an outcry, for the
man had the reputation of having, in the Parliament of
James II, favoured even such measures of that prince as
had been of doubtful legality. Yet the majority for him was
so large that it was unnecessary to count the votes.

The King's speech from the throne expressed his confidence
that in the pressing affairs which lay before it the new Parliament would support him better than its predecessor had done.
He had found himself hindered in his purpose of undertaking
the reduction of Ireland in person; he hoped now to meet
with zealous support in it: his revenue had not been settled;
he might hope that it would be settled now, and that with as
much regard for the dignity of the crown as had been shown
under earlier governments. ' How often,' he continues, ' have
I recommended an Act of Indemnity to the last Parliament!
. . . Debates of that nature must take up more of your
time than can now be spared from the despatch of those other
things which are absolutely necessary for our common safety;
I intend to send you an Act of Grace, with exceptions of some
few persons only, but such as may be sufficient to show my
great dislike of their crimes, and at the same time my readiness to extend protection to all my other subjects . . . who
will thereby see that they can recommend themselves to me
by no other methods than what the laws prescribe, which
shall always be the only rule of my government. . . . I am
desirous to leave no colour to any of my subjects for the
raising of disturbances in the government, and especially in
the time of my absence.'

This programme for the next session contrasted with the
course of that which had gone before, and the majority of the
new House of Commons agreed with the King.

The House did not hesitate to acknowledge that the hereditary revenue of the crown, which James II had enjoyed, was its
inalienable property, and had passed over with it to William
III. The views of the Tories, which had previously been over-
borne, now prevailed. The Act contains the continuation, as
it were, of the hereditary property of the crown over the in-
terlude of the Revolution. The other revenues were divided
into two classes : the half of the excise which Charles II and

James II had drawn was promised to their present Majesties
and to the survivor of them; the customs, the old tonnage
and poundage, were also to pass to William and Mary to the
same amount with that bestowed on the two previous kings,
with the limitation, however, that they were only granted for
four years [1]. The parliamentary point of view, that the King
ought not to be made independent of Parliament for too long
a time, was maintained even by the Tories; they produced,
however, a reason for the limitation which sounded plausible.
The King had declared himself willing that a part of his
revenue should be employed for the guarantee of a loan; it
was remarked to him that a grant limited to a definite number of years would form a surer basis for the credit to be
opened than one made for the duration of a life which must
always be uncertain.

The Tories thus granted what the Whigs had refused; the
King's answer to their concessions was the comprehensive
Act of Grace which had been announced. The exceptions
which it made affected only those who had become infa-
mous as the most confidential advisers and tools of James II,
and had already made their escape from popular vengeance
during the storm of the Revolution. We find the names of
the members of the Catholic Camarilla, Petre, Powis, Castlemaine, Dover, Melfort, and their assistants, but also some
names of men who had at last separated from them, especially
that of Robert Earl of Sunderland : on this occasion, as on an
earlier one, a dead man was included, the Chancellor Jeffreys ;
but the world was now spared a repetition of the disgusting
horrors which had followed the Restoration. Was not this
owing in part to the century's having become more humane?
—The main object and effect of the Act of Grace lay in this,
that a limit was set to the party-reaction contemplated by the
zealous Whigs : the Act was especially advantageous to the
Tories. So wonderfully had the relations of parties become
complicated that, as after the Restoration the Presbyterians

---

[1] Burnet says 'for five years,' which is explained by the fact that the provision
of the Act runs ' for the term of four years fiom Christmas next.' Burnet added
the current year, writing from memory, as was generally the case.

had to be secured against the Episcopalians, so after the
Revolution the Episcopalians had to be secured against the
Presbyterians. Both had taken part in both events, and the
subsequent history of England depended upon their opposition
and their co-operation.

The Whigs then sought to procure a new validity and a
new guarantee for their political point of view, by bringing in
a bill which prescribed an oath of abjuration of King James.
Not only was it to be taken by every one who was in the
public service, but it was to be possible to tender it to all
private persons also. In opposition to this proposal, however,
it was remarked that criminal attempts against the king's
person would certainly not be hindered by this oath, while on
the other hand, many quiet and conscientious men who were
obedient to the actual king, would be driven by scruples of
conscience into the opposite camp. Thus it had happened
with the bishops : the oath imposed upon them had led to the
formation of the party of the Nonjurors. Besides this, the
measure would have introduced an inquisition into men's
political sentiments which it was not desired should be
allowed to strike root. The bill, after being rejected by the
Commons, was brought in, with alterations which mitigated its
rigour, in the Lords; but there it experienced so many new
abatements of its harshness that it no longer possessed any.
value for the authors of the proposal, and the whole affair
fell to the ground [1]. The King, too, had declared himself
against the measure.

On one question however, in which only a word, no doubt,
but a very important word, was concerned, the Whigs secured
acceptance for their view. That question affected the validity
of the laws which had been passed in the Convention and in
the Convention Parliament. Not that any one had thought
of revoking them : the question was, whether the Parliament
which now sat, after being summoned in accordance with the
usual forms, should confirm or merely recognise the acts of
the previous assembly, in the case of which those forms had

---

[1] Its import may be learned in Macaulay, who saw the draft in the archives of
the House of Lords.

not been observed. The Tories were in favour of a confirmation, the Whigs of a recognition. The latter demanded
that the form should run that the acts in question 'were and
are good laws;' the former would only hear of a statement
'that they are good laws,' according to the precedent set by
the first Parliament of the Restoration. But they were reminded that the state of the case was different now from what
it had been then, as King Charles had issued the writs on the
ground of his hereditary right, whereas the authority of King
William rested upon the resolutions of the previous assembly
itself. In this dispute the position of the Whigs was clearly
in itself the stronger. It was remarked that the least doubt
of the absolute validity of the acts of the past year would
bring the new order of things into question, and that this
might become very dangerous if the King went away as he
just then intended to do. The argument that the nation ought
not to be disturbed worked on this occasion in favour of the
Whigs. The wording, which embodied a recognition of the
lawfulness of the acts in question rather than a confirmation
of them, was accepted in both Houses, first in the Lords, then
in the Commons also. The latter did not even think it
necessary to deliberate on the subject in committee.

As the government of William III had been founded by
a renewed combination of both parties, both had also to co-
operate in its administration.

It is asserted that the Whigs' object in bringing in the oath
of abjuration had been to exclude the Tories again from high
offices[1]. Danby repeatedly encountered the bitterest personal
attacks: an attempt was even made to get his name mentioned among the exceptions from the Act of Grace: but
how completely futile an attempt it was! At that very time
he took up his abode in Whitehall, and might be regarded
as the first minister.

The King had removed the most turbulent Whigs, such as
Mordaunt and Delamere, from their offices; but he did not
therefore wish to break with the party as such. He was

---

[1] Burnet: 'The Whigs hoped to have all the places of trust and profit, and by
consequence the government, again in their hand.' (First draft.)

much annoyed that Shrewsbury, who might be regarded as the head of its moderate section, tendered his resignation from jealousy of Danby's influence. The King sent to him first Bentinck and then Tillotson, in order to bring him to another mind; finally he spoke with him himself. Shrewsbury told him at the audience that he was his warmest adherent, that he would live and die for him. William interrupted him with the remark that in that case he must remain at his post, as it was just there that Shrewsbury's services were indispensable. The mental agitation itself caused Shrewsbury, who often referred to his weak health, to fall seriously ill. The King could not refuse to accept the seals which his minister sent back to him: but he would not bestow them upon any one else.

Not a little surprise was caused by William's separating himself from the Whigs, who passed for his own party: his friends were perplexed, his enemies took courage in consequence; but the separation could not have been avoided; and its result, in spite of the objections urged against it, was that the agitation which had sprung from the one-sided policy of the Whigs was calmed. The King had the majority in the Parliament, and it made him sufficient grants both for his own needs and for the campaign which was at hand.

Although surrounded by a thousand embarrassments, he had yet won a solid basis of operations over against his enemies, who, on their side likewise, assumed an imposing position.

CHAPTER IX.

THE COURT AT DUBLIN. RIVALRY OF THE FRENCH
AND ENGLISH NAVIES.

WE are reminded once more of the relation of the old Irish chiefs to the supreme king at Tara, when we hear how the descendants of those chiefs, who prided themselves on their lineage, attached themselves to a king who had been driven from England, and who, like them, could boast of descent from old Irish princes. They had organised themselves for war after the fashion of the seventeenth century. The heads of the septs appeared as colonels; their relations, according to the claims of their descent, as higher or lower officers: the common people attached themselves to them from a feeling of clanship. Strict military subordination could not be enforced under such circumstances any more than it had been possible to enforce it among the Russians as long as the *Me'stnitchestvo* [1] still prevailed among them. The relationship of the officers to each other, and even to their soldiers, forbade the establishment of any strict discipline. The captain could not seriously reprove the sergeant who was his cousin, nor the latter the soldier whom he considered to be about his equal, and who did not submit to any harsh usage. The natives were all equally unacquainted with military service, yet they would only be commanded by each other, for no foreigner was sup-

---

[1] [This word means a 'right of precedence,' military or official, based upon birth. Feodore, elder brother of Peter the Great, destroyed the evidences upon which such rights could be claimed. This note is condensed from an explanation of the meaning of the term, most kindly furnished to the translator by W. R. Morfill, Esq, M.A., of Oriel College. Tr.]

posed to love the country. The officers who had come over
from France were at first in a difficult position in ·dealing with
this rude and distrustful people. The Irish treated their king
with confidential familiarity. As he passed through a room
they even caught hold of him by the sleeve of his coat, in
order to lay their petitions before him ; they did not fear to
appear before his face even if they had come to Dublin contrary to his order. The English exiles, who continued to
reverence in the King the majesty of the supreme power,
could not conceal their astonishment on the subject[1]. With
the slender means which the Jacobites possessed — for the
only money seen was copper coins, to which the government
had assigned the value of shillings and half-crowns, with a
promise to redeem them at some future time according to
their nominal value—they lived magnificently and joyfully.
The town had never been more sociable and cheerful, nor at
the same time, more debauched and immoral. One day after
another was carelessly enjoyed : the Jacobites, self-satisfied
with being the defenders of religion and of legitimacy, neglected nevertheless to prepare themselves for the struggle in
which they would have to engage on behalf of their cause : just
as though being the defenders of a good cause were enough to
secure a special divine protection. More serious men objected
that immoral life in individuals, and the vices of which they
were guilty, might, in spite of their good cause, be visited by
divine punishments. But the natives hardly felt the contradiction of professing to fight for a great idea, and living frivolously
and thoughtlessly withal. The events of the last autumn had
doubled their self-confidence. In the Dublin journals they
boasted that the great Schomberg, the general of universal
celebrity, had not ventured with his veteran forces to resist in
the open field the Irish regiments which had only just received
the most indispensable training[2]. Recollections of the last
months formed the subject of every day's conversation, and

---

[1] For instance, the author of the Irish journal in Sir T. Phillipps' Library, from
which I take this and the following notices.

[2] There was even then a newspaper in Dublin, which however has utterly disappeared. I refer here to an account printed at the time, which O'Callaghan mentions in his Notes to the Macariae Excidium, p. 330.

together with them, the accounts which arrived from England ;
for communications had not been broken off for a moment :—
accounts of the resistance offered to the Prince of Orange—
for so the new king was still described in Ireland, as in
France ; of the combinations which on the other hand were
being formed for King James ; of the prospects of return which
he had, and which were certain : names and places were mentioned without consideration that all this might be reported
to England.

The principal hope of the Jacobites was always placed in
the King of France, who in March 1690 sent over an auxiliary
corps under Count Lauzun, not without taking an equal
number of Irish into his service in exchange. Ireland certainly lost nothing by the transaction. For the Irish were
half naked and could hardly be called soldiers ; the French
seemed to be the very flower of the army of Louis XIV.
The corps consisted of six regiments of infantry, 6,300 men
in number without counting the officers. A fine train of
artillery and considerable stores of ammunition were also
sent into the country.

Avaux had made himself intolerable to King James by his
exclusive connexion with the Irish ; he was recalled on the
request of James : Rosen also returned to France. In their
place Nompar de Caumont, Count Lauzun, was entrusted with
the direction both of political and military affairs—a choice
which was mainly owing to his having acquired the absolute
confidence of the court of St. Germains by the part which he
had taken in the flight of the Queen [1].

Yet Lauzun also met with manifold difficulties at Dublin.
He felt so uncomfortable in the council of ministers to which
James admitted him, that he begged that he might be heard
by the King in company with Tyrconnel only. It cost him
some trouble even to gain Tyrconnel. He had first to efface
the unfavourable impression which had been produced by
the accounts given of him by Avaux to the effect that he
would seek to be sole ruler [1].

---

[1] The despatches of Lauzun, which are in the archives of the French Ministry
of War, were of the greatest value to me for the comprehension of the events
of the year 1690.

Lauzun then put together in a special memoir a statement of all that was needed to defend Ireland against the great attack which might be expected, and which was contemplated in England : he specified above all the fortification of some tenable places of which Dublin must be the centre; but in addition to this a better organisation of the army according to its several arms, the formation of a park of artillery which should be able to follow it into the field, the establishment of magazines, and much else.

Not nearly all these measures, however, were actually carried out. The King was much inclined to set his hand to one or more of the measures suggested without delay; the necessary orders were given; but everything depended upon the Treasury, where not only the necessary means, but good will also was wanting.

Among the members of the old court who had followed King James to Ireland, and among the higher officials, a strong antipathy showed itself against the French, necessary as their presence was. Lord Dover took offence at the proposals for facilitating the trade between France and Ireland which Lauzun, like his predecessor, brought forward; he would even then have held it better to try whether an accommodation could not be made with William III. But how was that to be attained, or how was a dissolution of the connexion entered into with France to be brought about? Dover at last sued for his discharge and betook himself to the Spanish Netherlands.

The great struggle must go on as it had begun.

War had been declared on both sides; by England against Louis XIV on account of his proceedings, which were hostile to the freedom and religion of England, not against the French; by Louis XIV, not against the English but against the usurper and his adherents. It could not be at all expected that the French would at this time renounce the cause of their King; the remains of the Huguenots at most would have been capable of doing so, but they were disarmed and humbled to the dust. On the other hand it seemed quite possible to detach the English commonwealth by force from William III; the accounts which were received daily from

England and Scotland justified such an expectation; it was the great design which arose out of the complication of affairs : James II held it fast with undoubting confidence. At that time he interrupted Lauzun's advice about the next campaign with the demand that he would carry him over to England as soon as possible, for then everything would be decided.

That project however was in turn connected with the preponderance at sea which France seemed to be on the point of acquiring, if not to have already acquired it.

The secretary of state for the Marine, the Marquess of Seignelay, who had been carefully and strictly educated for public business[1] by his father, Colbert, had his attention entirely engrossed by maritime projects which had been chiefly directed against Holland. He was one of those enterprising ministers who, agreeing with the ideas of their princes, and having a complete control over the business especially entrusted to them, promote it with zeal as great as they could show if the public welfare depended solely upon it. He made the absolute will which animated the whole as effective in the administration of the navy as Louvois his rival did in the administration of the army. Seignelay undertook in the first instance to give practical effect to his father's thought that the sovereignty of the Mediterranean belonged by right to the French. He directed the bombardment of Genoa, and was himself present at it. The Spaniards were compelled by an undisguised exercise of force to salute the white flag on their way from Naples to Catalonia ; one town of the Moors of Barbary after another was punished for its piracies. Seignelay thought that he could get access to the East Indies through Turkey, where the French then exercised great influence. Nothing accordingly could run more directly counter to his designs than the increasing extension and activity of the Dutch marine. In the year 1688 a war with Holland seemed to be at hand for that reason alone. Seignelay then on his own responsibility commissioned

---

[1] This appears from the extracts from their correspondence which Father Clement has published : 'Travaux de l'académie des sciences morales, Juin 1865.'

the commanders of French squadrons to seize Dutch ships
wherever they might meet with them, on pretence of reprisals.
He fitted out a small expedition in order to capture Dutch
vessels on the coasts of Italy, Sicily, and Asia Minor: it was
especially their intercourse with Messina and with Smyrna that
he would not tolerate. French shipowners were encouraged to
get their vessels ready for sea, on the ground that there would
soon be much to be won; the three leading ministers,
Seignelay, Croissy, and Louvois themselves fitted out a vessel
with this object. At that time they reckoned on the neutrality of England, or even on an alliance with that power:
had their calculations proved correct, Holland would doubtless have had to yield to their demands[1]. It made then a
most serious change in the aspect of affairs that, in consequence of the Revolution, England and Holland were allied
so closely as to seem like one power. That was one reason
why the French took such a zealous interest in James II.
It was of inestimable service to them that he had a party
devoted to him which undermined and found occupation for
the power of the new King of England and, above all, that
James maintained himself in Ireland. Cork and Kinsale might
be considered as French ports. It was regarded not only as a
momentary advantage but as a pledge of future successes that
in the first encounter on the Irish coast (in Bantry Bay)
the French got the better of the English.. One of the most
famous seamen of the time, Tourville, who had distinguished
himself in all those undertakings in the Mediterranean, which
had been directed against Genoa, Spain, and the Moors of
Barbary, was transferred from the eastern to the western seas.
He was not yet fifty years old, but had already spent thirty
at sea. Seignelay, who appeared in person in the harbours on
the west coast of France, and showed especial zeal in providing for the construction of new galleys at Rochefort, held
Tourville to be the right man to conduct the war according
to his views in the waters of the Atlantic, as he had conducted
it in the Mediterranean. Passing over an older seaman he

---

[1] 'Principes de M. le Marquis de Seignelay sur la marine.' Printed in E. Sue
iv. 700. [qy. 392. Tr.]

gave Tourville the command-in-chief over the united French fleet, which had now become very numerous. While a small squadron remained on the coasts of France in order to repel any hostile attack that might take place, Tourville was to seek out the English in their harbours, at Plymouth and Portsmouth, to do them as much harm as possible, and then to take up his position off the mouths of the Thames and Southwold Bay in order to hinder the communication between the Dutch and the English. One division of his fleet was to destroy the trade between England and the North. It was intended to blockade Britain in order to produce an interruption of trade which was expected to react immediately upon English feeling. All neutral ships coming from the ports of England and Holland were laid under an embargo.

It was under these circumstances that William III prepared for his Irish undertaking; all around him were the smouldering symptoms of a revolt which might break out as soon as his back was turned ; and he had to meet in the field a combination of forces before which his own had been obliged to retire in the previous year, both on land and on the sea. But he could not hesitate. He said that he must go through with his undertaking or perish in the attempt. On the 4th of June he left London, on the 11th he left England.

He had entrusted the government to the hands of his wife, to assist whom he appointed a council, consisting of nine members ; four of them were Whigs, five were Tories. Such pretty nearly was at this moment the relation of the parties in the country[1]. And it was not an unfavourable circumstance that the party whose principles might most readily make it inclined to go over to James II was precisely that which had promoted the enterprise against Ireland, and had now the preponderance in the government. The Tories could not engage in a general revolt against an administration in which Danby and Nottingham had the chief authority. As for the Whigs it is evident that their very principles prevented

---

[1] Dalrymple has published a very remarkable portion of the correspondence between Mary and William, which throws equal light on their personal relations and on the general political relations of the time.

their attaching themselves to King James. They could not at least, any more than the Tories, do so on a great scale.

And yet the agitation which spread through London when the news arrived that the French had appeared off the English coasts was indescribable. There were plenty of people among whom the declaration of Louis XIV that his fleet should not wage war against England, but should make it possible for the English people to return to their allegiance to their legitimate sovereign, found a good reception. In the walks in Hyde Park words and exclamations were heard which breathed the spirit of Dublin. It was said even in Whitehall that the rightful master of the house would soon return and enter it. The government did not long hesitate to have the most suspicious personages taken into custody. Even Lord Clarendon, the uncle of the Queen Regent, was among them : she herself, however much the step grieved her, held it to be indispensable.

The government was by no means so sure even of the great Whigs that it could have counted on their unconditional obedience. Admiral Herbert, now Lord Torrington, was discontented in a high degree at having been excluded from the naval administration on the occasion of the last ministerial change ; it was with great displeasure that he saw his rival Russell in the Council of Nine ; people were almost terrified when they considered that it was to this man, who was naturally wilful and obstinate, and who moreover had received a slight, that the destiny of the kingdom, or, as was said, of three kingdoms, was to be entrusted.

Yet this could not be avoided. Tourville had been originally instructed to avoid an encounter. But subsequently the information which had come in about the ferment in England and Scotland, as well as about the condition of the English fleet, had raised Seignelay's spirits. With an impetuous vehemence peculiar to him, he now pressed Tourville to attack the English fleet wherever he found it, and that before William III could yet have undertaken anything in Ireland [1]. The English

---

[1] 'De tâcher engager l'action avant la jonction du prince d'Orange' (I understand 'avec Schomberg'): so runs the extract from the instructions as it is found

government also now desired an engagement. Not that it
had concealed from itself the superiority of the French fleet ;
but according to the accounts which reached it the latter was
not so strong as to be more than a match for the English and
Dutch united. If Tourville were left unassailed he would be
in a position to throw men and arms into Scotland, where
such aid was expected by the Jacobites in order that they
might bring to an outbreak the revolt which had been long
prepared [1] : on the other side the merchantmen coming from
Cadiz would fall into his hands. King William had made the
remark that the combined fleet must fight, even at the risk of
a defeat : for that in any case the French fleet would suffer
so much injury thereby that it would not be able to keep
the sea, or even to put out again during the year. Queen
Mary and the Council of Nine issued the most precise orders
to Torrington to sail to meet the enemy. Torrington, who
feared to risk his reputation in a doubtful affair, was then
engaged in a retreating movement. He now said that he
disapproved the plan, but would obey the order given him.
Without further delay he directed his course with the two
squadrons which he commanded, the blue and the red, and
with the Dutch squadron which had just arrived, about fifty
ships of the line in all, towards Beachy Head, not far from
Hastings Roads, near which the French lay at anchor. It
was on the 30th of June Old, on the 10th of July New, Style.

Tourville also seems not to have approved of the orders of
his government ; the tone of the despatches which he received
had put him out of humour. And commanders of fleets, even
where no special grounds for discontent exist, are usually, on
account of the peculiar conditions to which naval warfare is
subjected, even more impatient of interference on the part of

---

in the 'Principes de Seignelay.' The fleet left Brest on June 13/23. No information could yet have been received in France of the departure of William from
Highlake to Ireland.

[1] I take this reason from the letter of Nottingham to William, of June 28
(Sir T. Phillipps' Library) : 'The French would have opportunity of sending what
men and armes they please to Scotland, where such assistance was expected.' He
mentions the King's 'opinion formerly declared,' though the success of the engagement should be (of) some disadvantage at our side, because the French would at
least be disabled by a fight to keep the seas.

the home government than are generals by land. The difference between the behaviour of the two commanders was, that
Tourville, accustomed to absolute monarchy and needing the
approval of his sovereign, submitted completely, resolved to
fight at any cost and under all circumstances, while Torrington, a wilful aristocrat, carried with him into the battle his
discontent about the orders which he had received, and which
he held to have been ill-considered. When the Dutch, to
whom even in general he had no good will, after opening the
engagement bravely, began to get the worst—perhaps not
without fault on their part—he left them unsupported. He
had even then no desire to attack the French. Tourville says
in so many words, in his account of the battle, 'that the
enemy's admiral had not been willing to fight with him[1].'
Torrington availed himself of a calm which set in to break
off the engagement and order a retreat. In the report which
he made upon the action his language is penetrated by a
conviction that all this was not his fault, but was only to be
ascribed to the wrong directions, as he thought them, which
had been given him : 'had he been left his freedom he would
certainly have defended the country and saved the merchantmen[2] : God only knew what would happen now.'

But the world did not regard his behaviour in this light.
In Whitehall it was regarded as intentional treason, and it was
thought necessary to have an insubordinate Whig sent to the
Tower, in addition to the suspected Tories who had been
previously arrested. The loudest complaints were made by
the Dutch : their crews had suffered severely, and they had
lost two officers of reputation ; their ships had almost all
become unserviceable or had fallen into the hands of the
enemy during the battle and during the subsequent pursuit.

The French also had important losses to lament, but they
had not become unable to keep the sea for the time. Seignelay

---

[1] 'Herbert ne vouloit pas me combattre et ne combattit pas avec aucun de mes
pavillons.'
[2] See his letter in Dalrymple. In Bonnet he appears proud and disorderly :
'Il est connu pour n'avoir ni religion ni vertus morales—il a eu un valet de
chambre français et papiste. Les moins passionnés croyent qu'il a esté vendu à la
France'

invited Tourville to join battle a second time or to attempt a landing on the coast of England.

The great impression which a victory won over Dutchmen and Englishmen produced was deepened by the fact that on another theatre of war, which, however, stood practically in the closest connexion with the island kingdoms—that in the Netherlands—the French had obtained an important success. At Fleurus the Prince of Waldeck had been obliged to retire from the field before them.

At this moment it was still expected that the enterprises undertaken against Britain would be completely successful. Queen Mary Beatrice declares to Admiral Tourville that if she and her husband should soon return to the throne, the glory of having opened the way to it for them would belong to him, the admiral [1].

It appeared, however, to herself and to her friends that their object would be promoted not so much by a speedy decision of the struggle between the two armies which stood opposed to each other in Ireland, as on the contrary by the delay of a decision—such delay being needed in order to allow the Jacobite faction in Scotland and England the time required for it to assemble and rise in insurrection.

---

[1] See Macpherson, in the note to i. 230.

CHAPTER X.

NONE but those who live later can take a general survey of the circumstances which, on occasion of a great event, touch and condition one another. At the moment of action no one can know them, consider them, and accommodate himself to them ; the work goes on for the most part in a twilight of true and false conceptions ; in order not to be unjust one must allow even for mistakes.

When James II prepared to take the field in the latter half of June 1690, he did not yet know that William III had arrived in Ireland. He only heard that the army which was stationed in Ulster was assembling at Newry and Armagh. Shortly before this Schomberg had wrested from him the strong place of Charlemont, principally owing to the garrison's having been too numerous to be able to live on the provisions which had been brought in. James then felt himself unable to relieve it. He now thought that the enemy's designs were directed against Dundalk, which he did not wish to let fail into their hands in like manner. He decided to assemble his army at that very place, not to fight, but to maintain possession of the country, and to employ its produce as long as possible, for his own support ; 'as soon as it should become necessary he would retire and throw himself upon the defensive, for which he thought he could avail himself of many important posts, till autumn should come, which might produce the same results as it had done in the previous year.'

It must not be supposed that Count Lauzun, who accompanied him both as an adviser and as general of the auxiliary troops, approved of this plan. He complains that none of all his recommendations have been carried out. The strong places had not been put in a state of defence ; there were no magazines anywhere ; the army on taking the field was hardly provided with corn for a month. Lauzun repeats that there was no one about King James, except Tyrconnel, who had attended to his representations ; every one else only followed his own special interest ; the King was on all sides deceived and even robbed ; he did not know how to say enough of the annoyances to which he was exposed. The main point, however, was that a defensive war such as was contemplated did not seem to him to suit the circumstances. The country, he said, had neither large rivers nor forests where a stand could be made ; the army must defend itself on the retreat, but even so would not be able to avoid a decisive battle[1]. Lauzun had been particularly warned, and one might almost say pledged, by Louvois not to allow himself to be hurried into such a battle, and we see from his letters that he was constantly thinking of that advice. As he felt that all was at stake, the thought arose in his mind of giving up the greater part of the country, of rather destroying the capital than seriously defending it, and of retiring to Connaught where the Shannon and one or two fortified places would offer the means necessary for protracted defensive operations. These proposals were as outrageous as any which Avaux and Rosen had made ; James II abhorred them, and Lauzun, least of all men, would have been able to secure their adoption. For it was the very object of his mission to keep up a good understanding with the King, in contrast to his predecessors.

Lauzun accordingly, though against his better military conviction, followed the King to Dundalk. James II showed no want of activity there, and was unweariedly busied, after his fashion, in putting the town in a state of defence, and in posting the troops ; on one day he was eighteen hours on horseback. Everything wore the best appearance. Lauzun reports that the Irish regiments were, not indeed all com-

---

[1] See Lauzun's correspondence, in which alone information is found on this point.

pletely disciplined, but composed of very fine men ; that his French troops were in the best condition that could be wished ; and that all were burning with eagerness to match themselves with the enemy. If everything had been in the same position as in the previous year, they would perhaps indeed have yielded to the advancing enemy, but would have disputed every foot of land with him. But things were not in the same position as in the previous year. Before James II had any news of the arrival of William III in Ireland, the latter was in full march against him.

Soon after mid-day on the 14th of June, directly after landing from his yacht at Carrickfergus, William mounted on horseback ; at about four o'clock he arrived at a country-house on the way to Belfast, where Schomberg and some other generals awaited him [1]. It was agreed that the troops which were already in the country, the regiments which were just arriving from Scotland, and the corps with which William III came over, should unite at Loughbrickland, not far from Armagh, in order to advance upon Newry and Dundalk. Artillery and provisions were ordered thither as they were brought on shore ; all this took place under the eyes of William, so that the 22nd of June had come before he arrived in the camp. When the Brandenburg ambassador congratulated him on having advanced matters so far, he replied that he thought that would please the Elector also, as it was for the common good. There was no clear notion, even in the camp of King William, of the position and force of the enemy, and some doubts were expressed whether an immediate advance would be advisable. William replied that he had not come to Ireland to let grass grow under his feet. It was necessary to remain inactive for two more days till the troops had all assembled, and the roads through the defiles had been to some extent got into a proper condition [2].

---

[1] The details furnished by O'Callaghan from the Villare Hibernicum cannot be altogether correct ; I adhere to the reports of the Brandenburg resident, Dankelmann, who sends a report home day by day of everything which occurred.

[2] His Majesty sent on some pioneers, and as many peasants as could be obtained, in order to improve as far as possible the roads to Newry, and especially those from that place to Dundalk, and to remove the many stones which were found in the track.

The army was one of the finest and most practised in war which have ever appeared in Ireland. It consisted of a similar mixture of nationalities to that which had been found in the army which had sailed over from Holland to England two years before. But there had now been added to it some Danes, whose name made a peculiar impression in Ireland where this nation had formerly begun the Teutonic immigration. A prophecy was circulated that they would also complete it, and bring the Irish name to utter ruin. Marshal Schomberg appears as Captain-General next to the King, his son Meinhard as general of the cavalry, Count Solms as general of the infantry; among the major-generals we find Dutch, German, and English names; the Danes were commanded by Prince Ferdinand William of Würtemberg. The army might number 36,000 men. On the 26th of June, early in the day, it set itself in motion against Dundalk.

It was only on the 24th of June that definite information reached the Irish camp that William III was in Ireland, and was advancing with an army far superior to that of his opponents. Lauzun sent a courier with the news to Louvois. He did not consider that the position which had been occupied near Dundalk was tenable, and now remarked that the army ought not to remain there a day longer, for fear of being obliged to quit it under the eyes of the enemy: the retreat began on the very same day. Yet it was conducted very slowly; James II lingered at Ardee, still under the influence of the unseasonable thought that the enemy would suffer great loss if the forage of the neighbouring districts were consumed before him. It was only after some days that he continued his retreat towards Drogheda, where he thought that he would find a defensible position behind the Boyne. The retreat had not been effected without disorder, yet the army was still in good spirits. It would, in its chivalrous feeling, have been best pleased to fight with the enemy upon the open plain; only because he was far superior in numbers did the Irish think it allowable to avail themselves of the advantage which the river offered.

The central districts of Ireland are level and marshy; on the coast it is in many places bordered by heights which, penetrated by little streams, give the country its charm. One of these streams is the Boyne, which in past times formed the boundary between Ulster and Leinster—a river neither particularly broad nor deep, but, after receiving other streams, tolerably well supplied with water; it runs down to the sea between heights wooded or cultivated as arable land, through meadows luxuriant in their vegetation. The tide runs up as far as the spot where James II took up his position. That spot is moreover the region of the oldest civilisation, of the old royal citadel of Tara, of a heathen necropolis, and of the first conversions by St. Patrick in the fifth century. A thread might perhaps be found connecting the events of that early epoch with those of the time we are describing; but the latter had incomparably more importance of their own for the world. It had now come to pass that the great religious and political controversy which divided Europe was to be decided by arms in the island of the farthest west. The principle represented by the King of the native party was still very powerful in spite of all that had passed; it had been embraced and was defended by the greatest monarchy of the age, and had just obtained some important successes. But, on the other hand, the man who had already succeeded in overpowering that principle, when it sought to make itself master of England and Scotland, had set out to combat it in Ireland by force of arms, and to expel it altogether from the island realm.

The muster-rolls of the combined Irish and French army show thirty-two battalions and fifty-five squadrons; when we consider that the Irish regiments were not usually kept up to their full strength, the estimate of the total number at 23,000 men, as the Duke of Berwick, the son of James II, who was present, gives it, will not be too low. This army, however, was engaged in a retreat in which it wavered every moment between hastening forward and halting. Lauzun would have wished to lead it back immediately to Dublin, which the enemy might otherwise reach by a flank march, or by a landing in its rear. But that was already becoming impossible: King William passed Dundalk with his army on the 27th of June; there on the neighbouring hills the troops of the different arms took up their position; on the 28th he already encamped beyond Ardee. He passed over a length of road in two days which was expected to detain him for four. For the decisive battle which Lauzun wished to avoid was precisely what William wished to bring on. When the Irish reached the Boyne, on the evening of the 28th of June, they feared that they would be attacked ; they remained under arms during the night, and ammunition was given out. On the 29th they crossed the river and took up a position on its right bank ; early on the morning of the 30th the troops of William III appeared on the hills of the left bank. He had succeeded in arresting his enemy's retreat. He was like the eagle who swoops with straight flight upon his prey and overtakes it [1].

The Irish had planted on a neighbouring height, which it is thought can still be distinguished, a small battery, from which they fired upon the hostile troops as they occupied the opposite shore in numbers which increased from hour to hour. William did not hesitate to pitch his camp within range of the enemy's cannon. Accordingly, as he rode along the line, a ball happened to graze his left shoulder. He only said that there was no need for it to have come nearer, and did not allow himself to be disturbed in his inspection by the occurrence [2]. Soon afterwards his artillery arrived, consisting of thirty-six field-pieces, half-carronades and howitzers. At the first discharge it was so fortunate as to dismount two of the enemy's cannon, whose fire thereon became silent. In order to contradict the report that the grazing shot had done him a serious injury, William again mounted his horse in the evening and rode through the camp which had then been pitched. He was everywhere received with joyful acclamations.

---

[1] See the Dutch report of Hope : ' De vyandt is daerdoer [i.e. by the march] buyten staet gebracht, om verters te konnen retireren.'

[2] Dankelmann : ' His Majesty having gone in his own high person to inspect the enemy's camp, had a part of his overcoat carried away, and his skin touched, by a cannon ball so that blood followed ; but he was not in the least affected by it, but rode on.' Every point in these events has been brought nearer to the imagination, but at the same time rendered unintelligible, by unauthenticated narratives, which attached themselves to the events upon the spot, and were then combined in history as well as might be, for which even George Story furnished a precedent. (Cp. Wilde, The Beauties of the Boyne, chap x.) I pass them over on purpose, and keep only to the most immediate and simple narrative.

William's plan for the battle was, with his main force to
pass the river in his front, where it offered some fords opposite
to the enemy's position, while at the same time he tried
whether he could not reach the other shore higher up in the
district of Slane, or lower down in the direction of Drogheda.
He attached great importance to the passage of the army at
the first of these two points, and it did in fact prove decisive.
Two battalions were posted so as to hinder the garrison of
Drogheda from taking part in the battle.

On that evening an extension of the enemy's right wing in
the direction of Slane was already noticed in the Jacobite
camp.   Lauzun feared that William would really effect his
passage there, and would thereby get before him on the road
to Dublin.   In order to hinder this, James and Lauzun decided
next morning to shift their camp in such a way that the left
wing of their army should advance to Slane, while the defence
of the passages over the Boyne should be left to the right
wing, which should draw up to the left.   Their purpose was
not even now to risk a serious engagement,—they did not feel
strong enough for that, in spite of the advantage which the
river offered them,—but only to defend the passages until the
pass of Duleek on the road to Dublin, which perhaps was still
tenable, should have been reached.

The first act of the great drama was performed by Count
Meinhard Schomberg, son of the marshal, who with a considerable division of cavalry and infantry received a commission
to pass the river higher up.   King William told him that the
fate of the day depended upon his movement ; Count Meinhard
answered that, as it was necessary, he would with God's help
carry it out.   It was about eight o'clock in the morning when
he reached the most important passage below Slane, Rosnaree,
for the protection of which the enemy had posted about 1200
men.   Count Meinhard sent on some horse-grenadiers to
begin skirmishing in the first instance : then the dragoons
threw themselves into the water, also under the enemy's
bullets.   They suffered considerable losses ; but it was soon
noticed that the fire of the enemy, who perhaps had exhausted
his ammunition, became weaker ; Count Meinhard then himself plunged into the river, sword in hand.   Under his lead the

dragoons succeeded in reaching the opposite bank; they overthrew the enemy; the infantry then likewise found means of
crossing over.

With this news an aide-de-camp, whose account we still
possess, hastened back to the King in his camp. William
asked if things were going on well. With a delight which
was seldom noticed in him he received the account of the
happy result of his plan. He had already, when he noticed
the movement of the hostile army, sent a very considerable
reinforcement, under General James Douglas, in support of his
right [1]. He now invited Meinhard Schomberg, through the
aide-de-camp, to press further forward: saying that he relied
on him completely at that point, that at his own he, the King,
would begin the attack in front at the same time [2].

King James had also appeared upon the other side, not in
order to fight there, but in order to hasten the march of the
troops up the river, thinking that the main attack was to be
expected in that quarter [3]. He entrusted the defence of the
passages at Oldbridge to Tyrconnel, with whom he left as
many men as seemed necessary for the purpose—more cavalry
than infantry, and hardly any artillery. These measures had
just been taken when the great body of troops which formed
William's centre reached the shore. The different divisions
vied with one another in eagerness to be the first to cross
over: the nature of the fords and their depth seemed to
trouble them little. The Danes first threw themselves into
the river; but they sank up to their shoulders in the water;
they were seen holding their fire-arms high over their heads;

---

[1] In Napier's Memoirs of Dundee (iii. 715) an account of Douglas' own is
printed, in which this is mentioned.

[2] This may be gathered beyond a doubt from the account of this aide-de-camp,
by name St. Felice; it is addressed to the wife of the count, and dated July 2;
Story's accounts often prove untrustworthy.

[3] From King James' own notes, which Clarke has copied: 'The King went
to the right (near Oldbridge) to hasten up the troops to follow Lauzun, believing
the main body of the enemies' army was following their right, which had passed
at Slane.' With this agrees the view of Hope, who knew nothing of the presence
of James II: the enemy had retired from the bank and drawn up his forces in
two lines, 'lætende verscheyde detachementen van Infanterie als Cavallerie' om de
onse het overkomen te disputeren.'

in ·this condition they could not cope with the resistance
which they encountered on the shore.   The first who got
over were the three battalions of the Dutch guard, under the
Count of Solms, and two divisions of French exiles: they
crossed close to the hamlet of Oldbridge.   But here an Irish
regiment of unexpected strength had posted itself behind the
walls and fences; it received the enemy's troops as they came
over with an effective fire of small arms, and twice drove
them back : the guard, however, succeeded at last in getting
a firm footing and maintaining itself [1].   The King, who was
near, thanked the officers on the next day for their brave
behaviour.   But victory was not yet secured, for the Irish on
their side were also energetically supported, when at the sight
of the constantly-renewed struggle the old fighting spirit
awoke in Marshal Schomberg.   He had sent warning to his
son just before not to expose himself too much to danger;
for himself he felt no anxiety.   The tradition is that he sought
to inspirit the body of refugees, the first troops which he fell
in with after crossing the river, by pointing out to them their
enemies, among whom there were many French, as their old
persecutors from France.   This measure of success had Schomberg attained : he was leading the exiles, whom Louis XIV
had driven out, against the troops of that very King in a
remote spot, but at the great crisis in which fortune again
declared for the Protestant cause.   Then, so to speak, his
mission was fulfilled, and the fortune of war claimed him as
a victim.   Two soldiers of the guard of James II, who took
the marshal, wearing as he did the blue ribbon of his order,
for King William, pressed in upon him, amid the tumult of
the encounter and put an end to his life by two sabre strokes
upon the head [2].

---

[1] The most intelligible general description is the report which Bentinck appended
to his letters, as it is found in the Melville Papers i. 459.   It is repeated in the
‘Lettres de Bussy Rabutin’ (vi. 298), but not without disfiguring mistakes.   To this
may be added the reports of Hope and of the Brandenburg resident, Dankelmann,
of July 2, which deserve notice because their authors were near King William.
On the other side I use the detailed narrative of Lauzun, which Macaulay could
. not find (it is printed in E. Sue's Histoire de la Marine iv. 332, but with many
mistakes), and the details of the Jacobite journal.

[2] The. occasion of his crossing is definitely ascertained from the reports of the

Meanwhile the left wing also had passed the river lower down ; there William III himself, on horseback with his drawn sword in his hand, crossed, though not without difficulty, and put himself at the head of the Enniskilleners.   The passage was effected at other places also.   Thereupon the Irish, who had till then fought bravely, lost courage : the yellow dragoons, seized by a sudden panic, were the first who took to flight ; they rode over their own infantry.

This action can hardly be called a battle ; it was the passage of a river, with some skirmishes on the other bank, against an enemy who was just then engaged in shifting his position and was thinking of retreat more than of serious resistance.

Lauzun and James still thought of attacking young Schomberg with their strengthened left wing, in spite of the reinforcement which he had then received, when they heard that William had crossed at Oldbridge. James II still advised that even then the attack should be undertaken before the enemy could receive news of the passage ; but the most experienced colonels declared it impracticable, on account of the nature of the ground and of the dykes and marshes between the two armies.   Only one thing still seemed possible, namely to reach Dublin before the enemy. With this object Tyrconnel with the remains of his right wing joined Lauzun and the left.

The armies moved in the most peculiar fashion.   The Jacobite forces were taken in the middle between the two divisions of that of William.   In advance on the right flank it had Meinhard Schomberg and his corps, somewhat more to the rear, on the left, William III himself and the troops which had effected the crossing at Oldbridge.   The Jacobites suffered a fire of light artillery and carbines on both sides ; they still replied, but they felt at every moment how great an advantage the enemy had over them.

In this position of affairs Lauzun advised King James to quit the army with an escort of two squadrons, and to

---

aide-de-camp.   As to the manner of Schomberg's death, he agrees precisely with Dankelmann ; and the tradition, which may be designated the Brandenbı dition, is confirmed by the narratives of the Jacobites, especially of Berwˉ we learn from Douglas that even from the beginning a story was als Schomberg had been hit by the bullet of a Frenchman ' by mistake.'

hasten to Dublin in order that he might not himself fall into the hands of the enemy. James resisted, as formerly in England, but he gave way. The commanders of the squadrons called Lauzun's attention to the fact that their departure would expose the retreating army to still greater danger; but he paid no regard to this, for everything, he thought, depended on the preservation of the King's person.

Lauzun himself held it his duty to abide with the army. For a while his Frenchmen took up a position near two huts between field-ditches, in order to bid defiance to the enemy. Tyrconnel covered them on both flanks with his cavalry; no serious attack, however, was made upon them: they could continue their retreat towards Dublin.

William III indeed and his troops were far too much exhausted by the day's exertions to think of an energetic pursuit. The soldiers were gratified with the plunder of various kinds which fell into their hands, together with the enemy's tents which had been removed from the field by the Jacobites; there were watches, silver plate, money and trinkets. It is said that a weapon was found which had on one side the effigies of Louis XIV and of St. Louis, on the other the inscription 'the King of France will have the Prince of Orange's head cut off.'

Such had been the result of the unlucky advance to Dundalk which had from the beginning implied the necessity of a retreat. King James and the Irish mutually accused each other of cowardice: the truth is that they had allowed themselves to be forced into such a desperate position that very different generalship from the King's, and a much more obstinate resistance than that of the Irish, would have been necessary to secure even an honourable fall. Detained against their will, yet at the same time making a stand by their own will, they were surprised by a determined and superior enemy in the positions to which they no longer attached much value, and driven from them. Without being strictly speaking beaten, they suffered a defeat.

King James, who regarded his undertaking in Ireland as a trial of what it would be possible to effect from that country with French help against England, felt no special inclination, after the loss of the battle even to defend the capital itself,

Lauzun had told him that he had to take care not only for himself, but also for his son : he should above all things save himself and return to France, then his cause would not be lost. No news had yet been received of the action off Beachy Head; but Lauzun stated with confidence that France was mistress of the sea at that moment. James found a letter from his wife awaiting him at Dublin Castle which gave him the news of the victory of Fleurus; he was strengthened thereby in the opinion that he would provide better for the preservation of his crown if he fled to his protector the victorious Louis in France than if he exposed himself in Ireland to the dangers of a war. Some members of the Privy Council whose opinion he asked, among them his old advisers Powis and Albeville, agreed with him as to this; but he had not spoken his last word when the news arrived at daybreak that the army had dispersed in all directions, and that the enemy was close at his heels [1]. Thereupon all scruples disappeared. James only took time enough to announce his decision to the members of the city magistracy, not without justifying it by bitter censure of the bad behaviour of the Irish at Oldbridge, which, he said, made it impossible for him to rely upon them any longer; he warned his hearers, however, not to bring complete ruin upon the capital by an useless resistance. He then hurried away as quickly as possible; within three days he embarked at Waterford in a ship of St. Malo, which took him to Kinsale, whence he sailed over to France.

The condition of the army was not altogether so bad as the message above mentioned had reported. Lauzun and Tyrconnel, who, it was said, had perished, were still living; but the troops which still kept together were nevertheless not capable of defending Dublin; they thought that they did enough in taking the cannon and the French military chest in safety to Limerick [2].

In Dublin the issue of the battle had been first made known by the return of the King, and the desperate position of his cause was inferred from his flight. A great panic seized on all who had adhered to his policy; not only did

---

[1] Narrative of a French officer.
[2] See Lauzun's report of July 3. Louvois had required an account on the point.

most of the civil officials, the judges, and the Catholics of most
consideration follow the King's example and leave the city,
but the military officers did the same, even the governor on
the same morning. Thereupon a complete revolution ensued.
The Protestants had kept themselves in their houses, those
who were most suspected had been shut up in Trinity College:
now, under the direction of Captain Robert Fitzgerald, a son
of the Earl of Kildare, they got possession of the keys of the
town, posted some of their number as watches at the gates
and even got the castle into their hands. Then they informed
King William that the town was at his service, but needed his
help in order to maintain itself against the turbulent multitude. The King, who received this message in his camp,
said that he saw he had friends in Dublin; he had long
corresponded in person with Fitzgerald especially. He sent
two regiments to Dublin without delay to maintain public
order there. On the following Sunday he himself reached
the town and attended service at St. Patrick's, the church in
which the remains of Schomberg found a resting-place [1].

Thus did William III get the better of James II in Ireland.
What were the chief personal differences between the two in
this struggle?

James was not without activity, nor without a certain
elevation of mind, but he moved amid illusions which never
left him, and he aimed at impossible things. During his
reign he wished to combine his schemes of toleration for
Catholicism with the parliamentary constitution which was
connected with the exclusive privileges of Protestantism;
during his exile he wished to combine the interest of France
with that of England, though they ran directly counter to
each other; finally, he wished to combine favour shown to
the natives of Ireland with his design of gaining the English,
who, however, only thought of keeping the Irish down. It
seems incredible, but it is true, that he hastened to get away
from Ireland in order not to be too late for the moment at
which the preponderance of the French navy might bring
him back to England.

On the other hand, William always kept his great idea
before his eyes amid the perplexing circumstances which

---

[1] See the letter and authentic reports in Harris.

surrounded him.   The decision which he displayed at every
moment rested on the fact that he had only one end and that
one imposed by the course of things.   James thought that he
could attain his end even without Ireland; for William the
conquest of Ireland was a vital question.

At that time, however, his work was far from having been
completed.

The rapidity and extent of the successes obtained by William certainly produced the impression that Ireland was lost
for James II in consequence of them.   Louis lamented the
sacrifices which he had made for the maintenance of that
island, and determined to recall his troops.   The only advantage which he still expected to derive from it consisted in
the reception into his service of the Irish who were fit for a
military life, with a view to the war on the Continent.

In like manner Lauzun and Tyrconnel also, when they had
arrived at Limerick, formed the opinion that that place—the
most important in Ireland—would not hold out a moment
after William III undertook the siege of it.

William III, penetrated on his side by the same thought,
decided to put off for some time longer his return to England,
which would on general grounds have been very expedient,
in the hope that, as Wexford, Waterford, and other places, had
fallen into his hands, so he would take Limerick also without
delay, and would thereby complete the conquest of Ireland
upon the spot.

But he was neither sufficiently master of the country, nor
sufficiently provided with necessary war material, to do so.
It happened that a train of artillery on its way to Limerick
was, at only a few miles' distance from that place, overpowered
and destroyed by an Irish force which issued from the mountains.   This was the first event which aroused the self-confidence of the Irish in the midst of their general despondency.
William made such progress in his siege that an assault
could be undertaken; but the French brigadier Boisselot,
who directed the defence after the departure of Lauzun and
Tyrconnel for Galway, had taken such good precautions, and
the Irish showed themselves again so brave, that the vehement
attack failed, and William was compelled to desist from his
siege.   He consoled himself in his religious way: 'that was

only,' said he, 'the will of God : he must content himself with the other successes which he had obtained during the campaign.'

Soon after his departure the English obtained a new and great success. The two harbours which proved most useful to the French for keeping up their connexion with Ireland, Cork and Kinsale, were conquered by the co-operation of an expedition fitted out at Portsmouth under the King's direction with the forces which had been left behind in Ireland. At the head of the first stood Churchill, who offered himself voluntarily, and now wished to be of some service ; the others were commanded by Ferdinand William, Duke of Wurtemberg [1], the leader of the Danes. They both of them had the rank of lieutenant - general, and the question to which of them precedence properly belonged seemed to create some difficulty ; this difficulty, however, could hardly become serious between the friend of the Princess of Denmark and the Danish general : they soon came to an agreement, and worked together with one mind and most vigorously. Neither in Cork nor in Kinsale did the defenders wait for an assault, but preferred to capitulate when such an attempt was at hand ; the whole undertaking was brought to an end in twenty-three days ; it was of great importance, inasmuch as the whole south coast of Ireland was thereby brought back into the hands of the Protestants and of the English.

But that was by no means enough to induce the Irish to yield and offer their submission. They repulsed successfully every attempt of the English to press further on by land. In the district on the Shannon, which had been specially assigned to them in Cromwell's time, in the province of Connaught, they thought that they could maintain themselves even without the help of the French. So they were first told by Sarsfield, who had executed the attack above mentioned on the siege-train which was moving against Limerick, and who was subsequently celebrated as the hero of the nation.

A perishing nationality has sometimes men granted to it in whom its virtues are represented. Sarsfield was a thorough soldier, of undoubted bravery in every danger, of an enterprising spirit which was ever fresh and indefatigable, and of

---

[1] Of the line of Neustadt, born in 1659.

an imposing presence : he was also inflexible in his attachment
to the Catholic religion and to the right of his king. The
ebullitions of Irish pride made the French and their leaders
wish very much to be able to return to their own country;
they found life among their old comrades intolerable. But it
was most welcome to the French court that everything in Ireland again looked as though a vigorous resistance would be
made. Tyrconnel, who crossed over to France with Lauzun,
placed the resolution and military capability of the Irish in such
a light that Louis *XIV* was again induced to support them
with ammunition, provisions, and money. He did not wish to
subject himself to the reproach of allowing an auxiliary force
like this, which offered itself to him spontaneously, to perish
unemployed. Tyrconnel, in whose place Berwick had in the
meanwhile remained in Ireland, returned thither in January
1691, and neglected nothing which might serve to organise
the Irish army afresh, and to place the country in a state of
defence [1]. He brought with him for his adversaries and rivals
tokens of the favour of James II, among them the title of
Earl of Lucan for Sarsfield, and James himself at least
was convinced that his grants of such favours had an excellent effect in helping to allay the mutual animosities
of the Irish. The army was not again to be commanded
by Tyrconnel : he appeared as the deputy of James II, and
was recognised as such throughout the region which had
not yet been subjugated. A court formed itself around him
at Galway, resembling that which in the previous winter had
formed itself around the King at Dublin. In spite of the
existing deficiency in the most necessary materials, a considerable army nevertheless stood in readiness to repel the
advancing enemy : it held fast the conviction that there would
yet once more be a great revolution of fortune in its favour.

While the Irish, after a great defeat, and although confined
within a district of limited extent, yet retained spirit for resistance, the case was the same to some extent in the Scottish
Highlands also.

General Mackay, after the retreat of the revolted Scots to

---

[1] 'Macariae excidium' is the work of an adversary not only of James but also of
Tyrconnel, and is very welcome as a record of the internal dissensions existing
among the Irish.

their mountains, had succeeded in pressing forward among the hills and in hastily building a fortress, which he named after his king. It was built at Inverlochy. Eleven days were sufficient for the erection of a small work twenty feet high and surrounded with a ditch; it was rude indeed, and showed little skill in its construction, but was tenable against such an enemy as the Highlanders. Mackay left a garrison there which might, in combination with some other garrisons in the north, keep the country in check; he is convinced that he has thereby made it impossible for the natives to combine in any large bodies [1]. They, however, did not yet feel themselves in the least either conquered or inclined to submission; they remained in correspondence with James II. The new government established at Dublin found it necessary to watch over the relations of the Highlanders to the native party in Ireland.

In spite of these stirrings of opposition in the one country, and of this continued resistance in the other, the success of William III was decisive for the destiny of both. His restoration of political power in Ireland to the Protestants, who had been excluded from it, is the transaction which has done most to keep his memory alive. Even at this day parties quarrel there around his statue: they struggle to destroy or to preserve it. His strength lay altogether in the fact that he grasped in his hand the lawful authority which had been the growth of many centuries in Britain. In the modified form which that authority had assumed owing to the Revolution, it was again sovereign over the three British kingdoms: although not completely sovereign, though still exposed to attacks, and still very far from being firmly established. The movements of its opponents could not be suppressed so long as the general war of the great powers of the world, with which those movements had been connected from the beginning, still held out hopes of a result corresponding to the wishes of the disaffected.

---

[1] Mémoires de Maquay. ' Quoique quelques uns de leurs chefs se tinssent dans leurs cachettes et retraites des montagnes,—ils n'ont jamais depuis pu former quelques corps.

END OF VOL. IV.

Lightning Source UK Ltd.
Milton Keynes UK
UKHW020817241218
334505UK00012B/1010/P